T0211820

Lecture Notes in Computer Science 12936

More information about this subseries at http://www.springer.com/series/7409

Carmelo Ardito · Rosa Lanzilotti ·
Alessio Malizia · Helen Petrie ·
Antonio Piccinno · Giuseppe Desolda ·
Kori Inkpen (Eds.)

Human-Computer Interaction – INTERACT 2021

18th IFIP TC 13 International Conference
Bari, Italy, August 30 – September 3, 2021
Proceedings, Part V

 Springer

Editors
Carmelo Ardito ⓘ
Department of Electrical and Information
Engineering
Polytechnic University of Bari
Bari, Italy

Alessio Malizia ⓘ
Computer Science Department
University of Pisa
Pisa, Italy

University of Hertfordshire
Hatfield, United Kingdom

Antonio Piccinno ⓘ
Computer Science Department
University of Bari Aldo Moro
Bari, Italy

Kori Inkpen ⓘ
Microsoft Research
Redmond, WA, USA

Rosa Lanzilotti ⓘ
Computer Science Department
University of Bari Aldo Moro
Bari, Italy

Helen Petrie ⓘ
Department of Computer Science
University of York
York, UK

Giuseppe Desolda ⓘ
Computer Science Department
University of Bari Aldo Moro
Bari, Italy

ISSN 0302-9743   ISSN 1611-3349   (electronic)
Lecture Notes in Computer Science
ISBN 978-3-030-85606-9   ISBN 978-3-030-85607-6   (eBook)
https://doi.org/10.1007/978-3-030-85607-6

LNCS Sublibrary: SL3 – Information Systems and Applications, incl. Internet/Web, and HCI

This Springer imprint is published by the registered company Springer Nature Switzerland AG
The registered company address is: Gewerbestrasse 11, 6330 Cham, Switzerland

Welcome

It is our great pleasure to welcome you to the 18th IFIP TC13 International Conference on Human-Computer Interaction, INTERACT 2021, one of the most important conferences in the area of Human-Computer Interaction at a world-wide level. INTERACT 2021 was held in Bari (Italy) from August 30 – September 3, 2021, in cooperation with ACM and under the patronage of the University of Bari Aldo Moro. This is the second time that INTERACT was held in Italy, after the edition in Rome in September 2005. The Villa Romanazzi Carducci Hotel, which hosted INTERACT 2021, provided the right context for welcoming the participants, thanks to its liberty-period villa immersed in a beautiful park. Due to the COVID-19 pandemic, INTERACT 2021 was held in hybrid mode to allow attendees who could not travel to participate in the conference.

INTERACT is held every two years and is well appreciated by the international community, attracting experts with a broad range of backgrounds, coming from all over the world and sharing a common interest in HCI, to make technology effective and useful for all people in their daily life. The theme of INTERACT 2021, "Sense, Feel, Design," highlighted the new interaction design challenges. Technology is today more and more widespread, pervasive and blended in the world we live in. On one side, devices that sense humans' activities have the potential to provide an enriched interaction. On the other side, the user experience can be further enhanced by exploiting multisensorial technologies. The traditional human senses of vision and hearing and senses of touch, smell, taste, and emotions can be taken into account when designing for future interactions. The hot topic of this edition was Human-Centered Artificial Intelligence, which implies considering who AI systems are built for and evaluating how well these systems support people's goals and activities. There was also considerable attention paid to the usable security theme. Not surprisingly, the COVID-19 pandemic and social distancing have also turned the attention of HCI researchers towards the difficulties in performing user-centered design activities and the modified social aspects of interaction.

With this, we welcome you all to INTERACT 2021. Several people worked hard to make this conference as pleasurable as possible, and we hope you will truly enjoy it.

Paolo Buono
Catherine Plaisant

Preface

The 18th IFIP TC13 International Conference on Human-Computer Interaction, INTERACT 2021 (Bari, August 30 – September 3, 2021) attracted a relevant collection of submissions on different topics.

Excellent research is the heart of a good conference. Like its predecessors, INTERACT 2021 aimed to foster high-quality research. As a multidisciplinary field, HCI requires interaction and discussion among diverse people with different interests and backgrounds. The beginners and the experienced theoreticians and practitioners, and people from various disciplines and different countries gathered, both in-person and virtually, to learn from each other and contribute to each other's growth.

We were especially honoured to welcome our invited speakers: Marianna Obrist (University College London), Ben Shneiderman (University of Maryland), Luca Viganò (King's College London), Geraldine Fitzpatrick (TU Wien) and Philippe Palanque (University Toulouse 3 "Paul Sabatier").

Marianna Obrist's talk focused on the multisensory world people live in and discussed the role touch, taste and smell can play in the future of computing. Ben Shneiderman envisioned a new synthesis of emerging disciplines in which AI-based intelligent algorithms are combined with human-centered design thinking. Luca Viganò used a cybersecurity show and tell approach to illustrate how to use films and other artworks to explain cybersecurity notions. Geraldine Fitzpatrick focused on skills required to use technologies as enablers for good technical design work. Philippe Palanque discussed the cases of system faults due to human errors and presented multiple examples of faults affecting socio-technical systems.

A total of 680 submissions, distributed in 2 peer-reviewed tracks, 4 curated tracks, and 3 juried tracks, were received. Of these, the following contributions were accepted:

- 105 Full Papers (peer-reviewed)
- 72 Short Papers (peer-reviewed)
- 36 Posters (juried)
- 5 Interactive Demos (curated)
- 9 Industrial Experiences (curated)
- 3 Panels (curated)
- 1 Course (curated)
- 11 Workshops (juried)
- 13 Doctoral Consortium (juried)

The acceptance rate for contributions received in the peer-reviewed tracks was 29% for full papers and 30% for short papers. In the spirit of inclusiveness of INTERACT, and IFIP in general, a substantial number of promising but borderline full papers, which had not received a direct acceptance decision, were screened for shepherding.

Interestingly, many of these papers eventually turned out to be excellent quality papers and were included in the final set of full papers. In addition to full papers and short papers, the present proceedings feature's contributions accepted in the shape of posters, interactive demonstrations, industrial experiences, panels, courses, and descriptions of accepted workshops.

Subcommittees managed the reviewing process of the full papers. Each subcommittee had a chair and a set of associated chairs who were in charge of coordinating the reviewing process with the help of expert reviewers. Two new sub-committees were introduced in this edition: "Human-AI Interaction" and "HCI in the Pandemic". Hereafter we list the sub-committees of INTERACT 2021:

- Accessibility and assistive technologies
- Design for business and safety-critical interactive systems
- Design of interactive entertainment systems
- HCI education and curriculum
- HCI in the pandemic
- Human-AI interaction
- Information visualization
- Interactive systems technologies and engineering
- Methodologies for HCI
- Social and ubiquitous interaction
- Understanding users and human behaviour

The final decision on acceptance or rejection of full papers was taken in a Programme Committee meeting held virtually, due to the COVID-19 pandemic, in March 2021. The technical program chairs, the full papers chairs, the subcommittee chairs, and the associate chairs participated in this meeting. The meeting discussed a consistent set of criteria to deal with inevitable differences among many reviewers. The corresponding track chairs and reviewers made the final decisions on other tracks, often after electronic meetings and discussions.

We would like to express our strong gratitude to all the people whose passionate and strenuous work ensured the quality of the INTERACT 2021 program: the 12 sub-committees chairs, 88 associated chairs, 34 track chairs, and 543 reviewers; the Keynote & Invited Talks Chair Maria Francesca Costabile; the Posters Chairs Maristella Matera, Kent Norman, Anna Spagnolli; the Interactive Demos Chairs Barbara Rita Barricelli and Nuno Jardim Nunes; the Workshops Chairs Marta Kristín Larusdottir and Davide Spano; the Courses Chairs Nikolaos Avouris and Carmen Santoro; the Panels Chairs Effie Lai-Chong Law and Massimo Zancanaro; the Doctoral Consortium Chairs Daniela Fogli, David Lamas and John Stasko; the Industrial Experiences Chair Danilo Caivano; the Online Experience Chairs Fabrizio Balducci and Miguel Ceriani; the Advisors Fernando Loizides and Marco Winckler; the Student Volunteers Chairs Vita Santa Barletta and Grazia Ragone; the Publicity Chairs Ganesh D. Bhutkar and Veronica Rossano; the Local Organisation Chair Simona Sarti.

We would like to thank all the authors, who chose INTERACT 2021 as the venue to publish their research and enthusiastically shared their results with the INTERACT community. Last, but not least, we are also grateful to the sponsors for their financial support.

Carmelo Ardito
Rosa Lanzilotti
Alessio Malizia
Helen Petrie
Antonio Piccinno
Giuseppe Desolda
Kori Inkpen

IFIP TC13 – http://ifip-tc13.org/

Established in 1989, the Technical Committee on Human–Computer Interaction (IFIP TC 13) of the International Federation for Information Processing (IFIP) is an international committee of 34 member national societies and 10 Working Groups, representing specialists of the various disciplines contributing to the field of human–computer interaction. This includes (among others) human factors, ergonomics, cognitive science, and multiple areas of computer science and design.

IFIP TC 13 aims to develop the science, technology and societal aspects of human–computer interaction (HCI) by

- encouraging empirical, applied and theoretical research
- promoting the use of knowledge and methods from both human sciences and computer sciences in design, development, evaluation and exploitation of computing systems
- promoting the production of new knowledge in the area of interactive computing systems engineering
- promoting better understanding of the relation between formal design methods and system usability, user experience, accessibility and acceptability
- developing guidelines, models and methods by which designers may provide better human-oriented computing systems
- and, cooperating with other groups, inside and outside IFIP, to promote user-orientation and humanization in system design.

Thus, TC 13 seeks to improve interactions between people and computing systems, to encourage the growth of HCI research and its practice in industry and to disseminate these benefits worldwide.

The main orientation is to place the users at the center of the development process. Areas of study include:

- the problems people face when interacting with computing devices;
- the impact of technology deployment on people in individual and organizational contexts;
- the determinants of utility, usability, acceptability, accessibility, privacy, and user experience ...;
- the appropriate allocation of tasks between computing systems and users especially in the case of automation;
- engineering user interfaces, interactions and interactive computing systems;
- modelling the user, their tasks and the interactive system to aid better system design; and harmonizing the computing system to user characteristics and needs.

While the scope is thus set wide, with a tendency toward general principles rather than particular systems, it is recognized that progress will only be achieved through both general studies to advance theoretical understandings and specific studies on practical issues (e.g., interface design standards, software system resilience, documentation, training material, appropriateness of alternative interaction technologies, guidelines, integrating computing systems to match user needs and organizational practices, etc.).

In 2015, TC13 approved the creation of a Steering Committee (SC) for the INTERACT conference series. The SC is now in place, chaired by Anirudha Joshi and is responsible for:

- promoting and maintaining the INTERACT conference as the premiere venue for researchers and practitioners interested in the topics of the conference (this requires a refinement of the topics above);
- ensuring the highest quality for the contents of the event;
- setting up the bidding process to handle the future INTERACT conferences (decision is made at TC 13 level);
- providing advice to the current and future chairs and organizers of the INTERACT conference;
- providing data, tools, and documents about previous conferences to the future conference organizers;
- selecting the reviewing system to be used throughout the conference (as this affects the entire set of reviewers, authors and committee members);
- resolving general issues involved with the INTERACT conference;
- capitalizing on history (good and bad practices).

In 1999, TC 13 initiated a special IFIP Award, the Brian Shackel Award, for the most outstanding contribution in the form of a refereed paper submitted to and delivered at each INTERACT. The award draws attention to the need for a comprehensive human-centered approach in the design and use of information technology in which the human and social implications have been taken into account. In 2007, IFIP TC 13 launched an Accessibility Award to recognize an outstanding contribution in HCI with international impact dedicated to the field of accessibility for disabled users. In 2013, IFIP TC 13 launched the Interaction Design for International Development (IDID) Award that recognizes the most outstanding contribution to the application of interactive systems for social and economic development of people in developing countries. Since the process to decide the award takes place after papers are sent to the publisher for publication, the awards are not identified in the proceedings. Since 2019 a special agreement has been made with the *International Journal of Behaviour & Information Technology* (published by Taylor & Francis) with Panos Markopoulos as editor in chief. In this agreement, authors of BIT whose papers are within the field of HCI are offered the opportunity to present their work at the INTERACT conference. Reciprocally, a selection of papers submitted and accepted for presentation at INTERACT are offered the opportunity to extend their contribution to be published in BIT.

IFIP TC 13 also recognizes pioneers in the area of HCI. An IFIP TC 13 pioneer is one who, through active participation in IFIP Technical Committees or related IFIP groups, has made outstanding contributions to the educational, theoretical, technical, commercial, or professional aspects of analysis, design, construction, evaluation, and use of interactive systems. IFIP TC 13 pioneers are appointed annually and awards are handed over at the INTERACT conference.

IFIP TC 13 stimulates working events and activities through its Working Groups (WGs). Working Groups consist of HCI experts from multiple countries, who seek to expand knowledge and find solutions to HCI issues and concerns within a specific domain. The list of Working Groups and their domains is given below.

WG13.1 (Education in HCI and HCI Curricula) aims to improve HCI education at all levels of higher education, coordinate and unite efforts to develop HCI curricula and promote HCI teaching.

WG13.2 (Methodology for User-Centred System Design) aims to foster research, dissemination of information and good practice in the methodical application of HCI to software engineering.

WG13.3 (HCI, Disability and Aging) aims to make HCI designers aware of the needs of people with disabilities and encourage development of information systems and tools permitting adaptation of interfaces to specific users.

WG13.4 (also WG2.7) (User Interface Engineering) investigates the nature, concepts and construction of user interfaces for software systems, using a framework for reasoning about interactive systems and an engineering model for developing UIs.

WG 13.5 (Resilience, Reliability, Safety and Human Error in System Development) seeks a framework for studying human factors relating to systems failure, develops leading edge techniques in hazard analysis and safety engineering of computer-based systems, and guides international accreditation activities for safety-critical systems.

WG13.6 (Human-Work Interaction Design) aims at establishing relationships between extensive empirical work-domain studies and HCI design. It will promote the use of knowledge, concepts, methods and techniques that enable user studies to procure a better apprehension of the complex interplay between individual, social and organizational contexts and thereby a better understanding of how and why people work in the ways that they do.

WG13.7 (Human–Computer Interaction and Visualization) aims to establish a study and research program that will combine both scientific work and practical applications in the fields of human–computer interaction and visualization. It will integrate several additional aspects of further research areas, such as scientific visualization, data mining, information design, computer graphics, cognition sciences, perception theory, or psychology, into this approach.

WG13.8 (Interaction Design and International Development) is currently working to reformulate their aims and scope.

WG13.9 (Interaction Design and Children) aims to support practitioners, regulators and researchers to develop the study of interaction design and children across international contexts.

WG13.10 (Human-Centred Technology for Sustainability) aims to promote research, design, development, evaluation, and deployment of human-centered technology to encourage sustainable use of resources in various domains.

New Working Groups are formed as areas of significance in HCI arise. Further information is available at the IFIP TC13 website: http://ifip-tc13.org/.

IFIP TC13 Members

Officers

Chairperson

Philippe Palanque, France

Vice-chair for Awards

Paula Kotze, South Africa

Vice-chair for Communications

Helen Petrie, UK

Vice-chair for Growth and Reach out INTERACT Steering Committee Chair

Jan Gulliksen, Sweden

Vice-chair for Working Groups

Simone D. J. Barbosa, Brazil

Vice-chair for Development and Equity

Julio Abascal, Spain

Treasurer

Virpi Roto, Finland

Secretary

Marco Winckler, France

INTERACT Steering Committee Chair

Anirudha Joshi, India

Country Representatives

Australia
Henry B. L. Duh
Australian Computer Society

Austria
Geraldine Fitzpatrick
Austrian Computer Society

Belgium
Bruno Dumas
IMEC – Interuniversity
Micro-Electronics Center

Brazil
Lara S. G. Piccolo
Brazilian Computer Society (SBC)

Bulgaria
Stoyan Georgiev Dentchev
Bulgarian Academy of Sciences

Croatia
Andrina Granic
Croatian Information Technology
Association (CITA)

Cyprus
Panayiotis Zaphiris
Cyprus Computer Society

Czech Republic
Zdeněk Míkovec
Czech Society for Cybernetics
and Informatics

Finland
Virpi Roto
Finnish Information Processing
Association

France
Philippe Palanque and Marco Winckler
Société informatique de France (SIF)

Germany
Tom Gross
Gesellschaft fur Informatik e.V.

Ireland
Liam J. Bannon
Irish Computer Society

Italy
Fabio Paternò
Italian Computer Society

Japan
Yoshifumi Kitamura
Information Processing Society of Japan

Netherlands
Regina Bernhaupt
Nederlands Genootschap
voor Informatica

New Zealand
Mark Apperley
New Zealand Computer Society

Norway
Frode Eika Sandnes
Norwegian Computer Society

Poland
Marcin Sikorski
Poland Academy of Sciences

Portugal
Pedro Campos
Associacão Portuguesa para o
Desenvolvimento da Sociedade da
Informação (APDSI)

Serbia
Aleksandar Jevremovic
Informatics Association of Serbia

Singapore
Shengdong Zhao
Singapore Computer Society

Slovakia
Wanda Benešová
The Slovak Society for Computer
Science

Slovenia
Matjaž Debevc
The Slovenian Computer Society
INFORMATIKA

Sri Lanka
Thilina Halloluwa
The Computer Society of Sri Lanka

South Africa
Janet L. Wesson & Paula Kotze
The Computer Society of South Africa

Sweden
Jan Gulliksen
Swedish Interdisciplinary Society for
Human-Computer Interaction
Swedish Computer Society

Switzerland
Denis Lalanne
Swiss Federation for Information
Processing

Tunisia
Mona Laroussi
Ecole Supérieure des Communications de
Tunis (SUP'COM)

United Kingdom
José Abdelnour Nocera
British Computer Society (BCS)

United Arab Emirates
Ahmed Seffah
UAE Computer Society

ACM

Gerrit van der Veer
Association for Computing
Machinery

CLEI

Jaime Sánchez
Centro Latinoamericano de Estudios en
Informatica

Expert Members

Julio Abascal, Spain
Carmelo Ardito, Italy
Nikolaos Avouris, Greece
Kaveh Bazargan, Iran
Ivan Burmistrov, Russia
Torkil Torkil Clemmensen, Denmark
Peter Forbrig, Germany
Dorian Gorgan, Romania

Anirudha Joshi, India
David Lamas, Estonia
Marta Kristin Larusdottir, Iceland
Zhengjie Liu, China
Fernando Loizides, UK/Cyprus
Ochieng Daniel "Dan" Orwa, Kenya
Eunice Sari, Australia/Indonesia

Working Group Chairpersons

**WG 13.1 (Education in HCI
and HCI Curricula)**

Konrad Baumann, Austria

**WG 13.2 (Methodologies
for User-Centered System Design)**

Regina Bernhaupt, Netherlands

WG 13.3 (HCI, Disability and Aging)

Helen Petrie, UK

**WG 13.4/2.7 (User Interface
Engineering)**

José Creissac Campos, Portugal

**WG 13.5 (Human Error, Resilience,
Reliability, Safety and System
Development)**

Chris Johnson, UK

**WG13.6 (Human-Work
Interaction Design)**

Barbara Rita Barricelli, Italy

WG13.7 (HCI and Visualization)

Peter Dannenmann, Germany

**WG 13.8 (Interaction Design
and International Development)**

José Adbelnour Nocera, UK

**WG 13.9 (Interaction Design
and Children)**

Janet Read, UK

**WG 13.10 (Human-Centred
Technology for Sustainability)**

Masood Masoodian, Finland

Conference Organizing Committee

General Conference Co-chairs

Paolo Buono, Italy
Catherine Plaisant, USA and France

Advisors

Fernando Loizides, UK
Marco Winckler, France

Technical Program Co-chairs

Carmelo Ardito, Italy
Rosa Lanzilotti, Italy
Alessio Malizia, UK and Italy

Keynote and Invited Talks Chair

Maria Francesca Costabile, Italy

Full Papers Co-chairs

Helen Petrie, UK
Antonio Piccinno, Italy

Short Papers Co-chairs

Giuseppe Desolda, Italy
Kori Inkpen, USA

Posters Co-chairs

Maristella Matera, Italy
Kent Norman, USA
Anna Spagnolli, Italy

Interactive Demos Co-chairs

Barbara Rita Barricelli, Italy
Nuno Jardim Nunes, Portugal

Panels Co-chairs

Effie Lai-Chong Law, UK
Massimo Zancanaro, Italy

Courses Co-chairs

Carmen Santoro, Italy
Nikolaos Avouris, Greece

Industrial Experiences Chair

Danilo Caivano, Italy

Workshops Co-chairs

Marta Kristín Larusdottir, Iceland
Davide Spano, Italy

Doctoral Consortium Co-chairs

Daniela Fogli, Italy
David Lamas, Estonia
John Stasko, USA

Online Experience Co-chairs

Fabrizio Balducci, Italy
Miguel Ceriani, Italy

Student Volunteers Co-chairs

Vita Santa Barletta, Italy
Grazia Ragone, UK

Publicity Co-chairs

Ganesh D. Bhutkar, India
Veronica Rossano, Italy

Local Organisation Chair

Simona Sarti, Consulta Umbria, Italy

Programme Committee

Sub-committee Chairs

Nikolaos Avouris, Greece
Regina Bernhaupt, Netherlands
Carla Dal Sasso Freitas, Brazil
Jan Gulliksen, Sweden
Paula Kotzé, South Africa
Effie Lai-Chong Law, UK

Philippe Palanque, France
Fabio Paternò, Italy
Thomas Pederson, Sweden
Albrecht Schmidt, Germany
Frank Steinicke, Germany
Gerhard Weber, Germany

Associated Chairs

José Abdelnour Nocera, UK
Raian Ali, Qatar
Florian Alt, Germany
Katrina Attwood, UK
Simone Barbosa, Brazil
Cristian Bogdan, Sweden
Paolo Bottoni, Italy
Judy Bowen, New Zealand
Daniel Buschek, Germany
Pedro Campos, Portugal
José Creissac Campos, Portugal
Luca Chittaro, Italy
Sandy Claes, Belgium
Christopher Clarke, UK
Torkil Clemmensen, Denmark
Vanessa Cobus, Germany
Ashley Colley, Finland
Aurora Constantin, UK
Lynne Coventry, UK
Yngve Dahl, Norway
Maria De Marsico, Italy
Luigi De Russis, Italy
Paloma Diaz, Spain
Monica Divitini, Norway
Mateusz Dolata, Switzerland
Bruno Dumas, Belgium
Sophie Dupuy-Chessa, France
Dan Fitton, UK
Peter Forbrig, Germany
Sandnes Frode Eika, Norway
Vivian Genaro Motti, USA
Rosella Gennari, Italy

Jens Gerken, Germany
Mareike Glöss, Sweden
Dorian Gorgan, Romania
Tom Gross, Germany
Uwe Gruenefeld, Germany
Julie Haney, USA
Ebba Þóra Hvannberg, Iceland
Netta Iivari, Finland
Nanna Inie, Denmark
Anna Sigríður Islind, Iceland
Anirudha Joshi, India
Bridget Kane, Sweden
Anne Marie Kanstrup, Denmark
Mohamed Khamis, UK
Kibum Kim, Korea
Marion Koelle, Germany
Kati Kuusinen, Denmark
Matthias Laschke, Germany
Fernando Loizides, UK
Andrés Lucero, Finland
Jo Lumsden, UK
Charlotte Magnusson, Sweden
Andrea Marrella, Italy
Célia Martinie, France
Timothy Merritt, Denmark
Zdeněk Míkovec, Czech Republic
Luciana Nedel, Brazil
Laurence Nigay, France
Valentina Nisi, Portugal
Raquel O. Prates, Brazil
Rakesh Patibanda, Australia
Simon Perrault, Singapore

Lara Piccolo, UK
Aparecido Fabiano Pinatti de Carvalho, Germany
Janet Read, UK
Karen Renaud, UK
Antonio Rizzo, Italy
Sayan Sarcar, Japan
Valentin Schwind, Germany
Gavin Sim, UK
Fotios Spyridonis, UK
Jan Stage, Denmark
Simone Stumpf, UK
Luis Teixeira, Portugal

Jakob Tholander, Sweden
Daniela Trevisan, Brazil
Stefano Valtolina, Italy
Jan Van den Bergh, Belgium
Nervo Verdezoto, UK
Chi Vi, UK
Giuliana Vitiello, Italy
Sarah Völkel, Germany
Marco Winckler, France
Dhaval Vyas, Australia
Janet Wesson, South Africa
Paweł W. Woźniak, Netherlands

Reviewers

Bruno A. Chagas, Brazil
Yasmeen Abdrabou, Germany
Maher Abujelala, USA
Jiban Adhikary, USA
Kashif Ahmad, Qatar
Muneeb Ahmad, UK
Naveed Ahmed, United Arab Emirates
Aino Ahtinen, Finland
Wolfgang Aigner, Austria
Deepak Akkil, Finland
Aftab Alam, Republic of Korea
Soraia Meneses Alarcão, Portugal
Pedro Albuquerque Santos, Portugal
Günter Alce, Sweden
Iñigo Aldalur, Spain
Alaa Alkhafaji, Iraq
Aishat Aloba, USA
Yosuef Alotaibi, UK
Taghreed Alshehri, UK
Ragaad Al-Tarawneh, USA
Alejandro Alvarez-Marin, Chile
Lucas Anastasiou, UK
Ulf Andersson, Sweden
Joseph Aneke, Italy
Mark Apperley, New Zealand
Renan Aranha, Brazil
Pierre-Emmanuel Arduin, France
Stephanie Arevalo Arboleda, Germany
Jan Argasiński, Poland

Patricia Arias-Cabarcos, Germany
Alexander Arntz, Germany
Jonas Auda, Germany
Andreas Auinger, Austria
Iuliia Avgustis, Finland
Cédric Bach, France
Miroslav Bachinski, Germany
Victor Bacu, Romania
Jan Balata, Czech Republic
Teresa Baldassarre, Italy
Fabrizio Balducci, Italy
Vijayanand Banahatti, India
Karolina Baras, Portugal
Simone Barbosa, Brazil
Vita Santa Barletta, Italy
Silvio Barra, Italy
Barbara Rita Barricelli, Italy
Ralph Barthel, UK
Thomas Baudel, France
Christine Bauer, Netherlands
Fatma Ben Mesmia, Canada
Marit Bentvelzen, Netherlands
François Bérard, France
Melanie Berger, Netherlands
Gerd Berget, Norway
Sergi Bermúdez i Badia, Portugal
Dario Bertero, UK
Guilherme Bertolaccini, Brazil
Lonni Besançon, Australia

Julie Doyle, Ireland
Philip Doyle, Ireland
Fiona Draxler, Germany
Emanuel Felipe Duarte, Brazil
Rui Duarte, Portugal
Bruno Dumas, Belgium
Mark Dunlop, UK
Sophie Dupuy-Chessa, France
Jason Dykes, UK
Chloe Eghtebas, Germany
Kevin El Haddad, Belgium
Don Samitha Elvitigala, New Zealand
Augusto Esteves, Portugal
Siri Fagernes, Norway
Katherine Fennedy, Singapore
Marta Ferreira, Portugal
Francesco Ferrise, Italy
Lauren Stacey Ferro, Italy
Christos Fidas, Greece
Daniel Finnegan, UK
Daniela Fogli, Italy
Manuel J. Fonseca, Portugal
Peter Forbrig, Germany
Rita Francese, Italy
André Freire, Brazil
Karin Fröhlich, Finland
Susanne Furman, USA
Henrique Galvan Debarba, Denmark
Sandra Gama, Portugal
Dilrukshi Gamage, Japan
Jérémie Garcia, France
Jose Garcia Estrada, Norway
David Geerts, Belgium
Denise Y. Geiskkovitch, Canada
Stefan Geisler, Germany
Mirko Gelsomini, Italy
Çağlar Genç, Finland
Rosella Gennari, Italy
Nina Gerber, Germany
Moojan Ghafurian, Canada
Maliheh Ghajargar, Sweden
Sabiha Ghellal, Germany
Debjyoti Ghosh, Germany
Michail Giannakos, Norway

Terje Gjøsæter, Norway
Marc Gonzalez Capdevila, Brazil
Julien Gori, Finland
Laurent Grisoni, France
Tor-Morten Gronli, Norway
Sebastian Günther, Germany
Li Guo, UK
Srishti Gupta, USA
Francisco Gutiérrez, Belgium
José Eder Guzman Mendoza, Mexico
Jonna Häkkilä, Finland
Lilit Hakobyan, UK
Thilina Halloluwa, Sri Lanka
Perttu Hämäläinen, Finland
Lane Harrison, USA
Michael Harrison, UK
Hanna Hasselqvist, Sweden
Tomi Heimonen, USA
Florian Heinrich, Germany
Florian Heller, Belgium
Karey Helms, Sweden
Nathalie Henry Riche, USA
Diana Hernandez-Bocanegra, Germany
Danula Hettiachchi, Australia
Wilko Heuten, Germany
Annika Hinze, New Zealand
Linda Hirsch, Germany
Sarah Hodge, UK
Sven Hoffmann, Germany
Catherine Holloway, UK
Leona Holloway, Australia
Lars Erik Holmquist, UK
Anca-Simona Horvath, Denmark
Simo Hosio, Finland
Sebastian Hubenschmid, Germany
Helena Vallo Hult, Sweden
Shah Rukh Humayoun, USA
Ebba Þóra Hvannberg, Iceland
Alon Ilsar, Australia
Md Athar Imtiaz, New Zealand
Oana Inel, Netherlands
Francisco Iniesto, UK
Andri Ioannou, Cyprus
Chyng-Yang Jang, USA

Gokul Jayakrishnan, India
Stine Johansen, Denmark
Tero Jokela, Finland
Rui José, Portugal
Anirudha Joshi, India
Manjiri Joshi, India
Jana Jost, Germany
Patrick Jost, Norway
Annika Kaltenhauser, Germany
Jin Kang, Canada
Younah Kang, Republic of Korea
Jari Kangas, Finland
Petko Karadechev, Denmark
Armağan Karahanoğlu, Netherlands
Sukran Karaosmanoglu, Germany
Alexander Kempton, Norway
Rajiv Khadka, USA
Jayden Khakurel, Finland
Pramod Khambete, India
Neeta Khanuja, Portugal
Young-Ho Kim, USA
Reuben Kirkham, Australia
Ilan Kirsh, Israel
Maria Kjærup, Denmark
Kevin Koban, Austria
Frederik Kobbelgaard, Denmark
Martin Kocur, Germany
Marius Koller, Germany
Christophe Kolski, France
Takanori Komatsu, Japan
Jemma König, New Zealand
Monika Kornacka, Poland
Thomas Kosch, Germany
Panayiotis Koutsabasis, Greece
Lucie Kruse, Germany
Przemysław Kucharski, Poland
Johannes Kunkel, Germany
Bineeth Kuriakose, Norway
Anelia Kurteva, Austria
Marc Kurz, Austria
Florian Lang, Germany
Rosa Lanzilotti, Italy
Lars Bo Larsen, Denmark
Marta Larusdottir, Iceland

Effie Law, UK
Luis Leiva, Luxembourg
Barbara Leporini, Italy
Pascal Lessel, Germany
Hongyu Li, USA
Yuan Liang, USA
Yu-Tzu Lin, Denmark
Markus Löchtefeld, Denmark
Angela Locoro, Italy
Benedikt Loepp, Germany
Domenico Lofù, Italy
Fernando Loizides, UK
Arminda Lopes, Portugal
Feiyu Lu, USA
Jo Lumsden, UK
Anders Lundström, Sweden
Kris Luyten, Belgium
Granit Luzhnica, Austria
Marc Macé, France
Anderson Maciel, Brazil
Cristiano Maciel, Brazil
Miroslav Macík, Czech Republic
Scott MacKenzie, Canada
Hanuma Teja Maddali, USA
Rui Madeira, Portugal
Alexander Maedche, Germany
Charlotte Magnusson, Sweden
Jyotirmaya Mahapatra, India
Vanessa Maike, USA
Maitreyee Maitreyee, Sweden
Ville Mäkelä, Germany
Sylvain Malacria, France
Sugandh Malhotra, India
Ivo Malý, Czech Republic
Marco Manca, Italy
Muhanad Manshad, USA
Isabel Manssour, Brazil
Panos Markopoulos, Netherlands
Karola Marky, Germany
Andrea Marrella, Italy
Andreas Martin, Switzerland
Célia Martinie, France
Nuno Martins, Portugal
Maristella Matera, Italy

Florian Mathis, UK
Andrii Matviienko, Germany
Peter Mayer, Germany
Sven Mayer, Germany
Mark McGill, UK
Donald McMillan, Sweden
Lukas Mecke, Germany
Elisa Mekler, Finland
Alessandra Melonio, Italy
Eleonora Mencarini, Italy
Maria Menendez Blanco, Italy
Aline Menin, France
Arjun Menon, Sweden
Nazmus Sakib Miazi, USA
Zdeněk Míkovec, Czech Republic
Tim Mittermeier, Germany
Emmanuel Mkpojiogu, Nigeria
Jonas Moll, Sweden
Alberto Monge Roffarello, Italy
Troels Mønsted, Denmark
Diego Morra, Italy
Jaime Munoz Arteaga, Mexico
Sachith Muthukumarana, New Zealand
Vasiliki Mylonopoulou, Sweden
Frank Nack, Netherlands
Mohammad Naiseh, UK
Vania Neris, Brazil
Robin Neuhaus, Germany
Thao Ngo, Germany
Binh Vinh Duc Nguyen, Belgium
Vickie Nguyen, USA
James Nicholson, UK
Peter Axel Nielsen, Denmark
Jasmin Niess, Germany
Evangelos Niforatos, Netherlands
Kent Norman, USA
Fatima Nunes, Brazil
Carli Ochs, Switzerland
Joseph O'Hagan, UK
Takashi Ohta, Japan
Jonas Oppenlaender, Finland
Michael Ortega, France
Changkun Ou, Germany
Yun Suen Pai, New Zealand

Dominika Palivcová, Czech Republic
Viktoria Pammer-Schindler, Austria
Eleftherios Papachristos, Denmark
Sofia Papavlasopoulou, Norway
Leonado Parra, Colombia
Max Pascher, Germany
Ankit Patel, Portugal
Fabio Paternò, Italy
Maria Angela Pellegrino, Italy
Anthony Perritano, USA
Johanna Persson, Sweden
Ken Pfeuffer, Germany
Bastian Pfleging, Netherlands
Vung Pham, USA
Jayesh Pillai, India
Catherine Plaisant, USA
Henning Pohl, Denmark
Margit Pohl, Austria
Alessandro Pollini, Italy
Dorin-Mircea Popovici, Romania
Thiago Porcino, Brazil
Dominic Potts, UK
Sarah Prange, Germany
Marco Procaccini, Italy
Arnaud Prouzeau, France
Parinya Punpongsanon, Japan
Sónia Rafael, Portugal
Jessica Rahman, Australia
Mikko Rajanen, Finland
Nimmi Rangaswamy, India
Alberto Raposo, Brazil
George Raptis, Greece
Hanae Rateau, Canada
Sebastian Rauh, Germany
Hirak Ray, USA
Traian Rebedea, Romania
Yosra Rekik, France
Elizabeth Rendon-Velez, Colombia
Malte Ressin, UK
Tera Reynolds, USA
Miguel Ribeiro, Portugal
Maria Rigou, Greece
Sirpa Riihiaho, Finland
Michele Risi, Italy

Radiah Rivu, Germany
Mehdi Rizvi, Italy
Judy Robertson, UK
Michael Rohs, Germany
Marco Romano, Italy
Anton Rosén, Sweden
Veronica Rossano, Italy
Virpi Roto, Finland
Debjani Roy, India
Matthew Rueben, USA
Vit Rusnak, Czech Republic
Philippa Ryan, UK
Thomas Ryberg, Denmark
Rufat Rzayev, Germany
Parisa Saadati, UK
Adrian Sabou, Romania
Ofir Sadka, Israel
Juan Pablo Saenz, Italy
Marco Saltarella, Italy
Sanjit Samaddar, UK
Ivan Sanchez Milara, Finland
Frode Eika Sandnes, Norway
Leonardo Sandoval, UK
Carmen Santoro, Italy
Pratiti Sarkar, India
Guilherme Schardong, Brazil
Christina Schmidbauer, Austria
Eike Schneiders, Denmark
Maximilian Schrapel, Germany
Sabrina Scuri, Portugal
Korok Sengupta, Germany
Marta Serafini, Italy
Marcos Serrano, France
Kshitij Sharma, Norway
Sumita Sharma, Finland
Akihisa Shitara, Japan
Mark Shovman, Israel
Ludwig Sidenmark, UK
Carlos Silva, Portugal
Tiago Silva da Silva, Brazil
Milene Silveira, Brazil
James Simpson, Australia
Ashwin Singh, India
Laurianne Sitbon, Australia

Mikael B. Skov, Denmark
Pavel Slavik, Czech Republic
Aidan Slingsby, UK
K. Tara Smith, UK
Ellis Solaiman, UK
Andreas Sonderegger, Switzerland
Erik Sonnleitner, Austria
Keyur Sorathia, India
Emanuel Sousa, Portugal
Sonia Sousa, Estonia
Anna Spagnolli, Italy
Davide Spallazzo, Italy
Lucio Davide Spano, Italy
Katta Spiel, Austria
Priyanka Srivastava, India
Katarzyna Stawarz, UK
Teodor Stefanut, Romania
Mari-Klara Stein, Denmark
Jonathan Strahl, Finland
Tim Stratmann, Germany
Christian Sturm, Germany
Michael Svangren, Denmark
Aurélien Tabard, France
Benjamin Tag, Australia
Federico Tajariol, France
Aishwari Talhan, Republic of Korea
Maurizio Teli, Denmark
Subrata Tikadar, India
Helena Tobiasson, Sweden
Guy Toko, South Africa
Brianna Tomlinson, USA
Olof Torgersson, Sweden
Genoveffa Tortora, Italy
Zachary O. Toups, USA
Scott Trent, Japan
Philippe Truillet, France
Tommaso Turchi, UK
Fanny Vainionpää, Finland
Stefano Valtolina, Italy
Niels van Berkel, Denmark
Jan Van den Bergh, Belgium
Joey van der Bie, Netherlands
Bram van Deurzen, Belgium
Domenique van Gennip, Australia

Partners and Sponsors

Partners

International Federation for Information Processing

In-cooperation with ACM   In-cooperation with SIGCHI

Sponsors

EULOGIC

eusoft
more than a LIMS

Experis™
ManpowerGroup

exprivia

openwork
Just solutions

ORA ZERO
GROUP

sincon
ICT SOLUTIONS

Contents – Part V

Courses

Industrial Experiences

Panels

Posters

Workshops

User Studies

Effects of Personal Characteristics on Temporal Response Patterns in Ecological Momentary Assessments

Tomu Tominaga$^{(\boxtimes)}$, Shuhei Yamamoto, Takeshi Kurashima, and Hiroyuki Toda

NTT Service Evolution Laboratories, NTT Corporation, Yokosuka, Japan
{tomu.tominaga.hm,shuhei.yamamoto.ea,takeshi.kurashima.uf, hiroyuki.toda.xb}@hco.ntt.co.jp

Abstract. Response rates to Ecological Momentary Assessment (EMA) questions vary among individuals, which inevitably results in a disproportionate distribution of the volume of EMA data to personal characteristics. Previous research has explored how response rates are influenced by subjects' characteristics; however, few studies focused on temporal patterns of responses to EMA questions. In this study, we examined the relationship of personal characteristics with temporal response patterns by using StudentLife dataset. From this dataset, we adopted scales of personality traits (neuroticism, extraversion, openness, agreeableness, conscientiousness) and mental status (depression, stress, loneliness, life satisfaction) as subjects' personal characteristics, and analyzed how these characteristics relate to the subjects' temporal response patterns for EMA questions. Primary results of our analyses using regression models and latent growth curve models indicated that the subjects who reported high stress levels had a higher total number of EMA responses, but the number of responses from these subjects tended to decrease strongly throughout the experiment, especially after a stressful event such as the midterm examination. We also found that the subjects who reported low extraversion had a weak tendency to decrease the number of EMA responses throughout the experiment, but the number of EMA responses of these subjects decreased strongly after a social event such as the school festival. Based on our results, we discussed how the data collected with EMA studies are biased not only in terms of personal characteristics but also with timings.

Keywords: Ecological Momentary Assessment · StudentLife · Human factors

1 Introduction

Ecological Momentary Assessment (EMA), also known as Experience Sampling Method, is a longitudinal research methodology that asks study subjects in natural environments to continuously report their current thoughts, feelings, behaviors, or experiences in real-time [29]. Unlike traditional questionnaire surveys

Published by Springer Nature Switzerland AG 2021
C. Ardito et al. (Eds.): INTERACT 2021, LNCS 12936, pp. 3–22, 2021.
https://doi.org/10.1007/978-3-030-85607-6_1

in a lab setting, EMA captures within-subject fluctuations of perceived states (e.g., emotion) while improving ecological validity and reducing recall bias. Thus, the EMA data have been widely used for various applications (medical validations [32, 36], mood predictions [22, 27, 28], and so on) as ground truth data of the time-series changes in the values of people's subjective evaluations of their states.

In order to construct reliable EMA datasets, it is important for EMA to obtain a large number of responses uniformly covering various conditions (e.g., subjects, situations, etc.); however, past studies have shown that it is difficult to collect responses from subjects with specific characteristics [19, 23, 30, 37]. For example, subjects with mental illness [19] or young subjects [20, 37] were found to have low response rates. A response rate refers to the number or ratio of responses to the EMA questions from a subject within some duration. These previous studies show the conditions that bias EMA data against personal characteristics. Describing such conditions is a fundamental issue in EMA research, because it enables us to correctly evaluate and discuss the limitations and reliability of findings drawn from EMA data.

Although prior work has examined the relationships between subjects' personal characteristics and their EMA response rates, the effect of personal characteristics on temporal changes in response rates (e.g., slopes of EMA response frequency over time) has not been well studied yet. In our assumption, when stressed people experience a tense or anxious event, they may spend less time answering EMA questions because they are focused on dealing with that event. Examining this issue has the fundamental contribution of describing in detail the conditions that cause bias in EMA data, not only in terms of personal characteristics but also in terms of timing. If we understand when subjects with certain characteristics will not respond, it becomes possible to design experiments that encourage those subjects to respond at those times. This will contribute to the original purpose of EMA, which is to collect data uniformly under various conditions.

To understand how EMA data can be biased by the subjects' personal characteristics and time, this paper analyzes the relationship between subjects' personal characteristics and their temporal patterns of EMA responses. For the analysis, we used four metrics to characterize the temporal response patterns: (1) *continuity*: how long a subject kept responding to the EMA questions, (2) *frequency*: how many EMA questions a subject responded to per day, (3) *overall slope*: how the number of EMA responses per day for a subject increase/decrease over time, and (4) *period-separated slopes*: how the increase/decrease in EMA response numbers per day over time for a subject vary between time periods. Therefore, this paper addresses the following research questions.

RQ1 *What kind of personal characteristics affect continuity?*
RQ2 *What kind of personal characteristics affect frequency?*
RQ3 *What kind of personal characteristics affect overall slope?*
RQ4 *What kind of personal characteristics affect period-separated slopes?*

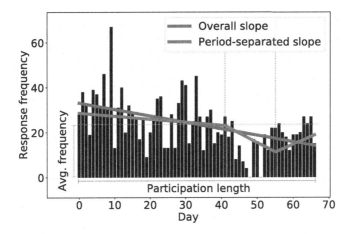

Fig. 1. A sample case of a subject: relationship of *continuity* (participation length), *frequency* (average of daily frequency), *overall slope*, and *period-separated slopes* with daily frequency of EMA responses (the bar colored in black). For period-separated slopes, three periods are given: week #1–#6 (day 0–41), week #6–#8 (day 42–55), and week #8–#10 (day 56–67). Note that overall slope is introduced from daily frequency, and that period-separated slopes are calculated from daily frequency per week.

The four metrics extracted from the daily frequency of EMA responses are shown in Fig. 1. We measured *continuity* as the difference between the first and the last response time to the EMA in order to assess how long subjects keep participating in the experiment, and *frequency* as the average number of EMA responses per day to elucidate how active subjects were in making EMA responses. We scaled *overall slope* as a linear trend component of daily frequency of EMA responses throughout the experiment to understand the overall trend in the number of responses to EMA over time. Moreover, we quantified *period-separated slopes* as linear trend components of week-level daily frequency of EMA responses in each of the periods stipulated for discovering how slopes differ between the periods (we set the periods by considering the events of the university (e.g., the midterm examination and the school festival) and the validity of the models used for the analysis).

For our analyses, we used StudentLife dataset [38]. StudentLife [38] followed 48 students at Dartmouth University over 10 weeks to collect responses for EMA questions, answers to questionnaire surveys, and passively-sensed data (e.g., wifi logs). The dataset also contains information about the school events including the examination period and the school festival at the university. In this paper, we used all of the EMA data to measure response rates of subjects. We also used the questionnaire data of personality traits (neuroticism, extraversion, openness, conscientiousness, and agreeableness) and mental status (depression, perceived stress, loneliness, and flourishing) as personal characteristics.

To address RQ1, RQ2, and RQ3, we run a series of regression analyses to explain a participation length (i.e., continuity), an average of daily frequency of

EMA responses (i.e., frequency), and a linear trend component of daily frequency of EMA responses (i.e., overall slope) from personal characteristics (i.e., scales of personality traits and mental status). Concerning RQ4, we used week-level daily frequency of EMA responses to account the influence of the midterm examination and the school festival, which are week-level events. We then adopted latent growth curve models to define the periods so that the trend components in each period (i.e., period-separated slopes) is well fitted to the week-level daily frequency, and to examine how the period-separated slopes are explained by personal characteristics.

Primary results indicated that subjects who reported high stress levels had a higher total number of EMA responses, but those subjects tended to strongly decrease the number of responses throughout the experiment, especially after the midterm examination. We also found that the subjects who reported low extraversion exhibited a slight decrease in the number of EMA responses throughout the experiment, but the number of EMA responses of these subjects decreased strongly after the school festival. Based on these results, we discussed the disproportion of EMA data in terms of subjects and timings, and described implications for understanding the limitations of EMA studies.

2   Related Work

EMA has been recognized as a powerful method for recording people's subjective states such as emotions, thoughts, and experiences over time. The nature of EMA is that the experimenter intermittently sends questions to the subjects through portable devices, and the subjects answer the questions in real time in the situation. Therefore, EMA has less recall bias and higher ecological validity than conventional questionnaire surveys. The data collected with EMA have been used for various purposes such as identifying behavioral patterns [11, 26, 38], predicting life outcomes [8, 40], and understanding human relationships [10, 13].

As shown above, many studies have been developed on the basis of EMA data, but it has been pointed out that EMA data contain various biases [19]. There are three primary types of factors behind the bias: subject factors, contextual factors, and design factors. Subject factors refer to the characteristics of the subject of the EMA experiment, including demographic attributes [20, 37], psychological state [30, 37], and mental health status [14, 37]. For example, male subjects [20, 37], young subjects [20, 37], subjects with high alcohol consumption [30], subjects with negative emotions [30], and subjects with psychotic disorder [19, 30, 37] are known to have lower response rates. Vachon et al.'s meta-analysis [37] also found that including more males and subjects with psychotic disorders yielded lower response rates. These findings indicate that EMA data is biased by such subject-dependent factors.

Contextual factors, which are properties of the environment in which the experiment is carried out (e.g., time [3, 5], place [5], daily occurrences [3], etc.), also create a bias. According to an investigation of temporal and spatial distributions of EMA responses, subjects were more likely to respond in the middle of the night than in the morning, and more likely to respond in places such as hospitals and restaurants rather than on the move [5]. Moreover, van Berkel et al. [3] examined how the probability of individual EMA questions being answered is influenced by contextual factors (e.g., number of notifications received in the last 15 min), and found that high-compliance subjects were likely to respond to EMA questions if they received recent notifications frequently. In this way, environmental properties can distort the distributions of EMA data.

Design factors refer to the characteristics of the experimental design of EMA, including the incentives [20, 37], frequency of questions [30], and methods of data sampling [37]. The experimental conditions under which EMA is carried out can lead to biased EMA data. For example, more EMA responses are collected if EMA questions are sent when the phone screen unlock event is detected than if they are sent randomly or periodically [4]. However, Lathia et al. [17] pointed out that controlling the timing of EMA questions by triggers based on passively-sensed data also causes a bias in that the number or values of EMA answers vary unevenly over time. A previous study that conducted sampling based on information captured by accelerometer, GPS, microphone sensor, smartphone screen usage status, and telephone/email, found that 25% of all responses were recorded between 10:00 and 13:00 [17]. This is different from the other result [5] which found that the response rate is highest in the middle of the night when EMA questions are sent randomly with respect to time. This discrepancy indicates that bias in EMA data can be caused by the experimental design.

These previous works on EMA data bias examined the number (probability) of EMA responses of subjects; however, trajectories of response rates have seldom been analyzed. Additionally, the effect of subject factors on the trajectories have not been well studied. In other words, the issue of which subjects' data are missing at which time has not been adequately examined. By clarifying this, we will be able to understand how EMA data is missing and biased, not only in terms of personal characteristics, but also in terms of time. These findings can also support optimization of EMA experiment design to determine which subjects should be asked to respond and when with the goal of securing more unbiased responses. Therefore, this study aims to examine how personal characteristics relate to the temporal variation of the response rates and to derive new knowledge about the bias of EMA data against time.

3   Dataset

To accomplish our research goals, we used the StudentLife dataset [38]. StudentLife [38] conducted traditional questionnaire surveys to identify personal characteristics, adopted EMA to observe ongoing situations or experiences, and used built-in sensors of smartphones to measure activities automatically. The obtained data was published as the StudentLife dataset for third parties. From the dataset, we used the records that paired questionnaire survey answers with EMA responses to assess how personal characteristics are associated with EMA responses. Details of these records are explained below.

3.1   EMA Data

The StudentLife dataset has subjects' responses to EMA questions concerning emotions, stress, sleep, and so on. We used all of the responses to introduce continuity, frequency, overall slope, and period-separated slopes. In total, 20,027 EMA responses were used for our analyses.

3.2   Personal Characteristics

This study describes personal characteristics with personality traits and mental status. The scales of personality traits follow the Big Five personality traits [21], defining personality from five dimensions: *neuroticism* (sensitive/nervous vs. resilient/confident), *extraversion* (outgoing/energetic vs. solitary/reserved), *openness* (inventive/curious vs. consistent/cautious), *conscientiousness* (efficient/organized vs. extravagant/careless), and *agreeableness* (friendly/compassionate vs. challenging/callous) [24]. The scales of depression, stress, loneliness, and life satisfaction were, respectively, measured using PHQ-9 [15], Perceived Stress Scale [6], UCLA Loneliness Scale [25], and Flourishing Scale [9]. In the StudentLife project, these surveys were conducted twice: at the beginning and the end. We used the scales obtained at the beginning (pre-survey).

For our analysis, we excluded subjects who did not answer all questionnaire items; 42 subjects remained. Table 1 shows the descriptive statistics of the measured values of the 42 subjects.

4   Analysis

We conducted a series of regression analyses for RQ1, RQ2, and RQ3, assessing how personal characteristics influence continuity, frequency, and overall slope. We also used latent growth curve models to examine how personal characteristics affect period-separated slopes. These procedures are explained below.

4.1   Personal Characteristics vs. Continuity, Frequency, and Overall Slope

In the series of regression analyses, continuity, frequency, and overall slope were used as objective variables, while personal characteristics are introduced as explanatory variables. The explanatory variables were standardized so that the mean is 0 and the standard deviation is 1. We took the partial regression coefficients yielded by these analyses as the effects of personal characteristics on the continuity, frequency, and overall slope of EMA responses. We considered the statistically significant partial regression coefficients in discussing the impact of personal characteristics.

Table 1. Left: descriptive statistics of scales of personal characteristics. Right: the number of questions (#) and the scales of answer options (answer scales) of each questionnaire. Concerning depression scale, the score ranges from 0 to 27 and is transferred into five levels of severity: 1. minimal (0–4), 2. minor (5–9), 3. moderate (10–14), 4. moderately severe (15–19), and 5. severe (20–27). We used the levels in our analyses.

Measure	Mean	S.D.	Min	1st Q.	Med.	3rd Q.	Max.	#	Scales
Mental status									
Depression scale	2.25	0.98	1	2.00	2.00	3.00	5	9	0–3[a]
Perceived stress scale	20.60	3.99	9	18.75	20.00	24.00	28	10	0–4[b]
Flourishing scale	41.20	10.90	25	32.00	39.50	50.25	64	8	1–7[c]
Loneliness scale	42.40	7.87	16	37.00	45.00	48.00	54	20	1–4[d]
Personality traits									
Neuroticism	23.78	5.63	14	20.00	23.00	27.25	36	8	1–5[e]
Extraversion	23.40	6.33	13	18.75	23.00	27.25	36	8	1–5[e]
Openness	35.88	4.85	25	33.00	36.00	38.25	46	10	1–5[e]
Agreeableness	32.83	5.62	12	30.00	34.00	37.00	41	9	1–5[e]
Conscientiousness	30.85	6.45	17	26.00	31.00	34.25	43	9	1–5[e]

[a]not at all – very often, [b]never – very often, [c]strongly disagree – strongly agree
[d]never – often, [e]disagree strongly – agree strongly

4.2 Personal Characteristics vs. Period-Separated Slopes

To assess how personal characteristics affect the period-separated slopes, we adopted latent growth curve (LGC) models. In this analysis, we used the week-level daily frequency of EMA responses. LGC models enable us to examine normative and individual-level changes in EMA responses over the weeks covered by the EMA experiment. In the following part, we firstly described LGC models. We then explained how to use LGC models for assessing the normative and individual-level changes.

Latent Growth Curve (LGC) Models. LGC modeling is a statistical technique based on the structural equation modeling framework to estimate growth trajectories of observed data. There are two types of the estimated variables: intercept and slopes. Intercept refers to the initial value of the growth trajectory. Slopes represent the linear trends of the growth trajectory. To represent the observed data, LGC models introduce several latent variables, which are equivalent to the intercept and slopes of the observed data.

To capture the trajectory more finely, piecewise LGC modeling is adapted. This approach separates the observation duration into multiple periods and fits linear models to the observed data in each period. The separation approach can be based on visual inspection or interpretability of results. For example, if the trajectory explicitly shows different trends before and after at a time point or if some influential events occur at multiple time points, the observation duration can be separated by the point(s).

According to the separation, LGC models automatically determine the number of latent variables. If the duration is separated into two periods, the number of the latent variables is three: the intercept and the slopes in each period. When inferring the latent variables, LGC models generally assume that values of the observation data grow or decline linearly. Based on this assumption, LGC models determine effects of the slopes on the observation data in the corresponding periods.

Afterward, LGC models infer the latent variables so that the models fit the observed data. Overall model fit is measured by RMSEA (Root Mean Square Error of Approximation) [31], CFI (Comparative Fit Index) [2], and TLI (Tucker-Lewis Index) [35].

LGC Models for Normative Changes. To model normative dynamics of EMA responses, we used piecewise LGC models. In this study, we separated the observation duration by week #6 and #8 into three periods: period I (week #1-#6), period II (week #6-#8), and period III (week #8-#10). We then adopted the LGC model according to this separation, leading the model to infer four latent variables: the initial status at week #1 (intercept) and the slopes in the period I, II, and III. There are two reasons for this separation.

First, we hypothesized that the way of responding to EMA questions is influenced by the midterm examination and the school festival, as indicated by prior work [11,39]. The examination was conducted from week #3 to #5 and the festival was held during week #7. To capture differences in EMA responses before and after these events, we separated the duration by week #6 and #8. The scheme of the separation enables us to reasonably interpret our results because we can discuss how slopes are different according to such influential events.

Second, we confirmed that the LGC model separating the duration by week #6 and #8 fits the observed data the best. Other than the #6-and-#8 separation, we have candidates of separation by 1 knot (e.g., separating by week #4), 2 knots (e.g., separating by week #5 and #7), or 3 knots (e.g., separating by week #3, #6, and #8). To avoid over-fitting, we excluded the strategies of 3-knots separations. For models based on 1-knot and 2-knots separations, we calculated the model fit measures. As a result, the model separating the duration by week #6 and #8 was the best for all model fit measures among those models.

For the above reasons, we adopted the LGC model separating the observation duration by week #6 and #8. For simplicity, the LGC model for normative changes of EMA responses is called unconditional model later in this paper.

LGC Models for Individual-Level Changes. To build LGC models for individual-level change, we introduced the factor of interest (personal characteristics here) into the unconditional model. LGC models can use the factor of interest to explain variances in each latent variable with regression. This model is called the conditional model.

Table 2. Regression models explaining (1) continuity, (2) frequency, and (3) overall slope of EMA responses from personal characteristics. Note that β is a partial regression coefficient, S.E. is standard error, and p is p-value (***...$p < 0.001$, **...$p < 0.01$, *...$p < 0.05$).

Measure	Continuity			Frequency			Overall slope		
	β	S.E.	p	β	S.E.	p	β	S.E.	p
(Intercept)	55.91	2.83	***	436.65	47.82	***	−0.120	0.012	***
Mental status									
Depression scale	−2.56	3.43		−107.60	57.94		−0.004	0.014	
Perceived stress scale	4.82	3.37		119.23	57.06	*	−0.033	0.015	*
Flourishing scale	1.71	3.58		15.82	60.57		0.013	0.015	
Loneliness scale	1.03	4.21		77.63	71.15		−0.025	0.018	
Personality traits									
Neuroticism	0.20	4.28		55.25	72.36		−0.011	0.018	
Extraversion	−1.74	3.73		11.06	63.01		−0.035	0.016	*
Openness	1.04	3.18		−3.63	53.85		0.026	0.014	
Agreeableness	−3.75	3.96		45.98	67.05		−0.001	0.016	
Conscientiousness	1.25	3.49		25.07	59.08		−0.034	0.015	*

Our analyses considered nine personal characteristics, thus we built nine kinds of conditional models. As for the unconditional model, the model fit of the conditional model is calculated using RMSEA, CFI, and TLI.

5 Results

5.1 Personal Characteristics vs. Continuity, Frequency, and Overall Slope

Table 2 shows the partial regression coefficients of personal characteristics for continuity, frequency, and overall slope. The intercept in the models represents values of the objective variables of a subject whose all explanatory variables are 0 (i.e., average). Thus, on average, the subjects made 436.65 EMA responses, participated in the experiment for 55.91 days, and reduced the number of responses by 0.12 per day. Betas mean the effect of personal characteristics on the continuity, frequency, and overall slope of EMA responses.

We found a significantly positive coefficient of the perceived stress scale for the frequency of responses to EMA questions ($\beta = 119.23^*$). This means that subjects with higher perceived stress make more responses in total than those with lower perceived stress. Furthermore, we found that perceived stress scale, extraversion, and conscientiousness have significantly negative effects on the overall slope of the daily frequency of EMA responses ($\beta = -0.033^*, -0.035^*, -0.034^*$). These results indicated that the higher the subject's perceived stress,

Table 3. Unconditional and conditional latent growth curve models for EMA responses (note that all predictors are scaled so that the mean is 1 and standard deviation is 0). M. is the mean value of the latent variables (intercept, slopes in period I, II, and III) of the unconditional model. V. represents the variance of the latent variables of the unconditional model. β and S.E. mean, respectively, the partial regression coefficient and its standard error of predictors in the conditional models (***...$p < 0.001$, **...$p < 0.01$, *...$p < 0.05$).

Model/Predictor	Model Fit Measures			Intercept		Slope in period I		Slope in period II		Slope in period III	
	RMSEA	CFI	TLI	M./β_0	V./S.E.	M./β_1	V./S.E.	M./β_2	V./S.E.	M./β_3	V./S.E.
Unconditional model	0.149	0.923	0.915	10.82 ***	25.79 ***	−0.96 ***	0.61 **	−0.84 **	2.03 **	−0.79 **	2.26 **
Mental status											
Depression scale	0.140	0.922	0.909	0.14	0.90	−0.16	0.15	−0.25	0.26	0.25	0.27
Perceived stress scale	0.142	0.921	0.908	1.88 *	0.85	−0.04	0.15	−0.68 **	0.24	0.26	0.27
Flourishing scale	0.142	0.920	0.906	−0.54	0.89	0.18	0.15	0.20	0.26	−0.13	0.27
Loneliness scale	0.139	0.923	0.910	1.50	0.86	−0.29	0.15	0.16	0.26	−0.14	0.27
Personality traits											
Neuroticism	0.146	0.916	0.901	0.71	0.89	0.02	0.15	−0.11	0.26	−0.12	0.27
Extraversion	0.146	0.916	0.902	0.13	0.90	−0.27	0.15	0.03	0.26	0.52 *	0.26
Openness	0.138	0.923	0.910	−0.29	0.89	0.11	0.15	0.17	0.26	−0.10	0.27
Agreeableness	0.145	0.918	0.904	−1.48	0.86	0.31 *	0.15	0.00	0.26	0.33	0.26
Conscientiousness	0.151	0.911	0.896	1.11	0.88	−0.19	0.15	−0.17	0.26	−0.24	0.27

extraversion, and conscientiousness, the stronger the decrease in EMA frequency for the total duration. We did not find significant coefficients of personal characteristics for continuity, implying that personal characteristics were not effective in explaining variances of the participation length.

5.2 Personal Characteristics vs. Period-Separated Slopes

Table 3 shows results obtained from LGC models. The unconditional model shows significantly negative slopes for all periods ($M. = -0.96^{***}$ (period I), -0.84^{**} (period II), -0.79^{**} (period III)). This is consistent with the result that the overall slope of daily EMA frequency is negative, which was obtained in answering RQ3. Moreover, the variances in the intercept and slopes in each period were significantly large ($V. = 25.79^{***}$ (intercept), 0.61^{**} (period I), 2.03^{**} (period II), 2.26^{**} (period III)). These results mean that overall, the frequency of EMA responses decreased over time, but the values of initial status (i.e., intercept) and the slopes significantly varied among the subjects.

The conditional models can explain the variations of the initial values and the slopes among the subjects. The perceived stress scale was found to have a positive effect on the initial value ($\beta_0 = 1.88^*$) and a negative effect on the slope in period II ($\beta_2 = -0.68^{**}$). The positive effect is consistent with the result that subjects with higher perceived stress respond to EMA questions more frequently, which was obtained in answering RQ2. The negative effect means that the higher the perceived stress, the more strongly the EMA response rate decreased after the end of the examination period.

We also found that extraversion had a positive effect on the slope in period III ($\beta_3 = 0.52^*$). It means that the lower the extraversion (i.e., the higher introversion), the more strongly the EMA response rate decreased after the school festival.

Moreover, our results showed that agreeableness had a positive effect on the slope in period I ($\beta_1 = 0.31^*$). It indicates that, in the initial duration of the experiment, subjects with higher agreeableness decreased the EMA response rates more strongly.

6 Discussion

6.1 Influential Factors

As indicated by our results, perceived stress, extraversion, conscientiousness, and agreeableness are influential factors for EMA response rates. Here, we discussed why these factors were significant.

Effects of Perceived Stress. Indicated by our results, subjects with higher perceived stress entered EMA responses at higher levels of daily frequency. According to the previous research [18], stressful individuals prefer disclosing themselves to machines (e.g., virtual agents) rather than to real people. In the context of EMA studies, answering EMA questions can be an activity of disclosing themselves to machines such as entering their emotions with the portable devices. Therefore, the EMA response rates of subjects with higher perceived stress were generally higher.

Subjects with higher perceived stress were also found to have stronger negative overall slopes. As mentioned above, such subjects tended to have a larger volume of EMA responses. This corresponds to a large amount of decrease margin, which may simply yield stronger decreasing trends.

The slope of response rates of subjects with higher perceived stress was found to be strongly negative particularly after the examination period. As discussed in prior work [11], the midterm examination might create extreme pressure for the students. Such stress often makes people disclose themselves to machines than to real people [18]. Considering this background, subjects with higher perceived stress may have disclosed themselves less frequently in the EMA questions after the examination, because they were released from their stress imposed by the tense event.

Effects of Extraversion (Introversion). We found that subjects with higher extraversion showed a stronger negative overall slopes. It was also seen that subjects with higher extraversion showed a stronger positive slope after the school festival (i.e., in period III). These results seem to be contradictory. We start by explaining how to interpret these results.

As shown in Table 3, the period-separated slopes of the conditional model with extraversion in period I, II, and III are -0.27, 0.03, and 0.52. From these values, we can derive that an overall effect of extraversion on the slope at week level is -0.25 ($-0.27 \cdot 5 + 0.03 \cdot 2 + 0.52 \cdot 2$). As shown in Table 2, the effect of extraversion on the overall slope at a day level is -0.035. Both are consistently negative. Therefore, extraversion was found to have a significantly positive effect on the slope in period III; however, it totally has a negative effect considering the period-separated slopes and the duration of each period.

We here explain why subjects with lower extraversion (i.e., higher introversion) showed a stronger negative slope in period III. Introverted people prefer reflecting on their internal aspects [1,34]. Answering EMA questions such as telling their mood or behaviors can be an activity indicative of reflection. According to the prior work [33], such reflection needs their psychological energy. However, the psychological energy is limited: it is consumed by social interactions [12]. Considering this, we assumed that introverted subjects depleted their psychological energy through social interaction such as the school festival, which led to a decrease in the EMA response rate.

To see whether introverted subjects engaged in social interaction, we examined the duration of subjects' daily conversations. The conversation durations were estimated by audio classification of microphone data [16,22]. They are stored in the StudentLife dataset. Following the prior work [11], we used the data as indicators of social activities.

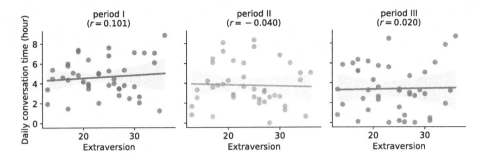

Fig. 2. Extraversion and daily averages of conversation time in each period. Note that each subject has three points (conversation time in period I, II and III). r represents correlation coefficients between extraversion and conversation time in each period.

Figure 2 shows the relationship between the conversation duration (the y-axis) and the extraversion (the x-axis) for each period. Extraversion and daily conversation time show slightly positive correlations in period I and III, but a slightly negative correlation in period II. Considering that highly extroverted people prefer social interaction, we can expect to see the same trend in period II as in period I and III. Contrary to this expectation, the association in period II shows a negative correlation. This means that the introverted subjects engaged in social interaction more than expected. However, it should be noted that these correlations are weak and not statistically significant. Therefore, our assumption was not completely supported, though it was confirmed in a weak trend.

Effects of Conscientiousness. Subjects with higher conscientiousness were found to have stronger negative slopes of the frequency of EMA responses, but conscientiousness did not have any significant effect on continuity and frequency. In general, people with high conscientiousness are known to show self-discipline, act dutifully, and aim for achievement [7]. Thus, subjects with high conscientiousness are expected to make many responses continuously, which is inconsistent with our results.

To understand this, we extracted top-5 subjects and bottom-5 subjects in terms of conscientiousness, and compared their week-level daily frequencies. Figure 3 shows the week-level daily frequency of these subjects. The daily frequency at week #1 of the top-5 subjects is higher than that of the bottom-5 subjects. Considering that continuity was not associated with conscientiousness, this means that subjects with a conscientious personality entered EMA responses in the early stage of the experiment, but not in the following period.

Moreover, the top-5 subjects showed a strong decrease in the EMA frequency from week #5 to #6, which is included in the examination period. After the event, the daily frequency of these subjects also gradually decreased. According to the previous work, the subjects with higher conscientiousness had higher GPA scores [39]. This implies that these subjects gave more weight on the midterm

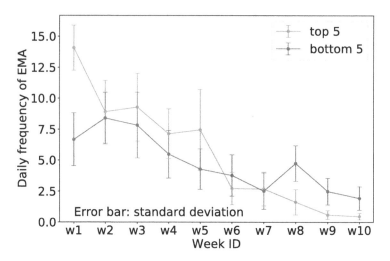

Fig. 3. Week-level daily frequency of top-5 and bottom-5 subjects in terms of conscientiousness.

examination than the EMA experiment. This might lead them to make fewer responses around this event.

To sum up, the highly conscientious subjects made more EMA responses in the early stage of the experiment but not in the following period. They also avoided answering EMA questions during (and after) a part of the examination period because they concentrated on the examination. As a result, conscientious personality had negative influence on the overall slope, but did not significantly affect frequency or continuity.

Effects of Agreeableness. Agreeableness was found to weaken the slope in period I. To understand this more deeply, we first separated the subjects into two groups by the mean value of agreeableness: high $(N = 24)$ and low $(N = 18)$ groups. We then compared the week-level daily EMA frequency of these groups. As shown in Fig. 4(a), the high group shows a strong increase from week 1 to week 2. We assumed that the subjects in the high group tended to delay making their initial EMA response.

To assess our assumption, we compared the time from the start of the experiment to the first time of making EMA response across these groups. Figure 4(b) shows the distributions of the number of subjects for the time between the start of the experiment and the first EMA response. For these distributions, we conducted Welch's t-test to see whether the mean values of the time are statistically different across these groups. As a result, we confirmed the mean value of the high group was higher than that of the low group $(t = 2.245, p < 0.05)$. Therefore, our assumption was confirmed. However, we could not understand why the subjects with higher agreeableness delayed making their initial responses to EMA questions. Assessing this issue is a future task.

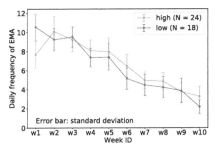

(a) Daily EMA frequency in each week.

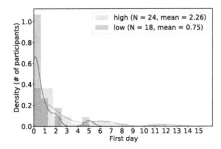

(b) Distributions and density curves of time from the start of the experiment to the first EMA response.

Fig. 4. Comparison of week-level EMA frequency and initial response time by high and low groups of agreeableness.

6.2   Theoretical Implications

Based on the above results and discussion, we discussed here how EMA data is biased according to personal characteristics and timing. In this discussion, the bias in EMA data can be divided into two types: *overall bias* and *local bias*. Overall bias refers to the fact that the EMA responses collected are biased toward subjects with certain characteristics. Local bias refers to the fact that the collected EMA responses are biased toward subjects with certain characteristics at a particular period or timing. The implications of overall bias and local bias are summarized in Table 4.

Among the personal characteristics in this study, perceived stress can be a factor behind overall bias, because it yields differences in the frequency of daily EMA responses among subjects. More specifically, it means that the EMA data is more likely to contain responses from subjects with higher perceived stress levels. The other personal characteristics were not found to cause overall bias, indicating that the overall proportion of EMA data is not biased by the personal characteristics other than perceived stress.

Local bias refers to the fact that the collected EMA responses are biased toward subjects with certain characteristics at a particular period or timing. The extent of local bias can be explained by the steepness of overall slopes of response rates. Our results indicated that subjects with higher perceived stress, extraversion, and conscientiousness had stronger negative overall slopes. This means that the EMA responses of subjects with these personal characteristics decrease over time strongly. In other words, the percentage of responses from subjects with a high degree of these personal characteristics is high in the early period of the survey, compared to the percentage in the later period of the survey. In this manner, the distribution of these personal characteristics in the EMA data is skewed for time.

The extent of local bias can be also explained by period-separated slopes, that is, the slopes of response rates in specific period. In the early stage of the

Table 4. EMA data bias and personal characteristics.

Bias type	Personal characteristic	Description (In the EMA data collected, ...)
Overall bias	Perceived stress	% responses from subjects with high degree of it is large
Local bias	Perceived stress	% responses from subjects with high degree of it decreases over time
	Extraversion	% responses from subjects with high degree of it decreases over time
	Conscientiousness	% responses from subjects with high degree of it decreases over time
Local bias	Perceived stress	% responses from subjects with a high degree of it strongly decrease after tense events
	Extraversion	% responses from subjects with a low degree of it strongly decreases after social experience
	Agreeableness	% responses from subjects with a high degree of it strongly increases in the early stage (they are late for making an initial EMA response)

EMA study, subjects with higher agreeableness were found to delay making an initial EMA response. Therefore, the EMA responses from subjects with high agreeableness tend to be missing in the early stage. After tense events such as the midterm examination, the proportion of EMA responses from subjects with high perceived stress may decrease. Similarly, the EMA responses of subjects with low extraversion are likely to be missed after they have social experiences.

The results of the overall bias are similar to those of previous studies [19,23, 30,37]. This is because they show the relationship between the characteristics of the subjects and the frequency of their responses throughout the experiment. However, the present study certainly shows a new finding, since previous studies did not verify the stress level of the subjects. More importantly, the results for local bias describe how the heterogeneity of EMA data due to individual characteristics varies by timing. The results differ from the findings of previous studies and are the main contribution of this study.

6.3   Recommendations

As shown by the present study and previous works, EMA data is inevitably biased in terms of personal characteristics and timing. However, the data collected by EMA are widely used for both academic and practical purposes. This is because they are accepted as true data that represent changes in people's subjective states.

Therefore, we encourage prospective EMA studies to describe the variance of EMA response rates as determined by individual characteristics and time, and to discuss the biases present in the data. These studies include, for example, studies that use EMA data to predict people's future moods, and studies that compare methods for increasing response rates to EMA.

In EMA studies involving human subjects, determining the nature of the study sample and assessing its impact are important to confirm the reproducibility of the findings. Such individual-level analyses will become increasingly important in the future development of HCI research. However, it is challenging for EMA studies to control study subjects and timing. Therefore, future EMA studies should share their findings on the bias of their respective EMA data and discuss, in depth, the limitations and generality of their work.

6.4   Limitations

Our study is a case study that points out bias in EMA data in a specific situation. Thus, our findings will be valid when one has similar conditions as to events, subjects, study design, and environments, particularly when subjects experience influential events in social contexts in the community (e.g., final examinations for students, salary increase interview for working adults, etc.).

We considered such influential events (a midterm examination and a school festival) that most of the subjects encountered, and did not focus on purely personal experiences. For example, if a subject had a negative experience such as troubles with family or traffic accidents, the subject would lose his/her energy regardless of his/her degree of perceived stress or introverted personality. Our research did not take this point into account, because our focus is the effect of personal characteristics.

Moreover, our results are based entirely on the StudentLife dataset. However, as discussed above, prospective EMA studies need to share their findings on the biases of their EMA data to understand the limits and the generality of EMA studies. The present study certainly contributes to these issues.

6.5   Future Work

To understand the effects of such personal experiences on response rates, it might be useful to examine passively-sensed data such as locations, mobility, phone logs, and so on. This contextual information can be used for inferring subjects' experiences. Our future work will investigate how response rates are associated with this contextual information to better understand individual differences in response rates from the viewpoint of personal ongoing experience.

To achieve the general goal of understanding how EMA data is biased, it is necessary to carry out experiments individually under various conditions in which each factor is controlled, and to perform a meta-analysis that aggregates the data of each experiment. For example, EMA experiments will be conducted in different cultures (e.g., Western vs. Eastern) and with different social statuses (e.g., students vs. workers). It is expected that generalized findings will be derived by comparing the results of the present study with those results, or by integrated analyses based on the experimental data of the present study.

7   Conclusion

EMA data is inherently heterogeneous. However, it is currently recognized and utilized as true data that represents the changes in people's subjective state over time. Therefore, it is important to discuss how the EMA data is biased. In this study, unlike previous studies, we analyzed the temporal changes in the response rate of EMA data.

Primary results indicated that the subjects with high perceived stress had a higher frequency of EMA responses, but the frequency of EMA responses from these subjects tended to decrease strongly throughout the experiment, especially after the midterm examination. We also found that the subjects with low extraversion had a weak tendency to decrease the number of EMA responses throughout the experiment, but the number of EMA responses of these subjects decreased strongly after the school festival. In addition, conscientiousness had a negative effect on the overall slope of EMA frequency. Subjects with high agreeableness were found to show a strong increase in EMA frequency at the initial stage of the experiment. We discussed the reasons behind these significant results, and provided new insights into the biasing of EMA data.

In the future, we will consider individual contextual information to understand the effect of purely personal experience on data bias, and conduct meta-analysis using multiple datasets to derive more general findings. Future EMA research should describe how the collected EMA data are biased with regard to individual characteristics and time, and advance the discussion on the limitations and generality of EMA research. We hope that this study will be one of such contributions.

References

1. The Myers & Briggs Foundation. Extraversion or Introversion (2014). https://www.myersbriggs.org/my-mbti-personality-type/mbti-basics/extraversion-or-introversion.htm. Accessed 24 May 2021
2. Bentler, P.M.: Comparative fit indixes in structural models. Psychol. Bull. **107**(2), 238–246 (1990)
3. van Berkel, N., Goncalves, J., Hosio, S., Sarsenbayeva, Z., Velloso, E., Kostakos, V.: Overcoming compliance bias in self-report studies: a cross-study analysis. Int. J. Hum. Comput. Stud. **134**, 1–12 (2020)
4. van Berkel, N., Goncalves, J., Lovén, L., Ferreira, D., Hosio, S., Kostakos, V.: Effect of experience sampling schedules on response rate and recall accuracy of objective self-reports. Int. J. Hum. Comput. Stud. **125**, 118–128 (2019)
5. Boukhechba, M., et al.: Contextual analysis to understand compliance with smartphone-based ecological momentary assessment. In: Proceedings of the 12th EAI International Conference on Pervasive Computing Technologies for Healthcare, pp. 232–238. ACM, New York (2018)

6. Cohen, S., Kamarck, T., Mermelstein, R.: A global measure of perceived stress. J. Health Soc. Behav. **24**(4), 385 (1983)

7. Costa, P.T., MacCrae, R.R.: Revised NEO Personality Inventory (NEO-PI-R) and NEO Five-Factor Inventory (NEO-FFI) Manual. Psychological Assessment Resources, Incorporated (1992)

8. Dejonckheere, E., et al.: Complex affect dynamics add limited information to the prediction of psychological well-being. Nat. Hum. Behav. **3**(5), 478–491 (2019)

9. Diener, E., et al.: New well-being measures: short scales to assess flourishing and positive and negative feelings. Soc. Ind. Res. **97**(2), 143–156 (2010)

10. Eagle, N., Pentland, A., Lazer, D.: Inferring friendship network structure by using mobile phone data. Proc. Natl. Acad. Sci. **106**(36), 15274–15278 (2009)

11. Harari, G.M., Gosling, S.D., Wang, R., Chen, F., Chen, Z., Campbell, A.T.: Patterns of behavior change in students over an academic term: a preliminary study of activity and sociability behaviors using smartphone sensing methods. Comput. Hum. Behav. **67**, 129–138 (2017)

12. Helgoe, L.A.: Introvert Power: Why Your Inner Life is Your Hidden Strength. Sourcebooks, Inc. (2013)

13. Hsieh, H.P., Li, C.T.: Inferring social relationships from mobile sensor data. In: Proceedings of the 23rd International Conference on World Wide Web, pp. 293–294. ACM, New York (2014)

14. Jones, A., et al.: Compliance with ecological momentary assessment protocols in substance users: a meta-analysis. Addiction **114**(4), 609–619 (2019)

15. Kroenke, K., Spitzer, R.L., Williams, J.B.W.: The PHQ-9. J. Gen. Intern. Med. **16**(9), 606–613 (2001)

16. Lane, N., et al.: BeWell: a smartphone application to monitor, model and promote wellbeing. In: Proceedings of the 5th International ICST Conference on Pervasive Computing Technologies for Healthcare. IEEE (2011)

17. Lathia, N., Rachuri, K.K., Mascolo, C., Rentfrow, P.J.: Contextual dissonance: design bias in sensor-based experience sampling methods. In: Proceedings of the 2013 ACM International Joint Conference on Pervasive and Ubiquitous Computing, pp. 183–192. ACM, New York (2013)

18. Lucas, G.M., et al.: Reporting mental health symptoms: breaking down barriers to care with virtual human interviewers. Front. Robot. AI **4**(51), 1–9 (2017)

19. Messiah, A., Grondin, O., Encrenaz, G.: Factors associated with missing data in an experience sampling investigation of substance use determinants. Drug Alcohol Depend. **114**(2–3), 153–158 (2011)

20. Morren, M., Dulmen, S., Ouwerkerk, J., Bensing, J.: Compliance with momentary pain measurement using electronic diaries: a systematic review. Eur. J. Pain **13**(4), 354–365 (2009)

21. Mount, M.K., Barrick, M.R.: The Big Five personality dimensions: implications for research and practice in human resources management. Res. Pers. Hum. Resour. Manag. **13**(3), 153–200 (1995)

22. Rabbi, M., Ali, S., Choudhury, T., Berke, E.: Passive and In-Situ assessment of mental and physical well-being using mobile sensors. In: Proceedings of the 13th International Conference on Ubiquitous Computing, pp. 385–394. ACM, New York (2011)

23. Rintala, A., Wampers, M., Myin-Germeys, I., Viechtbauer, W.: Response compliance and predictors thereof in studies using the experience sampling method. Psychol. Assess. **31**(2), 226–235 (2019)

24. Roccas, S., Sagiv, L., Schwartz, S.H., Knafo, A.: The big five personality factors and personal values. Pers. Soc. Psychol. Bull. **28**(6), 789–801 (2002)

25. Russell, D.W.: UCLA loneliness scale (version 3): reliability, validity, and factor structure. J. Pers. Assess. **66**(1), 20–40 (1996)
26. Sadri, A., Salim, F.D., Ren, Y., Shao, W., Krumm, J.C., Mascolo, C.: What will you do for the rest of the day? An approach to continuous trajectory prediction. Proc. ACM Interact. Mob. Wearable Ubiquit. Technol. **2**(4), 1–26 (2018)
27. Saha, K., Chan, L., De Barbaro, K., Abowd, G.D., De Choudhury, M.: Inferring mood instability on social media by leveraging ecological momentary assessments. Proc. ACM Interact. Mob. Wearable Ubiquit. Technol. **1**(3), 1–27 (2017)
28. Servia-Rodríguez, S., Rachuri, K.K., Mascolo, C., Rentfrow, P.J., Lathia, N., Sandstrom, G.M.: Mobile sensing at the service of mental well-being: a large-scale longitudinal study. In: Proceedings of the 26th International Conference on World Wide Web, pp. 103–112 (2017)
29. Shiffman, S., Stone, A.A., Hufford, M.R.: Ecological momentary assessment. Annu. Rev. Clin. Psychol. **4**(1), 1–32 (2008)
30. Sokolovsky, A.W., Mermelstein, R.J., Hedeker, D.: Factors predicting compliance to ecological momentary assessment among adolescent smokers. Nicotine Tob. Res. **16**(3), 351–358 (2014)
31. Steiger, J.H.: Statistically based test for the number of common factors. In: The Annual Meeting of the Psychometric Society (1980)
32. Thewissen, V., et al.: Emotions, self-esteem, and paranoid episodes: an experience sampling study. Br. J. Clin. Psychol. **50**(2), 178–195 (2011)
33. Thompson, E.R.: Development and validation of an international English big-five mini-markers. Personality Individ. Differ. **45**(6), 542–548 (2008)
34. Toegel, G., Barsoux, J.L.: How to become a better leader. MIT Sloan Manag. Rev. **53**(3), 51–60 (2012)
35. Tucker, L.R., Lewis, C.: A reliability coefficient for maximum likelihood factor analysis. Psychometrika **38**(1), 1–10 (1973)
36. Udachina, A., Varese, F., Myin-Germeys, I., Bentall, R.P.: The role of experiential avoidance in paranoid delusions: an experience sampling study. Br. J. Clin. Psychol. **53**(4), 422–432 (2014)
37. Vachon, H., Viechtbauer, W., Rintala, A., Myin-Germeys, I.: Compliance and retention with the experience sampling method over the continuum of severe mental disorders: meta-analysis and recommendations. J. Med. Internet Res. **21**(12) (2019)
38. Wang, R., et al.: StudentLife: assessing mental health, academic performance and behavioral trends of college students using smartphones. In: Proceedings of the 2014 ACM International Joint Conference on Pervasive and Ubiquitous Computing, pp. 3–14. ACM, New York (2014)
39. Wang, R., Harari, G., Hao, P., Zhou, X., Campbell, A.T.: SmartGPA: how smartphones can assess and predict academic performance of college students. In: Proceedings of the 2015 ACM International Joint Conference on Pervasive and Ubiquitous Computing, pp. 295–306 (2015)
40. Yao, H., Lian, D., Cao, Y., Wu, Y., Zhou, T.: Predicting academic performance for college students: a campus behavior perspective. ACM Trans. Intell. Syst. Technol. **10**(3), 1–21 (2019)

Jammify: Interactive Multi-sensory System for Digital Art Jamming

Sachith Muthukumarana[1]([⊠]), Don Samitha Elvitigala[1], Qin Wu[1],
Yun Suen Pai[2], and Suranga Nanayakkara[1]

[1] Augmented Human Lab, Auckland Bioengineering Institute,
The University of Auckland, Auckland, New Zealand
{sachith,samitha,qin,suranga}@ahlab.org
[2] Empathic Computing Laboratory, Auckland Bioengineering Institute,
The University of Auckland, Auckland, New Zealand
pai@kmd.keio.ac.jp

Abstract. As social distancing is becoming the new normal, technology holds the potential to bridge this societal gap through novel interaction modalities that allow multiple users to collaborate and create content together. We present Jammify, an interactive multi-sensory system that focuses on providing a unique digital art-jamming experience with a visual display and a wearable arm-sleeve. The 'jamming-canvas' visual display is a two-sided LED light wall ($2\,\text{m} \times 6\,\text{m}$) where users can draw free-hand gestures on either side and switch between two view modes: own-view and shared-view. The arm-sleeve uses shape-memory-alloy integrated fabric to sense and re-create a subtle and natural touch sensation on each other's hands. We describe the details of the design and interaction possibilities based on the diverse combinations of both input and output modalities of the system, as well as findings from a user study with ten participants.

Keywords: Digital drawings · Large displays · Collaborative drawing · Crowd and creativity · I/O Interface · Haptics · Touch

1 Introduction

Dynamic media jamming interfaces allow users to engage and compose improvised artworks [11]. Collaborative drawing can be considered as one potential jamming application that promotes creativity between individuals [38]. When two individuals are engaged in collaborative drawing, the shared-canvas is converted into a common-platform in which they can communicate their creativity and emotions [7,44,75]. Previous studies reveal that large displays enable interactions from afar [61], as well as interactions that are simple [30,66]. Therefore, enabling collaborative drawings in a large display could be used to provide a unique art-jamming experience for users [65].

Electronic supplementary material The online version of this chapter (https:// doi.org/10.1007/978-3-030-85607-6_2) contains supplementary material, which is available to authorized users.

Fig. 1. Jammify comprised of a jamming-canvas based on a two-sided large LED display (a, b) that enables collaborative drawing with free-hand gestures (c). A wearable forearm augmentation (d) provides additional feedback by recreating natural touch sensations.

Building upon prior work on large displays towards collective playful interactions [14,45] and the current state of the world, we present Jammify. Our system comprises a shared drawing canvas based on a two-sided large-scale LED display. Two individuals can use Jammify to draw with free-handed gestures on each side, creating a novel system for playful, open-ended interactions, and casual creativity for everyday pedestrians in public spaces. Both users are interconnected through a wearable arm-sleeve which can sense and recreate a natural touch sensation on the skin. The arm-sleeve, that extends prior work [52], acts as an integrated [49] communication channel between the two users, allowing them to sense and share subtle affective touch reactions on each other's forearms while maintaining appropriate social distancing. For the visual modality, two users can switch between different modes: own-view and shared-view, through the two conversely connected displays. We see this as an important aspect to consider in collaboration, given that shifts to using remote-based systems largely lack a multi-sensory experience. Although remote tools have vastly improved over the years, we are looking towards an assistive augmentation [34], that also facilitates multi-sensory feedback among users for shared content creation.

In this paper, we describe the technical implementation and the interaction possibilities of the system. In addition, we discuss how Jammify enables multiple interaction possibilities, such as collaborative, competitive, and exploratory tasks. Finally, we evaluated the effects of Jammify on user perception and experience across various proposed interaction modalities. In summary, we contribute with: 1) a system that allows user to experience a unique digital art-jamming experience based on visual feedback and the sensation of touch. 2) user evaluation of the Jammify with ten users to understand users' perception of the digital art jamming experience.

2   Related Work

Our research is based upon prior work on (1) haptic-affect interfaces that empower person-to-person interaction, (2) jamming interfaces that allow users to engage in improvised collaborative tasks, as well as (3) interactive large displays that enable multi-user interactions in-the-wild.

2.1   Haptic-Affect Interfaces

There has been a significant amount of work focusing on haptic interfaces that enable interactions between multiple users to express affections [21,50]. Particularly, interacting with multi-modal affective feedback methods, such as visual and haptic modalities, has been proven to be more influential in enabling an immersive user experience [2,36,74]. Previous research [8,9] imply the possibility of making people co-present by sharing and communicating touch feelings through abstract interfaces. Technological advancements with vibration motors renders vibrotactile feedback as one of the most utilised modes to convey affect-related information [57,58,71]. However, non-vibrating interfaces, such as Shape-Memory Alloy (SMA) based wearable interfaces [28,31,42,51,52,54,67] are becoming a popular alternative for vibrotactile interfaces as they are more natural and expressive [31]. Moreover, SMA demonstrates multiple advantages, such as efficiency in large-amplitude actuation [35], competitive Power-to-Weight ratio [41], and a smaller form factor. Some of the early explorations concerning SMAs such as Sprout I/O [16], HapticClench [29], and Tickler [43] exhibit insights about using SMAs in the research domain. Nakao et al. proposed Share-Haptics [55], an SMA-based haptic system that allowed multiple remote participants to share haptic sensations via the hands and feet depending on the application. Recently, *Springlets* [31] explored six expressive sensations on the skin using a single flexible sticker based on SMA springs. *Touch me Gently* [52] proposes a forearm augmentation that can mimic the natural touch sensations on the forearm by applying shear-forces on the skin using an SMA matrix configuration. In this work, we build upon *Touch me Gently* [52] to sense touch and share emotive information between a pair of users.

2.2   Art Jamming Interfaces

Dynamic media jamming interfaces allow multiple users to engage with generative multimedia systems to compose impromptu artworks, particularly in the audiovisual domain [11]. They mainly focus on multi-user interaction and the interfaces associated with collaborative interactions. These have gained an increasingly important role over single-user multimodal interfaces in human-centered designs, as they facilitate multiple users to work in group tasks [6,20]. For example, VJing is a format of real-time visual performance art that conducts concurrently with music sessions as a visual backdrop, allowing users to manipulate different video streams in real-time [69]. Meanwhile, drawing can be a potential collaborative platform for users to perform jamming sessions. Even before the invention of languages, drawing was one of the earliest ways in which humans conveyed expressions and ideas [12,24]. Nowadays, users generally have the tools to become digital artists by adjusting several parameters in the particular system using graphical or physical controller interfaces [11,33]. For instance,

BodyDiagrams [37] proposes an interface that enables the communication of pain symptoms via drawing. Similarly, considerable work has been done in the medicinal domain to evaluate the expressiveness of drawing in aiding interpretations, diagnosis, and recovery [26,27,64]. Drawing has also been used as a tool to interpret certain emotions of users [25,48,72], essentially demonstrating the influence of drawing in affective communication. Our work adds to this body of work by having the display act as a bridge between socially distanced individuals and as an interactive medium to connect them.

2.3   Interactive Large Displays

Amongst the multiple advantages of large displays, recent past work has also considerably highlighted performance benefits [62] and user satisfaction [17]. Additionally, psychological gains are also among the significant advantages of large displays as they aid memory improvement [18], peripheral awareness [17], and spatial knowledge [5], etc. Alternatively, large displays have been employed in shared surfaces across multiple users as they trigger and boost communication among unknown persons [10,46], enhance co-located collaborative activities [53,63], and facilitate the sense of community [15,63]. For instance, Zadow et al. [70] explored the multi-user interaction between personal devices and large displays. In addition, Graffito [65] presents a case study that explored the ways crowd-based performative interaction happens with large-scale displays. Generally, interactive displays invite users to creatively express themselves through the display. Although most interaction methodologies share texts or images over a personalised device, such as a mobile phone [3,14,23,45,56,70,73], there has been considerable interest in the HCI community to blend the natural gestures of users with large display interactions [1,39]. Sensing mechanisms such as motion tracking systems [47], mid-air gestures [10], and gaze estimations [40] have already been deployed in large displays. In this work, we combine sensing with natural touch sensation feedback for a multi-sensory experience.

3   Jammify

The goal of Jammify was to encourage users to engage in spontaneous and impromptu interactions, either with each other or with the system itself. We see this being especially useful currently, given that the ongoing pandemic has negatively affected human interaction. Jammify facilitates these interactions by being a bridge that provides both visual and haptic modalities while maintaining social distance. Moreover, one of our primary considerations while designing Jammify was to prevent users from physically contacting the wall or with each other while interacting with the system.

The overall design architecture of Jammify has two main components, the jamming canvas (public visual feedback) and the arm-sleeve (private haptic feedback). The jamming-canvas is the platform where two users can perform digital drawings using simple mid-air hand gestures. The augmented arm sleeve (see Fig. 1*d*) connects users with a channel to share remote touch sensations between them.

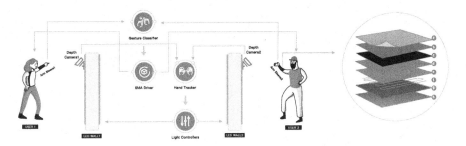

Fig. 2. Jammify System Architecture: Two large displays visualize the illustrations users draw. Light controllers control the two large displays according to the gesture classifier and hand tracker sensed by two depth cameras. The augmented arm-sleeve incorporates an 8-layer design; a) Electrical insulation layer, b) Copper layer 1, c) Velostat sheet, d) Copper layer 2, e) Thermal dissipation layer, f) SMA wire layout, g) Adhesive and stretchable textile, h) Thermal and electrical insulation layer.

3.1 Jamming Canvas

The jamming-canvas consists of a large LED display and a pair of depth cameras that can track and detect free-hand gestures. The light display controllers and the depth cameras are controlled by a central computer.

Light Display: The Jammify canvas is a two sided $2\,m \times 6\,m$ large canvas made using ten light panels. Each panel has four strands, illuminating 180 iColor Flex LMX LEDs installed to a plywood panel as shown in Fig. 1a. Altogether, the entire canvas has 1800 individually addressable, full-color LED nodes. Each node produces a maximum of 6.56 candela of light output while consuming just 1W of power. The light strands were connected to 8 Philips color kinetic light controllers with an inbuilt Ethernet controller that allowed individual nodes to be addressed. We deployed the jamming-canvas right beside the main entrance of a building, facilitating impromptu interactions with Jammify among people who pass through. Initial observations show that users were curious to examine the inside of the wall to see how it is made. Therefore, we integrated a 'behind-the-scene' into our design by keeping an opening for the light display (see Fig. 1b) for people to see inside.

The shared jamming-canvas operates in two modes: (1) *Own-View (OV)* allows two users to draw on the light display individually as two separate drawings, and (2) *Shared-View (SV)* enables both users to work on the same drawing simultaneously, as shown in Fig. 3e and 3f. In the *OV* setting, two users work on their own illustration independently on the two-sided light displays. For instance, the *OV* mode is more suitable for a competitive task, whereas the *SV* mode is more suitable for a collaborative task. When no participants are present, all the lights of the display start fading in and out slowly, creating an appealing effect [32] for the people passing by.

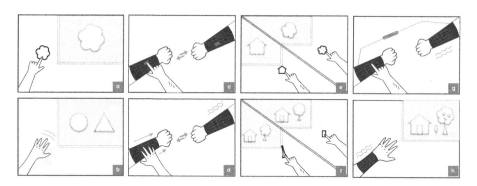

Fig. 3. Jammify enables multi-user interaction possibilities based on the diverse combinations of the following modes; (a) *One-to-One (O2O)*, (b) *Gestures-to-Shapes (GTS)*, (c) *Touch-to-Touch (T2T)*, (d) *Gestures-to-Gestures (G2G)*, (e) *Own-View (OV)*, (f) *Shared-View (SV)*, (g) *Feeling-User (FU)*, and (h) *Feeling-Drawing (FD)*.

Depth Camera: To control lights using hand gestures, we mounted two Intel RealSense D435 depth cameras [13] on top of both sides of the canvas (see Fig. 2). To track hand movements, we wrote a Unity application using Nuitrack SDK [59]. The position of the hand is mapped to the corresponding pixel coordinates of the light display. To enable drawings on the canvas, we interfaced the Intel depth cameras with iColor Flex LMX LEDs by using a software controller implemented using 'color kinetics' Java Processing API, along with a TCP library to interface with Unity.

We propose two ways of transforming the interaction in front of the display (see Fig. 3a *and* 3b) based on the geometrical location of the hand: (1) *One-to-One (O2O)* maps the position of the hand to the one-to-one pixel coordinate of the display, and (2) *Gestures-to-Shapes (G2S)* maps the free-hand gestures, namely *swipe-up*, *swipe-down*, *swipe-left*, and *swipe-right* to approximations of pre-defined shapes, namely circles, triangles, squares, and lines respectively to create collage type illustrations. Both users can switch between different modes by performing a *hand-waving* gesture. Holding the hand in the same spatial location for a period of three seconds would allow the user to choose different colours for the drawing. Furthermore, users can reset the jamming-canvas by performing a *push* gesture. Jammify supports one user per side of the set-up. We marked a specific location in front of the display where users can interact. When a user interacts with the system, other people, such as onlookers, are filtered out based on the horizontal distance from the display.

3.2   Augmented Arm Sleeve

We propose the inclusion of arm sleeves for two key reasons. Firstly, we wanted to pair a haptic modality with the jamming canvas to transmit subtle touch sensations among users. Secondly, we are looking towards an easy-to-put-on wearable device with a relatively large surface area for interaction with the hands. Arm sleeves [52] is one such device that enables users to pass subtle emotive touch responses among each other. Furthermore, it is easy to wear, as the forearm is a suitably large surface area without being obtrusive. The arm sleeve comprises of two main components; (1) *Sensing Layer Stack* to sense and classify the touch gestures performed on the forearm using a Force-Sensitive Resistor (FSR) matrix, and (2) *Actuation Layer Stack* to recreate the touch sensation of the skin by actuating an SMA-based plaster matrix, placed on top of each other on the forearm of the user.

Sensing Layer Stack: The sensing layer stack is based on 15 FSRs in a 5×3 matrix that covers most of the forearm area. A pressure sensitive conductive sheet (*Velostat*) was placed in between two non-attached copper layers (see Fig. 2a to 2d). Depending on the applied force on the node, the Velostat changes the conductivity and the connectivity of the two non-attached copper nodes. An overall sampling rate of $50Hz$ was achieved by switching between five rows of digital outputs and three analog inputs. The topmost layer is an electric insulation layer to eliminate direct contact between the copper nodes and the skin.

The sensing layer stack of the augmented arm-sleeve incorporates the real-time 2D coordinates associated with the touch gestures performed on the forearm. Based on these touch locations, Jammify allows users to interact in two ways (see Fig. 3c and 3d): (1) *Touch-to-Touch (T2T)* that maps the touch locations of the hand to the exact SMA patch on the augmented arm-sleeve of the other user, and (2) *Gestures-to-Gestures (G2G)* that classify six touch gestures performed on the forearm (*stroking down the arm, stroking up the arm, grabbing the arm, grabbing the wrist, encircling on the arm, and encircling on the wrist*) and activates the same actuation pattern in the SMA matrix.

Actuation Layer Stack: We developed the actuation part of the forearm-sleeve based on recent research work that demonstrated recreating the perception of natural touch sensation on the skin [52]. This was implemented with an SMA-based flexible plaster matrix design with four layers, as shown in Fig. 2 e to h, to generate shear-forces on the skin. In Jammify, we added a top layer to allow both sensing and feedback.

The arm-sleeve interface of Jammify also has two operating modes: (1) *Feeling-User (FU)* mode that allows users to share touch responses via the forearm augmentation, and (2) *Feeling-Drawings (FD)* mode that enables users to feel the artworks drawn on the jamming-canvas (see Fig. 3g and 3h). In *FU*, a user can receive haptic responses in the form of feedback, guidance, or reaction

	Single-user Interaction		Two-user Interaction	
	Depth Camera	Light Display	Depth Camera	Light Display
With the Augmented Arm-sleeve	One-to-One (O2O)	Own-View (OV)	One-to-One (O2O)	Own-View (OV)
	Gestures-to-Shapes (G2S)		Gestures-to-Shapes (G2S)	Shared-View (SV)
	FSR matrix	SMA matrix	FSR matrix	SMA matrix
	-	Feeling-Drawing (FD)	Touch-to-Touch (T2T)	Feeling-Drawing (FD)
			Gestures-to-Gestures (G2G)	Feeling-User (FU)
Without the Augmented Arm-sleeve	Depth Camera	Light Display	Depth Camera	Light Display
	One-to-One (O2O)	Own-View (OV)	One-to-One (O2O)	Own-View (OV)
			Gestures-to-Shapes (G2S)	Shared-View (SV)
	FSR matrix	SMA matrix	FSR matrix	SMA matrix
	-	-	-	-

Fig. 4. Jammify's Interaction space composes two dimensions: Number of users (*Single-user Interactions* versus *Two-user Interactions*) and the employment of the augmented arm-sleeve (*With the Augmented Arm-sleeve* versus *Without the Augmented Arm-Sleeve*).

for the drawn elements shared by the other user. We identified this mode as most suitable for a collaborative task where users can share several responses, such as emotions via haptic reactions. In the *FD* mode, we activate the SMA plaster matrix when the user hovers the hand over the boundaries (edges) of the drawn elements. This mode is more suited for single-user interactions.

3.3   Interaction Space

Jammify incorporates a combination of two types of inputs to the system (depth camera and FSR matrix), as well as two output modalities controlled by the system (light display and SMA matrix), as mentioned above. In this section, we suggest how these interactions can be combined: *Single-user Interactions* versus *Two-user Interactions* in terms of the number of users, and *With the Augmented Arm-sleeve* versus *Without the Augmented Arm-Sleeve* in terms of the utilization of the Augmented Arm-sleeve. Depending on the design requirements, Jammify can refer to different combinations of operation modes (as shown in Fig. 4) to facilitate various types of applications. We choose three potential types of applications that Jammify can assist; Collaborative tasks where users can work together or a single user can collaborate with Jammify, Competitive tasks in which two users can compete with each other or a single user can compete with Jammify, and Exploratory tasks where single users can free-play with Jammify.

Collaborative Tasks: Research work on collaborative drawing runs back several decades [60,68], and its potential to support creativity is well established [19,76]. In Jammify, when a pair of users interact with the system in a collaborative task, we propose *One-to-One (O2O)* as the depth camera mapping mechanism to draw on the canvas freely, *Shared-View (SV)* as the display mode for the shared view, *Gestures-to-Gestures (G2G)* mapping of the FSR matrix, and *Feeling-User (FU)* mode as the SMA matrix configuration to share real-time haptic responses. Similarly, a single user can also accomplish a collaborative task with Jammify. In this case, Jammify provides a prepared low-resolution image, allowing the user to modify the drawing as needed. In contrast to the two-user condition, we suggest maintaining the light display mode as the *Own-View (OV)* mode and the depth camera mapping as *One-to-One (O2O)* in the single-user mode. When a single-user uses an augmented arm-sleeve, it can only operate in the *Feeling-Drawing (FD)* mode.

Competitive Tasks: Competition tends to have positive effects on creativity [4,22]. For a competitive task, such as two users engaging in a drawing competition with each other, we propose *Gestures-to-Shapes (G2S)* as the mapping mechanism to collage abstract illustration, *Own-View (OV)* as the display mode for having two independent views, and *Feeling-Drawing (FD)* mode as the SMA matrix setting for users to feel the drawing in an abstract way independently. One person can compete with Jammify to complete a given abstract illustration as quickly as possible. The combination of *One-to-One (O2O)* depth camera mapping mechanism, *Own-View (OV)* display mode, and *Feeling-Drawing (FD)* mode is an exemplar for a single user interaction in this case.

Exploratory Tasks: Exploratory interactions associated with drawings have been shown to be applicable in playful interactions [23,77]. Likewise, in the exploratory mode of Jammify, such as a free-hand drawing interaction, users can free-play with the system without a particular objective. We propose *One-to-One (O2O)* as the depth camera configuration, *Own-View (OV)* as the display mode for the individual view, and *Feeling-Drawing (FD)* mode as the SMA matrix setting for the user to feel the drawing on the forearm. In the same way, users can engage in a simpler interplay with *Gestures-to-Shapes (G2S)* depth camera mode to create more abstract artworks by performing free-hand gestures mentioned above.

4   Evaluation

The goal of this user study is to understand users' perception of the digital art jamming experience Jammify provides. Ten participants (8 males and 2 females) aged between 22 and 38 years ($M = 29.7$, $SD = 4.29$) were recruited, and among them, four participants had previous experience with interactive displays. The jamming-canvas was deployed right beside the entrance of our institute and the user study was also conducted at the same location. At the beginning of the study, we explained the study details, instructions, and objectives to each participant. We explore several configurations including: *Arm-sleeve availability* (*With the Augmented Arm-sleeve, Without the Augmented Arm-sleeve*), and *Types of the task* (*Collaborative, Competitive, Exploratory*). Altogether, each participant went through six different scenarios; 2 *Arm-sleeve availability* × 3 *Types of the tasks* (See Fig. 5). In *Collaborative* tasks, an experimenter acted as the external person behind the screen. However, participants were unaware of this. We only

Fig. 5. Participants were engaged in three types of tasks: *Collaborative*, *Competitive*, and *Exploratory*. a) In the *Collaborative* task, users were given a partly completed drawing to complete as a collaborator. b) We provided a monochrome image to fill with colours in 30 s in *Competitive* tasks. c) The *Exploratory* task allowed the participants to interact with the jamming-canvas as they wish. d) All of the above mentioned tasks were conducted in two conditions With and Without the arm-sleeve.

informed them that an anonymous external person would be collaborating with them. In *Competitive* tasks, participants were asked to fill a monochrome image with colors within 30 s. To increase the competitiveness, we told them that their colouring will be evaluated. In *Exploratory* tasks, participants were allowed to interact with the display freely. The study took approximately one-hour per participant. After each condition, the participants filled out a questionnaire, asking about the emotions expressed through the interactions, negative and positive experiences, and comments on drawn illustrations. The quotes were collected using a questionnaire where participants were asked to select the most preferred mode and the reason for the selection at the end of the user study.

4.1   Results and Discussion

Exploratory Mode Preferred by Most Participants: When we asked participants about their favourite digital art jamming mode, the majority (nine out of ten) declared that they enjoyed the *Exploratory* task with the augmented arm-sleeve the most. They reported the reason as being the *"freedom"* they had during the task. For example, P1: *"I had complete freedom"*, and P4 : *" It gave me freedom of drawing, so I was able to draw what came into my mind"*. The freedom that the *Exploratory* mode gives may also have awakened their creativity, which the majority of participants enjoyed. P8: *"I like exploratory mode. It doesn't have an explicit task. So no pressure, more creativity"*. Only one participant felt that the *Exploratory* task required more effort since they needed to complete the drawing solely by themselves. The majority of participants preferred the *Collaborative* task, as it was less difficult. They specifically mentioned that users could acquire more support for the drawings in this mode, especially for those who lack the confidence in their artistic skill. P2: *"I'm not good at drawing. Therefore, drawing with someone else gave me confidence and help me to do a better job at drawing"*. None of the participants mentioned that they liked *Competitive* mode. The reason behind this could be the induced temporal cognitive load created by asking them to finish the task within 30 s, which was not a lot of time to awaken their creativity, compared to *Exploratory* or *Collaborative* (For example, refer

P8's statement above). Furthermore, many participants found that they could not enjoy the touch feedback during the *Competitive mode*. P4 : *"Competitive felt hurried so I really was not able to respond to the touch feedback, but I could respond accordingly for the other modes. I enjoyed it"*.

Augmented Arm-Sleeve Enhanced the Experience: In terms of the user experience with the augmented arm-sleeve combined with digital art jamming, all participants identified this as the most preferred mode compared to *Without the Augmented Arm-sleeve* setting. This was also reflected during the questionnaire when participants used terms such as *"nice haptic feedback"* (P8), *"great combination"* (P5), and *"amusing feedback"* (P7) to describe the haptic sensations generated by the arm-sleeve. Participants also noted that the haptic sensation blended with the visual stimulations induced a unique interactive experience. For example, P6: *"It felt more interactive. I felt I can explore stuff in a new way. It allowed me to be more creative and play around"*, P7: *"amusing feedback generated by the arm sleeve made it more interactive"*. Moreover, the participant who liked the *Collaborative* task mentioned that the arm sleeve gave him a feeling of the presence of his counterpart, who interacts with him from the other side of the wall (in this case, experimenter). This shows that the augmented arm sleeve enhanced the participants' experience in two main ways: increased the liveliness of the jamming experience, and increased the sense of presence of a partner interacting from the other side of the wall. Therefore, the participants' comments further confirm that the augmented arm-sleeve did not help them during the *Competitive* task (P2, P5). The greater focus on the competitive visual task caused users not to perceive the haptic sensation, thus making Jammify less entertaining. Moreover, some of the participants enjoyed the warmth generated in the arm-sleeve as a pleasing add-on. P6: *"warmth generated in the arm-sleeve felt pleasant as the environment was cold"*. This could also be due to users perceiving the warm sensation as a touch from a physical hand, allowing us to close the perceived gap between users, even with social distancing.

Other Observations: We observed several notable incidents while implementing the jamming-canvas at our institute's entrance and during the user studies. As the researchers in our institute passed by, they approached us with many queries about the set-up and the technological aspects of Jammify. These inquiries led us to believe that, despite the fact researchers generally lean towards science and technology as opposed to art, Jammify could nevertheless spark a sense of curiosity regarding its implementation and deployment. After the deployment of the set-up, even individuals from non-technical backgrounds, such as cleaners, delivery persons, and security guards tried to interact with the jamming-canvas. Although we thought participants would be overwhelmed after the one-hour user study, most were still interested in playing with the system post-study. These instances showcase that peoples' desire to interact with Jammify can potentially bridge two important gaps; the first is the gap of social distancing by allowing multi-sensory interaction between users, and the second being the gap between users who are and are not artistically or technologically inclined.

Design Implications: We discuss the design implications derived using the observations and results extracted during the design process and user study of Jammify. We learned that users did not have to physically touch the display necessarily; however, it is essential to support multiple users and show the resulting interaction between the users. Thus, when designing multi-user performative interactions [65], sharing the resulting outcome among all the users would improve the overall interaction depending on the context. Also, the illustrations projected on the large display need not be realistic. Greater abstraction in patterns are suitable as long as users can make a connection to their actions. With simple, yet never ending abstract patterns, users will find the system playful, and it would support attracting users to engage with the system. Similarly, we found that any form of pre-assigned tasks for the interaction should be minimised; rather, free-form interplay should be prioritised. Also, a system such as an interactive public wall should have easy access and allow for simple casual creativity among multiple users. The interaction should reflect this.

Nevertheless, employing an augmented arm-sleeve to enable a touch interface showed that users prefer a multi-modal feedback approach. However, there are challenges when incorporating a wearable device that users share in a crowd-based system. An ideal solution would be providing the device in the form of a disposable layer, such as a skin wrap. Such an alternative approach would remove hygiene concerns, necessity of sanitizing hands, and cleaning the device each time. Although it has practical challenges, haptics, in particular, provide enormously beneficial opportunities amidst the pandemic.

Limitations and Future Work: We acknowledge that our current number of participants is lacking for an in-depth quantitative analysis, largely due to the pandemic situation. Thus, we plan to reserve that for future works, including a study on long-term deployment. With the forearm augmentation, we employed the same pair of forearm sleeves for all the participants to wear. We spent a significant amount of time ensuring they were sufficiently hygienic. Hygiene concerns made us realise the challenging task of re-designing the system to be either easily sterilisable or disposable. Furthermore, users may sense a slight warmth on the skin from the heat generated in the SMA wires, although there is a thermal protective layer in the forearm augmentation just above the skin. Additionally, some of participants commented on the brightness of the jamming-canvas in low light conditions. In the future, this can be resolved by employing an ambient light sensor in the implementation. Currently, the system does not restrict the drawing privileges of users. Users are permitted to draw anything in public, potentially resulting in obscene drawings. In the future, these concerns can be avoided using a machine learning algorithm.

The current implementation of the arm-sleeve can be problematic for hygiene, yet from an interaction design standpoint, we find the subtle touch sensation from the sleeves to be quite crucial while social distancing. Although this proof-of-concept augmented arm-sleeve provides many advantages, improving the system usability in the real-world context requires more work. Those limitations can be overcome by manufacturing and designing the device in a sterilisable or disposable manner. In the user study, we ensured that our current implementation was sufficiently disinfected for users to interact with Jammify.

5   Conclusion

We developed Jammify, a multi-sensory system that enable users to share their remote touch sensations via an augmented arm-sleeve, while they engage in a collaborative drawing activity on a jamming-canvas that consists of a two-sided light display. The overall system provides multi-user interaction possibilities by enabling users to interact with free-hand gestures on each side of the wall in several modes, such as own-view and shared-view. The user interactions were promising, as this unique art-jamming system delivers an assertive experience to the users. We evaluated Jammify with ten participants in three different modes: Collaborative, Competitive, and Exploratory. We found that the Exploratory mode was most preferred by participants. Also, based on the findings, we concluded that the augmented arm sleeve enhanced the user experience with Jammify. As it maintains appropriate social distancing, we envision the concept of Jammify as a blend of haptic and visual modalities in large scale public interactive designs so that users may still create content together in these troubling times.

Acknowledgement. This work was supported by Assistive Augmentation research grant under the Entrepreneurial Universities (EU) initiative of New Zealand. We thank Peter Cleveland, Robyn Walton, and Prasanth Sasikumar for their assistance in constructing the LED display.

References

1. Ackad, C., Tomitsch, M., Kay, J.: Skeletons and silhouettes: comparing user representations at a gesture-based large display. In: Proceedings of the 2016 CHI Conference on Human Factors in Computing Systems, CHI 2016, pp. 2343–2347. Association for Computing Machinery, New York (2016). https://doi.org/10.1145/2858036.2858427
2. Akshita, Alagarai Sampath, H., Indurkhya, B., Lee, E., Bae, Y.: Towards multimodal affective feedback: interaction between visual and haptic modalities. In: Proceedings of the 33rd Annual ACM Conference on Human Factors in Computing Systems, CHI 2015, pp. 2043–2052. Association for Computing Machinery, New York (2015). https://doi.org/10.1145/2702123.2702288
3. Ananny, M., Strohecker, C., Biddick, K.: Shifting scales on common ground: developing personal expressions and public opinions. Int. J. Continuing Eng. Educ. Life Long Learn. **14**(6), 484–505 (2004)

4. Baer, M., Leenders, R.T.A., Oldham, G.R., Vadera, A.K.: Win or lose the battle for creativity: the power and perils of intergroup competition. Acad. Manag. J. **53**(4), 827–845 (2010)
5. Bakdash, J.Z., Augustyn, J.S., Proffitt, D.R.: Large displays enhance spatial knowledge of a virtual environment. In: Proceedings of the 3rd Symposium on Applied Perception in Graphics and Visualization, APGV 2006, pp. 59–62. Association for Computing Machinery, New York (2006). https://doi.org/10.1145/1140491.1140503
6. Barthelmess, P., Kaiser, E., Lunsford, R., McGee, D., Cohen, P., Oviatt, S.: Human-centered collaborative interaction. In: Proceedings of the 1st ACM International Workshop on Human-Centered Multimedia, HCM 2006, pp. 1–8. Association for Computing Machinery, New York (2006). https://doi.org/10.1145/1178745.1178747
7. Boehner, K., DePaula, R., Dourish, P., Sengers, P.: Affect: from information to interaction. In: Proceedings of the 4th Decennial Conference on Critical Computing: Between Sense and Sensibility, CC 2005, pp. 59–68. Association for Computing Machinery, New York (2005). https://doi.org/10.1145/1094562.1094570
8. Bonanni, L., Vaucelle, C.: Affective touchcasting. In: ACM SIGGRAPH 2006 Sketches, SIGGRAPH 2006, p. 35-es. Association for Computing Machinery, New York (2006). https://doi.org/10.1145/1179849.1179893
9. Brave, S., Dahley, A.: Intouch: a medium for haptic interpersonal communication. In: Extended Abstracts on Human Factors in Computing Systems, CHI 1997, CHI EA 1997, pp. 363–364. Association for Computing Machinery, New York (1997). https://doi.org/10.1145/1120212.1120435
10. Brignull, H., Rogers, Y.: Enticing people to interact with large public displays in public spaces. In: Proceedings of INTERACT, Brighton, UK, vol. 3, pp. 17–24 (2003)
11. Brown, A.R., Sorensen, A.: Dynamic media arts programming in impromptu. In: Proceedings of the 6th ACM SIGCHI Conference on Creativity & Cognition, pp. 245–246 (2007)
12. Burkitt, E., Barrett, M., Davis, A.: Effects of different emotion terms on the size and colour of children's drawings. Int. J. Art Ther. **14**(2), 74–84 (2009)
13. Depth Cameras Intel RealSense (2020). https://www.intelrealsense.com/depth-camera-d435/. Accessed 10 Apr 2020
14. Cheok, A.D., et al.: BlogWall: social and cultural interaction for children. Adv. Hum.-Comput. Interact. **2008** (2008)
15. Churchill, E.F., Nelson, L., Denoue, L., Helfman, J., Murphy, P.: Sharing multimedia content with interactive public displays: a case study. In: Proceedings of the 5th Conference on Designing Interactive Systems: Processes, Practices, Methods, and Techniques, pp. 7–16 (2004)
16. Coelho, M., Maes, P.: Sprout I/O: a texturally rich interface. In: Proceedings of the 2nd International Conference on Tangible and Embedded Interaction, TEI 2008, pp. 221–222. Association for Computing Machinery, New York (2008). https://doi.org/10.1145/1347390.1347440
17. Czerwinski, M., Robertson, G., Meyers, B., Smith, G., Robbins, D., Tan, D.: Large display research overview. In: Extended Abstracts on Human Factors in Computing Systems, CHI 2006, CHI EA 2006, pp. 69–74. Association for Computing Machinery, New York (2006). https://doi.org/10.1145/1125451.1125471
18. Czerwinski, M., Smith, G., Regan, T., Meyers, B., Robertson, G.G., Starkweather, G.K.: Toward characterizing the productivity benefits of very large displays. In: Interact, vol. 3, pp. 9–16 (2003)

19. Davis, N., Hsiao, C.P., Singh, K.Y., Lin, B., Magerko, B.: Creative sense-making: quantifying interaction dynamics in co-creation. In: Proceedings of the 2017 ACM SIGCHI Conference on Creativity and Cognition, C&C 2017, pp. 356–366. Association for Computing Machinery, New York (2017). https://doi.org/10.1145/3059454.3059478

20. Duarte, L., Carriço, L.: The collaboration platform: a cooperative work course case-study. In: 2010 Eighth International Conference on Creating, Connecting and Collaborating through Computing, pp. 19–25. IEEE (2010)

21. Eid, M.A., Al Osman, H.: Affective haptics: current research and future directions. IEEE Access **4**, 26–40 (2015)

22. Eisenberg, J., Thompson, W.F.: The effects of competition on improvisers' motivation, stress, and creative performance. Creat. Res. J. **23**(2), 129–136 (2011)

23. Elvitigala, S., Chan, S.W.T., Howell, N., Matthies, D.J., Nanayakkara, S.: Doodle daydream: an interactive display to support playful and creative interactions between co-workers. In: Proceedings of the Symposium on Spatial User Interaction, SUI 2018, p. 186. Association for Computing Machinery, New York (2018). https://doi.org/10.1145/3267782.3274681

24. Fan, J.E., Dinculescu, M., Ha, D.: Collabdraw: an environment for collaborative sketching with an artificial agent. In: Proceedings of the 2019 on Creativity and Cognition, pp. 556–561. Association for Computing Machinery, New York (2019). https://doi.org/10.1145/3325480.3326578

25. Fan, L., Yu, C., Shi, Y.: Guided social sharing of emotions through drawing art therapy: generation of deep emotional expression and helpful emotional responses. In: Proceedings of the Seventh International Symposium of Chinese CHI, Chinese CHI 2019, pp. 65–78. Association for Computing Machinery, New York (2019). https://doi.org/10.1145/3332169.3333571

26. Felix, E.R., Galoian, K.A., Aarons, C., Brown, M.D., Kearing, S.A., Heiss, U.: Utility of quantitative computerized pain drawings in a sample of spinal stenosis patients. Pain Med. **11**(3), 382–389 (2010)

27. Ghinea, G., Gill, D., Frank, A., De Souza, L.: Using geographical information systems for management of back-pain data. J. Manag. Med. (2002)

28. Gupta, A., Irudayaraj, A.A.R., Balakrishnan, R.: HapticClench: investigating squeeze sensations using memory alloys. In: Proceedings of the 30th Annual ACM Symposium on User Interface Software and Technology, UIST 2017, pp. 109–117. Association for Computing Machinery, New York (2017). https://doi.org/10.1145/3126594.3126598

29. Gupta, A., Irudayaraj, A.A.R., Balakrishnan, R.: HapticClench: investigating squeeze sensations using memory alloys. In: Proceedings of the 30th Annual ACM Symposium on User Interface Software and Technology, pp. 109–117 (2017)

30. Gutwin, C., Greenberg, S.: A descriptive framework of workspace awareness for real-time groupware. Comput. Supported Cooper. Work (CSCW) **11**(3–4), 411–446 (2002)

31. Hamdan, N.A.H., Wagner, A., Voelker, S., Steimle, J., Borchers, J.: Springlets: expressive, flexible and silent on-skin tactile interfaces. In: Proceedings of the 2019 CHI Conference on Human Factors in Computing Systems, CHI 2019. Association for Computing Machinery, New York (2019). https://doi.org/10.1145/3290605.3300718

32. Harrison, C., Horstman, J., Hsieh, G., Hudson, S.: Unlocking the expressivity of point lights. In: Proceedings of the SIGCHI Conference on Human Factors in Computing Systems, CHI 2012, pp. 1683–1692. Association for Computing Machinery, New York (2012). https://doi.org/10.1145/2207676.2208296

33. Hettiarachchi, A., Nanayakkara, S., Yeo, K.P., Shilkrot, R., Maes, P.: Fingerdraw: more than a digital paintbrush. In: Proceedings of the 4th Augmented Human International Conference, AH 2013, pp. 1–4. Association for Computing Machinery, New York (2013). https://doi.org/10.1145/2459236.2459237

34. Huber, J., Shilkrot, R., Maes, P., Nanayakkara, S.: Assistive Augmentation, 1st edn. Springer, Heidelberg (2017)

35. Ilievski, F., Mazzeo, A.D., Shepherd, R.F., Chen, X., Whitesides, G.M.: Soft robotics for chemists. Angew. Chem. Int. Ed. **50**(8), 1890–1895 (2011)

36. Indurkhya, B.: Towards multimodal affective stimulation: interaction between visual, auditory and haptic modalities. In: Stojanov, G., Kulakov, A. (eds.) ICT Innovations 2016. AISC, vol. 665, pp. 3–8. Springer, Cham (2018). https://doi.org/10.1007/978-3-319-68855-8_1

37. Jang, A., MacLean, D.L., Heer, J.: BodyDiagrams: improving communication of pain symptoms through drawing. In: Proceedings of the SIGCHI Conference on Human Factors in Computing Systems, CHI 2014, pp. 1153–1162. Association for Computing Machinery, New York (2014). https://doi.org/10.1145/2556288.2557223

38. Journeaux, J., Gorrill, H. (eds.): Collective and Collaborative Drawing in Contemporary Practice. Cambridge Scholars Publishing, UK (2017)

39. Kettebekov, S., Sharma, R.: Toward natural gesture/speech control of a large display. In: Little, M.R., Nigay, L. (eds.) EHCI 2001. LNCS, vol. 2254, pp. 221–234. Springer, Heidelberg (2001). https://doi.org/10.1007/3-540-45348-2_20

40. Khamis, M., Hoesl, A., Klimczak, A., Reiss, M., Alt, F., Bulling, A.: EyeScout: active eye tracking for position and movement independent gaze interaction with large public displays. In: Proceedings of the 30th Annual ACM Symposium on User Interface Software and Technology, UIST 2017, pp. 155–166. Association for Computing Machinery, New York (2017). https://doi.org/10.1145/3126594.3126630

41. Kheirikhah, M.M., Rabiee, S., Edalat, M.E.: A review of shape memory alloy actuators in robotics. In: Ruiz-del-Solar, J., Chown, E., Plöger, P.G. (eds.) RoboCup 2010. LNCS (LNAI), vol. 6556, pp. 206–217. Springer, Heidelberg (2011). https://doi.org/10.1007/978-3-642-20217-9_18

42. Knoop, E., Rossiter, J.: The tickler: a compliant wearable tactile display for stroking and tickling. In: Proceedings of the 33rd Annual ACM Conference Extended Abstracts on Human Factors in Computing Systems, CHI EA 2015, pp. 1133–1138. Association for Computing Machinery, New York (2015). https://doi.org/10.1145/2702613.2732749

43. Knoop, E., Rossiter, J.: The tickler: a compliant wearable tactile display for stroking and tickling. In: Proceedings of the 33rd Annual ACM Conference Extended Abstracts on Human Factors in Computing Systems, pp. 1133–1138 (2015)

44. Leahu, L., Schwenk, S., Sengers, P.: Subjective objectivity: negotiating emotional meaning. In: Proceedings of the 7th ACM Conference on Designing Interactive Systems, pp. 425–434 (2008)

45. Martin, K., Penn, A., Gavin, L.: Engaging with a situated display via picture messaging. In: Extended Abstracts on Human Factors in Computing Systems, CHI 2006, pp. 1079–1084 (2006)

46. McCarthy, J.: Using public displays to create conversation opportunities. In: Proceedings of Workshop on Public, Community, and Situated Displays at CSCW 2002 (2002)

47. Michelis, D., Müller, J.: The audience funnel: observations of gesture based interaction with multiple large displays in a city center. Int. J. Hum.-Comput. Interact. **27**(6), 562–579 (2011)

48. Moon, B.L.: The Role of Metaphor in Art Therapy: Theory, Method, and Experience. Charles C Thomas Publisher (2007)

49. Mueller, F.F., et al.: Next steps for human-computer integration. In: Proceedings of the 2020 CHI Conference on Human Factors in Computing Systems, CHI 2020, pp. 1–15. Association for Computing Machinery, New York (2020). https://doi.org/10.1145/3313831.3376242

50. Mullenbach, J., Shultz, C., Colgate, J.E., Piper, A.M.: Exploring affective communication through variable-friction surface haptics. In: Proceedings of the SIGCHI Conference on Human Factors in Computing Systems, CHI 2014, pp. 3963–3972. Association for Computing Machinery, New York (2014). https://doi.org/10.1145/2556288.2557343

51. Muthukumarana, S., Elvitigala, D.S., Cortes, J.P.F., Matthies, D.J., Nanayakkara, S.: PhantomTouch: creating an extended reality by the illusion of touch using a shape-memory alloy matrix. In: SIGGRAPH Asia 2019 XR, SA 2019, pp. 29–30. Association for Computing Machinery, New York (2019). https://doi.org/10.1145/3355355.3361877

52. Muthukumarana, S., Elvitigala, D.S., Forero Cortes, J.P., Matthies, D.J., Nanayakkara, S.: Touch me gently: recreating the perception of touch using a shape-memory alloy matrix. In: Proceedings of the 2020 CHI Conference on Human Factors in Computing Systems, CHI 2020, pp. 1–12. Association for Computing Machinery, New York (2020). https://doi.org/10.1145/3313831.3376491

53. Mynatt, E.D., Igarashi, T., Edwards, W.K., LaMarca, A.: Flatland: new dimensions in office whiteboards. In: Proceedings of the SIGCHI Conference on Human Factors in Computing Systems, CHI 1999, pp. 346–353. Association for Computing Machinery, New York (1999). https://doi.org/10.1145/302979.303108

54. Nakao, T., Kunze, K., Isogai, M., Shimizu, S., Pai, Y.S.: FingerFlex: shape memory alloy-based actuation on fingers for kinesthetic haptic feedback. In: 19th International Conference on Mobile and Ubiquitous Multimedia, MUM 2020, pp. 240–244. Association for Computing Machinery, New York (2020). https://doi.org/10.1145/3428361.3428404

55. Nakao, T., et al.: ShareHaptics: a modular haptic feedback system using shape memory alloy for mixed reality shared space applications. In: ACM SIGGRAPH 2019 Posters. SIGGRAPH 2019. Association for Computing Machinery, New York (2019). https://doi.org/10.1145/3306214.3338597

56. Nanayakkara, S., Schroepfer, T., Wyse, L., Lian, A., Withana, A.: SonicSG: from floating to sounding pixels. In: Proceedings of the 8th Augmented Human International Conference, AH 2017. Association for Computing Machinery, New York (2017). https://doi.org/10.1145/3041164.3041190

57. Nanayakkara, S., Taylor, E., Wyse, L., Ong, S.H.: An enhanced musical experience for the deaf: design and evaluation of a music display and a haptic chair. In: Proceedings of the SIGCHI Conference on Human Factors in Computing Systems, CHI 2009, pp. 337–346. Association for Computing Machinery, New York (2009). https://doi.org/10.1145/1518701.1518756

58. Nanayakkara, S.C., Wyse, L., Ong, S.H., Taylor, E.A.: Enhancing musical experience for the hearing-impaired using visual and haptic displays. Hum.-Comput. Interact. **28**(2), 115–160 (2013). https://doi.org/10.1080/07370024.2012.697006

59. Nuitrack (2020). https://nuitrack.com/. Accessed 10 Feb 2020

60. Peng, C.: Survey of collaborative drawing support tools. Comput. Supported Cooper. Work (CSCW) **1**(3), 197–228 (1992)
61. Reetz, A., Gutwin, C., Stach, T., Nacenta, M.A., Subramanian, S.: Superflick: a natural and efficient technique for long-distance object placement on digital tables. Graph. Interface **2006**, 163–170 (2006)
62. Robertson, G., et al.: The large-display user experience. IEEE Comput. Graph. Appl. **25**(4), 44–51 (2005)
63. Rogers, Y., Lindley, S.: Collaborating around vertical and horizontal large interactive displays: which way is best? Interact. Comput. **16**(6), 1133–1152 (2004)
64. Shaballout, N., Neubert, T.A., Boudreau, S., Beissner, F.: From paper to digital applications of the pain drawing: systematic review of methodological milestones. JMIR mHealth uHealth **7**(9), e14569 (2019)
65. Sheridan, J., Bryan-Kinns, N., Reeves, S., Marshall, J., Lane, G.: Graffito: crowd-based performative interaction at festivals. In: Extended Abstracts on Human Factors in Computing Systems, CHI 2011, CHI EA 2011, pp. 1129–1134. Association for Computing Machinery, New York (2011). https://doi.org/10.1145/1979742.1979725
66. Shoemaker, G., Tang, A., Booth, K.S.: Shadow reaching: a new perspective on interaction for large displays. In: Proceedings of the 20th Annual ACM Symposium on User Interface Software and Technology, UIST 2007, pp. 53–56. Association for Computing Machinery, New York (2007). https://doi.org/10.1145/1294211.1294221
67. Suhonen, K., Väänänen-Vainio-Mattila, K., Mäkelä, K.: User experiences and expectations of vibrotactile, thermal and squeeze feedback in interpersonal communication. In: The 26th BCS Conference on Human Computer Interaction 26, pp. 205–214 (2012)
68. Tang, J.C., Minneman, S.L.: Videodraw: a video interface for collaborative drawing. In: Proceedings of the SIGCHI Conference on Human Factors in Computing Systems, CHI 1990, pp. 313–320. Association for Computing Machinery, New York (1990). https://doi.org/10.1145/97243.97302
69. Taylor, S., Izadi, S., Kirk, D., Harper, R., Garcia-Mendoza, A.: Turning the tables: an interactive surface for VJing. In: Proceedings of the SIGCHI Conference on Human Factors in Computing Systems, pp. 1251–1254 (2009)
70. Von Zadow, U.: Using personal devices to facilitate multi-user interaction with large display walls. In: Adjunct Proceedings of the 28th Annual ACM Symposium on User Interface Software and Technology, pp. 25–28 (2015)
71. Wilson, G., Brewster, S.A.: Multi-moji: combining thermal, vibrotactile and visual stimuli to expand the affective range of feedback. In: Proceedings of the 2017 CHI Conference on Human Factors in Computing Systems, CHI 2017, pp. 1743–1755. Association for Computing Machinery, New York (2017). https://doi.org/10.1145/3025453.3025614
72. Yalom, I.D.: The gift of therapy: an open letter to a new generation of therapists and their patients. J. Soc. Work Pract. (2002)
73. Yeo, K.P., Nanayakkara, S.: SpeechPlay: composing and sharing expressive speech through visually augmented text. In: Proceedings of the 25th Australian Computer-Human Interaction Conference: Augmentation, Application, Innovation, Collaboration, OzCHI 2013, pp. 565–568. Association for Computing Machinery, New York (2013). https://doi.org/10.1145/2541016.2541061

74. Yoo, T., Yoo, Y., Choi, S.: An explorative study on crossmodal congruence between visual and tactile icons based on emotional responses. In: Proceedings of the 16th International Conference on Multimodal Interaction, ICMI 2014, pp. 96–103. Association for Computing Machinery, New York (2014). https://doi.org/10.1145/2663204.2663231

75. Zhao, M., Wang, Y., Redmiles, D.: Using collaborative online drawing to build up distributed teams. In: 2017 IEEE 12th International Conference on Global Software Engineering (ICGSE), pp. 61–65. IEEE (2017)

76. Zhao, M., Wang, Y., Redmiles, D.: Using collaborative online drawing to build up distributed teams. In: 2017 IEEE 12th International Conference on Global Software Engineering (ICGSE), pp. 61–65 (2017). https://doi.org/10.1109/ICGSE.2017.3

77. Zhao, M., Wang, Y., Redmiles, D.: Using playful drawing to support affective expressions and sharing in distributed teams. In: 2017 IEEE/ACM 2nd International Workshop on Emotion Awareness in Software Engineering (SEmotion), pp. 38–41 (2017). https://doi.org/10.1109/SEmotion.2017.3

Opportunities and Challenges for Reflective Data-Objects in Long-Distance Relationships

Maria Karyda[1]([🖂]) [ID] and Andrés Lucero[2] [ID]

[1] University of Southern Denmark, Kolding, Denmark
mkaryda@sdu.dk
[2] Aalto University, Espoo, Finland

Abstract. Personal data representations have been used to support acts of self-reflection, a topic that has received little attention in the context of long-distance relationships (LDRs). To explore a design space for reflective data representations in the LDR context, first-person methods have been employed together with nine generative sessions with people who had been or were in LDRs. Unlike previous work, the generative sessions were part of an autoethnographic exploration. The participants interpreted the first author's visualizations, sketched their own visualizations, and imagined their data as data objects. The insights from those sense-making sessions were then analyzed in a card sorting activity between the first author and their partner where seven themes around communication of long-distance couples emerged. Furthermore, based on the data-object ideas and the various sense making sessions, design opportunities and challenges are drawn related to the transformative nature of relationships, negative reflection and aspects of privacy. In conclusion, personal data are seen as co-evolving with humans constantly transforming people's impression of their romantic relationships in mundane environments.

Keywords: Data-objects · Reflection · Long-distance relationships

1 Introduction

People have been experimenting with their personal data through different formats, e.g., by producing visualizations [23,27,37,47], or physicalizations [1,21,33]. Those explorations are outcomes of numerous data assemblages [29] a person produces throughout time. Research on digital data practices have explored the temporal and emotional qualities of personal data to understand how people make sense of their data assemblages, but also, how they feel about them. This sense making process that relates to feelings has been discussed by scholar within the HCI community [10,11,28], however, it remains an ongoing challenge. The work in this paper sets out to further explore affective qualities of digital data, and furthermore, to imagine data objects [50] that may exist in people's everyday environments in the context of communication in LDRs.

© IFIP International Federation for Information Processing 2021
Published by Springer Nature Switzerland AG 2021
C. Ardito et al. (Eds.): INTERACT 2021, LNCS 12936, pp. 42–62, 2021.
https://doi.org/10.1007/978-3-030-85607-6_3

In this paper, the lens is set on communication data extending previous work by examining personal data as an inherently social phenomenon [9, 29]. Furthermore, the LDR research context has been selected as romantic partners already experiment with their data-sets pointing to an area for further exploration. For instance, we can find examples of this type of experimentation in online forums, such as Reddit[1] where couples share visualizations of their messaging data. The act of synthesizing [2, 41] personal data into alternative formats can help couples reflect on their shared past data-sets [10]. In those cases, data acquire characteristics of memorabilia. While acts of self-reflection have been broadly discussed in data representations, they have received little attention within the context of romantic relationships [15, 44]. Exploring data representations in that context may open up a path towards more reflective technologies supporting romantic relationships over time. In this paper reflection [3] is understood as data experiences and stories put together in ways that couples can better understand or gain some kind of insight through their communication data about their LDRs.

To explore that area, I[2] have inquired into LDR couples as their communication routine usually entails constantly keeping in touch through digital means (e.g., texting) producing large amounts of information. In fact, Stafford [43], puts emphasis on the need of LDR couples for continuous close communication, *"relationships are considered to be long distance when communication opportunities are restricted because of geographic parameters and the individuals within the relationship have expectations of continued close communications."*

Thus, I tried to make sense of Facebook messaging data between my LDR partner and I through visualizations and cardboard prototypes. Then, I invited nine people who were themselves in LDRs – or they had been in one – to generative sessions combined with semi-structured interviews where the visualizations from the previous step were discussed and further reflected upon inspiring the participants to imagine data-objects – in that last part people stretched their understandings about their data by starting to think about them as design material [42]. Data-objects [50] are artifacts in the intersection of industrial design and data physicalization [21].The coupling of personal data and everyday objects can make objects more affective and able to provoke reflection in everyday life.Last, my LDR partner was involved in a one-to-one card sorting activity to make sense of the outcomes of the first and second step. Unlike previous work [7,18,46], the generative sessions were integral to the autoethnographic exploration. Furthermore, that lengthy and detailed sense making process contributes to the corpus or research [9,12,30] that aims at understanding how people make sense of their data using qualitative methods, but also, reflects a typical Research through Design process [24].

I pose the following research questions: *How can LDR partners make sense of their communication data? How can we invite LDR partners to imagine their communication data in physical forms? Do data-objects offer opportunities for design in the area of romantic relationships?* Through this research I gained

---

[1] https://www.reddit.com/r/dataisbeautiful.

[2] First-person singular narrative will be sustained throughout the paper as this research heavily draws from first-person methods.

an understanding of the types of data-objects that people imagined in their homes and, I illustrated opportunities for design which view data-objects as living things that co-evolve with humans and help them conceptualize themselves and their actions. That is in line with Lupton and Watson's [31] research on more-than-human perspective which "positions personal data as lively human–data assemblages that are constantly changing as humans move through their everyday worlds". The contributions of this work are first methodological, where I have approached the broader context of this research on LDRs and fit that into a unique, idiosyncratic and private setting (i.e., a single couple) leveraging an interplay between an autoethnographic and a participatory approach. Second, this work contributes to *personal visualizations research* [47] as visualizations were used in novel ways e.g., sketching, and last, I offer opportunities for design in the context of LDR couples.

2   Relationships of Data Representations and Reflection

2.1   Making Sense of Reflective Representations of Personal Data

As described by Baumer et al. [3], in personal informatics [26], reflection is an element that can lead to self-knowledge through numbers. Whilst it is yet unknown how people self-reflect when triggered by data representations, previous works have illustrated various ways through which people make sense of their data and how these sense making processes might relate to self-reflection. For instance, in personal data physicalization [21], self-reflection may be triggered through association between personal data and different material-structures. However, due to emotional and temporal qualities of personal data there is much more depth in those processes which I attempt to illustrate below.

Barrass [1] has created sonifications of his personal data, a singing bowl. The interaction with the sonification triggers novel associations between data and sound. Barrass went through several iterations of the sonification. From that, I can speculate that reflection may occur during an iterative design process, and through the interaction with final sonification. In another example, Huron et al.'s [19] constructive visualizations, build upon constructive theories of learning, arguing that physical data construction is connected with learning and reflection, since reflective thought is common in education and learning [40]. In Karyda et al.'s [22] work on narrative physicalizations, three tailor-made physicalizations allowed for bodily interactions with people's data demonstrating how by involving the body people may arrive in nuanced understandings about the self.

Involving the body in data physicalization has been a way through which people can synthesize past data to then reflect on them both individually [19,22] and collectively [33]. In Data-things [33] people explored their personal data through knitting. Each participant formed a visualization through sensors placed on their knitting needles. Later, the same people were involved in the digital fabrication of their visualizations during which, they reflected on their data not only through construction but also by comparing and discussing with the rest of the group. That project illustrated the role of the social in self-reflections.

While in these examples the acts of constructing and comparing data may provoke self-reflections, there are social aspects that are rarely discussed in current literature on data physicalization. For instance, Data-objects [42,50] are inherently social opening up opportunities to explore reflection through data in mundane environments as they can become part of people's routines. As Li et al. [25] argue *"In comparison to creating completely new devices, augmenting current technologies and integrating them into users' communication ecology could be more easy and beneficial than introducing totally new devices."* I argue that, while integrating any device to people's communication ecology might be destructive for the couple, data-objects could blend into the background providing feedback only when people want to interact with them, and therefore, are appropriate for the context of this research.

In the context of InfoViz, one of the goals of personal visualization is to enable multi-faceted insights with one of them being *reflective insights* [37]. In *Dear Data* projects by Lupi and Posavec's [27] that goal of personal visualizations is very distinguishable. That project employed a manual approach to gathering and analyzing data. For a year and every week, the two authors would exchange postcards. Every week both authors agreed on a topic and then focused on gathering data based on that. Some of their topics were clocks, number of thank yous, smiles and more. The postcards included in their front drawings of each topic and on the back, they contained the address and instructions on how the receiver should read the drawing. As the authors described, the process of gathering but also visualizing the data was labor intensive and very slow. However, that process helped the author to realize things they do they were not aware of such as, Posavec's who realised that she tells more often *thank you* to strangers compared to her family and friends.

2.2   Data Sharing and Reflection in Romantic Relationships

In the context of LDRs there are several examples of tangible user interfaces (TUIs) [8,34,39,49] that explore remote communication between couples in an attempt to bridge the physical distance yet none explicitly discuss aspects of reflection. As Jansen et al. [21] argue while there is an overlap between TUIs [20] and data physicalization, the former focuses on input and manipulation while the latter is meant to explore and gain insights so it is more focused on output and exploration tasks. The focus on insights is interlinked with reflection and therefore, data physicalization appears to be appropriate for exploring reflection in the context of LDRs. Below, I present examples which focus on data sharing between romantic partners. While in most examples it is not apparent how and if reflection has occurred, when possible, I attempt to speculate on how the designed artifacts in those works might have triggered people's reflective thinking.

Thudt et al.'s [45] work is at the intersection of data physicalization [21] and romantic relationships. Thudt created ceramic tableware on which she represented communication of data (e.g., Skype) between herself and her partner. The purpose of those objects was for data to become part of everyday life in a meaningful way during mundane tasks for the purpose of self-reflection. As Heinicker [35] argues, *"being in a long distance relationship requires a thoughtful way of communication."* For that purpose he created an SMS necklace as a gift for his long-distance partner where he physicalized Goodnight SMSs that were exchanged between the two partners. Heinicker views text messages as manifestations of the self in his partner's life while in a long-distance situation.

Similarly, Helms [18] developed the leaky objects where implicit information is shared between couples through everyday objects. For instance, a lamp that is left switched on in someone's apartment shows presence of someone else, or a warm stove indicates that someone has used it recently. The leaky objects is an autobiographical design project where Helms builds upon the notion of implicit information shared between them and their partner enabling *"expressive communication and ambiguous speculation."* In that project reflection is not discussed, however, implicit information may have triggered reflections about the routine of the couple or even other unforeseen thoughts. Differently Branham et al.'s project, Diary Built For Two [4] focuses on reflection. In that project, the authors investigate reflection and restorying through exchange of selected diary entries between romantic partners. Similarly, Thieme et al. [44] developed the Lovers' box through which couples exchanged video messages. In that project the video messages became *"mirrors and sources of reflection"* about the couples' relationship and the videos became meaningful artifacts.

Away from the physical, Griggio et al. [15] study couples' communication through different streams of data. Those streams illustrate closeness to home, battery level, steps and more. One of the findings of that study was that there were no patterns on how couples used the app as couples appropriated the app and reflected on those data streams in their own idiosyncratic way. This finding supports the idea of how unique intimate relationships are for those experiencing them [13], a fact that provides researchers with a great opportunity to develop something for uniqueness within that research context. In fact, in research about intimate relationships there are several examples of autobiographical design exploration [7,18,46], yet none of those examples explore the prospect of reflective artifacts which is aimed through this paper.

3   Methodology

This research investigates how can we use communication data to inform the design of data objects in the context of LDRs. To conduct this research, I have used an RtD approach [24] which involved several interlinked sense making activities. Unlike previous work, I have combined first-person methods with co-design design activities. Traditionally an auto-ethnographic approach would focus on the individual. In my work, following an RtD approach where iterative thinking and doing is central, I contextualized nine one-to-one generative sessions as part of a broader (iterative) sense-making process (three levels of sense-making) which were all part of the autoethnographic exploration. In particular, this research started as an autoethnographic exploration where I used the messaging data of

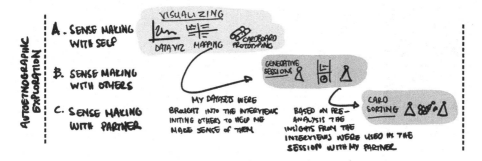

Fig. 1. Three levels of sense making took place throughout the stud. In level A, I explored the Facebook messaging data-sets by myself. In level B, I explored the data-sets with nine people who were themselves, or had been, in LDRs. In level C, I conducted an analysis with my LDR partner of steps A and B in a card sorting activity.

my long-distance partner and I in different sense making activities with the purpose to design data-objects. One of those sense making activities involved nine people to interpret and sketch visualization based on their own LDR communication data, which then helped them to imagine their data in material forms. *"Couples build their own idiosyncratic universe which is different from others"* [6]. Building upon this notion, I used interviews with people who had been or were in LDRs. The purpose of this mixed method approach Fig. 1 was to enrich the autoethnographic accounts by taking into consideration a broader perspective yet adjusted to the unique communication routines of a single couple. Prior to participation, my partner, as well as, all participants of the study read a detailed description of the project and signed consent forms.

3.1   Visualizing Messaging Data Between My LDR Partner and I

Thus, based on nine months of Facebook messaging data at the beginning of my LDR relationship, data visualizations were created in traditional graphs but also in exploratory ways (Fig. 2a, 1b). During those months I was in [European Country A] and my partner was living in [European Country B] therefore, we were in the same time zone.

To make sense of those data sets, I formed a mapping (Fig. 2c) where the traditional visualizations were juxtaposed with questions such as, *what are the main thoughts the graph brings to me?* Three main categories were generated based on the mapping. *Intensity, togetherness* and *flow-maintenance.* Following that activity, I did cardboard prototypes which reflected the categories of the mapping. After my initial explorations, I realised I needed input to better understand my research context, both from people who were themselves in a LDR, as well as from my partner. The reason was that I needed to better understand the data I had extracted from Facebook, as well as, the potential of designing for data representations in the context of LDRs.

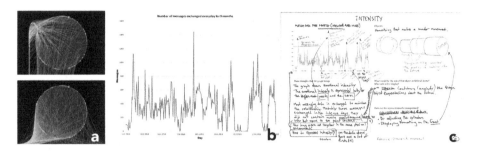

Fig. 2. (a) InfoViz of the messages using processing, (b) Traditional Visualization of the nine months LDR graph and (c) Data Visualization Mapping.

3.2   Generative Sessions with People in LDRs

For the second part of this research, I invited nine people (6 female, 3 male) who were in LDRs, to individual generative sessions that included semi-structured interviews. Since I was set to explore a sensitive topic such as, individuals' romantic relationship and also reveal information about my relationship to them, I intentionally reached to people with who I was acquainted with and I knew they were or had been in long-distance relationships. Sharing personal information mutually, created an environment of trust where the participants were comfortable to reveal personal information. Three of the participants were in a cross-continental relationships (P1, P2, P9), the other six were either in the same time zones (P3) or an hour apart (P4, P5, P6, P7, P8). All the participants apart from P6 and P7 (25–30) were in the 30–35 age group. All the participants were in heteronomrative relationships. In my view, it was irrelevant to aim for a more diverse sample as online communication data between couples should not be seen as something that is affected by sexual orientation. The main goal of the generative sessions were to help me better understand my data-sets as those people were or had been themselves in LDRs.

The generative sessions were split into three parts and seven out of nine were conducted through Skype. Throughout, I used slides as a visual aid. In the first part, I invited the participants to help me reflect on my nine-month messaging data visualizations. I showed three visualizations to them, all presented in Fig. 3. One that shows the amount and frequency of messages of each person (Fig. 3a), another that illustrates the overall amount and frequency of messages (Fig. 3b), and a last that showed the amount of messages sent over day and night (Fig. 3c). I asked the participants open questions such as, *what comes to mind when you see this graph?*, similar to the questions I asked myself while I was doing the mapping. In addition, questions that were related to the topics that emerged in my mapping (e.g. intensity) were added, *do you see intensity in the graph?* During the second part of the session, I asked the participants to pick one of the messaging visualizations that were discussed earlier and sketch out on paper a similar visualization to reflect on their own communication data (Fig. 4). The sketches were an interpretation of what the participants thought their communication

Fig. 3. From left to right the visualizations show: a) amount and frequency of messages of each person, b) overall amount and frequency of messages, c) the average of the amount of messages sent over day and night.

data might look like resulting into subjective visualizations [47]. After, the participants completed their sketches I asked them to present them. Next, I asked participants questions about the concepts that were discussed previously about my visualizations (e.g. intensity, maintenance). In the last part of the generative sessions, I challenged the participants' perception about their visualization by inviting them to think of the data as an artifact that has three dimensions and can be placed somewhere in the participants' personal environments. This last part of the generative sessions was also supported by visual inputs, which were gradually helping the participants to imagine *the kind of data-object they wanted, the texture it would have, the type of modality it would use to show the data, the interaction it would facilitate,* and *if or how the participants' partners would use that artifact.*

3.3 Card Sorting Activity with My LDR Partner

In the third part, a card sorting activity was conducted face-to-face between my partner and I where our messaging data visualizations, as well as, some of the concepts from the generative sessions were discussed and reflected upon. Concepts and quotes were selected from the interviews by conducting a pre-analysis [48]. To reflect, I used three sets of hexagonal cards. The first set included visualizations and raw data from the nine-month messaging data. The second set included concepts around messaging derived from the generative sessions in the form of provocative statements or direct quotes. The third set were blank cards used to write down our reflections from synthesizing the other two sets of cards. The data visualizations, the concepts and our reflections were discussed and organized in an open-ended way. Though this activity I wanted to combine a broader understanding about the communication of long-distance couples and see how those practices were reflected in my own relationship.

3.4 Analysis

All the qualitative data collected from the generative sessions and the card sorting activity was transcribed. I open coded the generative session data and

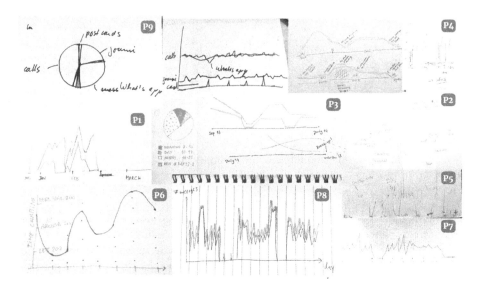

Fig. 4. In this collage I present the visualizations the participants produced during the generative sessions.

organised it in thematic categories following abductive reasoning [5]. Then, the categories were challenged by the second author to validate the results. Parts of the generative session data was also analysed, reflected upon, and categorised during the card sorting activity. The clusters formed in the latter provide a more in-depth analysis of the communication practices of the nine participants with their partners and are presented below.

4   Results

In this section, I present how the participants interpreted, sketched, presented and reflected on the visualizations. Then, I present the results from the card sorting activity that illustrates current communication practices of the participants with their partners' and what that meant from the point of view of my relationship. Last, I present what purpose the participants assigned to the data-objects and which aspects of communication appeared relevant to materialize.

Notably, six participants reflected on their current or former relationships already from the beginning of the generative sessions. For instance, P3 reflected on how she used to communicate 15 years ago with her long-distance partner. *"There wasn't even like MSN chat. We had to go into like chat rooms offered by specific portals and private mode to be able to talk over chat once a week."* P4 would link almost every question to the communication practices with her partner. P1 and P2 compared the second part of the session to therapy with P1 using the word "cathartic" to describe how she felt visualizing a former-relationship of hers. Overall, the participants were of the opinion that my graphs were too open for interpretation since the peaks and lows opened up for multiple explanations. For instance, the peaks in the first visualization were translated as emotional support (P1, P9), doing an activity together (P8, P1), meaningful discussions/special days (P1, P2, P4, P5, P9) and arguments (P1, P6, P7, P9). The lows of the graph or the *"valleys"* (P3) were translated as busy days (P1, P9), silence due to arguments (P1, P7, P8, P9) and holidays together (P1, P3, P6, P7, P9). My graphs were described as having a certain *"balance"* (P1, P8). The communication is described as frequent, homogenic (P6), constant (P1, P3) and consistent (P9). My second graph showed separately my amount and frequency of messages and my partner's too. In that case a discussion was raised around the length of the messages, about who is *"feeding the chat"* (P6) meaning who initiates the discussions and about how the communication appears to be balanced between me and my partner since *"the two lines follow each other"* (P7) in a consistent way.

Overall, my Facebook data visualizations provided enough information for the participants to guess texting habits such as, to understand that one follows the other, that the communication is balanced, to understand when my partner and I were physically together and to guess important moments in the data-set while they knew nothing about the content of the messages.

In the second part of the generative sessions, when the participants were sketching their communication graphs, the sketches showed a person's own truth and a subjective image of their communication with current and former partners. P1 said *"It's funny to..to think of.. because I'm imagining, right? I'm telling the story I want to. Not necessarily what happened because we're not checking the data sets."* Not all of the graphs resonated with all the participants. Depending on the type and state of each relationship the participants selected different graphs to sketch. For instance, P1 created a communication visualization of her former relationship where the communication was one-sided, her writing to him a lot, and him not responding. That made her pick graph B because graph A in her case would not make sense. P2 who was in a cross-continent relationship selected graph C because through that she could show the different time zones for her and her partner. P9 was also in a cross-continent relationship however, in her relationship she uses different channels to communicate with her partner thus, she came up with her own visualization style.

Topics such as, the communication rituals of each couple, special days of texting, stand by messages and other practices related to digital data were also discussed. In relation to communication routines P4 who uses a lot of texting in her relationship said *"...and I have our little messenger open and we just write the whole day basically."* P6 in an almost ritualistic way waits for the weekend to talk to her partner. During the week her and him discuss casual topics and *"the weekend is the time for meaningful conversations."* (P6) Those meaningful conversations might have been initiated during the week with stand by messages. P4 also talks about messages that might be answered even two hours later but for her it is fine because this is how the couple communicates. P9 talks about messages that, due to the time difference, her partner will only

Fig. 5. This Figure shows, (a) the first cluster that was formed during the session, while in (b) we can see the entire mapping. (c) is an example of marking the cards to connect the with cards in other clusters (d) the order in which the clusters were formed.

see nine hours later: *"so you can send a text message but you won't receive a reaction. Only nine hours later."* In the case of P6, those stand by messages that are also important become long and concise and the communication begins to become slow since each partner takes time to reflect and then reply. Or for P2 whose partner lives in North America there are periods when she is worried and then their communication changes since she starts texting more: *"for instance September is the hurricane season in [...]. So, I guess in September we talk much more because then you to constantly check where the thunder and hurricanes are going."* Last the participants talked about other digital communication practices apart from texting they use in their daily life such as, the journi application[3] that P9 uses with her partner and both update every week with pictures from their days, which gives a glimpse into each other's life.

4.1   Card Sorting Activity

The card sorting activity was conducted between my partner and I, using graphs from our communication data, building upon the concepts and ideas that were discussed in the generative sessions. In this activity, a visualization would be picked and juxtaposed with another and with the concepts from the generative sessions. Visualizations, concepts and our reflections were all clustered. The outcome of that process was a physical mind map of seven clusters which are presented in Fig. 5b which we see as aspect of communication data that could be further extended to design for reflection. In Fig. 5d we illustrate the order in which the clusters were formed. We present them below accordingly.

Balanced Communication. The session started by discussing the day and night visualization (Fig. 3c). That graph made my partner think of three main qualities revolving around communication between couples. The graph presented the communication between the two of us involving a natural external condition such as, day and night. That led to a discussion of how external factors may

---

[3] https://www.journiapp.com.

influence the communication between a couple. Despite external factors, she and I learned how to communicate with each other and we co-constructed our normality through messaging. In that respect, the day and night graph illustrates a balance of communication between us. The graph illustrates a balance not in the sense of evenness but in terms of how a couple builds its own normality of communication. Our normality included a large amount of messages and a distinguishable difference between day and night. For other couples, this might appear extreme. However, the normality of the communication between partners perhaps can always be seen as a product that is co-constructed depending on external factors and the behavioral traits of the people involved.

Four more data sets were included under this cluster. Those were four of the days that my partner and I exchanged the most messages which would be about 1000 messages per day. Two of those data sets had exactly the same amount of messages which at first glance was an odd finding. However, when further discussed, we realised that indeed, in terms of balanced messaging *"if you speak around the same time, everyday, it's very likely for this to happen,"* to have the same amount of messages. Linking this back to the idea of balanced communication, there was a routine which was built over time. Thus, although that finding appeared to be odd in the beginning, in essence it was very likely that the numbers would repeat. While discussing the dates with the largest amount of messages, my partner and I were trying to remember what happened in those days. For most of the cases it was quite easy to recall the events. *"Do you remember? It was the day that I was sending you voice messages,"* my partner said. *"You were going somewhere, you were hitting the road I remember,"* I replied. Thus, together based on an event we remembered the reason behind the large amount of messages. At some point I asked her to compare how the messages sent on January were different from those sent in August. She said that the first were messages of getting to know each other, while the second were messages of being already in the relationship. *"You know what, everything connects with each other,"* my partner said while thinking about where to place the cards. That happened when we were half way through the first cluster.

Meaningful Messages. The main data set of the second cluster was the day my partner and I had exchanged 1445 messages. That date was a very emotional day for us as we were texting until the next morning. Hence, we connected it with a card that we then wrote on top *"the peaks are meaningful days."* That led to a discussion of how that data, the number 1445, while it is raw data it was not perceived as such anymore. It acquired a sentimental, meaningful value for us. At that point we also discussed how sometimes we save messages by taking a screenshot, in essence capturing a picture of the communication between us. My partner and I keep screenshots to remember an important moment to be able to revisit when wanted. However, meaningful days were also discussed in relation to the concept of normality of a relationship. *"For instance, if the peak of a relationship are two messages per day, it is still a meaningful day,"* my partner said. At this point the aspects of how a couple constructs their communication, quantity versus quality and aspect of meaningfulness come together.

Important Events Feeding the Communication. *"When there is something good happening or something bad you indeed need support, and often in those two cases you talk a lot (with your partner)."* This sentence refers to the dates when most messages were exchanged. While the card that says *joy, sadness and support* is connected with the card that says *feeding the chat*, forming a separate cluster both of them connect to all dates with most messages exchanged from different clusters. To indicate that, we marked the card with different color dots and connected it with other cards, drawing the same annotation on them as illustrated in Fig. 5. When I asked my partner if she can find the same emotions in the days we exchanged less messages, she said, *"yes, but, I believe that one of them (joy, sadness and support) may feed the chat."* That statement indicated that emotions can be the reason for exchanging more messages than usual. The main reason is support. You reach to the other person because you want to share how you feel and find support.

Deception. In this cluster we discussed how the amount of messages may be deceiving. The visualization of this cluster was line graph which illustrates how many messages each of us send over time, as well as the relationship of those messages. There was also a bar graph that shows the overall amount of messages exchanged throughout the nine-month period. The line graph clearly shows that the person behind the pink line was constantly sending more messages than the other person. In the generative sessions this person was named as the one who was *"feeding the chat"* (P6). My partner thought the card *"who is feeding the chat"* was rather confusing, because, while in the visualization the pink line appeared to be leading the conversation, in reality things were different. As she said *"often you are the one who is feeding the chat. While you send much less messages, you often say more substantial things."* The point she was making initiated a discussion around content versus quantity. In relation to the line graph my partner said *"I think that depending who sees the graph may understand different things."* Thus, the story told through the visualization may have different interpretations since the content seems essential in this case to understand what this graph means.

Quantity vs Quality. While quantity vs quality is a theme that came up towards the end of the session it has been discussed indirectly throughout. *Quantity vs Quality* was written on a card when discussing the amount of messages and what those numbers meant in the context of our and other relationships too. That she and I exchange several messages says little about the relationship. Other couples might exchange fewer messages while the content is more dense and or complemented by phone calls, which is also reflected in the generative sessions (P2, P5, P6, P9). Again the theme of normality comes up as we discussed that couples construct their own normality when it comes to the amount of messages, content and frequency. My partner argued that the *"quantity vs quality"* should be placed in the middle of the mapping since it connects with everything we had discussed. Then she placed the card at the edge of the table because *"this is where everything starts from."*

My partner thinks that the amount of messages *"is irrelevant information about the communication of a couple."* The quantity does not provide us with much information. However, as a matter of fact, while the quantity does not say much about the relationship the interaction between the two lines on a graph (each line represents each one of the partners) reveal a lot about the relationship itself. If there is a disconnect between the two lines probably communication is failing (lack of communication also seen in P1 and P3), or when the two lines follow each other, it seems that there is a balance in the interaction.

Error Messages. This cluster very well connects back to the amount of messages. My partner defines several of her messages as *"error messages."* The reason is that as she writes messages very quickly often it is even hard for her to make sense of them if she reads them after a while. This happens due to mixed words, auto-correct, as well as, texting sentences that are not well thought through and do not connect very well with each other.

Zero Messages. *"When all the rest were happening (pointing to the mapping on the table) this happened too (16 days of 0 messages)."* It was intriguing that there were so few days without exchanging messages–we were in the same location. Reflecting on our communication over time we realised that even when we are together sometimes we might exchange messages. This fact perhaps illustrates how instant messaging is a great part of our communication routine. This may connect again to the normality of a relationship. The fact that my partner and I constantly exchange messages illustrates how using instant messaging is not only necessary due to the distance, but instant messaging is also an inseparable part of how we chose to communicate with each other.

4.2   Imagining Data-Objects

The third part of the generative sessions, which involved imagining the couples' communication data in material forms, highlighted different aspects around the meaning, significance and functionality of data objects, as well as, aspects related to privacy. While the data-object ideas could be separated into *data-objects for reminiscence* and *reflective data-objects*, P5's and P7's ideas were not included as they were not related to data practices. For instance, P5 imagined an artifact that would enable memories through the body (touch) as he said, he would touch e.g., Christmas, on his end, an she would feel it on the inner part of the thighs. He then described a story where him and his partner went sleighing and she fell off the sleigh resulting in *"a horrible blue spot"* on her leg. As for P7, his objects would remind him of the summer when the couple spends time together.

Separating the data objects ideas into data-objects for reminiscence and reflective data objects Fig. 6 does not mean that objects in the second category can provoke reflection while objects in the first category cannot. Reflection and remembering are two concepts that are tied together in the field of personal representations of data [10, 41], and thus, reflection is not exclusive to one. The first category relates to memory and the second sees data objects as artifacts that through ongoing synthesis of information can shape people's perspectives about their data.

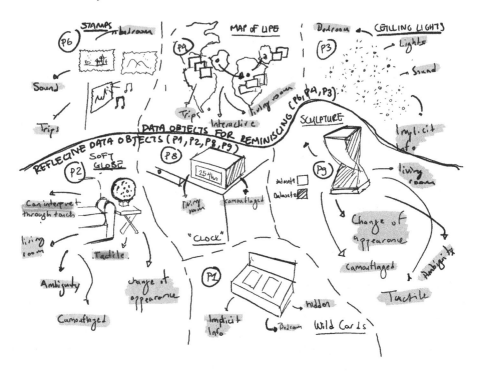

Fig. 6. An illustration of the two categories of data-objects.

Data-Objects for Reminiscence. P3, P4 and P6 thought of data-objects as reminders of their digital communication data. P3 imagined lights on her bedroom's ceiling representing humorous messages P3 exchanged with her partner in the beginning for their relationship. P3 acknowledges the design limitations such artifact might have, *"that period that I chose is the one that we have the most messages and the most exchange. If it would be light it would become very bright. – A lot means a lot and that wouldn't be pleasant."* While P4 imagined as she said, *"the map of our life"* (P4), which would show P4's and her partners story described through the different cities they have visited. Each city would be represented with a point on the map showing all the digital data (e.g. text, pictures, etc.) the couple produced to organize each trip. P6's data-object was a stamp that would symbolize the trips of the couple similar to the P4's data-object but it would also include sound. P6 referred to the limitation such artifact might have. As P6 said "I don't want to be reminded all the time that I'm missing him", which means that she would require control over the artifact.

Data-Objects to Reflect. Lupton's characterized personal data assemblages as companion species [28] suggesting recognizing the interdependency between humans and data. The type of objects that are presented in this category could be described as 'companion species' mainly because they allow transformation from the side of data that is independent from what the person might want, and thus, demonstrates characteristics of a co-evolving relationship. In particular, P1, P2, P8 and P9 imagined data-objects that would help them synthesize their communication data in novel ways rather than just remember past digital data. The data-objects, as described by the participants, would synthesize the data and present it back to them in different ways. For instance, P1 imagined an artifact that would symbolically relate to the communication P1 had with her former partner. The artifact would have a "didactic" (P1) function which would show that the communication was one-sided through, among other ideas, bouncing dice. P2 imagined a soft globe which she could hold between her hands. That object would surface the aspect of care and show the transformative nature of a relationship since it would change overtime depending on the communication data of the couple. P8's artifact would present "the time of the time" (P8) of their communication. He imagined a clock which would show the total of their communication time. This number would change daily providing the average of each day. P9 imagined of a data sculpture which would represent two timelines of pictures, one for each partner. The data-object would present an abstract version of the pictures. The viewers could only see the interaction between the timelines rather than pictures in full resolution.

5   Discussion

This research involved several sense making activities in which personal digital data took various formats e.g., different types of visualization. In the second activity, the visualizations of communication data helped the participants interpret and reflect on their LDRs, while viewing data as design material helped them imagine data-objects. In terms of using data as design material, Sosa et al. [42] argue that as sketching, modeling and prototyping are all intended to help the designer make-sense of the materials they want to manipulate, the same rational could be applied to the processes required to shape data as a design material. The findings of this study illustrated how unique but also how multi-faceted couples' communication data can be. For instance, communication data cannot always be *pleasing* [47] (P1, P3) as it represents a social bond that transforms over time illustrating both positive but also negative aspects. Below I present design opportunities that emerged through the study related to *the transformative nature of relationships, negative reflection and aspects of privacy*. The design opportunities I present below draw from the data-objects the participants envisioned. I speculate that the design opportunities combined with the seven aspects around communication that were discussed previously could be used as departure points for designing for reflection in the context of long-distance relationships.

5.1   Long-Term Use of Data-Objects

Couples reveal themselves over time [38]. Some of the participants talked about former relationships (P1, P3), others were just living temporarily apart from their partners (P9) and last, most of the participants were in LDRs for a long time (P4, P5, P6, P7, P8). Due to that diversity, the way the participants thought of the data-objects changed depending on the state of their relationship. This indicates a path for exploration on the long-term use of data-objects focusing on the transformative nature of relationships. Mazé and Redström explore what means to design a relationship with a computational thing that will last and develop over time [32]. In essence, they investigated objects whose forms are constituted by their temporal manifestations. While that demonstrates the natural cycle of a product in the case of data objects the transformation of the form over time may affect the relationship people will develop with those artifacts.

In particular, to support transformation, data-objects may grow or transform in ambiguous ways, depending on the communication of the couple. This would require the device to constantly keep track of the data, translate and represent it through the properties of the object. For instance, the example of the soft globe (P2) indicates transformations such as, change of size over-time. Based on Hassenzahl et al.'s joint action [17] a device that shows live time data, indeed implies that each partner's behavior has implications for the other and by extension for the data-set itself. Thus, the couple by exchanging messages sustain the lifespan of the device, as well as, affect its physical expression which may be perceived differently by the respective partners while the relationship evolves.

However, engineering such device may come with limitations. Intimate relationships, have a beginning and an end. Therefore, it is valuable to critically reflect on the possible impact of such objects when in use. A data-object that transforms with the relationship becomes a unique creation bounded between the respective partners. When a relationship ends, an object like that most likely will be discarded, as P3 indicated or as P1 suggested, it would be kept somewhere that P1 would only stumble upon it rarely. However, how people would treat those objects cannot be predicted, as what happens to the object after the relationship ends mostly depends on the intricacies of the relationship itself. Most certainly an object that represents live time data and connects to a 'living' relationships will pass through a lot of transformations. Grosse-Hering et al. [16] argue that many objects people acquire for their functional aesthetics are eventually discarded while still being fully functional. In that case, the data objects could be imagined as something similar which in the future might eventually be discarded, or alternatively kept. As Petrelli et al. argue in their research, 80% of people had at least one object related to sad events such as death or divorce but they never displayed those sad mementos in public rooms [36]. Most certainly an object that represents live time data and connects to a 'living' relationships will pass through a lot of transformations.

5.2   Camouflaged Data in the Home

In the data-object ideas of P9, P8, P2 and P1, the information represented through the object would be *"camouflaged"* by the form and format of the objects providing privacy of information for the couples. Notably, those participants who imagined *data-objects to reflect* decided that their object would be placed in their living rooms - except for P1 who thought of an object representing a former relationship - which would allow others (e.g., visitors) to see them. Perhaps that their information would be camouflaged allowed the participant to imagine the data-objects in environments (e.g., living rooms) open to acquaintances, family and friends. On the other hand, P3, P4 and P6 imagined their data-objects placed in their bedrooms with P4 arguing that she would choose the place of the data-object depending on the level of privacy in the information.

In terms of privacy, through the generative sessions I found out that data-objects may offer another layer to the data, which is the aspect of privacy when the physicalization is placed in real-world settings. Thus, data physicalization may offer opportunities to revisit the data without *"seeing"* the data, benefiting from the ambiguity of the form. Gaver et al. [14] argue that ambiguity is a key aspect for letting people imagine and interpret things in an open-ended way. Similarly, Thieme et al. [44] address this ambiguity in their designs for romantic partners. Thieme et al. [44] argue that the open-ended digital artifact played a role in provoking reflection to the respective partners. When thinking of data-objects in LDRs perhaps, systems that allow for this kind of re-visiting may facilitate reflection on the LDR in a way that is detached (in terms of format) yet connected (in terms of data) to the actual data. For instance, the content of important days may become abstract in a way that only the couple recognizes, the days when zero messages were sent can be shown through long pauses.

6   Conclusion

Reflecting on the methodology, during the generative sessions the roles switched between participant and interviewee in several moments. The generative sessions were conducted in an equal ground as the participants were free to ask more information about the content of my graphs and the other way around. The sessions made me realize a lot about my own relationships too. P1 said, *"who is interviewing whom now?"* when one of her comments triggered a reflection about me asking for more attention from my partner, while she is the one who was always more active in the chat. The personal tone in the generative sessions was enhanced by the fact that I knew the participants. This fact made it easier to create an environment of trust. Besides, them feeling comfortable to share, it was also easier for me to talk about my personal information to non-strangers.

In this paper, I presented a project on designing for reflection in the context of LDR. I set up several sense making session. In the first, I tried to make sense of data-sets myself; then I invited others who had experience with LDRs to help me make sense of my messaging data visualization, sketch and reflect on their own visualization, and imagine data-objects; last, I made sense of data from the previous two steps in a session with my LDR partner. Overall, the different sense making sessions allowed me to work with personal data as my design material. To further explore data as such, I plan to develop data-objects for my LDR and observe my partner's and my response to them over time.

References

1. Barrass, S.: Acoustic sonification of blood pressure in the form of a singing bowl. In: Proceedings of the Conference on Sonification in Health and Environmental Data, vol. 12 (2014)
2. Baumer, E.P., Khovanskaya, V., Matthews, M., Reynolds, L., Schwanda Sosik, V., Gay, G.: Reviewing reflection: on the use of reflection in interactive system design. In: Proceedings of the 2014 Conference on Designing Interactive Systems, pp. 93–102 (2014)
3. Baumer, E.P., Khovanskaya, V., Matthews, M., Reynolds, L., Schwanda Sosik, V., Gay, G.: Reviewing reflection: on the use of reflection in interactive system design. In: Proceedings of the 2014 Conference on Designing Interactive Systems, DIS 2014, pp. 93–102. Association for Computing Machinery, New York (2014). https://doi.org/10.1145/2598510.2598598
4. Branham, S.M., Harrison, S.H., Hirsch, T.: Expanding the design space for intimacy: supporting mutual reflection for local partners. In: Proceedings of the Designing Interactive Systems Conference, pp. 220–223 (2012)
5. Brinkmann, S.: Doing without data. Qual. Inq. **20**(6), 720–725 (2014)
6. Cheal, D.: 'Showing them you love them': gift giving and the dialectic of intimacy. Sociol. Rev. **35**(1), 150–169 (1987)
7. Chien, W.C., Hassenzahl, M.: Technology-mediated relationship maintenance in romantic long-distance relationships: an autoethnographical research through design. Human-Comput. Interact. **35**, 1–48 (2017)
8. Chien, W.C., Hassenzahl, M., Welge, J.: Sharing a robotic pet as a maintenance strategy for romantic couples in long-distance relationships. An autobiographical design exploration. In: Proceedings of the 2016 CHI Conference Extended Abstracts on Human Factors in Computing Systems, pp. 1375–1382 (2016)
9. Elsden, C., Durrant, A.C., Chatting, D., Green, D., Kirk, D.S.: Abacus datagraphy: a speculative enactment. In: 3rd Biennial Research Through Design Conference (2017)
10. Elsden, C., Kirk, D.S., Durrant, A.C.: A quantified past: toward design for remembering with personal informatics. Human-Comput. Interact. **31**(6), 518–557 (2016)
11. Fors, V., Pink, S., Berg, M., O'Dell, T.: Imagining Personal Data: Experiences of Self-tracking. Routledge, Milton Park (2020)
12. Friske, M., Wirfs-Brock, J., Devendorf, L.: Entangling the roles of maker and interpreter in interpersonal data narratives: explorations in yarn and sound. In: Proceedings of the 2020 ACM Designing Interactive Systems Conference, pp. 297–310 (2020)
13. G.), S.E.C.: Intimate Objects. Leonardo **13**(1), 47 (2006). https://doi.org/10.2307/1577924
14. Gaver, W.W., Beaver, J., Benford, S.: Ambiguity as a resource for design. In: Proceedings of the SIGCHI conference on Human factors in computing systems, pp. 233–240. ACM (2003)
15. Griggio, C.F., Nouwens, M., Mcgrenere, J., Mackay, W.E.: Augmenting couples' communication with lifelines: shared timelines of mixed contextual information. In: Proceedings of the 2019 CHI Conference on Human Factors in Computing Systems, p. 623. ACM (2019)
16. Grosse-Hering, B., Mason, J., Aliakseyeu, D., Bakker, C., Desmet, P.: Slow design for meaningful interactions. In: Proceedings of the SIGCHI Conference on Human Factors in Computing Systems, pp. 3431–3440 (2013)

17. Hassenzahl, M., Heidecker, S., Eckoldt, K., Diefenbach, S., Hillmann, U.: All you need is love: current strategies of mediating intimate relationships through technology. ACM Trans. Comput.-Human Interact. **19**(4), 1–19 (2012). https://doi.org/10.1145/2395131.2395137

18. Helms, K.: Leaky objects: implicit information, unintentional communication. In: Proceedings of the 2017 ACM Conference Companion Publication on Designing Interactive Systems, pp. 182–186 (2017)

19. Huron, S., Carpendale, S., Thudt, A., Tang, A., Mauerer, M.: Constructive visualization. In: Proceedings of the 2014 Conference on Designing Interactive Systems, pp. 433–442 (2014)

20. Ishii, H., Ullmer, B.: Tangible bits: towards seamless interfaces between people, bits and atoms. In: Proceedings of the ACM SIGCHI Conference on Human Factors in Computing Systems, pp. 234–241 (1997)

21. Jansen, Y., et al.: Opportunities and challenges for data physicalization. In: Proceedings of the 33rd Annual ACM Conference on Human Factors in Computing Systems, pp. 3227–3236 (2015)

22. Karyda, M., Wilde, D., Kjærsgaard, M.: Narrative physicalization: supporting interactive engagement with personal data. IEEE Comput. Graph. Appl. **41**, 74–86 (2020)

23. Kim, N.W., Im, H., Henry Riche, N., Wang, A., Gajos, K., Pfister, H.: DataSelfie: empowering people to design personalized visuals to represent their data. In: Proceedings of the 2019 CHI Conference on Human Factors in Computing Systems - CHI '19 (Chi), pp. 1–12 (2019). https://doi.org/10.1145/3290605.3300309. http://dl.acm.org/citation.cfm?doid=3290605.3300309

24. Koskinen, I., Zimmerman, J., Binder, T., Redstrom, J., Wensveen, S.: Design Research Through Practice: From the Lab, Field, and Showroom. Elsevier, Amsterdam (2011)

25. Li, H., Häkkilä, J., Väänänen, K.: Review of unconventional user interfaces for emotional communication between long-distance partners, pp. 1–10 (2018). https://doi.org/10.1145/3229434.3229467

26. Li, I., Dey, A.K., Forlizzi, J.: Understanding my data, myself: supporting self-reflection with ubicomp technologies. In: Proceedings of the 13th International Conference on Ubiquitous Computing, UbiComp 2011, pp. 405–414, ACM, New York (2011). https://doi.org/10.1145/2030112.2030166. http://doi.acm.org/10.1145/2030112.2030166

27. Lupi, G., Posavec, S.: Dear Data. Chronicle Books, San Francisco (2016)

28. Lupton, D.: Digital companion species and eating data: implications for theorising digital data-human assemblages. Big Data Soc. **3**(1), 2053951715619947 (2016)

29. Lupton, D.: Personal data practices in the age of lively data. Digit. Sociol. **2016**, 335–50 (2016)

30. Lupton, D.: Feeling your data: touch and making sense of personal digital data. New Media Soc. **19**(10), 1599–1614 (2017)

31. Lupton, D., Watson, A.: Towards more-than-human digital data studies: developing research-creation methods. Qual. Res. 1468794120939235 (2020)

32. Mazé, R., Redström, J.: Switch! energy ecologies in everyday life. Int. J. Des. **2**(3) (2008)

33. Nissen, B., Bowers, J.: Data-things: digital fabrication situated within participatory data translation activities. In: Proceedings of the 33rd Annual ACM Conference on Human Factors in Computing Systems, pp. 2467–2476. ACM (2015)

34. Pan, R., Neustaedter, C., Antle, A.N., Matkin, B.: Puzzle space: a distributed tangible puzzle for long distance couples. In: Companion of the 2017 ACM Conference on Computer Supported Cooperative Work and Social Computing, CSCW 2017 Companion, pp. 271–274. ACM, New York (2017). https://doi.org/10.1145/3022198.3026320. http://doi.acm.org/10.1145/3022198.3026320
35. Paul, H.: goof night sms (2015). http://paulheinicker.com/goodnightsms/
36. Petrelli, D., Whittaker, S., Brockmeier, J.: Autotopography: what can physical mementos tell us about digital memories? In: Proceedings of the SIGCHI conference on Human Factors in computing systems, pp. 53–62 (2008)
37. Pousman, Z., Stasko, J., Mateas, M.: Casual information visualization: depictions of data in everyday life. IEEE Trans. Vis. Comput. Graph. **13**(6), 1145–1152 (2007)
38. Reiss, I.L.: Toward a sociology of the heterosexual love relationship. Marriage Fam. Living **22**(2), 139–145 (1960)
39. Samani, H.A., Parsani, R., Rodriguez, L.T., Saadatian, E., Dissanayake, K.H., Cheok, A.D.: Kissenger: design of a kiss transmission device. In: Proceedings of the Designing Interactive Systems Conference, pp. 48–57. ACM (2012)
40. Schön, D.A.: Educating the reflective practitioner (1987)
41. Selby, M., Kirk, D.: Experiential manufacturing: the earthquake shelf. In: Proceedings of RTD 2015 Conference on Research Through Design (2015)
42. Sosa, R., Gerrard, V., Esparza, A., Torres, R., Napper, R.: Data objects: design principles for data physicalisation. In: Proceedings of International Design Conference, DESIGN, vol. 4, pp. 1685–1696 (2018). https://doi.org/10.21278/idc.2018.0125
43. Stafford, L.: Maintaining Long-distance and Cross-residential Relationships. Routledge, Milton Park (2004)
44. Thieme, A., Wallace, J., Thomas, J., Le Chen, K., Krämer, N., Olivier, P.: Lovers' box: designing for reflection within romantic relationships. Int. J. Hum Comput Stud. **69**(5), 283–297 (2011)
45. Thudt, A., Hinrichs, U., Carpendale, S.: Data craft: integrating data into daily practices and shared reflections (2017)
46. Thudt, A., Hinrichs, U., Huron, S., Carpendale, S.: Self-reflection and personal physicalization construction. In: Proceedings of the 2018 CHI Conference on Human Factors in Computing Systems, p. 154. ACM (2018)
47. Thudt, A., Lee, B., Choe, E.K., Carpendale, S.: Expanding research methods for a realistic understanding of personal visualization. IEEE Comput. Graph. Appl. **37**(2), 12–18 (2017)
48. Visser, F.S., Stappers, P.J., Van der Lugt, R., Sanders, E.B.: Contextmapping: experiences from practice. CoDesign **1**(2), 119–149 (2005)
49. Werner, J., Wettach, R., Hornecker, E.: United-pulse: feeling your partner's pulse. In: Proceedings of the 10th International Conference on Human Computer Interaction with Mobile Devices and Services, MobileHCI '08, pp. 535–538. ACM (2008)
50. Zhu, C.L., Agrawal, H., Maes, P.: Data-objects: re-designing everyday objects as tactile affective interfaces. In: 2015 International Conference on Affective Computing and Intelligent Interaction, ACII 2015, pp. 322–326 (2015). https://doi.org/10.1109/ACII.2015.7344590

Supporting Sensor-Based Usability Studies Using a Mobile App in Remotely Piloted Aircraft System

Antonio Esposito[1]($\boxtimes$) , Giusy Danila Valenti[1] , Fabrizio Balducci[2] ,
and Paolo Buono[2]

[1] Università degli Studi di Enna Kore, Enna, Italy
{antonio.esposito,giusy.valenti}@unikore.it
[2] Università degli Studi di Bari "Aldo Moro", Bari, Italy
{fabrizio.balducci,paolo.buono}@uniba.it

Abstract. Monitoring user workload during task performance is a relevant and widely investigated topic in the aviation field of study due to its associations with the level of safety and number of human errors. The current study aims at assessing the workload of pilots wearing sensors while performing typical fly operations. To this purpose, a mobile app able to record physiological measures while performing usability studies with multiple users, even remotely, is provided. Results coming from a preliminary test with three pilots reveal the usefulness of the app in the evaluation of the workload level for each participant and each task.

Keywords: Human factors · Physiological measures · Evaluation

1 Introduction and Related Work

Aviation safety is a complex domain that can be improved not only by taking into account the reliability of the aircraft and its systems, but also by considering and monitoring the crew performances. 75% of aircraft accidents are related to human errors that in most cases derive from the mental workload and fatigue of pilots and aircraft operators [18]. Human error can be a consequence of design flaws, inadequate training, incorrect procedures, old manuals and other technical, environmental and organizational factors [11].

The problem is increased in the context of *Remotely Piloted Aircraft Systems* (RPAS) that ranges from small devices, used for play purposes, to large aircraft, configured with sophisticated equipment and with extremely heterogeneous performances, dimensions and characteristics. A common element between these devices is represented by the absence of a pilot on board, since they are controlled by a ground operator from a remote station.

Aeronautics is one of the most interested field to issues related to Human Factors. Understanding the psycho-physical state of pilots and real-time monitoring of the mental workload during simulator training or in real flight can

© IFIP International Federation for Information Processing 2021
Published by Springer Nature Switzerland AG 2021
C. Ardito et al. (Eds.): INTERACT 2021, LNCS 12936, pp. 63–72, 2021.
https://doi.org/10.1007/978-3-030-85607-6_4

improve the efficiency of a crew and the safety of air operations. Workload refers to the measurement of mental processing requests placed on a person during the execution of a task [15] and it can affect flight performance predisposing crews to mistakes [6,20,21]. The required amount of cognitive resources varies with the current activity. For example, operational phases like landing and take-off, which are the most critical [19] with the highest workload.

When humans have to perform physical and/or mental tasks, their cognitive state varies and many parameters such as fatigue, attention and memory must be monitored [16] measuring, for example, if person A is working harder than person B or whether task A requires more work than task B by defining practical and reasonable limits for the workload.

The contributions of this work are: i) a mobile app that interfaces with physiological sensors allowing to support user-based perform usability studies even remotely; ii) a pilot study that exploits the acquired data to evaluate the workload of drone pilots.

The paper is structured as follows: studies in the field of workload evaluation through behavioral, subjective and objective techniques are presented in Sect. 2; Sect. 3 introduces materials and methods to perform experimental evaluation through a mobile app and an electrocardiogram (ECG) sensor. In Sect. 4 there are results about the evaluation of the proposed approach; Sect. 5 provides conclusions and future works.

2   Evaluation Techniques

There are several ways to estimate mental workload: 1) Behavioral measurements: performance indices based on reaction times and the number of errors related to the task; 2) Subjective measurements: provided by the operator once the task is completed through specific questionnaires; 3) Physiological measurements: made with specific equipment that analyzes objective data like heart rate, respiratory rate, eye movements.

A study conducted by Alaimo et al. [2] analyzed the workload level during a flight mission performed using a simulator correlating Heart Rate Variability (HRV) biometric data with the subjective information collected through the NASA-TLX questionnaire. In particular, heart rhythm was used to determine the body's natural response to stressful situations, whereas subjective measures were used to analyze how the pilot perceives these workloads. From this perspective, more than one methodology should be considered for workload evaluation.

2.1   Behavioral Measures

Behavioral measures are directly related to the definition of performance provided by Paas et al. [22] that can be defined as the effectiveness in completing a particular task. Typical examples relating to the performance measurements can be considered: i) the detection of the reaction time or the time elapsed between a stimulus and the execution of a response; ii) the pace to perform the activity; iii) the accuracy of the performance or the percentage of errors carried out during the tasks. In such a way, the workload can be assessed by analyzing the decrease in the subject performances. Nevertheless, according to Wilson et al. [27], the performance measures do not adequately reflect the level of workload experienced since the quality of behavioral measures does not always result in the operator's ability/inability to react adequately to the required task.

2.2 Subjective Measurements

Subjective measures are low cost and non-invasive assessment tools for evaluating workload [2,9,21].

Inspection methods involve expert evaluators and results depend on their own experience, sensitivity and personal preferences. For this reason, experts produce their evaluation individually and independently, then they meet and redact a final report that considers all of them. An example of an inspection technique is the 'Cognitive Walkthrough' which evaluates the task considering that users usually prefer to learn a system by using it rather than studying a manual [2,9]. Answering questions for each action allows evaluators to analyze the problems that a user encounters in formulating objectives to perform a task, associating the correct action with the aim of carrying out actions.

User-based techniques allow to mitigate the subjectivity of the evaluations with experts. They consist of groups of users performing tasks in a controlled environment. A sample of users that is representative of the category to which the system is addressed is selected and everyone is asked to perform the same tasks separately. The expert observes and analyzes their behavior to understand if, where and why they have encountered difficulties. In the "Thinking aloud" technique users comment aloud thoughts while performing the tasks. Comments are related to the difficulties, and since the causes of such difficulties may not be evident, the observer must take notes, recording the situations in which the user is uncertain or commits some mistakes in order to review them later and identify issues and propose corrections.

Interviews and questionnaires are part of subjective techniques. They are usually employed in the aeronautical field to measure the user workload [17]. The *NASA-TLX (Task Load Index)*, [11,24] the *Modified Cooper-Harper Workload Rating Scale* [26], and the SWAT (Subjective Workload Assessment Technique) are among the most common used questionnaires.

2.3 Physiological Measurements

Physiological measures, based on the detection of several physiological parameters, can be considered as a very powerful technique for assessing workload, and they are widely applied in numerous studies [3,7,25]. Using physiological measures in the aviation field of study is advantageous for several reasons. First, these kinds of measures, which are also tested and used in the medical sector, have a high level of validity and reliability. In addition, they provide an objective assessment since their evaluation does not depend on subjective perceptions. Moreover, the detection of physiological parameters can allow a real-time workload assessment, leading to continuous monitoring of variations in the amount of physical and mental effort experienced while performing a task [27]. The electroencephalogram (EEG), electrocardiogram (ECG), pupil size, and the eye movement are very useful methods for measuring workload, and they seem to overcome some of the shortcomings of both subjective and behavioral measurements [8] and have been successfully employed to evaluate human aspects like emotions [4].

From this perspective, the shift from low to high workload can be evaluated in terms of changes of the activity of the Autonomous Nervous System (ANS), which can be linked to specific physiological responses. Among the different physiological measures used in this specific sector, indexes based on Heart Rate Variability (HRV) measurement are very popular thanks to their high level of sensitivity and efficiency in assessing changes in mental workload [2,13,21]. [10]. HRV is inversely associated with workload: individuals experiencing high levels of mental effort tend to show a decrease of HRV due to the activation of Sympathetic Nervous System (SNS) and/or to the Parasympathetic (PNS) withdrawal [23].

The indexes based on HRV measurements can be distinguished into different categories, and the most common are based on: i) the time domain analysis, ii) the frequency domain (or power spectral density) analysis, and iii) the non-linear indexes analysis. The time-domain parameters quantify the amount of variability in measurements of the Interbeat Interval (IBI), meant as the time period between two consecutive heartbeats. Some of the most common time-domain metrics are the Standard Deviation of NN intervals (SDNN) and the Root mean square of successive RR interval differences (RMSSD). The frequency domain indexes involve defining ECG waves as different spectral components through power spectral density and they can be divided into four frequency bands: HF (High Frequency) frequencies between 0.15 and 0.4 Hz; LF (Low Frequency) frequencies between 0.04 and 0.15 Hz; VLF (Very Low Frequency) frequencies between 0.003 and 0.04 Hz; ULF (Ultra Low Frequency) the band falls below 0.003 Hz. Given the very low frequency of the oscillations, the ULF band's contribution can only be appreciated in 24-hour acquisitions. Nonlinear indexes used in HRV analysis include Poincaré plot, detrended fluctuation analysis, approximate entropy, and sample entropy calculation [12].

3 Materials and Methods

We developed a mobile app to support usability experts to carry out evaluation studies. The app allows to evaluate the subject's mental load during the performance of real tasks by measuring physiological data produced by specific devices. In this work ECG data detected by a Polar H10 sensor have been used.

3.1   The ECG Sensor

The Polar H10 is equipped with an elastic strap with integrated electrodes. It records data relating to inter-beat times and Pulse-to-Pulse Interval (PPI) like ECG, with a sample rate 130 Hz and an impedance of $2M\Omega$ in a range of $\pm20,000\,\mu V$. The signal quality of RR intervals (distance between two R peaks of ECG wave) of a Holter device and the Polar H10 chest strap at rest and during exercise both measurement systems are valid for RR intervals detection [14]. The sensor uses Bluetooth (BLE) or Ant + technologies to communicate and allows the connection to multiple devices simultaneously. Polar software libraries allows developers to extract live data directly from the sensors, in order to acquire in real-time *HR data* (bpm), *RR interval* data (1/1024 format), *electrocardiogram data* (μV), with timestamp, and *record HR and RR data* in the device internal memory using a sample time of 1 s.

3.2   The Mobile App

The app connects to the Polar H10 sensor through the Bluetooth BLE connection supporting test sessions with two non-exclusive configurations: *On-site*: users take the experimental device one at a time wearing the sensor while carrying out their tasks. The evaluator manages different participant sessions through the app; *Remote*: the information about the tasks to perform are sent to the participant's device who wears the sensor, so that it can record ECG data. Data are sent to the evaluator upon completion of all the tasks in a session.

Data coming from local users are combined with the remote ones, flowing neatly into the experimenter's device and thus building the global dataset. The final results is the performing of a hybrid user-test session. When a configuration file is opened on a device, the tasks to be performed are loaded into the app and the device is ready to start the test. Once all the tasks have been carried out, the file containing the measurements is saved and, in case of a remote user, is sent to the evaluator. The data of the session and tasks are stored in an SQLite DBMS and the app exports data in raw format as .csv file and as human-readable tables. Everything is compressed in a .zip file that the evaluator can easily manage.

The initial screen of the app shows the list of the sessions. In sessions created in the device, the evaluator can add participants. The app displays the list of subjects (local and remote) who participated in a specific session and the time to complete each task. Each participant sees only personal tasks and those already completed (Fig. 1a), displayed with a check on the left of the task name and the duration time taken to complete it on the right (Fig. 1b). Figure 1c shows an example of results in the frequency domain, in addition to the values (top), the Power Spectral Density of the signal (bottom) is given.

To create a new experimental session the evaluator specifies the name of the test and the number of tasks to perform, then it is possible to rename them or keep the automatic names as TASKi (i = 1,..., n). In order to carry out a task where data from the sensor are recorded, a message shows the status of the connection and, once established, values are shown in real-time with a graph

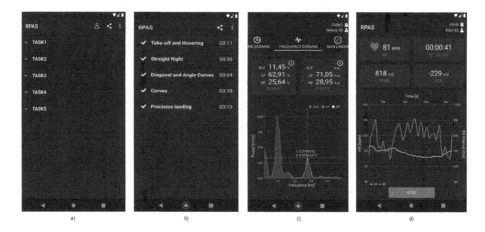

Fig. 1. Four screenshots of the app showing, respectively a) the task list, b) the same list after the task have been renamed by the evaluator, c) the sensor details in the frequency domain and d) the real-time HR and RR data produced by the sensor.

that depicts the HR values in bpm on the left Y axis while on the right Y axis are the RR values in ms (Fig. 1d). At the end of a task, by pressing the "STOP" button on the panel the file is saved.

4   Experiments and Results

A user study to examine the app effectiveness on the HRV acquired measurements was carried out. Three drone pilots, all having an official drone pilot's license, were engaged for a flight mission based on five different tasks. In the following section, the drone missions success rates are presented, and successively, an example of the physiological measurements for the evaluation of workload during two different flight phases is described.

4.1   Drones Flight Experiment

The evaluation of the usability of piloting systems has been performed exploiting two types of drones: *DJI Fly* app for the *DJI Mavic Mini* drone and *FIMI Navi* app for the *Xiaomi Fimi X8 SE* drone. After having interviews with the subjects regarding their previous experience with drones, five tasks with different complexity were designed to stress specific functions. The tests were conducted individually with three participants, one at a time, and were carried out in the open field. Each pilot used a drone with active stabilizer and Global Positioning System (GPS). The task to execute were:

1. *Take-off and Hovering*: take altitude up to about 10 m for a few seconds and then descend

2. *Straight flight*: proceed straight at constant altitude for 30 m and go back to the starting position by turning (use of the inverted controls)
3. *Diagonal and Angle curves*: from a low altitude made a diagonal climb of 45°, draw a rectangle in flight and then make a diagonal descent of 45°
4. *Curves*: fly to the agreed point, circle around it and return to the starting point
5. *Precision Landing*: land the drone at a designated point

Table 1. Results of the evaluation. For each on the five tasks, the colored cells report the performance results for a participant *Pi* where S indicates *Success*, F indicates *Failure* and P indicates *Partial* success in the task correct execution.

	Task-1	Task-2	Task-3	Task-4	Task-5
P1	S	S	S	S	F
P2	S	S	S	S	P
P3	S	S	F	S	S

As visible in Table 1, while most of the tasks were successfully completed, two failures and one partial success were recorded. Partial success was attributed in the event that unforeseen external factors influenced the difficulty.

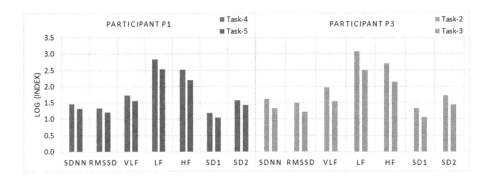

Fig. 2. HRV indexes between task 4 and task 5.

4.2 Pilot Workload Evaluation

During the drone flight phases, the heart rate variability of the pilots was recorded and monitored by the app. The measurements of HRV indexes can usefully estimate the workload levels associated with the task's difficulty. Indeed, the pilot's emotional state influences the HRV when the participant is not able to complete the task successfully. To analyze this effect and compare a successful task with a failure task, participants P1 and P3 are considered. The results in Fig. 2 for Task-4 and Task-5, and Task-2 and Task-3 are given respectively for P1 and P3. Results are reported as logarithmic values in the y-scale to compare the HRV indexes on the same amplitude scale. The HRV indexes taken into account are inversely associated with the levels of workload (for more details the reader could refer to [1]). Concerning the results, it is worth noting that for all the HRV indexes, Task 5-is associated with lower values than Task-4; and the same effect is found for Task-3 and Task-2. These results can be read as an increase in the workload level while accomplishing the task or increasing mental workload levels due to the failure. Moreover, in particular, the workload associated with the precision landing flight phase is higher than other maneuvers as reported in [2,21]; additionally, the level flight can be considered as a lower demand maneuver and therefore associated with higher HRV values as shows in Fig. 2 for the Task-2.

5   Conclusion and Future Work

This paper is focused on the support to evaluators in conducting usability study involving participants that wear physiological sensors. An app that connects to the sensors, collects the physiological data, makes the computation, shares the data to the evaluator and creates a basic report that summarizes the main collected data has been developed and briefly presented. We conducted a test with three pilots that wore a Polar H10 sensor and performed five typical tasks having different difficulty.

The use of an app to monitor physiological data has several advantages: the evaluator is leveraged in taking the task execution times; the data collected from the sensors are computed and stored directly by the app; the data of the test are easily shared between the user and the evaluator, also in the case that they are not co-located; the setting works well also in real scenarios and does not require a lab. Indeed, the tests with pilots presented in this paper were performed in an open field. Several apps capable of manipulating the sensor data are available but, to the best of our knowledge, none also directly connect to the sensor, support usability studies, store the data and show both real-time information and the final report of the session.

We plan to integrate new sensors to increase the subjective data, such as ECG and Galvanic Skin Response. We also plan to add subjective evaluations in the app (e.g. questionnaires). The integration the two types of workload assessment will help better estimating the human factors and associated practices for the workload in aircraft crews. The results presented in this work may also be useful to the evaluation and improvement of Smart Interactive Experiences [5] (in the Cultural Heritage domain), and in general when the subject is at the center of experience and IoT sensors help collecting data.

Acknowledgments. This work is partially supported by the projects "Integrazione dei Sistemi Aeromobili a Pilotaggio Remoto nello spazio aereo non segregato per servizi" (RPASinAir ARS01_00820 CUPJ66C18000460005), funded by Italian Ministry of Education, Universities and Research (MIUR) and "Gestione di oggetti intelligenti per migliorare le esperienze di visita di siti di interesse culturale" funded by the Apulia Region under the program Research for Innovation (REFIN) POR Puglia FESR FSE 2014–2020. The authors thank Edilio Formica for his help in the app implementation.

References

1. Alaimo, A., Esposito, A., Orlando, C.: Cockpit pilot warning system: a preliminary study. In: 2018 IEEE 4th International Forum on Research and Technology for Society and Industry (RTSI), pp. 1–4 (2018). https://doi.org/10.1109/RTSI.2018.8548518

2. Alaimo, A., Esposito, A., Orlando, C., Simoncini, A.: Aircraft pilots workload analysis: heart rate variability objective measures and Nasa-task load index subjective evaluation. Aerospace **7**(9), 137 (2020). https://doi.org/10.3390/aerospace7090137

3. Baevsky, R.M., Chernikova, A.G.: Heart rate variability analysis: physiological foundations and main methods. Cardiometry (10) (2017)

4. Balducci, F., Grana, C., Cucchiara, R.: Classification of affective data to evaluate the level design in a role-playing videogame. In: 7th International Conference on Games and Virtual Worlds for Serious Applications (VS-Games), pp. 1–8 (2015). https://doi.org/10.1109/VS-GAMES.2015.7295766

5. Balducci, F., Buono, P., Desolda, G., Impedovo, D., Piccinno, A.: Improving smart interactive experiences in cultural heritage through pattern recognition techniques. Pattern Recognit. Lett. **131**, 142–149 (2020). https://doi.org/10.1016/j.patrec.2019.12.011. http://www.sciencedirect.com/science/article/pii/S0167865519303745

6. Boff, K.R., Kaufman, L., Thomas, J.P.: Handbook of perception and human performance (1986)

7. Borghini, G., Astolfi, L., Vecchiato, G., Mattia, D., Babiloni, F.: Measuring neurophysiological signals in aircraft pilots and car drivers for the assessment of mental workload, fatigue and drowsiness. Neurosci. Biobehav. Rev. **44**, 58–75 (2014)

8. Brookhuis, K.A., De Waard, D.: Monitoring drivers' mental workload in driving simulators using physiological measures. Accid. Anal. Prev. **42**(3), 898–903 (2010)

9. Cao, X., et al.: Heart rate variability and performance of commercial airline pilots during flight simulations. Int. J. Environ. Res. Public Health **16**(2), 237 (2019)

10. Delliaux, S., Delaforge, A., Deharo, J.C., Chaumet, G.: Mental workload alters heart rate variability, lowering non-linear dynamics. Front. Physiol. **10**, 565 (2019)

11. Dumitru, I.M., Boşcoianu, M.: Human factors contribution to aviation safety. Sci. Res. Educ. Air Force-AFASES **2015**(1), 49–53 (2015)

12. Electrophysiology, Task Force of the European Society of Cardiology the North American Society of Pacing: Heart rate variability: standards of measurement, physiological interpretation, and clinical use. Circulation **93**(5), 1043–1065 (1996)

13. Fuentes-García, J.P., Clemente-Suárez, V.J., Marazuela-Martínez, M.Á., Tornero-Aguilera, J.F., Villafaina, S.: Impact of real and simulated flights on psychophysiological response of military pilots. Int. J. Environ. Res. Public Health **18**(2), 787 (2021)

14. Gilgen-Ammann, R., Schweizer, T., Wyss, T.: RR interval signal quality of a heart rate monitor and an ECG Holter at rest and during exercise. Eur. J. Appl. Physiol. **119**(7), 1525–1532 (2019). https://doi.org/10.1007/s00421-019-04142-5

15. Gopher, D., Donchin, E.: Workload: an examination of the concept (1986)
16. Hancock, P.A., Matthews, G.: Workload and performance: associations, insensitivities, and dissociations. Hum. Factors **61**(3), 374–392 (2019). https://doi.org/10.1177/0018720818809590
17. Hart, S.G., Staveland, L.E.: Development of NASA-TLX (task load index): results of empirical and theoretical research. In: Hancock, P.A., Meshkati, N. (eds.) Human Mental Workload, Advances in Psychology, North-Holland, vol. 52, pp. 139–183 (1988). https://doi.org/10.1016/S0166-4115(08)62386-9
18. Kharoufah, H., Murray, J., Baxter, G., Wild, G.: A review of human factors causations in commercial air transport accidents and incidents: from to 2000–2016. Prog. Aerosp. Sci. **99**, 1–13 (2018). https://doi.org/10.1016/j.paerosci.2018.03.002
19. Lee, Y.H., Liu, B.S.: Inflight workload assessment: comparison of subjective and physiological measurements. Aviat. Space Environ. Med. **74**, 1078–84 (2003)
20. Liu, J., Gardi, A., Ramasamy, S., Lim, Y., Sabatini, R.: Cognitive pilot-aircraft interface for single-pilot operations. Knowl.-Based Syst. **112**, 37–53 (2016). https://doi.org/10.1016/j.knosys.2016.08.031
21. Mansikka, H., Virtanen, K., Harris, D.: Comparison of NASA-TLX scale, modified cooper-harper scale and mean inter-beat interval as measures of pilot mental workload during simulated flight tasks. Ergonomics **62**, 1–22 (2018). https://doi.org/10.1080/00140139.2018.1471159
22. Paas, F.G.W.C., Merriënboer, J.J.G.V.: The efficiency of instructional conditions: an approach to combine mental effort and performance measures. Hum. Factors **35**(4), 737–743 (1993). https://doi.org/10.1177/001872089303500412
23. Taelman, J., Vandeput, S., Vlemincx, E., Spaepen, A., Van Huffel, S.: Instantaneous changes in heart rate regulation due to mental load in simulated office work. Eur. J. Appl. Physiol. **111**(7), 1497–1505 (2011). https://doi.org/10.1007/s00421-010-1776-0
24. Valdehita, S., Ramiro, E., García, J., Puente, J.: Evaluation of subjective mental workload: a comparison of SWAT, NASA-TLX, and workload profile methods. Appl. Psychol. **53**, 61–86 (2004). https://doi.org/10.1111/j.1464-0597.2004.00161.x
25. Wanyan, X., Zhuang, D., Zhang, H.: Improving pilot mental workload evaluation with combined measures. Bio-Med. Mater. Eng. **24**(6), 2283–2290 (2014)
26. Wierwille, W.W., Casali, J.G.: A validated rating scale for global mental workload measurement applications. In: Proceedings of the Human Factors Society Annual Meeting, vol. 27, no. 2, pp. 129–133 (1983). https://doi.org/10.1177/154193128302700203
27. Wilson, G.F., Russell, C.A.: Real-time assessment of mental workload using psychophysiological measures and artificial neural networks. Hum. Factors **45**(4), 635–644 (2003)

Understanding the Stakeholders' Expectations About an Adherence App: A Case Study

Anna Spagnolli[✉] [iD], Luciano Gamberini[iD], Enrico D'Agostini, and Giulia Cenzato

Human Inspired Technologies Research Centre, Università degli Studi di Padova, via Venezia 8, 35131 Padua, Italy
{anna.spagnolli,luciano.gamberini}@unipd.it,
giulia.cenzato@studenti.unipd.it

Abstract. Digital health assistants are increasingly used to improve adherence to pharmaceutical treatments because of their intuitiveness, timeliness, and ubiquity. These applications serve the goals of different kinds of stakeholders, all interested in ensuring adherence: the patients, the physicians treating the patient, the pharmaceutical companies sponsoring the treatment, and the software developers selling the application. If unquestioned, different expectations can be reflected in digital assistants pursuing erratic, confusing goals.

In this case study, we focus on an application called PatchAi (PA), which assists the collection of patients' data during medical treatments; we aimed to understand the way in which different stakeholders conceive the role of PA. We carried out 14 interviews, with patients, physicians, pharmaceutical companies, and software developers. The interviews were recorded, transcribed, and analyzed with a two-stage thematic analysis, yielding in the end 76.8% inter-coders' agreement.

We identified six roles of PA, i.e., guide, interlocutor, safe box, lifesaver, secretary, and travel mate. We also break down the frequency with which each role is mentioned by the different classes of stakeholders involved in the interviews. We conclude with some formative design implications.

Keywords: Digital health assistant · Adherence apps · Stakeholders · Interviews · Expectations

1 Introduction

Successful medical therapy is based on patient's medication adherence that, according to Cramer et al. [8], can be defined as the "act of conforming to the recommendations made by the provider with respect to timing, dosage, and frequency of medication-taking during the prescribed length of time" (p.46). The World Health Organization in 2003 defined adherence as a global problem of striking magnitude both in terms of the number of patients affected and of the costs it involves for the health system [14]. Non-compliance with a treatment includes taking incorrect doses, taking medications at

© IFIP International Federation for Information Processing 2021
Published by Springer Nature Switzerland AG 2021
C. Ardito et al. (Eds.): INTERACT 2021, LNCS 12936, pp. 73–81, 2021.
https://doi.org/10.1007/978-3-030-85607-6_5

wrong times, being discontinuous in taking the treatment as well as stopping the treatment too soon; these behaviors can result from involuntary forgetfulness of medication, miscommunication with the care-provider, the complexity of medication, wrong beliefs and lack of motivation [11].

Smartphone applications are increasingly used to improve adherence [6]. As opposed to applications that provide medical recommendations and are often questioned for the authenticity and reliability of their sources [1, 17], adherence applications pursue the adherence to the treatment prescribed by a physician. Adherence applications support the daily routine of treatment by reminding patients to take their medication, recording all taken and missed doses, and sharing the patients' medication regimens and medication-taking with the physician [9].

Ahmed et al. (2018) identified three strategies currently implemented by adherence apps: reminders, education and behaviors. Reminders include alerts, notifications and text messages to the patients' phones informing them that the time has come to take a given medication or provide some data. Reminders improve the accuracy of the data collected because they help overcome the typical memory biases plaguing other data collection methods [2]. Educational tools provide information about the medicine prescribed in order to dispel misbeliefs; the reliability and authenticity of the application's sources are crucial in this case [17]. Behavioral strategies are persuasive strategies meant to motivate adherence, hopefully driving the patient towards the state where they feel empowered [13]. Behavioral strategies include tracking the treatment progress, setting goals and receiving scores and badges. Data illustrating the patients' treatment history also was found to increase treatment adherence significantly [10, 20]. A recent meta-analysis by Wiecek et al. [21] suggests that a comprehensive multi-component mobile intervention is the most effective long-term solution, considering that non-adherence is a complex phenomenon with several determinants.

One strategy to improve the effectiveness of adherence apps is the use of a conversational format. A meta-analysis by Wald et al. [19] compared eight randomized trials using text messages to improve treatment adherence, either as one-way reminders or as two-way reminders. In the latter case, the patient would send replies confirming whether a given medication has been taken. A 23% improvement in adherence was found when this last strategy was applied, compared with a 4% improvement using one-way reminders. For these reasons, adherence apps use conversational interfaces. Some can interpret and respond to the patients' input delivered as free text (or speech), using natural language processing; other conversational interfaces use predetermined messages in both the application's turns and the patient's replies [7]. Conversational agents deployed in health services and applications do not "chat" with patients but engage in goal-oriented transactions with them. These transactions aim to support the patients' treatment (i.e., treatment implementation, management, adherence, support, and monitoring) or a behavior change program; connect patients to health care services; answer health-related queries or establish a diagnosis/triage [7]. Regardless of their goals, they are generally well-received, especially for their timeliness and ease of use [7].

The patient is typically considered the target of adherence application; however, physicians and pharmaceutical companies study the data collected, or prepare the treatment protocols. The heterogenous agendas of these different stakeholders can be conveyed in the app and make the nature of the transaction with the app confusing to the user. A formative evaluation to identify and compare the stakeholders' expectations can help avoid such confusion.

1.1 Study Goal

In the present study, we focus on one adherence app, called PatchAi, henceforth PA. PA can be installed on the patients' smartphones to report their health conditions during the whole duration of a treatment. Its companion web application allows physicians to monitor their patient's data remotely. The smartphone interface relies on an intuitive interface to improve the patients' retention in the monitoring program. In particular, it uses a conversational digital assistant to prompt data collection with a set of predefined options, for instance, asking which symptom was experienced that day and how acutely. It also ushers the patients to the various features relevant to them or reminds them of data that was scheduled to be provided. The conversation interface resembles an instant messaging application. (Screenshots can be found here: https://patchai.io/en). Formative evaluations are carried out on a product while still formed, often with qualitative methods [4]. Our study has a formative goal, i.e., identifying the stakeholder's expectations about PA role and possible frictions or gaps between them.

2 Method

2.1 Participants

Four classes of stakeholders had a direct interest in PA: patients, researchers or physicians monitoring the patient's treatment, pharmaceutical companies sponsoring a treatment, and developers working at the application. The main requirement when recruiting members of those classes was having a familiarity with treatments involving data monitoring. We could not reach any patient who was using PA at the time because they were bound to confidentiality constraints established before the start of our study. Therefore, the kind of patient's expectations we collected here are those of patients who would consider using the application prospectively. They were explained the basic features of the application during a hands-on demonstration meeting organized some weeks earlier by the company. Only one of them gathered the information on the app from the website. Physicians, pharmaceutical representatives and developers were already familiar with PA, being its direct stakeholders.

The stakeholders reached for this study were 14: six patients familiar with clinical trials involving data monitoring (oncological patients and patients suffering from migraine); three physicians running a medical trial with the PA at the time of the interview; three developers from PA company; two representatives of pharmaceutical companies using PA. No compensation was given to participate in the study.

2.2 Interviews

The interviews took place in August and September 2020. They were carried out individually and remotely, at a time agreed upon with the participants. Each interview lasted about 30 min, and the audio was recorded. The interviews focused on the application in general and on the virtual assistant in particular. The interviewees were encouraged to answer from their perspectives. The interview format was semi-structured, with a few predefined questions and additional follow-up questions to clarify or elaborate. The predefined questions were:

- what do you think could be the usefulness of an application like PA?
- do you think that PA application can be useful also to other categories such as physicians/patients?
- what are the advantages/disadvantages of using this application compared with other tools you used to collect health data in the past?
- why would patients discontinue sending their data via PA?
- what would be the perfect digital health assistant?

    Then the participant was thanked and greeted.

2.3 Ethics

The study complies with the Declaration of Helsinki (2013) and the European General Data Protection Regulation (2016/679, GDPR). Before the interview, each participant received the information note and a consent form via email; they agreed to participate by signing the consent and returning it via email to the principal investigator. No interviewee was obliged to participate; participation or withdrawal did not affect their participation in future or current treatments. The information note described the goal of the study (i.e., improving PA), the focus, modality, and duration of the interview, the data protection policy, the participants' rights, and the contact information of the research team carrying out the study. The interview transcripts are anonymous, and their association with participants' identification data was deleted at the end of the study; also, the audio files were deleted once transcribed.

2.4 Analysis

A two-stage thematic analysis [5, 18] was carried out on the transcribed interviews to identify the roles attributed to PA. The first phase proceeded in a bottom-up direction: the principal investigator and another research team member read aloud the interviews together and identified their recurring themes. Six different themes (i.e., PA roles) were found. The second phase was top-down. Two members of the research team who did not participate in the bottom-up phase served as independent coders. They were trained on two interviews and then coded the remaining 12 interviews autonomously. For each sentence in the interviews, they decided whether it mentioned any of the six roles or not; they were instructed to create a new role if the six predefined ones did not fit the sentence. No new theme emerged during the coding process, thereby indicating that data saturation was reached. The agreement between coders was 76.8%. Then, the two coders jointly decided how to code the sentences on which they initially disagreed. Overall, 352 sentences were coded, containing 373 mentions to PA roles.

3 Results

Overall, the stakeholders referred to six possible roles of PA in the interviews; we named them "guide," "interlocutor," "safe box," "lifesaver," "secretary," and "travel mate." We described them using a rhetorical storyline and some extracts exemplifying them. Rhetorical storylines are "synthetic statements which parsimoniously summarize the unique topics invoked in the corpus" [12].

Secretary: Interviewees refer to PA as an assistant to overloaded physicians, taking on the burden of collecting, storing, and analyzing the data from the patients. "At any point in time, we can say 'let see how that patient is doing, let's see how that other patient is doing" or "I'm interested in knowing, for instance, the frequency and length of the events in a given month, the medicines taken, everything, in a blink." Such an assistant is void of any medical responsibility.

Guide: Interviewees refer to PA as a guide supporting the patients in providing health data. It helps the patients keep their intended data collection schedule and simplify the data entry process through a usable interface. This remark is expressed by sentences such as "[PA] can guide the patient who might have some difficulties in using an application" or "PA is patient-friendly as they say, I mean it is very close to their [the patients'] language."

Interlocutor: Interviewees refer to PA as an interlocutor due to the conversational format. This role transpires from sentences such as: "PA can communicate with some empathy, through which one perceives some sort of closeness." Being an interlocutor, PA would also enliven the data collection routine by making it more personal and various, "there must be some variation…or some personalization even, so it is not always the same over and over."

Safe Box: Interviewees refer to PA as a means to collect and preserve data. The emphasis is here on the data and the quality of their collection, storage, and access. PA allows collecting accurate data, keeping them safely in compliance with privacy norms, and making them conveniently inspectable from both patients and physicians. This role transpires from sentences such as "not to lose, or squander, relevant information about their symptoms" or "data are managed really accurately, and are always used for positive goals, for their stated goals."

Lifesaver: Interviewees refer to PA as a necessary component of the treatment allowing the patients to play an active role, become more aware of their health condition, and be useful to themselves and others. This role is expressed by sentences such as "having to provide regular information becomes part of the treatment itself" or "the patient feels that their opinion, judgment, disclosures – so to speak – matter."

Travel Mate: Interviewees refer to PA as a companion being always with the patients during their sickness. "Surely, a support like a chatbot makes you feel constantly assisted." The installation on personal smartphones and the regular opening of conversations with the patient contribute to this impression.

For each class of stakeholders, we calculated the number of mentions to each role; then, we averaged it by the number of stakeholders in that class. The average frequency per stakeholder class is reported in Table 1 and allows to appreciate the emphases given by different stakeholders to each role.

Table 1. The average number of mentions to the six roles within each stakeholder class (a mention is a transcripts' sentences referring to a role).

	Guide	Interlocutor	Safe box	Lifesaver	Secretary	Travel mate
Patients	5.33	6.00	2.17	1.33	6.50	2.50
Physicians	5.67	0.67	8.67	6.33	10.67	0.00
Pharma rep.	5.50	4.00	3.50	2.00	16.50	5.50
Developers	5.33	8.67	1.67	2.00	2.00	0.33

Given the scope of this study and its small sample size, the data in Table 1 will be commented qualitatively. It seems that no role is paramount or exclusive to a specific stakeholder class; at the same time, each class puts a different emphasis on each role. The patients mainly referred to three roles: PA as a guide, interlocutor, or secretary; less often did they mention safe box and lifesaver roles. Conversely, safe box and lifesaver are frequently mentioned by the physicians, in addition to the secretary role; this suggests that physicians are very interested in the medical data provided by PA and in being relieved from the burden of collecting them. Secretary is also the role that the representatives of the pharmaceutical companies mentioned more often; this reflects their interest in making the application useful to the physicians, the class of PA with which they are more in touch. Finally, the developers seem to mention the role of guide and interlocutor more often than the other roles; this suggests their great concern with the usability and intuitiveness of the interface as a key strategy to obtaining adherence. In the next section, we will discuss these results and propose some formative recommendations.

4   Discussions and Conclusions

The previous section highlights the multifacetedness of the application, whose advantages are distributed over a complex ecology of parties with different, interconnected objectives. This multifacetedness is demonstrated by the six roles that emerged from the analysis of our interviews. At the same time, Table 1 suggests that these roles are perceived differently by different stakeholders. PA can be conceived as a "boundary object" [16] shared by four classes of stakeholders: it represents not only an object they have in common but also one they invest in with different sets of expectations. Our formative contribution to the improvement of this application is then to highlight what roles coexist in the same application and whether there are gaps or frictions between them.

Some roles could become more evident to make adherence more effective. In particular, two roles that physicians already appreciate in PA could be made more visible to patients as well: the creation of a safe dataset of health data, on the one hand, and the close monitoring of a given treatment on specific patients, on the other hand. We named these roles "safe box" and "lifesaving," respectively. In both cases, the application puts patients in control of the monitoring process and makes them responsible for the treatment's outcome. These roles then provide a motivational boost to retain the patient in the treatment they contribute to building. Interestingly, however, the "safe box" and "lifesaving box" roles do not come forward in the interviews with the patients. We can assume that it might be even less so to patients who – unlike the ones we interviewed - are administered a treatment without being part of a clinical trial: they are not instructed to appreciate the considerable advantages of constant monitoring. To improve the visibility of these roles to patients, PA could stress the importance of each data received from the patient. The app, for example, could quantify the advancement in the monitoring process enabled by the patients' data; and the physicians' and scientists' access to this data could become visible to the patients, proving to them that their effort is of immediate use.

Some frictions between roles could be prevented from blossoming to keep expectations realistic. For example, there is a potential conflict between the "interlocutor" and "secretary" roles, which could mislead some stakeholder's expectations. PA is an interlocutor because it adopts a conversational format; this is one critical feature making PA intuitive and pleasant to use and is often mentioned by the patients and developers in our interviews. PA is also a secretary because it alleviates a burden from the physicians' shoulders by taking over the most mechanical parts of the monitoring process. This role is very often mentioned by the physicians and the representatives of the pharmaceutical companies in our interviews. The friction between these two roles can be generated by the PA's conversational format and the immediacy of its interactional style, which might lead to overestimating its agency beyond the capabilities of a secretary. The patients might attribute the app the ability to interpret the data collected and even intervene upon them. Indeed, one patient in our sample expected the PA to be backed up by a medical team ready to intervene after receiving bad health updates. To avoid this misunderstanding, PA reminds the user that the app should not be considered an emergency alert. The realistic perception of PA's skills can also be obtained by checking the way in which the digital health assistant describes itself and its activities during the conversation with the patient, avoiding the impression of having some clinical agency.

Our sample was heterogeneous but small and did not include patients using or having used PA. Regardless of these limits, this study can provide insights that can be extended to other adherence apps using a digital assistant to address the patients/users. Some of the expectations that emerged from our interviews can be tracked back to functions that PA shares with other applications (i.e., sending reminders, storing data, engaging the user with a conversational interface) and are then likely to appear in similar apps. The same goes for the formative recommendations we provided in this section. Of general relevance outside this case study is also the method we have adopted, which gives a voice to the expectations of the different stakeholders having a close role in the application.

Digital assistants could pave the way to more patient-centered treatment [15]; in order to do so, their design must have a good user model and consider the different groups of users involved [3].

Acknowledgments. We are very grateful to the informants who accepted to be interviewed and shared their thoughts with us. We also thank Valentina Irene Missaggia and Marina Smorto for their help in coding the data. The study was sponsored by PatchAi via the research agreement "Supporto al design e allo sviluppo dell'app. PatchAi®".

References

1. Alamoodi, A.H., et al.: A systematic review into the assessment of medical apps: motivations, challenges, recommendations and methodological aspect. Health Technol. 1–17 (2020). https://doi.org/10.1007/s12553-020-00451-4
2. Anghel, L.A., Farcas, A.M., Oprean, R.N.: An overview of the common methods used to measure treatment adherence. Med. Pharm. Rep. **92**(2), 117 (2019). https://doi.org/10.15386/mpr-1201
3. Bath, P.A.: Health informatics: current issues and challenges. J. Inf. Sci. **34**(4), 501–518 (2008). https://doi.org/10.1177/0165551508092267
4. Baxter, K., Courage, C., Caine, K.: Understanding Your Users: A Practical Guide to User Research Methods. Morgan Kaufmann, Burlington (2015)
5. Braun, V., Clarke, V.: Using thematic analysis in psychology. Qual. Res. Psychol. **3**(2), 77–101 (2006)
6. Car, J., Tan, W.S., Huang, Z., Sloot, P., Franklin, B.D.: eHealth in the future of medications management: personalisation, monitoring and adherence. BMC Med. **15**(1), 1–9 (2017). https://doi.org/10.1186/s12916-017-0838-0
7. Car, L.T., et al.: Conversational agents in health care: scoping review and conceptual analysis. J. Med. Internet Res. **22**(8), e17158 (2020). https://doi.org/10.2196/17158
8. Cramer, J.A., et al.: Medication compliance and persistence: terminology and definitions. Value Health **11**(1), 44–47 (2008). https://doi.org/10.1111/j.1524-4733.2007.00213.x
9. Dayer, L., Heldenbrand, S., Anderson, P., Gubbins, P.O., Martin, B.C.: Smartphone medication adherence apps: potential benefits to patients and providers. J. Am. Pharm. Assoc. **53**(2), 172–181 (2013). https://doi.org/10.1331/JAPhA.2013.12202
10. Demonceau, J., et al.: Identification and assessment of adherence-enhancing interventions in studies assessing medication adherence through electronically compiled drug dosing histories: a systematic literature review and meta-analysis. Drugs **73**(6), 545–562 (2013). https://doi.org/10.1007/s40265-013-0041-3
11. Jin, J., Sklar, G.E., Oh, V.M.S., Li, S.C.: Factors affecting therapeutic compliance: a review from the patient's perspective. Ther. Clin. Risk Manag. **4**(1), 269 (2008). https://doi.org/10.2147/tcrm.s1458
12. Montiel, C.J., Uyheng, J., Dela Paz, E.: The Language of Pandemic Leaderships: Mapping Political Rhetoric During the COVID-19 Outbreak. Political Psychology (in press)
13. Pereira, J., Diaz, Ó.: Using health chatbots for behavior change: a mapping Study. J. Med. Syst. **43**(5), 135 (2019). https://doi.org/10.1007/s10916-019-1237-1
14. Sabatè, E.: Adherence to Long-Term Therapies: Evidence for Action. Geneva, Switzerland: World Health Organization (2003). https://www.who.int/chp/knowledge/publications/adherence_report_fin.pdf?ua=1

15. Sharma, T., Bamford, M., Dodman, D.: Person-centred care: an overview of reviews. Contemp. Nurse **51**(2–3), 107–120 (2015). https://doi.org/10.1080/10376178.2016.1150192

16. Star, S., Griesemer, J.: Institutional ecology, 'translations' and boundary objects: amateurs and professionals in Berkeley's museum of vertebrate zoology, 1907–39 (PDF). Soc. Stud. Sci. **19**(3), 387–420 (1989)

17. Subhi, Y., Bube, S.H., Bojsen, S.R., Thomsen, A.S.S., Konge, L.: Expert involvement and adherence to medical evidence in medical mobile phone apps: a systematic review. JMIR Mhealth Uhealth **3**(3), e79 (2015). https://doi.org/10.2196/mhealth.4169

18. Thomas, D.R.: A general inductive approach for analyzing qualitative evaluation data. Am. J. Eval. **27**(2), 237–246 (2006)

19. Wald, D.S., Butt, S., Bestwick, J.P.: One-way versus two-way text messaging on improving medication adherence: meta-analysis of randomized trials. Am. J. Med. **128**(10), 1139.e1-1139.e5 (2015)

20. van Heuckelum, M., van den Ende, C.H., Houterman, A.E., Heemskerk, C.P., van Dulmen, S., van den Bemt, B.J.: The effect of electronic monitoring feedback on medication adherence and clinical outcomes: a systematic review. PLoS ONE **12**(10), e0185453 (2017). https://doi.org/10.1371/journal.pone.0185453

21. Wiecek, E., Tonin, F.S., Torres-Robles, A., Benrimoj, S.I., Fernandez-Llimos, F., Garcia-Cardenas, V.: Temporal effectiveness of interventions to improve medication adherence: a network meta-analysis. PLoS ONE **14**(3), e0213432 (2019). https://doi.org/10.1371/journal.pone.0213432

Welicit: A Wizard of Oz Tool for VR Elicitation Studies

Andrea Bellucci$^{(\boxtimes)}$ [ID], Telmo Zarraonandia[ID], Paloma Díaz[ID], and Ignacio Aedo[ID]

Universidad Carlos III de Madrid (UC3M),
Avenida de la Universidad, 30, 28911 Leganés, Madrid, Spain
{andrea.bellucci,telmo.zarraonandia,paloma.diaz,ignacio.aedo}@uc3m.es

Abstract. Recent advances and availability of consumer hardware has enabled the proliferation of voice, head-gaze, haptic and gesture-based interactions in VR applications. However, interactions are often the result of idiosyncratic designs and little has been investigated about user preferences and behaviour. Elicitation and Wizard of Oz (WOz) studies showed potential to design user-informed intuitive and discoverable interactions in a wide range of domains. In this paper we introduce Welicit, a WOz tool to support researchers in running VR elicitation studies. The system provides tools to adapt the elicitation methodology to immersive environments by allowing users to experience the result of proposed interactions. We discuss a use case in which the tool has been used to uncover multimodal speech+gesture interactions in VR.

Keywords: Elicitation studies · Wizard of Oz · Design tools

1   Introduction

The development of interactive systems outside the desktop pushed the narrative of hand gestures, body movement and voice as natural forms of interacting with a computer. However, the desired "naturalness" does not solely rely on the properties of an interaction modality, technique or device: it is delivered by a skilfully crafted user interface that makes the interaction feeling seamless and meaningful in the context it is performed [11]. Early research on gestures, voice and body movement was heavily influenced by technological limitations (e.g., Charade [1]) and designers prioritized interactions that were easy to recognize by the system, but that did not reflect user preferences and behaviour. Wizard of Oz (WOz) [9,19] and elicitation methodologies [20] were proposed to counter this issue and gather feedback from the user to investigate an interaction space we don't know much about. Modern consumer VR hardware provides voice, head-gaze, haptic and gesture-based interactions that are manufacturer- or application-specific. As research has not yet developed a common framework and guidelines for designing interactions with 3D virtual objects, elicitation and WOz studies could help

ⓒ IFIP International Federation for Information Processing 2021
Published by Springer Nature Switzerland AG 2021
C. Ardito et al. (Eds.): INTERACT 2021, LNCS 12936, pp. 82–91, 2021.
https://doi.org/10.1007/978-3-030-85607-6_6

to understand users' preferences, expectations and behaviours in different VR scenarios. Our work contributes to tools for interaction design in the form of enabling technology [8]. We present a visual tool that aims at helping researchers to setup (pre-experiment), conduct (during the experiment), and analyse (post-experiment) WOz studies for exploring user interaction for VR experiences. We discuss a walkthrough use case in which the tool has been used to uncover user preferences for speech+gesture interaction in immersive VR editing.

2   Background

The design of the tool has been informed by previous research on interaction elicitation and Wizard of Oz studies as well as software tools that support such methodologies.

2.1   Elicitation Studies and Tools

Elicitation studies refer to a methodology, originally designed for surface comput-ing [20], in which the experimenter shows a referent —the effect of an action— and ask a participant to perform the interaction that would produce that effect. The methodology, not only aims at producing unique interaction vocabularies that are easier for the users to discover, use and remember [20]. More broadly, it has been used in think-aloud experiments to establish a dialog with the par-ticipants and learn about novel or underexplored interaction spaces [14,16,17]. While various elicitations studies on AR interactions can be found in the liter-ature [11,17,18], very few studies have explored user-defined immersive interac-tions for VR [15]. Running elicitation studies for novel interactive environments, such as the immersive VR medium, can be a non-trivial task: a substantial tech-nical effort and time is required to setup and run the experiment as well as to analyse the results [13].

2.2   Wizard of Oz Studies and Tools

In WOz studies, the experimenter, through a purposefully crafted interface, sim-ulates systems' functionality that is not already implemented, thus giving partic-ipants the illusion they are interacting with a functioning system. Researchers have used this approach to conduct user studies in a wide array of contexts [3,4,9,12,19]. Relevant for this work is the combination of WOz simulation with the interaction elicitation methodology to inform the design of interactions for AR/VR/MR [7,18]. WOz interfaces allow the experimenter to manipulate 3D objects in the virtual environment [11], which can be used to present the referent and, more importantly, to show participants the result while they are perform-ing the proposed interaction [18]. The literature of WOz elicitation studies is, however, still scarce. Current studies primarily discuss the resulting interaction vocabulary without providing insights on the technical and methodological con-siderations of WOz tools [7]. Common issues of WOz systems can be amplified when the methodology is applied to immersive VR environments and the WOz system has to be specifically designed to reduce the cognitive and physical load of the wizard [6].

3 The Welicit System

Based on the review of the literature and our own experience in conducting WOz studies, we identified the following design requirements (R) for a WOz tool to support elicitation studies for VR.

R1. Reduce Technical Knowledge. Researchers might not have the technical knowledge needed to install and run complex scripts or plugins, tweak configuration files, or to setup the environment to cast the VR experience from standalone headsets as well as send commands. The WOz system should be easy to install and configure (possibly no installation) and it should work with known technology (e.g., web-based applications in a browser).

R2. Support Collocated as Well as Remote Studies. VR environments enable different time/space configurations, e.g., single user [4], collocated multi-users [5], remote multi-users [10]. The system should support the researcher in the definition of a wide range of experiment configurations, including the case in which multiple users are interacting in different cross-reality interactions between physical and virtual worlds [2].

R3. Contextual Richness. Novel interactions in VR are not limited to gestures, but they encompass a wide range of modalities that can be combined in multimodal interfaces. Very little is known about how best combine different modalities or to what extent the semantic of the objects would affect the user interaction. A WOz tool, therefore, should support exploration of different modalities, e.g., hand-free, controller-based, voice, or head-gaze, as well as interaction with tangible objects. To this end, the tool should also implement strategies to reduce the effects of legacy bias, such as encouraging participants to propose more than one interaction for each referents, or priming participants towards to the use of a new device or sensing modality.

R4. Reduce the Experimenter/Wizard Cognitive and Motor Load. The major drawback of the WOz technique is the high cognitive and physical demands it introduces [4]. WOz interfaces can be difficult for the experimenter to manipulate, and, in order to provide meaningful results, the wizard has to provide responses as quick and accurate as possible. The system should support the experimenter in the definition of the wizard interface, possibly providing tools to easily modify the interface and support more than one wizard. In elicitation studies, the experimenter has also to show the referents to the users, take note of the different interactions proposed for the referents as well as the user ratings for the interactions (questionnaires). The system, therefore, should support the experimenter in these tasks.

R5. Facilitate Data Analysis. The literature stresses that analysing results from an elicitation study is a complex task [13]. The situation is even more complex for multimodal interaction in VR: the experimenter has to analyse data from different sources such as audio/video recording as well as the resulting interaction in the virtual world. The system should provide an interface that facilitates this process and help the experimenter to organize data for analysis.

R6. Generate Interaction Datasets. Contributions to the field also comes with the generation of datasets of interactions in different application contexts that other researchers can use and compare. Generated data can be used to train AI recognition algorithm, and also to speed the design of the user experience in case developers do not have access to an actual device.

3.1   Architecture and Implementation

The Welicit tool is built on top of the A-Frame Inspector[1], an opensource visual tool that provides user interface widgets to build 3D scenes and tweak entities' components and properties. We wanted to integrate a flexible tool to support WOz interfaces into a design environment for prototyping VR experiences, with the goal to reduce the technical setup (R1) and provide a unique interface to build a 3D scene, and define the wizard interface as well as the connections between

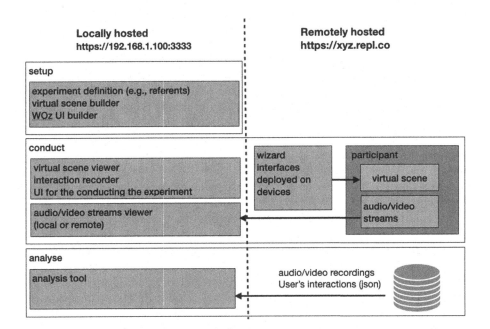

Fig. 1. Architecture of the Welicit system.

---

[1] https://github.com/aframevr/aframe-inspector.

widgets' behaviour and 3D objects (R3). Figure 1 shows the architecture of the system. On a local server runs the application that the experimenter uses to design the virtual environment, define the details of the experiment, and build the wizard interface. The system exposes the local development server for other computers to access, as well as to stream the audio and video (R2). The virtual scene, the wizard interfaces as well as the interface to run the experiment are exposed as web applications through a Node.js server, which can be locally or remotely hosted (e.g., on services such as Replit.com). Having a remote server with a fixed URL eases the setup of collocated studies (R1). At the same time, it offers the possibility to have more than one human wizard (R4), and it allows to run WOz experiment with multiple participants accessing from remote locations (R2) as well as to run remote users studies with one participant (R2), without requiring extra configurations (R1). The tool has been implemented using Web technologies such as React for building the user interface, Node.js for the server, Websocket and WebRTC API for the communication, WebXR API for hand joints visualization and recording on supported hardware, and Sensor API to retrieve data from the absolute orientation sensor of mobile devices.

3.2   System Design

The Welicit system provides tools to setup and conduct an experiment as well as to analyse data.

Setup. The system provides a step-by-step interface to define details of the study (R1), such as the study id, the name, the starting and closing date and the list of participants. In the next screen, the experimenter enters the list of referents, the maximum number of alternative interactions, the post-interaction questions, and the number of scenarios to test. We decided to include scenarios because we envision that for VR interactions it would be meaningful to test the same set of referents under different conditions, as also reported in [17]. In case of multiple conditions, the system will automatically counterbalance the conditions in the experiment to avoid learning bias. Figure 2 shows the main interface of Welicit for building WOz interfaces. The system supports cross-device distributed interfaces, that is, the experimenter can select different WOz components and widgets to compose an interface across different devices. This has the goal to enable multiple human wizards at the same time, provide extra flexibility to the interface setup and avoid to clutter the interface of a single device with too many widgets (R4). Welicit implements a WYSIWYG visual editor for the composition of the wizard interface (R1): widgets are selected from a dropdown list and they can be (re)arranged through drag-and-drop interaction. Once a 3D object in the scene has been selected (mouse click), a panel appears with the properties of the object that can be controlled through the widgets of the wizard interface. The widgets that are currently implemented are: button, toggle, sliders (linear and circular), digital thumbpad, canvas for $1 gesture recognizer (R3, R4). Additionally, quaternion data from the absolute orientation sensor of mobile devices (using the Sensor Web API) are supported. This has the goal to

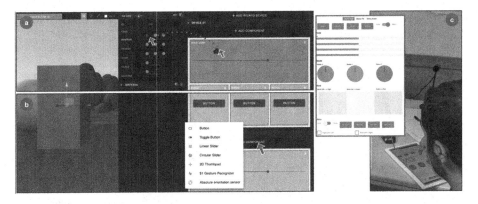

Fig. 2. The Welicit user interface to build the Wizard interface. (a) Drag-and drop properties of a 3D object to a component of the Wizard interface that will be used to control the property. (b) Add a new component to the Wizard interface. (c) An example of a deployed Wizard interface.

enable embodied controls for the experimenters (R4). Each widget has its own attributes that can be defined by the experimenter. For example, for a slider, the following attributes can be defined from the interface: the default value, the type (continuous or discrete), the step, the min and max values and the orientation.

Conduct. Once the experimenter has defined the virtual scene and the wizard interface, all the code is automatically generated and made available on the remote server. A URL is generated to open the virtual scene on a VR device. Other URLs are generated and codified into QRCodes to access the wizard interface from the browser of the target devices (Fig. 2c). When running the experiment, the locally hosted server receives data from the virtual scene as well as audio and video streams from remote or local clients, which the experimenter will use to observe the interaction of the user (R1, R2). During this phase, Welicit provides an interface to view the interaction of the participant in the virtual scene, local as well as remote video streams and buttons to go to the next referent and to record the interaction. The system implements a functionality to record the interaction as it takes place in the virtual world, exploiting the motion capture tools of the A-frame Inspector, which allows to save *json* files describing *xyz* position and rotation of camera and tracked controllers with timestamps. The motion capture tool was extended to record hands joint data on the Oculus Quest 2 (WebXR API) and Oculus Rift (Leap Motion), and it was tweaked to support two modes of recording: automatic and manual. In the automatic mode, interactions in the virtual world are recorded as long as hands or controllers movements are in the field of view of the participants. Auto recording could lower the cognitive load of the experimenter (R4) and it facilitates unsupervised recording of interactions [16]. However, it does not capture camera-only movements, which are important to study head-gaze interaction.

To give the experimenter more control over recordings, the manual mode allows to start and stop recording by pressing the <space> key.

Fig. 3. The Welicit interface to analyse video, audio and VR interaction recordings.

Analyse. In this last stage, the Welicit system offers an interface (Fig. 3) that shows video and audio streams matched with the interaction performed in the virtual world. This functionality aims at supporting analysis of complex interactions (R5), for instance multimodal interactions with speech, head-gaze and gestures, for which the experimenter needs to observe, at the same time, the participant interaction in the real world and the resulting interaction in the virtual world. The analysis tool automatically organizes recordings according to the referents and produces one set of recordings for each scenario.

4   Walkthrough Use Case and Lessons Learned

We used the Welicit tool to run a WOz study to understand user preferences for multimodal speech+gesture interactions for VR editing environments. Our initial goal was to understand how properties of the objects, such as their size and position with respect to the user (within or out of reach) would affect the interaction. We discuss the user study as a walkthrough scenario and to describe the potential of the tool to support WOz studies as well as lessons learned.

Setup. In the setup stage, we designed a 3D scene of a small flat apartment with a cup on table and a bed, using existing 3D models. Two researchers defined the referents to use in the study, namely: select, clone, delete, change color, move, scale, rotate and undo. Two scenarios were also defined: one for the small object close to the participant (the cup) and another one for the big object out of reach (the bed). We then built the user interface for the WOz to run on tablet device, with two tabs, one for each object, and widgets that allowed to perform manipulations of the objects: linear sliders for changing the xyz scale, circular sliders for xyz rotation, 2D digital thumbpads for moving the object on xy-, xz-, and yz-axis and buttons to hide/show, duplicate or delete the objects. We also designed a fake menu: an object with buttons that would appear close to the object in case the participants felt the need to use virtual UIs. Welicit proved useful in this phase, since it allowed the two experimenters to quickly run pilot studies to decide the final design of the virtual environment and the wizard interface and, at the same time, gain experience in the use of the interface itself.

Conduct. We conducted the experiment with 16 participants, using the Oculus Rift VR headset and Leap Motion for hand-tracking. Automatically counterbalancing the scenarios as well as presenting the next referent on button press was helpful: it reduced the cognitive load of the experimenter, who did not have to worry about remembering or reading on a piece of paper what was the next referent. We also discovered that, in cases when experiments are not conducted by the same researcher, the interaction to show to the user should be pre-recorded. This would assure consistency among studies, since different researchers could show the interaction in a slightly different way, which could bias the study. Recording the interaction to present for a referent would also allow to show only *before* and *after* states of an object, and not an animated transition [17]. As we expected, allowing participants to experience their interactions encouraged them to think out loud and to propose more than one interaction for each referent.

Analyse. The manual recording feature was helpful to extract the audio corresponding to an interaction in VR and the visualization tool allowed to easily identify and classify it. We discovered that it would be useful to provide the experimenter with an interface to add time-based annotation during the study. In the case of voice interaction only, in fact, it was difficult to find when they were performed and such annotations would solve this problem.

5   Limitations and Future Development

The Welicit tool has technological limitation that will be addressed in future development. The system supports only single-user immersive experiences on Oculus Quest 2 and Oculus Rift. There is no mechanism to easily extend the tool to support additional widgets and sensors; new components could be added but this would require programming work and we do not describe in this paper how it could be accomplished. Lastly, user studies with researchers outside our lab are needed to evaluate the effectiveness of the tool.

6   Conclusions

We introduced a tool to setup, conduct and analyse elicitation studies with the Wizard of Oz paradigm. Easing the technical and methodological issues of these studies is an important step to generate user and interaction requirements for novel VR interactions in different contexts. To this end, we plan on making the tool available under open-source license and create a space where researchers and designers can contribute by sharing their data and experience.

Acknowledgments. This work was supported by the Spanish State Research Agency (AEI) under grants Sense2MakeSense (PID2019-109388GB-I00) and Cross-Colab (PGC2018-101884-B-I00).

References

1. Baudel, T., Beaudouin-Lafon, M.: Charade: remote control of objects using free-hand gestures. Commun. ACM **36**(7), 28–35 (1993)
2. Bellucci, A., Zarraonandia, T., Díaz, P., Aedo, I.: End-user prototyping of cross-reality environments. In: Proceedings of the Eleventh International Conference on Tangible, Embedded, and Embodied Interaction, pp. 173–182 (2017)
3. Connell, S., Kuo, P.Y., Liu, L., Piper, A.M.: A wizard-of-Oz elicitation study examining child-defined gestures with a whole-body interface. In: Proceedings of the 12th International Conference on Interaction Design and Children, pp. 277–280 (2013)
4. Dow, S., Lee, J., Oezbek, C., MacIntyre, B., Bolter, J.D., Gandy, M.: Wizard of Oz interfaces for mixed reality applications. In: CHI 2005 Extended Abstracts on Human Factors in Computing Systems, pp. 1339–1342 (2005)
5. Grandi, J.G., Debarba, H.G., Nedel, L., Maciel, A.: Design and evaluation of a handheld-based 3D user interface for collaborative object manipulation. In: Proceedings of the 2017 CHI Conference on Human Factors in Computing Systems, pp. 5881–5891 (2017)
6. Grill, T., Polacek, O., Tscheligi, M.: ConWIZ: a tool supporting contextual wizard of Oz simulation. In: Proceedings of the 11th International Conference on Mobile and Ubiquitous Multimedia, pp. 1–8 (2012)
7. Höysniemi, J., Hämäläinen, P., Turkki, L.: Wizard of Oz prototyping of computer vision based action games for children. In: Proceedings of the 2004 Conference on Interaction Design and Children: Building a Community, pp. 27–34 (2004)
8. Hudson, S.E., Mankoff, J.: Concepts, values, and methods for technical human–computer interaction research. In: Olson, J.S., Kellogg, W.A. (eds.) Ways of Knowing in HCI, pp. 69–93. Springer, New York (2014). https://doi.org/10.1007/978-1-4939-0378-8_4
9. Klemmer, S.R., Sinha, A.K., Chen, J., Landay, J.A., Aboobaker, N., Wang, A.: SUEDE: a wizard of Oz prototyping tool for speech user interfaces. In: Proceedings of the 13th Annual ACM Symposium on User Interface Software And Technology, pp. 1–10 (2000)
10. Lang, T., MacIntyre, B., Zugaza, I.J.: Massively multiplayer online worlds as a platform for augmented reality experiences. In: 2008 IEEE Virtual Reality Conference, pp. 67–70. IEEE (2008)
11. Lee, M., Billinghurst, M.: A wizard of Oz study for an AR multimodal interface. In: Proceedings of the 10th International Conference on Multimodal Interfaces, pp. 249–256 (2008)
12. MacIntyre, B., Gandy, M., Dow, S., Bolter, J.D.: DART: a toolkit for rapid design exploration of augmented reality experiences. In: Proceedings of the 17th annual ACM Symposium on User Interface Software and Technology, pp. 197–206 (2004)
13. Magrofuoco, N., Vanderdonckt, J.: Gelicit: a cloud platform for distributed gesture elicitation studies. Proc. ACM Hum.-Comput. Interact. **3**(EICS), 1–41 (2019)

14. Morris, M.R.: Web on the wall: insights from a multimodal interaction elicitation study. In: Proceedings of the 2012 ACM International Conference on Interactive Tabletops and Surfaces, pp. 95–104 (2012)

15. Nanjappan, V., Liang, H.N., Lu, F., Papangelis, K., Yue, Y., Man, K.L.: User-elicited dual-hand interactions for manipulating 3d objects in virtual reality environments. Hum.-Cent. Comput. Inf. Sci. **8**(1), 1–16 (2018)

16. Nebeling, M., Ott, D., Norrie, M.C.: Kinect analysis: a system for recording, analysing and sharing multimodal interaction elicitation studies. In: Proceedings of the 7th ACM SIGCHI Symposium on Engineering Interactive Computing Systems, pp. 142–151 (2015)

17. Pham, T., Vermeulen, J., Tang, A., MacDonald Vermeulen, L.: Scale impacts elicited gestures for manipulating holograms: implications for AR gesture design. In: Proceedings of the 2018 Designing Interactive Systems Conference, pp. 227–240 (2018)

18. Piumsomboon, T., Clark, A., Billinghurst, M., Cockburn, A.: User-defined gestures for augmented reality. In: Kotzé, P., Marsden, G., Lindgaard, G., Wesson, J., Winckler, M. (eds.) INTERACT 2013. LNCS, vol. 8118, pp. 282–299. Springer, Heidelberg (2013). https://doi.org/10.1007/978-3-642-40480-1_18

19. Salber, D., Coutaz, J.: Applying the wizard of Oz technique to the study of multimodal systems. In: Bass, L.J., Gornostaev, J., Unger, C. (eds.) EWHCI 1993. LNCS, vol. 753, pp. 219–230. Springer, Heidelberg (1993). https://doi.org/10.1007/3-540-57433-6_51

20. Wobbrock, J.O., Morris, M.R., Wilson, A.D.: User-defined gestures for surface computing. In: Proceedings of the SIGCHI Conference on Human Factors in Computing Systems, pp. 1083–1092 (2009)

Virtual Reality

A Proposal for Discreet Auxiliary Figures for Reducing VR Sickness and for Not Obstructing FOV

Masaki Omata[✉] and Atsuki Shimizu

University of Yamanashi, 4-3-11 Takeda, Kofu, Yamanashi, Japan
{omata,atsuki18}@hci.media.yamanashi.ac.jp

Abstract. We aim to reduce the virtual reality (VR) sickness by superimposing discreet auxiliary figures: "gazing point" on the center of the user's field of view, "dots" on the four corners of the field of view, "user's horizontal line" links a line to the user's head movement, and "real world's horizontal line" links to the real-world horizontal line. We conducted an experiment to evaluate the degree to which these figures could reduce VR sickness in a VR environment on a head-mounted display (HMD) by using Simulator Sickness Questionnaire (SSQ) and skin conductance (SC) on the user's palm. The results show that the VR sickness tended to reduce by the superimposition of "dots."

Keywords: Virtual reality sickness · Auxiliary figure · Simulator Sickness Questionnaire · Skin conductance

1 Introduction

In recent years, the market size for virtual reality (VR) technologies, such as head-mounted displays (HMDs) and VR contents, has been increasing. Major VR manufacturers have released stand-alone low-cost HMDs. Therefore, users who previously avoided VR devices because of their complexity and high price have started using them.

However, the spread of VR devices, has also given rise to certain specific health concerns. A number of users have been affected by VR sickness, and this number is expected to increase in the coming years. VR sickness refers to the deterioration of HMD user's health because of operating the virtual space on a large display and viewing 360° videos on an HMD. The typical symptoms of VR sickness are mild headache and heartburn followed by dizziness and nausea, which eventually leads to vomiting. These symptoms and processes are very similar to motion sickness [1].

The cause of motion sickness has not yet been completely elucidated, but one powerful theory is the sensory conflict theory proposed by Reason and Brand [2]. Sensory conflicts theory classifies motion sickness into two parts: a conflict between the ear canal and otoliths and a conflict between the vision and the vestibular system. Other theories concerning the causes of motion sickness include the subjective vertical conflict theory [3] and the ecological theory of motion sickness [4].

C. Ardito et al. (Eds.): INTERACT 2021, LNCS 12936, pp. 95–104, 2021.
https://doi.org/10.1007/978-3-030-85607-6_7

Sensory conflicts are considered a major cause of VR sickness as in the case of motion sickness. In a VR environment in which HMDs and other visual systems are the main stimuli, the vestibular system does not perceive the acceleration of motion even when the visual system perceives the motion. To solve this problem, researchers have proposed methods of moving the user's body directly to stimulate the vestibular system [5, 6]; another methods have been proposed of presenting a visual effect to reduce the degree of conflict in the visual system [7–15]. Moving a user's body is a costly method that requires a large space. On the other hand, presenting a visual effect does not require a large space and costs.

Based on this reasoning, we aim to reduce the VR sickness by superimposing discreet auxiliary figures (see Fig. 1), such as dots and a horizontal line, in a VR space on an HMD. We hypothesized that the superimposition of the figures could reduce the VR sickness without disturbing the user's FOV too much.

Then, we conducted an experiment to measure the degree of VR sickness in a VR environment on an HMD by using Simulator Sickness Questionnaire (SSQ) and skin conductance (SC) to measure mental sweating [16–18] on the user's palm as evaluation metrics to confirm the reduction effect of each of the auxiliary figures. In the following sections, we describe some related studies, the designs of the four auxiliary figures, the details of our experiment, and the results.

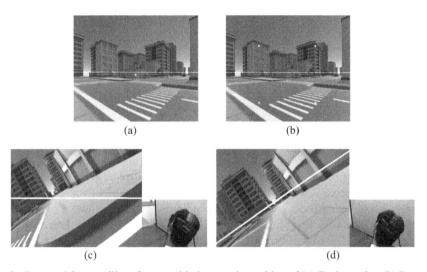

(a)   (b)

(c)   (d)

Fig. 1. Proposed four auxiliary figures with the superimposition of (a) Gazing point, (b) Dots, (c) User's horizontal line, and (d) Real world's horizontal line.

2   Related Work

As a method to change a user's field-of-view, Bos et al. hypothesized that appropriate visual information on self-motion was beneficial in a naval setting and conducted and experiment a ship's bridge motion simulator with three visual conditions: an Earth-fixed outside view, an inside view that moved with the subjects, and a blindfolded condition [7]. As the results, sickness was highest in the inside viewing condition, and no effect of sickness on task performance was observed. Norouzi et al. investigated use of vignetting to reduce VR sickness when using amplified head rotations instead of controller-based input and whether the induced VR sickness is a result of the user's head acceleration or velocity by introducing two different modes of vignetting, one triggered by acceleration and the other by velocity [8]. The results show generally indicating that the vignetting methods did not succeed in reducing VR sickness for most of the participants and, instead, lead to a significant increase. Duh et al. suggested that an independent visual background (IVB) might disturbance when conflicting visual and inertial cues [9]. They examined 3 levels of independent visual background with 2 levels of roll oscillation frequency. As the results, there were statistically significant effects of IVB and a significant interaction between IVB and frequency. Sargunam et al. compared three common joystick rotation techniques: traditional continuous rotation, continuous rotation with reduced field-of-view, and discrete rotation with fixed intervals for turning [10]. Their goal is to investigate whether there are tradeoffs for different joystick rotation techniques in terms of sickness, preferences in a 3D environment. The results showed no evidence of differences in orientation, but sickness ratings found discrete rotations to be significantly better than field-of-view reduction. Fernandes et al. explored the effect of dynamically, yet subtly, changing a physically stationary person's field-of-view in response to visually perceived motion in a virtual environment [11]. Then, they could reduce the degree of VR sickness perceived by participants, without decreasing their subjective level of presence, and minimizing their awareness of the intervention. Budhiraja et al. proposed Rotation Blurring, uniformly, uniformly blurring the screen during rotational movements to reduce cyber-sickness caused by character movements in a First Person Shooter game in virtual environment [12]. The results showed that the blurring technique led to an overall reduction in sickness levels of the participants and delayed its onset.

On the other hand, as a method to add a figure on user's field-of-view, Whittinghill et al. placed a three-dimensional model of a virtual human nose in the center of the fields of view of the display in order to observe that placing a fixed visual reference object within the user's field of view seems to somewhat reduce simulator sickness [13]. As the results, users in the Nose experimental group were able, on average, to operate the VR applications longer and with fewer instances of stop requests than were users in the no-nose control group. Cao et al. designed a see-through metal net surrounding users above and below as a rest frame to reduce motion sickness reduction in an HMD [14]. They showed that subjects feel more comfortable and tolerate when the net is included than when there was no rest frame. Buhler et al. proposed and evaluated two novel visual effects that can reduce VR sickness with head-mounted displays [15]. The circle effect is that the peripheral vision shows the point of view of a different camera. The border between the outer peripheral vision and the inner vision is visible as a circle. The dot effect adds artificial motion in peripheral vision that counteracts a virtual motion. The results showed lower means of sickness in the two effects; however, the difference is not statistically significant across all users.

As mentioned above, in many studies, entire view is changed, or figures are conspicuously superimposed. There are some superimposed figures that imitate the user's nose, which are not so obvious, but it is not effective in some situations, or can only be used for a first-person's view. Therefore, we designed a more discreet static figure in virtual space and a scene-independence figure connecting the virtual world and the real world.

3 Design of Discreet Auxiliary Figures

We designed four types of discreet auxiliary figures to reduce VR sickness (see Fig. 1).

3.1 Gazing Point

The gazing point is superimposed on the center of the virtual space on an HMD (see Fig. 1a). The aim is to suppress eye movements of the user. We subjectively selected the size and color of the point so that it would most likely not interfere with the user's content-viewing experience and was also not difficult to see. Sprite is the knob of the Unity standard [19]. The distance from the avatar in the virtual space was 0.31; the coordinates of the point were x = 0.05, y = 0.05 in the Unity scale, and it was white in color.

3.2 Dots

Four dots, one at each corner, are superimposed on the four corners of the view of virtual space (see Fig. 1b). By making the user aware of the center of the relative view from the four dots, it is expected that eye movement can be suppressed as well as the gazing point. Additionally, unlike the display of the gazing point, nothing is displayed at the center of the view, so it does not interfere with the content viewing, and it is thought that the decline in the sense of immersion can be suppressed. The size and color of each dot is the same as the gazing point. The positions of the dots are at x = 2.5 or −2.5 and y = 2.5 or −2.5 in the Unity scale.

3.3 User's Horizontal Line

The horizontal line linked to the user's head movement was superimposed on the center of field of view (see Fig. 1c). When the user tilts his/her head, a conflict occurs between the user's memorized information of the horizon of the real world and the vestibular and visual information of the tilt of the virtual space. Therefore, the superimposed horizontal line linked to the user's head movement can reduce the conflict. The horizontal line passes from the screen edge to the screen center and reaches the opposite screen edge. We subjectively selected the thickness and color of the line so that it would not be bothersome or hard to view. Sprite is the knob of the Unity standard. In the virtual space, the distance from the avatar was 0.31; the coordinates were x = 5, y = 0.0025 in the Unity scale, and the color was white.

3.4 World's Horizontal Line

In the virtual space, we superimposed a line that always showed the horizontal line of the real world (see Fig. 1d). This line clarified how much of the user's head was tilted from the real world's horizon by always presenting the real world in the virtual space. The user could correct his/her autonomous head tilt and become aware of the degree of the tilt. The size and color of the line was the same as that of the user's horizontal line.

4 Evaluation Experiment

We verified the hypothesis that the SSQ score, which is an index of VR sickness, could be significantly reduced by superimposing each of the auxiliary figures on the field of view in the VR space. Therefore, we investigated the SSQ scores of the five conditions by including the condition without superimposition for the four types of auxiliary figures described in the Sect. 3.

SSQ is a metric that can calculate three sub-scores (oculomotor, nausea, and disorientation) and the total score by asking the participants to score approximately 16 symptoms caused by VR sickness on a four-point scale [20]. These scores have different calculation methods, and it is difficult to compare the extent to which the scores differ. In this experiment, the results were expressed as a percentage with the upper limit value being 100% in each score.

We also measured the palmar sweating as an objective psychophysiological metric (see Fig. 2). The reason for using SC as one of the indexes of sickness is that it is known that motion sickness induces sweating [16, 17], and that emotional sweating is caused by stress and anxiety [21].

Fig. 2. Experimental equipment and scene.

4.1 Equipment and the VR Space

We used a computer (Intel Corei36100 3.70 GHz, GeForce GTX 1050 Ti, Windows10) to construct and output two 3D VR spaces: a dark tunnel generated from "Modular Metro Tunnels [22]" and a bright cityscape generated from "Simple Town Pack [23]"; these spaces were published on Unity Asset Store. We used Unity (ver. 2018.3.1f1) [19] for the construction of 3D spaces and superimposition of the auxiliary figures. The HMD was GALAX VISION Developer Edition (1920 × 1080 pixels, 60 Hz); it had a viewing angle of 100° and a delay of 25 ms. This device was equipped with an input high-definition multimedia interface, a gyroscope, and an accelerometer. Typical in-ear type earphones (Final, E-1000) were used to play environmental sounds in the spaces.

For the SC measurement, two electrodes of an SC sensor (Thought Technology Ltd.) were attached to the forefinger and the ring finger of the participant's non-dominant hand during the experiment.

To eliminate the influence of temperature on VR sickness, the room temperature was adjusted to a constant 20 °C using an air conditioner.

4.2 Task

The experimental task was to find white boxes with numbers in the VR spaces. The movement of the avatar in the spaces was automatic, and the participant was only allowed to rotate the view by head tracking. The task of using only head rotations to search for a box forced the participants to look around in the VR spaces.

The avatar first moved automatically in the dark tunnel, and when it reached a specific point, the scene changed to a bright cityscape. Then, the avatar also moved automatically in the cityscape. Finally, the movement stopped when the avatar reached a specific point, and the task was finished. We added a pitch of 1.5 Hz to the view all the time. The pitch is a frequency that easily induces motion sickness [24]. The amplitude was set subjectively so that it was natural similar to the head pitching.

4.3 Procedure

The experiment was conducted as a within-subject design; therefore, all the participants performed the experimental task under five conditions. We randomized the order of the five conditions for each participant.

The task performance time for each condition was approximately 10 min and 30 s. To avoid the influence of the immediately preceding condition, we introduced a rest time of approximately 40 min between conditions. If the participant did not recover even after 40 min, the rest time was extended. However, even if 40 min had not passed, when the participant recovered, the rest time was shortened, and the task was performed in the following condition. The conditions were spread over two days to avoid lengthening the experiment. Two experiments were performed on the first day, and the remaining three were performed on the second day. In addition, to avoid the influence of ingested food, the participants were asked to refrain from eating one hour before the start of the experiment.

At the start of the experiment, the experimenter took the informed consent of each participant and told the participant that he/she could immediately stop the task at any time if he/she felt unwell during the experiment. Then, each participant was asked to respond to the Motion Sickness Susceptibility Questionnaire (MSSQ) [25], and the questionnaire survey on the participant's VR experience. Then, the experimenter attached an SC sensor to the participant's non-dominant hand and measured the sweating data on his/her palm for 2 min at rest; this was the baseline data.

The experimental scene is shown in Fig. 2. The participants answered the SSQ before and after the task execution under each condition. In the SSQ before the execution, the experimenter asked the participants to fill in '1' for all the items and to memorize their current physical conditions. The SSQ was used to evaluate how much the physical condition deteriorated after the task execution. After all the conditions were performed by the participants, each participant ranked the five conditions of "difficulty of developing VR sickness" and "immersion in VR environment."

4.4 Participants

The participants were nine undergraduates (six men and three women) aged 20 to 33 years who did not have any history of problems with vision and vestibular sensations.

5 Results and Discussions

5.1 Difficulty Rankings to VR Sickness

Figure 3 shows the results of the responses of all participants based on the order of difficulty of developing VR sickness. From this figure, although we can say that the dots condition was less likely to develop VR sickness as a high-order tendency, there was no significant difference between the conditions (Friedman's test, $N = 9$, $df = 4$, $p > .05$).

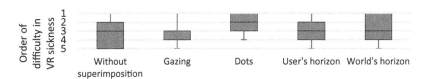

Fig. 3. Results for the order of difficulty in developing VR sickness.

5.2 SSQ

Figure 4 shows the results of the SSQ. No significant difference was found between the conditions (Friedman's test, $N = 9$, $df = 4$, $p > .05$), but the without-superimposition condition had the largest symptom of VR sickness, and the dots condition had the smallest symptom.

By grouping the rankings for the difficulty to develop VR sickness, we found that the SSQ was affected by the participants' preferences for difficulty. Moreover, we found that the dots condition relatively reduced the VR sickness, although there were no major differences among the conditions.

The results of the grouping based on the total scores of SSQ were probably influenced by the presence or the absence of the presentation in the center of the field of view. In our proposed auxiliary figures, only the dot condition was not superimposed on the center of the field of view. Therefore, the participants who do not easily develop VR sickness felt uncomfortable about the obstruction more than the reduction effect of VR sickness.

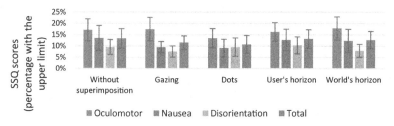

Fig. 4. SSQ total score percentages.

5.3 Sweating Rate

Figure 5 shows the changes in the sweating rates from the state of rest for each auxiliary figure. Although no significant difference was found, the superimposition of auxiliary figures tended to suppress sweating. In particular, under the user's and world's horizontal conditions, the sweating was suppressed to almost the same level as that at rest.

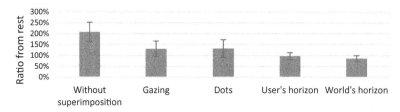

Fig. 5. Result of the sweating ratio of each condition from the state of rest.

6 Conclusion

We designed the discreet auxiliary figures to aim to reduce the VR sickness and not to obstruct the field of view on an HMD. In the evaluative experiment, although there was no significant difference between the without-superimposition group and the auxiliary figures-imposed groups, we found that the VR sickness tended to reduce by the super-imposition of dots design. Although there were individual differences in whether or not the dots were suitable, VR sickness did not increase for the dots superimposition case even when the participants did not think the dots useful.

The experimental results were classified according to the SSQ scores although it was possible to reduce the sickness of the participants who easily got sick when the auxiliary figures were used. The sickness of the participants who did not easily get sick became strong. From these results, we concluded that the presence of an auxiliary figure in the central field of view influenced intensity of the VR sickness; the VR sickness did not intensify even in participants who did not easily develop VR sickness under the dots condition.

References

1. Andrew, B., Gresham, C.: Prevention and treatment of motion sickness. Am. Fam. Physician **90**(1), 41–46 (2014)
2. Reason, J.T., Brand Joan, J.: Motion Sickness. Academic Press (1975)
3. Bles, W., Bos, J.E., de Graaf, B., Groen, E., Wertheim, A.H.: Motion sickness: only one provocative conflict? Brain Res. Bull. **47**(5), 481–487 (1998)
4. Riccio, G.E., Stoffregen, T.A.: An ecological theory of motion sickness and postural instability. Ecol. Psychol. **3**(3), 195–240 (1991)
5. Nakayama, Y., et al.: Zentei denki shigeki ga VR-yoi ni ataeru koka no kento. In: The 23rd Annual Conference of the Virtual Reality Society of Japan, 14B-5 (2018). (in Japanese)
6. Virtual Reality Lab. in University of Tukuba. String Walker. http://intron.kz.tsukuba.ac.jp/str ingwalker/stringwalker.html. Accessed 11 Apr 2021
7. Bos, J.E., MacKinnon, S.N., Patterson, A.: Motion sickness symptoms in a ship motion simulator: effects of inside, outside, and no view. Aviat. Space Environ. Med. **76**(12), 1111–1118 (2005)
8. Norouzi, N., Bruder, G., Welch, G.: Assessing vignetting as a means to reduce VR sickness during amplified head rotations. In: Proceedings of the 15th ACM Symposium on Applied Perception (SAP 2018), Article 19, pp. 1–8. Association for Computing Machinery, New York (2018)
9. Duh, H.B., Parker, D.E., Furness, T.A.: An "independent visual background" reduced balance disturbance envoked by visual scene motion: implication for alleviating simulator sickness. In: Proceedings of the SIGCHI Conference on Human Factors in Computing Systems (CHI 2001), pp. 85–89. Association for Computing Machinery, New York (2001)
10. Sargunam, S.P., Ragan, E.D.: Evaluating joystick control for view rotation in virtual reality with continuous turning, discrete turning, and field-of-view reduction. In: Proceedings of the 3rd International Workshop on Interactive and Spatial Computing (IWISC 2018), pp. 74–79. Association for Computing Machinery, New York (2018)
11. Fernandes, A.S., Feiner, S.K.: Combating VR sickness through subtle dynamic field-of-view modification. In: IEEE Symposium on 3D User Interfaces (3DUI), Greenville, pp. 201–210 (2016)
12. Budhiraja, P., Miller, M.R., Modi, A.K., Forsyth, D.: Blurring: use of artificial blurring to reduce cybersickness in virtual reality first person shooters. arXiv preprint arXiv:1710.02599 (2017)
13. Whittinghill, D.M., Ziegler, B., Moore, J., Case, T.: Nasum Virtualis: a simple technique for reducing simulator sickness. https://www.gdcvault.com/play/1022287/Technical-Artist-Boo tcamp-Nasum-Virtualis. Accessed 11 Apr 2021
14. Cao, Z., Jerald, J., Kopper, R.: Visually-induced motion sickness reduction via static and dynamic rest frames. In: IEEE Conference on Virtual Reality and 3D User Interfaces (VR), Reutlingen, pp. 105–112 (2018)
15. Buhler, H., Misztal, S., Schild, J.: Reducing VR sickness through peripheral visual effects. In: IEEE Conference on Virtual Reality and 3D User Interfaces (VR), Reutlingen, pp. 517–519 (2018)
16. Takov, V., Prasanna, T.: Motion Sickness. StatPearls, StatPearls Publishing (2020)
17. Golding, J.F.: Motion sickness. Handb. Clin. Neurol. **137**, 371–390 (2016)
18. Laviola Jr., J.J.: A discussion of cybersickness in virtual environments. SIGCHI Bull. **32**(1), 47–56 (2000)
19. Unity Technologies. Unity. https://unity.com/. Accessed 11 Apr 2021
20. Kennedy, R.S., Lane, N.E., Berbaum, K.S., Lilienthal, M.G.: Simulator sickness questionnaire: an enhanced method for quantifying simulator sickness. Int. J. Aviat. Psychol. **3**(3), 203–220 (1993)

21. Wilke, K., Martin, A., Terstegen, L., Biel, S.S.: A short history of sweat gland biology. Int. J. Cosmetic Sci. **29**(3), 169–179 (2007)

22. Unity Technologies. Unity Asset Store, Modular Metro Tunnels. https://assetstore.unity.com/packages/3d/environments/urban/modular-metro-tunnels-130591. Accessed 11 Apr 2021

23. Unity Technologies. Unity Asset Store, Simple Town Pack. https://assetstore.unity.com/packages/3d/environments/urban/simple-town-pack-91947. Accessed 11 Apr 2021

24. Ikuko, T., et al.: The analysis of global motion for videos inducing motion sickness. In: Proceedings of the Institute of Image Information and Television Engineers Annual Convention, pp. 8–3 (2004)

25. Golding, J.F.: Predicting individual differences in motion sickness susceptibility by questionnaire. Pers. Individ. Differ. **41**(2), 237–248 (2006)

A Trajectory Model for Desktop-Scale Hand Redirection in Virtual Reality

Flavien Lebrun[✉], Sinan Haliyo[✉], and Gilles Bailly[✉]

Sorbonne Université, CNRS, ISIR, Paris, France
{flavien.lebrun,sinan.haliyo,gilles.bailly}@sorbonne-universite.fr

Abstract. In Virtual Reality, visuo-haptic illusions such as hand redirection introduce a discrepancy between the user's hand and its virtual avatar. This visual shift can be used, for instance, to provide multiple virtual haptic objects through a single physical proxy object. This low-cost approach improves the sense of presence, however, it is unclear how these illusions impact the hand trajectory and if there is a relationship between trajectory and the detection of illusion. In this paper, we present an empirical model predicting the hand trajectory as a function of the redirection. It relies on a cubic Bézier curve with 4 control points. We conduct a two alternative forced choice (2AFC) experiment to calibrate and validate our model. Results show that (1) our model predicts well the hand trajectory of each individual using a single parameter; (2) the hand trajectory better explains the detection of the illusion than the amplitude of the redirection alone; (3) a user specific calibration allows to predict per-user redirected trajectories and detection probabilities. Our findings provide a better understanding of visuo-haptic illusions and how they impact the user's movements. As such they may provide foundations to design novel interaction techniques, e.g. interacting in a scene with multiple physical obstacles.

Keywords: Visuo-haptic illusion · Hand redirection · Detection threshold · Trajectory estimation

1 Introduction

The Central nervous system integrates inputs from all senses to construct a unified percept of reality. Virtual Reality (VR) through *Head Mounted Displays* gives means to subtly distort the sense of vision, which can be used to skew the integration with other modalities such as haptic to create various illusions. Among these visuo-haptic illusions, *hand redirection* (e.g. haptic retargeting [2]), affects the virtual location of the hand so that users reach for a certain physical target in a different position than its virtual counterpart. This is especially useful in *passive haptics*, where a single physical prop can be used for 2 or more virtual neighboring objects.

© IFIP International Federation for Information Processing 2021
Published by Springer Nature Switzerland AG 2021
C. Ardito et al. (Eds.): INTERACT 2021, LNCS 12936, pp. 105–124, 2021.
https://doi.org/10.1007/978-3-030-85607-6_8

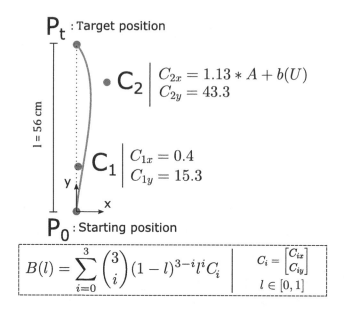

Fig. 1. Model overview. Our hand trajectory model is a Bézier curve. The resulting trajectory $B(l)$ is defined by 4 control points: P_0, C_1, C_2 and P_t. We show that the redirection can be accounted for by only adjusting the x coordinate of point C_2. This adjustment depends on the redirection amplitude A and a user-dependent factor $b(U)$.

Several empirical studies have been conducted showing that these illusions are imperceptible when the amplitude of redirection is below a certain threshold [14,37]. However, the effect of different amplitudes of illusion on motor control has not been investigated.

In this article, we investigate how the amplitude of the redirection alters the hand trajectory. We make the hypothesis that the detection of the illusion stems from users observing the distortion of their own movement. The detection of the illusion can then be predicted from a geometric description of the hand trajectory. In this prospect, we propose an analytic model of the hand trajectory using cubic Bézier curves, constructed with four control points (see Fig. 1). In this model, under the approximation that the trajectory is planar, 2D coordinates of these 4 points are sufficient to describe the hand movement, regardless of the coordinate system.

We conduct a two-alternative-forced-choice (2AFC) experiment on a target reaching task under hand redirection illusion. Collected data are used to refine and validate the model as well as to explore the relationship between trajectory adjustment, and the ability of the users to detect the illusion.

Our main findings are (1) our model predicts well the adjusted hand trajectory of each individual using a single parameter (see Fig. 1); (2) the hand trajectory better explains the detection of the illusion than the redirection amplitude alone; (3) a user specific calibration allows to predict per-user redirected trajectories and the probability to detect the illusion.

Our findings provide a better understanding of visuo-haptic illusions and how they impact users' movements. They also provide foundations to design novel interaction techniques, e.g. interacting in a scene with multiple physical obstacles or to develop low-cost calibration tasks without exposing the users to the illusions.

2   Related Work

2.1   Visuo-Haptic Illusions

The brain integrates information from different senses to construct a robust percept [12,13]. The sense with the best reliability will be favored in this integration. This model of integration has been verified for the combination of vision and vestibular cues for the perception of displacement [28] and for the localization of body parts with vision and proprioception [4,5,10]. Vision is often more reliable than other senses and thus generally favored by the brain. This phenomenon is called *visual dominance* [7,17].

Several VR interaction techniques leverage visual dominance to influence users' experience in a virtual environment (VE). For example in *redirected walking* [30], users have the feeling to walk along a straight line while they are made to follow a curved path. It's achieved through a non-strict mapping between head rotation and orientation in the real and virtual world.

Manipulating virtual representations induce visio-haptic illusions. These illusions trick the user to perceive different shapes [3] or mechanical characteristics such as weight or stiffness [11,24,33], or to overrate a haptic device's performance [1]. Hand redirection is one of the most popular techniques to induce such illusions.

2.2   Hand Redirection

Hand redirection refers to an alteration of the mapping between users' real hands and their virtual avatars. One of the main application of hand redirection is in passive haptics, where a single physical object – prop – is used as haptic proxy to several virtual objects in neighboring locations [2,9,23,26]. During the movement toward a virtual object, users' virtual hands are gradually shifted from their real hands. Users' unwittingly correct this shift. This leads to the redirection of users' real hands toward the physical prop.

A critical aspect of this approach is the *amplitude of redirection*, i.e. the degree of mismatch between the real hands and their avatars. Indeed with an appropriate amount of redirection users remain unaware of the mismatch. However, when this one is too large, the illusion is detected and affects negatively the user experience [21]. It is thus important to determine the maximum amplitude of redirection – detection threshold – beyond which users do notice the illusion.

2.3   Detection Threshold

Several methods have been proposed to determine the detection threshold of visuo-haptic illusions. One method consists of asking if participants perceived a manipulation of their visual feedback during the interaction [1,8,20,25,31]. However, participants might have difficulties to judge a barely perceptible phenomena. This method thus requires a large safety margin.

Another method relies on a two-alternative forced-choice experiment (2AFC) where the participants are only asked in which direction they think the visual feedback was manipulated. This forced choice approach is more robust to participants' subjectivity and provides a lower bound threshold (by using a psychometric function). This method has been used for instance to study redirect walking [22,34] and visuo-haptic conflicts [27].

Previous work exploiting these methods investigate hand redirection detection threshold at the *population* level [14,37]. However, humans have different perceptual abilities and this detection threshold differs from user to user. In this paper, we study whether this detection threshold can be adapted to each *individual* with a simple calibration task.

2.4   Redirected Hand Velocity and Trajectory

Some works took an interest on the effect of the redirection on the hand velocity and trajectory. Gonzalez et al. looked at tangential velocities and noted that the minimum jerk model (MJM) [16] doesn't hold for large amplitudes of redirection [18]. They did not however analyse the evolution of hand trajectory. The correction of the hand trajectory under redirection has been *qualitatively* mentioned by Azmandian et al. [2]. They observed the general shape of the trajectory and pointed out that it generally exhibits a kink towards the end. In this paper, we propose a trajectory model linking the amplitude of redirection and the shape of the real hand trajectory.

3   Approach

Hand redirection has been shown to enrich the interaction in VR, especially when users explore different haptic features [1,11,24,33] or manipulate several objects [2,26]. However, it remains unclear how hand trajectory is affected by redirection, and if there is a relation between the hand trajectory and the detection of the illusion. Our approach consists of elaborating a mathematical model to explain and predict the hand trajectory as a function of the amplitude of redirection (*i.e.* the angle defined between the virtual hand, the real hand and the starting position; Fig. 2). We then use this model to explore the relationship between the users' detection of the illusion and his hand trajectory.

Beyond a better understanding of hand redirection, the model has several implications for design. For instance, it can serve to define a light calibration task to estimate the appropriate detection threshold for each participant. It can also provide theoretical foundations to design novel interaction techniques, e.g. it would be possible to dynamically adapt the amplitude of redirection to control the hand trajectory and avoid physical obstacles while maintaining the illusions.

3.1   Research Questions

We investigate the relationship between the trajectory (T) of the hand movement, the amplitude of redirection (A) and the Detection Threshold (A_{DT}).

- **RQ1:** *What is the influence of the amplitude of redirection on hand trajectory?* $(A \rightarrow T)$
- **RQ2:** *Does the detection threshold depend on the features of the trajectory?* $(T \rightarrow A_{DT})$. In particular, we aim to study whether the probability to detect the illusion is better explained by the deformation of the trajectory under redirection $(A + T)$, instead of A alone.

3.2   Problem Formulation

Hand Trajectory. Let $T = P_0, P_1, ...P_n$ the trajectory of the hand movement where p_0 is the starting point and $P_n = P_t$ the position of the target (t). We assume it exists a function f such as:

$$T = f(u, P_t, P_0, A) \tag{1}$$

where T is the trajectory produced by the participant u, when reaching the target t at the location P_t, from the position P_0, with an amplitude of redirection A. We aim to determine the function f to answer the first research question (**RQ1**).

Model of Gesture Trajectory. We model hand trajectory as a Bézier curve. A Bézier curve is a polynomial parametric curve, and is defined as:

$$B(l) = \sum_{i=0}^{k} \binom{k}{i} (1-l)^{k-i} l^i C_i \tag{2}$$

where k is the degree of the Bezier curve and $C_0, ..., C_k$ the control points.

  This parametric model is widely used in mechanical design and computer graphics and has also been used to model hand trajectories [15]. This formulation has several advantages. First, it considerably reduces the complexity of the description of a trajectory as the number of control points is small in comparison with the number of points of the trajectory $k << n$. Moreover, the description is smooth, continuous and invariant to the user speed and sampling rate. Finally, the position of the control points provides a convenient and geometrical interpretation of the trajectory (see Fig. 1). In particular the first and last control points are the start and end point of the trajectory, so these are fixed in our modeling.

$$C_0 = P_0; C_K = P_t \tag{3}$$

  Figure 4 shows the impact of moving the control point C_2 (while keeping the three other controls fixed) on the Bézier curve.

Number of Control Points. A choice must be made regarding the degree k of the Bézier curve, i.e. the number of control points. A higher k better describes a given trajectory, but it increases the complexity of the model and reduces its interpretability. Moreover, it is important to use the same k for different trajectories in the purpose to compare them. Based on pilot studies, we found that cubic Bézier curves with 4 controls points ($k = 4$) was sufficient to well describe, compare and explain the different trajectories.

Based on the Eqs. 1 and 3, we can then reformulate our problem as estimating the function g such as (see 1):

$$C_{1x}, C_{1y}, C_{2x}, C_{2y} = g(u, P_t, P_0, A) \tag{4}$$

where C_{ix} and C_{iy} are the x and y coordinates of the control point C_i. To achieve this, we conducted a user experiment to collect data and to identify the model parameters (see Sect. 4). Validation of the model will allow us to predict the trajectory for a given user u, under any redirection A.

Detection Threshold. Based on the literature [34,37], the population model predicting the probability P of detecting the illusion given the amplitude of redirection (A) is a psychometric function:

$$P(A) = \frac{1}{1 + \exp{-\frac{A - PSE_G}{\sigma}}} \tag{5}$$

where PSE_G is the global point of subjective equality, i.e. the amplitude such as $P(PSE_G) = 50\%$. It can be seen as the amplitude where the participants estimate that no redirection is applied and is usually different than 0. σ is the spread (inverse slope). A_{LT} and A_{RT} are two other specific values such as $P(A_{LT}) = 25\%$ and $P(A_{RT}) = 75\%$. The detection threshold A_{DT} is then defined as:

$$A_{DT} = A_{RT} - A_{LT} \tag{6}$$

The smaller σ the steeper the slope of the psychometric curve is and, in our case, the smaller A_{DT} is. The same methodology can be applied for the whole population (population model) or each individual (individual model).

So, the second research question (**RQ2**) has the objective to estimate PSE_G and σ as a function of the trajectory T:

$$P(A, T) = \frac{1}{1 + \exp{-\frac{A - PSE_G(T)}{\sigma(T)}}} \tag{7}$$

4   Data Collection

Our user experiment is similar to Zenner et al. [37] where participants perform a pointing task in VR while experiencing visuo-haptic illusions. Their primary objective was to investigate the probability to detect the illusion depending on the amplitude of redirection. In this experiment, we also investigate hand trajectory to refine, calibrate and test our model. This experiment has been approved by the IRB 2020-CER-2020-61.

4.1 Participants

10 participants (8 male and 2 female, between 25 and 30 years old) took part in the study. 2 participants were left-handed, 8 were right-handed. 4 participants wore glasses and one wore contact lenses. They did not report any other visual impairment or neuromuscular disorder. All the participants except 2 had experienced a VR headset before, but all less than three times. None were familiar with VR.

4.2 Apparatus

Physical Setup. Participants were seated in front of a standard table and with a fixed position seat. They wore an HTC Vive head-mounted-display (HMD), a white-noise headphones and a right-hand glove with a cluster of optical markers on the index finger. Both positions and orientations of the HMD and the glove were tracked by a motion capture system (Optitrack) providing submillimeter precision. We thus saved 3D positions of the real hand and projected them on a horizontal plane. We used a sampling rate of 0.03s resulting in around 40 points per trajectory.

On the table, there was an haptic marker for "starting position", a joystick placed on the left of the starting position and 6 cylindrical targets located along a semi-circular arc illustrated Fig. 2-left. Only the 4 central targets were actually touched by participants, the targets at the two extremities of the arc were just used as lures. These targets are located at 30 cm distance from the starting position. The 30 cm distance was chosen to be easily reachable by participants while they are seated on the chair. The angular distance between targets is 15°. It is large enough to avoid accidental physical collisions and to study the influence of target orientation on hand trajectory and illusion detection.

Virtual Scene. The virtual scene is illustrated on Fig. 2-right. It mimics the real set-up. It is implemented with the *Unity3D* game engine and shows the table, the starting position, one virtual target as well as an avatar of the participant' right hand. The virtual target has the same color and shape as the real one.

Hand Redirection Implementation. The virtual target's position was computed from the position of the chosen real target and the amplitude of redirection (see Fig. 2). The shift between the virtual and the real hands was implemented such as it increases linearly during the reaching motion and the real hand reaches the real target simultaneously as the virtual hand reaches the virtual target. As such, users effectively touch a real object which provides a *haptic confirmation*. Participants compensate the shift while reaching the target, resulting in a curved trajectory (see Fig. 2). Note that in our implementation, the hand is considered as a single point, the forefinger tip.

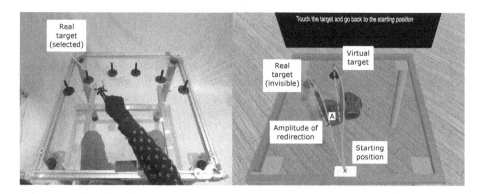

Fig. 2. Left: the experimental table with 6 physical targets. Right: the virtual scene as seen by participants during the experiment. The phantom of the real hand (left) is displayed for illustration purpose but was not visible during the experiment. The dashed lines represent the straightest reach toward the target for the real hand (orange) and the virtual hand (purple). The curved lines is a representation of the actual trajectory of the two hands. (Color figure online)

4.3 Experimental Design

Stimulus and Task. The experiment is a *two-alternative forced choice* (2AFC): Once the right arm of the participants is in the starting position, the trial starts and the virtual target is displayed. The participants are asked to touch the target with their right hand and then to come back to the starting position (we made this choice to minimize task difference among participants, thus we restrain even left handed participants in using their right arm). The participants are asked to move naturally toward the target as we do not know the effect of speed on the illusion detection. If the participants are too fast or too slow the experimenter asks them to slow down or to accelerate. After they came back to the starting position, they move the joystick in the corresponding direction with their left hand to indicate whether their real hand was positioned on the left or the right of its virtual avatar. No feedback is provided.

Conditions. In this experiment, we controlled two factors. The primary factor is AMPLITUDE of redirection with 15 levels from $-13°$ to $13°$ ($-13°$, $-10°$, $-8°$, $-6°$, $-5°$, $-4°$, $-2°$, $0°$, $2°$, $4°$, $5°$, $6°$, $8°$, $10°$, $13°$). The second factor is TARGET Orientation from $-22.5°$ to $22.5°$ (step of $15°$).

Procedure. The participants were first instructed about the goal of the experiment and the task to perform. In particular, the concept of hand redirection was explained in these terms: *"A virtual hand that follows the position of your hand is displayed in the VE. During the reaching task an offset will be gradually introduced between this virtual hand and your real hand. The virtual hand will be located either on the left or the right of your real hand"*.

Participants put on the glove, HMD and headphone. They then performed a training phase. It consists of 2 blocks of 10 trials where they experience hand redirection with an amplitude of either $-13°$ or $+13°$ (corresponding to the highest amplitudes in the main experiment). During the training phase, participants received feedback at the end of the trial regarding the direction (left or right) of the redirection. They were also informed about the trial time as they have to calibrate their speed so that the trial time is between 1s and 2s. Finally, during the first block, the position of the *real* hand was displayed in the virtual scene in addition to the hand avatar to understand the concept of hand redirection.

Design. We used a within-subject design. Each participant completed 4 blocks. In each block, the participants tested the 60 combinations of AMPLITUDE and TARGET in a randomized order. In summary, the experimental design is: 10 participants × 4 blocks × 15 AMPLITUDES × 4 TARGETS = 2400 trials.

Dependent Variables. The two dependent variables are CHOICE (left or right) and Hand TRAJECTORY, i.e. the sequence of points to reach the target.

5   Analysis 1: Trajectory and Amplitude of Redirection

In this section, we analyze how the amplitude of redirection influences the position of the two control points C_1 and C_2. We first describe our empirical findings. We then refine our model and compare four model variants.

5.1   Empirical Results

Method. We first removed 60 (2.5%) outliers trajectories. We calculated for each amplitude of redirection the distance (MSE) between a given trajectory and the mean trajectory. Each trajectory with a MSE larger than a threshold was plotted for a verification of their wrong shape. For the resulting 2340 trajectories, we estimated the four parameters C_{1x}, C_{1y}, C_{2x}, C_{2y} of the Bézier curve that minimize the Dynamic Time Warping (DTW) distance [32,35]. DTW is appropriate as it is independent of the user speed. We use the python package DTAIDistance for calculating the DTW distance and the function "minimize" of the "scipy.optimize" package with the Nelder-Mead algorithm for the optimization method. The resolution of the Bézier curve is 250 points per trajectory.

Result. The Fig. 3 shows the mean value of the four parameters with 95% confidence Interval (CI) as a function of the amplitude of redirection. We were expecting that the four parameters vary with the amplitude, but the results show that three parameters can be approximated by a constant: $C_{1x} = 0.35$ cm ($ci = [-0.0, 0.8]$), $C_{1y} = 15.3$ cm ($ci = [15.2, 15.4]$), $C_{2y} = 43.4$ cm ($ci = [42.6, 44.2]$). However, C_{2x} linearly increases with the amplitude ($R^2 = 0.99$, $MSE = 1.9$).

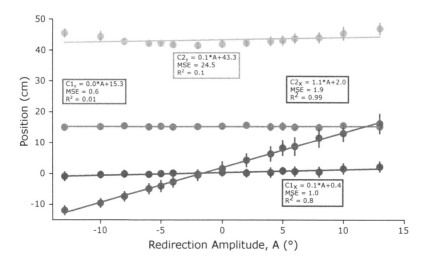

Fig. 3. The value of the four parameters C_{1x}, C_{1y}, C_{2x}, C_{2y} as a function of the amplitude of redirection. Error bars show 95% confidence interval.

Discussion. We learned three things. First, as C_1 is fixed and aligned with $\overrightarrow{P_0 P_T}$, it confirms that the initial direction of the user's movement is towards the virtual target. Second, as only one parameter varies, these results suggest that using a Cubic Bézier curve model is appropriate. Third, it exists a simple and elegant linear relationship between C_{2x} and the amplitude of redirection. We can thus revisit our model, reduce its complexity and improve its explainability.

5.2   Refining and Evaluating the Model

Based on our findings, we revisit our model (Eqs. 3 and 4) and propose four model variants summarized in Table 1. Three parameters (C_{1x}, C_{1y}, C_{2y}) are fixed. We introduce two novel parameters a and b to approximate the x coordinate of C_2:

$$C_{2x} = aA + b \tag{8}$$

where A is the amplitude of redirection, a is the slope, i.e. the sensitivity to the amplitude and b, the intercept, reflects the natural human bias at doing curved trajectories even when no hand redirection is applied [36]. To study whether these two parameters are the same for all participants (population parameter) or participant dependent (individual parameter), we defined four model variants (Table 1) reflecting the four configurations.

5.3   Model Comparison

We compare the capacity of the model variants to accurately predict the trajectories of each class C_A^u where A is the Amplitude of redirection and u a

Table 1. Comparisons of four model variants in terms of fixed and free (population and individual) parameters, number of free parameters (k), distance (DTW), Likelihood and BIC. The model with b as user-dependent parameter has the lowest BIC score.

Model	Fixed parameters	Population parameters	Individual parameters	k	DTW	-LL	BIC
M	$C_{1x}\ C_{1y},$ C_{2x}	a, b	–	2	670	501	1012
M_b	$C_{1x}\ C_{1y},$ C_{2x}	a	b	11	576	401	857
M_a	$C_{1x}\ C_{1y},$ C_{2x}	b	a	11	661	457	969
$M_{a,b}$	$C_{1x}\ C_{1y},$ C_{2x}	–	a, b	20	559	396	896

user (participant). To achieve this, we first define $d(A, u, m)$ the average DTW distance between the predicted trajectory $T_{pred}(A, u, m)$ and all observed trajectories $T_{obs}^0(A, u)...T_{obs}^N(A, u)$ of the class C_A^u for a given model m:

$$d(A, u, m) = \frac{1}{N} \sum_{i=0}^{N} DTW\left(T_{pred}(A, u, m), T_{obs}^i(A, u) \right) \tag{9}$$

We can then use a Boltzmann soft-max function to transform the distance $d(A, u, m)$ into probability $P(C_A^u \mid A, u, m)$:

$$P(C_A^u | A, u, m) = \frac{e^{-\beta\, d(A,u,m)}}{\sum_a e^{-\beta\, d(A,u,m)}} \tag{10}$$

where the parameter β indicates how much the probability distribution is concentrated around the positions of the smallest distance. We chose $\beta = 1$.

Model Likelihood. Based on the Eq. 10, we now compare the result of models fitness function. In Bayesian terms, we compare the likelihood of the data given the model, that is the maximum probability $P(C_A^u)$ that the model chooses the correct class of trajectories C_A^u. Formally, we estimate:

$$LL(m) = \sum_{A,u} \log P(C_A^u | A, u, m, \theta_m^p) \tag{11}$$

where θ_m^u is the set of parameters of the model m for the participant u.

BIC Score. In the process of model selection, it is common to include a penalty term for model complexity, i.e. for the number of parameters [29]. The Bayesian Information Criterion (BIC score) is commonly used. It is estimated as $BIC = -2LL + k \times log(N)$ where LL is the likelihood (Eq. 11), k, the number of parameters (i.e. individual parameters + population parameters), and $N = 150$ ($10\, participants \times 15\, amplitudes$), the number of points to predict.

Result. The Table 1 indicates that the model $M_{a,b}$ better fits the data. It is not surprising as it has much more parameters than the other model variants. When penalizing for the number of parameters, the BIC score suggests that M_b better explains the data. This result indicates that a is not sensitive to the user id. In contrast, model prediction benefits the estimation of b for each user.

5.4   Discussion

RQ1: *What is the influence of the amplitude of redirection on hand trajectory?* Our analysis showed a clear impact of amplitude of redirection on hand trajectory. More precisely, we learned that 1) if we model hand trajectory as a simple cubic Bézier curve, the amplitude of redirection **only affects** the x coordinate of a single control point (C_2). This makes the model highly interpretable (Fig. 4). Moreover, 2) this x coordinate increases linearly with the amplitude of the redirection; 3) the slope is independent of the participant, i.e. increasing the amplitude by $1°$ moves C_{2x} of 1.13 cm on the right; 4) the intercept is user dependent (mean $= 2.1$ cm, std $= 3.9$). This result is inline with [36] indicating that even when no redirection is applied humans perform curved trajectories (due to visual perceptual distortion). The degree and direction of curvature depends on the participant.

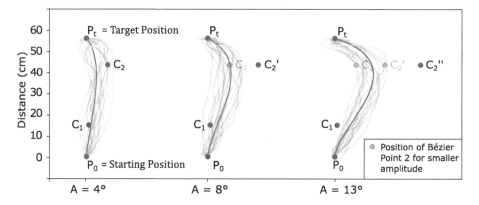

Fig. 4. Visualisation of all the trajectories for three different amplitudes of redirection and for the same participant. We display the Bezier curve resulting from the model M_b. All the control point are fixed except C_2 that have a linear relation with the amplitude.

Interestingly, the calibration of the model is easy to perform. Indeed, the individual parameter b is the intercept, i.e. it is the value of C_{2x} when $A = 0$ (Eq. 8). It is thus possible to estimate b for each participant **without** experiencing hand redirection. b can be estimated by simply performing a reaching task without illusion.

6   Analysis 2: Detection Threshold

In this section we study the second research question RQ2: *Does the detection threshold depend on the features of the trajectory?*. We first evaluate the probability to detect the illusion as a function of the amplitude of redirection and then as a function of the deformation of the hand trajectory.

6.1   Amplitude of Redirection and Detection Threshold

Figure 5-Left illustrates the probability $P(A)$ to detect the illusion as a function of the amplitude of redirection A (psychometric function corresponding to the Eq. 5) for the whole population. We found $PSE_G = -1.13°$, $A_{LT} = -4.52°$, $A_{RT} = 2.27°$. We compute the detection threshold $A_{DT} = A_{RT} - A_{LT} = 6.79°$. Our results are in the same order of magnitude than Zenner et al. study [37] ($PSE_G = -0.28°$, $R = 8.19°$). The difference can be due to the experimental setup and/or the absence of haptic confirmation at the end of the movement.

6.2   Hand Trajectory and Detection Threshold

We now investigate the link between the hand trajectory and the probability to detect the illusion. As C_{2x} is sufficient to describe the hand trajectory, we analyze the probability to detect the illusion $P(C_2x)$ as a function of C_{2x} with the same methodology of Sect. 6.1. We discriminated C_{2x} into 15 groups based on its magnitude. We made this choice to compare the two psychometric functions, $P(A)$ and $P(C_{2x})$ of the Fig. 5.

Figure 5-right shows the result of the psychometric fit for $P(C_{2x})$ ($MSE = 64.0$) which is better than the one of $P(A)$ ($MSE = 68.3$), Fig. 5-Left. It shows that the more the hand trajectory is curved the easier the illusion is detected. This result was expected given the linear relation between A and C_{2x} outlined in Sect. 5. However, the fact that both the amplitude of redirection and the trajectory explain the illusion detection requires further explanations.

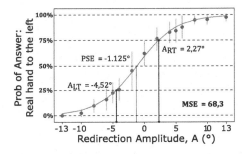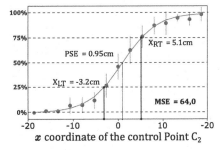

Fig. 5. Psychometric fit of the answer of the 2AFC experiment. Left: detection according to the amplitude of redirection. Right : detection of the illusion according to the C_{2x} coordinate.

6.3 Further Explanations

To better understand the role of C_{2x} on illusion detection, we analysed its magnitude as a function of the absolute amplitude of redirection ($|A|$) and whether the participants answer correctly (detection of the illusion) or not (the illusion works) to the 2AFC task. We removed extreme amplitudes $0°$ as there was no error and $\pm 13°$ as all participants detected the illusion for these amplitudes.

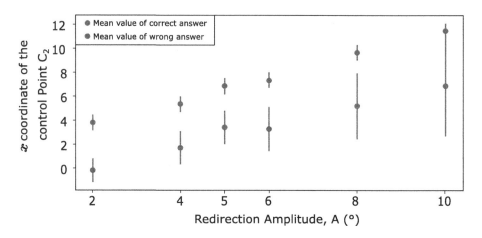

Fig. 6. x coordinate of C_2 as a function of the redirection amplitude and whether the answer of participants is correct or false.

Our results are illustrated Fig. 6. A two-way ANOVA confirmed the effect of AMPLITUDE on the amplitude of C_{2x} ($F_{5,45} = 109.4$, $p < .0001$). ANOVA also revealed an effect of ANSWER (Correct vs., False) on the amplitude of C_{2x} ($F_{1,9} = 7.6$, $p < .05$). A post Tukey-test indicates that at a given amplitude, C_{2x} is larger when the illusion is detected (mean = 3.4 cm) than when the illusion is not detected (mean = 7.4 cm). ANOVA does not reveal AMPLITUDE × ANSWER interaction effect.

Discussion. The amplitude of redirection is the primary factor to explain and predict whether the participants will detect or not the illusion. However, given an amplitude of redirection, we demonstrate that the curvature of the hand trajectory, i.e. the magnitude of C_{2x}, refines the prediction. Indeed, participants performing low curved trajectories (i.e. small C_{2x}) are less likely to detect the illusion. The user dependent parameter b reflects this natural tendency to perform curved trajectories (to the right ($b > 0$) or to the left ($b < 0$)) under no redirection. We thus decided to study more precisely the influence of b on the detection threshold.

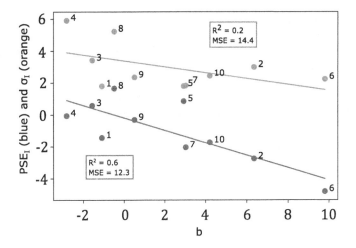

Fig. 7. Evaluation of PSE_I (in blue) and σ_I (in orange) for each participant (1–10) according to parameter b. (Color figure online)

6.4   User-Dependent Detection Threshold

We now evaluate the relation between the user-dependent parameter b and the probability to detect the illusion expressed in Eqs. 5 and 7:

$$P(A, b) = \frac{1}{1 + \exp -\frac{A - PSE_I(b)}{\sigma_I(b)}} \tag{12}$$

where PSE_I is the Point of Subjective Equality for each Individual (PSE_G was the Point of Subjective Equality global, i.e. for the whole population). Figure 7 illustrates PSE_I and σ_I as a function of b. While no clear relationship is revealed regarding σ_I ($R^2 = 0.25$; $MSE = 14.39$), there is a weak relationship between b and PSE_I ($R^2 = 0.63$; $MSE = 12.32$):

$$PSE_I = -0.39 \times b - 0.19 \tag{13}$$

Thus there is a relation between the value of C_{2x} when no redirection is applied $C_{2x} = b$ and PSE_I. In other words, a user performing naturally a curved trajectory to the right ($b > 0$) will be more sensitive to a redirection to the right ($PSE_I < 0$). This result is important, because after estimating b, a designer can estimate PSE_I of a user and know in which direction (left or right) the user is less likely to detect the illusion. The designer can also measure b of each individual of a given population and estimate the *unique* range of amplitude of redirection that best fit this population.

This is what is illustrated Fig. 8. On the left, we see the range of amplitude of redirection (blue) which is not detected for each participant. The intersection is small: The vertical surface inficates the maximal ranges for which the illusion is not detected for respectively 70%, 80% and 90% of the population. It results that only the amplitudes of redirection in $[-0.7°; 0.7°]$ is not detected for 70% of the population.

However, when b is known for each participant, it is possible to choose a unique range of amplitude of redirection and to adapt it to each participant (based only on the parameter b). This is what is illustrated on Fig. 8-right where each range of amplitude is virtually re-centered based on b, offering a range of $[-1.7°, 1.7°]$ which is almost four times larger.

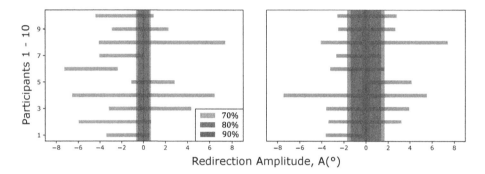

Fig. 8. Left: the horizontal blue rectangles depict the range of redirection amplitudes for which the illusion is not detected for each participant. The vertical surfaces indicate the maximal ranges for which the illusion is not detected for respectively 70% (green), 80% (red) and 90% (yellow) of the population. The wider are these ranges, the more flexibility is offered to the designers. However, increasing the number of participants decreases this population range. Right: when taking individual differences, i.e. b into account, we can artificially recenter their range, increasing the range of amplitudes for the whole population. (Color figure online)

7   Discussion

7.1   Main Findings

We revisit our two research questions from Sect. 3.

RQ1: *What is the influence of the amplitude of redirection on hand trajectory?* We have shown that a cubic Bézier curve constructed using four control points C_i, $i \in [0; 3]$ approximates the hand trajectory quite faithfully. Moreover, the coordinates of 3 out of 4 control points do not depend on the redirection for a given user. The control point C_2 is the only one which is modified by the amplitude of redirection: C_{2x} linearly increases with the amplitude such as $C_{2x}(A) = 1.13A + 1.97$ at the population level. At the individual level, further analysis revealed that the intercept is user dependent, $C_{2x}(A, u) = 1.13A + b(u)$. These results demonstrate that 1) the amplitude of redirection influences *only* a single feature of the trajectory when described with a Bézier curve; 2) the trajectory can be better approximated when considering the parameter b which 3) can be easily estimated for each user. Indeed, b indicates the curvature of the trajectory when users do not experience an illusion.

RQ2: *Does the detection threshold depend on the features of the trajectory?*
It was well known that the detection threshold depends on the amplitude of redirection. We demonstrated that it also depends on the trajectory. In particular, we demonstrated that once the amplitude of redirection is given, users performing trajectories with low curvature (*i.e.* smaller C_{2x}) are less likely to detect the illusion. Our hypothesis is that users detect the illusion through observing the distortion of their hand motion.

To determine individual detection thresholds, we used a psychometric function with two parameters PSE_I and σ_I. Our analysis shows a relationship between PSE_I and b but not with σ_I. In other words, estimating b for each participant can increase the range of amplitudes of redirection of 258% without risking the illusion to be detected by at least 70% of our participants.

7.2   Implications for Design

Our findings on **RQ1** suggest a method for designers to anticipate user hand trajectory during a redirected reaching task. In particular, designers can *easily* elaborate a calibration task to estimate b and refine the trajectory model as it does not require to expose the users to the illusion ($A = 0$). This trajectory model can for instance be exploited advantageously to make users unwittingly circumvent obstacles or encountered-type haptic devices [6,19]. Our findings on **RQ2** indicate a simple way of adapting the range of amplitude of redirection to each user. The knowledge of the parameter b allows the computation of individual PSE_I. The designer can then center the population range of amplitudes around the PSE_I to minimize the risk of detecting the illusion. Again, this only requires to estimate b without exposing the user to the illusion.

7.3   Limitation and Future Work

Future studies should be conducted to validate the robustness of the model. First, left-handed participants had to reach for targets with their right hand. This choice was made to facilitate the comparison of data between participants. Even though we interact with the environment with both hands, we favor our dominant hand for reaching tasks. Thus this could have impacted the hand trajectory and their illusion detection threshold. Moreover, the speed of the hand can have an impact on the detection of the illusion and was not constant among participants. Then, participants were informed about the illusion at the beginning of the experiment, thus the calculated detection threshold is likely bigger.

Furthermore, concerning the trajectory model, we assumed that 3 of the 4 coordinates of the Bézier control points are fixed. However the Fig. 3 shows that C_{1x} and C_{2y} are slightly affected by the amplitude of redirection. As future work, we plan to refine our model to investigate whether it significantly improves the prediction of the beginning and the end of the trajectory. The distance to the target is fixed in our task and different distances should be tested as well.

Finally, the use of a 2AFC experiment for the determination of detection threshold is debatable. On one hand, users can sense that something is odd in their movement, without being able to pinpoint the relative position of their real and virtual hand. On the other hand, if users do not focus on the position of their hands we would certainly find a larger range of non-detection. We hypothesize that there is not a clear breaking point of the illusion. In particular, we plan to investigate whether user involvement might have an impact on *sigma* and thus on the ability to detect the illusion.

Acknowledgments. We would like to thank Benoit Geslain and Hugues Lebrun for their valuable feedback, as well as the participants of experiments.

References

1. Abtahi, P., Follmer, S.: Visuo-haptic illusions for improving the perceived performance of shape displays. In: Proceedings of the 2018 CHI Conference on Human Factors in Computing Systems, CHI 2018, pp. 150:1–150:13. ACM, New York (2018). https://doi.org/10.1145/3173574.3173724
2. Azmandian, M., Hancock, M., Benko, H., Ofek, E., Wilson, A.D.: Haptic retargeting: dynamic repurposing of passive haptics for enhanced virtual reality experiences. In: Proceedings of the 2016 CHI Conference on Human Factors in Computing Systems, CHI 2016, pp. 1968–1979. ACM, New York (2016). https://doi.org/10.1145/2858036.2858226
3. Ban, Y., Kajinami, T., Narumi, T., Tanikawa, T., Hirose, M.: Modifying an identified curved surface shape using pseudo-haptic effect. In: 2012 IEEE Haptics Symposium (HAPTICS), pp. 211–216, March 2012. https://doi.org/10.1109/HAPTIC.2012.6183793
4. van Beers, R.J., Wolpert, D.M., Haggard, P.: When feeling is more important than seeing in sensorimotor adaptation. Curr. Biol. **12**(10), 834–837 (2002). https://doi.org/10.1016/S0960-9822(02)00836-9
5. Block, H.J., Sexton, B.M.: Visuo-proprioceptive control of the hand in older adults. bioRxiv (2020). https://doi.org/10.1101/2020.01.18.911354
6. Bouzbib, E., Bailly, G., Haliyo, S., Frey, P.: CoVR: a large-scale force-feedback robotic interface for non-deterministic scenarios in VR. CoRR abs/2009.07149 (2020). https://arxiv.org/abs/2009.07149
7. Burns, E., Razzaque, S., Panter, A., Whitton, M., McCallus, M., Brooks, F.: The hand is slower than the eye: a quantitative exploration of visual dominance over proprioception. In: 2005 IEEE Proceedings of Virtual Reality, VR 2005, pp. 3–10 (2005). https://doi.org/10.1109/VR.2005.1492747
8. Burns, E., Razzaque, S., Panter, A.T., Whitton, M.C., McCallus, M.R., Brooks, F.P.: The hand is more easily fooled than the eye: users are more sensitive to visual interpenetration than to visual-proprioceptive discrepancy. Presence: Teleoper. Virtual Environ. **15**(1), 1–15 (2006). https://doi.org/10.1162/pres.2006.15.1.1
9. Cheng, L.P., Ofek, E., Holz, C., Benko, H., Wilson, A.D.: Sparse haptic proxy: touch feedback in virtual environments using a general passive prop. In: Proceedings of the 2017 CHI Conference on Human Factors in Computing Systems, CHI 2017, pp. 3718–3728. Association for Computing Machinery, New York (2017). https://doi.org/10.1145/3025453.3025753

10. van Dam, L.C.J., Ernst, M.O.: Knowing each random error of our ways, but hardly correcting for it: an instance of optimal performance. PLOS One **8**(10), 1–9 (2013). https://doi.org/10.1371/journal.pone.0078757
11. Dominjon, L., Lecuyer, A., Burkhardt, J., Richard, P., Richir, S.: Influence of control/display ratio on the perception of mass of manipulated objects in virtual environments. In: 2005 IEEE Proceedings of Virtual Reality, VR 2005, pp. 19–25, March 2005. https://doi.org/10.1109/VR.2005.1492749
12. Ernst, M.O., Banks, M.S.: Humans integrate visual and haptic information in a statistically optimal fashion. Nature **415**(6870), 429–433 (2002). https://doi.org/10.1038/415429a
13. Ernst, M.O., Bülthoff, H.H.: Merging the senses into a robust percept. Trends Cogn. Sci. **8**(4), 162–169 (2004). https://doi.org/10.1016/j.tics.2004.02.002
14. Esmaeili, S., Benda, B., Ragan, E.D.: Detection of scaled hand interactions in virtual reality: the effects of motion direction and task complexity. In: 2020 IEEE Conference on Virtual Reality and 3D User Interfaces (VR), pp. 453–462 (2020). https://doi.org/10.1109/VR46266.2020.00066
15. Faraway, J.J., Reed, M.P., Wang, J.: Modelling three-dimensional trajectories by using bézier curves with application to hand motion. J. Roy. Stat. Soc.: Ser. C (Appl. Stat.) **56**(5), 571–585 (2007). https://doi.org/10.1111/j.1467-9876.2007.00592.x. https://rss.onlinelibrary.wiley.com/doi/abs/10.1111/j.1467-9876.2007.00592.x
16. Flash, T., Hogan, N.: The coordination of arm movements: an experimentally confirmed mathematical model. J. Neurosci. **5**(7), 1688–1703 (1985). https://doi.org/10.1523/JNEUROSCI.05-07-01688.1985
17. Gibson, J.J.: Adaptation, after-effect and contrast in the perception of curved lines. J. Exp. Psychol. **16**(1), 1 (1933)
18. Gonzalez, E.J., Abtahi, P., Follmer, S.: Evaluating the minimum jerk motion model for redirected reach in virtual reality. In: The Adjunct Publication of the 32nd Annual ACM Symposium on User Interface Software and Technology, UIST 2019, pp. 4–6. Association for Computing Machinery, New York (2019). https://doi.org/10.1145/3332167.3357096
19. Gonzalez, E.J., Abtahi, P., Follmer, S.: REACH+: extending the reachability of encountered-type haptics devices through dynamic redirection in VR, pp. 236–248. Association for Computing Machinery, New York (2020)
20. Gonzalez, E.J., Follmer, S.: Investigating the detection of bimanual haptic retargeting in virtual reality. In: 25th ACM Symposium on Virtual Reality Software and Technology, pp. 1–5 (2019)
21. Gonzalez-Franco, M., Lanier, J.: Model of illusions and virtual reality. Front. Psychol. **8**, 1125 (2017). https://doi.org/10.3389/fpsyg.2017.01125. https://www.frontiersin.org/article/10.3389/fpsyg.2017.01125
22. Grechkin, T., Thomas, J., Azmandian, M., Bolas, M., Suma, E.: Revisiting detection thresholds for redirected walking: combining translation and curvature gains. In: Proceedings of the ACM Symposium on Applied Perception, SAP 2016, pp. 113–120. ACM, New York (2016). https://doi.org/10.1145/2931002.2931018
23. Han, D.T., Suhail, M., Ragan, E.D.: Evaluating remapped physical reach for hand interactions with passive haptics in virtual reality. IEEE Trans. Vis. Comput. Graph. **24**(4), 1467–1476 (2018). https://doi.org/10.1109/TVCG.2018.2794659
24. Jauregui, D.A.G., Argelaguet, F., Olivier, A., Marchal, M., Multon, F., Lecuyer, A.: Toward "pseudo-haptic avatars": modifying the visual animation of self-avatar can simulate the perception of weight lifting. IEEE Trans. Vis. Comput. Graph. **20**(4), 654–661 (2014). https://doi.org/10.1109/TVCG.2014.45

25. Kasahara, S., et al.: Malleable embodiment: changing sense of embodiment by spatial-temporal deformation of virtual human body. In: Proceedings of the 2017 CHI Conference on Human Factors in Computing Systems, CHI 2017, pp. 6438–6448. ACM, New York (2017). https://doi.org/10.1145/3025453.3025962

26. Kohli, L.: Redirected touching: warping space to remap passive haptics. In: 2010 IEEE Symposium on 3D User Interfaces (3DUI), pp. 129–130, March 2010. https://doi.org/10.1109/3DUI.2010.5444703

27. Lee, Y., Jang, I., Lee, D.: Enlarging just noticeable differences of visual-proprioceptive conflict in VR using haptic feedback. In: 2015 IEEE World Haptics Conference (WHC), pp. 19–24, June 2015. https://doi.org/10.1109/WHC.2015.7177685

28. MacNeilage, P.R., Banks, M.S., Berger, D.R., Bülthoff, H.H.: A Bayesian model of the disambiguation of gravitoinertial force by visual cues. Exp. Brain Res. **179**(2), 263–290 (2007)

29. Raftery, A.E.: Bayesian model selection in social research. Sociol. Methodol. 111–163 (1995)

30. Razzaque, S., Kohn, Z., Whitton, M.C.: Redirected walking. In: Eurographics 2001 - Short Presentations. Eurographics Association (2001). https://doi.org/10.2312/egs.20011036

31. Rietzler, M., Geiselhart, F., Gugenheimer, J., Rukzio, E.: Breaking the tracking: enabling weight perception using perceivable tracking offsets. In: Proceedings of the 2018 CHI Conference on Human Factors in Computing Systems, CHI 2018, pp. 128:1–128:12. ACM, New York (2018). https://doi.org/10.1145/3173574.3173702

32. Sakoe, H., Chiba, S.: Dynamic programming algorithm optimization for spoken word recognition. IEEE Trans. Acoust. Speech Signal Process. **26**(1), 43–49 (1978). https://doi.org/10.1109/TASSP.1978.1163055

33. Samad, M., Gatti, E., Hermes, A., Benko, H., Parise, C.: Pseudo-haptic weight: changing the perceived weight of virtual objects by manipulating control-display ratio. In: Proceedings of the 2019 CHI Conference on Human Factors in Computing Systems, CHI 2019, pp. 320:1–320:13. ACM, New York (2019). https://doi.org/10.1145/3290605.3300550

34. Steinicke, F., Bruder, G., Jerald, J., Frenz, H., Lappe, M.: Estimation of detection thresholds for redirected walking techniques. IEEE Trans. Visual Comput. Graph. **16**(1), 17–27 (2010). https://doi.org/10.1109/TVCG.2009.62

35. Velichko, V., Zagoruyko, N.: Automatic recognition of 200 words. Int. J. Man Mach. Stud. **2**(3), 223–234 (1970). https://doi.org/10.1016/S0020-7373(70)80008-6

36. Wolpert, D.M., Ghahramani, Z., Jordan, M.I.: Perceptual distortion contributes to the curvature of human reaching movements. Exp. Brain Res. **98**(1), 153–156 (1994)

37. Zenner, A., Krüger, A.: Estimating detection thresholds for desktop-scale hand redirection in virtual reality. In: 2019 IEEE Conference on Virtual Reality and 3D User Interfaces (VR), pp. 47–55 (2019). https://doi.org/10.1109/VR.2019.8798143

Complex Contexts and Subtle Actions: Design and Evaluation of a Virtual Coach for Utilitarian Cycling

Matthias Wunsch[✉] and Geraldine Fitzpatrick

TU Wien, 1040 Vienna, Austria
mail@matthiaswunsch.com, geraldine.fitzpatrick@tuwien.ac.at
http://igw.tuwien.ac.at/hci/

Abstract. The role of HCI to support cyclists has been researched for many years. However, there has been relatively little work on the interaction with and acting within real-world traffic situations. We collaborated with professional cycling instructors to understand experiences of (novice) cyclists in complex real-world urban traffic situations and existing coaching and teaching strategies. Building on this understanding, we designed a system informed by these strategies: an on-the-bike Virtual Cycling Coach (VCC), a system aware of its user's actions and context that delivers coaching interventions in appropriate moments. In a qualitative in-the-wild study with 25 participants we evaluated if the VCC – as Wizard-of-Oz prototype – can offer a coaching experience. Our findings show that the VCC enables processes such as reflection and learning comparable to conventional coaching settings. We discuss limitations and implications for similar designs in complex, highly context-dependent realms.

Keywords: Mobile HCI · Virtual coach · Cycling

1 Introduction

Cycling as a low-emission and space-efficient urban mobility option can contribute to ecologically sustainable development in an urbanizing world [20,49]. The benefits of utilitarian cycling in urban contexts are also substantial on an individual level. Cycling is often a time efficient mode of transportation and has lower costs than other transportation options [16]. It offers immediate health benefits, lowering the risks of cardiovascular disease, cancer, and other causes of mortality [7]. It even brightens one's mood [27,30]. However, these intrinsic benefits only weakly relate to the actual experience of adopting urban cycling for commuting or other personal transportation needs, as making it a routine activity means more hurdles to clear [37]. To exemplify this: In a recent study about cycling, a population of 3.000 persons from 50 U.S. metropolitan areas was

© IFIP International Federation for Information Processing 2021
Published by Springer Nature Switzerland AG 2021
C. Ardito et al. (Eds.): INTERACT 2021, LNCS 12936, pp. 125–146, 2021.
https://doi.org/10.1007/978-3-030-85607-6_9

surveyed. Therein, 10% had used a bicycle for transportation in the last 30 days, and over 50% of the respondents were categorized as "interested but concerned", that is: they are physically able to ride, but are uncomfortable with biking on a major street without or with a bike lane, and neutral to interested in riding more [11]. This gap represents an opportunity for design to meet preferences and reduce existing friction in adopting cycling. While this is most typically tackled by civil engineering and transportation research, previous HCI research has also contributed to supporting cycling through exploring technology for navigation, context awareness and behavior change via different modalities (for example [1, 9, 14]). However, there is little research that considers the interplay between an interactive system, a complex context – such as traffic, street design, other road participants, etc. –, and the actions of a cyclist. Hence, the experience of urban cycling is mostly dependent on and left to the design of the built environment.

We report on a series of studies to create an interactive system capable of providing situated, in-the-moment coaching support for cyclists. This paper is structured in two sections following our research trajectory: In the first section we present our studies on novice cyclists and how they are supported by professional cycling instructors. We explore the coaching strategies used in these settings and the experiences of the cyclists. We also highlight limitations of these programs and the opportunities for a technical system to provide situated support. In the second section, we describe the design and evaluation of the subsequent mobile HCI intervention: the "Virtual Cycling Coach" (VCC), an on-the-bike virtual coach, that is aware of its user's actions and context. To provide *in situ* support to cyclists on their bike in real contexts, it delivers coaching interventions in appropriate moments.

2   Related Work

As cyclists have to act within and interact with a complex context, they need to exercise skillful control over their bicycle, while applying knowledge and being exposed to a variety of potentially dangerous situations [34, 35]. Transportation research shows a positive relation between the available dedicated bicycle infrastructure – such as a network of separated bike lanes – and the degree to which citizens choose cycling [12, 36]. Starkly simplified, this can be viewed as the built infrastructure being designed for ease of use, thereby reducing the level of proficiency needed to cycle.

A large theme in HCI research is interactive technology for supporting cyclists through navigational guidance. De Waard et al. [50] compare a map displayed on a smartphone, auditory route guidance and a dedicated system with flashing lights for supporting navigation. Modes of interactions such as tactile feedback for navigation support have been studied in detail [2, 35, 43, 48]. The use of projections from the bicycle has been explored for both navigation by projecting a map [9] and to project turn signals on the street [10]. On bicycle navigation has also been studied with the goal of supporting excursions and the exploration of unfamiliar environments by bicycle [33, 35].

Previous studies do show that the experiential quality of a route plays a role in navigation and people trade maximum directness for lower stress [8]. Route choices can also differ dependent on the level of cycling experience, with inexperienced cyclists being more sensitive to factors related to separation from automobiles, whereas experienced cyclists are more likely to choose routes with shorter travel times [44]. This relation between a navigation support system and the cyclist's experience of built infrastructure has not been studied so far in HCI research. Context awareness in this area of transportation and mobile HCI has been almost exclusively limited to geolocation data. Providing feedback on action on a bike has been studied in multiple ways: Okugawa [32] explored training systems that provide immediate feedback on the pedalling cadence in sports-oriented cycling. Matviienko et al. [28,29] compared the effectiveness of visual, auditory or vibrotactile cues to warn children while cycling. There is also research on how such warnings could be realized in real-world settings using vehicular ad-hoc network technologies [19]. Context aware sensing has been used to help cyclists regulate their speed to cross all traffic lights on green, taking into account both the context and actions of the cyclist [1].

Cycling has also been studied from a behaviour change agenda. In a recent review, Klecha and Gianni [22] outline commonly used approaches: Supporting eco-friendly choices such as cycling is done with information and guidance using journey planning services [21,25,40]. Game-like designs are used in "sustainability challenges", as well as rewards, that usually are virtual points [6,14,51,55]. Social influence and social comparison are used and instantiated e.g. with leader boards [13,21,25,51,54]. Another approach is self-monitoring, often enabled through graphical, statistical representations of reported or logged mobility behaviour [6,14,40,51,55]. As these studies focus on choices, none have been concerned with the experience of a mobility practice and how technology could be used to offer in-the-moment support within the complex context often found when cycling in an urban environment.

As for coaching, we understand it broadly 'as a collaborative solution-focused, result-orientated and systematic process in which the coach facilitates the enhancement of life experience and goal attainment in the personal and/or professional life of normal, nonclinical clients' [17]. Existing meta-reviews on the effectiveness of coaching show that it has significant positive effects on performance/skills, well-being, coping, work attitudes, and goal-directed self-regulation [46]. There is the subset of virtual coaching or e-coaching, characterized by using information and communication technologies as means to facilitate coaching. In a meta-analysis for health care, coaching has been shown to improve outcomes in supporting and motivating chronically ill adolescents [47]. Another study on virtual coaching – including ones fully executed by systems through a set of pre-defined questions – did produce comparable outcomes to conventional interpersonal coaching [15]. There are no studies so far that investigated a coaching approach in the domain of utilitarian cycling.

3   Existing Teaching and Coaching Strategies

To inform the design of our technology intervention, we focus on users that are beginning to ride bicycles to fulfil their transportation needs. To gain a better understanding of the experiences of (novice) cyclists, we worked together with a local bike advocacy group in Vienna, Austria, that offers classes for beginning and for advanced cyclists. Furthermore, we worked with a cycling coach from the same region specialized in supporting his customers to learn cycling for utilitarian purposes.

3.1   Methods

Empathetic participant observation is key for gaining knowledge about the experiences of people in this situation [53]. For this, we conducted one observation lasting for two hours in the beginner's class with five students, unstructured *in situ* ethnographic interviews with the students as well as *in situ* interviews with the three cycling instructors. We also conducted two observations in the advanced class, which, at that point had nine participants and two instructors, each lasting for one hour. The two cycling instructors – one being the same as the one in the beginner's class – were interviewed *in situ*. Field notes and memory protocols were used to record our observations and interviews.

In addition to the cycling classes and to gain insights into a more coaching-oriented approach, we had two 1.5 h long expert interviews with the cycling coach. He furthermore provided video material demonstrating his coaching approach. Notes and the provided video material were used here as primary data.

Analysis. Thematic analysis was used to identify and structure emerging themes regarding the experiences of urban cycling [3,4]. The collected notes and descriptions where coded, analyzed and structured by a pair of researchers to produce the results described in Sect. 3.2. Given the qualitative paradigm, our own subjectivity was part of that analysis process. Particularly, we had to reflect on our own knowledge about urban cycling, and how they are similar or different to our data. In reflection on and engaging with the data, we could emphasize with the experiences of urban cyclists we observed in the teaching settings.

3.2   Findings: Existing Support Strategies

To answer, how professional instructors teach and support cyclists we present the course structures, course curricula, strategies for scaffolding of learning experiences, framings, the use of feedback and motivational support, the student's agency and the role of reflection in the trainings.

Course Structures. There are different courses for a beginner and an advanced level. The former prepares the students for recreational cycling in traffic-free areas, the latter prepares them to ride their bikes for everyday trips in an urban environment. The classes consist of ten sessions, held weekly, each lasting for two hours. The number of students per class could go up to 20. As not all of them attend all sessions, some sessions have had only five attendees. In the coaching setting, the coach has only one student for usually three to five sessions, each lasting for two hours and being typically about one to two weeks apart. While the coach did also offer trainings on a beginner and advanced level, the content was mainly driven by the student's needs.

Training Content. The curriculum for the beginner level covers various exercises to practice basics of riding a bicycle, such as balancing, controlled steering and braking, riding along given paths, e.g. a straight line or around obstacles, shifting gears or viewing technique. At the advanced level, students practice riding in more complex situations, such as riding on streets according to traffic laws, including right-of-way, signalling, turning at intersections, entering and exiting separated bike-infrastructure or interacting with motorists. Hence, students have to be able to handle their bicycle well enough to participate in the advanced level trainings, including being able to stop and start riding without falling over, braking sufficiently if necessary and being physically capable of riding a bicycle for several kilometres.

Scaffolded Learning Experiences. The training at the beginner level take place in socially and spatially safe spaces. The novice cyclists are provided with an accepting, patient and open-minded social space where students do not have to feel ashamed when they have problems or fail to do certain exercises and "where it is okay, to learn cycling as an adult" [Instructor 1]. These trainings are conducted within recreational areas with no motorized traffic. For the cyclists this prevented feeling overwhelmed by the complexity of the surroundings. For beginners the physical and mental effort of controlling a bike, such as balancing, adjusting speed, pedalling also takes away mental capacity, with beginners often riding at low speeds and basically just trying not to fall. This mental depletion reduces the cognitive capacity for coping with interacting in complex situations (also see [5,52]).

For the advanced level, the instructors or coach select routes that are appropriate to the current level of competencies of the student(s). The selection of these routes is done very deliberately, to provide the right sort of experience – or teachable moments – to the students. An example is riding within a lane with shared traffic, i.e. together with motorized vehicles and next to parked cars. The loud, heavy and fast-moving vehicles are stress-inducing and typically result in negative emotional responses. We observed that defensively riding cyclists tend to ride at the very right side of the lane. However, if there are parking cars next to the lane this means riding within the "dooring zone", i.e. being in danger of colliding with a car door while it is opened. Hence, the intuitive response of the cyclists – riding on the very right side of the street to give way to faster moving traffic – results in a more dangerous situation for her. Coaching can help here by both pointing out the risk of opening doors when riding too close to parked cars and by offering reassurance that a cyclist can ride within the lane to have sufficient safety distances. However, giving such feedback in the moment was hardly possible for the instructors as the moving group and noisy surroundings did not provide an opportunity to do so.

Re-Framing. Metaphors and re-framings are deliberately used, especially in the coaching sessions. For example, motorized vehicles are often perceived as dangerous and scary, resulting in an overall negative experience of cycling close to them. The coach would use phrases to re-frame this experience, for example: "Cars are easy. They are loud and fast, but you can predict them. They cannot move suddenly or change direction at once". Another example is fear, which is a negative emotion commonly experienced by novice cyclists. The coach would acknowledge that and frame it as a signal. His students should understand this signal as "telling them that something is not right", and how to act upon it. The instruction was to slow down or pull over and stop if one is scared. Beyond that, with their own behaviour and attitude towards cycling, the instructors and coach act as a role model. They convey a defensive, aware and anticipatory way of riding a bicycle and the joy and simplicity of doing so. In talking to their students, they also share their attitude towards cycling in the city, as being a sometimes challenging but mostly a rewarding mode of transportation to them.

Feedback and Motivational Support. In the beginner's class, the instructors observed the students and provided feedback to them. This was possible as the students stayed mostly within a small physical area – typically not more than 30 m away from the instructor. Critical feedback such as "take care" or "that was not so good" was given when students acted in ways that could result in minor accidents or fall-overs. This was often followed up by advice, verbally and in most cases by example, i.e. the instructor demonstrating an exercise. More often than that, positive and reinforcing feedback was used such as "that was good" or "you are doing much better now than the last time". This was often followed-up with an instruction to keep doing this exercise or that the student would be now "ready for more". Besides that, the instructors of the class are also trying to keep the mood up and to keep their students motivated to keep trying and practising.

The advanced class also rode as a group in traffic, which made it difficult for the instructors to give feedback immediately. Even the coach, who typically only has one student to take care of, was challenged by the lack of immediacy. He was therefore at the time experimenting with providing students with annotated video recordings of their rides for them to analyse and reflect upon later.

Agency. We observed that the setup as a group with an instructor riding up-front reduced the agency of individual students. They were mostly focused on following and imitating the rider in front of them, being less aware and less considerate than when riding on their own. In contrast, in the coaching sessions, the student typically rode ahead with the coach riding behind them, creating a situation where learners could not rely on someone else to guide their actions and had to take more responsibility for their decisions.

The coach also highlighted the need "to read" traffic situations, that is the capability to anticipate actions of other cyclists, motorists and pedestrians. It also included to ability to see what the built infrastructure enables and requires from the cyclist, to detect possible sources of danger, and to ride as effortless and safe as possible. With this he emphasises cyclists to see themselves as being in control of their situation.

Reflection. During the rides, the coach would stop whenever he "felt it to be appropriate or necessary", to discuss and give feedback on what just happened. This reflection-on-action [39] is a main instrument in his teaching approach and according to him it should happen as often and as immediate as possible to create a strong learning experience for the student. He also used photos from the ride with the students to support them re-living the experience and thereby reflecting on and learning from it. The time between the individual sessions – one to two weeks – was meant to help students reflect and to let the learning "sink in".

Limitations. Both the class and coaching settings struggle with providing feedback in the moment while being in traffic. In classes, the instructors had to wait for the whole group to come to a safe stop before giving feedback. This delay made the feedback hard to understand, as the situation it was referring to (1) had often happened minutes before and (2) was experienced differently dependent on each cyclist's position within the group. Teachable moments mostly occurred for individuals and not the entire group. Hence, even though the group allows more students to practice at the same time, the lack of intermediate feedback on an individual's teachable moments likely results in a less effective learning setup.

The one-on-one coaching setting offered more tailored and adaptive training to students. This however could not scale to the needs of the students in the classes. There, the needs and problems could vary substantially between students. E.g. a set of students did have a drivers licence and were therefore familiar with traffic rules and signs, but struggled with handling the bike and fear from motorized vehicles. Within the same class, other students were handling the bicycle proficiently but failed to follow the traffic signs and general traffic rules.

Another limitation regarding scale was the actual spatial context of the sessions. The coach tried to ride in areas that his student would be riding in the future as well. Organizationally this was not possible for the classes. Therefore, the students could never practice riding where they live or riding a route they would need in their everyday routines. This points to a more general limitation of the transferability of the learned skills into different contexts. For example, one participant in the class reported that she is taking it already for the second time and does really enjoy it but does not feel confident enough yet to ride in the area she is living in.

4 In-Action-Support for Challenging Experiences: The Virtual Cycling Coach

Based on the studies presented above, we designed the Virtual Cycling Coach (VCC) – a system that acts as a virtual coach on the bike with the goal of supporting the development of a general urban cycling competence. We follow the definition outlined by Siewiorek [24, 41]: "A virtual coach system is an always-attentive personalized system that continuously monitors user's activity and surroundings and delivers interventions – that is, intentional messages – in the appropriate moment". The VCC is designed to explicitly create a learning and practicing opportunity out of an occurring experience or teachable moment. The concept of a virtual coach tackles the limitations found in the existing teaching approaches: As it is always present, a virtual coach can give immediate feedback in a teachable moment and do so within a spatial context most relevant to a user. It also scales up the tailored approach found by the cycling coach.

4.1 Design

Monitoring User's Actions and Context-Awareness. The design of a virtual coach was chosen to enable individualized, in-the-moment and on-the-bicycle support for its users. For this, the VCC has to have the capability to "understand" both the context of the rider as well as her actions within it, with no input from a user. Building a system capable of such an awareness was beyond the scope and resources of this research project. To avoid limiting the design by that, we used a Wizard-of-Oz-prototype, where a present researcher would control the VCC. On the bicycle, a web-application running on a regular smartphone acted as a software client. The present researcher would trigger the VCC using the GUI of a web-based controller. A web-backend enabled the communication between controller and client. Using such a Wizard-of-Oz-prototype allowed us to focus on the effect of the VCC on the study participants and gain insights into the feasibility of such a design.

Interaction Design. For the output, we chose an audio-based voice user interface (VUI). Its ubiquitous use in navigation systems and prior studies with cyclists repeatedly reported this as being the preferred interaction mode [23, 26, 28, 38]. The VUI of the prototype used pre-recorded audio messages and did not offer an option to freely communicate with the cyclist.

Coaching Interventions of the Virtual Cycling Coach. The VCC should be offering support similar to the advanced level training described above, i.e. persons that can balance, steer and control a bicycle and knew essential traffic rules. The curriculum was created for typical situations in which cyclists felt they needed reassurance. Our knowledge on which situations these are was grounded in the study on existing coaching and teaching settings. The interventions – examples are shown in Table 1 – are informed by the insights reported from the exploratory studies presented above. Additionally, guidelines for cyclists from Boston (MA), educational material from bike advocacy groups[1] and textbooks used for cycling education in primary schools in Austria have been used to design the individual interventions.

Coaching Strategy. The coaching interventions target the "manoeuvring level" of cycling [52], that includes e.g. decisions are made about the course and tactics in traffic, selection of appropriate speeds in a specific situation or interaction with other traffic participants. They span from easy to more challenging exercises to allow the VCC to scaffold learning by providing exercises that are challenging, but not too challenging [42]. A session could start with riding on a quiet street and looking back or giving hand signals. Later on, more complex contexts can be combined with more difficult exercises, e.g. doing a left turn on a busy street intersection. An excerpt of the curriculum developed for the VCC is shown in Table 1.

Similar to the professional cycling coach, the VCC should promote an overall defensive, aware and anticipatory way of cycling. The messages should convey this approach of cycling while also including questions to provoke reflection-in-action [39]. For example, while riding in traffic the VCC would prompt awareness and anticipation, but also reflection with messages such as "What can you anticipate? Hear! Look around!" Other messages were "Think! What could be a danger to you? How can you react to that?" or "Do you think that the current distance to the parked cars is sufficient?" This approach also allowed us to include a set of generic messages. Those enable the VCC to stimulate reflection beyond pre-defined situations.

4.2 Methods for Evaluation

The prototype of the Virtual Cycling Coach was qualitatively evaluated to study the experiences created by using it in a real-world scenario to see if the coaching reflection-in-action approach could be achieved. Prior to conducting this study, a formal ethical review by the Committee on the Use of Humans as Experimental Subjects (COUHES) at the Massachusetts Institute of Technology (MIT) has been completed. The evaluation was conducted in two subsequent rounds, in Greater Boston, MA, US and Vienna, Austria. Both cities do see a

---

[1] http://www.bikeleague.org/ridesmart, last accessed at Feb 2021.

Table 1. Excerpt from the curriculum for the Virtual Cycling Coach.

Coaching intervention	Triggers and simulated inputs	Voice interface output
Bicycle handling techniques, e.g. looking back during riding, accelerating and braking precisely	Riding in a safe space (e.g. no motorized vehicles, little complexity) Simulated input: geolocation, object detection	"Now speed up a little and try to brake as hard as you can." "Watching out is crucial for cycling. Now try to ride in a straight line while looking behind you from time to time"
Raise awareness in traffic: Prompt awareness and anticipation; trigger reflection on own awareness	When entering more crowded context, e.g. entering an area with motorized traffic Simulated input: geolocation, object detection	"What can you anticipate? Hear! Look around!" and "Think! What could be a danger to you? How can you react to that?"
Re-framing negative emotions as helpful indicator: Using fear as a signal; practicing slowing down and stopping as a behavioural strategy to cope with fear	When in a crowded traffic situation Simulated input: object detection, noise levels	"I want you to know: Fear is good! It tells you that something might be wrong." "If you are scared slow down or stop"
Own actions in traffic: Teaching safe practices for right and left turns	Participant is approaching an intersection Simulated input: geolocation	"Let's practice right turns. The sequence is: Look back, signal, turn if possible"
Reassurance: Provide support and reassurance to take space on the road to have sufficient safety distances (e.g. to overtaking or unpredictably moving vehicles)	Participant has been riding too close to a pedestrian, parked vehicle or a physical obstacle Simulated input: object detection and sonar/radar/LIDAR based distance measurements	"Take your space, there has to be room for error." "Try to have more safety distance around you or slow down"
Riding next to parked cars/dooring prevention: Reflect on how they ride next to parked cars and the danger of opening doors.	Participant riding on a street next to parked vehicles. Participant riding with sufficient space to parked vehicle (under 1.2 m) Simulated input: same as above	"Let us focus on riding next to the parked cars. Do you think that the current distance is sufficient?" "Good, you are currently riding with enough distance to the parked cars"
Provide situated, in-the-moment feedback to reinforce desired actions	Participant actively follows instruction by VCC Simulated input: comparison between current state and desired state	"Good" "Good, let's repeat this"
Provide critical feedback on an undesired action of a participant	Participant rides close to a pedestrian Participant did not anticipate other vehicles	"Try to do this better the next time"

steady increase in bicycle ridership.[2] Both provide dedicated cycling infrastructure. However, this is mostly retrofitted to existing streets resulting in complex negotiations with other road users, particularly at intersections.

The sessions using the VCC lasted between 20 to 45 min. Each session began with an introduction to the idea of the Virtual Cycling Coach and a short semi-structured interview to assess the participants level of experience and confidence in urban cycling. Depending on those, we adjusted the time spent with exercises of the coaching curriculum to the participant. E.g., a novice cyclist would have been given all basic exercises and doing those in a traffic-free or low-traffic area, whereas an experienced cyclist would have started to ride within denser traffic right from the beginning.

Participants were recorded and asked to think aloud to collect data on thoughts that occur in-the-moment. Observational material was collected as well, including the choices of the participant such as the speed, the distance to other vehicles or pedestrians as well as their overall handling of the bike. Participants did not know from the start of the session that the output of the VCC was directly controlled by the researcher.

First Evaluation Round: Cambridge, MA, United States. Fifteen adults were recruited in the Greater Boston area (MA, United States) using mailing lists from the Massachusetts Institute of Technology (MIT). Six of the participants were MIT students. Seven participants were female, eight were male, their age ranged from early 20 to early 60. The evaluation study took place in Cambridge over a period of two weeks. In this round, the participants put a smartphone with the VCC client in a pocket and could hear the VCC via earphones they wore.[3] The present researcher followed the participants on a bike controlling the VCC and partially instructed participants where to go. Furthermore, he used traffic related stops (e.g. at red lights, stop signs, etc.) to gather *in situ* feedback from participants about their experience using the VCC. A voice recorder with a clip-on microphone was given to the participants to record better quality audio of them thinking aloud during the rides and talking with the researcher(s). The sessions were recorded using two GoPro action cameras, one on the handlebar recording the participant and one on the participant's helmet. In the second week of the study, we added a third camera which was mounted on the researcher's bike to record the participant with more distance from behind. While starting the video a live timecode from the VCC server was shown into the camera for syncing with the log-files of the VCC stored at the server. The log-files – containing when

---

[2] https://www.nast.at/leistungsspektrum/verkehrsmanagement-und-verkehrssteue rung/verkehrsdaten/, https://www.cambridgema.gov/CDD/Transportation/getting aroundcambridge/bikesincambridge/biketrends, both last accessed at Feb 2021.

[3] The earphones did not block outside noise. The volume of the VCC was set to a level so that participants were able to hear traffic while the VCC was talking to them. This setup with a low audio volume was chosen for obvious safety reasons and participants did not find it distracting. However, at times they could not hear messages from the VCC.

which message was said to the participant – where later combined with the video and audio recordings in a single video file used for analysis.

Follow-up interviews have been conducted three months after the sessions. Those were semi-structured open-question interviews reflecting on the experience of using the VCC and cycling thereafter. Those follow-up interviews were conducted via Skype or phone and lasted between 12 and 30 min. We were able to conduct those interviews with all but one of the 15 participants of this evaluation round.

Second Evaluation Round: Vienna, Austria. The main reason to conduct this second evaluation round was to examine if an observer effect has been introduced due to the researcher riding behind participants. To reduce such a possible observer effect, the VCC client smartphone was put in a casing, mounted on a bicycle's handlebar. The casing – shown in Fig. 1 – included a second smartphone that would live-stream a video to the researcher showing the current location and environment. This eliminated the need to follow the study participants as the VCC could now be controlled remotely by the researcher who stayed at the meeting point, using a laptop to use the VCC controller. The casing housed a speaker, thereby eliminating the need for study participants to wear earphones and the need to synchronise the log-files with the videos for analysis as the VCC messages were recorded on video. A 360° camera was mounted on top to record the sessions.

Ten adults living in Vienna were recruited using university mailing lists and via social media. Two of the participants were university students. Eight participants were female, two were male, age ranged from between 20 and 40 years.

Fig. 1. The hardware iteration of the Virtual Cycling Coach used in the second evaluation round: Mounted on the handlebar, the casing housed a front-facing camera that live-streamed a video feed to the controlling researcher (the wizard), a smartphone with an attached loudspeaker for outputs of the audio interface, and a 360° camera on top for recording the session.

The evaluation study took place in Vienna over a period of eight weeks. The researcher instructed participants to ride for about 20 min without any more specific information regarding the route.

Sample. The overall study sample included 15 women and 10 men. 12 participants reported public transport as their main mode of transportation, 11 reported bicycling, one was primarily walking, and one did primarily use her car. As for their experience with urban cycling, one participant had none, 13 participants had some experience – i.e. they rode a bike a few times per year in the city – and 11 had substantial experience in urban cycling.

Analysis. The collected data ranged from interview recordings, field notes and video-recordings shown in Fig. 2. The latter offered detailed, contextualized information on the experiences of the study participants which were annotated along with the transcripts. The data was partially transcribed and summed up by three researchers. A thematic analysis was used to provide a detailed account within the data [4]. The coding of the data was also informed by the exploratory studies, however unexpected themes that emerged from the data have been taken into account as well. We aimed at finding "repeated patterns of meaning" [4] across the data set. Those identified themes and presented in the results lean towards the semantic end on the spectrum from semantic to latent themes.

Fig. 2. Combined video and log data used for analysis of the rides using the Virtual Cycling Coach (VCC) from the first evaluation round (left). 360° video from second evaluation round (right).

4.3 Findings from Qualitative Evaluation of the Virtual Cycling Coach

Using the Virtual Cycling Coach was overall appreciated by the study participants. They found the idea interesting and saw value in the in the moment feedback. Participating in the VCC evaluation study already affected the anticipation of the cycling experience. The bicycle ride was about "learning", "coaching" and "support", thereby changing the framing of cycling from a generic everyday experience to a deliberate learning experience. As creating a learning and practicing opportunity out of an occurring experience or teachable moment, in-the-moment guidance was a prominent feature – allowing users to gain procedural knowledge. For example, to teach a turn sequence when a participant approached an intersection, the VCC would provide this message: "Let us practice right turns. (pause) The sequence is: Look back, signal, turn if possible". This framing was reported back by the study participants, as they all viewed using the VCC as a learning or coaching experience.

Participants were often prompted by the VCC to repeat exercises and those could take place in several different locations. E.g., the VCC would prompt to focus on the viewing technique and signalling whenever participants made turns at intersections, or would prompt them to keep enough safety distance to pedestrians as soon as there were interactions with those. Repetition also resulted in a strong memory of the actual coaching messages: Even in the follow-up interviews which took place three months after the VCC sessions, participants could recall the VCC's messages and often even the exact wording of those. Repetition and reinforcement in the use of the VCC added a quality of learning to the overall cycling experience, similar to the existing non-technological approaches outlined in Sect. 3.2.

Furthermore, the VCC was designed to scaffold the learning experience for its users, e.g. by doing certain exercises in safe or less complex environments. Scaffolding was important for the challenge to be at the right level in relation to the competences of the participant, that is being not too easy but also not too hard [42]. A typical session therefore started in areas with little or no traffic from motorized vehicles, as shown in Fig. 3. We could observe how this helped participants develop competencies like looking back while riding or riding with one hand on the handlebar to signal turns. *"I didn't look back much because I was scared. I thought that I would lose control. But after doing it a few times in a safe environment it was fine". [Judd—follow-up interview—all names are changed for anonymity]*.

Fig. 3. Start of a session with the VCC in an area without motorized vehicles to reduce overall complexity of the context.

Effective Feedback and Reassurance. Feedback from the virtual cycling coach was given repeatedly based on the quality of a participant's actions. Less experienced cyclists noted that this was helpful for them to understand what is the right or safe thing to do. This reduced the feeling of uncertainty for novice cyclists. Deliberately riding and reflecting on cycling in urban traffic also led participants to ask themselves specific questions. Those were mostly legal questions regarding the rules of traffic that emerged during the sessions or related to best practices, e.g., in what areas cycling is allowed, how much space a cyclist is allowed to take or different types of signalling turns by hand. Having the external support structure during the ride can provide answers to such specific questions.

The more experienced cyclists expressed that the VCC was a way to reassure them that they were right with their own thinking or, in other words, that the strategies they had created based on experience were right. *"I think of some of this confusion what the best practices are. [...] There are things to know like what are the legal obligations and what is the safest". [John—during session].*

An instance for that was how to interact with motorized vehicles in tight spaces, where many cyclists had a feeling that they were blocking cars and supposed to ride on the very right side of the road. The focus on how and why to act in a certain way further reduced uncertainty and increased confidence in acting according to the guidelines used to inform the curriculum. The VCC reassured them that they should always keep a 1-meter (3 foot) safety distance to parked cars, often meaning that they had to use the full lane. *"I remember particularly [...] needing to make sure that you take over the road. If there is a road that you sharing with a car. So that you don't feel shy". [Sara—follow-up interview].*

During these rides the participants often raised additional questions on laws, best practices and guidance. This indicates that the VCC promoted the engagement with "how" one was cycling in the given urban environment. Participants also developed a more pronounced view of themselves within urban traffic. The language used to express that points at a strong feeling of agency for their actions and that they view those actions and themselves situated within traffic. Using the VCC is by design a reflective activity. This might result in developing a more pronounced outside view of seeing one's actions from the perspective of others as well. *"And still, everyday things! Thinking about: where are my relations to other cyclists, vehicles? Am I being predictable, visible? It's something that it [the VCC session] certainly made me aware of: my physical surroundings and how I fit into those and to ensuring my own safety". [John—follow-up interview].*

Reflection. While it is difficult for the cycling instructors and the coach to give in the moment feedback as well as to prompt reflection-in-action, technology makes it possible to deploy that. Participants knew upfront that the aim of this study was to support them in urban cycling by setting up an explicit learning structure, with the participant being in the role of the learner and the VCC as well as the present researcher taking up the role as coach. Even without the Virtual Cycling Coach being active, the very presence of this structure led to reflection-in-action. Participants said they were more aware of how they were riding and that they acted more deliberately, knowing that their actions were observed. So, with and without the VCC being active, a reflection-in-action was present as illustrated in the excerpt above. Our analysis did not reveal differences between the two study waves that would based on an observer-effect.

The messages from the Virtual Cycling Coach were mostly understood by participants as advice on what to do, rather than prompts for reflection-in-action. However, here, it is of relevance how specific the VCC messages are. A message can contain specific advice such as: "Always keep a safety distance of at least 1 m to pedestrians". This was expected by the participants. But the VCC could also prompt a participant with general and unspecific messages such as: "Think! What could be a danger to you? How can you react to that?" We found that those did help to further trigger reflection, with the first step being a participant finding what to reflect on in the specific moment.

The following description of a segment from a evaluation session highlights the role of reflection: The participant is riding in an area with other cyclists and pedestrians and no motorized traffic. The VCC says "Let us practice some basics". The participant is riding at a low speed while thinking aloud: *"Make sure you don't get in the way of other bikers"*. Then, the VCC says "Watching out is crucial for cycling. Now try to ride in a straight line while looking behind you from time to time". The exercise is meant to deliberately practice looking back without loosing control or balance. The participant is trying to ride in a straight line while looking back, which at first he does not achieve. While doing so, he is thinking aloud: *"Ok, the straight line, that's difficult, because you don't really know where you are going."* Now, another cyclist and a pedestrian enter the area and pass close by. The participant continues to think aloud: *"Watch out for this biker and this person. But let's try it again. Let's try it again. Looking back, looking forward. That one went well. So after about three times it got a lot better"*. Repeating the exercise did improve his ability to ride straight. Here, the previously established reflection process made the participant continuously improve his actions without the VCC intervening in any particular moment.

Development of Competences. With coaching being an essential aspect of the VCC it does not come as a surprise that a theme of developing competencies is a result of interacting with it. Especially in the follow-up interviews participants reported a rise of their overall awareness during urban cycling. They were supported by the VCC to cycle in a defensive, aware and anticipatory way. The Virtual Cycling Coach also helped to develop particular competencies and change specific aspects of how participants rode within the city. Those competencies were directly related to the curriculum of the VCC, for example instructions and feedback on riding along pedestrians or viewing technique.

"I felt better checking for cars behind me as we kept biking. That was a helpful one." [Macy—follow-up interview].

"[I] also remember [the VCC] telling me to look around occasionally. Which I've been doing, but I try to be a little more aware of how I get information. When

there is not much traffic I still usually rely on my ears [. . .] but I am trying to make a more conscious effort to pay attention". [Anna—follow-up interview].

We included regular cyclists to uncover differences between them and less experienced cyclists. From those experienced cyclists, two did mention that the VCC experience did not have had any effects on their competencies or behaviours. Other experienced cyclists reported that using the VCC had more relevance to them than they initially expected. The *in situ* approach of the VCC made them aware on aspects of cycling that they had either not considered before or had not embedded in their cycling routines yet.

"I've had a lot of experience cycling before. But there were some things that I took away from it – that have actually stayed with me as I am cycling. Kind of remembering some of the instructions, you know, look back when I am turning right and things like that. So in a kind of surprising way I am remembering it even though I didn't think I would get much out of it back at that time". [Sam— follow-up interview].

5   Discussion

We used a prototype that simulates understanding of context, actions of users and is able to provide relevant *in situ* interventions in-the-wild. Our findings show that the tight coupling between real experiences of users and the interventions by the virtual coach enabled meaningful learning and reflection.

Technologically, there is currently no system capable of understanding traffic contexts, human actions and human experiences. Especially not one that could be fitted and used on a bicycle. Resorting to safe spaces like a design studio [39] or even a cycling simulator would be a way to study a system in a more controlled and safe environment. However, this would not generate comparably realistic experiences [29], while the Wizard-of-Oz prototype did sufficiently simulate the system and allowed us to study the interplay between the real contexts, the user's in-the-moment real actions and experiences. As there are fast advancements in the field of autonomous systems [18], especially regarding systems capability to understanding contexts, technology will eventually be suitable to be used on a bicycle eliminating the need for the Wizard-of-Oz prototype. Our insights allow to inform the design of such systems already today.

In line with existing research on interaction design for cycling, participants generally liked the audio-based voice user interface (VUI). But there were instances, particularly when riding in loud traffic, where instructions could become difficult to hear. Future work using voice user interfaces on bicycles should therefore offer a way for users to easily change the playback volume. Failures of the system, such as providing an inappropriate message, where seen as flaws of the prototypical setup by participants within the evaluation study. However, future work could explore the trust between riders and such a coaching system and how it is affected by failures. Similar designs for support systems in real settings could also be improved by adding turn-by-turn navigation. And the other way around, bicycle navigation systems could benefit from a VCC, i.e. by guiding novice cyclists to traffic free areas or offering a routing suitable for the cyclists current level of experience and competence. This could help to reduce the mental load of its user, and would likely be anyway in line with preferences of unexperienced cyclists for potentially slower routes if they offer a more pleasant experience [8,44].

A future approach might be to always offer a virtual coach. This would allow to extend existing learning contexts, i.e. by being always present if a person wants to have some support or feedback in everyday settings, similar to existing advanced driver assistance systems. This would allow the VCC to provide coaching interventions over an extended period of time and when suitable situations and teachable moments occur, as these moments produce the reported processes of learning and reflection-in-action.

With the two rounds for evaluating the VCC we have also seen limitations of the system compared to human interaction. Compared to real cycling instructors or coaches, the VCC is lacking the flexibility and capability to react to every event in some form. It also lacks the depth of the emotional support possible in communication between humans. However, our findings show that the VCC can create comparable learning experiences and reflection. A real system could very well complement, rather than replace, existing class or coaching settings. This is very similar to the use of virtual coaches e.g. in health care, where they are deployed in addition to conventional care [24,31]. Beyond the domain of health our work can also inform research in care for elderly, social-emotional-learning, or on-the-job coaching.

6   Conclusion

By studying professional cycling instructors conducting their classes, we uncovered both how novice cyclists are taught to develop their urban cycling competences. We designed and built a prototype of a Virtual Cycling Coach, with our evaluation showing it can be a meaningful support that can generate similar processes to existing teaching settings. It can enable a deliberate learning experience, provide effective immediate feedback and reassurance, prompt reflection and support the development of competences. These findings have implications for similar designs and the development of mobile applications with dependencies to both context of use and actions of users.

Acknowledgements. We thank Agnis Stibe, Alexandra Millonig and Stefan Seer for their help in conducting this study. We thank Petr Slovak for his feedback and input for both the study and early drafts on this paper.

References

1. Andres, J., Kari, T., Von Kaenel, J., Mueller, F.: Co-riding with my eBike to get green lights. In: Proceedings of the 2019 on Designing Interactive Systems Conference, pp. 1251–1263 (2019)
2. Bial, D., Appelmann, T., Rukzio, E., Schmidt, A.: Improving cyclists training with tactile feedback on feet. In: Magnusson, C., Szymczak, D., Brewster, S. (eds.) HAID 2012. LNCS, vol. 7468, pp. 41–50. Springer, Heidelberg (2012). https://doi.org/10.1007/978-3-642-32796-4_5
3. Braun, V., Clarke, V.: Reflecting on reflexive thematic analysis. Qual. Res. Sport Exercise Health **11**(4), 589–597 (2019)
4. Braun, V., Clarke, V.: Using thematic analysis in psychology. Qual. Res. Psychol. **3**(2), 77–101 (2006)
5. Brisswalter, J., Collardeau, M., René, A.: Effects of acute physical exercise characteristics on cognitive performance. Sports Med. **32**(9), 555–566 (2012)
6. Broll, G., et al.: Tripzoom: an app to improve your mobility behavior. In: Proceedings of the 11th International Conference on Mobile and Ubiquitous Multimedia, pp. 1–4 (2012)
7. Celis-Morales, C.A., et al.: Association between active commuting and incident cardiovascular disease, cancer, and mortality: prospective cohort study. BMJ **357**, j1456 (2017). https://doi.org/10.1136/bmj.j1456
8. Crist, K., Schipperijn, J., Ryan, S., Appleyard, B., Godbole, S., Kerr, J.: Fear factor: level of traffic stress and GPS assessed cycling routes. J. Transp. Technol. **9**(1), 14–30 (2018)
9. Dancu, A., Franjcic, Z., Fjeld, M.: Smart flashlight: map navigation using a bike-mounted projector. In: Proceedings of the SIGCHI Conference on Human Factors in Computing Systems, pp. 3627–3630 (2014)
10. Dancu, A., et al.: Gesture bike: examining projection surfaces and turn signal systems for urban cycling. In: Proceedings of the 2015 International Conference on Interactive Tabletops & Surfaces - ITS 2015, pp. 151–159. ACM Press, Madeira (2015)
11. Dill, J., McNeil, N.: Revisiting the four types of cyclists: findings from a national survey. Transp. Res. Rec. **2587**(1), 90–99 (2016)
12. Fishman, E.: Cycling as transport. Transp. Rev. **36**(1), 1–8 (2016)
13. Gabrielli, S., Maimone, R.: Are change strategies affecting users' transportation choices? In: Proceedings of the Biannual Conference of the Italian Chapter of SIGCHI, CHItaly 2013, pp. 9:1–9:4. ACM, New York (2013)
14. Gabrielli, S., et al.: Designing motivational features for sustainable urban mobility. In: CHI 2013 Extended Abstracts on Human Factors in Computing Systems, CHI EA 2013, pp. 1461–1466. ACM, New York (2013)
15. Geissler, H., Hasenbein, M., Kanatouri, S., Wegener, R.: E-coaching: conceptual and empirical findings of a virtual coaching programme. Int. J. Evid. Based Coach. Mentor. **12**(2), 165–187 (2014)
16. Gössling, S., Choi, A.S.: Transport transitions in Copenhagen: comparing the cost of cars and bicycles. Ecol. Econ. **113**, 106–113 (2015)
17. Grant, A.M.: The impact of life coaching on goal attainment, metacognition and mental health. Soc. Behav. Personal. Int. J. **31**(3), 253–263 (2003)
18. Harel, D., Marron, A., Sifakis, J.: Autonomics: in search of a foundation for next-generation autonomous systems. Proc. Natl. Acad. Sci. **117**(30), 17491–17498 (2020)

19. Heinovski, J., et al.: Modeling cycling behavior to improve bicyclists' safety at intersections-A networking perspective. In: 2019 IEEE 20th International Symposium on "A World of Wireless, Mobile and Multimedia Networks" (WoWMoM), pp. 1–8. IEEE (2019)
20. IPCC, Climate Change 2014: Synthesis Report. Contribution of Working Groups I, II and III to the Fifth Assessment Report of the Intergovernmental Panel on Climate Change. Technical report. IPCC, Geneva (2014)
21. Kazhamiakin, R., et al.: Using gamification to incentivize sustainable urban mobility. In: 2015 IEEE First International Smart Cities Conference (ISC2), pp. 1–6 (2015)
22. Klecha, L., Gianni, F.: Designing for sustainable urban mobility behaviour: a systematic review of the literature. In: Mealha, Ó., Divitini, M., Rehm, M. (eds.) SLERD 2017. SIST, vol. 80, pp. 137–149. Springer, Cham (2018). https://doi.org/10.1007/978-3-319-61322-2_14
23. Lee, C.-L., Lee, D., Cheng, Y.-M., Chen, L.-C., Chen, W.-C., Sandnes, F.E.: On the implications of sense of control over bicycling: design of a physical stamina-aware bike. In: Proceedings of the 22nd Conference of the Computer-Human Interaction Special Interest Group of Australia on Computer-Human Interaction, pp. 13–16 (2010)
24. Lete, N., Beristain, A., García-Alonso, A.: Survey on virtual coaching for older adults. Health Inf. J. **26**(4), 3231–3249 (2020)
25. Magliocchetti, D., Gielow, M., De Vigili, F., Conti, G., de Amicis, R.: Ambient intelligence on personal mobility assistants for sustainable travel choices. J. Ubiquit. Syst. Pervasive Netw. **4**(1), 1–7 (2012)
26. Marshall, J., Dancu, A., Mueller, F.: Interaction in motion: designing truly mobile interaction. In: Proceedings of the 2016 ACM Conference on Designing Interactive Systems, DIS 2016, pp. 215–228. Association for Computing Machinery, New York (2016)
27. Martin, A., Goryakin, Y., Suhrcke, M.: Does active commuting improve psychological wellbeing? Longitudinal evidence from eighteen waves of the British household panel survey. Prev. Med. **69**, 296–303 (2014)
28. Matviienko, A., Ananthanarayan, S., El Ali, A., Heuten, W., Boll, S.: NaviBike: comparing unimodal navigation cues for child cyclists. In: Proceedings of the 2019 CHI Conference on Human Factors in Computing Systems, CHI 2019, pp. 1–12. Association for Computing Machinery, New York (2019)
29. Matviienko, A., Ananthanarayan, S., Sadeghian Borojeni, S., Feld, Y., Heuten, W., Boll, S.: Augmenting bicycles and helmets with multimodal warnings for children (2018)
30. Morris, E.A., Guerra, E.: Mood and mode: does how we travel affect how we feel? Transportation **42**(1), 25–43 (2014). https://doi.org/10.1007/s11116-014-9521-x
31. Nussbaum, R., Kelly, C., Quinby, E., Mac, A., Parmanto, B., Dicianno, B.E.: Systematic review of mobile health applications in rehabilitation. Arch. Phys. Med. Rehabil. **100**(1), 115–127 (2019)
32. Okugawa, R., Murao, K., Terada, T., Tsukamoto, M.: Training system of bicycle pedaling using auditory feedback. In: Proceedings of the 12th International Conference on Advances in Computer Entertainment Technology, pp. 1–4 (2015)
33. Pielot, M., Poppinga, B., Heuten, W., Boll, S.: Tacticycle: supporting exploratory bicycle trips. In: Proceedings of the 14th International Conference on Human-Computer Interaction with Mobile Devices and Services, pp. 369–378 (2012)
34. Pooley, C.G., et al.: Policies for promoting walking and cycling in England: a view from the street. Transp. Policy **27**, 66–72 (2013)

35. Poppinga, B., Pielot, M., Boll, S.: Tacticycle: a tactile display for supporting tourists on a bicycle trip (2009)
36. Pucher, J., Buehler, R.: Making cycling irresistible: lessons from the Netherlands, Denmark and Germany. Transp. Rev. **28**(4), 495–528 (2008)
37. Pucher, J., Dill, J., Handy, S.: Infrastructure, programs, and policies to increase bicycling: an international review. Prev. Med. **50**(Supplement), S106–S125 (2010)
38. Rowland, D., et al.: Ubikequitous computing: designing interactive experiences for cyclists. In: Proceedings of the 11th International Conference on Human-Computer Interaction with Mobile Devices and Services, p. 21. ACM (2009)
39. Schön, D.A.: The Reflective Practitioner: How Professionals Think in Action. Basic Books, New York (1983)
40. Semanjski, I., Lopez Aguirre, A.J., De Mol, J., Gautama, S.: Policy 2.0 platform for mobile sensing and incentivized targeted shifts in mobility behavior. Sensors **16**(7), 1035 (2016)
41. Siewiorek, D.P.: Invited talk: virtual coaches in health care. In: IEEE/IFIP International Conference on Dependable Systems and Networks Workshops (DSN 2012), p. 1 (2012)
42. Slovak, P., Frauenberger, C., Fitzpatrick, G.: Reflective practicum: a framework of sensitising concepts to design for transformative reflection. In: Proceedings of the 2017 CHI Conference on Human Factors in Computing Systems, pp. 2696–2707. ACM (2017)
43. Steltenpohl, H., Bouwer, A.: Vibrobelt: tactile navigation support for cyclists. In: Proceedings of the 2013 International Conference on Intelligent user Interfaces, pp. 417–426 (2013)
44. Stinson, M.A., Bhat, C.R.: A comparison of the route preferences of experienced and inexperienced bicycle commuters. In: TRB 84th Annual Meeting Compendium of Papers (2005)
45. Telfer, B., Rissel, C., Bindon, J., Bosch, T.: Encouraging cycling through a pilot cycling proficiency training program among adults in central Sydney. J. Sci. Med. Sport **9**(1), 151–156 (2006)
46. Theeboom, T., Beersma, B., Vianen, A.E.M.V.: Does coaching work? A meta-analysis on the effects of coaching on individual level outcomes in an organizational context. J. Posit. Psychol. **9**(1), 1–18 (2014)
47. Tornivuori, A., Tuominen, O., Salanterä, S., Kosola, S.: A systematic review on randomized controlled trials: coaching elements of digital services to support chronically ill adolescents during transition of care. J. Adv. Nurs. **76**(6), 1293–1306 (2020)
48. Tsukada, K., Yasumura, M.: ActiveBelt: belt-type wearable tactile display for directional navigation. In: Davies, N., Mynatt, E.D., Siio, I. (eds.) UbiComp 2004. LNCS, vol. 3205, pp. 384–399. Springer, Heidelberg (2004). https://doi.org/10. 1007/978-3-540-30119-6_23
49. United Nations, D.o.E.a.S.A.: World Urbanization Prospects: The 2014 Revision Highlights (2014)
50. de Waard, D., Westerhuis, F., Joling, D., Weiland, S., Stadtbäumer, R., Kaltofen, L.: Visual map and instruction-based bicycle navigation: a comparison of effects on behaviour. Ergonomics **60**(9), 1283–1296 (2017)
51. Wernbacher, T., Pfeiffer, A., Platzer, M., Berger, M., Krautsack, D.: Traces: a pervasive app for changing behavioural patterns. In: European conference on games based learning, p. 589. Academic Conferences International Limited (2015)
52. Wierda, M., Brookhuis, K.A.: Analysis of cycling skill: a cognitive approach. Appl. Cogn. Psychol. **5**(2), 113–122 (1991)

53. Wright, P., McCarthy, J.: Empathy and experience in HCI. In: Proceedings of the SIGCHI Conference on Human Factors in Computing Systems, pp. 637–646. ACM (2008)

54. Wunsch, M., Stibe, A., Millonig, A., Seer, S., Chin, R.C.C., Schechtner, K.: Gamification and social dynamics: insights from a corporate cycling campaign. In: Streitz, N., Markopoulos, P. (eds.) DAPI 2016. LNCS, vol. 9749, pp. 494–503. Springer, Cham (2016). https://doi.org/10.1007/978-3-319-39862-4_45

55. Wunsch, M., et al.: What makes you bike? Exploring persuasive strategies to encourage low-energy mobility. In: MacTavish, T., Basapur, S. (eds.) PERSUASIVE 2015. LNCS, vol. 9072, pp. 53–64. Springer, Cham (2015). https://doi.org/10.1007/978-3-319-20306-5_5

Exploring How Saliency Affects Attention in Virtual Reality

Radiah Rivu[1]([✉]), Ville Mäkelä[1,2,3], Mariam Hassib[1], Yomna Abdelrahman[1], and Florian Alt[1]

[1] Bundeswehr University Munich, Munich, Germany
{sheikh.rivu,mariam.hassib,yomna.abdelrahman,florian.alt}@unibw.de
[2] LMU Munich, Munich, Germany
ville.maekelae@ifi.lmu.de
[3] University of Waterloo, Waterloo, Canada

Abstract. In this paper, we investigate how changes in the saliency of the Virtual Environment (VE) affect our visual attention during different tasks. We investigate if users are attracted to the most salient regions in the VE. This knowledge will help researchers design optimal VR environments, purposefully direct the attention of users, and avoid unintentional distractions. We conducted a user study ($N = 30$) where participants performed tasks (video watching, object stacking, visual search, waiting) with two different saliency conditions in the virtual environment. Our findings suggest that while participants notice the differences in saliency, their visual attention is not diverted towards the salient regions when they are performing tasks.

Keywords: Virtual Reality · Saliency · Visual attention

1 Introduction

Virtual Reality (VR) has become an important research topic in human-computer interaction. Over the years, researchers have studied various topics in VR like perception (immersion, presence, cognition) [5], novel input devices [13], locomotion [3], navigation [27], and avatars and virtual humans [21]. More recently, researchers have looked into how VR could be used to simulate real-world situations, for example, for research purposes [14,15] and training [7], and looked in more detail into VR study methodologies [19].

However, our understanding is still limited as to how the design of the virtual environment (VE) influences human *visual attention* and behavior. Though factors affecting visual attention in the real world have been studied [12,22], we know very little about its effects in VR. One of the key factors affecting visual attention is *saliency*, termed as "the tendency of humans to be drawn to areas or objects that stand out amongst the background, when viewing natural scenes" [10].

© IFIP International Federation for Information Processing 2021
Published by Springer Nature Switzerland AG 2021
C. Ardito et al. (Eds.): INTERACT 2021, LNCS 12936, pp. 147–155, 2021.
https://doi.org/10.1007/978-3-030-85607-6_10

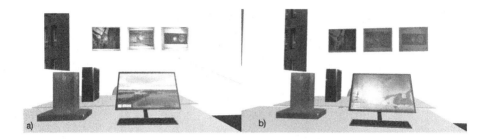

Fig. 1. We explored how different levels of saliency in a virtual environment affect the user's attention while performing tasks. a) Saliency condition 1: original paintings, b) Saliency condition 2: color of the paintings changed. (Color figure online)

Saliency is potentially a confounding variable in VR studies, and understanding its effects will help researchers design their experiment. Saliency is both a challenge and an opportunity for almost any VR experience, ranging from games [16] to cinematic virtual reality [20]. Salient parts of the environment may distract players and viewers unintentionally; however, saliency can also be used to subconsciously direct users' attention towards relevant objects in the environment [2]. Therefore, understanding how saliency affects visual attention in VR is useful for many purposes.

Prior work explores saliency in virtual reality [1,4,17,23], but we lack an investigation into how saliency affects visual attention during various tasks, and whether this has an effect on task performance and behavior. Therefore, in this paper we conduct a preliminary exploration to understand if the saliency of VEs influences the user's visual attention while performing different tasks. Saliency is an umbrella term that consists of many factors such as color, shape, illumination and texture. Investigating each factor is out of scope for this paper, thus as a first-step towards research in this direction we study saliency in VR using *color*.

To this end, we conducted an experiment (N = 30) where users performed tasks in VR (stacking 3D objects, searching for a specified object, watching a video, and waiting), while we manipulated the saliency of certain objects (paintings) in the environment. Our primary **research question** was: *Does saliency in a virtual environment affect visual attention and task performance?*

Our findings show that although participants notice changes in saliency, their visual attention is not diverted towards the salient regions when they are performing tasks. Participants also completed their tasks as efficiently in both saliency conditions, showing that saliency did not affect task performance.

2   Background

Saliency affects our visual attention [29]. Researchers have widely explored the effects of saliency in real-world environments and built saliency-based models. A popular saliency-based search model was presented by Itti and Koch [8]. The authors applied the model to a demanding search task and results show that saliency has a great impact on our visual attention and behaviour. Following this work, Underwood et al. [24] studied if saliency dominantly determines the visual attention given to objects, and if a cognitively demanding task can overtake this effect. Their findings suggest that when building saliency models, one should consider cognitive load as a metric [24].

Studies have also investigated whether saliency can be used to direct the user's attention. For example, Vig et al. [26] used machine learning to model how modifying the saliency of videos can redirect attention. Veas et al. [25] used visual saliency modulation to make subtle changes in videos, and were able to unobtrusively direct the viewer's attention to the modified regions. However, Meur et al. [11] found that saliency-based distortion of videos had only a moderate effect on which regions received the viewers' attention.

In this paper, we are motivated to understand how saliency functions in VR. Due to the diversity in graphics, art style, lighting, and hardware, VR can be salient in many ways. We argue that exploring such effects in VR is important because we are yet unaware how this may affect user behaviour in VR.

3   Study: Investigation of Saliency in VR

To answer our research question, we conducted a user study in VR where participants performed tasks with a varying degree of saliency in the virtual environment. We implemented a virtual office room with paintings, tables, chairs and a screen. The VR environment was built using Unity and SteamVR. As the head-mounted display (HMD), we used the HTC VIVE Pro. The VIVE Pro has an integrated eye tracker from which we obtained gaze data.

3.1   Design

We used a within-subjects design where all participants experienced all conditions. We had two independent variables: 1) task and 2) level of saliency.

Tasks. We selected the following four tasks (Fig. 2), as these represent typical tasks in VR [18] and were also different in nature, ranging from physical tasks to more passive tasks. Participants performed each task twice (with and without change of saliency) in a counterbalanced order.

- **Manipulation Task:** Participants used the VR controllers to stack numbered cubes on the table (Fig. 2a).
- **Search Task:** Participants searched for a hidden object (a red cube) in the room. They needed to use the controller to grab it and move it on the table (Fig. 2b).
- **Video Watching Task:** Participants watched a one-minute video on the screen in front of them (Fig. 2c).
- **Waiting Task:** This was a deceptive task where the participants were told to wait for the experimenter's instructions. This one-minute task was used to allow the participants to observe the environment (Fig. 2d).

Fig. 2. Participants performed four kinds of tasks: a) Manipulation task where participants stack the numbered colored blocks, b) Visual search task where participants look for a hidden red cube, c) Video watching where participants watch a one minute video on the screen, d) Waiting task where participants wait for further instructions. (Color figure online)

Saliency. We used two saliency levels *(original, changed saliency)* as shown in Fig. 1. Prior work explored several approaches to measure and quantify the saliency of an image or video [6]. To identify the salient regions of the virtual environment for our study, we used Saliency Toolbox [28]. The saliency maps show that when the color of the paintings is changed to red, they become more salient. We measured the saliency for three colors (red, blue and green) but red showed the highest increase, thus we selected it for our experiment.

3.2 Participants and Procedure

We recruited 30 participants (18 males, 12 females) with an average age of 27 (SD = 4.04) through university mailing lists and social media. 25 participants were students, five were professionals in different fields. 12 participants had no experience with VR or eye tracking.

Upon arrival, participants filled their demographic information (age, gender, background, experience with VR), signed a consent form, and were explained the tasks in the study. The task order was balanced using Latin square. After the study, they filled in the final questionnaire in which we asked open-ended questions about the objects they noticed in the environment, if they felt distracted while performing the tasks, and if their visual attention was diverted. The study lasted approximately 30 min. During the experiment, we recorded gaze data from the participants. Each participant was awarded 5 EUR.

4 Results

4.1 Attention Towards the Salient Regions

We quantified and visualized the number of times participants glanced at the salient regions (the paintings) between the conditions. This was calculated using the number of times the gaze ray intersected with the observed virtual objects. To eliminate false positives, we only considered measurements from the moment the user's gaze left the initial starting point, similar to prior work [9]. After the study, we asked participants which objects in the room attracted their attention. 15 participants mentioned the paintings on the wall.

There was no significant difference in glance counts among any of the tasks between saliency levels (Table 1). This indicates that the saliency conditions of the VE did not affect the participants when they were focused on a task. We visualized the glances as colored dots as shown in Figs. 3, 4, 5, and 6. The figures show that in both environments, users were focused on the tasks. We see greater variation for the *search task* and *waiting task*. This is because in *search task* participants were looking for a specified hidden object, and in the *waiting task* participants did not have anything particular to focus on.

Table 1. Result of the Friedman Test for gaze on the paintings, between two different saliency conditions.

Rating	Manipulation	Searching	Video	Waiting
Chi-Square $\chi^2(2)$	2.778	3.333	.043	2.133
ρ	.96	.068	.835	.144

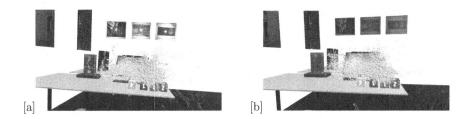

Fig. 3. Gaze visualization for the manipulation task between a) Original saliency and b) Changed saliency.

4.2 Task Completion Time

The average task completion times show no significant difference between the two saliency levels. Table 2 shows the results from comparing the original and changed saliency and its effect on task completion time. Given the *waiting* task and the *video watching* task were of fixed length, we see no difference in completion time between the two conditions (original and changed saliency). For the *manipulation task* and *search task*, there is also no statistically significant difference between saliency levels (Table 2), although there is a slight difference in the average completion times.

We also asked participants if they noticed anything unusual in the room. 16 out of 30 participants replied that they noticed the paintings on the wall changed color between tasks.

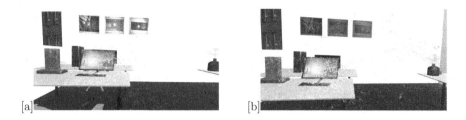

Fig. 4. Gaze visualization for the search task between a) Original saliency and b) Changed saliency.

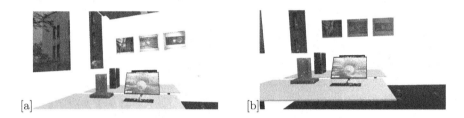

Fig. 5. Gaze visualization for the video watching task between a) Original saliency and b) Changed saliency

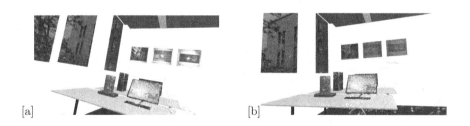

Fig. 6. Gaze visualization for waiting task between a) Original saliency and b) Changed saliency.

Table 2. Friedman Test between original and changed saliency condition for task completion time.

Rating	Manipulation	Searching	Video	Waiting
Chi-Square $\chi^2(2)$	1.2000	.133	1.33	2.133
ρ	.273	.715	.715	.144

5   Discussion and Future Work

In our study, participants noticed the most salient VR regions in their field of view. This is in line with existing literature, that suggest that humans attend to the most salient regions of their surrounding [29]. Therefore, this preliminary investigation suggests that participants pay attention to saliency in virtual environments similar to real environments. We investigated how the salient regions would attract attention during different tasks. Tasks are frequently performed in VR (for example, user studies in VR, gaming, and other virtual experiences). Hence, it is important to understand how the virtual environment affects our behavior during VR experiences.

We found that the participants were unaffected by the saliency during the tasks. In both saliency conditions, participants did not noticeably glance at the salient regions during their tasks. They also performed their tasks equally fast in both settings. The short duration required to complete each task may have impacted the viewing behaviour of the participants. It is possible that if each task required a substantially longer time to complete then the participants would have been likely to also glance more at their surroundings during the tasks. In the future, we wish to investigate how different categories of tasks as well as task duration may be affected by saliency.

Saliency can be used to highlight information to users in VR, which is beneficial for many applications like virtual advertisements, storytelling, gaming, and shopping. However, based on our results, designers should be aware that salient regions do not gain the user's constant attention while they are focused on other tasks, even if the salient regions are located within their field of view. Therefore, designers should consider utilizing the more relaxed periods in their VR experiences (e.g., after a task has been finished) to guide users through saliency.

Our early investigation had some limitations and therefore there is room for more in-depth studies in the future. First, we only explored one type of subtle change in saliency and we only focused on the most salient objects in the environment (the paintings on the wall). The saliency of a VE can be manipulated in various other ways—and to a varying extent—and these should be investigated in the future. In particular, research should investigate the effect of combining other forms of saliency to understand its effect in VR, mainly combining color with shape and illumination as all these play a role in the design of VR environments. Second, visual attention could be further investigated by considering additional measures such as eye blinking and fixation time. Third, we wish to explore visual attention during a more diverse set of tasks. In particular, we plan to include VR tasks of varying cognitive requirements to see if saliency plays a bigger role in cognitively demanding tasks.

6   Conclusion

To explore the effect of saliency on visual attention and task performance in VR, we conducted a preliminary study where participants performed several tasks in VR while we manipulated the saliency of the environment. We learned that although participants do notice different saliency levels in the VE, it has no significant effect on visual attention or task performance. Rather, participants focus on the objects relevant to their task, and are more prone to detecting the salient regions in the environment between the tasks. We believe that our work helps us understand how saliency affects attention in VR. For example, designers of virtual environments and virtual experiences who want to use saliency changes to guide users, could consider leveraging the downtime between tasks for more effective guidance.

References

1. Albayrak, D., Askin, M.B., Capin, T.K., Celikcan, U.: Visual saliency prediction in dynamic virtual reality environments experienced with head-mounted displays: an exploratory study. In: 2019 International Conference on Cyberworlds (CW), pp. 61–68 (2019)
2. Bailey, R., McNamara, A., Sudarsanam, N., Grimm, C.: Subtle gaze direction. ACM Trans. Graph. **28**(4), 14 (2009), Article 100. https://doi.org/10.1145/1559755.1559757
3. Boletsis, C.: The new era of virtual reality locomotion: a systematic literature review of techniques and a proposed typology. Multimodal Technol. Interact. **1**(4), 24 (2017)
4. De Abreu, A., Ozcinar, C., Smolic, A.: Look around you: saliency maps for omnidirectional images in VR applications. In: 2017 Ninth International Conference on Quality of Multimedia Experience (QoMEX), pp. 1–6 (2017)
5. Diemer, J., Alpers, G.W., Peperkorn, H.M., Shiban, Y., Mühlberger, A.: The impact of perception and presence on emotional reactions: a review of research in virtual reality. Front. Psychol. **6**(2015), 26 (2015)
6. Fang, Y., Wang, J., Narwaria, M., Le Callet, P., Lin, W.: Saliency detection for stereoscopic images. IEEE Trans. Image Process. **23**(6), 2625–2636 (2014)
7. Gorecky, D., Khamis, M., Mura, K.: Introduction and establishment of virtual training in the factory of the future. Int. J. Comput. Integr. Manuf. **30**(1), 182–190 (2017). https://doi.org/10.1080/0951192X.2015.1067918
8. Itti, L., Koch, C.: A saliency-based search mechanism for overt and covert shifts of visual attention. Vis. Res. **40**(10–12), 1489–1506 (2000)
9. Judd, T., Ehinger, K., Durand, F., Torralba, A.: Learning to predict where humans look. In: 2009 IEEE 12th International Conference on Computer Vision, pp. 2106–2113 (2009)
10. Koehler, K., Guo, F., Zhang, S., Eckstein, M.P.: What do saliency models predict? J. Vis. **14**(3), 14 (2014)
11. Le Meur, O., Ninassi, A., Le Callet, P., Barba, D.: Overt visual attention for free-viewing and quality assessment tasks: impact of the regions of interest on a video quality metric. Sig. Process. Image Commun. **25**(7), 547–558 (2010)
12. Logan, G.D., Gordon, R.D.: Executive control of visual attention in dual-task situations. Psychol. Rev. **108**(2), 393 (2001)
13. Maggioni, C.: A novel gestural input device for virtual reality. In: Proceedings of IEEE Virtual Reality Annual International Symposium, pp. 118–124. IEEE (1993)

14. Mäkelä, V., et al.: Virtual field studies: conducting studies on public displays in virtual reality. In: Proceedings of the 2020 CHI Conference on Human Factors in Computing Systems (CHI 2020), New York, NY, USA, pp. 1–15. Association for Computing Machinery (2020). https://doi.org/10.1145/3313831.3376796

15. Moussaïd, M., et al.: Crowd behaviour during high-stress evacuations in an immersive virtual environment. J. R. Soc. Interface **13**(122), 20160414 (2016)

16. Ordaz, N., Romero, D., Gorecky, D., Siller, H.R.: Serious games and virtual simulator for automotive manufacturing education & training. Procedia Comput. Sci. **75**(2015), 267–274 (2015)

17. Oyekoya, O., Steptoe, W., Steed, A.: A saliency-based method of simulating visual attention in virtual scenes. In: Proceedings of the 16th ACM Symposium on Virtual Reality Software and Technology, pp. 199–206 (2009)

18. Regian, J.W., Shebilske, W.L., Monk, J.M.: Virtual reality: an instructional medium for visual-spatial tasks. J. Commun. **42**, 136–149 (1992)

19. Rivu, R., et al.: Remote VR studies - a framework for running virtual reality studies remotely via participant-owned HMDs. CoRR abs/2102.11207 (2021)

20. Rothe, S., Hußmann, H.: Guiding the viewer in cinematic virtual reality by diegetic cues. In: De Paolis, L.T., Bourdot, P. (eds.) AVR 2018. LNCS, vol. 10850, pp. 101–117. Springer, Cham (2018). https://doi.org/10.1007/978-3-319-95270-3_7

21. Steed, A., Pan, Y., Zisch, F., Steptoe, W.: The impact of a self-avatar on cognitive load in immersive virtual reality. In: 2016 IEEE Virtual Reality (VR), pp. 67–76. IEEE (2016)

22. Sun, Y., Fisher, R.: Object-based visual attention for computer vision. Artif. Intell. **146**(1), 77–123 (2003)

23. Sung, M., Choi, S.: Selective anti-aliasing for virtual reality based on saliency map. In: 2017 International Symposium on Ubiquitous Virtual Reality (ISUVR), pp. 16–19 (2017)

24. Underwood, G., Foulsham, T., van Loon, E., Underwood, J.: Visual attention, visual saliency, and eye movements during the inspection of natural scenes. In: Mira, J., Álvarez, J.R. (eds.) IWINAC 2005. LNCS, vol. 3562, pp. 459–468. Springer, Heidelberg (2005). https://doi.org/10.1007/11499305_47

25. Veas, E.E., Mendez, E., Feiner, S.K., Schmalstieg, D.: Directing attention and influencing memory with visual saliency modulation. In: Proceedings of the SIGCHI Conference on Human Factors in Computing Systems (CHI 2011), New York, NY, USA, pp. 1471–1480. Association for Computing Machinery (2011). https://doi.org/10.1145/1978942.1979158

26. Vig, E., Dorr, M., Barth, E.: Learned saliency transformations for gaze guidance. In: Human Vision and Electronic Imaging XVI, vol. 7865, p. 78650W. International Society for Optics and Photonics (2011)

27. Vinson, N.G.: Design guidelines for landmarks to support navigation in virtual environments. In: Proceedings of the SIGCHI conference on Human Factors in Computing Systems, pp. 278–285 (1999)

28. Walther, D., Koch, C.: Modeling attention to salient proto-objects. Neural Netw. **19**(9), 1395–1407 (2006)

29. Zhang, F.J., Dai, G.Z., Peng, X.: A survey on human-computer interaction in virtual reality. Sci. Sin. Inform. **46**(12), 1711–1736 (2016)

Global Scene Filtering, Exploration, and Pointing in Occluded Virtual Space

Yuan Chen[1,2(✉)], Junwei Sun[2], Qiang Xu[2], Edward Lank[1], Pourang Irani[3], and Wei Li[2]

[1] University of Waterloo, Waterloo, ON, Canada
{y2238che,lank}@uwaterloo.ca
[2] Huawei Technologies, Markham, ON, Canada
{junwei.sun,qiang.xu1,wei.li.crc}@huawei.com
[3] University of Manitoba, Winnipeg, MB, Canada
irani@cs.umanitoba.ca

Abstract. Target acquisition in an occluded environment is challenging given the omni-directional and first-person view in virtual reality (VR). We propose Solar-Casting, a global scene filtering technique to manage occlusion in VR. To improve target search, users control a reference sphere centered at their head through varied occlusion management modes: Hide, SemiT (Semi-Transparent), Rotate. In a preliminary study, we find SemiT to be better suited for understanding the context without sacrificing performance by applying semi-transparency to targets within the controlled sphere. We then compare Solar-Casting to highly efficient selection techniques to acquire targets in a dense and occluded VR environment. We find that Solar-Casting performs competitively to other techniques in known environments, where the target location information is revealed. However, in unknown environments, requiring target search, Solar-Casting outperforms existing approaches. We conclude with scenarios demonstrating how Solar-Casting can be applied to crowded and occluded environments in VR applications.

1 Introduction

While Virtual Reality (VR) presents end-users with rich 3D environments, an on-going challenge within VR involves the acquisition of targets to support subsequent manipulation. As a result, 3D selection in VR remains an active research area, particularly given the variety of possible 3D environment configurations

---

Y. Chen—The work was done when the author was an intern at Huawei Canada.

Electronic supplementary material The online version of this chapter (https://doi.org/10.1007/978-3-030-85607-6_11) contains supplementary material, which is available to authorized users.

necessitating interactive support [2]. Most VR systems use some variant of Ray-Casting for 3D pointing [5], which enables users to select using a virtual ray.

Among the many concerns with 3D target acquisition, targeting occluded objects is a significant challenge with Ray-Casting [2,20]. Two types of occlusion exist within virtual environments: an object is either partially-occluded or fully-occluded by other objects in the scene. Each type of occlusion has its own issues. While a partially-occluded target can be seen, selecting it efficiently and accurately is challenging because of distracting neighbour targets [9,23]. An example of partial occlusion might be selecting a single piece of data from a 3D visualization. As for fully-occluded scenarios, since targets are completely hidden, it is hard to locate targets, resulting in subsequent difficulties selecting and interacting. Examples of this include tasks such as browsing 3D models [34] or interacting with 3D scenes.

To motivate this work, we have identified two design requirements (DRs) absent from existing Ray-Casting techniques based on the presented literature. These are **(1)** the lack of ability to handle both partial-occlusion and full-occlusion in virtual environments; and **(2)** the need to explore the environment and dynamically control the interaction space to overcome visual occlusion. These DRs are absent because target acquisition techniques that require some augmentation to control depth [4,20] or progressive refinement [9,23] demand one degree of control such that adding another degree of control (to limit or overcome occlusion visually or trajectorially) on the occlusion space will increase the complexity of manipulating the controller. It is also difficult to manage visual occlusion and selection-based disambiguation because target selection is a local interaction, whereas visual occlusion – and techniques to allow users to overcome it – require global interaction in the immersive environment.

Motivated by these design requirements, we propose Solar-Casting, a 3D pointing technique designed to support rapid, and low-error target selection across different levels of occlusion. We use a reference sphere or *Solar* that is centered at the user's head and works as an interactive volume. Users can effortlessly control the radius of *Solar* with a touch enabled surface. The sphere plays a vital role. It first filters inner items, by either hiding (Hide) or turning them semi-transparent (SemiT). This has the effect of making items outside the egocentric sphere visible to users, thereby reducing the effects of occlusion. In one variant (Rotate), a simple manipulation on the touch surface rotates items on *Solar*'s surface; in another a ray or other interaction metaphor can be used to select objects on the surface. Finally, since this occurs uniformly, by simply looking around, the user can identify items of interest.

To evaluate Solar-Casting, we conducted two experiments using different occlusion levels. In the first study, we compared Solar-Casting with existing Ray-Casting techniques in an occluded environment where a visual cue was presented so users could quickly locate the target. Our results showed that Solar-Casting had competitive performance to competing techniques. In the second study, we evaluated Solar-Casting without any visual cues such that users needed to search for occluded targets. The results highlight Solar-Casting's strengths in occluded environments, particularly increasing accuracy in dense and highly-occluded instances. In summary, our contributions include: (1) proposing an efficient pointing technique for selecting targets at different occlusion levels; (2) conducting experiments to evaluate and investigate Solar-Casting's pros and cons in occluded environments with/without visual guidance.

2 Related Work

Numerous techniques have been proposed for 3D selection in virtual environments [2]. Ray-Casting [24] and the virtual hand [27] appear as two key 3D pointing metaphors [36]. Bowman et al. [7] introduce Ray-Casting with reeling to add a single degree of freedom, making it possible to change the length of the ray. In the ray-depth technique [37], users are able to adjust control display (C/D) ratio while adjusting the depth of the ray. Both Ray-Casting and virtual hand techniques offer complementary strengths and weaknesses [12,36,43]. Ray-Casting works well with distant objects, but the virtual hand needs augmentations, such as the Go-Go technique [35] to acquire out-of-reach objects. Argelaguet et al. [1] propose Ray-Casting from the eye, where a ray originates from the user's eye, yet is controlled by their hand. They found that Ray-Casting from the eye was helpful for selection tasks in cluttered environments. A variation of using the head as a focal point for cursor manipulation has also been adopted in AR headsets such as the Microsoft HoloLens.

While the majority of techniques are tuned for selecting visible targets virtual environments [2], techniques for selecting occluded targets through transparency or cut-outs have received some attention. Considering first, transparency, the BalloonProbe [15] uses an invisible or transparent (wireframe) sphere that forces distortion in a 3D virtual environment, reducing occlusion. XPointer [41] is an X-ray mouse cursor technique for 3D selection, which enables users to select initially hidden objects via object-based transparency by changing the cursor's penetration. Tilt-Casting [33] uses a virtual plane as a filtering surface, and objects above the surface are invisible, allowing objects on and below the plane to be seen and selected, and Sun et al. [42,44] propose a layer-based transparency technique to select and manipulate objects that are originally fully occluded. Finally, Elmqvist et al. [16] propose an image space algorithm to achieve dynamic transparency for managing occlusion of important target objects in 3D. Cut-away techniques [13,34] permit a user to look "through" occluding objects by interactively cutting holes into the occluding geometry. Similarly, the Cut Plane technique [30] uses a plane to split the entire scene, makes one side of the plane translucent, and reveals occluded targets on the other side. Many of these techniques are either geared toward 3D views [33], are tuned to select occluded targets at a known location [15,41], or provide limited support for visual search during selection tasks [42,44].

Beyond transparency and cut-outs, there exist a number of other input or view manipulations that allow users to select partially occluded targets or that rearrange targets spatially to handle occlusion. For example, the flexible pointer [18] bends a ray to avoid obstacles, thus allowing the user to select partially, but not fully occluded objects. Similarly, Outline Pursuits [40] enables users to select a partly occluded target by following its outline with their gaze. Flower ray [20] presents all intersected targets with a ray in a marking menu and allows users to select the intended target. SQUAD [3,23] adopts a similar design. Users first specify a spherical volume containing all targets of interest and then refine the initial selection progressively by selecting the subset of objects containing the desired one from a four-item menu until the target is finally selected. Expand [9] is an extension of SQUAD, where objects are placed in a grid for users to choose from. In a more dense environment (e.g. point clouds), the Slicing Volume [28] supports selection of occluded targets by first defining a specific region, followed by intersecting desired targets with a slicing plane. Most recently, Yu et al. [52] propose various Ray-Casting techniques to select fully occluded targets, including filtering targets globally or rearranging targets in a local space. However, all of these view manipulation techniques are designed based on the assumption that targets are either always at least partially visible to the users, that their location is known a priori, or that their location context can be disrupted without cost. In many scenarios, we cannot make any of these assumptions.

Regardless of how a previously occluded target becomes visible, the next step is to acquire it precisely. This is challenging for Ray-Casting techniques in virtual reality due to unintentional hand tremor and distant target location magnifying small rotation changes into large-scale distant movements. Grossman et al. [20] adopt various disambiguation mechanisms (e.g. depth-aware bubble cursor, and two-step selection) into Ray-Casting techniques so users can disambiguate different targets along a ray and select targets effectively. The bubble cursor is perhaps the most popular selection facilitation technique [19,47]. Alongside its use by Vanacken [47], in RayCursor [4], a 3D bubble cursor is implemented to select the closest object to the cursor when users manually move a cursor on the ray to disambiguate object selection, and Moore et al. [29] find that choosing the closest target (de facto a bubble cursor technique) performs the best for virtual hand pointing. More recently, Lu et al. [25] investigate multiple variants of the bubble mechanism for Ray-Casting, i.e., selecting the closest object to the ray or cursor, and argue that the bubble mechanism significantly improves the performance and preference for Ray-Casting selection.

Other selection mechanisms have also been explored. Sun et al. [45] proposed a manual disambiguation mechanism for positioning 3D objects in depth. Multiple degrees-of-freedom (DOF) are often implemented to manipulate a ray or other virtual representations, such as a plane or sphere, and then perform precise 3D target acquisition [21,22,33]. Finally, multiple devices have also been explored: ARPen [48] uses a pen and smartphone to perform image plane selection [32] in a AR system; and Slicing Volume [28] uses controllers, a pen and a tablet to select targets intersecting with a plane in a scalable region. In contrast, our technique, Solar-Casting, uses a single touch surface (in our case, a smartphone display that also drives the VR display) to control the necessary degrees-of-freedom to simultaneously control the interaction space, remove occlusion, explore the scene, and, finally, select targets precisely in an occluded VR environment.

3   Solar-Casting

Our Solar-Casting technique is built in several steps. We begin by creating our own instance of the Ray-Casting technique with an interactive sphere to support global filtering and pointing with one control action. We design three global interaction modes: SemiT (Semi-Transparent), Hide and Rotate, and then evaluate these modes in a preliminary study. Last, We add head control to constrain the interaction region of the global occlusion function and two facilitation techniques for fast and stable manipulation of the cursor and the ray, as in [4]. This section describes each of these aspects of Solar-Casting in turn.

Fig. 1. Illustration of Solar-Casting with SemiT mode: (a) a red sphere is occluded by blue spheres, when *Solar* turns on (b) and users move up on the touchscreen to increase *Solar*'s radius, objects inside *Solar* and within field-of-view (fov) become translucent (c&d), so users can easily select the occluded target. For objects inside *Solar* but outside fov, their status will automatically update after entering fov (e). (Color figure onine)

3.1   Solar Metaphor

As we observe the evolution of pointing and selecting in 3D environments, we see a clear progression from using rays [4,18,41], to surfaces [30,33] and volumes [28] to enable filtering and target selection. As existing Ray-Casting techniques that support depth manipulation already require a degree of control [4,20], one challenge is that to support occlusion management, at least one other degree of control is required; otherwise, the occlusion management space is local and fixed [47] to the ray. This means that, while users can easily select a target when its location is revealed, it is difficult to identify occluded desired targets at unknown locations if some mechanism for visual search of the virtual space is not supported.

To achieve dynamic global filtering and local pointing with only one degree of control, we use a semi-transparent sphere (*Solar*) centered at the user's head.

Solar's status depends on touch events, provided by the entire touchscreen of the connected device. When the touch area is held over $T_{trigger}$ (*Solar* trigger time), *Solar* turns on and users observe the virtual environment through it. When fingers leave the touch surface, *Solar* turns off and users are able to observe objects with their original appearance. $T_{trigger}$ is set to 300 ms, a value that reduces Heisenberg effect [6] and works well in practice.

With *Solar* on, a ray and a cursor are defined in relation to *Solar*'s volume. When a ray does not intersect with any object, the ray extends to the inner surface of *Solar* (Fig. 3(2)). However, if the extension of the ray beyond *Solar*'s surface intersects with an object *outside* the sphere, the ray snaps to the intersected object (Fig. 3(3)). Furthermore, when *Solar* is activated, users can either rotate or scale the translucent sphere to interact with occluders. By integrating these motions with progress refinement [9,20,23] and a virtual x-ray [2,17], we propose three modes to handle occlusion using *Solar*: Rotate, Hide and Semi-Transparent (SemiT). Users perform defined interactions as described in the following section to enter modes and the corresponding outcome is preserved even when *Solar* is off.

We can envision manipulating *Solar* in one of two ways, either by rotating it, sheering the display space such that hidden objects become visible; or by expanding and contracting it, i.e. by scaling *Solar* along its radius. As with flower-ray [20] and Expand [9], **Rotate** mode rearranges objects in the environment to minimize occlusion. With **Rotate** mode, objects that intersect with *Solar*'s surface can rotate around *Solar*'s center, similar to the Arcball Rotation [38] (Fig. 2). Therefore, when the environment is not fixed and a target is occluded by multiple objects, it is easier to point at the target after rotating the object away from the occluders.

Alongside **Rotate**, *Solar* can also be scaled, and objects inside *Solar* can be filtered using complete or partial transparency. We introduce **Hide** and **SemiT** modes, a virtual x-ray metaphor [2,17,28,33]. This metaphor presents two alternative filters that permits users to see through objects between the user and the surface of the sphere, thus making the occluded (beyond the sphere's surface) objects visible. As their names suggest, Hide is used to hide occluders while SemiT turn occluders semi-transparent. We use a similar design as [28,33] where the spatial relation between objects and the *Solar*'s surface defines objects' selectability. When Hide is on, objects intersecting with *Solar* or outside of it are visible and selectable while inside *Solar*, they are invisible and unselectable. When SemiT is on, objects inside *Solar* become semi-transparent and unselectable. Figure 2 shows these filter mechanisms.

3.2   Interaction Mapping

To support filtering with *Solar*, the user must be able to control rotation or scaling. To rotate objects intersecting with *Solar*, we map the horizontal movement of a finger on the touchscreen (Δ_h) with their rotation (θ, in degrees) on *Solar* around its Yaw axis using the following function: $\theta = f(v_{\Delta_h}) \cdot \Delta_h$. Here, v_{Δ_h} is the finger speed and $f(v_{\delta_h})$ is a transfer function for both movement mapping and gain control of rotation. When users want to point at a occluded object but not move its neighbour objects too far, they should move their fingers horizontally on the touch surface slowly. Therefore, $f(v_{\Delta_h})$ is designed as a bounded linear interpolation depending on finger speed [4].

The scaling of Solar has a similar design, where the vertical movement of a finger on the touchscreen (Δ_v) maps to the radius of the *Solar* (R, in meters). When a finger moves up/down on the touchscreen, the radius increases/decreases correspondingly. We use the distance from the head position to the position of the connected device when Solar is initialized, defined as R_o. Solar's mapping function is, therefore, defined as:

$$R = \begin{cases} R_o & \text{R is initialized or smaller than } R_o \\ R + g(V_{\Delta_v}) \cdot \Delta_v & \text{otherwise} \end{cases} \quad (1)$$

Similar to $f(v_{\Delta_h})$, $g(V_{\Delta_v})$ is also a bounded linear interpolation gain function. They both depend on the finger speed but not the cursor position, as gain functions on finger speed are more reliable and faster [4].

Fig. 2. Left: moving up/down on the touchscreen of a smartphone scales up/down Solar (Hide or SemiT). Mid: moving left/right on the touchscreen rotates objects intersecting with *Solar* left/right around *Solar*'s yaw axis (Rotate). Right: modes will only be applied to targets within *Solar* and a user's fov.

3.3   Facilitation Techniques

To facilitate selection, *Solar* can include pointing facilitation. We include both a bubble cursor mechanism [19] and jitter filtering, as follows.

Bubble Mechanism. Solar-Casting's bubble mechanism is implemented by selecting the nearest on- or outside-Solar targets by calculating their Euclidean distance from the point where the ray intersects the Solar to surrounding targets when the ray does not intersect with any object. The target selected by the bubble mechanism is highlighted with a different colour (Fig. 3 (2&4)).

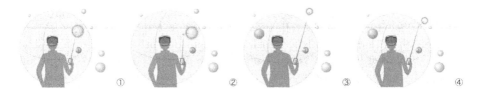

Fig. 3. Bubble mechanism in ray: (1) If a ray intersects with an object on *Solar*, the object is highlighted; (3) If a ray intersects with an object outside of *Solar*, the cursor snaps to the target and the ray gets extended; (2&4) If a ray does not intersect with any object, the closest target to the cursor will be highlighted.

Ray Filtering. Jitter is a common issue in Ray-Casting for 3D target acquisition, especially when pointing at small and distant targets, due to unintentional hand tremor and noisy sensing from input devices. Ray filtering smooths ray related movement during selection. In the Solar-Casting technique, we use the 1€filter [10] as it offers a good trade-off between precision and latency.

3.4 Preliminary Study on Solar-Casting Mode

We conducted informal preliminary tests with 5 adults for feedback on our three occlusion mitigation modes (Hide, SemiT, and Rotate) and their combinations using Solar-Casting (Fig. 4).

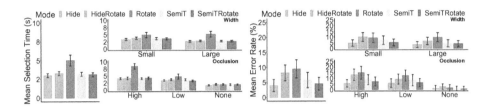

Fig. 4. Mean selection time (left) and error rate (right) results for the preliminary study, with 95% confidence intervals.

The results showed that, among all modes, Hide, SemiT and their combinations with Rotate had similar, good performance in terms of selection time, but Hide had a trend to lower error rate than all other modes. This is consistent with previous findings [2], suggesting that semi-transparency might compromise the task as spatial relationships between semi-transparent targets and unfiltered targets become unclear. However, for Hide, as context is removed, participants have more difficulty searching for targets. As P2 commented, *Hiding is bad for real UI, how will you know things are hidden?*

Rotate was slower than other modes because two steps were needed to handle occlusion. Participants first moved vertically on the touchscreen to scale *Solar* such that it intersected with occluders. Then, they moved horizontally to rotate occluders away. Participants reported that Rotate was difficult to use if a goal target was occluded not only by its neighbors but also by other distant targets that blocked the intersecting ray. Unlike Hide and SemiT, which provided straightforward visual feedback, sometimes it was hard for participants to identify intersecting objects on *Solar*'s surface.

Regarding mode combinations, some participants felt that they caused unexpected results: when they intended to use Hide or SemiT, Rotate was triggered by accident as they carelessly swiped horizontally, and objects intersecting with *Solar*'s surface were rotated away. Essentially, when in combination, Rotate was difficult to use and resulted in mode errors. Rotate alone was also slower than other visualizations.

4   General Experimental Setup

We designed and conducted two studies to evaluate Solar-Casting for selecting targets in 3D virtual environments, at different occlusion levels. Given the results of the pilot study, we eliminated *Solar* rotation and used SemiT in both studies, as Hide partially sacrifices context by suppressing part of the virtual environment (inside Solar's sphere).

In Study 1, a visual indicator (orange triangle) was provided and a small portion of targets were noticeable even in the high occlusion environment (Fig. 5 (left)) to investigate how visual guidance influences selection in an occluded environment [31]. In Study 2, the visual indicator was removed and targets were fully blocked in the full-occlusion environment (Fig. 5 (right)). Aside from this significant difference, the two studies had a similar experimental design and protocol.

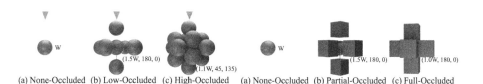

(a) None-Occluded (b) Low-Occluded (c) High-Occluded   (a) None-Occluded (b) Partial-Occluded (c) Full-Occluded

Fig. 5. Three occlusion levels in Study 1 (left) and Study 2 (right): a red sphere (target) is surrendered by blue occluders, which are generated around the target in a spherical coordinate system (r, θ, ϕ), r in meter, θ, ϕ are in degree. (Color figure online)

4.1   Apparatus

We used a Huawei VR Glass as the head-mounted display (HMD) in both studies. It has a resolution of 3200 px × 1600 px, with a pixel density of 1058 ppi. The display of this VR Glass is rendered by a connected smartphone, which conveniently provides both a touch surface and a Ray-Casting device for use in the VR environment. We note that smartphones are frequently explored as an input device for selection [11] and manipulation [51], and current VR controllers generally include a touchpad or joystick which can be used for controlling *Solar*.

4.2   Procedure

In both studies, participants were welcomed to the experiment room and sat in a swivel chair. They first read the study instructions and verbal consent was obtained. Before the study, they were first asked to answer a questionnaire on demographic information (gender, age) and daily and weekly usage of mobile and VR devices. Participants were warned about potential motion sickness induced from VR, and were allowed to have breaks between experimental blocks. If they felt uncomfortable at any time during the study, the study immediately stopped.

After sanitizing the VR glass and phone with alcohol wipes, participants wore the VR glass, and started a training session to practice each technique with 6 trials. They then entered the experimental scene and finished the study with the provided techniques. Techniques were counter-balanced using a Latin square [49]. When participants completed the study, they removed the VR glasses and completed a survey of 7-scale Likert items grading their experience.

5   User Study 1: With Visual Guidance

In the first study, our goal was to evaluate Solar-Casting's performance in dense and occluded environments, where visual cues can help to identify objects.

We designed a comparative study including four interaction techniques: Solar-Casting, Expand [9], Depth Ray with a localized transparency function [47] and Depth-Casting, a technique similar to Tilt-Casting [33] or Slicing-Volume [28], which were chosen because of their characteristics (Table 1).

Table 1. Characteristics of the selected baseline techniques.

Technique	Interaction space	Strategy
Expand	Limited	Progressive refinement
Depth ray	Limited	Visual filtering (virtual X-ray)
Depth-Casting	Scaled	Visual filtering (virtual X-ray)

While Expand, Depth Ray and Tilt-Casting were all previously used in physical displays for occlusion management, and Slicing Volume used two controllers for volume control, we adapted them to a VR HMD and a phone-control environment with the following modification:

- Depth Ray: The cursor movement along the ray was controlled by the phone by moving the finger on the touchscreen and any target within 0.1 m to the cursor is rendered as semi-transparent while the closest one is highlighted via a bubble cursor mechanism [19].
- Expand: A semi-transparent sphere with radius 0.1 m, is rendered when a ray is intersecting with any target. When a finger is moving down on the touchscreen, i.e. a pull gesture, targets intersecting with the sphere are cloned, arranged into a grid, and presented in front of the user.
- Depth-Casting: The tilted plane is always displayed in front of the user vertically, which dynamically scales and occupies over 90% of the view frustum based on the depth. Targets in front the plane are rendered semi-transparent and only targets intersecting with the tilted plane are selectable. Second, tilting of the phone changes the depth of the plane instead of rotating the plane around its pitch axis [33,46]; third, as the cursor is restricted to the tilted plane, cursor position is controlled by the head movement. We also implemented a relative mapping [39] on the phone to accommodate one-hand use and target positions which are hard to acquire with the head.

5.1   Experimental Design

Participants were instructed to perform a sequential pointing task as quickly and accurately as possible. A block design was adopted. In each block, given the technique, participants were asked to perform selection on 10 goal targets for each occlusion level (Fig. 5) and targets of all occlusion levels were generated around users at the same time (all were at least 0.6 m away from users).

Participants first pointed to a white sphere (dummy target) in order to fix the initial cursor position and start the timer for measuring the selection time of the sequential trials. Target width was 0.06 m and the distance D between two consecutive goal target was chosen from $(0.4\,\text{m}, 1.0\,\text{m}, 1.6\,\text{m})$, so ID ranged from 2.94 to 4.79 bits [26]. To select a target, participants either had to position the cursor over it or move the cursor as close as possible, to allow selection with the bubble mechanism. When either hovering over a target or moving as close as possible to it, the target would be highlighted (in orange), indicating it was selectable. The pointing task moved to the next trial only when the target was correctly selected. If participants made an erroneous selection, a misclick was recorded. Once a goal target was correctly selected, this goal target became blue and the next goal target became red. There was only one goal target in red at a time and an orange indicator was shown above it to help participants quickly locate where they should point to. The connected phone would vibrate for 0.1 s and 1 s when participants completed a block and a technique respectively.

In summary, we designed a within-subjects experiment with independent variables: *Technique* (Depth Ray, Depth-Casting, Expand, Solar-Casting), *Occlusion* (None-Occluded, Low-Occluded, High-Occluded), and *Block* (1–4). Therefore, each participant needed to perform 4 *Technique* × 3 *Occlusion* × 4 *Block* × 10 trials = 480 trials.

5.2   Participants

We recruited 12 participants from our organization, of which 11 reported their ages (22 to 26, $\mu = 23.6$, $\sigma = 1.3$). Among 12 participants, 1 was female, all were right-handed and 1 an experienced VR user. The study lasted about 60 min.

5.3   Results

We conducted a multi-way repeated-measure ANOVA ($\alpha = 0.05$) for selection time (ST) and error rate ($\%_{Err}$) respectively on three independent variables: *Technique*, *Occlusion* and *Block*. ST refers to the time elapsed between selections while $\%_{Err}$ refers to the percentage of erroneous trials among 10 trials. Taking into account the non-normal distribution of ST and $\%_{Err}$, a Box-Cox transformation [8] and Aligned Rank Transform (ART) [14,50] was applied to the data respectively. Greenhouse-Geisser corrections was applied to the DoFs when sphericity was violated using Mauchly's test. Pairwise tests with Bonferroni corrections were conducted when significant effects were found. Effect sizes were reported as partial eta squared (η_p^2) values.

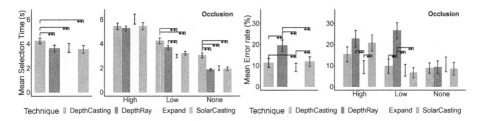

Fig. 6. Mean selection Time (left) and error Rate (right) for *Technique* and its interaction effect with *Occlusion*. Statistical significances are marked ($++$ = $p < 0.01$). Error bars represent 95% confidence intervals.

Learning Effect. With Box-Cox transformation ($\lambda = -0.1$) and Aligned Rank Transform (ART) on ST and $\%_{Err}$ respectively, we found only a significant effect of *Block* ($F_{3,33} = 4.46$, $p < 0.05$, $\eta_p^2 = 0.03$) on ST. Pairwise t-test did not report any significance between blocks. Therefore, all 4 blocks were kept.

Selection Time. We found a significant effect of *Technique* on ST ($F_{3,33} = 14.83$, $p = 0.001$, $\eta_p^2 = 0.28$). As shown in Fig. 6 (left), the pairwise t-test showed that Depth-Casting (mean = 4.23 s) took significantly longer ($p < 0.001$) than other techniques: Solar-Casting (3.53 s), Depth Ray (3.60 s) and Expand (3.66 s). We also found a significant effect of *Occlusion* on ST ($F_{2,22} = 1312.59$, $p < 0.001$, $\eta_p^2 = 0.85$). It took participants significantly longer ($p < 0.001$) selecting targets in high-occlusion environments (5.53 s) than in low-occlusion environments (3.52 s) and non-occluded environments (2.20 s). We also found a significant interaction effect of *Technique* $\times$ *Occlusion* ($F_{6,66} = 40.11$, $p < 0.001$, $\eta_p^2 = 0.28$) on ST. In non- and low-occlusion environments, Solar-Casting (1.93 s & 3.21 s respectively) was significantly faster ($p < 0.001$) than Depth-Casting (3.03 s & 4.23 s), but in high-occlusion environments, they had similar performance.

Error Rate. We found a significant effect of *Technique* on $\%_{Err}$ ($F_{3,553} = 33.03$, $p < 0.001$, $\eta_p^2 = 0.15$). The pairwise comparison showed that Solar-Casting (11.87%), Depth-Casting (11.26%) and Expand (9.12%) caused significantly less erroneous selection than Depth Ray (19.45%, $p < 0.001$). Meanwhile, Expand caused significantly ($p < 0.005$) less erroneous selection than Solar-Casting and Depth-Casting. We found a significant effect of *Occlusion* on $\%_{Err}$ ($F_{3,553} = 27.71$, $p < 0.001$, $\eta_p^2 = 0.09$). Obviously, participants made significantly more erroneous selection ($p < 0.001$) in the high-occlusion environment (16.97%) than in the non- and low-occlusion environments (9.20% & 12.60% respectively). We also found a significant interaction effect between *Technique* and *Occlusion* ($F_{3,553} = 15.23$, $p < 0.001$, $\eta_p^2 = 0.14$). Looking at Fig. 6 (right), in both non- and low-occlusion environments, Solar-Casting (8.42% & 6.50%) and Depth-Casting (8.77% & 9.68%) had relatively low error rates, and in the high-occlusion environments, the error rate increased (Solar-Casting: 20.67% and Depth-Casting: 15.32%); while Expand kept relatively low-error rate across three levels of occlusion environments (Fig. 7).

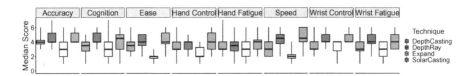

Fig. 7. The median score and lower/upper quartiles are visualized for each measure. Lower scores indicate worse performance.

Preference. Friedman tests reported a significant effect of *Technique* on all attributes except for *Hand Fatigue*: $\chi^2_{Accuracy}(4) = 15.13$, $p < 0.005$, $\chi^2_{Cognition}(4) = 8.70$, $p < 0.05$, $\chi^2_{Ease}(4) = 21.11$, $p < 0.001$, $\chi^2_{HandControl}(4) = 8.50$, $p < 0.05$, $\chi^2_{Speed}(4) = 21.28$, $p < 0.001$, $\chi^2_{WristControl}(4) = 12.79$, $p < 0.01$, $\chi^2_{WristFatigue}(4) = 13.02$, $p < 0.001$. The pairwise Wilcox test showed that participants felt Solar-Casting significantly easier and faster to use ($p < 0.05$) and had better accuracy, hand and wrist control ($p < 0.05$) than Expand. Regarding user feedback, P1 commented that it would be better if Solar's sphere could reset after each successful selection. P1, P4, and P8-9 mentioned that Expand did not work well with high occlusion scenes, as it was difficult to intersect the desired region where the target object was. P2, and P10 complained about the wrist fatigue in Depth-Casting, as users needed to precisely control the plane tilt using their wrist. P1-P3, and P6-P10 mentioned that it was difficult to move the cursor in Depth Ray (P3: *It would be nice to filter all objects along the ray*). In the non-occluded condition, participants indicated a preference for selecting the target directly rather than moving the cursor along the ray.

Discussion. Solar-Casting was at least as fast and accurate as the other three techniques. However, note that the target indicator was the dominant factor in selection performance, which drastically decreased the visual search time in the task. Users were given the visual cue of the low- and high-occluded targets and they only needed to reveal and select them. Therefore Solar-Casting's visual search benefits were not represented in the above analysis. As expected, occlusion level had a significant impact on selection time. All four techniques performed more slowly in high-occlusion environments. Although users were informed of the target's location by the target indicator, it still took longer for them to reveal the occluded target for subsequent selection. In terms of error rate, Expand had a consistently low error rate through different occlusion levels. This is understandable given the characteristics of progressive refinement, considering that the visual representation of objects during selection is consistent in Expand. Meanwhile for the other three techniques, occlusion had a more significant impact on error rate.

6   User Study 2: Without Visual Guidance

Different from the former study, in the second study, the visual cue was removed and a new occlusion design (Fig. 5 (right)) was adopted so that participants needed to use the provided technique to explore the scene and point at targets across different occlusion levels.

In our pilots, in the full-occlusion environment, Expand was extremely time-consuming and demanded significant effort, as participants needed to try every cluster with a pull gesture on the touchscreen. Without a visual cue, users felt dizzy quickly rotating their head and turning around to search for occluded targets. Therefore, Expand was eliminated from User Study 2 and targets were all presented in front of the participants. Since targets were all presented in front of participants, the front cube might block the user's view, therefore, for the partial-occlusion environment, we slightly rotated cubes round the goal target to a random degree (0° - 45°) to ensure that at least a small portion of a target was visible to participants.

6.1 Experimental Design

Similar to Study 1, a within-subjects experiment was designed with independent variables: *Technique* (Depth Ray, Depth-Casting, Solar-Casting), *Occluded* (None-Occluded, Partial-Occluded, Full-Occluded), and *Block* (1–4). As targets were all presented in front the user (at least 0.6 m away from users), the distance D between two consecutive goal target was chosen from 0.3 m, 0.6 m, 0.9 m, so ID ranged from 2.58 to 4.00 bits given that target width was still 0.06 m. Given the difficulty of the task, the number of trails per condition was reduced to 8. Therefore, each participant performed 3 *Technique* × 3 *Occlusion* × 4 *Block* × 8 trials = 288 trials.

6.2 Participants

We recruited 12 participants, exclusive from User Study 1, from our organization, aged from 21 to 31 ($\mu = 25.5$, $\sigma = 3.1$), of which 4 were female, all were right-handed and 2 were experienced VR users. The study lasted about 90 min.

6.3 Results

Learning Effect. With Box-Cox transformation ($\lambda = -0.1$), a repeated measures ANOVA found a significant effect of *Block* ($F_{3,33} = 2.79$, p = 0.04, $\eta_p^2 = 0.05$) on ST. However, pairwise t-test did not report any significance between blocks. Therefore, all 4 blocks were kept.

Selection Time. We found a significant effect of *Technique* on ST ($F_{2,22} = 23.13$, p < 0.001, $\eta_p^2 = 0.39$). As shown in Fig. 8 (left), the pairwise t-test showed that Depth-Casting (mean = 8.02 s) took significantly longer (p < 0.001) than other techniques: Solar-Casting (6.77 s), Depth Ray (6.78 s). We found a significant effect of *Occlusion* on ST ($F_{2,22} = 593.98$, p < 0.001, $\eta_p^2 = 0.90$). The pairwise t-test showed that participants spent significantly longer time in a partial-occluded environment (4.94 s) than in a none-occluded environment

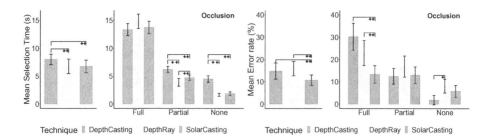

Fig. 8. Mean selection Time (left) and error Rate (right) for *Technique* and its interaction effect with *Occlusion*. Statistical significances are marked (++ = p < 0.01, + = p < 0.05). Error bars represent 95% confidence intervals.

(2.67 s, p < 0.001), yet significantly shorter time than in a full-occlusion environment (13.96 s, p < 0.001). We also found a significant interaction effect between *Occlusion* and *Technique* on ST ($F_{4,44} = 57.00$, p < 0.001, $\eta_p^2 = 0.38$). In both non- and partial-occluded environments, Depth-Casting (4.48 s & 6.23 s respectively) was significantly slower (p < 0.001) than Solar-Casting (1.88 s & 4.70 s respectively) and Depth Ray (1.65 s & 3.88 s respectively) while in the full-occlusion environment, there was no significant difference though Depth Ray (14.81 s) was relatively slower than Depth-Casting (13.34 s) and Solar-Casting (13.72 s).

Error Rate. We found a significant effect of *Technique* on $\%_{Err}$ ($F_{2,412} = 9.19$, p < 0.001, $\eta_p^2 = 0.04$). The pairwise comparison showed that Solar-Casting (10.72%) was significantly more accurate than Depth-Casting (14.85%) and Depth Ray (15.96%). We also found a significant effect of *Occlusion* on $\%_{Err}$ ($F_{2,412} = 62.77$, p < 0.001, $\eta_p^2 = 0.23$). Obviously, error rate increased while the occlusion level increased. Participants performed significantly more accurate selection in the non-occluded environment (5.21%) than in the partially- (14.14%) and fully-occluded (22.18%) environments. We also found a significant interaction effect of *Technique* and *Occlusion* on $\%_{Err}$ ($F_{4,412} = 10.83$, p < 0.001, $\eta_p^2 = 0.10$). While Depth-Casting and Depth Ray made significantly more erroneous selections in the full-occlusion environment than in the partial-occlusion environment, Solar-Casting still achieved high accuracy in both environments (fully-occluded: 13.41%, partially-occluded: 13.02%).

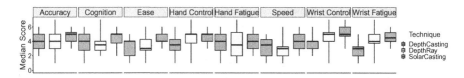

Fig. 9. The median score and lower/upper quartiles are visualized for each measure. Lower scores indicate worse performance.

Preference. Friedman tests reported a significant effect of *Technique* on Wrist Control and Fatigue: $\chi^2_{WristControl}(4) = 14.00$, $p < 0.001$, $\chi^2_{WristFatigue}(4) = 12.19$, $p < 0.01$. The pairwise Wilcox test reported that DepthCasting demanded significantly ($p < 0.05$) more wrist control and caused significantly ($p < 0.05$) more wrist fatigue than Solar-Casting. Figure 9 also showed that Solar-Casting had relatively high scores across all attributes.

Given the local transparency function of Depth Ray, some participants reported that it was difficult to see where the goal target was in the full-occlusion environment as targets outside the transparency volume and in front of the goal target in depth might block the view. To handle this issue, some participants (P1,P3-P6,P9) believed that a global filtering mechanism along the ray would be much welcome in Depth Ray, instead of on the cursor. As Solar-Casting supported global filtering, P5 and P7 felt Solar-Casting needed careful manipulation, (P5: *I like Solar-Casting, but I found Depth-Casting very fast at searching targets*). Similarly, P3 commented that the tilting mechanism in Depth-Casting was better than finger swiping in Solar-Casting or Depth Ray, yet P6 prefer swiping over tilting.

Discussion. In this study, we noted that, across all occlusion levels, Solar-Casting outperformed Depth-Casting in terms of speed, and outperformed both Depth-Casting and Depth Ray in terms of error rate. While Solar-Casting's and Depth Ray's speed was near identical in our experiment – their speeds differ by less than 2%, not significant – Solar-Casting's lower overall error rate argued for the effectiveness of SolarCasting for elegantly supporting selection regardless of level of occlusion.

Looking, specifically, at levels of occlusion, we saw that Solar-Casting's significant accuracy advantage was particularly acute for the full occlusion condition, and that Depth Ray was consistently less accurate. Further, we saw that, regardless of occlusion level, Depth-Casting was significantly slower than both Solar-Casting and Depth Ray. Solar-Casting's and Depth Ray's speed parity holds across occlusion levels (see Fig. 8).

7   Overall Discussion

As we note in our second study, our final Solar-Casting design supports high accuracy, particularly for fully-occluded contexts, and its speed is at least as good as competing techniques regardless of occlusion levels. Together, these results demonstrate that Solar-Casting achieved our design goals.

The target layouts, Fig. 5, were initially inspired by [47], and serve to create occluding distractors around targets. We noted that occlusion in VR could happen with/without visual guidance, and within/outside the fov; therefore, our designs in both studies were, essentially, a generalized version of [52]. This balance between preserving aspects of prior study design while seeking more representative tasks is challenging, and does represent a potential limitation.

While Solar-Casting appears highly effective for supporting selection despite occlusion, there are ways that Solar-Casting could be enhanced, particularly with respect to control of the Solar's volume. Compared with techniques using a spherical volume [9, 23] at the end of a ray, Solar-Casting required increased effort to point at occluded objects at a large distance because users needed to perform repeated scaling actions, i.e. *clutching*, to increase the volume of *Solar* and filter occluders. We continue to explore clutching-mitigation strategies, including tuned CD gain functions for controlling Solar's radius, which may reduce clutching and further speed performance.

Looking specifically at Depth Ray and Solar-Casting, we discovered that compared with local filtering, global filtering greatly increased the accuracy but not speed of selection. During the search-point process, participants' attention was limited regardless of the filtering range, while this range controlled the presence of occluders. Meanwhile, comparing results in two studies, we observed that visual guidance not only greatly increased the accuracy but also the speed of selection. This is understandable as visual guidance is a strong stimulus to improve participants' attention. Therefore, future work also includes investigating approaches to improve users' attention with Solar-Casting.

We used the Huawei VR glass, a system in which the connected phone serves as both the computing and input device. One advantage of this setup is simpler configuration (the smartphone is "at hand") and our smartphone-based implementation of Depth Ray and Expand is useful as it demonstrates their performance on smartphones (as opposed to a dedicated controller). However, Solar-Casting is independent of the input device or HMD. It can be generalized using any other headsets and input devices with suitable mapping on *Solar*'s scaling and rotation parameters. Exploring optimal mappings for varied hardware controllers is another avenue of future work.

To highlight Solar-Casting's benefits in virtual environments with occlusion, we conclude by demonstrating Solar-Casting's use in two scenarios to manage occlusion. In Fig. 10 (a), we created an interior design example, where SemiT is applied to the environment globally such that pillars become translucent so users can easily point at the partially occluded chair. Similarly, in a fully-occluded environment, like a refrigerator in Fig. 10 (b), users can gradually scale *Solar*, filter unwanted food items and then point at the occluded bowl.

(a) Pointing at a partially occluded chair   (b) Acquiring a fully occluded bowl

Fig. 10. Two typical scenarios in virtual environment: Solar-Casting can easily be applied in either (a) a partial-occlusion environments or (b) full-occlusion environments to achieve fast and stable target acquisition.

8 Conclusion

In this paper, we present Solar-Casting, a dynamic pointing technique for global filtering and selection in occluded virtual environments. Solar-Casting uses a scalable, semi-transparent sphere as the reference for object manipulation and filtering to address occlusion. In a pilot study evaluating three filtering modes – Rotate, Hide and SemiT – we find that Hide and SemiT have better performance, and SemiT improves users' awareness of the environment. We then evaluate Solar-Casting's performance in two formal experiments. In the first, we compare Solar-Casting with several techniques with a visual cue pointing to occluded targets. We find that Solar-Casting has competitive performance. However, the advantage of Solar-Casting is that it supports search and selection concurrently, even when target locations are not known *a priori*. To highlight Solar-Casting's search advantages, in a second experiment we evaluate Solar-Casting without visual guidance. We find that Solar-Casting achieves significantly more accurate selection without any degradation in speed, regardless of occlusion level. Overall, these findings demonstrate that Solar-Casting is an effective tool to support search and target acquisition in cluttered virtual environments.

Acknowledgements. We would like to thank Roger Luo and Shino Che Yan for their help in creating Figs. 1–3, Chaoran Chen for his help in organizing and conducting studies remotely, all participants for their help in this difficult time, and reviewers for their valuable feedback. This research received ethics clearance from the Office of Research Ethics, University of Waterloo. This research was funded by a grant from Waterloo-Huawei Joint Innovation Laboratory.

References

1. Argelaguet, F., Andujar, C.: Efficient 3d pointing selection in cluttered virtual environments. IEEE Comput. Graph. Appl. **29**(6), 34–43 (2009)
2. Argelaguet, F., Andujar, C.: A survey of 3d object selection techniques for virtual environments. Comput. Graph. **37**(3), 121–136 (2013)
3. Bacim, F., Kopper, R., Bowman, D.A.: Design and evaluation of 3d selection techniques based on progressive refinement. Int. J. Hum. Comput. Stud. **71**(7–8), 785–802 (2013)
4. Baloup, M., Pietrzak, T., Casiez, G.: Raycursor: a 3d pointing facilitation technique based on raycasting. In: Proceedings of the 2019 CHI Conference on Human Factors in Computing Systems, pp. 1–12 (2019)
5. Bowman, D., Kruijff, E., LaViola, J.J., Jr., Poupyrev, I.P.: 3D User Interfaces: Theory and Practice. Addison-Wesley, CourseSmart eTextbook (2004)
6. Bowman, D., Wingrave, C., Campbell, J., Ly, V.: Using pinch gloves (tm) for both natural and abstract interaction techniques in virtual environments (2001)
7. Bowman, D.A., Hodges, L.F.: An evaluation of techniques for grabbing and manipulating remote objects in immersive virtual environments. In: Proceedings of the 1997 Symposium on Interactive 3D Graphics, pp. 35-ff (1997)
8. Box, G.E.P., Cox, D.R.: An analysis of transformations. J. Roy. Stat. Soc. Ser. B (Methodol.) **26**(2), 211–252 (1964)

9. Cashion, J., Wingrave, C., LaViola, J.J., Jr.: Dense and dynamic 3d selection for game-based virtual environments. IEEE Trans. Vis. Comput. Graph. **18**(4), 634–642 (2012)

10. Casiez, G., Roussel, N., Vogel, D.: 1€filter: a simple speed-based low-pass filter for noisy input in interactive systems. In: Proceedings of the SIGCHI Conference on Human Factors in Computing Systems, pp. 2527–2530 (2012)

11. Chen, Y., Katsuragawa, K., Lank, E.: Understanding viewport-and world-based pointing with everyday smart devices in immersive augmented reality. In: Proceedings of the 2020 CHI Conference on Human Factors in Computing Systems, pp. 1–13 (2020)

12. Chen, Y., Sun, J., Xu, Q., Lank, E., Irani, P., Li, W.: Empirical evaluation of moving target selection in virtual reality using egocentric metaphors. In: IFIP Conference on Human-Computer Interaction. Springer (2021)

13. Coffin, C., Hollerer, T.: Interactive perspective cut-away views for general 3d scenes. In: 3D User Interfaces (3DUI 2006),pp. 25–28. IEEE (2006)

14. Elkin, L.A., Kay, M., Higgins, J.J., Wobbrock, J.O.: An aligned rank transform procedure for multifactor contrast tests (2021)

15. Elmqvist, N.: BalloonProbe: reducing occlusion in 3d using interactive space distortion. In: Proceedings of the ACM symposium on Virtual Reality Software and Technology, pp. 134–137 (2005)

16. Elmqvist, N., Assarsson, U., Tsigas, P.: Employing dynamic transparency for 3d occlusion management: design issues and evaluation. In: Baranauskas, C., Palanque, P., Abascal, J., Barbosa, S.D.J. (eds.) INTERACT 2007. LNCS, vol. 4662, pp. 532–545. Springer, Heidelberg (2007). https://doi.org/10.1007/978-3-540-74796-3_54

17. Elmqvist, N., Tsigas, P.: A taxonomy of 3d occlusion management for visualization. IEEE Trans. Vis. Comput. Graph. **14**(5), 1095–1109 (2008)

18. Feiner, A.O.S.: The flexible pointer: an interaction technique for selection in augmented and virtual reality. Proc. UIST. **3**, 81–82 (2003)

19. Grossman, T., Balakrishnan, R.: The bubble cursor: enhancing target acquisition by dynamic resizing of the cursor's activation area. In: Proceedings of the SIGCHI Conference on Human Factors in Computing Systems, pp. 281–290 (2005)

20. Grossman, T., Balakrishnan, R.: The design and evaluation of selection techniques for 3d volumetric displays. In: Proceedings of the 19th Annual ACM Symposium On User Interface Software and Technology, pp. 3–12 (2006)

21. Katzakis, N., Kiyokawa, K., Takemura, H.: Plane-casting: 3d cursor control with a smartphone. In: Proceedings of the 11th Asia Pacific Conference on Computer Human Interaction, pp. 199–200 (2013)

22. Katzakis, N., Teather, R.J., Kiyokawa, K., Takemura, H.: INSPECT: extending plane-casting for 6-DOF control. HCIS **5**(1), 22 (2015)

23. Kopper, R., Bacim, F., Bowman, D.A.: Rapid and accurate 3d selection by progressive refinement. In: 2011 IEEE Symposium on 3D User Interfaces (3DUI), pp. 67–74. IEEE (2011)

24. Liang, J., Green, M.: Geometric modeling using six degrees of freedom input devices. In: 3rd Int'l Conference on CAD and Computer Graphics, pp. 217–222. Citeseer (1993)

25. Lu, Y., Yu, C., Shi, Y.: Investigating bubble mechanism for ray-casting to improve 3d target acquisition in virtual reality. In: 2020 IEEE Conference on Virtual Reality and 3D User Interfaces (VR). IEEE (2020)

26. MacKenzie, I.S.: Fitts' law as a research and design tool in human-computer interaction. Hum.-Comput. Interact. **7**(1), 91–139 (1992). https://doi.org/10.1207/s15327051hci0701_3

27. Mine, M.R.: Virtual environment interaction techniques. UNC Chapel Hill CS Dept. (1995)

28. Montano, R., Nguyen, C., Kazi, R.H., Subramanian, S., DiVerdi, S., Martinez-Plasencia, D.: Slicing volume: hybrid 3d/2d multi target selection technique for dense virtual environments. In: 2020 IEEE Conference on Virtual Reality and 3D User Interfaces (VR). IEEE (2020)

29. Moore, A., Kodeih, M., Singhania, A., Wu, A., Bashir, T., McMahan, R.: The importance of intersection disambiguation for virtual hand techniques. In: 2019 IEEE International Symposium on Mixed and Augmented Reality (ISMAR), pp. 310–317. IEEE (2019)

30. Mossel, A., Koessler, C.: Large scale cut plane: An occlusion management technique for immersive dense 3d reconstructions. In: Proceedings of the 22nd ACM Conference on Virtual Reality Software and Technology, pp. 201–210 (2016)

31. Ouramdane, N., Otmane, S., Davesne, F., Mallem, M.: FOLLOW-ME: a new 3d interaction technique based on virtual guides and granularity of interaction. In: Proceedings of the 2006 ACM International Conference on Virtual Reality Continuum and Its Applications, p. 137–144. VRCIA 2006, Association for Computing Machinery, New York, NY, USA (2006). https://doi.org/10.1145/1128923.1128945

32. Pierce, J.S., Forsberg, A.S., Conway, M.J., Hong, S., Zeleznik, R.C., Mine, M.R.: Image plane interaction techniques in 3d immersive environments. In: Proceedings of the 1997 Symposium on Interactive 3D Graphics, pp. 39-ff (1997)

33. Pietroszek, K., Wallace, J.R., Lank, E.: Tiltcasting: 3D interaction on large displays using a mobile device. In: Proceedings of the 28th Annual ACM Symposium on User Interface Software and Technology, pp. 57–62 (2015)

34. Pindat, C., Pietriga, E., Chapuis, O., Puech, C.: Drilling into complex 3D models with gimlenses. In: Proceedings of the 19th ACM Symposium on Virtual Reality Software and Technology, p. 223–230. VRST 2013, Association for Computing Machinery, New York, NY, USA (2013). https://doi.org/10.1145/2503713.2503714

35. Poupyrev, I., Billinghurst, M., Weghorst, S., Ichikawa, T.: The go-go interaction technique: non-linear mapping for direct manipulation in VR. In: Proceedings of the 9th Annual ACM Symposium on User Interface Software and Technology, pp. 79–80 (1996)

36. Poupyrev, I., Ichikawa, T., Weghorst, S., Billinghurst, M.: Egocentric object manipulation in virtual environments: empirical evaluation of interaction techniques. In: Computer Graphics Forum, vol. 17, pp. 41–52. Wiley Online Library (1998)

37. Ro, H., et al.: A dynamic depth-variable ray-casting interface for object manipulation in ar environments. In: 2017 IEEE International Conference on Systems, Man, and Cybernetics (SMC), pp. 2873–2878. IEEE (2017)

38. Shoemake, K.: ARCBALL: a user interface for specifying three-dimensional orientation using a mouse. Graph. Interface **92**, 151–156 (1992)

39. Siddhpuria, S., Malacria, S., Nancel, M., Lank, E.: Pointing at a distance with everyday smart devices. In: Proceedings of the 2018 CHI Conference on Human Factors in Computing Systems, pp. 1–11 (2018)

40. Sidenmark, L., Clarke, C., Zhang, X., Phu, J., Gellersen, H.: Outline pursuits: gaze-assisted selection of occluded objects in virtual reality (2020)

41. Sun, C.: Xpointer: an x-ray telepointer for relaxed-space-time wysiwis and unconstrained collaborative 3d design systems. In: Proceedings of the 2013 Conference on Computer Supported Cooperative Work, pp. 729–740 (2013)

42. Sun, J., Stuerzlinger, W.: Selecting invisible objects. In: 2018 IEEE Conference on Virtual Reality and 3D User Interfaces (VR), pp. 697–698. IEEE (2018)

43. Sun, J., Stuerzlinger, W.: Extended sliding in virtual reality. In: 25th ACM Symposium on Virtual Reality Software and Technology, pp. 1–5 (2019)

44. Sun, J., Stuerzlinger, W.: Selecting and sliding hidden objects in 3D desktop environments. In: Proceedings of the 45th Graphics Interface Conference on Proceedings of Graphics Interface 2019, pp. 1–8. Canadian Human-Computer Communications Society (2019)

45. Sun, J., Stuerzlinger, W., Shuralyov, D.: Shift-sliding and depth-pop for 3d positioning. In: Proceedings of the 2016 Symposium on Spatial User Interaction, pp. 69–78 (2016)

46. Sun, M., Cao, M., Wang, L., Qian, Q.: PhoneCursor: improving 3d selection performance with mobile device in AR. IEEE Access **8**, 70616–70626 (2020)

47. Vanacken, L., Grossman, T., Coninx, K.: Exploring the effects of environment density and target visibility on object selection in 3d virtual environments. In: 2007 IEEE Symposium on 3D User Interfaces. IEEE (2007)

48. Wacker, P., Nowak, O., Voelker, S., Borchers, J.: Arpen: Mid-air object manipulation techniques for a bimanual AR system with pen and smartphone. In: Proceedings of the 2019 CHI Conference on Human Factors in Computing Systems, pp. 1–12 (2019)

49. Williams, E.: Experimental designs balanced for the estimation of residual effects of treatments (1949). https://doi.org/10.1071/CH9490149

50. Wobbrock, J.O., Findlater, L., Gergle, D., Higgins, J.J.: The aligned rank transform for nonparametric factorial analyses using only anova procedures. In: Proceedings of the SIGCHI Conference on Human Factors in Computing Systems, pp. 143–146 (2011)

51. Wu, S., Chellali, A., Otmane, S., Moreau, G.: TouchSketch: a touch-based interface for 3d object manipulation and editing. In: Proceedings of the 21st ACM Symposium on Virtual Reality Software and Technology. p. 59–68. VRST 2015, Association for Computing Machinery, New York, NY, USA (2015). https://doi.org/10.1145/2821592.2821606

52. Yu, D., Zhou, Q., Newn, J., Dingler, T., Velloso, E., Goncalves, J.: Fully-occluded target selection in virtual reality. IEEE Trans. Vis. Comput. Graph. **26**(12), 3402–3413 (2020). https://doi.org/10.1109/TVCG.2020.3023606

Real vs Simulated Foveated Rendering to Reduce Visual Discomfort in Virtual Reality

Ariel Caputo[1]([✉])[ID], Andrea Giachetti[1][ID], Salwa Abkal[2], Chiara Marchesini[2], and Massimo Zancanaro[2,3][ID]

[1] Department of Computer Science, University of Verona, Verona, Italy
ariel.caputo@univr.it
[2] Department of Psychology and Cognitive Science, University of Trento, Trento, Italy
[3] Fondazione Bruno Kessler, Trento, Italy

Abstract. In this paper, a study aimed at investigating the effects of real (using eye tracking to determine the fixation) and simulated foveated blurring in immersive Virtual Reality is presented. Techniques to reduce the optical flow perceived at the visual field margins are often employed in immersive Virtual Reality environments to alleviate discomfort experienced when the visual motion perception does not correspond to the body's acceleration. Although still preliminary, our results suggest that for participants with higher self-declared sensitivity to sickness, there might be an improvement for nausea when using blurring. The (perceived) difficulty of the task seems to improve when the real foveated method is used.

Keywords: Virtual Reality · Motion sickness · Foveated rendering

1 Introduction

The perceptual mismatch in sensory cues between the vestibular and the visual systems is known to induce in human subjects the so-called motion sickness that may strongly affect users' experience in Virtual Reality (VR) where they navigate synthetic environments while being still [9]. The visual discomfort can harm the diffusion and acceptance of immersive VR applications [13].

As discomfort is often related to the optical flow perceived at the margins of the field of view, a potential solution to reduce this effect is to reduce the amount of this optical flow. A reasonable way to do this consists of blurring or obscuring the images at the margins of the field of view (marginal blurring/FOV reduction). An approximation of foveated rendering can be obtained by assuming that the user's gaze is consistently directed along the virtual camera axis. Therefore, image quality is varied with the distance from the center of the viewpoint [12].

Nowadays, low-cost eye-tracking devices are integrated into several Head Mounted Displays for Virtual Reality, making it possible to implement a truly

© IFIP International Federation for Information Processing 2021
Published by Springer Nature Switzerland AG 2021
C. Ardito et al. (Eds.): INTERACT 2021, LNCS 12936, pp. 177–185, 2021.
https://doi.org/10.1007/978-3-030-85607-6_12

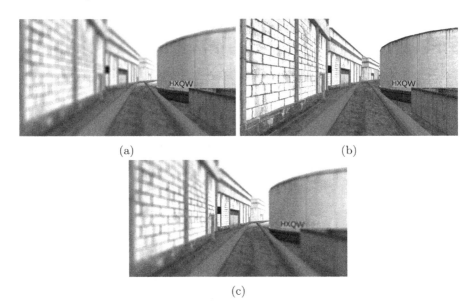

(a)   (b)

(c)

Fig. 1. The three rendering methods used in the study. (a) (Real) foveated: the user is looking at the visual target on the right (in focus), and the rest of the image is blurred. (b) No effects: everything is in focus. (c) Marginal blur (simulated foveated): the gaze is assumed in the center of the image, and pixels far from it, including the visual target, are blurred

foveated rendering, modifying the image's appearance far from the actual user's gaze point. A few recent papers [1,11] proposed the use of eye-tracking to implement foveated rendering for the reduction of motion sickness.

There is some empirical evidence on the positive effect of optical flow reduction techniques (for example, [1,5]). Yet, the advantage of using a foveated approach by tracking the user's gaze rather than a simulated one (assuming that the gaze point coincides with the image center) has not been thoroughly investigated, at least for the blurring technique.

In this work, we explicitly investigated the differences between real and simulated foveated blurring rendering while moving on a roller coaster in an immersive VR environment. Figure 1 exemplifies the effect seen by users in the two foveated conditions with respect to a view when no effects have been applied. To engage participants in being actively scanning the environment, we asked them to perform a recognition task. We did not expect improvements in the recognition task since it was just designed to engage participants visually. The blurring effect was not so strong to prevent recognition of the surroundings.

We expected that both real and simulated foveated blurring reduced in some respect visual discomfort or the task difficulty and real foveated being better than the simulated one. Specifically, we measured visual discomfort using a reduced version of the validated questionnaire proposed by Sevinc and colleagues [15] that consider three scales for nausea, oculomotor fatigue and disorientation.

2   Related Work

A large amount of research work has been dedicated to the study of visually-induced motion sickness (VIMS) [9,14]. Several authors agree on the necessity of finding good strategies to reduce this effect in virtual environments, and different approaches based on specifically designed rendering solutions have been proposed.

Carnegie and Rhee [5] proposed a dynamic depth of field blurring to reduce the amount of perceived motion showing a reduction of nausea and disorientation discomfort in a user study.

Fernandes and Feiner [7] proposed a dynamic reduction of the field of view that seems to help the participants of a user study to stay in the Virtual Environment longer and feel more comfortable than they did in the control condition.

Buhler et al. [3] proposed two visual effects: the "circle effect" (blending the view of a different static camera outside a circle) and the "dot effect", (adding rendered dots in peripheral vision that counteracts the virtual motion of the environment when the user is moving), to alter the visualization in the peripheral area of the perceived visual image aiming at reducing effective optical flow. The study did not show significant effects for reducing VR sickness due to the large variability of the effects.

Cao et al. [4] proposed the addition of static rest frames and dynamic rest frames (with velocity-dependent opacity) to limit sickness. Nie et al. [10] used adaptive blurring of the background. The method detects not salient regions and applies selective blurring only to them.

FOV reduction, DOF blurring, and rest-frame have been compared in a racing game task in [16]. A comparison of some of those techniques is proposed in [6]. The study suggested a weaker effect of the rest frame with respect to other methods.

A selection of the methods has also been implemented in a Unity toolkit and made available in an open-source repository [2].

As suggested in [11], gaze estimation might be an effective approach to select the regions where applying optical flow reduction. The use of eye-tracking to control sickness reduction algorithms has been proposed first in [1]. In this work, the authors compare foveated vs non-foveated large FOV reductions without specific tasks performed by the users.

In this work, we aimed to assess the effect on real vs. simulated foveated blurring empirically. Our study complement and extend the results provided by Carnegie and Rhee [5] on foveated blurring while offering empirical support to the approach of using "real" foveated as initially proposed by Pai and colleagues [11].

3   VR Environment and Task

The VR environment used for the study realizes a roller coaster simulation with a heavily textured scene with a relevant optical flow at the margins of the visual field to foster sickness (Fig. 2). This setting has been chosen because of its natural form of constrained navigation, limiting possible biases related to user control.

The simulation program was implemented in the Unity framework. The VR experience was created to use HTC Vive Pro Eye Head-Mounted Display (HMD) equipped with 120 Hz eye-tracking technology. In each ride, the user goes through a VR roller coaster experience in which they are sitting in a cart, moving automatically through the course that consisted of a set of rails organized in a closed loop. The course features a variety of turns, uphill and downhill sections, and speed variations introduced to induce motion sickness. A full lap around the course track takes about 160 s.

The simulation can be executed with three different visualization modes: *foveated blurring*, in which only a circular area is in focus (centered on the actual user's gaze point as tracked by an eye-tracking device embedded in the HMD) while the rest of the image is blurred; *simulated foveated blurring*, similar to the above but the gaze point is assumed fixed in the middle of the rendered frame; and *no effects*, on which no blurring effects are applied and all the scene in focus.

For both the blurring modes, the in-focus area is a circle with radius r while, outside of it, a Gaussian blur with standard deviation σ is applied. The effect is smoothed from the edge of the in-focus circle with a ramp up parameter that scales linearly with the distance from the center of the circle. The parameters r and σ have been tuned in a set of pilot studies with participants not involved in the main study.

A set of 35 visual targets (similar to those visible in Fig. 1) are placed at different heights and angles on the sides of the track. Each one displays a string of 4 letters. Five of the targets contain the "X" character, and they have to be identified by the users while riding the roller coaster. This recognition task is relatively easy, but it requires active visual search and attention.

Acknowledging the limitations of the eye-tracking device [17], the recognition task has been designed in such a way that visual search does not require frequent and fast head movements.

Fig. 2. View of the roller coaster environment. The user position is anchored to a cart moving on the red rail track surrounded by heavily textured buildings. (Color figure online)

4   The Study

The study design was a full factorial experiment with three within-subject conditions based on the visualization modes described above: (i) *(Real) Foveated*, (ii) *Simulated foveated*, and (iii) *No effects* The study was carried out in the VIPS lab at the University of Verona and received ethical clearance by the Human Research Approval Committee of the same university. The hypotheses were the following:

- *H1*: in general, foveated blurring reduces visual discomfort and the (perceived) task difficulty, with respect to the *no effects* condition (as partially demonstrated by Carnegie & Rhee [5]);
- *H2*: the real foveated blurring technique reduces visual discomfort and task difficulty with respect to simulated blurring (as proposed, without empirical evidence, by Pai et al. [11])

4.1   Participants and Procedure

Thirty-eight (38) participants have been recruited (20 females with age between 18 to 25, 18 males with age between 18 to 25, and 2 males with age between 26 to 30). All of them had normal or corrected to normal vision. Twenty (20) participants had no previous experience with VR, and 13 had only one previous experience.

Each participant was tested individually. Upon arrival, s/he received the informed consent form, the privacy form, and the information about the COVID-19 procedure adopted. S/he was also informed that the experiment can be interrupted at any moment (nobody actually did) and was asked to fill the pre-task questionnaire.

Then, the participant was invited to wear the HMD and perform the eye tracker's calibration. This procedure provided an initial exposition to VR for the participants without previous experience and assessed their willingness to continue the study.

The participant was then assigned to a randomized order and repeated the roller coaster experience in the three conditions. The positions of the targets to recognize were also randomized within the conditions and the participants. Each condition involved one single ride in the roller coaster in one of the visualization modes described above, followed by a 3-min break before starting the next ride. For the recognition task, the participants had to verbally report to the experimenter when they located a target with an "X" inside.

The participant was eventually thanked and dismissed. No compensation was provided for the participation.

4.2   Measurements

A pre-task questionnaire was used to collect demographic information (gender and age), previous experience with VR, self-reported vision problems, self-reported sensitivity to sickness (measured on a 4-item scale from never to very often).

Measures of visual discomfort and task difficulty have been collected after each condition. For measuring visual discomfort, a reduced version of the Simulator Sickness Questionnaire (SSQ) [15] has been used. Specifically, we used the items General discomfort, Fatigue, Eyestrain, Difficulty focusing, Sweating, Nausea, Blurred vision (all 4-point Likert scales from none to severe) which correspond to the scales of Nausea, Oculomotor, and Disorientation.

In order to measure the perceived task difficulty, a single item on a 4-point Likert scale (from very simple to very difficult) has been used.

5   Results

Although the variability in the data is very high (see Table 1), the three SSQ scales have a good level of reliability (their Cronbach's alpha values are 0.71 for the *Nausea* scale, 0.84 for the *Oculomotor* scale and 0.76 for the *Disorientation scale*). It is worth noting that at least part of the variability is due to the self-declared sensitivity to sickness: its Pearson correlation with the *Nausea* scale is $r = 0.48$, $p < 0.01$; with the *Oculomotor* scale is $r = 0.56$, $p < 0.01$ and with the *Disorientation* scale is $r = 0.59$, $p < 0.01$.

A first attempt to fit a Linear Mixed Effect Model on each scale by using both condition and the pre-test variables of gender, sight, and sensitivity to sickness as fixed effects with the individual participants as random effects confirms a statistically significant effect of sickness on each scale and also an effect of condition on the *Nausea* and *Disorientation* scales (but not for *Oculomotor* scale). Neither gender nor sight have statistically significant effects.

Friedman non-parametric tests (using the individuals as grouping variable) revealed a difference between the three conditions on the *Nausea* scale (Friedman, $f = 10.84$, $p < 0.01$), and Conover post-hoc tests confirm a significant difference between the *no effects condition* and the other two (respectively $p = 0.0054$ for *foveated* vs *no effects* and $p = 0.0054$ for *simulated* vs *no effects*) but no difference between *foveated* and *simulated*. No statistical differences were found for the other two scales (respectively, Friedman $f = 1.54$, $p = 0.46$ for *Oculomotor* and Friedman $f = 3.36$, $p = 0.19$ for *Disorientation*). A significant effect has been found for the difficulty of task (Friedman $f = 12.12$, $p < 0.01$). Conover post-hoc tests confirm a difference between *foveated* and *simulated* conditions ($p < 0.01$) and between *no effects* and *simulated* ($p < 0.01$) but not between *foveated* and *no effects*.

To better discount the effect of self-declared sensitivity to sickness, we decided to categorize sickness as low when the value of self-declared sensitivity to sickness was equal to 1 and high for the values 2, 3 and 4. This procedure partitioned the data into two groups of 21 participants with *low sensitivity to sickness* and 17 participants with *high sensitivity to sickness*.

Among the participants with *low sensitivity to sickness*, a Friedman non-parametric tests (using the individuals as grouping variable) revealed a difference among the three conditions for the *Nausea* scale (Friedman, $f = 9.29$, $p < 0.01$), and Conover post-hoc tests confirm a significant difference between the

Table 1. Means and standard deviations in the different conditions and levels of sensitivity of sickness. The values displayed in bold have statistical significant difference with the others across the same condition.

	Scale nausea			Scale oculomotor			Scale disorient.			Task difficulty		
	All	Low sick	High sick	All	Low sick	High sick	All	Low sick	High sick	All	Low sick	High sick
Foveated	1.90	1.74	2.92	2.02	1.87	3.00	1.83	1.68	**2.83**	2.07	1.96	2.50
	(.74)	(.67)	(.17)	(.67)	(.53)	(.41)	(.72)	(.56)	**(.88)**	(.69)	(.66)	(.50)
No effects	**2.07**	**1.91**	3.08	2.01	1.85	3.06	1.89	1.72	3.00	2.13	2.03	2.25
	(.79)	**(.70)**	(.57)	(.71)	(.55)	(.83)	(.71)	(.54)	(.72)	(.63)	(.60)	(.50)
Simulated	1.92	1.74	3.08	2.08	1.88	3.38	1.96	1.78	**3.08**	**2.40**	**2.31**	3.00
	(.77)	(.66)	(.32)	(.77)	(.58)	(.60)	(.74)	(.60)	**(.63)**	**(.77)**	**(.74)**	(.82)

no effects condition and the other two (respectively $p < 0.05$ for *foveated* vs *no effect* and $p < 0.01$ for *simulated* vs *no effects*) but no difference between *foveated* and *simulated*. No statistical differences were found for the other two scales (respectively, Friedman $f = 0.12$, $p = 0.94$ for *Oculomotor* and Friedman $f = 0.047$, $p = 0.98$ for *Disorientation*). A significant effect has been found for *difficulty of task* (Friedman $f = 8.16$, $p = 0.01$). Conover post-hoc tests confirm a difference between *foveated* and *simulated* conditions and between *no effects* and *simulated* but not between *foveated* and *no effects*.

For the participants with (self-declared) *high sensitivity on sickness*, there is no difference for the *Nausea* scale (Friedman $f = 2.63$, $p = 0.27$) nor for the *Oculomotor* scale (Friedman $f = 4.38$, $p = 0.11$) and the *task difficulty* item (Friedman $f = 4.8$, $p = 0.09$). There is a statistically significant effect for the *Disorientation* scale (Friedman $f = 7.66$, $p < 0.05$). Conover post-hoc tests reveal a difference between *foveated* and *simulated* but not between those two and no effect. As expected, there are no differences in the recognition task: 94% of the participants recognized more than 4 targets and only 5 participants recognized 3 or less.

6   Discussion

Our results, although still preliminary, provide evidence that both techniques of foveated blurring reduce visual discomfort (hypothesis H1), specifically for nausea, while the real foveated reduces the perceived task difficulty (hypothesis H2), but only for users with low sensitivity to sickness. Participants with high sensitivity for sickness do not seem to benefit from the blurring techniques for reducing nausea or the perceived task difficulty. Still, we found a small effect on reducing disorientation.

Although still preliminary, our results consider the moderating effect of individual sensitivity to sickness and provide some evidence that it plays a role in the foveated rendering effect. In this respect, it contributes with new evidence to the growing body of research. Indeed, the variations in the scores, although small, were, at least for the *Nausea* and *Disorientation* scales in line with those found in other studies [1,5].

Differently from previous works, we had noticeable effect only on the *Nausea* and *Disorientation* scale and not on the *Oculomotor* scale for the SSQ. That might be due to the constrained navigation or the short duration of the ride that could have limited the VR experience's sickness effect. Another explanation might be that our task required more cognitive attention than simple navigational tasks used in other studies, and that may have an impact on the perception of ocular strain [8].

Another novel result is that we also measured the effect on the perceived task difficulty and observed a small but significant effect, particularly in differentiating real from simulated foveated blurring.

Our experiment had some weaknesses and limitations that we plan to overcome in future studies. The single session duration was perhaps too short to create a relevant sickness on many subjects. The number of subjects tested was higher than in other studies but still limited;. It would be better to have a larger number of participants would allow to using more powerful statistical tools. Both the sensitivity level of sickness and the experienced sickness were self-reported while in further studies they should be objectively measured.

For active recognition, it would also be helpful to use a more challenging task. Although we still believe that an active task helps control the participants' engagement with the environment, our task was probably too easy.

Finally, an important issue to be considered is related to the accuracy and the latency of the eye tracker. Recent studies [17] revealed that the device we used is less precise and accurate far from the center of the headset FOV. The latency of the tracking could, in principle, also limit the sickness reduction.

7   Conclusion

In conclusion, our results suggest that for participants with higher self-declared sensitivity to sickness, we found some evidence that the foveated technique provides a small benefit on disorientation for simulated blurring but not enough to improve with respect to applying no effects. For participants with lower sensitivity to sickness, there might be an improvement for nausea when using blurring. Still, the specific technique does not matter, although the (perceived) difficulty of the task seems to improve when the real foveated method is used.

The effects of the differences are minimal (and the sample is small); therefore, the present study results should be considered an indication for further research rather than robust evidence. Nevertheless, we believe that this study contributes to the ongoing discussion on the effects of foveated techniques and, in particular, on the opportunity to implement "real" foveated using eye-tracking. The difference found in our study between participants with different levels of sensitivity to sickness has never been reported in the literature and deserves further investigation.

References

1. Adhanom, I.B., Griffin, N.N., MacNeilage, P., Folmer, E.: The effect of a foveated field-of-view restrictor on VR sickness. In: 2020 IEEE Conference on Virtual Reality and 3D User Interfaces (VR), pp. 645–652. IEEE (2020)
2. Ang, S., Quarles, J.: GingerVR: an open source repository of cybersickness reduction techniques for unity. In: 2020 IEEE Conference on Virtual Reality and 3D User Interfaces Abstracts and Workshops (VRW), pp. 460–463. IEEE (2020)
3. Buhler, H., Misztal, S., Schild, J.: Reducing VR sickness through peripheral visual effects. In: 2018 IEEE Conference on Virtual Reality and 3D User Interfaces (VR), pp. 517–519. IEEE (2018)
4. Cao, Z., Jerald, J., Kopper, R.: Visually-induced motion sickness reduction via static and dynamic rest frames. In: 2018 IEEE Conference on Virtual Reality and 3D User Interfaces (VR), pp. 105–112. IEEE (2018)
5. Carnegie, K., Rhee, T.: Reducing visual discomfort with HMDs using dynamic depth of field. IEEE Comput. Graph. Appl. **35**(5), 34–41 (2015)
6. Choroś, K., Nippe, P.: Software techniques to reduce cybersickness among users of immersive virtual reality environments. In: Nguyen, N.T., Gaol, F.L., Hong, T.-P., Trawiński, B. (eds.) ACIIDS 2019. LNCS (LNAI), vol. 11431, pp. 638–648. Springer, Cham (2019). https://doi.org/10.1007/978-3-030-14799-0_55
7. Fernandes, A.S., Feiner, S.K.: Combating VR sickness through subtle dynamic field-of-view modification. In: 2016 IEEE Symposium on 3D User Interfaces (3DUI), pp. 201–210. IEEE (2016)
8. Iskander, J., Hossny, M., Nahavandi, S.: A review on ocular biomechanic models for assessing visual fatigue in virtual reality. IEEE Access **6**(17), 19345–19361 (2018)
9. Kennedy, R.S., Drexler, J., Kennedy, R.C.: Research in visually induced motion sickness. Appl. Ergon. **41**(4), 494–503 (2010)
10. Nie, G.Y., Duh, H.B.L., Liu, Y., Wang, Y.: Analysis on mitigation of visually induced motion sickness by applying dynamical blurring on a user's retina. IEEE Trans. Visual Comput. Graph. **26**(8), 2535–2545 (2019)
11. Pai, Y.S., Tag, B., Outram, B., Vontin, N., Sugiura, K., Kunze, K.: GazeSim: simulating foveated rendering using depth in eye gaze for VR. In: ACM SIGGRAPH 2016 Posters, pp. 1–2 (2016)
12. Patney, A., et al.: Towards foveated rendering for gaze-tracked virtual reality. ACM Trans. Graph. (TOG) **35**(6), 1–12 (2016)
13. Sagnier, C., Loup-Escande, E., Lourdeaux, D., Thouvenin, I., Valléry, G.: User acceptance of virtual reality: an extended technology acceptance model. Int. J. Hum. Comput. Interact. **36**(11), 993–1007 (2020)
14. Saredakis, D., Szpak, A., Birckhead, B., Keage, H.A., Rizzo, A., Loetscher, T.: Factors associated with virtual reality sickness in head-mounted displays: a systematic review and meta-analysis. Front. Hum. Neurosci. **14**, 96 (2020)
15. Sevinc, V., Berkman, M.I.: Psychometric evaluation of simulator sickness questionnaire and its variants as a measure of cybersickness in consumer virtual environments. Appl. Ergon. **82**, 102958 (2020)
16. Shi, R., Liang, H.N., Wu, Y., Yu, D., Xu, W.: Virtual reality sickness mitigation methods: a comparative study in a racing game. arXiv preprint arXiv:2103.05200 (2021)
17. Sipatchin, A., Wahl, S., Rifai, K.: Accuracy and precision of the HTC VIVE PRO eye tracking in head-restrained and head-free conditions. Investig. Ophthalmol. Visual Sci. **61**(7), 5071 (2020)

Using Technology to Visualize Gender Bias

Sara Tranquada[1,2]($\boxtimes$) ®, Nuno Correia[2] ®, and Karolina Baras[3]

[1] ITI/LARSys, 9020-105 Funchal, Portugal
[2] Nova LINCS, FCT Universidade Nova de Lisboa, Lisbon, Portugal
nmc@fct.unl.pt
[3] Universidade da Madeira, Funchal, Ilha da Madeira, Portugal
karolina.baras@staff.uma.pt

Abstract. Science and technology have been typically associated with masculinity. Research contradicting this belief has been mainly focused on our unconscious awareness. In this paper, we propose two interactive systems designed to make gender bias noticeable. One that combines physical and virtual environment and present the numbers of college applications (Gender by Numbers, that interacts with our conscious mind) and one that uses QR codes to visualize a gender bias riddle (Riddle Me This QR, that interacts with our unconscious mind). We conducted a study that aimed to infer which of the strategies could trigger a difference using the conscious and unconscious measures. We found that Gender by Numbers only reinforced the mentality that men should pursue engineering and women should go into a more characteristic job like kindergarten teacher or nursing. Riddle Me This QR uncover the possibility of mentality change. The next step is up to each individual to have the will to break that prejudice.

Keywords: Gender bias · Technology · High school · Tangible · Riddle

1 Introduction

Social biases have long affected our society [1]. Currently, our global marketplace is more and more guided by technology [2] and men still dominate, despite the vast growth in the number of women in science, technology, engineering and math (STEM) fields [3, 4]. This is a common phenomenon that has long been held true, creating beliefs and assumptions that specific occupations require either masculine or feminine traits – it is what we perceive as a stereotype, matching society's collective knowledge [5, 6]. Whereas prejudice is observed as the operation of social stereotypes [7]. If women enter a technology area, we consider it a win-win for them as the world gains new perspectives on problem-solving [4]. Diversity in the working classes leads to creativity, productivity, and innovation [8]. Research on ways to reduce prejudice has been primarily focused on intergroup interactions with different groups. Gordon Allport was one of those researchers who focused on conscious response and self-reporting. Patricia Devine and others, on the other hand, observed that bias can be engaged in unconscious awareness, hypothesizing that to break the bias habit there must be awareness, motivation and

C. Ardito et al. (Eds.): INTERACT 2021, LNCS 12936, pp. 186–194, 2021.
https://doi.org/10.1007/978-3-030-85607-6_13

training [9–11]. There are at least two ways to raise awareness about implicit bias: one is to openly inform people of its presence with lectures and workshops; the second is making the bias salient, that is, calling attention to the likelihood of a specific bias in others can boost self-awareness of their own biases [9].

2 Related Work

Implicit cognition can be measured using a simple test named The Implicit Association Test (IAT). This test detects our stronger pairs of associations, identifying implicit stereotypes. To understand IAT, imagine you have a basket of apples, both green and red, and you need to separate them as fast as you can, green to the left and red to the right. As the difference between them is the colour, the task is easily done. Now imagine you need to separate them by condition, fresh or rotten (regardless of the colour). Your sorting speed would decline. The IAT uses this tactic to associate our speed with tasks about race, gender, religion, age, and so on [12, 13].

Devine assumed that the implicit bias is identical to a habit, that can be diminished over a mixture of self-awareness, involvement about the hurtful effects of the bias and the deliberated use of strategies to overcome them. In a study, all participants were requested to complete the Race Implicit Association Test, getting their results in the end. While the control group went home, the other group watched a 45-min interaction slideshow that included an education and training piece. In the educational part information was brought in the sense that prejudice was a habit that could be overcome, the development of the implicit bias and its damaging effects. While in the training part strategies were introduced to reduce implicit bias, the acquirer of information about our-group members and it was explained that those strategies needed to be practiced to break the prejudice habit. All participants repeated the measurement in the following two, four, six and eight weeks later. Devine found that those who participated in the intervention had lower their implicit values than the control group, maintaining it, through the eight weeks. The study did not affect the racial attitude nor the motivation, however participants did increase their involvement about discrimination and awareness of their self-bias. In the end, giving the participants strategies to overcome their own bias is not enough, they need to have confidence in themselves that they could use the strategies to overcome their bias [10].

Our work focused on the design and evaluation of two prototypes that uses technology make the bias salient. To that effect, we explored studies related to the extent of the message persuading someone. Baesler and Burgoon [14] were interested in the impact of messages. They bestowed messages centered on statistical evidence and narratives in three time periods (i.e., immediate, 48 h later, one week later). Both demonstrated persuasive power; however, to last at least one week of persuasion, the message had to be composed of statistical and memorable content. A study by Woolley [15], showed evidence that when a group of people cooperate among themselves, their intelligence is greater than a group of individuals. Furthermore, that inclination to cooperate efficiently is related to the number of women in the group. However, when the problem is associated with gender, the efficiency stops. The author Skorinko [16], thought that students could learn about stereotypes if riddles (surgeon is male, surgeon is female) were used in the classroom, discovering first-hand if their ability to solve problems is influenced by stereotypes. "A father and son are in a horrible car crash that kills the dad. The son is rushed to the hospital; just as he's about to go under the knife, the surgeon says, 'I can't operate – that boy is my son!' Who is the surgeon?". In four studies she explored the cognitive performance (time taken to solve and recognition of difficulty), subjective learning (if they learn) and objective learning (knowledge) about gender stereotypes with the use of opposite riddles. Her results showed that both riddles indicated an increased understanding about gender stereotypes (subjective learning). As for the riddle comparison, when the solution was female, students were slower and rated the riddle as difficult, but it provoked a better performance in the quiz (objective learning), unlike when the solution was male.

One study used the combination of the virtual and physical environment to create a preliminary concept to display a gender imbalance of the student's choice for an academic career. Named Gender By Number, with the physical environment as the selection of the sex and academic career of the student while its results would show in the virtual environment show in statistic view [18].

Even though there are studies focused on improving gender inclusiveness in computation [19, 20], some of them believed that the software that people used is the problem: by disrupting the female problem-solving capabilities [21–23]. One example is this study that created the GenderMag (Gender-Inclusiveness Magnifier). This technique aids the creators to detect problems with their software with a "gender-specialized cognitive walkthrough" and a group of Gender Mag personality within the five factors in problem-solving approach: *Motivations*, *Information Processing Styles*, *Computer Self-Efficacy*, *Attitudes toward Risk*, and style of *Learning* new technologies [22].

The present article's goal is to test which type of intervention (Gender by Numbers: conscious or Riddle Me This QR: unconscious) has the demonstrated potential to change stereotypes views on occupation and gender. We predict that Riddle Me This QR that interacts with our unconscious mind would indicate a change in the stereotype views on occupation and gender. For this purpose, we conducted a study with forty-five students to interact with one of the prototypes that will be better explained in the next section.

3   Prototypes

In this study, two prototypes were developed centered on our conscious (Gender by Numbers) and unconscious (Riddle Me This QR) mind. Our aim is to explore how a combined environment (physical and virtual) can facilitate a clear reflection of the uneven number of genders, through statistic (Gender by Numbers) or the answer to a riddle (Riddle Me This QR).

3.1   Measurement of Our Conscious and Unconscious Mind – IAT

As we were interested in one of the topics: Gender - Science (generally associating liberal arts with females and science with males), we reproduced that topic to create a measurement of our conscious and unconscious mind (IAT) about two departments currently available in our hometown University: Exact Sciences and Arts and Humanities. We transformed the eight words [24] into five words to assimilate the degrees available in our hometown University. The five Exact Sciences words (biology, biochemistry, economics, engineering and mathematics), the five Arts and Humanities words (culture, education, communication, languages and psychology), have the equivalent number of female and male gender words; five male gender words (father, uncle, man, grandfather and son) and five female gender words (mother, aunt, woman, grandmother and daughter). Both projects have the same instructions; a computer with a keyboard is needed; the "E" key should be pressed to associate to the group on the left side of the screen and the "I" key for the group on the right. The project is composed of seven parts, only two parts are important to measure the stereotype - part 4 and part 7 – with the rest being mainly for practice (see Appendix A).

The purpose of this project is to measure the time participants take to associate engineering/male and engineering/female, as well as their counterparts, humanities/female and humanities/male. Each word appears 500 ms after interacting with a key, registering the time the user takes to press the correct button (time in milliseconds) and the number of mistakes the user makes. After part 7, the participant's time is calculated by the difference between the time for Engineering/Male against Engineering/Female. At the end of the IAT, the participant is presented with four questions (based on Project Implicit [24], see Appendix B). All the information was saved in a text file.

3.2   Gender by Numbers - Conscious

Gender by Numbers has been recreated based on [18] with the data from our home country. From 1063 degrees, we created 23 names to use as tags (based on the areas established by the Education/Training and Course Area [25]) for example, for the degree Computer Science, we had the name Engineering and Related Areas and 2 tags for sex. All we needed was to associate each tag with the amount of data for each institution. A raspberry pi three and the Phoenix MFRC-522 RFID tags used as the physical environment to show the data in the virtual environment, screen. To interact with the prototype, the user only had to choose a tag corresponding to a course and a tag corresponding to their sex to see the numbers. (See Fig. 1).

Fig. 1. On the left the interface of Gender by Numbers, with the example of the number of male students' applicants in the area of Humanities. The inside of Gender by Numbers. In the middle, we can see the power bank connected to the raspberry pi 3, and on the right, we see the back part of the tag readers.

3.3 Riddle Me This QR – Unconscious

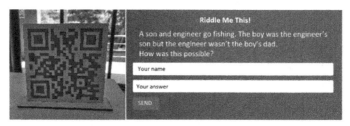

Fig. 2. The two components of Riddle Me This QR. To visualize the riddle, participants had only to access the wifi connection created by the raspberry pi and scan the QR code to access the riddle.

Riddle Me This QR was inspired by [16] but with a different implementation, using QR codes to transmit the riddle. A QR (Quick Response) code is a form of barcode that allows us access to a web information, in this case, a riddle (see Fig. 2). The information of the riddle is stored in the previously mentioned raspberry pi. The QR code generator was used to open a website where the riddle is shown – through the raspberry pi [26]. All answers and participants' names were saved in the raspberry pi.

4   Method

Our study aimed to answer the following questions: *Can the mindset of gender bias of students be changed with technology? Which type of intervention (Gender by Numbers or Riddle Me This QR) has the demonstrated potential to change stereotypes views on occupation and gender?*

4.1 Design

Forty-five students at the local high school (15 female, Mage = 16.71, SDage = 0.99) participated in this study (15 students for each experiment). The study used a between-participants design with a control group (just waits), experiment 1 (Gender by Numbers) group, experiment 2 (Riddle Me This QR), registering the time they took to complete the IAT (milliseconds) and their responses to the explicit test serving as the dependent variables. The study is composed by: (a) IAT, (b) Interaction with one of the prototypes (A or B) or just wait (each with 15 min), (c) IAT.

4.2 Procedure

Before the study, students were asked to take home a written consent form for them and their parents to sign. On the day of the study, students were randomly assigned to three groups: the control group, the Gender by Numbers group and the Riddle Me This QR group. The experiment consisted of three phases. In the first phase, the student had to do the IAT. In the second phase, the student had to interact with one of the prototypes with a maximum duration of 15 min: In experiment 1 (Gender by Numbers), students participated together (based on the fact that when a group of people cooperate among themselves their efficiently is greater than working alone, especially if there are of opposite genders [15]). Interacting with the pieces, to see the real numbers of each course. In experiment 2 (Riddle Me This QR), students interacted with the riddle individually (to learn by themselves about the stereotypes). Finally, in the third phase the student does the IAT.

5 Results

The times of the measurements for the three studies are shown in Table 1. The best result outcome would be in the intervals of −5 to 5 s, i.e., take for example in Table 1, in the control group, the number −12.14 means that the students took 12 s more on average to associate engineering/female than to associate engineering/male. While if the number were positive, the opposite would happen, on average, the students would have taken 12 s more to associate engineering/male than associate engineering/female. As said before the intervals between −5 to 5 are the best outcome as they would associate to any professions as female or male occupation.

Table 1. The average times in seconds for each group in the pre-study, post-study and its difference.

	Pre-study	Post-study	Difference
Control group	−12.14	−11.41	0.73
Gender by numbers	−3.69	−8.25	−4.56
Riddle me this QR	−10.37	1.44	11.80

Table 2. The average time in seconds of each in the pre-study and post-study and its difference in the engineering/male on the left and engineering/female on the right.

Engineering/Male	Pre-study	Post-study	Difference	Engineering/Female	Pre-study	Post-study	Difference
Control group	42.54	36.37	−6.17	Control group	54.68	47.78	−6.90
Gender by numbers	52.96	50.24	−2.72	Gender by numbers	56.65	58.49	1.84
Riddle me this QR	54.51	57.75	3.24	Riddle me this QR	64.88	56.31	−8.57

In the control group, there was not much difference, improving their times by only 1 s. In Gender by Numbers, there was an increase by almost 5 s, and finally, in Riddle Me This QR, we see a very significant improvement, by almost 12 s. Table 2 presents the analysis regarding the engineering/male and engineering/female. With this separation of engineering/male and engineering/female, we better analysed the reason for the previous results (Table 1). In Table 2 on the left, we see that in the control group and the Gender by Numbers group, the average times decrease, this was not observed for the Riddle Me

This QR. In Table 2 on the right, the same happens with the control group, decreasing their times as the Riddle Me This QR group, with an improvement of 9 s.

A Mann-Whitney test was conducted to analyse if there was any difference in the post-study. In the unconscious measure, the times associating engineering/male of the control group (Mdn = 36210 ms) were significantly less than those in the other two groups after interacting with the Gender by Numbers (Mdn = 48945 ms) U = 49, p = 0.008, r = −0.481 and Riddle Me This QR (Mdn = 47790 ms) U = 46, p = .005, r = −0.504. However, only between the experiences was found a significance for the conscious measure, specifically in the third question ("Do you associate engineering to female or male?"). In experiment 1 (Gender by Numbers), students were associating engineering/male (Mdn = 3), while in experiment 2 (Riddle Me This QR), they were associating engineering/ female (Mdn = 4) U = 55, p = .016, r = −0.456.

Analysing the groups individually, the pre-test and post-test with a Wilcoxon Signed Ranks Test, we found that in the control group, the times in engineering/female was compared with the times in engineering/male, the pre-test and post-test. In the pre-test, milliseconds were significantly higher on engineering/female (Mdn = 51577 ms) than on engineering/male (Mdn = 42062 ms), T = 14, p = .009, r = −0.675. The same happened on the post-test, the times in milliseconds were significantly higher on engineering/female (Mdn = 44850 ms) than on engineering/ male (Mdn = 36210 ms), T = 15, p = .011, r = −0.66. For the experiment groups, no significant difference was found for the times they took to associate engineering with females or engineering with males. Nor was the significance found between the explicit questionnaires.

6 Discussion

Our study addresses whether any of the interventions (Gender by Numbers or Riddle Me This QR) shows the potential to change stereotype views on occupation and gender. For this purpose, we collaborated with a high school to interact with their students to answer this question. Our results showed that for the unconscious measure, the students in the control group in the post-study were significantly faster-associating male/engineering than the other two groups (Gender by Numbers and Riddle Me This QR). By analysing the difference between the pre-study and post-study, we can see the effects in implicit measure, while in the control group, the difference is small, in the experiments group, we can see a much larger difference. In the Gender by Numbers, by showing the real numbers of engineering application, it reinforced the mentality that only men should pursue engineering. While in Riddle Me This QR, the opposite happened, the mentality that a woman can pursue engineering appears to be started to get noticed. In the conscious measure, only a significant association was detected between the two experiment groups (Gender by Numbers and Riddle Me This QR). That association was found on the third question ("Do you associate engineering to female or male?"). While in one experiment, an association of engineering/male was detected (Gender by Numbers), in the other (Riddle Me This QR), the opposite was detected, an association of engineering/female. This difference can be explained because each experiment highlights a different part of our mind (unconscious and conscious). While Gender by Numbers highlights the present situation, as there are more men than women in engineering areas, Riddle Me This QR highlights that male are not the only ones that can pursue engineering.

7   Conclusions and Future Work

Tonso and Adichie tell us about their view on what was happening with women and engineering, the very low enrolling numbers, perpetuating it as a male career [27, 28]. High school students used one of the two prototypes mentioned above to visualize which had the demonstration potential to type views on occupation and gender. Both interventions raised interest and curiosity among students. This study suggested that Riddle Me This QR has the potential to drive the change in stereotype views, and the next moves are the individuals' desire or motivation to change. We believe that the use of technology to make the bias salient is a promising new direction for that end. Future work will explore a new prototype that combines the two presented prototypes to combine the best of the two approaches - the numbers and the riddle, the conscious and the unconscious.

Acknowledgment. This research was supported by ARDITI (Agência Regional para o Desenvolvimento da Investigação, Tecnologia e Inovação), Doctoral Grant under the Project M14-20 - 09-5369-FSE-000001.

References

1. Keene, S.: Social bias: prejudice, stereotyping, and discrimination. **1**(3), 5 (2011)
2. National Coalition for Women and Girls in Education: 'Title IX at 45:Advancing Opportunity through Equity in Education' (2017). https://www.ncwge.org/
3. Beede, D.N., Julian, T.A., Langdon, D., McKittrick, G., Khan, B., Doms, M.E.: Women in STEM: a gender gap to innovation. SSRN J. (2011). https://doi.org/10.2139/ssrn.1964782
4. Morrow, M.: Why Our Future Depends on Women in Technology. HuffPost 2017. https://www.huffpost.com/entry/women-in-technology-prospects_b_6102040. Accessed 17 Jun 2020
5. White, M.J., White, G.B.: Implicit and explicit occupational gender stereotypes. Sex Roles **55**(3–4), Article no. 3–4 (2006). https://doi.org/10.1007/s11199-006-9078-z
6. Aronson, J.: The Threat of Stereotype - Educational Leadership (2004). http://www.ascd.org/publications/educational-leadership/nov04/vol62/num03/The-Threat-of-Stereotype.aspx. Accessed 03 May 2021
7. Hilton, J.L., von Hippel, W.: Stereotypes. Annu. Rev. Psychol. **47**(1), 237–271 (1996). https://doi.org/10.1146/annurev.psych.47.1.237
8. Corbett, C., Hill, C.: Solving the Equation: The Variables for Women's Success in Engineering and Computing. AAUW, Washington (2015)
9. Lee, C.: 2017 Awareness as a first step toward overcoming implicit bias. SSRN Electron. J. https://doi.org/10.2139/ssrn.3011381
10. Devine, P.G., Forscher, P.S., Austin, A.J., Cox, W.T.L.: Long-term reduction in implicit race bias: a prejudice habit-breaking intervention. J. Exp. Soc. Psychol. **48**(6), 1267–1278 (2012). https://doi.org/10.1016/j.jesp.2012.06.003
11. Allport, G.W.: The Nature of Prejudice, pp. xviii, 537. Addison-Wesley, Oxford (1954)
12. Greenwald, A.G., Banaji, M.R.: Implicit Social Cognition: Attitudes, Self-esteem, and Stereotypes, p. 24 (1995)
13. Ratliff, K.A., Nosek, B.A.: Negativity and outgroup biases in attitude formation and transfer. Pers. Soc. Psychol. Bull. **37**(12), 1692–1703 (2011). https://doi.org/10.1177/0146167211420168

14. Baesler, E.J., Burgoon, J.K.: The temporal effects of story and statistical evidence on belief change. Commun. Res. **21**(5), 582–602 (1994). https://doi.org/10.1177/009365094021005002
15. Woolley, A.W., Chabris, C.F., Pentland, A., Hashmi, N., Malone, T.W.: Evidence for a collective intelligence factor in the performance of human groups. Science **330**(6004), 686–688 (2010). https://doi.org/10.1126/science.1193147
16. Skorinko, J.L.M.: Riddle me this: using riddles that violate gender stereotypes to demonstrate the pervasiveness of stereotypes. Psychol. Learn. Teach. **17**(2), 194–208 (2018). https://doi.org/10.1177/1475725717752181
17. Wang, T.-L., Tseng, Y.-K.: The comparative effectiveness of physical, virtual, and virtual-physical manipulatives on third-grade students' science achievement and conceptual understanding of evaporation and condensation. Int. J. Sci. Math. Educ. **16**(2), 203–219 (2016). https://doi.org/10.1007/s10763-016-9774-2
18. Tranquada, S., Correia, N., Caraban, A.: Gender by numbers: is your education course dominated by your opposite gender? Presented at the Proceedings of the 32nd International BCS Human Computer Interaction Conference, July 2018. https://doi.org/10.14236/ewic/HCI2018.186
19. Otterbacher, J.: Crowdsourcing stereotypes: linguistic bias in metadata generated via GWAP. In: Proceedings of the 33rd Annual ACM Conference on Human Factors in Computing Systems, Seoul Republic of Korea, April 2015, pp. 1955–1964 (2015). https://doi.org/10.1145/2702123.2702151
20. Metaxa-Kakavouli, D., Wang, K., Landay, J.A., Hancock, J.: Gender-inclusive design: sense of belonging and bias in web interfaces. In: Proceedings of the 2018 CHI Conference on Human Factors in Computing Systems, Montreal QC Canada, April 2018, pp. 1–6 (2018). https://doi.org/10.1145/3173574.3174188
21. Burnett, M., Peters, A., Hill, C., Elarief, N.: Finding gender-inclusiveness software issues with GenderMag: a field investigation. In: Proceedings of the 2016 CHI Conference on Human Factors in Computing Systems, San Jose California USA, May 2016, pp. 2586–2598 (2016). https://doi.org/10.1145/2858036.2858274
22. Hill, C., Ernst, S., Oleson, A., Horvath, A., Burnett, M.: GenderMag experiences in the field: the whole, the parts, and the workload. In: 2016 IEEE Symposium on Visual Languages and Human-Centric Computing (VL/HCC), September 2016, pp. 199–207 (2016). https://doi.org/10.1109/VLHCC.2016.7739685
23. Beckwith, L., Burnett, M., Wiedenbeck, S., Cook, C., Sorte, S., Hastings, M.: Effectiveness of End-User Debugging Software Features: Are There Gender Issues?, p. 10 (2004)
24. Ratliff, K., Bar-Anan, Y., Lai, C., Smith, C.T., Nosek, B., Greenwald, T.: Project Implicit (2011). https://implicit.harvard.edu/implicit/. Accessed 19 June 2020
25. DGES: Acesso ao Ensino Superior 2021 - Índices de Cursos (por área de estudos e curso) (2021). https://www.dges.gov.pt/guias/indarea.asp. Accessed 21 May 2021
26. QR Code Generator (2021). https://app.qr-code-generator.com/site/login#!/?folder=all. Accessed 26 Jan 2021
27. Adichie, C.N.: We Should All Be Feminists, 1st published. Fourth Estate, London (2014)
28. Tonso, K.L.: Engineering Gender - Gendering Engineering: What About Women in Nerd-DOM?, p. 50 (1998)

VRSketch: Investigating 2D Sketching in Virtual Reality with Different Levels of Hand and Pen Transparency

Jonas Auda[✉], Roman Heger, Uwe Gruenefeld, and Stefan Schneegass

University of Duisburg-Essen, Schützenbahn 70, 45127 Essen, Germany
{jonas.auda,roman.heger,uwe.gruenefeld,stefan.schneegass}@uni-due.de
https://www.hci.wiwi.uni-due.de/

Abstract. Sketching is a vital step in design processes. While analog sketching on pen and paper is the defacto standard, Virtual Reality (VR) seems promising for improving the sketching experience. It provides myriads of new opportunities to express creative ideas. In contrast to reality, possible drawbacks of pen and paper drawing can be tackled by altering the virtual environment. In this work, we investigate how hand and pen transparency impacts users' 2D sketching abilities. We conducted a lab study ($N = 20$) investigating different combinations of hand and pen transparency. Our results show that a more transparent pen helps one sketch more quickly, while a transparent hand slows down. Further, we found that transparency improves sketching accuracy while drawing in the direction that is occupied by the user's hand.

Keywords: Virtual Reality · Sketching · Transparency · Occlusion

1 Introduction

Virtual Reality (VR) headsets have become increasingly popular for both consumers and professionals in recent years. While some use their headsets only for entertainment purposes, VR looks promising for serious tasks such as 3D modeling [4], note taking [18], or exploring spreadsheets [7], among others. Bringing existing applications to VR is not restricted to implementing their original functionalities. For sketching, VR allows one to implement new ideas and features that are not feasible in the real world e.g. 3D modeling [11] or sketching in mid-air [4]. Moreover, VR enables users to be immersed in their favorite surroundings without any visual distractions as they would appear, for example, in an open

Electronic supplementary material The online version of this chapter (https://doi.org/10.1007/978-3-030-85607-6_14) contains supplementary material, which is available to authorized users.

C. Ardito et al. (Eds.): INTERACT 2021, LNCS 12936, pp. 195–211, 2021.
https://doi.org/10.1007/978-3-030-85607-6_14

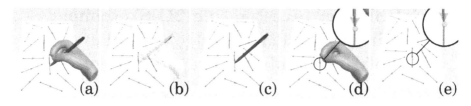

Fig. 1. The five transparency variations of hand and pen for sketching in VR: (a) both opaque $H_{100}P_{100}$, (b) both semitransparent $H_{50}P_{50}$, (c) hand invisible and pen opaque H_0P_{100}, (d) hand opaque and pen is replaced by a cursor $H_{100}P_0$, and (e) only the cursor with invisible pen and hand H_0P_0. *Best seen in color.*

office space. Further, VR allows the investigation of creative content in 3D space alone or together with others [6]. For example, an artist could get an impression of how a painting appears in a museum, gallery, or to viewers. Designers could quickly sketch a logo and add it to a product to get first impressions of their work [12] or feedback from customers. Engineers could sketch ideas, discuss implications of different design decisions in the context of technical drawings. Moreover, physics laws do not restrict the possibilities of such a sketching environment, enabling, for example, a transparent hand or pen which are not prone to occlusion. Nevertheless, while hand or pen transparency for sketching in VR sounds promising, to our knowledge, its effect on user performance has not been investigated in research thus far. Insight into the application of transparency to sketching utilities or the user in VR and its influence on the performance of the user could help VR designers and developers to improve future applications and experiences and enhance user performance by applying transparency to certain virtual objects.

Previous work has frequently explored hand transparency for integrating physical keyboards in VR, enabling occlusion-free typing [13,27]. Their study results look promising, suggesting that novice users benefit most from transparent hands [13]. For sketching in VR, different commercial solutions exist (e.g., Google Tilt Brush[1] and Gravity Sketch[2]). Additionally, some researchers explored sketching experiences in VR [4,5]. However, all existing solutions focus on 3D sketching only, using VR controller-input (e.g., Gravity Sketch) or pen-input with different types of haptic feedback [4,5]. So far, little research explored 2D sketching in VR, which remains relevant, for example, for early design stages or user interface design. More importantly, no existing studies provide a systematic evaluation of users' performance with controller/pen or hand transparency.

In this paper, we investigate the effect of different levels of hand and pen transparency on 2D sketching in Virtual Reality. To enable accurate sketching in VR, we developed a sketching system called *VRSketch* that allows tracking of a physical pen, the user's hand, and a sheet of paper to sketch on. The tracked items are integrated into the Virtual Reality experience in real-time, enabling fluid sketching. In a user study, we compare sketching performances for different

---

[1] Google Tilt Brush. https://www.tiltbrush.com, last retrieved August 12, 2021.
[2] Gravity Sketch. https://www.gravitysketch.com, last retrieved August 12, 2021.

hand and pen transparency levels for drawing on a 2D surface; a sheet of paper (c.f., Fig. 1). Our results show that higher pen transparency allows users to sketch faster, while not losing accuracy. Moreover, while drawing participants achieved a mean deviation of slightly above 0.1 cm for each of the investigated techniques, indicating overall good performance for 2D sketching in VR.

1.1 Contribution

Our contribution is twofold: 1) we propose a system called *VRSketch* that allows sketching in Virtual Reality, and 2) conduct a comparative evaluation of five different levels of hand and pen transparency to understand the impact on users' 2D sketching performance.

2 Related Work

In the following, we review previous work exploring pen input for Augmented and Virtual Reality, and hand/pen occlusion for different input modalities.

2.1 Pen Input for Augmented and Virtual Reality

As pens offer users a familiar form of input, they have been frequently investigated for Augmented Reality (AR) and Virtual Reality (VR).

For AR, researchers explored how digital pen input can be used to annotate analog paper documents, augmented via either projection [10,22,28] or by using an Head-Mounted Display (HMD) [16]. Interestingly, annotations written with the help of an AR pen are processable with Optical Character Recognition (OCR), and the resulting text can serve as input to interact with applications [16]. Beyond written text, pen input also allows direct ways of interacting with AR applications, for example, to navigate menus [25]. Moreover, previous works investigated pen input in AR for 3D modeling, empowering users to design based on three-dimensional real-world objects [26].

For VR, researchers examined different interaction types with a digital pen in different scenarios. For example, for pointing and selecting interactions [17] in scenarios such as interacting with spreadsheets [7]. A interest of previous work is text input either by selecting letters on a virtual keyboard [3] or with the use of OCR [8]. Moreover, previous work studied sketching in VR using a pen as the input device. Here, an early approach is the Virtual Notepad by Poupyrev et al. [18]. The Virtual Notepad enables users to take notes and sketches in an Virtual Environment (VE), using a tracked tablet and pen. In later years, sketching with a pen in VR was primarily used for 3D sketching, often in the context of 3D modeling. In this context, either by expanding base sketches in the third dimension by lifting out single lines with pens [11] or by sketching lines mid-air [2,4,5]. The main focus of recent research on sketching mid-air is to create a believable haptic sensation for users. Results show that constraining the degrees of freedom by, for example, sketching on movable physical surfaces allows for higher accuracy [2,5] and can enhance interactions [4]. Further, virtual environments can provide other helpful features like gridlines that allow the user to draw 3D sketches by hand [19].

In sum, for sketching in VR, researchers focused mostly on 3D sketching, aiming for believable haptic sensations when drawing mid-air. Thus, typical 2D sketching experiences received little attention, while they remain relevant for many use-cases and allow for more straightforward to implement haptic feedback.

2.2 Hand and Pen Occlusion for Input

One problem when using pens for input is the obscuring of content or interface elements. When using a pen on a tablet, up to 47% of a 12″ display can be hidden by hand, pen, and arm [24]. Besides hiding parts of interface, it can also result in a loss of precision and speed during input [1,14]. To avoid occlusion, interfaces can detect occlusion and display content in visible areas [24,30] or add offsets to controls [23]. However, while this improves precision for targeting tasks, it decreases the precision for tracing operations like sketching [15].

Another approach to compensate for occlusion while sketching is replacing the hardware pen tip with a semitransparent one rendered on the tablet [14]. A semitransparent pen tip leads to a 40% reduction in error rate and an improvement in drawing speed of up to 26% [14]. We adopt this promising concept to VR and take it further by applying the transparency to the pen and the hand.

3   Sketching in Virtual Reality

The goal of our work is to understand the influence of hand and pen transparency on a user's 2D sketching performance in VR. Inspired by the idea of the Phantom-Pen [14], we extended the concept to include both the user's hand and the used pen. We hypothesize that transparency can improve performance, empowering users to sketch more precisely and quickly than they otherwise could. Furthermore, we are interested in optimizing the experience and precision of sketching in VR. To investigate VR sketching, we implemented the *VRSketch* system that allows real-time tracking of a physical pen, the user's hand, a sheet of paper, and a table.

To systematically explore the design space, we first identified pen and hand as two involved entities that may be improved by transparent rendering. Then, we continued by differentiating three levels of transparency (similar to the work of Knierim et al. [13]) that are invisible (0% opacity), semi-transparent (50% opacity) and opaque (100% opacity) for the hand and pen each. Semitransparency in particular has the potential to help with spatial orientation by displaying information without occlusion of content [29]. The complete design space and the selected evaluation conditions are presented in Fig. 2.

From the design space, we selected the following combinations of hand and pen transparency as conditions for our comparative study:

$\mathbf{H_{100}P_{100}}$ is our baseline condition in which we render the user's hand and pen fully opaque, similar to a real-world environment (see Fig. 1a).

$\mathbf{H_{50}P_{50}}$ renders both hand and pen semi-transparent, providing spatial information and paper content (see Fig. 1b).

$\mathbf{H_0P_{100}}$ shows the pen as fully opaque with no transparency, but it does not render the user's hand (see Fig. 1c).

$\mathbf{H_{100}P_0}$ displays the user's hand as opaque with no transparency, while the pen is reduced to a small cursor point, representing the pen's tip (see Fig. 1d).

$\mathbf{H_0P_0}$ removes all occlusion caused by hand and pen, rendering only the small cursor representing the tip of the pen (see Fig. 1e).

4   Evaluation

To investigate 2D sketching in VR and the benefits of semi- and full-transparency for pen and drawing hand, we conducted a comparative user study with the selected conditions from the design space (see Fig. 2). We opted for these conditions as they seemed promising to uncover the effects of transparency on sketching while keeping the experiment time within a reasonable limit. Especially the semi-transparency applied to the pen and hand seemed promising from the literature [13]. Future research might investigate the remaining conditions of the design space.

		Hand		
	Opacity	0%	50%	100%
Pen	0%	H_0P_0		$H_{100}P_0$
	50%		$H_{50}P_{50}$	
	100%	H_0P_{100}		$H_{100}P_{100}$

Fig. 2. The design space for hand and pen transparency and the five investigated conditions for 2D sketching in VR.

4.1   Study Design

To investigate different pen and hand transparency levels for sketching in VR, we conducted a within-subjects controlled laboratory user study in Virtual Reality with the Oculus Rift headset. Our independent variables were technique with five levels ($H_{100}P_{100}$ vs. $H_{50}P_{50}$ vs. H_0P_{100} vs. $H_{100}P_0$ vs. H_0P_0, see Fig. 1) and line type with two levels (*connected* vs. *unconnected*). Each technique was tested in a block consisting of four measured trials, with two trials evaluating *connected* lines and two trials evaluating *unconnected* lines. In each trial, participants had to draw a pattern consisting of 16 lines, drawing 64 lines for each block in total. To make the task more realistic, we varied the lines' orientation, introducing 16 different orientations (starting at 0-degree with 22.5-degree steps). Within each block, each line orientation was tested twice for each of both line types. We counterbalanced all blocks and the line types within each block using a Latin-square design to avoid learning effects. We used quantitative methods to evaluate sketching performance, taking pattern completion time, sketching accuracy, and the questionnaires as our dependent variables.

For this study, we asked: **(RQ) Which level of transparency for hand and pen results in the best sketching performance in Virtual Reality?** We posit the following hypotheses:

H_1 Semi-transparent rendering of the user's hand results in the shortest pattern completion times because it allows users to see the paper underneath while not losing spatial understanding.

H_2 We expect higher sketching accuracy for all conditions that render the pen semi-transparent or opaque compared to conditions in which it is fully transparent and replaced by a cursor because the cursor does not convey posture.

4.2 Apparatus

We implemented the *VRSketch* system to enable 2D sketching via pen in VR. We create an empty virtual room, centered around a sketching table, presented on the Oculus Rift headset. The scene was created using the Unity game engine 2018.2.20f1 and was running on a Windows PC with an Intel i7-7700K, 32 GB RAM, and an Nvidia Geforce GTX 1080 Ti. We spatially synchronized VR and reality by tracking the real-world scene with an OptiTrack system and its Motive 2.2.0 motion capture software. The tracking apparatus involved seven OptiTrack Prime^x 13W cameras near the sketching table to enable a high precision capturing of the sketching movements (see Fig. 3a). Furthermore, four additional OptiTrack Prime^x 13 cameras were placed at a greater distance for more general tracking. For the physical representations, we used a 3D printed pen and a DIN A4 sheet of paper, both shown in Fig. 3a. The paper was glued to a thin sheet of acrylic glass for durability and flatness. Both had a unique configuration of retro-reflective markers to get tracked as rigid bodies by the OptiTrack System. Besides, the user's hand was tracked by wearing a thin glove with markers. Thus, we could render both the hand's general position and the grip motion when picking up the pen. We also tracked the table, the chair, and the VR headset to complete the spatial synchronization. After initial positioning, the head movement was tracked by the sensors of the HMD. The lines, sketched by the user, are determined and rendered by the Unity application via calculating the pen tip's contact points with the paper. For measuring the sketching precision, the calculated line points were logged with timestamps. We controlled the degree of transparency for hand and pen via adjusting the alpha channel of according texture in the Unity game engine.

4.3 Participants

We recruited 20 volunteer participants (7 female), aged between 19 and 60 years (M = 33.3, SD = 13.7). None suffered from color vision impairments. Participants with corrected-to-normal vision were requested to wear their contacts or glasses during the study. We asked participants to rate their sketching skills on a 7-point

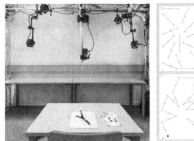

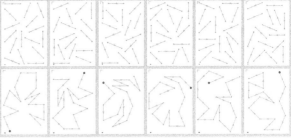

(a) Hardware setup.   (b) Overview of the test patterns.

Fig. 3. a) Hardware setup of the *VRSketch* system where hand, pen, paper, table, and chair are tracked via configurations of retro-reflective markers. Seven of the eleven OptiTrack cameras are close to the table for more precise tracking. b) Overview of the unconnected test patterns in the upper row and the connected ones in the lower row. The lines had to be drawn in the direction of the arrows.

Likert-scale from 1 (cannot sketch at all) to 7 (can sketch on a professional level). Participants stated that they had limited sketching skills (Md = 2.05, IQR = 2.0). Furthermore, we asked participants for their experience with Virtual Reality. Five participants had never tried VR before, three used it once, and twelve participants said they use a VR headset regularly (at least once a month).

4.4   Procedure

At the beginning of the study, we informed participants about the procedure and asked them to sign a consent form. Afterward, we collected the participant's demographic data, sketching skills, and experience with VR. We then introduced the participant to the Oculus Rift and adjusted the headset for optimal fit and correct interpupillary distance. Then, we started the study. The study was conducted in five blocks for each participant, with one technique tested in each block. We counterbalanced all blocks using a Latin-square design. In each block, participants first took a seat at the sketching table, put on the tracked glove, and the HMD and picked up the tracked pen. Each block started with a warm-up pattern, which participants could try until they indicated that they were familiar with that block's respective technique. After the warm-up, participants continued with the measured trails. Participants had to trace lines in four test patterns for each block, two unconnected, and two connected ones (see Fig. 3b). After one pattern was complete, the experimenter started the next pattern. After all four patterns were complete, the participants could take off the headset, pen, and glove, and fill out the questionnaires: UEQ-S [20], NASA Raw-TLX [9] and IPQ [21]. After completing all blocks, we conducted a final interview with the participants asking them about their impressions of sketching in VR and the individual techniques. Each participant took approximately 70 min to finish the experiment.

4.5   Data Preparation

In addition to the observations of users' impressions, sketching precision is used for the quantitative evaluation of the different techniques. We use the mean deviations of the drawn lines from the corresponding target lines of the patterns to measure precision. Four out of 400 (1%) recorded patterns were corrupted due to technical difficulties and replaced with the same participant's matching pattern of the same technique. We first corrected the lines' position and rotation according to the paper's position to calculate the mean deviations (see Fig. 4).

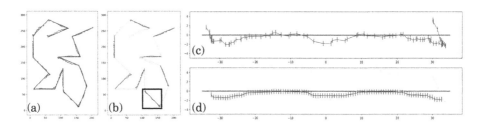

Fig. 4. To calculate the mean deviation, the points of the sketched lines (a) are assigned to the lines of the target pattern (b). The assigned points are rotated around the center of the target line and the center is moved to the origin (c). The points are restricted to the area between the start and end of the target line, and the sketched line is resampled with 100 equidistant points (d).

The line points were each assigned to a specific target line, as shown in Fig. 4b and c. A point was always assigned if its minimum distance to the target line was less than 1 cm, whereby in the case of connected lines, the bisector between two lines served as the limit for the assignment. The lines were resampled at 100 equidistant points in line with previous work [2,26] (see Fig. 4e). The mean deviation of a drawn line from its target line is then calculated as the arithmetic means of the Y-values' amounts at the measurement points.

4.6   Results

In the following, we present the results from our study analysis. We use mean (M), standard deviation (SD) to describe our data. We do not assume normal-distribution of our data, and thus, apply non-parametric tests. We ran Friedman tests and post-hoc Wilcoxon Signed-rank tests with Bonferroni correction to show significant differences.

Pattern Completion Time. To understand how quickly participants were able to sketch with each technique, we looked at their pattern completion times. The times in ascending order are: $H_{100}P_0 = 41.88$ s (SD $= 16.25$ s), $H_0P_{100} = 44.08$ s (SD $= 15.37$ s), $H_{50}P_{50} = 45.86$ s (SD $= 19.01$ s), $H_0P_0 = 48.32$ s (SD $= 23.13$ s),

Table 1. Significant comparisons of pattern completion times for the different techniques (with r: >0.1 small, >0.3 medium, and >0.5 large effect).

Comparison			W	Z	p	r
$H_{100}P_{100}$	vs.	$H_{50}P_{50}$	2291	3.22	0.011	0.25
$H_{100}P_{100}$	vs.	$H_{100}P_0$	2654	4.96	<0.001	0.39
$H_{50}P_{50}$	vs.	$H_{100}P_0$	2318	3.35	0.007	0.26
$H_{100}P_0$	vs.	H_0P_0	742	-4.21	<0.001	0.33

and $H_{100}P_{100} = 50.17\,\mathrm{s}$ (SD $= 21.66\,\mathrm{s}$). Figure 5 compares the pattern completion times. A Friedman test revealed a significant effect of technique on pattern completion time ($\chi^2(4) = 35.91$, p < 0.001, N $= 20$). Post-hoc tests showed significant differences between some of the evaluated conditions (see Table 1). For the completion time, we conclude: $H_{100}P_0 < H_{50}P_{50} < H_{100}P_{100}$ and $H_{100}P_0 < H_0P_0$. For H_0P_{100} we cannot make a statement.

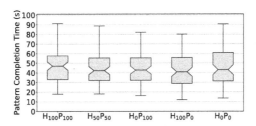

Fig. 5. Boxplots of pattern completion times for the different techniques.

Sketching Accuracy. Throughout the study, participants drew exactly 6400 lines. To evaluate the sketching accuracy of each technique, we applied our data preparation step described in Sect. 4.5. The mean deviations of each line within each technique in ascending order are: $H_{100}P_{100} = 1.02\,\mathrm{mm}$ (SD $= 0.55\,\mathrm{mm}$), $H_{50}P_{50} = 1.04\,\mathrm{mm}$ (SD $= 0.55\,\mathrm{mm}$), $H_0P_{100} = 1.06\,\mathrm{mm}$ (SD $= 0.55\,\mathrm{mm}$), $H_{100}P_0 = 1.06\,\mathrm{mm}$ (SD $= 0.6\,\mathrm{mm}$), and $H_0P_0 = 1.08\,\mathrm{mm}$ (SD $= 0.58\,\mathrm{mm}$). The mean deviations are compared in Fig. 6. We applied a Friedman test, which revealed no significant differences between the techniques ($\chi^2(4) = 8.23$, p $= 0.083$, N $= 20$).

Sketching Accuracy for Different Sketching Directions. The area in the direction of sketching can be occluded, for example, by the virtual pen or the hand of the VR user. Hence, the sketching direction could influence sketching performance. To gain further insides about the effect of the transparency, we reviewed the influence of the sketching direction on the sketching accuracy by clustering the different line orientation into quadrants. The quadrants are $Q1$:

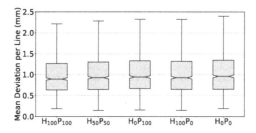

Fig. 6. Boxplot of the mean sketching deviations for the different techniques.

upper right, $Q2$: upper left, $Q3$: lower left, and $Q4$ lower right. For example, if a line is drawn towards the upper left relative to its starting point, it belongs to $Q2$. The edge cases are clustered as follows: drawing upwards $Q1$, drawing to the left $Q2$, drawing downwards $Q3$, and drawing to the right $Q4$. The mean deviations for each technique and quadrant are shown in Table 2. To analyze the data of the different quadrants, we compared both the different techniques in each quadrant and the different quadrants of each technique.

Table 2. The mean sketching deviation (in mm) per technique and quadrant.

Technique	$Q1$	$Q2$	$Q3$	$Q4$
$H_{100}P_{100}$	0.97 (SD 0.51)	0.96 (SD 0.46)	0.92 (SD 0.49)	1.06 (SD 0.54)
H_0P_{100}	1.04 (SD 0.53)	1.03 (SD 0.55)	0.94 (SD 0.49)	1.09 (SD 0.57)
$H_{100}P_0$	1.05 (SD 0.61)	1.08 (SD 0.51)	1.02 (SD 0.58)	1.09 (SD 0.65)
H_0P_0	1.05 (SD 0.61)	1.13 (SD 0.58)	1.06 (SD 0.6)	1.11 (SD 0.56)
$H_{50}P_{50}$	1.08 (SD 0.59)	1.15 (SD 0.61)	1.08 (SD 0.57)	1.14 (SD 0.61)

Comparison of Techniques within Quadrants. We performed Friedman tests for each quadrant. For $Q1$ ($\chi^2(4) = 4.15$, p = 0.386, N = 20) and $Q4$ ($\chi^2(4) = 3.88$, p = 0.422, N = 20), we observed no significant differences between the techniques. However, the Friedman tests for $Q2$ ($\chi^2(4) = 24.09$, p = 0, N = 20) and $Q3$ ($\chi^2(4) = 20.64$, p = 0, N = 20) revealed a significant effect of technique on the mean deviation. Post-hoc tests showed significant differences between some of the conditions (see Table 3). We conclude that $H_{100}P_{100}$ leads to significantly higher accuracy than $H_{50}P_{50}$, H_0P_{100}, and H_0P_0 in $Q2$ and that $H_{50}P_{50}$ and H_0P_{100} lead to significantly higher accuracy than $H_{100}P_0$ and H_0P_0 in $Q3$.

Comparison of Quadrants of Each Technique. For the comparison of mean deviations in the different quadrants for each technique the Friedman tests for the techniques $H_{100}P_0$ ($\chi^2(3) = 3.61$, p = 0.307, N = 20) and H_0P_0 ($\chi^2(3) = 6.3$, p = 0.098, N = 20) revealed no significant differences. For the techniques $H_{100}P_{100}$ ($\chi^2(3) = 12.1$, p = 0.007, N = 20), $H_{50}P_{50}$ ($\chi^2(3) = 19.19$, p = 0, N = 20), and

Table 3. Pairwise comparisons of mean deviations with significant results for the different techniques in the quadrants $Q2$ and $Q3$.

Quadrant	Comparison	W	Z	p	r
$Q2$	$H_{100}P_{100}$ vs. $H_{50}P_{50}$	20404	−3.19	0.014	0.13
$Q2$	$H_{100}P_{100}$ vs. $H_{0}P_{100}$	18443	−4.37	<0.001	0.17
$Q2$	$H_{100}P_{100}$ vs. $H_{0}P_{0}$	19110	−3.97	0.001	0.16
$Q3$	$H_{50}P_{50}$ vs. $H_{100}P_{0}$	20066	−3.39	0.007	0.13
$Q3$	$H_{50}P_{50}$ vs. $H_{0}P_{0}$	19947	−3.46	0.005	0.14
$Q3$	$H_{0}P_{100}$ vs. $H_{100}P_{0}$	20438	−3.16	0.015	0.13
$Q3$	$H_{0}P_{100}$ vs. $H_{0}P_{0}$	20780	−2.96	0.03	0.12

$H_{0}P_{100}$ ($\chi^2(3) = 14.79$, p $= 0.002$, N $= 20$) the Friedman tests revealed a significant effect of the quadrants on the mean deviation. Post-hoc tests showed significant differences between some of comparisons (see Table 4).

Table 4. Pairwise comparisons of mean deviations with significant results for the techniques $H_{100}P_{100}$, $H_{50}P_{50}$, and $H_{0}P_{100}$.

Technique	Comparison	W	Z	p	r
$H_{100}P_{100}$	$Q1$ vs. $Q4$	19307	−3.85	0.001	0.15
$H_{100}P_{100}$	$Q2$ vs. $Q4$	18994	−4.04	<0.001	0.16
$H_{100}P_{100}$	$Q3$ vs. $Q4$	21033	−2.81	0.03	0.11
$H_{50}P_{50}$	$Q1$ vs. $Q3$	31759	3.67	0.001	0.15
$H_{50}P_{50}$	$Q2$ vs. $Q3$	32367	4.04	<0.001	0.16
$H_{50}P_{50}$	$Q3$ vs. $Q4$	19011	−4.03	<0.001	0.16
$H_{0}P_{100}$	$Q2$ vs. $Q3$	33294	4.6	<0.001	0.18
$H_{0}P_{100}$	$Q3$ vs. $Q4$	19255	−3.88	0.001	0.15

Here we conclude that for technique $H_{100}P_{100}$ $Q4$ is significantly worse then for all other quadrants, that for $H_{50}P_{50}$ $Q3$ is significantly better then all other quadrants, and that for $H_{0}P_{100}$ $Q3$ is significantly better than $Q2$ and $Q4$.

Questionnaires. Furthermore, we asked participants to fill out three different questionnaires (NASA Raw-TLX, User Experience Questionnaire, and iGroup Presence Questionnaire) after each technique. In the following, we report on the gathered results using median and interquartile range (IQR).

NASA Raw-TLX. To evaluate the workload of the different techniques, we analyzed the results of the NASA-TLX. The median scores in ascending order are: $H_{100}P_{0} = 18.75$ (IQR $= 19.58$), $H_{0}P_{0} = 19.17$ (IQR $= 21.25$), $H_{0}P_{100} = 20.42$ (IQR $= 12.08$), $H_{100}P_{100} = 20.83$ (IQR $= 20.62$), $H_{50}P_{50} = 22.92$ (IQR $= 14.17$).

To compare the scores, we conducted a Friedman test that revealed no significant effect of technique on the NASA Raw-TLX score ($\chi^2(4) = 5.83$, p $= 0.212$, N $= 20$).

User Experience Questionnaire. For insights on the user experience, we conducted the short version of the UEQ (see Table 5).

Table 5. Results of the UEQ-S for the different techniques.

Technique	Pragmatic quality		Hedonic quality		Overall quality	
	Median	IQR	Median	IQR	Median	IQR
$H_{100}P_{100}$	1.0	2.31	1.62	1.0	1.19	1.56
$H_{50}P_{50}$	1.75	1.62	1.88	1.31	1.75	1.22
H_0P_{100}	1.62	2.12	2.0	1.31	1.62	1.28
$H_{100}P_0$	0.75	1.62	1.62	0.81	1.38	0.81
H_0P_0	1.5	1.81	1.5	0.81	1.62	1.22

To compare the overall quality for the individual techniques, we conducted a Friedman test which revealed a significant effect. However, a post-hoc tests did not reveal any significant differences.

iGroup Presence Questionnaire. The results of the iGroup Presence Questionnaire (IPQ) are shown in Table 6. A Friedman test revealed a significant effect of technique on overall score. Post-hoc tests showed a significant difference between $H_{100}P_{100}$ and H_0P_{100} (W $= 16$, Z $= -2.77$, p $= 0.04$, r $= 0.44$), meaning that rendering hand and pen opaque results in lower presence, than rendering only the pen opaque and not the hand.

Table 6. Results of the IPQ for the different techniques.

Technique	General presence		Spatial presence		Exp. realism		Involvement		Overall score	
	Median	IQR	Median	IQR	Median	IQR	Median	IQR	Median	IQR
$H_{100}P_{100}$	4.0	1.0	4.2	1.05	2.75	0.81	2.75	1.19	3.32	0.96
$H_{50}P_{50}$	4.0	1.0	4.3	1.25	2.75	1.31	2.75	0.88	3.54	1.07
H_0P_{100}	4.5	1.0	4.1	1.5	3.0	1.06	3.0	1.25	3.46	0.91
$H_{100}P_0$	4.0	1.0	4.0	1.1	2.75	1.25	2.75	0.75	3.39	0.68
H_0P_0	4.0	1.0	3.9	1.45	2.88	0.94	2.88	1.06	3.11	0.89

5 Discussion

In the following, we discuss the most important findings of our user study.

Pattern Completion Time. In our results, we found that the more the opacity of the pen is reduced, the faster participants were able to sketch. This result is in line with similar findings in previous work. For example, Lee et al. found that rendering the pen tip transparent also increases the sketching speed [14]. In contrast, reducing the opacity of the hand resulted in longer pattern completion times. However, in H_1, we expected a semi-transparent rendering of the user's hand would result in the shortest completion time. We could not verify this in our study, and hence, cannot accept our hypothesis H_1. However, mixing transparency and opacity, one on the hand and one on the pen, resulted in shorter completion times compared to both elements being fully transparent or fully opaque. This might indicate that providing both overview by transparent elements and spatial information by visible elements together could indeed be beneficial. In the future, further research could investigate more fine-grained levels of transparency to uncover its definite influence on completion time.

Sketching Accuracy. We found no significant influence of transparency on user's accuracy, neither for transparency of the hand nor for the pen. Therefore, we cannot accept our hypothesis H_2. While this result is in line with previous work (e.g., transparent hands for typing on physical keyboards [13]), we expected a higher sketching accuracy for semi-transparent rendering as it empowers users to see otherwise occluded sketch areas. Nonetheless, we think that we did not observe an effect because humans may have adapted to this constraint due to excessive practice (writing with a pen is one of the first skills we learn at school). Overall, the measurements with a maximum mean of 1.08 mm for mean deviation show the high precision of VR sketching with *VRSketch*. In comparison, Arora et al. [2] found a mean deviation of 2.54 mm (SD = 1.87 mm) for the data subset with the closest conditions of drawing straight, short lines on a horizontal writing surface using a VR-HMD. We downloaded the corresponding GitHub repository[3] and applied our algorithm shown in Fig. 4. The high precision of sketching with the *VRSketch* system confirms the positive effect of concrete writing surfaces and visual guidance aids, as shown by Arora et al. and Wacker et al. [2,26].

Accuracy and Sketching Direction. For example, for $H_{100}P_{100}$, sketching in Q4 (downright/below hand and arm) was significantly worse than in all other directions, which shows the influence of occlusion as described by Vogel et al. [24]. In general, from our results, we learned that fully seeing the hand makes it easier to sketch away from arm and hand, while eradicating the pen makes it more challenging to sketch towards the down left quarter. Based on our findings, we suggest that it may be beneficial to adapt the transparency, dependent on the sketching direction dynamically, to reach an optimal accuracy.

Perceived Workload. For the NASA Raw-TLX [9] questionnaires, we observed that not rendering the pen resulted in a lower workload. In contrast to previous work [13], we found that not rendering the hands did not lead to significantly higher workload. Quite the opposite, transparent and opaque hands and pen resulted in a higher workload. However, these results were not statistically significant.

---

[3] https://github.com/rarora7777/VRSketchingStudyCHI17.

User Experience and Presence. In the conducted UEQ-S questionnaires, we did not find any significant differences between the techniques. Nevertheless, our findings point in the direction that seeing the hand fully visible results in less pragmatic quality, while overall, the results indicate a good user experience. Seeing only the pen significantly increases presence compared to seeing the pen and virtual hand. This finding is very interesting and in line with some VR games[4] that as soon as one grabs an object, do not render the users' hands anymore but instead only show the object that the user is holding.

Limitations. Our work is limited by the rather complex setup that we used to implement our *VRSketch* system. It relies on several expensive OptiTrack sensors and enough space to set up the tracking system. Nonetheless, we argue that as VR advances tracking accuracy improves and in a few years, it may be possible to track physical objects in our surroundings to integrate them in the experience (as is demonstrated with integrated hand-tracking on the Oculus Quest).

6 Conclusion

In this work, we investigated five different levels of pen and hand transparency for sketching in VR. We proposed the *VRSketch* system that integrates users' hands and a pen into a virtual sketching environment. Our results show that drawing lines with our *VRSketch* system, on average, results in a mean deviation of slightly above 0.1 cm. Moreover, we could show that not seeing the pen, allows users to draw more quickly while not losing accuracy. In the future, we want to experiment with dynamic transparency that adjusts pen and hand rendering based on the user's current sketching or writing direction.

References

1. Annett, M., Bischof, W.F.: Hands, hover, and nibs: understanding stylus accuracy on tablets. In: Proceedings of the 41st Graphics Interface Conference, GI 2015, Toronto, ON, Canada, pp. 203–210. Canadian Information Processing Society (2015). http://dl.acm.org/citation.cfm?id=2788890.2788926. Event-place: Halifax, Nova Scotia, Canada
2. Arora, R., Kazi, R.H., Anderson, F., Grossman, T., Singh, K., Fitzmaurice, G.: Experimental evaluation of sketching on surfaces in VR. In: Proceedings of the 2017 CHI Conference on Human Factors in Computing Systems, CHI 2017, New York, NY, USA, pp. 5643–5654. ACM (2017). https://doi.org/10.1145/3025453.3025474. Event-place: Denver, Colorado, USA
3. Bowman, D.A., Rhoton, C.J., Pinho, M.S.: Text input techniques for immersive virtual environments: an empirical comparison. In: Proceedings of the Human Factors and Ergonomics Society Annual Meeting, Los Angeles, CA, vol. 46, pp. 2154–2158. SAGE Publications (2002). https://doi.org/10.3390/technologies7020031

---

[4] Job Simulator. https://store.steampowered.com/app/448280/Job_Simulator, last retrieved August 12, 2021.

4. Drey, T., Gugenheimer, J., Karlbauer, J., Milo, M., Rukzio, E.: VRSketchin: exploring the design space of pen and tablet interaction for 3D sketching in virtual reality. In: Proceedings of the 2020 CHI Conference on Human Factors in Computing Systems, CHI 2020, New York, NY, USA, pp. 1–14. Association for Computing Machinery (2020). https://doi.org/10.1145/3313831.3376628

5. Elsayed, H., et al.: VRSketchpen: unconstrained haptic assistance for sketching in virtual 3d environments. In: 26th ACM Symposium on Virtual Reality Software and Technology, VRST 2020, New York, NY, USA. Association for Computing Machinery (2020). https://doi.org/10.1145/3385956.3418953

6. Gerry, L.J.: Paint with me: stimulating creativity and empathy while painting with a painter in virtual reality. IEEE Trans. Vis. Comput. Graph. **23**(4), 1418–1426 (2017). https://doi.org/10.1109/TVCG.2017.2657239

7. Gesslein, T., et al.: Pen-based interaction with spreadsheets in mobile virtual reality. arXiv:2008.04543 [cs], August 2020

8. González, G., Molina, J.P., García, A.S., Martínez, D., González, P.: Evaluation of text input techniques in immersive virtual environments. In: Macías, J., Granollers Saltiveri, A., Latorre, P. (eds.) New Trends on Human-Computer Interaction, pp. 109–118. Springer, London (2009). https://doi.org/10.1007/978-1-84882-352-5_11

9. Hart, S.G., Staveland, L.E.: Development of NASA-TLX (Task Load Index): results of empirical and theoretical research. In: Advances in Psychology, vol. 52, pp. 139–183. Elsevier (1988). https://doi.org/10.1016/S0166-4115(08)62386-9. https://linkinghub.elsevier.com/retrieve/pii/S0166411508623869

10. Holman, D., Vertegaal, R., Altosaar, M., Troje, N., Johns, D.: Paper windows: interaction techniques for digital paper. In: Proceedings of the SIGCHI Conference on Human Factors in Computing Systems, pp. 591–599. ACM (2005). https://doi.org/10.1145/1054972.1055054

11. Jackson, B., Keefe, D.F.: Lift-off: using reference imagery and freehand sketching to create 3D models in VR. IEEE Trans. Vis. Comput. Graph. **22**(4), 1442–1451 (2016). https://doi.org/10.1109/TVCG.2016.2518099

12. Jetter, H.C., Rädle, R., Feuchtner, T., Anthes, C., Friedl, J., Klokmose, C.N.: "In VR, everything is possible!": sketching and simulating spatially-aware interactive spaces in virtual reality. In: Proceedings of the 2020 CHI Conference on Human Factors in Computing Systems, CHI 2020, New York, NY, USA, pp. 1–16. Association for Computing Machinery (2020). https://doi.org/10.1145/3313831.3376652

13. Knierim, P., Schwind, V., Feit, A.M., Nieuwenhuizen, F., Henze, N.: Physical keyboards in virtual reality: analysis of typing performance and effects of avatar hands. In: Proceedings of the 2018 CHI Conference on Human Factors in Computing Systems, p. 345. ACM (2018). https://doi.org/10.1145/3173574.3173919

14. Lee, D., Son, K., Lee, J.H., Bae, S.H.: PhantomPen: virtualization of pen head for digital drawing free from pen occlusion & #38; visual parallax. In: Proceedings of the 25th Annual ACM Symposium on User Interface Software and Technology, UIST 2012, New York, NY, USA, pp. 331–340. ACM (2012). https://doi.org/10.1145/2380116.2380159. Event-place: Cambridge, Massachusetts, USA

15. Lee, H., Ko, I., Tan, Y.R., Zhang, D., Li, C.: Usability impact of occlusion-free techniques on commonly-used multitouch actions. In: Proceedings of the 5th International ACM In-Cooperation HCI and UX Conference, CHIuXiD 2019, New York, NY, USA, pp. 96–105. ACM (2019). https://doi.org/10.1145/3328243.3328256. Event-place: Jakarta, Surabaya, Bali, Indonesia

16. Li, Z., Annett, M., Hinckley, K., Singh, K., Wigdor, D.: HoloDoc: enabling mixed reality workspaces that harness physical and digital content. In: Proceedings of the 2019 CHI Conference on Human Factors in Computing Systems, CHI 2019, New York, NY, USA, pp. 687:1–687:14. ACM (2019). https://doi.org/10.1145/3290605.3300917. Event-place: Glasgow, Scotland, UK

17. Pham, D.M., Stuerzlinger, W.: Is the pen mightier than the controller? A comparison of input devices for selection in virtual and augmented reality. In: 25th ACM Symposium on Virtual Reality Software and Technology, pp. 1–11. ACM, Parramatta NSW Australia, November 2019. https://doi.org/10.1145/3359996.3364264

18. Poupyrev, I., Tomokazu, N., Weghorst, S.: Virtual notepad: handwriting in immersive VR. In: Proceedings of the IEEE 1998 Virtual Reality Annual International Symposium (Cat. No. 98CB36180), pp. 126–132. IEEE (1998). https://doi.org/10.1109/VRAIS.1998.658467

19. Sandnes, F.E.: Panoramagrid: a graph paper tracing framework for sketching 360-degree immersed experiences. In: Proceedings of the International Working Conference on Advanced Visual Interfaces, AVI 2016, New York, NY, USA, pp. 342–343. Association for Computing Machinery (2016). https://doi.org/10.1145/2909132.2926058

20. Schrepp, M., Hinderks, A., Thomaschewski, J.: Design and evaluation of a short version of the user experience questionnaire (UEQ-S). Int. J. Interact. Multimed. Artif. Intell. 4(6), 103 (2017)

21. Schubert, T., Friedmann, F., Regenbrecht, H.: The experience of presence: factor analytic insights. Presence Teleoper. Virtual Environ. 10(3), 266–281 (2001). https://doi.org/10.1162/105474601300343603

22. Song, H., Guimbretiere, F., Grossman, T., Fitzmaurice, G.: MouseLight: bimanual interactions on digital paper using a pen and a spatially-aware mobile projector. In: Proceedings of the SIGCHI Conference on Human Factors in Computing Systems, CHI 2010, New York, NY, USA, pp. 2451–2460. ACM (2010). https://doi.org/10.1145/1753326.1753697. Event-place: Atlanta, Georgia, USA

23. Vogel, D., Baudisch, P.: Shift: a technique for operating pen-based interfaces using touch. In: Proceedings of the SIGCHI Conference on Human Factors in Computing Systems, CHI 2007, New York, NY, USA, pp. 657–666. Association for Computing Machinery (2007). https://doi.org/10.1145/1240624.1240727

24. Vogel, D., Cudmore, M., Casiez, G., Balakrishnan, R., Keliher, L.: Hand occlusion with tablet-sized direct pen input. In: Proceedings of the SIGCHI Conference on Human Factors in Computing Systems, CHI 2009, New York, NY, USA, pp. 557–566. ACM (2009). https://doi.org/10.1145/1518701.1518787. Event-place: Boston, MA, USA

25. Wacker, P., Nowak, O., Voelker, S., Borchers, J.: Evaluating menu techniques for handheld AR with a smartphone & mid-air pen. In: 22nd International Conference on Human-Computer Interaction with Mobile Devices and Services, MobileHCI 2020, New York, NY, USA. Association for Computing Machinery (2020). https://doi.org/10.1145/3379503.3403548

26. Wacker, P., Wagner, A., Voelker, S., Borchers, J.: Physical guides: an analysis of 3D sketching performance on physical objects in augmented reality. In: Proceedings of the Symposium on Spatial User Interaction, SUI 2018, New York, NY, USA, pp. 25–35. ACM (2018). https://doi.org/10.1145/3267782.3267788. Event-place: Berlin, Germany

27. Walker, J., Li, B., Vertanen, K., Kuhl, S.: Efficient typing on a visually occluded physical keyboard. In: Proceedings of the 2017 CHI Conference on Human Factors in Computing Systems, pp. 5457–5461. ACM (2017). https://doi.org/10.1145/3025453.3025783

28. Wellner, P.D.: Interacting with paper on the DigitalDesk. Technical report, University of Cambridge, Computer Laboratory (1994). https://doi.org/10.1145/159544.159630

29. Zhai, S., Buxton, W., Milgram, P.: The partial-occlusion effect: utilizing semitransparency in 3D human-computer interaction. ACM Trans. Comput. Hum. Interact. **3**(3), 254–284 (1996). https://doi.org/10.1145/234526.234532

30. Zhang, Y., et al.: Sensing posture-aware Pen+Touch interaction on tablets. In: Proceedings of the 2019 CHI Conference on Human Factors in Computing Systems, CHI 2019, New York, NY, USA, pp. 55:1–55:14. ACM (2019). https://doi.org/10.1145/3290605.3300285. Event-place: Glasgow, Scotland, UK

VRTactileDraw: A Virtual Reality Tactile Pattern Designer for Complex Spatial Arrangements of Actuators

Oliver Beren Kaul[✉], Andreas Domin, Michael Rohs, Benjamin Simon, and Maximilian Schrapel

Leibniz University Hannover, Am Welfengarten 1, 30167 Hannover, Germany
{kaul,domin,rohs,simon,schrapel}@hci.uni-hannover.de
http://www.hci.uni-hannover.de

Abstract. Creating tactile patterns on the body via a spatial arrangement of many tactile actuators offers many opportunities and presents a challenge, as the design space is enormous. This paper presents a VR interface that enables designers to rapidly prototype complex tactile interfaces. It allows for painting strokes on a modeled body part and translates these strokes into continuous tactile patterns using an interpolation algorithm. The presented VR approach avoids several problems of traditional 2D editors. It realizes spatial 3D input using VR controllers with natural mapping and intuitive spatial movements. To evaluate this approach in detail, we conducted a user study and iteratively improved the system. The study participants gave predominantly positive feedback on the presented VR interface (SUS score 79.7, AttrakDiff "desirable"). The final system is released alongside this paper as an open-source Unity project for various tactile hardware.

Keywords: Tactile patterns · Tactile pattern design · Tactile feedback · Design tool · Design interface · VR tool · Spatial input

1 Introduction

Beyond haptic renderings, which may be realized using physics simulations (e.g., contact or impact forces), tactile patterns (TPs) can be used for abstract concepts such as eliciting emotions or guidance during navigation. However, the design of tactile patterns for such abstract concepts requires manual exploration of the design space. It is also interesting for non-technical people (e.g., for personalized touch sensations between remote humans). With the emergence of high-fidelity haptic feedback, the demand for interfaces that can be used to design TPs and effects rose as well. Several works appeared in the recent past

Electronic supplementary material The online version of this chapter (https://doi.org/10.1007/978-3-030-85607-6_15) contains supplementary material, which is available to authorized users.

[6, 13, 20, 33, 36, 42] but none of these approaches is designed for a high number of actuators that may be spatially oriented in more complex shapes than just a 2D grid.

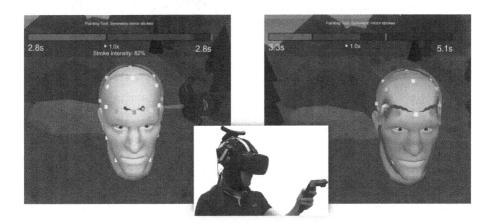

Fig. 1. The final version of *VRTactileDraw* in action. Users wear an HTC Vive Pro VR headset and a tactile display [26] (center). A user draws symmetric strokes on the 3D model head in VR (left) and then replays the resulting pattern (right). During drawing, the user can feel the resulting tactile actuation.

This work introduces a pattern design interface for tactile feedback systems that feature many actuators in complex spatial arrangements around the body (e.g., [3, 4, 10, 14, 26, 29, 32, 41]). The need for a pattern designer for systems, including many arbitrarily distributed actuators on the human body, can be further motivated by the wide range of novel use cases the systems above enable. For example, full-body suits potentially enable the feeling of physical closeness to a remote person by "distantly touching or brushing" a model body in any desired location, effectively creating a real-time TP. Another example would be creating TPs for an immersive movie where viewers wear a tactile system when watching action-packed scenes and feel specifically designed effects on their body. Imagine feeling the shockwave of an explosion or a giant spider crawling up your spine and over your head before finally becoming visible in the movie scene from above.

In our prior work [24], an iterative design process was followed, which includes several design and implementation phases and two think-aloud studies with feedback from technical and non-technical users. The goal was to develop two variants of an intuitive TP designer (see Fig. 2):

- A *curve interface*, which behaves like an audio/video editor, allowing the user to modify the intensity-over-time curve of each actuator.
- A *drawing interface*, which allows the user to directly draw actuation strokes onto a body part, with interpolation between the actuators.

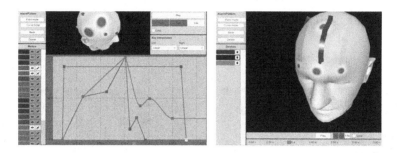

Fig. 2. Curve interface (left) and drawing interface (right) from prior work [24].

With the TP designer from our prior work [24], created patterns can be played while drawing. Heat maps provide a live visual representation of vibration intensity. Users who wear the tactile feedback system can simultaneously feel the created pattern. The two variants have different advantages and disadvantages, but we focused on improving the drawing interface, as users tended to prefer it over the rather complex curve interface. Some of the most severe disadvantages of the drawing mode are related to the 2D user interface. In particular, the following tasks are difficult to perform with the 2D interface:

- Drawing a stroke on a non-flat body part from a 2D camera perspective as this leads to distortions.
- Moving the camera around the modeled body part while drawing a stroke.
- Adjusting the stroke intensity level while drawing a stroke.

These issues with the 2D interface led us to develop a VR user interface for the same purpose. A VR interface can address the above challenges. It offers increased spatial awareness, ease of moving around a 3D model by simply walking around, and a more direct spatial mapping when drawing. While developing the VR interface, we had the following research questions in mind:

- RQ1 - Usability: What kinds of interactions are suited best for designing tactile patterns in VR? How can the required interface functionality be made as simple and intuitive as possible, and what levels of and usability does the designed VR interface achieve?
- RQ2 - Comfort: How can the VR experience be made comfortable for the user, and what levels of and comfort does the designed VR interface achieve?

The final version of the resulting *VRTactileDraw* system is shown in Fig. 1.

2   Background and Related Work

We first give an overview of tactile feedback systems without going into too much detail, as the specific actuator configurations and application areas are less relevant to this work. Then we discuss several TP editors and conclude with the specific prior work on which this paper is based.

2.1   Tactile Feedback

Early work on tactile displays appeared in 1957 by Geldard et al. [16] and was neatly summarized alongside newer work and general guidelines by Jones and Sarter [23]. Their research review in the area concludes that different levels of vibrotactile intensity and frequency are hard to distinguish and even interfere with each other. Simultaneously, stimulus location and duration are easier to identify and can thus achieve a higher bandwidth of communicated information.

A variety of tactile feedback systems appeared after the initial steps in this domain with a large number of different use cases, including situational awareness, navigation and guidance, vision substitution, obstacle avoidance, notification, target acquisition, and others:

- vibrotactile belts: e.g. [15, 34, 45]
- vibrotactile systems on the arm, wrist, or hand: e.g. [4, 33]
- vibrotactile systems on the head: e.g. [8, 11, 26]
- vibrotactile systems on the back: e.g. [22, 38]
- full body suits: e.g. [3, 10, 14, 29, 32]

Except for full-body, head-worn, and vision substitution systems, most of the systems above feature a relatively low number of actuators in a simple configuration and require only moderate work to define meaningful TPs manually. However, there are systems with large numbers of actuators or complex actuator arrangements [3, 4, 10, 14, 26, 29, 32, 41], which pose an obvious challenge to the design of TPs. They currently require a significant amount of manual work by a pattern designer or algorithmic support to generate meaningful TPs due to their complexity. In such situations and without the support of a suitable interface, creating high-quality TPs is a daunting task. These use cases are likely to profit most from the proposed system, as it is expected to drastically reduce the amount of work needed for generating meaningful TPs. It enables fast prototyping and allows even non-technical users of the system to define their own TPs.

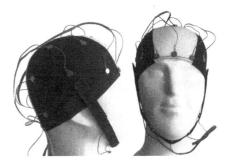

Fig. 3. *HapticHead* for vibrotactile feedback around the head [26].

One system that benefits from the *VRTactileDraw* system is *HapticHead* [26]. *HapticHead* is a vibrotactile interface with a total of 24 actuators located around the head in a sphere-like arrangement (see Fig. 3). The actuator type we used in this work is a common coin-style Precision Microdrives model 312-101 [35] (12500 rpm at 3.3V, 12 mm coin type, 2.6 g normalized amplitude, 40 ms lag time, 132 ms rise time, and 285 ms stop time). Combined with the high update rate of the *HapticHead* system 90 Hz, this actuator type can playback any tactile intensity, roughness, and rhythm within its limits (namely rise and stop time). Typical, predefined patterns such as sine or sawtooth are also possible.

2.2   Tactile Pattern Editors

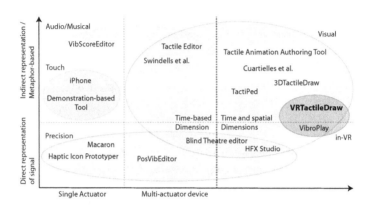

Fig. 4. Design space of TP editors after [33], modified to include *VRTactileDraw* and various other recent works.

Seifi et al. [42] evaluated three possible interfaces that allow users to define TPs for a single actuator in a Wizard of Oz study. They conclude that users want more control (intensity, roughness, and rhythm) over TPs than a simple choice among preset patterns. *Macaron* is a web-based TP editor for single actuator TP design [40]. Swindells et al. published an editor to merge simple haptics with audio and video channels [44].

Cuartielles et al. [6] briefly present four different approaches to TP editors and give recommendations on how a TP editor should allow interaction (touch-based, not overly complex, and allowing immediate replay of the created pattern). The "Blind Theatre Editor" (2009) mentioned in [6] is an approach to generate TPs for up to 64 haptic actuators. However, while it allows defining an intensity curve for each actuator individually on a timeline, like the curve mode in [24], it is also quite complex, shows just a rough indication of spatial actuator position, and can only be used by technicians [6].

The *posVibEditor* [36] aims to support TP design for multiple actuators and arbitrary waveforms but lacks in selecting a particular actuator from a large number of possibilities as the actuators are not visualized on the affected body part. Moreover, each actuator curve has to be defined individually, leading to a high degree of control on the generated pattern but is rather complex. The *bHaptics Designer* [3] by bHaptics Inc. is similar to the *posVibEditor*. It was released alongside a commercial tactile suit and accessorizes for VR gaming and also features grid and timeline editing of TPs using the mouse and keyboard [3].

TactiPEd [33] is a visual interface to easily prototype TPs for multiple actuators. [33] surveys several systems and approaches and discusses their strengths and weaknesses, including some of the ones above (see Fig. 4). The philosophy behind *TactiPEd* is closely related to this work, as the goal is to provide a simple visual interface to define TPs for multiple actuators. While [33] works for actuator arrangements of up to 6 to 8 actuators, such as in a wristband, it is unclear whether it scales to more complex spatial arrangements due to the missing spatial 3D mapping. The *Tactile Animation Authoring Tool*, presented with an algorithm to interpolate between actuators in grid displays, is similar to the algorithm used in this work. It allows users to draw strokes on a 2D grid representation of actuators, thus enabling rapid prototyping of TPs for 1D or 2D tactile grids [38]. It has not been released publicly nor validated in usability studies with standardized usability measures.

HFX Studio [7] is a haptic editor to design patterns for VR use cases with the human perceptual model in mind. The intention is to design haptic patterns for VR, but the actual pattern editing is performed outside of VR using Unity timelines with a mouse and keyboard. Thus, while the aim is related to the aims of *VRTactileDraw*, the interaction concept is very different. In principle, HFX Studio can design TPs of similar spatial complexity like the ones resulting from *VRTactileDraw*. However, the effort and time investments in designing such complex TPs are considerably higher than our approach. In Danieau et al.'s [7] study task of drawing a tactile arrow on a model, users took more than three minutes on average, while the same task takes just a few seconds with *VRTactileDraw*. Nevertheless, HFX studio is one of the most advanced haptic editors, as it aims for high precision and even allows defining effects for other modalities (like thermal and pressure) in addition to vibration.

VibroPlay [21] is the first short concept of an in-VR TP editor that allows direct manipulation of a pattern by touching actuators in a model (only supports binary on or off), which is distinct to our approach. The concept was neither fully documented nor tested in a usability study. Finally, *3DTactileDraw* [24], mentioned in the introduction, shows a first implementation of two possible user interfaces for designing TPs using strokes on a model for a large number of actuators in arbitrary configurations. The implemented curve interface (see Fig. 2, left) is closely related to many of the approaches above. The drawing interface (see Fig. 2, right) pursues a novel approach to define TPs. With the drawing interface, individual actuators no longer have to be defined separately. Instead, the user can draw a stroke on the model of a body part. An interpolation algorithm, first published in [25,26] and similar to *TactileBrush* [22,38], takes care of modeling the resulting TP. This drawing interface was preferred by most participants of the user studies that compared the curve interface, and the drawing interface [24]. However, due to the nature of a 2D user interface and mouse and keyboard input, this system has some inherent limitations. For this reason, we decided to realize the TP editor in a VR environment. Unlike most previous related works, the simple and intuitive design of *VRTactileDraw* focuses on novice users.

3   Iterative Design Process and Implementation

We started by reviewing TP design interfaces from related work. We settled on using the Unity IDE for VR scene modeling with the HTC VIVE Pro, including the wireless add-on, as the basis of our system. The HTC VIVE has left and right-hand controllers, which are used simultaneously. These controllers feature several buttons, including an analog trigger button and a touchpad, which offer various possibilities for the design of VR interfaces.

3.1   Virtual Reality Interface Design

Apart from appropriate hardware, a suitable user interface design is needed for effective tool selection and to prevent so-called VR sickness (in particular nausea) from occurring [30]. Previous work on VR sketching showed prototypes of, e.g., a color selector menu [9]. We mostly followed the guidelines by Sherman et al. [43] for general guidelines, Alger [1] for recent VR interfaces, and Lin et al. [31] for measures to prevent VR sickness. Lin et al. [31] recommend using *independent visual backgrounds* to reduce VR sickness. With RQ2 in mind, we implemented this by using a low-poly background from the Unity asset store. We chose a background with few environmental features (e.g., mountains and trees) to prevent distraction and for performance reasons. The VR environment should be rendered at least as fast as the VR headset refresh rate to reduce the likelihood of VR sickness and nausea [43,46]. Alger recommends using radial menus anchored on the controllers or hands themselves combined with a touchpad [1]. We found this a useful recommendation for implementing several different interface options for the HTC Vive controllers as we aimed to design our interface as simple and intuitive as possible (RQ1). The final mapping of interface functions to controller buttons is shown in Fig. 5. Because drawing in mid-air sometimes leads to inaccuracies, it is necessary to let users rapidly delete and re-draw a stroke in case of erroneous input.

3.2   Goals and Basic Features

We defined the following set of goals for the system, which originate from earlier work [24], VR interface design guidelines mentioned above, our research questions defined in the introduction, and pilot testing:

G1 Make the VR interface easy and intuitive to use so that non-technical and first-time VR users can still design their imagined TPs for a complex tactile interface on an experimental basis, without having to rely on external documentation or training.

G2 All settings within the interface should be within reach, and easily usable, comparable to *Tilt Brush* [17] and adhere to the design guidelines set by Alger [1].

We identified the following basic features of the VR TP design interface, which originate from pilot testing and adapting related work in VR [24]:

- Drawing strokes of varying intensity levels by "laser pointing" at a modeled body part.
- Instantly rendering the stroke that a user is currently drawing as a TP (the user should see real-time visual feedback and feel tactile feedback).
- Selecting existing strokes by pointing and clicking or through menu buttons.
- Replaying the entire pattern, which may consist of several strokes that may overlap in time.
- Changing the TP playback speed seamlessly within a certain range (e.g., 0.1–3.0 times the original speed).
- Jumping to a desired position within the TP and looping the TP.
- Changing the start time of a stroke relative to other strokes after drawing it.
- Deleting strokes and patterns.

3.3 Design and Implementation

Based on related work and the goals and essential functions outlined above, we started designing a VR interface for TPs from scratch. In our first sketching sessions, we came up with the concept of two radial controller menus as suggested by Alger [1], where one "draw" controller in the user's dominant hand would be responsible for the main functions (e.g., draw, delete stroke/entire pattern, return to the main menu). In contrast, the "select" controller in the user's non-dominant hand is mapped to secondary functions, such as stroke selection, pattern playback speed, start/pause, and current position in the pattern. Furthermore, we designed a simple main menu for choosing between the available patterns, specify global settings, and potentially delete patterns.

We used Unity v5.6.6f for the implementation. The project is designed so that it can easily be used with a variety of tactile interfaces.

We implemented the aforementioned basic features and made them accessible via two controller menus as shown in Fig. 5. To quickly delete multiple strokes, we implemented a multi-tap for the "delete stroke" button so that users can delete strokes in rapid succession without a confirmation dialog. We decided not to implement an undo function for this feature, as it is easy to draw a new stroke in case of accidental deletion. Deleting all strokes at once is also possible by deleting the entire pattern in the main menu.

As shown in Fig. 6, we designed a head-up display (HUD) embedded in the upper center of the user's field of view. The HUD shows the current and total time in the pattern, an overlay of all strokes with their respective colors, the selected pattern speed, and whether pattern looping is turned on. It also seamlessly shows the current position on the timeline while changing the current time. This HUD makes it easy to use these functions without looking at the controller. We also decided to show the current stroke intensity percentage as a hint that stroke intensity is proportional to force applied to the trigger button (hidden while no stroke is being drawn).

Since the user can draw multiple strokes which have to be visually distinguished, we select colors for our strokes by picking colors from a color alphabet

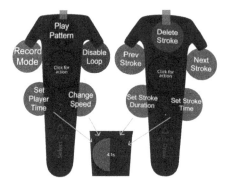

Fig. 5. Final mapping of the controller menu in the final prototype. Some functions were not yet present in the user study. Left: selection controller, right: drawing controller. Menu items can be selected by moving the thumb in the appropriate direction on the touch pad and then pressing down. Pressing down multiple times without fully lifting the thumb triggers the action repeatedly. Some menu items lead to an adjustable slider, which is confirmed by pressing down (bottom center).

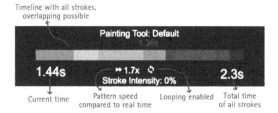

Fig. 6. First version of the head-up display with annotated elements.

designed by Green-Armytage [18]. It ensures a high contrast between the colors and works well on bright backgrounds.

We initially implemented the same interpolation algorithm for tactile actuation as in [24,26], but finally settled on a different algorithm. The original algorithm was targeted explicitly at guidance, whereas in this work, each actuator's intensity depends on one or more drawn strokes. The original guidance algorithm would sometimes stimulate an actuator farther away to get a person to move their head in that direction. In contrast, the new algorithm always picks the actuators closest to the stroke. The new interpolation algorithm works as follows: For a single position on a stroke, we gather the $N = 3$ closest actuators. These are driven at an intensity proportional to their distance to the stroke position, normalized over all N actuators, and multiplied by the stroke's intensity at the current position $(0..1)$. In case multiple stroke positions of different strokes affect an actuator at the same time, the results are added up per actuator and capped at the maximum intensity. This algorithm is less suitable for tactile interfaces that do not feature a dense layout of tactile actuators. For example, *HapticHead* has closely spaced actuators to take advantage of the tactile funneling illusion, which may cause users to perceive stimulations as smoother and in-between actuators [26,27]. The interpolation algorithm can easily be replaced by a more appropriate algorithm for less dense arrangements.

4 User Study

We validated our system in a user study with 17 participants from different backgrounds and gathered feedback on possible improvements.

4.1 Design and Study Tasks

We chose the think-aloud method [47] for our study as it helps to expose usability flaws. In a think-aloud study, the user interface should be self-descriptive so that the user can work on a given task without any advice from the experimenter [47].

To make participants fully explore the possibilities of the interface, we designed a set of 10 tasks. Most of these tasks are open so that the participants may take various approaches and may reach different results.

Specifically, the tasks ask the participants to design a TP which:

1. asks the user to stop,
2. notifies the user of an up-leading staircase,
3. asks the user to turn right,
4. asks the user to crouch,
5. lets the user feel a growing tension,
6. asks the user to look up,
7. warns the user of a future earthquake,
8. asks the user to run forward,
9. lets the user feel a slow heartbeat, and
10. lets the user feel a simultaneous vibration left and right.

Tasks 1–8 represent general use cases of the tactile interface. Task 9 was chosen so that users experiment with the "Loop" feature and task 10 requires users to experiment with the "set stroke time" feature.

4.2 Implementation

We implemented the aforementioned counterbalanced tasks in the interface by embedding the textual instruction statically in the scene's background. Users are constantly reminded of what they are currently working on.

4.3 Procedure

After reading and signing an informed consent form and optionally a photographic release form, we explained the think-aloud study method [47] to the participant. For hygienic reasons, participants wore a balaclava under the *HapticHead* prototype, which played the TP. On top of that, they wore the HTC

Vive Pro, which rendered the VR scenes. The only other instruction to each participant was that they are supposed to go back to the main menu after finishing a task, possibly take a break and then start the next task.

Before starting the actual experiment, we tested each of the 24 actuators of the *HapticHead* individually to make sure there were no defects. The participant then started working on the first task after tapping the appropriate "new pattern" button in the main menu. A balanced Latin Square counterbalanced tasks to distribute order effects. In case the participant gave us consent, we also recorded the entire session on video for later analysis. All participants gave us consent for video recording, at least for internal uses. In the end, the participant filled out a final questionnaire containing several Likert scales and comment fields about his or her experiences. Since we wanted to measure the final usability (RQ1) and comfort (RQ2) of our system, we used *system usability scale* (SUS) [5] questions in the final questionnaire, and users also filled out an *AttrakDiff* questionnaire [19]. The participants received a bar of chocolate as a small sign of gratitude.

4.4 Participants

We invited a total of 17 participants (one woman and 16 men, 12 technical and 5 non-technical backgrounds, mean age 24 years, SD 3.4 years). Eight participants had prior experiences with VR headsets, and 11 frequently use game controllers. Six participants indicated drawing about once a month, five about once a year, and the others never performed any drawing activity.

4.5 Results

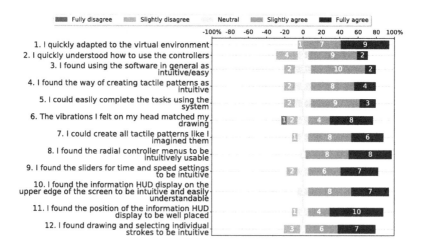

Fig. 7. Questionnaire on intuitiveness and interface design presented as a diverging stacked bar chart.

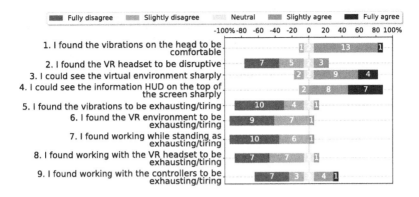

Fig. 8. Questionnaire on comfort presented as a diverging stacked bar chart.

The final questionnaire was split in SUS questions [5], questions on intuitiveness and the design of interface elements (Fig. 7), and the comfort of using the VR interface, *HapticHead*, and VR controllers (Fig. 8). The system usability scale (SUS) score of our system reached a mean of 79.7 (SD=11.2). The AttrakDiff questionnaire [19] was external as we used the official one[1]. Results of AttrakDiff are shown in Fig. 9.

Our participants generally designed quite different patterns, but some general similarities could be found among the responses as seen in Fig. 10.

4.6   Discussion

Generally, the VR TP designer was well received by the study participants. A SUS score of 79.7 is between "good" and "excellent" according to [2]. A meta-analysis of 5000 SUS evaluations showed that a system with a SUS score of 80.3 is better than 90 % of all evaluated systems [5,37]. The AttrakDiff scores show a similarly positive result. The system is generally rated as desirable (Fig. 9), with a little higher pragmatic than hedonic quality (answers RQ1). However, the AttrakDiff result is influenced by two questions that generally penalize VR systems: Since the system is a solo VR experience, it is more isolating than connective (the real world is completely shut out), and it separates the user from the world and other people around, instead of bringing them closer together (see Fig. 9, right). Without these two categories, the already good AttrakDiff scores would likely be even higher.

There are possible solutions to make users feel less isolated from the world and other people. For example, it is possible to put the entire experience into an AR context instead of VR, using a device like the Microsoft HoloLens. Doing this would make users feel more connected to the real world and further bring them closer to other people. Multiple users could collaboratively work together on a single pattern: All participating users could feel the pattern they collaboratively

---

[1] http://attrakdiff.de/index-en.html – accessed September 04, 2020.

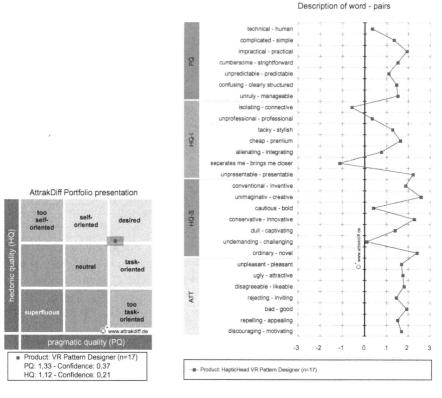

Fig. 9. AttrakDiff: Portfolio of results (left) and Diagram of word pairs (right).

created. Patterns could be discussed immediately. New ideas could be brain-stormed, explored, and refined together.

Figure 7 shows that the overwhelming majority of the participants liked the concept, implementation, and intuitiveness of the design (answers RQ1). Nonetheless, the following analysis concentrates on the few negative responses we got in the questionnaires.

P2 strongly disagreed that the vibrations he felt on his head were matching his drawing. This participant tried to specifically target individual actuators and insert pauses of no actuation, which was difficult with the prototype and chosen interpolation algorithm. It incorporated the $N = 3$ closest actuators instead of just one. While it is possible to add pauses with the "set stroke time" function, this is not as intuitive as a "record mode," which this participant suggested instead of stopping the time while a stroke is not being drawn. P8 was the other participant who was mostly negative on the questions shown in Fig. 7 and answered positively on some of the tiring questions in Fig. 8. At 33 years, P8 was the oldest participant and did not like the concept of vibrations on the head.

Regarding comfort, Fig. 8 shows that the majority of users were happy with the design and software prototype (answers RQ2). Some participants could not adjust the VIVE Pro headset in such a way that they could sharply see the

VR scene and interface. While we made sure that the headset was adequately adjusted at the beginning of the study, it may shift slightly on the head during the study, which leads to the display surface not being in focus. Also, three participants did not like the VR headset with *HapticHead* below it and described it as disruptive or annoying. Nevertheless, only one of our 17 participants would have preferred working with a standard 2D UI instead of a VR interface. Five of the participants agreed that working with the controllers was exhausting or tiring. We can relate this to the clunkiness and weight of the VIVE controllers (203 g each). Future systems might offer different controller types, e.g., Valve index controllers[2], which naturally fit around the hands without needing a permanent firm hand grip.

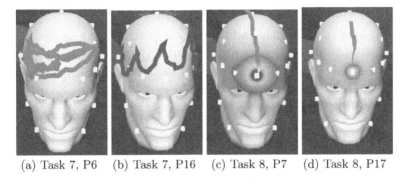

(a) Task 7, P6   (b) Task 7, P16   (c) Task 8, P7   (d) Task 8, P17

Fig. 10. Example TP designs by our participants. Task 7 was to design a pattern to notify the user of an earthquake, while task 8 encouraged the user to run forward. The heat map in (c) and (d) shows the stroke's start and intensity.

Another interesting finding is the appropriateness, complexity, and similarity of the TPs designed by our participants. While appropriateness is difficult to measure as it is highly individual, pattern complexity varied strongly between participants. Some used only a single short stroke, while others used multiple strokes of varying intensity for the same task. Not all of the designed patterns were similar, but certain tasks had a considerable level of agreement. Figure 10 shows a number of example designs. The task to design a TP for notifying the user of an earthquake evoked mostly high-intensity patterns, which spread over multiple regions of the head. Other tasks, e.g., the task to encourage the user to run forward, produced simpler lower intensity patterns. An interesting avenue for future research may be a study on how users define and recognize their own TPs and how the TP designs of different users differ in certain relevant aspects (e.g., intensity, complexity, and head region).

In terms of usability comparison vs. related work, we cannot directly compare our system's usability against other TP editors, as no other work we know of published standardized usability measures such as SUS or AttrakDiff. In terms of performance, our system is faster for rapid prototyping of complex TPs than

---

[2] https://www.valvesoftware.com/en/index/controllers – accessed August 20, 2020.

TP editors based on timelines or intensity curves for individual actuators. For example, HFX Studio [7], as one of the most sophisticated TP editors, conducted a study in which participants had to draw a tactile arrow on the back of a torso model. Their users took more than three minutes on average to complete the task, while the same task using *VRTactileDraw* is as simple as drawing an arrow in any drawing application and only takes a few seconds. The only other work using a similar algorithmic interpolation approach as *VRTactileDraw*, the *Tactile Animation Authoring Tool* [38], is likely to have a similar TP prototyping performance, but only in the case of a 1D or 2D tactile grid. However, we are not aware of a public release of the tool or any usability evaluation with standardized usability measures.

4.7   Improvements After the User Study

We implemented the following features that our participants suggested:

- *Set stroke duration* function: Allows changing the total duration of an individual stroke after drawing it with visual feedback (changing bar length) in the HUD. Eight participants suggested this.
- *Symmetric mirror drawing mode*: Strokes on one side of the model are simultaneously drawn on the other side of the model (symmetric relative to the mid-sagittal plane). This was requested by five participants and generalizes to other systems beyond *HapticHead* due to the human body's symmetry.
- *Show actuator positions* option: This option in the main menu shows the positions of all actuators so that users can consider actuator locations while drawing patterns. Four participants requested this.
- *Record mode*: While pushing a record menu button on the select (left-hand) controller, time moves on even while not drawing a stroke compared to the regular mode, in which pattern recording time stops when no stroke is being drawn. A red recording icon on the HUD shows whether the record mode is active at a given time. A single participant suggested this function. We still found it to be a worthwhile addition.

With these changes, there are two drawing modes: *normal* and *mirror*. Switching between these modes is performed by the VIVE controller grip button. Otherwise, most of the new functions can be reached through the controller menus' final mapping (see Fig. 5).

Fig. 11. Final version of the HUD. Recording mode is currently active and a stroke is being drawn.

We also polished the overall look and feel of the HUD by adding a vertical red time indicator, choosing appropriate background transparency, and hiding elements that are not strictly necessary in a given context (see Fig. 11).

Even though related work [38,39] found that users might want to manipulate created paths after initial creation, only three participants would have liked an option to manipulate stroke intensity after creation. No participant suggested altering the strokes spatially. Thus, we chose not to include an option to manipulate strokes, as the current implementation allows rapid deletion and re-drawing of a stroke, which is only marginally slower than selecting a different tool and manipulating a stroke.

5   Limitations

While our software prototype already received predominantly positive feedback, we did not conduct a follow-up study of the changes made after the user study. Since we implemented features that the participants suggested and that we considered valuable, we estimate the SUS and AttrakDiff scores to improve with these changes. We aim for the final verification of this hypothesis in future work.

Nine of our 17 participants in the user study had no prior experience with VR systems. Thus a novelty effect [28] cannot be precluded. Even if we had recruited only participants with prior VR experience, a novelty effect could still occur as the TP editor itself would be novel to them. Thus, the ratings of our TP editor are likely positively biased. The novelty effect wears off over time [28], so a long-term study in future work may procure more accurate ratings.

6   Open Source Release and Extension to Other Prototypes

The user study was conducted with a tactile display from prior work [25,26]. However, the prototype can easily be extended to support different body-worn tactile feedback systems, like tactile vests or full-body suits [3,4,10,14,26,29, 32,41]. We provide an open-source release[3] of *VRTactileDraw*. The interface is implemented in a modular, extensible way so that it is easy to replace the main components to fit specific requirements. In order to use the *VRTactileDraw* editor with a different tactile output system, a developer has to perform the following steps, further specified in the documentation:

- Replace the provided models of the head and human body with a targeted body part model (e.g., chest).
- Create copies of the *Actuator Prefab* model, assign unique ids, and position the actuators according to the tactile system's specification. This is all done inside the Unity editor.
- Implement a script to drive the new tactile system, including the system-specific communication protocol. The *RaspberryCommandSender* class may serve as an example.

---

[3] VRTactileDraw open-source release: https://github.com/obkaul/VRTactileDraw.

With the open-source release, we provide a documented framework for developers to use on their own tactile prototypes. The original software prototype for *HapticHead* is included in the framework. Besides, we provide other examples of tactile displays: two different tactile vests, including the respective 3D model of a complete human body.

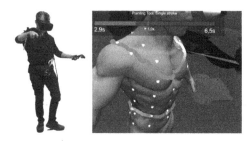

Fig. 12. *VRTactileDraw* driving a 52-actuator tactile vest mockup, and the users' view inside an HTC Vive

Figure 12, left, shows *VRTactileDraw* in action on a virtual tactile vest with 52 actuators around the torso and over the shoulders. The VR software components are fully implemented, but the tactile output system is currently a mockup only.

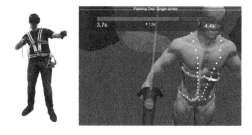

Fig. 13. *VRTactileDraw* driving the MultiWave prototype vest [41]: A wearable vibrotactile vest containing 76 actuators (left) and the user's view inside an HTC Vive (right). The user is replaying a TP and simultaneously feels vibrations as indicated by the heatmap.

Figure 13 shows *VRTactileDraw* driving a fully implemented tactile vest system [41]. *MultiWave* is an FPGA-based controller for multiple tactile actuators connected to a tactile vest prototype, which is intended for mobile haptic feedback in virtual or augmented reality [41]. It consists of 76 actuators controlled by *MultiWave* via Bluetooth or WiFi. *VRTactileDraw* can be used to generate TPs for *MultiWave* and the tactile vest, e.g., to realize navigation for visually impaired people and to provide orientation feedback and effects in VR environments.

7   Conclusion and Future Work

We present the first full-fledged design, implementation, and evaluation of a TP editor where the actual TP editing process is entirely conducted inside a virtual environment. VR interfaces are well suited for designing TPs for complex spatial arrangements of tactile actuators. Users can freely move around and generally have a better understanding of spatial relationships than in 2D UIs (see [12]). Our system is also more scalable in terms of the number of actuators and spatial actuator configurations than traditional timeline-based TP pattern design UIs. In traditional timeline-based TP editors, a designer has to define an intensity curve for each actuator. Simultaneously, in our approach, an interpolation algorithm takes care of calculating intensity curves of all actuators in real-time based on simple strokes drawn by potentially novice users.

VRTactileDraw is generally easy to use and understand, especially when considering the complexity of the created patterns generated out of simple strokes. Thus, we can answer the research questions defined in the introduction as follows: The presented VR interface with its minimalistic environment and self-explanatory interactions is indeed highly suitable to design tactile patterns as it allows rapid prototyping, the SUS, and AttrakDiff scores indicate a desirable system and most of our users were able to design TPs without any prior knowledge freely and rated it as generally intuitive (see Fig. 7 and 9, answers RQ1), and it was highly accepted amongst our study participants in terms of comfort (see Fig. 8, answers RQ2).

Apart from extending our system to other tactile prototypes, as mentioned in the previous section, another direction for future work was already hinted at in the discussion: Multiple users could collaboratively design TPs, either in the same VR environment and simultaneously experience the created patterns or in an AR variant that shows the natural environment, other users, as well as the designed TPs. This collaboration would make users feel less isolated from the world and their colleagues, facilitate discussion about and refine patterns, and probably lead to a better overall result. However, it would require that each user is equipped with a tactile feedback device.

These collaborating users would not even need to be at the same physical location but could be represented by avatars and work together at a distance, sharing the created patterns. Furthermore, one user could draw a tactile stroke on a body part, while another user would simultaneously feel the tactile feedback. This would allow for the exploration of novel use cases compared to simple TP design, like feeling the touch of another person, hugs, "cuddles," and possibly experiencing a faraway person's emotions. Future work may also investigate the effects of drawing TPs from a third-person perspective and experiencing the synchronous tactile sensation on the process of designing tactile patterns and the outcome.

All the use cases mentioned above of extending our concept to multiple users are another considerable advantage of our in-VR (or potentially AR) concept over traditional TP designers. These are not easily extended to multiple collaborating users working in the same environment.

References

1. Alger, M.: Visual Design Methods for Virtual Reality. Personal Website (September), 98 (2015). http://aperturesciencellc.com/vr/VisualDesignMethodsforVR_MikeAlger.pdf
2. Bangor, A., Kortum, P., Miller, J.: Determining what individual SUS scores mean. J. Usability Stud. **4**(3), 114–123 (2009)
3. BHaptics: bHaptics Tactot (2020). https://www.bhaptics.com/tactsuit/
4. Bloomfield, A., Badler, N.I.: A Low cost tactor suit for vibrotactile feedback a low cost tactor suit for vibrotactile feedback. Technical reports (CIS) (January), 7 (2003)
5. Brooke, J.: SUS?: a Retrospective. J. Usability Stud. **8**(2), 29–40 (2013)
6. Cuartielles, D., Göransson, A., Olsson, T., Stenslie, S.: Developing visual editors for high-resolution haptic patterns. In: The Seventh International Workshop on Haptic and Audio Interaction Design, pp. 42–44 (2012). http://www.forskningsdatabasen.dk/en/catalog/2389362226
7. Danieau, F., Guillotel, P., Dumas, O., Lopez, T., Leroy, B., Mollet, N.: HFX studio: haptic editor for full-body immersive experiences. In: Proceedings of the ACM Symposium on Virtual Reality Software and Technology, VRST (2018). https://doi.org/10.1145/3281505.3281518
8. de Jesus Oliveira, V.A., Brayda, L., Nedel, L., Maciel, A.: Designing a vibrotactile head-mounted display for spatial awareness in 3d spaces. IEEE Trans. Vis. Comput. Graphics **23**(4), 1409–1417 (2017). https://doi.org/10.1109/TVCG.2017.2657238, http://ieeexplore.ieee.org/document/7829406/
9. Deering, M.F.: HoloSketch: a virtual reality sketching / animation tool. ACM Trans. Comput.-Hum. Interact. (TOCHI) **2**(3), 220–238 (1995). https://doi.org/10.1145/210079.210087
10. Delazio, A., Nakagaki, K., Lehman, J.F., Klatzky, R.L., Sample, A.P., Hudson, S.E.: Force jacket: pneumatically-actuated jacket for embodied haptic experiences. In: Conference on Human Factors in Computing Systems - Proceedings 2018-April, pp. 1–12 (2018). https://doi.org/10.1145/3173574.3173894
11. Dobrzynski, M.K., Mejri, S., Wischmann, S., Floreano, D.: Quantifying information transfer through a head-attached vibrotactile display: principles for design and control. IEEE Trans. Biomed. Eng. **59**(7), 2011–2018 (2012). https://doi.org/10.1109/TBME.2012.2196433, http://ieeexplore.ieee.org/lpdocs/epic03/wrapper.htm?arnumber=6189750
12. Dünser, A., Steinbügl, K., Kaufmann, H., Glück, J.: Virtual and augmented reality as spatial ability training tools. In: ACM International Conference Proceeding Series vol. 158, pp. 125–132 (2006). https://doi.org/10.1145/1152760.1152776
13. Enriquez, M.J., MacLean, K.E.: The hapticon editor: A tool in support of haptic communication research. In: Proceedings - 11th Symposium on Haptic Interfaces for Virtual Environment and Teleoperator Systems, HAPTICS 2003, pp. 356–362. IEEE Computer Society (2003). https://doi.org/10.1109/HAPTIC.2003.1191310, http://ieeexplore.ieee.org/document/1191310/
14. Erp, J.B.F.V., Veen, H.A.H.C.V.: A Multi-purpose tactile vest for astronauts in the international space station. In: Proceedings of Eurohaptics, pp. 405–408 (2003)
15. Flores, G., Kurniawan, S., Manduchi, R., Martinson, E., Morales, L.M., Sisbot, E.A.: Vibrotactile guidance for wayfinding of blind walkers. IEEE Trans. Haptics **8**(3), 306–317 (2015). https://doi.org/10.1109/TOH.2015.2409980

16. Geldard, F.A.: Adventures in tactile literacy. Am. Psychol. **12**(3), 115–124 (1957). https://doi.org/10.1037/h0040416, http://content.apa.org/journals/amp/12/3/115
17. Google LLC: Tilt Brush by Google (2016). https://www.tiltbrush.com/
18. Green-Armytage, P.: A colour alphabet and the limits of colour coding. JAIC - J. Int. Colour Assoc. **5**, 1–23 (2010). https://www.aic-color.org/resources/Documents/jaic_v5_06.pdf
19. Hassenzahl, M., Burmester, M., Koller, F.: AttrakDiff: Ein Fragebogen zur Messung wahrgenommener hedonischer und pragmatischer Qualität, pp. 187–196. Vieweg+Teubner Verlag (2003). https://doi.org/10.1007/978-3-322-80058-9_19, http://link.springer.com/10.1007/978-3-322-80058-9_19
20. Hong, K., Lee, J., Choi, S.: Demonstration-based vibrotactile pattern authoring. In: Proceedings of the 7th International Conference on Tangible, Embedded and Embodied Interaction - TEI 2013, p. 219. ACM Press, New York, USA (2013). https://doi.org/10.1145/2460625.2460660
21. Huang, D.Y., et al.: VibroPlay: aaorind three-dimensional spatial-temporal tactile effects with direct manipulation. In: SA 2016 - SIGGRAPH ASIA 2016 Emerging Technologies (2016). https://doi.org/10.1145/2988240.2988250
22. Israr, A., Poupyrev, I.: Tactile brush. In: Proceedings of the 2011 Annual Conference on Human Factors in Computing Systems - CHI 2011, p. 2019. ACM Press, New York, USA (May 2011). https://doi.org/10.1145/1978942.1979235
23. Jones, L.A., Sarter, N.B.: Tactile displays: guidance for their design and application. Hum. Factors **50**(1), 90–111 (2008). https://doi.org/10.1518/001872008X250638, http://journals.sagepub.com/doi/10.1518/001872008X250638
24. Kaul, O.B., Hansing, L., Rohs, M.: 3DTactileDraw: a tactile pattern design interface for complex arrangements of actuators. In: Extended Abstracts of the 2019 CHI Conference on Human Factors in Computing Systems - CHI EA 2019, pp. 1–6. ACM Press, New York, USA (2019). https://doi.org/10.1145/3290607.3313030
25. Kaul, O.B., Rohs, M.: HapticHead: 3d guidance and target acquisition through a vibrotactile grid. In: Proceedings of the 2016 CHI Conference Extended Abstracts on Human Factors in Computing Systems - CHI EA 2016, pp. 2533–2539. ACM Press, New York, USA (May 2016). https://doi.org/10.1145/2851581.2892355
26. Kaul, O.B., Rohs, M.: HapticHead: a spherical vibrotactile grid around the head for 3d guidance in virtual and augmented reality. In: Proceedings of the 2017 CHI Conference on Human Factors in Computing Systems - CHI 2017, pp. 3729–3740. ACM Press, New York, USA (2017). https://doi.org/10.1145/3025453.3025684
27. Kaul, O.B., Rohs, M., Simon, B., Demir, K.C., Ferry, K.: Vibrotactile funneling illusion and localization performance on the head. In: Proceedings of the 2020 CHI Conference on Human Factors in Computing Systems - CHI 2020, pp. 1–13. Association for Computing Machinery (ACM), Honolulu, Hawaii, USA (April 2020). https://doi.org/10.1145/3313831.3376335
28. Koch, M., Von Luck, K., Schwarzer, J., Draheim, S.: The novelty effect in large display deployments-experiences and lessons-learned for evaluating prototypes. In: ECSCW 2018 - Proceedings of the 16th European Conference on Computer Supported Cooperative Work. European Society for Socially Embedded Technologies (EUSSET) (2018). https://dl.eusset.eu/handle/20.500.12015/3115
29. Konishi, Y., et al.: Synesthesia suit. In: Hasegawa, S., Konyo, M., Kyung, K.-U., Nojima, T., Kajimoto, H. (eds.) AsiaHaptics 2016. LNEE, vol. 432, pp. 499–503. Springer, Singapore (2018). https://doi.org/10.1007/978-981-10-4157-0_84

30. LaViola Jr, J.J.: A discussion of cybersickness in virtual environments. ACM SIGCHI Bull. **32**(1), 47–56 (2000). https://doi.org/10.1145/333329.333344, http://portal.acm.org/citation.cfm?doid=333329.333344

31. Lin, J.J.W., Abi-Rached, H., Kim, D.H., Parker, D.E., Furness, T.A.: A "natural" independent visual background reduced simulator sickness. In: Proceedings of the Human Factors and Ergonomics Society Annual Meeting, vol. 46, no. 26, pp. 2124–2128 (2002). https://doi.org/10.1177/154193120204602605, http://journals.sagepub.com/doi/10.1177/154193120204602605

32. Lindeman, R.W., Page, R., Yanagida, Y., Sibert, J.L.: Towards full-body haptic feedback: the design and deployment of a spatialized vibrotactile feedback system. In: Proceedings of the ACM Symposium on Virtual Reality Software and Technology, VRST, pp. 146–149 (2004)

33. Paneels, S., Anastassova, M., Strachan, S., Van, S.P., Sivacoumarane, S., Bolzmacher, C.: What's around me Multi-actuator haptic feedback on the wrist. In: 2013 World Haptics Conference, WHC 2013, pp. 407–412 (2013)

34. Pielot, M., Krull, O., Boll, S.: Where is my team? Supporting situation awareness with tactile displays. In: Proceedings of the 28th international conference on Human factors in computing systems - CHI 2010, p. 1705. ACM Press, New York, USA (April 2010). https://doi.org/10.1145/1753326.1753581

35. Precision Microdrives: Precision Microdrives 312–101 (2017). https://www.precisionmicrodrives.com/product/312-101-12mm-vibration-motor-3mm-type

36. Ryu, J., Choi, S.: posVibEditor: graphical authoring tool of vibrotactile patterns. In: 2008 IEEE International Workshop on Haptic Audio visual Environments and Games, pp. 120–125. IEEE (Oct 2008). https://doi.org/10.1109/HAVE.2008.4685310, http://ieeexplore.ieee.org/document/4685310/

37. Sauro, J.: A Practical Guide to the System Usability Scale: Background, Benchmarks & Best Practices. Measuring Usability LLC, Denver (2011)

38. Schneider, O.S., Israr, A., MacLean, K.E.: Tactile animation by direct manipulation of grid displays. In: Proceedings of the 28th Annual ACM Symposium on User Interface Software & Technology - UIST 2015, pp. 21–30. ACM Press, New York, USA (2015). https://doi.org/10.1145/2807442.2807470

39. Schneider, O.S., Maclean, K.E.: Improvising design with a haptic instrument. In: IEEE Haptics Symposium, HAPTICS, pp. 327–332 (2014). https://doi.org/10.1109/HAPTICS.2014.6775476

40. Schneider, O.S., MacLean, K.E.: Studying design process and example use with Macaron, a web-based vibrotactile effect editor. In: IEEE Haptics Symposium, HAPTICS 2016-April, pp. 52–58 (2016). https://doi.org/10.1109/HAPTICS.2016.7463155

41. Schrapel, M., Loewen, S., Rohs, M.: MultiWave: A Fully Customizable Mobile Function Generator For Haptic Feedback In VR. Contest (2019)

42. Seifi, H., Anthonypillai, C., MacLean, K.E.: End-user customization of affective tactile messages: a qualitative examination of tool parameters. In: 2014 IEEE Haptics Symposium (HAPTICS), pp. 251–256. IEEE (Feb 2014). https://doi.org/10.1109/HAPTICS.2014.6775463, http://ieeexplore.ieee.org/document/6775463/

43. Sherman, W.R., Craig, A.B.: Understanding virtual reality : interface, application, and design (2018). https://books.google.de/books?hl=en&lr=&id=D-OcBAAAQBAJ

44. Swindells, C., Pietarinen, S., Viitanen, A.: Medium fidelity rapid prototyping of vibrotactile haptic, audio and video effects. In: IEEE Haptics Symposium, HAPTICS, pp. 515–521 (2014). https://doi.org/10.1109/HAPTICS.2014.6775509

45. Tsukada, K., Yasumura, M.: ActiveBelt: belt-type wearable tactile display for directional navigation, vol. 3205 (2004). http://link.springer.com/chapter/10. 1007/978-3-540-30119-6_23

46. Unity Technologies: Unity - Manual: VR overview (2019). https://docs.unity3d. com/Manual/VROverview.html

47. Van Someren, M.W., Barnard, Y.F., Sandberg, J.A.C.: The Think Aloud Method: A Practical Approach to Modelling Cognitive Processes. London: AcademicPress, Cambridge (1994)

When Friends Become Strangers: Understanding the Influence of Avatar Gender on Interpersonal Distance in Virtual Reality

Radiah Rivu[1(⊠)], Yumeng Zhou[2], Robin Welsch[2], Ville Mäkelä[1,2,3], and Florian Alt[1]

[1] Universität der Bundeswehr München, Neubiberg, Germany
{sheikh.rivu,florian.alt}@unibw.de
[2] LMU Munich, Munich, Germany
{yumeng.zhou,robin.welsch,ville.makela}@ifi.lmu.de
[3] University of Waterloo, Waterloo, Canada

Abstract. In this paper, we investigate how mismatches between biological gender and avatar gender affect interpersonal distance (IPD) in virtual reality (VR). An increasing number of VR experiences and online platforms like Rec Room and VRChat allow users to assume other genders through customized avatars. While the effects of acquaintanceship and gender have been studied with regard to proxemic behavior, the effect of changed genders remains largely unexplored. We conducted a user study (N = 40, friends = 20, strangers = 20) where users played a two-player collaborative game in Rec Room using both male and female avatars. We found that with swapped avatar genders, the preferred distance increased between friends but not between strangers. We discuss how our results can inform researchers and designers in the domain of multi-user VR.

1 Introduction

In virtual reality (VR), users can embody avatars to represent themselves that are drastically different from their real selves. Social VR platforms such as Rec Room and VRChat allow the users to engage in immersive social interaction with each other through these avatars online. Interestingly, the virtual avatar can influence how their user is perceived by others and thus how they interact with each other. This creates a need to better understand the effect avatar appearance and how it may impact user behaviour in the context of social VR.

An important factor of social interaction is non-verbal behavior such as gaze, touch and proxemics, i.e., the distance to others [1]. Knowledge on non-verbal behavior change in VR as a function of avatar appearance is important because it guides the way we design VR spaces much like in the real world. For example,

© IFIP International Federation for Information Processing 2021
Published by Springer Nature Switzerland AG 2021
C. Ardito et al. (Eds.): INTERACT 2021, LNCS 12936, pp. 234–250, 2021.
https://doi.org/10.1007/978-3-030-85607-6_16

Fig. 1. The Rec Room setup. a) Participants starting the game. b) Participants playing in the game room. c) Collaboration between participants. d) Participant being interviewed in the second room.

in the real world we design meeting spaces at work in such a way that people can comfortably interact at a so-called social distance, whereas homes accommodate for personal distance.

Previous research has studied how the appearance and gender of agents affect proxemics in VR with virtual agents [1,29,36,42]. Specifically, the interpersonal distance (IPD) that users keep between themselves and a virtual, computer-controlled agent has been explored. Female agents produce shorter IPD than male agents. However, the influence of gender and *gender mismatches* (i.e., users embodying an avatar with a gender different from their own) on interpersonal distance in dyadic interaction between VR users has not yet been explored.

Moving from computer-controlled agents to user-controlled avatars also opens up the dimension of *familiarity* that is well-studied in real life [10] but not in social VR. It remains unclear how familiarity links to avatar appearance, i.e., does it matter whether the persons interacting in VR are acquaintances in the real world or whether they do not know each other, and how does avatar appearance mitigate familiarity?

In this paper we close this gap. Our work is driven by the following research questions: (**1**) How do mismatches between biological and avatar genders affect interpersonal distance in VR? (**2**) What is the influence of the relationship between users in the real world on the effects of a gender mismatch?

We conducted a user study (N = 40, friends = 20, strangers = 20), where participants played a collaborative two-player game in Rec Room[1]. Participants

---

[1] Rec Room: https://recroom.com/.

embodied avatars of both their own gender as well as the opposite gender. We measured the distance that participants kept to each other, and we especially focused on the distance they chose to stop at when approaching each other (called *preferred distance*).

We found that **(1)** the preferred distance increases between friends as a result of the mismatch between avatar and biological gender; **(2)** the preferred distance is not affected by gender mismatches between strangers; and **(3)** users are largely unaware of changes in their preferred distance.

Our findings are valuable for researchers and designers alike. Researchers should ideally be aware of the real-world relationship between users, and their gender, when studying proxemics and social interaction in VR. Both factors can influence proxemics and ultimately the results, particularly if participants embody avatars with a different gender. Designers of virtual environments can also benefit from this knowledge during the design of a VR experience; we provide a discussion on this at the end of this paper.

2 Background

Our work draws from previous work on 1) proxemics and social interaction, 2) proxemics in VR, and 3) gender swapping.

2.1 Proxemics

Hall [5] proposed that four circular regions of egocentric space, defined by increasing radii, are distinctly reserved for social interactions: intimate space for the partner or family (0–45 cm), personal space only reserved for interaction with close friends (45–120 cm), social space for interaction with strangers (120–365 cm), and public space for the general public (365–762 cm).

Further research has refined this concept and found that a multitude of other factors influence IPD during interaction between two humans such as ethnicity, culture, and age. In non-acquainted pairs, two males keep a greater distance from each other than mixed sex pairs, and female pairs prefer shortest distances [11]. Uzzell and Horne [33] identified that sexual identity and sexual orientation determine the sex effect on IPD, rather than biological sex. This is likely because sexual attraction can modulate IPD to a large degree [37].

Proxemic theory can be used to facilitate interaction and guide the design of space and has thus found use in HCI. For example, McDaniel et al. [22] used tactile rhythms to provide cues for appropriate IPD to blind individuals. Proxemics have also been used to facilitate novel digital play experiences [25], public display interaction [18,26], and cross-device interaction [9], among others. Marquardt et al. [20] developed a proximity toolkit aimed to provide fine-grained proxemic information and thus to allow for prototyping in proximity-aware devices.

2.2   Proxemics in VR

Prior research sought to understand and compare real-world behavioral concepts to the virtual world [4,19]. Welsch et al. [38] used VR to investigate how psychopathy impacts judgement on comfortable IPD when confronted with threatening social interactions. They found that psychopathy produces smaller IPD in such situations. Llobera et al. [17] observed that as distance between participants and virtual characters decreases, the level of physiological arousal increases. Therefore, VR can be considered a viable tool to study social interaction as it allows for experimental control but also realism of social interactions [3].

The effects of gender on interpersonal distance were studied using VR by Iachini et al. [15], which showed that the effects of sex seen in the real world are at times present in VR, but there is also evidence that they are sometimes absent [12,31]. This may be because gender effects on IPD are currently not fully understood. As VR allows for the manipulation of virtual avatars and their gender, it is possible to study the effect of gender independent from the real user gender, and thus attain a more nuanced understanding on gender effects on IPD.

2.3   Gender Switching

Proxemics have also been studied in computer games. A preference for personal space and effects of avatar gender are present in games such as Second Life [7,40] and thus proxemic theory also carries to this domain. While such games are not VR per se, they share many similarities in that players embody a customizable avatar, explore a virtual world, and socialize with other players.

Gender switching is often observed among online gamers, particularly those of massively multi-player online role-playing games (MMORPGs) [13,32,35]. Gender swapping is more often observed among male gamers [13,35], some reporting advantages of embodying a female in a male-oriented environment [13]. At the same time, women frequently suffer from harassment in online video games [6].

In VR, effects of gender have been studied extensively. For example, Yee et al. [41] examined the behavioral outcome of conflicting gender cues in the virtual world. In VR, gender switching (embodying avatars of different genders) has been explored in the context of sexual harassment [27] and violence [8]. Martens et al. [21] studied the similarities and differences in gender behaviour in a virtual environment by manipulating the participants' gender. However, we are unaware of studies that focus on gender switching and its effects on proxemics.

2.4   Summary

In summary, proxemics have been studied extensively in social encounters both in the real world and in VR. In VR, we know from existing research that a multitude of factors can affect IPD, like the appearance of avatars and the users' gender [14]. However, we currently lack an understanding of how *gender swapping* affects the IPD. It also remains unclear whether real-world acquaintanceship plays a role in gender swapping. Hence, we assess whether there is a difference between groups of friends and groups of strangers, and how they perceive other users in VR with different avatar genders.

3 Study

We ran a user study to understand how users maintain IPD in a VR environment. Participants attended the study in pairs and completed playful tasks together, embodying an avatar of their own gender as well as an avatar of another gender as shown in Fig. 2.

Fig. 2. Avatars used in the study. a) Male avatar. b) Female avatar.

We recruited 40 participants (35 males, 5 females; 15 male-male groups, 5 male-female groups) with an average age of 23.7 years (SD = 7.75). Due to a significantly higher number of males using Rec Room, there exists a possible gender imbalance among the set of participants. A more balanced gender distribution could have been more easily achieved in a lab setting. However, we opted for participant-owned HMDs and Rec Room. We ran the study in Rec Room because such online social platforms are where gender swapping takes place: users interact with each other, strangers and friends alike, and they have diverse avatars to choose from and can change them at will. Also, having users participate from home, with their own equipment, using a familiar online platform, is a far more natural setting than artificial settings typically seen in labs. For an in-depth discussion on the approach we used in this remote VR study, see Rivu et al. [30].

Half of the pairs were friends and half were strangers. Participants used various head-mounted displays, the most popular being PlayStation VR (45%),

Oculus Quest (25%) and HTC Vive (10%). Participants were mainly recruited online from the Rec Room community on Reddit and Facebook. The sessions took around 30 min, and each participant was awarded 5.

3.1 Study Design and Tasks

We conducted a mixed within and between subjects design with the following independent variables:

- **Relationship (between-subjects):** strangers, friends
- **Gender (within-subjects):** own gender, changed gender
- **Gender group (between-subjects):** male-male, male-female

Based on the availability of avatar design that Rec Room offers, we instructed the participants to change their avatar to represent either the male or the female gender of the avatar. We ran the study in the online VR platform Rec Room, in which we set up custom rooms where participants played a two-player collaborative game (Fig. 1). The game consisted of two tasks. Our game design was based on giving two players the opportunity to interact and move around, which is crucial for studying proxemics. Thus, our game was representative of what users do on such platforms.

The first task was "Find the password" where players needed to find a clue in the room to unlock a door with a three-digit password. Participants needed to collaborate by looking around the room together and picking up objects that might be related to the password.

The second task was a "Guess the color of the drawn object". Out of five differently colored key cards on a table, one would open the back door. One player, who was told the correct color (e.g., red) by the experimenter via chat, had to draw an item on the whiteboard using marker pen (feature available in Rec Room) that would have a characteristic color (e.g., a tomato), matching the color of the correct key card. The second player would guess the color from the drawn object and then pick the key card of that color. An example of the second task is shown in Fig. 1c). The two players decided between themselves who would draw. Both tasks were designed to maximize user interaction.

After each completed task, the participants were asked to walk up to each other and congratulate their partner on having done a good job. At this point we measured the distance between users (referred to as *preferred distance*). This type of approach to measuring interpersonal distance is commonplace in proxemics research and psychology [36,38,39].

The participants played both tasks in two sessions, thus completing both tasks twice. In the second round the gender of both participants was changed to the opposite gender (counter-balanced). The study was conducted completely virtually and participants attended from their homes. Thus, we had no control over the physical settings and the participants' arrangements. However, we reason that since participants use their own VR setups, and they are Rec Room users, they are familiar with their own physical space and understand the requirements of Rec Room.

3.2   Apparatus

We built two custom rooms for the study in Rec Room (Fig. 1). In one room, participants played the game. In the other room, participants were briefed before the start of the study and later filled in a questionnaire and answered interview questions. Each player was interviewed separately.

The experimenter was remotely present, using an avatar of their biological gender. During the tasks, she was outside the room where the game was taking place, but was available through the audio channel. In the instruction phase and the post-study interview the experimenter was visible to participants.

3.3   Data Collection

Demographics and Qualitative Measures. The demographics questionnaire consisted of 14 questions where we asked participants about their gender, age, country of origin, prior experience with VR, and relationship to the other player. We also conducted a post-study questionnaire and interview asking about their own perceived behavior and their perception of their game partner after the gender swap.

Proximity Detection. Since Rec Room does not allow the users' location to be logged and transmitted, we implemented eight virtual proximity sensors (using the look-at Gizmo and Rangefinder components available in Rec Room) in each corner of the game room. Each look-at gizmo followed one of the players and the rangefinder output the distance (in centimeters) between player and the proximity sensor in real-time on a screen which was placed outside of the game room. Each player had 4 proximity sensors assigned to track them. The output data for player 1 was indexed from A to D, starting clockwise from the upper-left corner (Fig. 3). Player 2 was indexed from E to H. During the experiment, the data output was screen-recorded in 30 FPS. The distance data was extracted from the video using the Optical Character Recognition API (OCR.Space).

The distance between participants was determined as follows. Taking the coordinates of 3 points $A(x1,y1)$, $B(x2,y2)$, $C(x3,y3)$ and their distance to player1 ($L1, L2, L3$), we calculate the coordinates for player1 using three functions:

$$(y4 - y1)^2 + (x4 - x1)^2 = L1^2$$
$$(y4 - y2)^2 + (x4 - x2)^2 = L2^2$$
$$(y4 - y3)^2 + (x4 - x3)^2 = L3^2$$

After obtaining the coordinates for each player, we calculate the distance between them using the distance formula: $d = \sqrt{(x2 - x1)^2 + (y2 - y1)^2}$, where $(x1,y1)$ and $(x2,y2)$ are the coordinates for each player.

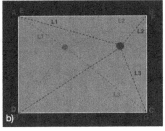

Fig. 3. Position tracking setup. a) Rangefinder to detect distance, b) Layout of position labels for each player between the Rangefinders.

Categories of Distance. We measured two distinct categories of distance:

- **Preferred distance:** distance between players at which they congratulated each other after each task.
- **Minimum distance:** overall minimum recorded distance between players. Only idle periods were counted where players remained stationary for more than four seconds. This decision was data-driven. We made an informed decision that if players were stationary even after four seconds, they were not moving and standing at x distance away from the other player which gave us the minimum distance between players.

3.4   Study Procedure

The procedure is illustrated in Fig. 4. The study started with participants entering the room where they were instructed. This room was separate from the room where the participants played the game. Participants first filled in the demographics questionnaire and gave their consent for data collection by pressing a virtual button (Fig. 1). We then started the video recording, and asked participants to move to the game room. The study was divided into two sessions, with each session consisting of the same two tasks. In each session, participants used an avatar of either their biological or opposite gender. At the beginning of each session, participants were asked to change their avatar before the game starts. At the end of each session, participants were asked to walk up to and congratulate their partner (*preferred distance measure*). Between the sessions, the experimenter reset the room and the clues for the tasks.

Finally, participants moved to the other room to respond to a questionnaire and interview questions. This phase was done individually, so the other participant waited in the game room while the first participant was interviewed. The interview was recorded.

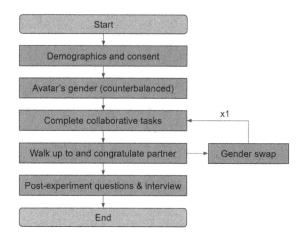

Fig. 4. Study procedure.

Table 1. Distance analysis consisting of preferred distance and minimum distance.

Distance (avg)	Male/Male	Male/Female	Friends	Strangers
Preferred distance (own gender)	1.64 m	1.58 m	1.45 m	1.80 m
Preferred distance (changed gender)	1.84 m	1.76 m	2.00 m	1.64 m
Minimum distance (own gender)	1.33 m	1.26 m	1.13 m	1.50 m
Minimum distance (changed gender)	1.11 m	0.79 m	1.09 m	0.97 m

4 Results

We present quantitative results from our statistical analysis on IPD as well as qualitative insights. Average distances of IPD measured as a function of relationship and gender switch are listed in Table 1.

4.1 Relationship (Stranger/Friend)

Friends (using their biological gender) maintained a preferred distance of 1.45 m which increased to 2.00 m with swapped gender. For strangers, the preferred distance using a biological gender was 1.80 m and 1.64 m with swapped gender.

We calculated a repeated measure ANOVA (Type III; alpha = .05) on both groups showing that for strangers, the difference is non-significant whereas for friends, there is a significant difference in the distance due to the gender swap of the avatars (p=0.031, F = 5.458). The distribution of preferred distance between each study condition is shown in Fig. 5. No significant effect was found for minimum distance ($p > .10$).

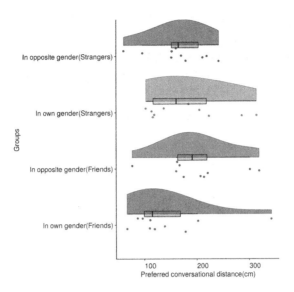

Fig. 5. Preferred distance between each relationship and gender.

4.2   Gender Group (Male–Male/Male–Female)

We compared the IPD between M/M groups and M/F groups (due to the high number of male participants, we did not have F/F groups). We ran repeated measures ANOVAs on both groups, in both minimum distance and preferred conversational distance. Neither the main effect of gender swap nor the paired gender was statistically significant (preferred distance: F = 0.003, p = .958, η^2 = 1.575e-4; minimum distance: F = 0.357, p = .558, η^2 = 0.019).

While we did not find an effect, it is known from prior work that generally differences exist between gender groups, although differences can be smaller between mixed groups and homogeneous groups [33], especially in VR [12].

4.3   Perceptions of Gender Swapping

Participants stated whether they believed changing the gender of the avatars had any effect on them in terms of behavior and experience (5-point Likert scale). The majority (72.5%) strongly believed changes in gender did not affect their own behavior or how they perceived their partner (Fig. 6). Only two participants (5%), belonging to the friends group, somewhat agreed their behavior changed. The remaining participants somewhat disagreed or were neutral about changes.

Similarly, the majority of participants strongly believed that changes in avatar gender did not affect their experience. However, out of the five female participants, two (40%) strongly agreed that the change in the other player's avatar affected their experience, whereas only three out of 35 male participants agreed (8.5%). This indicates that female players perceive their experience in social VR differently compared to males, but this cannot be reliably inferred due to the low number of female participants.

In the interview, we furthermore asked if the gender of the other person's avatar affected the distance participants chose to keep to them. Almost all participants, 37 out of 40 (92.5%), answered negatively. A few participants believed that this was because the avatars did not look realistic.

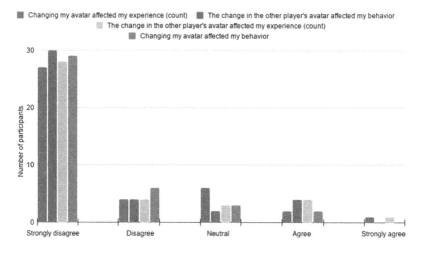

Fig. 6. Post-study questionnaire results.

4.4 Mismatch of Avatar Gender and Voice

When asked about their attitude towards the mismatch of voice and avatar gender, nine out of 40 participants (22.5%) expressed that they felt weird. Among those, only one person was from the friends group while eight were from the strangers group. This indicates that the mismatch of voice and gender may create more discomfort among strangers. Many found the mismatch acceptable though some believed it could cause confusion during social interaction. P7 stated: "It didn't bother me, but if we were to play paintball, I would be confused, I wouldn't register the voice to a different gendered avatar, so it would cause confusion' (friends group, female). P23 stated: "I don't like it very much, mostly people trying to deceive other people" (strangers group, male).

4.5 Gender Choice

When asked about how they generally choose the gender of their VR avatars, the majority of participants preferred using avatars of their own gender as it is what they identify with. Some participants preferred the male avatar as it potentially reduces chances of sexism and harassment within the social VR community. This again highlights the current attitude women face in online video gaming world [6,34]. Many participants stated to regularly use different genders. Two participants explained that they don avatars of different gender for a different experience. Three participants said they relate to both avatar genders. For some, virtual worlds allow self-exploration through different avatar appearances.

5   Discussion

Overall, our research shows that IPD in VR is affected by the gender of the users' avatars and the relationship between the users.

5.1   Gender Mismatches Increase the IPD Between Friends but Not Between Strangers

The preferred distance between friends was significantly larger when they embodied avatars with opposite gender. Preferred distance was measured after each task when the participants walked up to and congratulated each other. The appearance (e.g., gender) of the avatar affects how we perceive our friends in VR. We are likely seeing proxemics in action [1,10,29,42]: as a friend becomes less familiar in VR due to the unfamiliar visual appearance, the IPD transitions to what is commonly observed between strangers.

Despite the significant difference with preferred distance, there was no significant difference in overall minimum distance. One reason for this could be that when users are actively focusing on completing a task, changes in avatar appearance are less of a factor.

Between strangers, there was no significant difference in distance despite gender swapping. This is likely because there is no established familiarity between strangers, so gender mismatches are less pronounced. This is supported by the fact that with their own genders, the IPD was significantly greater between strangers than friends, so a more intimate IPD was never there.

5.2   Users Are Unaware of Gender Swapping Effects

The majority of participants believed that gender mismatches did not effect their behavior or experience. This strong consensus is interesting as we nonetheless found a clear difference, suggesting that changes in IPD in VR are subconscious. Due to gender mismatch, participants also experienced a mismatch of voices and among the ones who were affected by it, the majority belonged to the strangers group. This is interesting because avatar appearance affected friends more than voice mismatch, whereas strangers are more affected by voice mismatch.

There were also some interesting, generalized remarks about intentionally embodying avatars with a different gender. Some females find donning a male avatar to be more secure, and some see it as an opportunity to explore themselves with different appearances. Some also raised concerns about the intentions of another person if they are donning a different gender.

5.3   Own and Other Gender

We always swapped the gender of both participants, i.e., when two male participants met they were both assigned female avatars in the next round. We found an
effect of gender swap on IPD for friends but not for strangers. This leaves room
for interpretation on the subjectivity of the gender swapping effect on IPD. One
could argue that changing both the own gender but also seeing a change in the
other's gender could have produced the estrangement, accompanied with larger
distances, among friends because the perceived gender composition changed.

We argue that rather the perception of the other person than the change
of the own avatar produced the effect. First, rather the gender composition
than the own gender produces variation of IPD. Welsch [38] asked subjects to
position virtual characters in a third-person view. They found that both the sex
of the approached and the approaching character affected IPD. The real sex of
the participant did not contribute to understanding IPD. This interpretation of
a mere perceived sex effect runs counter to our data. Second, IPD for female
pairs is smaller than for male pairs [12,33]. Considering that the majority of
our sample was male, IPD should have been reduced following a gender swap.
We therefore believe that the mere effect of gender composition cannot account
for our results; rather the in-congruence of avatar gender and perception of real
gender in the other person, estranges friends.

Nonetheless, future work could vary the gender swap independently, i.e., only
one person from each pair changes their avatar gender. One could also change
other unique features of participants that are familiar with each other. Also,
one could add an embodiment phase in which the avatars and thus also the
perception of the own avatar gender is reinforced among the users.

5.4   Implications for Research and Design

Researchers should account for the effects of gender mismatches in their studies,
as they may affect results. Researchers should ideally report the real-world gender of the participants, their potential relationship with other participants, as
well as the appearance and gender of the avatar of each participant. Particularly
when participants are friends, gender mismatches may have a strong effect.

Designers have been using proxemics theory to aid in their work [2,23,28]. We
believe VE designers can similarly use the knowledge from our work to inform
their designs. Gender mismatches cause changes in IPD between friends, which
should be taken into account when creating collaborative virtual environments.
For example, VEs could consider how the interactive functions would remain
accessible to users who might be less than ideally positioned due to keeping more
distance to others (e.g., standing further away than intended). At the same time,
because users are largely unaware of changes in IPD, designers could consider
ways to attract and guide users to more ideal positions.

Designers should also consider the level of intimacy that arises from the context of the VE as well as the relationship between VR users. For example, in
therapy there may be a therapist present as an avatar alongside the patient.

Given the patient and the therapist are strangers, they may be positioned at a greater distance and overtime when acquaintanceship occurs, their selected positions should change. Another context of use can be rooms designed to facilitate corporate meetings and conference. In this context, design guidelines should adhere to the interaction models based on IPD.

5.5   Limitations and Future Work

We swapped genders by switching between pre-defined male and female avatars available on the Rec Room platform. While Rec Room allows changing avatars, there is no option for modulating the user's voice. Thus, when users donned avatars with a non-matching gender, there was a mismatch of voice and avatar characteristics. This may result in unfavorable evaluations [16, 24], increase the need for distance [36], and may be pronounced in people that are familiar with each other. Future work may explore this effect of voice mismatch on proxemics.

Given the low number of male-female pairs, and the lack of female-only pairs, we cannot make strong conclusions for mixed-gender pairs and especially female-only pairs. However, we argue that currently the majority of HMD owners are male [30] and therefore our study provides a representative sample of HMD users and motivates further research in the area. We further plan to explore the effect of gender mismatch in larger virtual groups instead of pairs.

6   Conclusion

In this paper, we explored how gender swapping affects interpersonal distance in VR. We conducted a user study using an online VR platform, Rec Room, with 40 participants (20 strangers, and 20 friends). Participants completed playful tasks in pairs, and used both male and female avatars.

Our findings show that with swapped genders, the preferred distance increases significantly between friends but not between strangers. Also, users are largely unaware of these effects, as they believe that their behavior does not change despite the gender swap.

We hope our findings to (a) raise awareness among researchers that gender mismatches might present an issue in VR studies focusing on proxemics and needs to be accounted for, (b) inform VE designers to account for (unconscious) changes in IPD between users, and (c) provide a starting point for future work, investigating in detail how VR environments could be designed for and adapted to cases where acquainted users might use avatars of various genders.

Acknowledgements. We thank the Rec Room tutor who aided in recruiting participants for our study. The presented work was funded by the German Research Foundation (DFG) under project no. 425869382 and by dtec.bw – Digitalization and Technology Research Center of the Bundeswehr [Voice of Wisdom].

References

1. Bailenson, J.N., Blascovich, J., Beall, A.C., Loomis, J.M.: Interpersonal distance in immersive virtual environments. Pers. Soc. Psychol. Bull. **29**(7), 819–833 (2003)
2. Ballendat, T., Marquardt, N., Greenberg, S.: Proxemic interaction: designing for a proximity and orientation-aware environment. In: ACM International Conference on Interactive Tabletops and Surfaces, pp. 121–130 (2010)
3. Blascovich, J., Loomis, J., Beall, A.C., Swinth, K.R., Hoyt, C.L., Bailenson, J.N.: Immersive virtual environment technology as a methodological tool for social psychology. Psychol. Inq. **13**(2), 103–124 (2002)
4. Boud, A.C., Haniff, D.J., Baber, C., Steiner, S.: Virtual reality and augmented reality as a training tool for assembly tasks. In: 1999 IEEE International Conference on Information Visualization (Cat. No. PR00210), pp. 32–36. IEEE (1999)
5. Edward, T.: Hall, the hidden dimension (1966)
6. Fox, J., Tang, W.Y.: Women's experiences with general and sexual harassment in online video games: rumination, organizational responsiveness, withdrawal, and coping strategies. New Media Soc. **19**(8), 1290–1307 (2017)
7. Friedman, D., Steed, A., Slater, M.: Spatial social behavior in second life. In: International Workshop on Intelligent Virtual Agents, pp. 252–263. Springer, Berlin, Heidelberg (2007). https://doi.org/10.1007/978-3-540-74997-4_23
8. Gonzalez-Liencres, C., Zapata, L.E., Iruretagoyena, G., Seinfeld, S., Perez-Mendez, L., Arroyo-Palacios, J., Borland, D., Slater, M., Sanchez-Vives, M.V.: Being the victim of intimate partner violence in virtual reality: first-versus third-person perspective. Front. Psychol. **11**, 820 (2020)
9. Grønbæk, J.E., Knudsen, M.S., O'Hara, K., Krogh, P.G., Vermeulen, J., Petersen, M.G.: Proxemics beyond proximity: designing for flexible social interaction through cross-device interaction. In: Proceedings of the 2020 CHI Conference on Human Factors in Computing Systems, p. 1–14. CHI 2020, Association for Computing Machinery, New York, NY, USA (2020). https://doi.org/10.1145/3313831.3376379
10. Hall, E.T., Birdwhistell, R.L., Bock, B., Bohannan, P., Diebold, A.R., Jr., Durbin, M., Edmonson, M.S., Fischer, J., Hymes, D., Kimball, S.T., et al.: Proxemics [and comments and replies]. Curr. Anthropol. **9**(2/3), 83–108 (1968)
11. Hayduk, L.A.: Personal space: where we now stand. Psychol. Bull. **94**(2), 293 (1983)
12. Hecht, H., Welsch, R., Viehoff, J., Longo, M.R.: The shape of personal space. Acta Physiol. (Oxf) **193**, 113–122 (2019)
13. Hussain, Z., Griffiths, M.D.: Gender swapping and socializing in cyberspace: an exploratory study. CyberPsychol. Behav. **11**(1), 47–53 (2008)
14. Iachini, T., Coello, Y., Frassinetti, F., Ruggiero, G.: Body space in social interactions: a comparison of reaching and comfort distance in immersive virtual reality. PloS one **9**(11), e111511 (2014)
15. Iachini, T., Coello, Y., Frassinetti, F., Senese, V.P., Galante, F., Ruggiero, G.: Peripersonal and interpersonal space in virtual and real environments: effects of gender and age. J. Environ. Psychol. **45**, 154–164 (2016)
16. Kuznekoff, J.H., Rose, L.M.: Communication in multiplayer gaming: examining player responses to gender cues. New Media Soc. **15**(4), 541–556 (2013)
17. Llobera, J., Spanlang, B., Ruffini, G., Slater, M.: Proxemics with multiple dynamic characters in an immersive virtual environment. ACM Trans. Appl. Percept. (TAP) **8**(1), 1–12 (2010)

18. Mäkelä, V., Heimonen, T., Luhtala, M., Turunen, M.: Information wall: evaluation of a gesture-controlled public display. In: Proceedings of the 13th International Conference on Mobile and Ubiquitous Multimedia, p. 228–231. MUM 2014, Association for Computing Machinery, New York, NY, USA (2014). https://doi.org/10.1145/2677972.2677998

19. Mäkelä, V., et al.: Virtual field studies: conducting studies on public displays in virtual reality. In: Proceedings of the 2020 CHI Conference on Human Factors in Computing Systems, p. 1–15. CHI 2020, Association for Computing Machinery, New York, NY, USA (2020). https://doi.org/10.1145/3313831.3376796

20. Marquardt, N., Diaz-Marino, R., Boring, S., Greenberg, S.: The proximity toolkit: prototyping proxemic interactions in ubiquitous computing ecologies. In: Proceedings of the 24th Annual ACM Symposium on User Interface Software and Technology, p. 315–326. UIST 2011, ACM, New York, NY, USA (2011). https://doi.org/10.1145/2047196.2047238

21. Martens, A.L., Grover, C.A., Saucier, D.A., Morrison, B.A.: An examination of gender differences versus similarities in a virtual world. Comput. Hum. Behav. **84**, 404–409 (2018)

22. McDaniel, T.L., Villanueva, D., Krishna, S., Colbry, D., Panchanathan, S.: Heartbeats: A methodology to convey interpersonal distance through touch. In: CHI '10 Extended Abstracts on Human Factors in Computing Systems, p. 3985–3990. CHI EA 2010, Association for Computing Machinery, New York, NY, USA (2010). https://doi.org/10.1145/1753846.1754090

23. McLaughlin, C., Olson, R., White, M.J.: Environmental issues in patient care management: proxemics, personal space, and territoriality. Rehabil. Nurs. **33**(4), 143–147 (2008). https://doi.org/10.1002/j.2048-7940.2008.tb00219.x

24. Mitchell, W.J., Szerszen Sr, K.A., Lu, A.S., Schermerhorn, P.W., Scheutz, M., MacDorman, K.F.: A mismatch in the human realism of face and voice produces an uncanny valley. i-Perception **2**(1), 10–12 (2011)

25. Mueller, F., et al.: Proxemics play: understanding proxemics for designing digital play experiences. In: Proceedings of the 2014 Conference on Designing Interactive Systems, p. 533–542. DIS 2014, Association for Computing Machinery, New York, NY, USA (2014). https://doi.org/10.1145/2598510.2598532

26. Mäkelä, V., Heimonen, T., Turunen, M.: Semi-automated, large-scale evaluation of public displays. Int. J. Hum.-Comput. Interact. **34**(6), 491–505 (2018). https://doi.org/10.1080/10447318.2017.1367905

27. Neyret, S., Navarro, X., Beacco, A., Oliva, R., Bourdin, P., Valenzuela, J., Barberia, I., Slater, M.: An embodied perspective as a victim of sexual harassment in virtual reality reduces action conformity in a later milgram obedience scenario. Sci. Rep. **10**(1), 1–18 (2020)

28. Obata, A., Sasaki, K.: OfficeWalker: a virtual visiting system based on proxemics. In: Proceedings of the 1998 ACM Conference on Computer Supported Cooperative Work, pp. 1–10 (1998)

29. Peña, J., Yoo, S.C.: Under pressure: Avatar appearance and cognitive load effects on attitudes, trustworthiness, bidding, and interpersonal distance in a virtual store. Presence **23**(1), 18–32 (2014)

30. Rivu, R., et al.: Remote VR studies - a framework for running virtual reality studies remotely via participant-owned HMDs. CoRR abs/2102.11207 (2021). https://arxiv.org/abs/2102.11207

31. Ruggiero, G., Frassinetti, F., Coello, Y., Rapuano, M., di Cola, A.S., Iachini, T.: The effect of facial expressions on peripersonal and interpersonal spaces. Psychol. Res. **81**(6), 1232–1240 (2016). https://doi.org/10.1007/s00426-016-0806-x

32. Schmieder, C.: World of maskcraft vs. world of queercraft? communication, sex and gender in the online role-playing game world of warcraft. J. Gaming Virtual Worlds **1**(1), 5–21 (2009)

33. Uzzell, D., Horne, N.: The influence of biological sex, sexuality and gender role on interpersonal distance. Br. J. Soc. Psychol. **45**(3), 579–597 (2006)

34. Vella, K., Klarkowski, M., Turkay, S., Johnson, D.: Making friends in online games: gender differences and designing for greater social connectedness. Behav. Inf. Technol. **39**(8), 917–934 (2020)

35. Wang, S.T., Kuo, W.C., Yang, J.C.: An empirical study on gender switching of MMORPG players. In: Proceedings of the 19th International Conference on Computers in Education (ICCE 2011). Chiang Mai, Thailand (2011)

36. Welsch, R., von Castell, C., Hecht, H.: Interpersonal distance regulation and approach-avoidance reactions are altered in psychopathy. Clin. Psychol. Sci. **8**(2), 211–225 (2020). https://doi.org/10.1177/2167702619869336

37. Welsch, R., von Castell, C., Rettenberger, M., Turner, D., Hecht, H., Fromberger, P.: Sexual attraction modulates interpersonal distance and approach-avoidance movements towards virtual agents in males. PloS one **15**(4), e0231539 (2020)

38. Welsch, R., Hecht, H., von Castell, C.: Psychopathy and the regulation of interpersonal distance. Clin. Psychol. Sci. **6**(6), 835–847 (2018)

39. Williams, J.L.: Personal space and its relation to extraversion-introversion. Can. J. Behav. Sci. **3**(2), 156 (1971)

40. Yee, N., Bailenson, J.N., Urbanek, M., Chang, F., Merget, D.: The unbearable likeness of being digital: the persistence of nonverbal social norms in online virtual environments. CyberPsychol. Behav. **10**(1), 115–121 (2007)

41. Yee, N., Ducheneaut, N., Yao, M., Nelson, L.: Do men heal more when in drag? conflicting identity cues between user and avatar. In: Proceedings of the SIGCHI Conference on Human Factors in Computing Systems, pp. 773–776 (2011)

42. Zibrek, K., Niay, B., Olivier, A.H., Hoyet, L., Pettre, J., McDonnell, R.: The effect of gender and attractiveness of motion on proximity in virtual reality. ACM Trans. Appl. Percept. **17**(4) (2020). https://doi.org/10.1145/3419985

Courses

Introduction to User-Centred Design Sprint

Marta Larusdottir[1]([✉]), Virpi Roto[2], and Åsa Cajander[3]

[1] Reykjavik University, Reykjavik, Iceland
marta@ru.is
[2] Aalto University, Helsinki, Finland
[3] Uppsala University, Uppsala, Sweden

Abstract. This course will introduce attendees to the challenges and benefits of integrating User-Centred Design (UCD) methods into the Google Design Sprint (GDS) process. The course will introduce this new User-Centred Design Sprint process, and participants will practice selected methods from the process during the course. By the end of the course, participants will know why, when and how to use User-Centred Design Sprint. Delivered by experienced members of IFIP TC13, this course will appeal to researchers and developers working in the early stages of designing software products.

Keywords: User-Centred Design methods · Google design sprint · Software design

1 Introduction

The Google Design Sprint process [1] has gained popularity in the software industry for being suitable for analysing user needs and designing a running prototype for a software system in five days. A team of 7–10 people collaborates through one week to better understand the users' needs and the suitability of the design for users. At the beginning of the process, the team has a relatively vague idea for the user needs for the software product, but on the fifth day, a running prototype is evaluated in think-aloud evaluations with five users to evaluate the users' experiences and the usefulness of the product.

This course's proposers have taught the Google Design Sprint process in an international, 2-week intensive course in 2018 and 2019 [2, 3]. During these courses, we combined the Google Design Sprint process, with User-Centred Design (UCD) methods, in a process called User-Centred Design Sprint, or UCD Sprint in short [3]. We developed the process through three editions of the intensive course, focusing on UCD methods in the first edition of the course [4] and integrating the Google Design sprint and the UCD processes in the second and third edition of the course [2, 3]. In the last version of our course, we saw that conducting three days of UCD activities before the Google Design Sprint process and two days after it significantly extended the course attendees' understanding of the user needs.

We want to introduce the challenges and benefits of integrating user-centred design methods into the Google Design sprint process to course attendees. The course will

© IFIP International Federation for Information Processing 2021
Published by Springer Nature Switzerland AG 2021
C. Ardito et al. (Eds.): INTERACT 2021, LNCS 12936, pp. 253–256, 2021.
https://doi.org/10.1007/978-3-030-85607-6_17

introduce the User-Centred Design Sprint process, and participants will practice four methods from the process during the course. At the conclusion of the course, participants will be introduced to how they can use the process professionally.

2 User-Centred Design and Google Design Sprint

User-Centred Design (UCD) is a rich and varied discipline. The primary aim is to combine design and evaluation in developing a software system and focus these activities on the prospective users of the system that is being developed. The literature includes extensive research on UCD concepts, principles and methods. One of the classical references provides an overview of the discipline [5]. Other references focus on the principles behind UCD [6] or identify how software practitioners define and work with UCD [7].

Teaching UCD is of crucial importance to increase its influence in software development. Software development will not change towards a more user-centred approach unless there are practitioners available with UCD skills. Nevertheless, the literature on the teaching of UCD is minimal. An early workshop aimed to produce a list of skills that are necessary and important for UCD practitioners. They see UCD as a process that should yield a high utility and usability level by developing good task flows and user interfaces. Therefore, UCD practitioners should have the knowledge, skills, and other characteristics needed for considering and involving users [8].

Created to better balance his time on the job and with his family, Jake Knapp optimized the different activities of a design process by introducing a process called the Google Design Sprint (GDS) [1]. Knapp noticed that despite the large piles of sticky notes and the collective excitement generated during team brainstorming workshops, the best ideas were often developed by individuals who had a big challenge and not too much time to work on them. Another key ingredient was to have people involved in a project all working together in a room, solving their part of the problem and ready to answer questions. Combining a focus on individual work, time to prototype, and an inescapable deadline, Knapp called these focused design efforts "sprints".

The GDS is a process to solve problems and test new ideas by building and testing a prototype in five days. The central premise for the process is seeing how customers react before committing to making an authentic product. It is a "smarter, more respectful, and more effective way of solving problems", one that brings the best contributions of everyone on the team by helping them spend their time on what matters [1].

3 Description of the Course

Total duration of the course is 3 h. The course will be scheduled in three sessions and the content of each session is described below.

The learning objectives are that:

- participants will gain knowledge on how the User Centred Design sprint process could be used in software development
- participants will gain skills in using four methods from the process
- participants will gain knowledge on how to further study the process

Content and Structure of the Course
Session 1 (50 min)

- Introduction to the course schedule and the presenters (10 min).
- Introduction to the User-Centred Design Sprint process (20 min).

  - How is the process?
  - How does it relate to the Google Design Sprint process?
  - How does the process relate to User-Centred Design?
  - How can it be used on software development?

- Introduction to the User Group Analysis method - one of the methods in the UCD sprint process. Participants do a short exercise in using the User Group Analysis method (20 min).

BREAK (15 min)
Session 2 (50 min)

- Introduction to UX goals, which is another UCD method in the UCD sprint process. Participants do a short exercise on stating UX goals (30 min).
- Introduction to the Mapping method. Participants do a short exercise on that method (20 min).

BREAK (15 min)
Session 3 (50 min)

- Introduction to the design and evaluation methods used in the User-Centred Design Process. Participants do a Crazy-4 exercise (30 min).
- Introduction to how the process could be used in industry and research.
  Q/A session at the end (20 min)

4 Intended Audience

Our intended audience are lecturers, IT professionals, researchers and students at the INTERACT conference who have done prototyping and evaluations with users. It is beneficial if the participants are familiar with the Google Design sprint process, but it is not a prerequisite.

Participants can be:

- Lecturers in interaction design, interested in including a User-Centred Design Sprint approach in their teaching,
- IT professionals that are interested in learning about the user-centred way of running a design sprint,
- Researchers and students interested in rapid user-centred design methods.

5   Reading List

Recommended reading is:

- About GDS: https://www.thesprintbook.com/the-design-sprint
- Also about GDS: https://www.gv.com/sprint/
- About UCD: https://www.interaction-design.org/literature/topics/user-centered-design

Addtionally, we would like to point your attention to a long paper published at INTERACT 2021 describing a study on the User Centred Design Sprint process [3].

References

1. Knapp, J., Zeratsky, J., Kowitz, B.: Sprint: How to Solve Big Problems and Test New Ideas in Just Five Days. Simon and Schuster, New York (2016)
2. Larusdottir, M., Roto, V., Stage, J., Lucero, A., Šmorgun, I.: Balance talking and doing! using google design sprint to enhance an intensive UCD course. In: Lamas, D., Loizides, F., Nacke, L., Petrie, H., Winckler, M., Zaphiris, P. (eds.) INTERACT 2019. LNCS, vol. 11747, pp. 95–113. Springer, Cham (2019). https://doi.org/10.1007/978-3-030-29384-0_6
3. Roto, V., Larusdottir, M.K., Lucero, A., Stage, J., Šmorgun, I.: Focus, structure, reflection! integrating user-centred design and design sprint. In: INTERACT 2021 Conference Proceedings (2021, to appear)
4. Larusdottir, M., Roto, V., Stage, J., Lucero, A.: Get realistic! - UCD course design and evaluation. In: Bogdan, C., Kuusinen, K., Lárusdóttir, M.K., Palanque, P., Winckler, M. (eds.) HCSE 2018. LNCS, vol. 11262, pp. 15–30. Springer, Cham (2019). https://doi.org/10.1007/978-3-030-05909-5_2
5. Norman, D.A., Draper, S.W. (eds.): User Centered System Design: New Perspectives on Human-Computer Interaction. Erlbaum, Hillsdale (1986)
6. Gulliksen, J., Göransson, B., Boivie, I., Blomkvist, S., Persson, J., Cajander, Å.: Key principles for user-centred systems design. Behav. Inf. Technol. 22(6), 397–409 (2003)
7. Gulliksen, J., Boivie, I., Persson, J., Hektor, A., Herulf, L.: Making a difference: a survey of the usability profession in Sweden. In: Proceedings of NordiCHI 2004, Tampere, Finland, pp. 207–215 (2004)
8. Dayton, T.: Skills needed by user-centered design practitioners in real software development environments: report on the CHI92 workshop. SIGCHI Bull. 25(3), 16–31 (1993)

Industrial Experiences

A Flexible and Adaptable Workflow to Develop and Visualise Industrial Digital Twins

Antonella Guidazzoli[✉], Silvano Imboden, Paolo Zuzolo, Daniele De Luca,
Eleonora Peruch, Eric Pascolo, Federica Farroni, and Maria Chiara Liguori

Cineca, Casalecchio di Reno, Italy
visitlab@cineca.it

Abstract. A workflow for building a Digital Twin with a 3D interface for VR
and desktop output was developed by focusing on the interaction with the virtual
model, an easy deployment of the framework and a straightforward reusability. The
case study was conceived for supercomputing datacenters, but its main strength
lies in flexibility and adaptability.

Keywords: Digital twin · Virtual reality · 3DWeb · Industry 4.0

1 Introduction

Replicating production entities, processes and systems as Digital Twins more than doubles the effectiveness attainable with design optimization, process control, life cycle management, predictive maintenance, risk analysis, and more [7, 8]. Anyway, the digitization of a "shadow" version [8] can be implemented through different solutions, from the simpler to the more complex and similar solutions can be adapted to radically different realities. Following the five-dimension digital twin model proposed in [2], a simple yet effective workflow was developed for the building of the digital twin of a physical entity. The workflow was tested first on an imaginary production chain, the Cube Cookies factory, then on the real test case, the CINECA supercomputing datacenter. Such workflow is focused on the interaction with the virtual model, the easy deployment of the framework and the straightforward reusability. The tool set is shaped in such a way that the system is deployed through a web-based application, thus without local software installation, and allowing easy-to-use interactions with the virtual environment by means of several input devices, such as the common keyboard and pointer, the extended reality devices as a cardboard using a smartphone or a virtual reality headset.

The dataset used for the supercomputing datacenter digital twin is taken by Examon [12] monitoring infrastructure, developed under the European project IoTwins [9]. IoTwins approach is based on a technological platform allowing a simple and low-cost

Electronic supplementary material The online version of this chapter (https://doi.org/10.1007/
978-3-030-85607-6_18) contains supplementary material, which is available to authorized users.

C. Ardito et al. (Eds.): INTERACT 2021, LNCS 12936, pp. 259–263, 2021.
https://doi.org/10.1007/978-3-030-85607-6_18

access to big data analytics functionality, AI services and edge cloud infrastructure for the delivery of digital twins in manufacturing and facility management sectors. This workflow enriches the Examon infrastructure with an easy-to-use visualization component.

2 Immersive Digital Twin, from 3D Web to VR

2.1 Workflow

As shown in Fig. 1, the workflow starts with the creation of a virtual model using Blender [1], a 3D Computer Graphics toolkit, where CAD and BIM models can be easily imported and simplified. Notwithstanding, Blender allows to obtain a faithful replica of the physical entity thanks to its several tools for realistic computer-generated imagery.

Fig. 1. The developed framework and workflow for the building of a digital twin.

Besides, Blender allows exporting 3D models on a webpage by means of an add-on for Verge3D [3], a real-time rendering engine and Computer Graphics toolkit used to produce immersive 3D web-based experiences. This tool has multiple functions within the framework: it allows to obtain high modularity and standardization of the virtual model, for instance creating arrays of identical object components of the physical entity without the need to model each of them in Blender. In this way the virtual model can more easily co-evolve with the constant changes in the physical world. In addition to the geometrical modeling, it enables the behavioural modeling of virtual environments and of the digital twin itself, defining a set of actions and logics that the virtual world must perform to fulfill functions, respond to changes and interact with the user. Thus, in general, Verge3D enables the attachment of value-adding services to the digital twin, such as the real-time monitoring and diagnosis and the visualization of the digital twin connection data. Moreover, Verge3D, used in combination with Javascript library JQuery [4] and front-end web programming toolkit BootStrap [5], allows to quickly design and customize responsive website and interact with the digital twin by means of keyboard and pointer or thanks to the WebXR Device API with extended reality devices. Finally, Verge3D can run on several devices such as desktop, smartphone or tablet by means of a web browser application. The back-end of the web application for the digital twin is based on Django [6], a high-level Python Web framework. Django allows the management of the application of the website, the communication with databases of several types, supporting as many features as possible on all database backends. In this way, taking advantage of the AJAX call allowed by JQuery, the virtual model can query the databases hosting the digital twin connection data.

The framework can be easily reused and adapted to several physical entities, thanks to the workflow, which is based on the abstractions of the main processes, features and purposes of a digital twin and to the flexibility of the proposed tool set.

Fig. 2. Production units with annotations in the Cube Cookies Factory. Navigation and interaction are performed with cardboard, through a smartphone.

2.2 The Implementation

Two applications of the workflow described above are presented: the production chain of an imaginary Cube Cookies factory and the datacenter of CINECA supercomputing center.

The geometrical modeling of the Cube Cookies factory can be seen in Fig. 2 where the status information panel is built through Verge3D functions and can be updated in real-time from the application interface. The behavioural modeling function of Verge3D can also be seen in Fig. 2: if one of the production chain units stops functioning in the physical world, the corresponding conveyor belt in the 3D model, which would normally be animated, stops accordingly, thanks to the animation management features of Verge3D.

The geometrical modeling of Cineca datacenter can be seen in Fig. 3. As in the previous application, if a node of a rack of the supercomputer has an issue in the physical world, the corresponding rack in the 3D model would be highlighted with a red flickering outline, thanks to the post-processing features of Verge3D. Regarding user-interaction with the virtual environment, in Fig. 3 the rack door is opened by double-clicking on it, showing the red outline of a node. This allows a system administrator to identify the location, both in the virtual and physical world, of the node having an issue. The digital twin can be navigated in two modalities: on the website or using Virtual Reality. In the first case, the navigation happens through the keyboard and pointer, while in the second case, using the WebXR Device API the user can access the scene and use the controllers of the virtual reality headset or the cardboard pointer to move within the virtual environment or, as shown in Fig. 2, to point to a production unit and click to show its status information panel.

Fig. 3. User interaction and issue tracking in the data center digital twin.

3   Conclusions

We have tested the workflow on two digital twins: first on an imaginary production chain, the Cube Cookies factory, then on the real test case, the CINECA supercomputing datacenter. Such workflow is focused on the interaction with the virtual model, that we exemplified through the control panel in the Cube Cookie factory, the easy deployment of the framework and the straightforward reusability, that we demonstrated by easily adapting the workflow to both a shop floor factory and a supercomputing center.

The next step is to link online the digital twin with the Examon database to visualize in real time the datacenter behaviour. According to an Agile approach [11], use cases will be collected among the final users of the applications in order to address the requirements with adequate interactions. The digital twin, including the visualization system, will be replicated and deployed on the new CINECA datacenter that will host Leonardo preEXASCALE supercomputer, the next CINECA HPC cluster [10]. The Leonardo digital twin will be a complete monitoring system used by CINECA system administrator and technician to improve the ease of maintenance and reduce the intervention time in the case of failure.

Acknowledgements. The present work has been developed under the IoTwins project (receiving funding from the European Union's Horizon 2020 research and innovation programme under grant agreement N. 857191) and the EUROCC project (Grant Agreement Number 951731 – EUROCC EU-H2020, Euro HPC JU).

References

1. Blender. https://www.blender.org/. Accessed 15 Apr 2021
2. Qi, Q., et al.: Enabling technologies and tools for digital twin. J. Manuf. Syst. **58**, Part B, 3–21 (2021). https://doi.org/10.1016/j.jmsy.2019.10.001
3. Verge3D. https://www.soft8soft.com/verge3d/. Accessed 15 Apr 2021
4. JQuery Javascript Library. https://jquery.com/. Accessed 15 Apr 2021
5. Bootstrap. https://icons.getbootstrap.com/. Accessed 15 Apr 2021
6. Django Web Framework. https://www.djangoproject.com/. Accessed 15 Apr 2021
7. Digital twins – rise of the digital twin in Industrial IoT and Industry 4.0, in i-SCOOP. https://www.i-scoop.eu/internet-of-things-guide/industrial-internet-things-iiot-saving-costs-innovation/digital-twins/. Accessed 15 Apr 2021
8. Weippl, E., Sanderse, B. (eds.): Digital Twins - Introduction to the Special Theme, in ERCIM NEWS, 114 July (2018). https://ercim-news.ercim.eu/images/stories/EN115/EN115-web.pdf
9. IoTwins. https://www.iotwins.eu/. Accessed 15 Apr 2021
10. https://eurohpc-ju.europa.eu/news/leonardo-new-eurohpc-world-class-pre-exascale-supercomputer-italy. Accessed 15 Apr 2021
11. Cohen, D., et al.: An introduction to agile methods. Adv. Comput. **62**, 1–66 (2004). https://doi.org/10.1016/S0065-2458(03)62001-2
12. https://github.com/EEESlab/examon. Accessed 15 Apr 2021

Improving the User Experience and the Trustworthiness of Financial Services

Giandomenico Cornacchia[1](✉) (iD), Fedelucio Narducci[1] (iD), and Azzurra Ragone[2]

[1] Politecnico di Bari, Bari, Italy
{giandomenico.cornacchia,fedelucio.narducci}@poliba.it
[2] EY, Milan, Italy
azzurra.ragone@it.ey.com

Abstract. Decision-making systems have been widely used in the Financial Services domain. AI is bringing both many innovations and opportunities as well as new risks linked to ethical considerations. Customer trust is at the forefront of customer retention. To build trust, there is the need to make the decision process Interpretable, Understandable, and Trustworthy for the end-user. Since products offered within the banking sector are usually of an intangible nature, customer trust perception is crucial to maintain a long-standing relationship and to ensure customer loyalty. To this end, in this paper we propose more insightful and user-friendly explanations for decisions made by AI systems in the financial domain.

Keywords: Trustworthy AI · Financial services · Credit scoring · Fairness · Explainability · Human-centered computing

1 Introduction

Artificial Intelligence (AI) has increasingly played a predominant role in the interaction with consumers, citizens, and patients in the last years. It has been capable of revolutionizing their daily lives and improving all those user-centered services that are expanding out from the back office into customer-facing applications[1]. However, users often interact with such systems without even knowing that life-changing decisions like mortgage grants, job offers, patients screenings, etc., are in the hand of an AI-based system. Sometimes, such decisions may result arbitrary or inconsistent and limit users' ability to access the opportunities for which they are indeed qualified [1]. In particular, AI adoption is growing rapidly in the financial sector. Financial firms have widely used it to monetize data

---

[1] https://www.fca.org.uk/publications/research/research-note-machine-learning-uk-financial-services.

© IFIP International Federation for Information Processing 2021
Published by Springer Nature Switzerland AG 2021
C. Ardito et al. (Eds.): INTERACT 2021, LNCS 12936, pp. 264–269, 2021.
https://doi.org/10.1007/978-3-030-85607-6_19

assets, improve customer experience, customize product and service offerings, drive business growth, and enhance operational efficiencies.

On the other hand, AI has shown its weakness by emphasizing social and ethical issues such as gender and demographic discrimination [3,4], and lack of interpretability and explainability. As these applications become key enablers and more deeply embedded in processes, financial services organizations need to cope with AI applications' inherent risks. This is true both from a compliance point of view (regulatory and ethical norms) and because the lack of trust is the leading barrier to AI adoption and acceptance by users. Building trust requires transparency and clear communication with internal stakeholders and customers, who should know when, how, and why AI is being used. This is especially true in a sector heavily regulated, such as the financial services one.

AI-based systems are increasingly attracting the attention of regulatory agencies and society at large, as they can cause, although unintentionally, harm. Indeed as reported by the Ethics guidelines for trustworthy AI from the European Commission's High-Level Expert Group on AI: *"The development, deployment, and use of any AI solution should adhere to some fundamental ethical principles such as respect for human autonomy, prevention of harm, fairness, and explainability"* [10]. Moreover, the GDPR set off the *right to explanation*: users have the right to ask for an explanation about an algorithmic decision made about them. In the UK, the Financial Conduct Authority (FCA) requires firms to explain why a more expensive mortgage has been chosen if a cheaper option is available. The G20 has adopted the OECD AI Principles[2] for a trustworthy AI where it is underline that users should not only understand AI outcomes but also be able to challenge them. In the financial sector, this is not an easy task to solve. As on one side, it is required to show how an outcome has been reached and whether it was fair and unbiased. On the other, not all the rationales behind a decision can be disclosed to prevent users from gaming the system.

In this paper, we propose an approach to provide more insightful explanations to make the interaction more user-friendly and, at the same time, to reinforce customer trust in the system.

2   What Does It Mean to Be Fair?

There is no single, globally accepted definition of fairness in AI [17]. However, being fair implies ensuring the same quality of service to all people, avoiding discriminating against minorities, and using protected characteristics like gender, nationality, age. AI-based systems should allocate opportunities, resources, or information fairly, thus avoiding societal or historical biases. The definition provided by Mehrabi et al. [13] summarizes well these concepts: *the absence of any prejudice or favouritism toward an individual or a group based on their inherent or acquired characteristics.*

In our analysis, we refer to Credit Scoring (CS) systems that compute the probability of a customer to repay a loan. We use this case study since for

---

[2] https://oecd.ai/ai-principles.

credit loan the concept of equal opportunity is crucial, and it lies very often in the hands of ML algorithms. Indeed, governments have addressed demographic, gender, and racial discrimination as regulatory compliance requirements since the 1960s [5,7,8]. Since those norms were not set to prevent discrimination in not-human decision making (as in the case of ML algorithms), "Ethics guidelines for a Trustworthy AI" [10] and "The White Paper"[3] were released to give guidelines for ethical and safe use of AI. Some critical keys requirements are "equity, diversity and not-discrimination" enclosed in the concept of fairness.

Going deeper with this analysis, the concept of fairness in CS could linked to one or more of these three criteria [11]: (i) *Independence* [6], (ii) *Separation* [9], and (iii) *Sufficiency* [3].

The (i) Independence guarantees that the fraction of customer classified as good-risks is the same in each sensitive groups. Therefore, if the gender is considered as sensitive, both men and women should have the same percentage of good-risk classification. The (ii) Separation criterion is related to the concepts of misclassification. Accordingly, the errors in classifying will be the same both in sensitive and non-sensitive groups. Finally, the (iii) Sufficiency criterion states that the probability that an individual belonging to the good-risk class is classified as good-risk will be the same for both sensitive groups. In this case, if the algorithm shows a gender bias, for example, a woman that belongs to the good-risk customer could be classified in the bad-risk class.

Once defined the concept of fairness and described the dimensions it is based on, the next question is: how can the customer be sure that the decision made by the algorithm is fair? We introduce now the next step that allows the customer to realize that the decision is fair. In particular, the person accountable for the AI system should be able to *explain* their outcome to the customer. The following section will address what explanation means and how to reach this goal.

3   From Model Fairness to End-User Explanation

Several definitions are provided in the literature on what *explainable* means when we talk about an ML algorithm. The most relevant one for our purpose is provided by Bracke et al. [2] *"explanations can answer different kinds of questions about a model's operation depending on the stakeholder they are addressed to"*. This definition introduces an interesting characteristic of the explanation that has to consider the point of view of a specific stakeholder. Accordingly, in a CS scenario, for example, the explanation for a given decision might be different if addressed to customers rather than to the risk management functions. From the customer's point of view, which is the most interesting in our analysis, the explanation should describe the motivations behind a decision in a way that is easy to understand. Naturally, as abovementioned, the decisions are made by algorithms thus, it is crucial to know how these algorithms work. The ML

---

[3] https://ec.europa.eu/digital-single-market/en/news/white-paper-artificial-intelligence-public-consultation-towards-european-approach-excellence.

Fig. 1. An example of generation of natural-language explanations

algorithms belong to two main classes: interpretable and uninterpretable. More specifically, the former implement a *white-box* model, the latter a *black-box* one.

On this perspective, Sharma et al. [15] distinguish *model-agnostic* and *model-specific* explanations. Model-agnostic methods provide an explanation that is not dependent on the ML model adopted and are generally used for *black-box* models. A *surrogate* model is thus implemented with the aim of *simulating* the behavior of the original algorithm.

Several methods have been proposed to explain black-box models. Two of the most important are LIME and SHAP. LIME trains local surrogate models explaining single data [14]. It generates a perturbation of initial data creating a new dataset and observing how the prediction changes through training an interpretable model. The analysis of the outcome of the perturbated data allows to interpret the original model. SHAP [12] is inspired by the cooperative game theory based on the Shapley Values. Each feature is considered a player that contributes differently to the outcome (i.e., the algorithm decision). SHAP does not compute all the possible combinations between all the features but performs only a random set of combinations for efficiency constraints. SHAP provides a ranked list of the features that contributed to the outcome ordered from the most to the less important. However, this explanation probably is not so clear for a customer who does not have experience with how an algorithm works. For this reason, if we want to improve the user's trust and general user experience with the system, we need to make the explanation more understandable. In that direction, we guess that an effective solution could be to transform the output produced by software like LIME or SHAP in a natural language sentence. We propose the pipeline described in Fig. 1. Customer characteristics are the input, then the algorithm makes a decision, e.g. the computation of the CS, and shows using SHAP the features that contributed the most to the decision. At this point, another module takes as input the decision and the SHAP output and generate a natural-language explanation: e.g. *Dear Giulio, your loan application has been rejected since you don't have an account with us, the credit amount you asked for is too high compared to your income, and the duration is too long.* An interesting opportunity in this context could be provided by a counterfactual explanation that explains how the output of the algorithm could be changed [16]. For example, the system can add: *In the case you decide to open an account with us, to reduce the credit amount to 10,000\$, and to reduce the duration to 12 months, the application will be probably accepted.* Conversely, model-specific explanations are based on the analysis of the structural information and the internal components of the algorithm that should be interpretable natively. From a technical perspective, these algorithms are easier to explain, but in this case, as well, most users will not be able to understand them. Therefore, the scenario is quite similar to the previous one and also here the exploitation of natural language can improve comprehensibility.

4   Future Directions and Challenges

In the credit risk context, we analyzed which fairness metrics can better evaluate the ML model and which explanation tools can get a better insightful interpretation of the decision process. For decision-making systems, it is necessary to understand the causality of learned representations, and visualization tools need to be human-centered through natural language. It turns out that Shapley values can help scientists to understand something more on what features have more influence on the outcome. However, no explanation has been developed specifically for the knowledge domain of the end-user. One of the possible future directions concerns the development of intelligent conversational systems that can adapt the explanation to the type of user they interface with, guaranteeing the fairness of the treatment received and proposing counterfactual analyses of their characteristics. The explanation needs to be more Human-centered and more user-friendly without disclosing all the financial institution's decision criteria, risking adverse actions from unfair users.

References

1. Barocas, S., Hardt, M., Narayanan, A.: Fairness and machine learning (2019). https://fairmlbook.org/
2. Bracke, P., Datta, A., Jung, C., Sen, S.: Machine learning explainability in finance: an application to default risk analysis (816) (2019)
3. Chouldechova, A.: Fair prediction with disparate impact: a study of bias in recidivism prediction instruments. Big Data 5(2), 153–163 (2017)
4. Cohen, L., Lipton, Z.C., Mansour, Y.: Efficient candidate screening under multiple tests and implications for fairness. In: FORC. LIPIcs, vol. 156, pp. 1:1–1:20. Schloss Dagstuhl - Leibniz-Zentrum für Informatik (2020)
5. Congress of the United States: Fair housing act (1968)
6. Dwork, C., Hardt, M., Pitassi, T., Reingold, O., Zemel, R.: Fairness through awareness. In: ITCS, pp. 214–226 (2012)
7. Federal Reserve Board: The truth in lending act (1968)
8. Federal Trade Commission: Equal credit opportunity act (1974)
9. Hardt, M., Price, E., Srebro, N.: Equality of opportunity in supervised learning. In: NIPS, pp. 3315–3323 (2016)
10. High-Level Expert Group on AI: Ethics guidelines for trustworthy AI. Report, European Commission, Brussels (2019)
11. Kozodoi, N., Jacob, J., Lessmann, S.: Fairness in credit scoring: assessment, implementation and profit implications. arXiv preprint arXiv:2103.01907 (2021)

12. Lundberg, S.M., Lee, S.: A unified approach to interpreting model predictions. In: NIPS, pp. 4765–4774 (2017)
13. Mehrabi, N., Morstatter, F., Saxena, N., Lerman, K., Galstyan, A.: A survey on bias and fairness in machine learning (2019)
14. Ribeiro, M.T., Singh, S., Guestrin, C.: "Why should I trust you?": explaining the predictions of any classifier. In: KDD, pp. 1135–1144. ACM (2016)
15. Sharma, R., Schommer, C., Vivarelli, N.: Building up explainability in multi-layer perceptrons for credit risk modeling. In: DSAA, pp. 761–762. IEEE (2020)
16. Stepin, I., Alonso, J.M., Catala, A., Pereira-Fariña, M.: A survey of contrastive and counterfactual explanation generation methods for explainable artificial intelligence. IEEE Access **9**, 11974–12001 (2021)
17. Verma, S., Rubin, J.: Fairness definitions explained. In: ICSE-FairWare, pp. 1–7 (2018)

ISCADA: Towards a Framework for Interpretable Fault Prediction in Smart Electrical Grids

Carmelo Ardito[1] , Yashar Deldjoo[1] , Eugenio Di Sciascio[1] ,
Fatemeh Nazary[1(✉)] , and Gianluca Sapienza[2]

[1] Politecnico di Bari, Bari, Italy
{carmelo.ardito,yashar.deldjoo,eugenio.sciascio,fatemeh.nazary}@poliba.it
[2] SmartGridLab e-distribuzione S.p.A., via Rubattino 84, Milano, Italy
gianluca.sapienza@e-distribuzione.com

Abstract. This paper reports ongoing research for the definition of a data-driven self-healing system using machine learning (ML) techniques that can perform automatic and timely detection of fault types and locations. Specifically, the proposed method makes use of spectrogram-based CNN modeling of the 3-phase voltage signals. Furthermore, to keep human operators informed about why certain decisions were made, i.e., to facilitate the interpretability of the black-box ML model, we propose a novel explanation approach that highlight regions in the input spectrogram that contributed the most for the prediction task at hand (e.g., fault type or location) - or *visual explanation*.

Keywords: Self-healing system · Interpretability · Fault prediction

1 Introduction and Context

Electrical grids are susceptible to a variety of electrical abnormalities, failures, and security threats, which if not tackled abruptly, in some cases they can leave a devastating impact on lives and the country's critical industries, leading to a national dilemma as the result of a cascading effect [5,6]. Over the last decade, the problem of automatic fault detection has been studied from various viewing angles using a combination of tools and techniques from computer science, electrical engineering, statistics, and artificial intelligence (AI) and in particular using automatic data-driven machine learning (ML) algorithms [2,7]. From a software point of view, the use of SCADA (Supervisory Control And Data Acquisition) has dominated the electrical industry. SCADA is a control system architecture composed of computers, networked data communications, and graphical user interfaces (GUIs) for high-level process supervisory management tasks [4]. The users of the SCADA, however, can be diverse ranging from electrical engineers to expert data-scientists, and lower professional-level workers.

F. Nazary—Authors are listed in alphabetical order.

© IFIP International Federation for Information Processing 2021
Published by Springer Nature Switzerland AG 2021
C. Ardito et al. (Eds.): INTERACT 2021, LNCS 12936, pp. 270–274, 2021.
https://doi.org/10.1007/978-3-030-85607-6_20

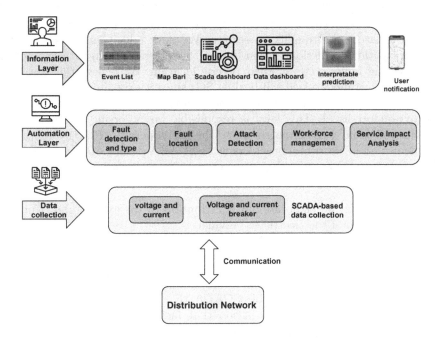

Fig. 1. The 3-layered management architecture of an electricity provider network. The red modules show our contribution.

2 Overview of the Self-healing Management System of an Electricity Provider Workflow

We model the self-healing management system of an electricity distributor as shown in Fig. 1 according to hierarchical architecture, where the lowest layer is the closest level to the input data (i.e., raw electrical signals), and the highest level is semantic data that are supposed to be understandable to the human observer, thus **bottom (data)→top (user)**. We describe the functionality of each layer below:

1. **Data-collection level:** The main role of the data collection layer is the acquisition of electrical, and logical data e.g., whether the fault breaker status is close (0) or open (1). The data collection task by an electricity provider is mainly managed by the SCADA (short for Supervisory control and data acquisition) system, which is a standard approach to different types of input data.

2. **Automation levels:** This level is responsible for automating the decision-making by the system. Fault classification is the functionality that is inside the operative center, however, traditionally it relies on the knowledge of specialists that analyze fault to understand if it is necessary to inspect the feeder. Attack detection (remote control part of smart grid), is mainly managed by the telecommunication network. The workforce management unit relates to the

crew who directly goes to check the problem. Service impact analysis deals with regulatory and quality of service. We have added an accurate data-driven location prediction system (where the latter is shown with red color) for isolating faulty zones or their precise location. We believe this can be a crucial part of modernized self-healing SGs since it expedites the dispatch of the crew members to the targeted (faulty) areas.

3. **Information level:** This level is responsible for reporting the monitoring status and fault decision outcomes to the user/operator. Practically, this is implemented in electricity providers using SCADA dashboard and data dashboard that can summarize data or give some detailed information to the user, depending on the type level of analysis he is interested in.

In the next section, we elaborate our contribution to the existing management self-healing system of the electricity provider.

3   Our Proposed Contribution

We propose *ISCADA*, interpretable SCADA that aims to augment fault prediction results in SGs with information that facilitates interpreting them to both experts and non-experts operators or users. To this end, we have built a deep-learning-based fault prediction system[1] that can provide accurate and interpretable fault type and location with relatively high precision. ISCADA extends the traditional SCADA by adding other components in the specific layers, as shown with red colors in Fig. 1. They include a fault location detection (automation layer) and interpretable fault prediction visualization (data layer). We now describe the main idea and the functioning mechanism behind the proposed work.

As shown in Fig. 2, starting from the raw 3-phase voltage signal collected from a hypothetical faulty area (zone A), we transform the data into a spectrogram representation, which will serve as a visual time-frequency representation of the original signal [3]. This representation is not only an efficient representation of the signal as it contains both time and frequency representation, but also a suitable technique for visual inspection of the fault prediction results according to time and frequency changes in the signal. For the fault prediction system, we build a data-driven classification system utilizing a powerful **deep convolutional neural network** (CNN). Furthermore, an approach based on gradient-weighted class activation mapping (Grad-CAM) [8] technique is utilized to highlight important regions in the spectrogram that can explain fault type and location, or **visual explanation**. The result of the explanation is a heatmap visualizing where on the spectrogram images the network was paying attention to. These can provide insightful visual cues to the human operator about the characteristics of the faults and can keep them in the loop.

A hypothetical extension of these results would involve how to turn such interpretable outcomes [1,2] into an explanation for non-expert users. In our

---

[1] This work is currently under review at a journal/transaction.

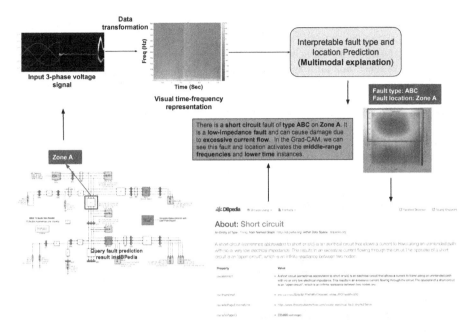

Fig. 2. Illustration of the principles behind the proposed intereptable fault prediction system

scenario, we can use the result of fault prediction as an input to a knowledge graph or other semantic repository of knowledge that can be also found freely on the web. An example of such freely available resource we can name of DBPedia, as shown in Fig. 2. The results are presented to the user in terms of **multi-modal explanation** using natural language (results returned from the KG) and visual outcome (the result of the automated fault prediction system shown with the red zone over the spectrograms).

4   Conclusion

In this paper, we have reported the results of an ongoing research work aiming at the definition of an interpretable and accurate data-driven self-healing system using machine learning (ML). The end goal on the one hand is to perform automatic and timely detection of fault types and locations; on the other hand, we aim to make the prediction results interpretable to the user. We discussed briefly the main insights behind our proposed CNN-based modelling of fault spectrograms and the Grad-CAM technique, and how the latter can be used to make the decisions made by the system more transparent.

Acknowledgments. This work has been partially funded by *e-distribuzione S.p.A* company, Italy, through a PhD scholarship granted to Fatemeh Nazary.

References

1. Ardito, C., Deldjoo, Y., Di Sciascio, E., Nazary, F.: Interacting with features: visual inspection of black-box fault type classification systems in electrical grids. In: Italian Workshop on Explainable Artificial Intelligence (XAI.it@AIxIA 2020) (2020)
2. Ardito, C., Deldjoo, Y., Di Sciascio, E., Nazary, F.: Revisiting security threat on smart grids: accurate and interpretable fault location prediction and type classification. In: The Italian Conference on CyberSecurity (ITASEC) (2021)
3. Birajdar, G.K., Patil, M.D.: Speech and music classification using spectrogram based statistical descriptors and extreme learning machine. Multimed. Tools Appl. **78**(11), 15141–15168 (2019). https://doi.org/10.1007/s11042-018-6899-z
4. Boyer, S.A.: SCADA: Supervisory Control and Data Acquisition. International Society of Automation, Research Triangle (2009)
5. Burpee, D., et al.: Us-Canada power system outage task force: final report on the implementation of task force recommendations (2006)
6. Majidi, M., Etezadi-Amoli, M., Fadali, M.S.: A sparse-data-driven approach for fault location in transmission networks. IEEE Trans. Smart Grid **8**(2), 548–556 (2017). https://doi.org/10.1109/TSG.2015.2493545
7. Raja, S., Fokoué, E.: Multi-stage fault warning for large electric grids using anomaly detection and machine learning. CoRR abs/1903.06700 (2019). http://arxiv.org/abs/1903.06700
8. Selvaraju, R.R., Cogswell, M., Das, A., Vedantam, R., Parikh, D., Batra, D.: Gradcam: visual explanations from deep networks via gradient-based localization. In: Proceedings of the IEEE International Conference on Computer Vision, pp. 618–626 (2017)

Let's Dance: An Exergame to Lead the Way in Parkinson Rehabilitation

Pierpaolo Di Bitonto[1], Angela la Forgia[2], Giovanni Melone[2], Ada Potenza[1(✉)],
Luca Rossetti[2], Antonio Ulloa Severino[1], and Felice Vitulano[2]

[1] Grifo Multimedia srl, Via B. Zaccaro, 17-19, 70126 Bari, BA, Italy
{p.dibitonto,a.potenza,a.ulloa}@grifomultimedia.it
[2] Exprivia S.p.A, Via A. Olivetti, 11, 70056 Molfetta, BA, Italy
{angela.laforgia,giovanni.melone,luca.rossetti,
felice.vitulano}@exprivia.com

Abstract. Healthy Ageing represents one of the most crucial topics that our society will face in the next decades, due to the progressive demographic ageing of the population, (e.g., in Italy old-age dependency ratio is estimated to reach 59,7% by 2065). These statistics highlights the need of a new paradigm for active and healthy ageing, as well as a healthcare system able to support elderly population in age-related diseases management.

In this work we present Let's dance, an innovative exergame that aims to provide a new way to deliver physiotherapy for mild or moderate Parkinson's disease patients. Within the game, the patients are asked to reproduce the choreography proposed, whose dance moves are aimed toward the achievement of specific therapeutic goals (e.g., optimize motor coordination, physical endurance, etc.). The game is part of a broader integrated platform that through sensors and actuators located on a robot device in the clinical environment and on patients themselves, can track in real-time both the game performance and the clinical KPIs and determine the assessment of patient's therapeutic progress.

In this paper we present the first prototype of Let's dance and a use-case scenario.

Keywords: Parkinson · Exergame · Rehabilitation

1 Introduction

According to the World Health Organization (WHO), noncommunicable diseases (NCDs) are responsible for almost 70% of all deaths worldwide [1].

The epidemic of NCDs poses devastating health consequences for individuals, families and communities, and threatens to overwhelm health systems. The socioeconomic costs associated with NCDs make the prevention and control of these diseases a major development imperative for the 21st century.

NCD management is the way to improve the quality of life for patients and their families and to reduce the costs of the treatment for health systems. Scientists, in fact, have proven that good management of NCD at home reduce drastically hospitalizations.

© IFIP International Federation for Information Processing 2021
Published by Springer Nature Switzerland AG 2021
C. Ardito et al. (Eds.): INTERACT 2021, LNCS 12936, pp. 275–279, 2021.
https://doi.org/10.1007/978-3-030-85607-6_21

NCD management implies adopting healthy lifestyles, eating healthy foods and practicing physical activity in order to reduce the risk of complication and prevent the problems related to the disease. The difficulty lies in how to persuade the patients and their families to change their habits. Patients need to be continuously motivated, monitored and supported during the therapy.

In order to support patient empowerment and improve compliance with the medical prescription, game dynamics can help. Games are very useful because they give further motivation to reach the therapeutics goals even if patients lack intrinsic motivations connected to their health. In other words, patients that usually resist adopting healthy behaviors, if involved in a game tend to be more willing to adopt the same behaviors. "Let's Dance" is an exergame used in rehabilitation for patients affected by Parkinson's Disease (P.D.). Usually, the rehabilitation activity for P.D. merges physical and cognitive activity: "Let's dance" game uses a rehabilitation protocol based on Irish dance [2] to involve patients in a joyful and engaging rehabilitation activity in two different game settings: at home and in the hospital. Game dynamics are inspired by the famous Ubisoft game "Just dance".

In this paper we present the game Let's dance and specifically section two describes how the motivational levers are used to engage patients and convince them to comply with the medical prescriptions; section three describes the game dynamics and software architecture; section four reports some conclusion and future work.

2 Engagement Design

One of the first problems faced in the design phase was how to engage patients in the hospital or at home. Elderly people often reject technology and tend to think that it is a further and useless complication in everyday life. The challenge needed to be overcome (1) how to make the game appealing in the eyes of the patient and (2) how to convince the patient to play it repeatedly.

The first challenge was approached by presenting to the patient the game as digital therapy. It is not just a game but also a way to undergo rehabilitation. The game, during the exercises, can "observe" patients, gaining implicit feedback and calculating scores about their health. At the end of each game, session feedbacks are released. They are used to show health improvement or to suggest to the therapist new exercises that best fit the patient's condition. The second challenge was approached including a game dynamic where two couples of patients face each other to win the title of best dancers. The collaborative/competitive dynamics is very useful to include patients who are not very competitive and play just for fun.

3 Game Description

"Let's Dance" is an exergame that aims to support patients suffering from mild or moderate Parkinson's disease in the rehabilitation process, by introducing a new way of approaching the therapy based on Irish dance. The game is used both at the hospital (within a specific clinical environment used for rehabilitation treatments) and at home, and it has been designed to ensure a rehabilitation protocol completely safe as regards to traumas and falls that may occur during physical activities.

3.1   Game Session at the Hospital

The game session at the hospital involves the participation of 1 to 4 users that can share similar therapeutic goals about motor and cognitive abilities. Prior to the game session, the users carry out a warm-up phase, preparatory to the correct execution of rehabilitation activities. Based on the specific users involved, the therapist can set a number of initial parameters, such as the music track, the exercise duration and, most importantly, the therapeutic goals on which to focus the session (see Fig. 1).

Fig. 1. Setting of initial parameter for the therapy.

Once the game level starts, each player has two key elements on the screen: a visual representation of steps (hereinafter the "Virtual Dance Teacher") that mimics the movements that the player will have to perform (each of which represents a game task), and a humanoid avatar (hereinafter the "Player"), that replicates each gesture made by the user in real space. During each game level, the Virtual Dance Teacher shows to the user a number of steps to perform: the user has to recreate precisely each movement, both in terms of correct physical performance and timing of execution. For each task performed, the game provides audio-visual (positive or negative) feedback relative to the player's performance (see Fig. 2).

Fig. 2. Game scene.

At the same time, as the users carry out the exercise, the range of sensors set up in the game environment (both artificial vision setting and biofeedback sensors) track the users' key kinematic and clinical parameters. These data, elaborated by the Data Analysis component, are used by the AI reasoner (alongside the game performance) to plan a new and subsequent task sequence to be performed by the user. In this way, the game is able to dynamically adapt both to the players' performance and clinical status, generating levels suitable for the correct users' rehabilitation and safety.

After the last task, users perform cool-down exercises, in order to allow a correct physical and energy recovery.

3.2 Game Session at Home

The exergame will be available also at home, where the patients will be able to execute rehabilitation sessions designed specifically for the domestic environment. This activity has been created for those patients that find it difficult to join the clinical activities, but may also be used as a strengthening activity between two clinical sessions. The exergame can be used under remote medical supervision.

The game session may be realized in two different modes: single player (the player carries out a game session without other participants); 2) multi-player (the player carries out a game session with other users remotely connected). The latter approach may be used to encourage the players' interaction and engagement, as well as to stimulate the competition among the participants. As it will happen in the clinic, the game session will be recorded, in order to be shared among the users and provided to the therapist for further analysis.

3.3 Personalization Logic

Each game session can be set up and personalized according to the type of users involved. A preliminary customization of the level may be carried out by the therapist, and concerns the setup of parameters such as music track, exercise duration and therapeutic goals. These settings, alongside with the user data, will lay the ground for the AI reasoner to plan a first sequence of tasks to provide to the users.

The sequence setup will be realized starting from a pool of approved steps, that have been identified and enumerated (i.e. Forward step, Backward step, Alternated steps forward, etc.). Each of these movements is self-consistent, i.e., it brings back the user to a rest position, and therefore is potentially linkable with other movements. Steps can involve both the use of a single limb (e.g. upper limb or lower limb) or both limbs.

In each level, the Virtual Dance Teacher provides to the player a sequence of steps. The player will have to perform the same movements as closely as possible.

The key parameters analyzed during the game session are listed below:

1. Game performance: step execution, rhythm (meant as step execution in the expected time frame in terms of bpm).
2. Kinematic parameters: gait analysis, centre of gravity position, upper and lower limb symmetry, degree of torso angle, cadence, etc.
3. Physiological parameters: heart rate, respiratory rate, blood pressure, etc.

3.4   A Middleware to Facilitate Module Interaction

During the game, the kinematic and clinical parameters of the patient are monitored by a middleware platform that reads the values transmitted by the environmental and wearable sensors, and processes the data through artificial intelligence algorithms, thus obtaining information on the state of health with a high degree of accuracy, supporting the physiotherapist in evaluating the patient's playing performance.

In more infrastructural terms, the platform can be defined as IoT Cloud and Edge combined with IoT Smart Gateway and IoT Device. Instead of sending information back to the cloud for analysis, IoT devices, using the Edge processing architecture, send information directly to IoT Smart Gateway to effectively reduce response time, while also saving cloud resources and bandwidth and providing better connection security.

In Let's dance scenario, the middleware platform allows the integration of the exergame with the following components: *(1) Environment Camera Gateway*: captures video frames from the cameras placed in the environment and sends them, via TCP protocol, to other middleware components for their processing. *(2) Wearable Sensor Gateway*: collects data from meters worn by patients and sends them to the module in charge of an initial processing through the TCP protocol. *(3) Event Bus Interoperability Framework*: through a system of connectors and topics and the adoption of the publish /subscribe architectural pattern, it manages the messages that circulate within the robotic platform, redistributing them to other components that express the need. *(4) Stream & Batch Processing*: allows to execute data analysis scripts/jobs in streaming or batch mode. The events produced can be lost-stored as data as well as sent as new events to the Event Bus module so that they can be consumed by other modules interested in them. *(5) Persistence Layer*: it allows to provide persistence to the circulating information: contextualized sensor data (internal and external to the robot), events produced by streaming and batch processing video.

4   Conclusion and Future Works

The present paper describes the first prototype of the exergame developed for the treatment of PD. A great effort has been spent to improve the appeal of the game for the target users. The first prototype will be tested in a trial in order to evaluate the usability. The project's ambition is to certify the game as a medical device.

References

1. WHO. https://www.who.int/health-topics/noncommunicable-diseases#tab=tab_1. Accessed 23 Apr 2021
2. Petzinger, G.M., Fisher, B.E., McEwen, S., Beeler, J.A., Walsh, J.P., Jakowec, M.W.: Exercise-enhanced neuroplasticity targeting motor and cognitive circuitry in Parkinson's disease. Lancet Neurol. **12**(7), 716–726 (2013). https://doi.org/10.1016/S1474-4422(13)70123-6

S.A.M.I.R.: Supporting Tele-Maintenance with Integrated Interaction Using Natural Language and Augmented Reality

Fabio De Felice[✉], Anna Rosa Cannito, Daniele Monte, and Felice Vitulano

Exprivia S.p.A., Molfetta, Italy
Fabio.DeFelice@exprivia.com

Abstract. Remote maintenance is becoming a crucial aspect in the industrial life cycle, especially in context where different countries, languages, and time zones are involved. Supplying on-site operators with smart tools to rapidly and easily request support can boost maintenance procedure execution times and solving of unexpected problems, can reduce the number of interventions and can speed up novice training, resulting in cost reduction and equipment use maximization. Authoring tools are needed to properly create new multimedia content and to process, organize and index legacy company knowledge, regardless of type. In this paper the SAMIR solution is presented, it defines a SaaS platform integrating Augmented Reality and Natural Language Processing to supply an effective support during maintenance intervention together with authoring tools to create multimedia content and procedures.

Keywords: Augmented reality · Tele-maintenance · Architecture for AR services · Middleware · Natural language processing · Natural language interaction

1 Introduction

Today, the interaction between production and maintenance is gaining importance in the "Industry 4.0" context. Proper maintenance management helps maximize utilization of equipment, to maintain a constant level of productivity, to reduce the number and timing of interventions, leading to costs reduction [1]. The tele-presence approach for remote maintenance, also because of the current pandemic emergency, is gaining the attention of companies in the manufacturing industry. In this context, the use of Virtual Reality/Augmented Reality (AR/VR) combined with multimodal Human-Machine Interaction, such as using gestures or natural language with text or voice [2, 3], allows effective reduction of execution times. Stress and weariness can be reduced enhancing security [4] and human error [5] and intervention costs can be minimized. Knowledge sharing of specialized skills is also enhanced facilitating continuous learning of operators.

In this paper we present SAMIR (Smart Assistance for Maintenance with Intelligent Research), developed for the Italian project FINDUSTRY4.0 – Future Internet for

© IFIP International Federation for Information Processing 2021
Published by Springer Nature Switzerland AG 2021
C. Ardito et al. (Eds.): INTERACT 2021, LNCS 12936, pp. 280–284, 2021.
https://doi.org/10.1007/978-3-030-85607-6_22

Industry 4.0 (PON FESR 2014–2020 project code F/080002/01–04/X35, from MISE–Ministero dello Sviluppo Economico), a SaaS platform aimed at supplying integrated tools to support on-site operators during maintenance, remotely and in real time. SAMIR also defines authoring tools to easily create multimedia contents (video, text, image, 3D models) and uploads legacy company content.

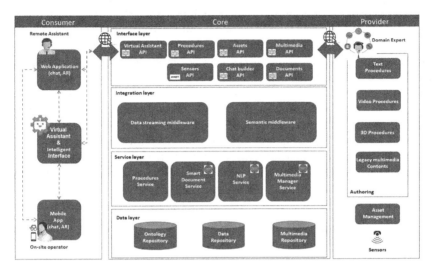

Fig. 1. The SAMIR architecture

On-site operators interact with the system by using natural language during dialogue with remote human experts, by means of chat or video call, and with an AI Virtual Assistant by means of chat or Voice/Vocal User Interface (VUI). The adoption of VUI in conjunction with normal chats allows keeping the hands and eyes focused on the task at hand, speeding up the intervention, as the speech recognition process is at least three times faster than keyboard input on smartphones [6]. Remote human experts can enhance their explanation by the use of 3D symbols, predefined or drawn in freehand, visualized by the operator in AR mode, moreover, AR can be used to represent entire maintenance procedures. The closer the interaction between human and real object, as in the maintenance case, the more virtuality should be non-invasive and constructive by enriching the real world with virtual contents, for this reason the AR approach is preferable to VR [7, 8].

The rest of the paper is organized as follows: in Sect. 2 an overview of the main architecture components is given with focus on interaction implementation, in Sect. 3 the interaction design is described, while in Sect. 4 and 5 a real use case and conclusions are reported respectively.

2   SAMIR Architecture

In this section the SAMIR architecture, depicted in Fig. 1, is described highlighting how contents are created and consumed. The architecture is organized in three main areas, the Provider, including tools used by the domain expert to create and organize contents, the Consumer, with tools to request and use contents, and the Core implementing the back-end, which integrates processing services and stores data.

The Provider tier contains applications to create maintenance procedures in different formats (text, video, 3D) by means of authoring tools and to upload legacy multimedia contents to populate the solution company knowledge. Also, sensors monitoring the equipment fall in this area as they provide live data that can be visualized by the operator during intervention or can be used to trigger condition-based maintenance procedures.

On the Consumer side there are three main components, the mobile app used by the on-site operator, running on smartphone or tablet, the web application used by the remote expert, and the Virtual Assistant which provides an intelligent interface to interact directly with the search engine of the system. The Core tier is based on a three-tiers architecture, extended with an integration layer to decouple interface and service layers in order to promote extensibility and modularity. In the Service Layer the Multimedia Manager Service (MMS) is responsible for the semantic segmentation and indexing of uploaded videos and for successively retrieving them as results of user queries. The Smart Document Service (SDS) handles the textual contents, both generic and procedures, and retrieves them when queried, while Procedures Service handles both video and 3D procedures. The NLP Service is responsible for processing user requests in natural language both syntactically and semantically to create a formal query to be used in input to the MMS and SDS.

3   Interaction Design

Two types of interactions take place, Provider interaction, involving authoring activities, and Consumer interaction, involving how operators interact with each other and with the system. In Provider interaction, to create video or text procedures, intuitive interfaces are available; videos can be subdivided into tasks and steps, analogously a given text can be annotated to create an index and to mark section of interests. This preprocessing step allows direct access to the portion of interests of a given procedure. Generic contents can also be uploaded, after tagging them, for free research.

In the Consumer interaction the on-site operator is first guided by the Virtual Assistant to the required information, if this support does not satisfy the user needs the dialogue can switch to a human operator. The Virtual Assistant tries to understand user requests by grouping them into three categories: Planned Procedures, Live Data and Contents Research. The user asks for Planned Procedures during scheduled maintenance to find a particular procedure about particular equipment, the assistant guides the user by showing the procedures available for that equipment and the format available for a given procedure (text, video or AR), at the end of this dialogue the procedure is shown to the user in the chosen modality. In an analogue dialog, Live Data requests show sensor data and other quantitative measurements to the user. Finally, Contents Research allows the user to submit a generic request using natural language, this is the case when NLP comes in by extracting the key words needed to make formal queries to the MMS and SDS to retrieve contextual information based on videos and text.

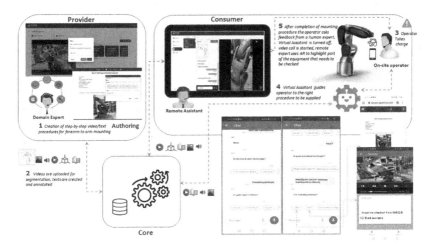

Fig. 2. Forearm to arm mounting scenario

4   Use Case

The ongoing development of the solution is constantly tested within a real use case. The application has been deployed in the industrial automation domain with the collaboration of the project partner Comau [9], a leading company in the field. Maintenance procedures about robotic equipment have been created and some user experiences have been conducted as depicted in Fig. 2. In this image the case of the Racer7 robot is depicted concerning the procedure of robot forearm to arm mounting.

The implementation integrates two existent solutions, while the integration back-end is developed from scratch in Exprivia [10]. The Scotty application from Wideverse [11] is used for AR interaction and authoring for video and 3D procedures, while Algho Virtual Assistant from Quest-it [12] is used for VUI, dialogues and NLP, with a proprietary algorithm [13].

5   Conclusions

In this paper the SAMIR solution has been presented with focus on integrated interaction combining NLP and AR supporting on-site operators with effective contextual information research during maintenance operations. Multimodal procedures can be supplied in real time created with appropriate authoring tools used by domain experts. Also, live data from sensors and free contents research based on requests submitted in natural language are possible. The development is in progress and constantly tested in real use cases in collaboration with a leading company in the domain of industrial automation. The interest from a real stakeholder proves how such approach is a real need from the industry field, and allows better understanding of final user requirements in order to realize a quality product.

References

1. Mourtzis, D., Zogopoulos, V., Vlachou, E.: Augmented reality application to support remote maintenance as a service in the robotics industry. Procedia CIRP **63**, 46–51 (2017)
2. Flatt, H., Koch, N., Röcker, C., Günter, A., Jasperneite, J.: A context-aware assistance system for maintenance applications in smart factories based on augmented reality and indoor localization. In: 20th Conference on Emerging Technologies & Factory Automation (ETFA). IEEE, Luxemburg (2015)
3. Gorecky, D., Schmitt, M., Loskyll, M., Zühlke, D.: Human-machine-interaction in the Industry 4.0. In: 12th IEEE International Conference on Industrial Informatics (INDIN), pp. 289–294. IEEE, Porto Allegre (2014)
4. Kaasinen, E., et al.: Empowering and engaging industrial workers with Operator 4.0 solutions. Comput. Ind. Eng. (2020)
5. Gavish, N., et al.: Evaluating virtual reality and augmented reality training for industrial maintenance and assembly tasks. Interact. Learn. Environ. **23**(6), 778–798 (2015)
6. Ruan, S., Wobbrock, J.O., Liou, K., Ng, A., Landay, J.A.: Comparing speech and keyboard text entry for short messages in two languages on touchscreen phones. In: Proceedings of the ACM on Interactive, Mobile, Wearable and Ubiquitous Technologies, vol. 1, no. 4, pp. 1–23 (2018)
7. Krupitzer, C., et al.: A survey on human machine interaction in Industry 4.0. Human Comput. Interact. (1), 1–45 (2020)
8. Eschen, H., Kötter, T., Rodeck, R., Harnisch, M., Schüppstuhl, T.: Augmented and virtual reality for inspection and maintenance processes in the aviation industry. Procedia Manuf. **19**, 156–163 (2018)
9. Comau. https://www.comau.com/it. Accessed 20 Apr 2021
10. Exprivia. https://www.exprivia.it/it/. Accessed 20 Apr 2021
11. Wideverse. https://www.wideverse.com/it/home-it/. Accessed 20 Apr 2021
12. Algho. https://www.alghoncloud.com/. Accessed 15 Apr 2021
13. Melacci, S., Globo, A., Rigutini, L.: Enhancing modern supervised word sense disambiguation models by semantic lexical resources. In: Proceedings of the Eleventh International Conference on Language Resources and Evaluation (2018)

Supporting the Analysis of Inner Areas of a Territory

Paolo Buono[1]([⊠])[iD], Maria Francesca Costabile[1][iD], Palmalisa Marra[2],
Valentino Moretto[2], Antonio Piccinno[1][iD], and Luca Tedesco[2]

[1] IVU Lab, Department of Computer Science, University of Bari Aldo Moro,
Bari, Italy
{paolo.buono,maria.costabile,antonio.piccinno}@uniba.it
[2] Links Management and Technology S.p.A., Lecce, Italy
{palmalisa.marra,valentino.moretto,luca.tedesco}@linksmt.it
http://www.springer.com/gp/computer-science/lncs

Abstract. This paper addresses the problem of supporting public decision makers in the data analysis of the territory they are responsible for. Most of the Italian territory consists of the so-called inner areas, which are primarily rural areas usually far from main centers that provide education, health and mobility services. A project that analyzes inner areas is reported; it has two main objectives. A first one is to identify proper clusters of such areas so that smaller areas can be grouped together in order to share important services in the best and more economic way; different algorithms are used to identify relevant parameters and to cluster inner areas. The second objective is to create proper visualizations of data of such inner areas, in order to better support decision makers in understanding the data and taking more informed decisions. It is remarked that using visualization techniques without adequate knowledge of their possibilities greatly limits the support that analysts may get from them.

Keywords: Smart territories · Urban development planning ·
Clustering algorithms · Data visualization

1 Introduction and Motivations

The emphasis on smart cities keep increasing with a major focus on large metropolitan cities. Other important components of the European territory are the so-called inner areas. In Italy, inner areas are rural areas characterized by their distance from main service centers; such centers are municipalities able to provide education, health and mobility services that inner areas may lack, for example schools with a full range of secondary education, emergency care hospitals and silver category railway stations. In Italy, inner areas refer to more than 50% of Italian municipalities, are home of about 25% of the Italian population and cover about 60% of the national territory. Thus, they require specific attention by public administration managers and politicians.

© IFIP International Federation for Information Processing 2021
Published by Springer Nature Switzerland AG 2021
C. Ardito et al. (Eds.): INTERACT 2021, LNCS 12936, pp. 285–289, 2021.
https://doi.org/10.1007/978-3-030-85607-6_23

The models considered for the analysis of smart cities cannot be directly used for analyzing inner areas since they have different characteristics. Such models could be used only after selecting the right indicators for inner areas. The data resulting from the analysis can then be presented to the decision makers so that they can identify proper strategies for the development of such marginalized territories [8]. Several attempts have been developed to categorize inner areas [1, 2,10]). For example, data engineering, data visualization and intelligent data analytics methods are used to create a decision support system to be used by technical and/or political decision makers [6]. In Italy, a national strategy for inner areas was introduced with the objective of improving the quality of life of people living in inner areas and inverting the demographic trend of such areas, see e.g. [14]. Several indicators describing the social, economic and territorial environment have been proposed [5,7,13]. The census of inner areas performed in 2013 classifies the peripheral level according to two main criteria: the offered services and the distance of an inner area from the centers that provide the essential services.

This paper briefly reports about a project that Links Management and Technology S.p.A. is carrying out in the South of Apulia region, the Salento area, with the municipality of Galatone, a town in that area. The project involves researchers of the IVU Lab of the Computer Science Department of the University of Bari Aldo Moro, since one of the objectives is to analyze data with the support of visualization techniques, of which these researchers are expert. The overall goal of the project is to improve the potentialities of inner areas, based on the idea that inner areas can join to provide together more essential services. Some activities of the project are briefly described in Sects. 2 and 3. Section 4 concludes the paper.

2   Clustering Inner Areas

One of the objectives of the project is to analyze how inner areas can be joined so that, together, can provide a set of essential services. For this analysis, several aspects have been considered, such as geo-demography, economy, innovation and sustainable development [11]. For each aspect, several indicators have been defined, reaching a total of about 50. Using such indicators, several clustering algorithms have been applied to cluster inner areas in order to identify those that can be grouped together. The results showed that the most useful algorithms are K-means++, Skater and an ensemble algorithm; however, they provide different classifications of the inner areas. Specifically, K-means++ reveals more irregular distribution of municipalities and classifies them in four clusters, while Skater takes more into account the distance and creates 5 clusters. The ensemble method shows the most similar municipalities to a reference one, so that all similar municipalities are selected at once and can be classified more easily.

The clustering techniques have been selected empirically, taking into account the knowledge of the analyst. In order to support the analyst on the correct choice of the method or the parameters, a visual tool may help. Some authors

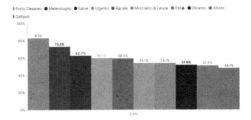

Fig. 1. Occupied houses by municipalities

use visual techniques to compare predictive models (e.g., see [4,9]). Pister et al. [12] propose PK-clustering to support the user choosing the best method compared to the user's prior knowledge. However, visual techniques are useful not only for complementing other analytical methods, they are very powerful as visual analysis tools themselves, as described in the next section.

3   Visual Analysis of Inner Areas

Several tools are available in the market, which provide different visualization techniques. One of these is Kibana[1], that is used in the project with Galatone municipality. However, the collaboration with researchers of the IVU Lab of the University of Bari was instrumental for a more valuable use of the techniques in Kibana, as reported in the following. In addition, IVU researchers discussed with Links researchers the importance of the validation with real users of the adopted visualizations, as for example done in [3].

In this project, a first report was produced by Links consisting of 26 dashboards (a dashboard is a set of visualizations proposed for a certain goal); such visualizations referred to data relative to various aspects of the inner areas: environment and territory; economy; infrastructures and mobility; socio-demographic, tourism. An example of visualization using one of the technique in

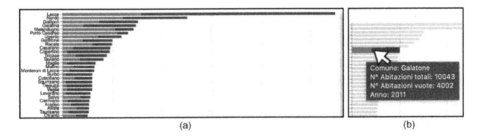

Fig. 2. (a) Salento municipalities ordered by the number of houses; orange color indicates empty houses and blue color indicates occupied houses. (b) Details of Galatone municipality when hovered with the mouse

---

[1] https://www.elastic.co/kibana, last visited: July 2021.

Kibana is in Fig. 1: it visualizes the top 10 municipalities of Salento in terms of occupied houses; each column represents the percentage of houses occupied by people; the legend at the top of the figure associates the color of each bar with the referred municipality.

Let us discuss now how this data visualization was redesigned by the IVU experts in order to allow the analyst to be faster in the data analysis and get more information, possibly discovering new and unexpected patterns.

Figure 2(a) still uses a histogram as in Fig. 1 but, being rotated of 90 degrees, it may visualizes all 97 municipalities in Salento (for the sake of space, the image is cropped and only the top 28 municipalities are visible here). In addition, each bar presents two colors because each color codifies an attribute: the blue color indicates houses occupied in the municipality and the orange color indicates empty houses. The length of the colored bar is proportional to the number of houses. This is an interactive visualization. As shown in Fig. 2(b), the visualization changes when hovering with the mouse on one bar: all the other municipalities are grayed and a popup shows detailed information about the selected municipality (Galatone, in the case of Fig. 2(b)). The municipalities can be shown in the histogram in various orders chosen by the user. In Fig. 2, the data are ordered by the number of houses. It is immediately visible that the proportion of occupied and free houses in the municipalities is different in the municipalities. For example, the three municipalities above Galatone (reported by eighth bar from the top in Fig. 2(a)) have much more empty houses than occupied ones. By further investigating on these three municipalities, the analyst finds that they refer to the most touristic towns in Salento, located on the sea, and the empty houses are a lot since they are occupied only during summer.

4   Conclusions

This paper discussed the problem of analyzing inner areas with clustering techniques as well as visualizations techniques, in order to better support the the decision maker of public administrations to group them in larger areas that are more efficient from the point of view of the available services. An on-going project is illustrated, on which Links Management and Technologies is working on, also collaborating with researchers of the IVU Lab of the University of Bari Aldo Moro. There is still a significant work to do on different directions, including the identification of the best clustering algorithms and the investigation of additional visualization techniques, not only to improve the comprehension of the analyzed data but also to provide new perspectives or analysis dimensions. A future plan is also to provide citizens with dashboards they may directly use. This is a challenging task because the visualizations must be understandable for the mass without requiring any training or specific expertise.

Acknowledgments. The authors thank Andrea De Matteis for his contribution in the implementation of the dashboards.

References

1. Battaglia, M., Annesi, N., Pierantoni, I., Sargolini, M.: Future perspectives of sustainable development: an innovative planning approach to inner areas. experience of an Italian alpine region. Futures **114**, 102468 (2019)

2. Bertolini, P., Pagliacci, F.: Quality of life and territorial imbalances. a focus on Italian inner and rural areas. Bio-based Appl. Econ. **6**(2), 183–208 (2017). https://doi.org/10.13128/BAE-18518, https://oaj.fupress.net/index.php/bae/article/view/3312

3. Buono, P., Costabile, M., Lanzilotti, R.: A circular visualization of people's activities in distributed teams. J. Vis. Lang. Comput. **25**(6), 903–911 (2014). https://doi.org/10.1016/j.jvlc.2014.10.025

4. Buono, P., Legretto, A., Bertini, E., Costabile, M.F.: Visual techniques to compare predictive models. In: Proceedings of the 13th Biannual Conference of the Italian SIGCHI Chapter: Designing the next Interaction. CHItaly 2019, Association for Computing Machinery, New York, NY, USA (2019). https://doi.org/10.1145/3351995.3352035

5. Cazzato, F.: Le politiche di sviluppo rurale in italia: un'analisi territoriale alla luce dei nuovi programmi comunitari. Le politiche di sviluppo rurale in Italia: un'analisi territoriale alla luce dei nuovi programmi comunitari, pp. 79–106 (2007)

6. Conejero, J.M., Preciado, J.C., Prieto, A.E., Bas, M., Bolós, V.J.: Applying data driven decision making to rank vocational and educational training programs with TOPSIS. Decis. Support Syst. **142**, 113470 (2021)

7. Girard, L.F.: Multidimensional evaluation processes to manage creative, resilient and sustainable city. Aestimum, pp. 123–139 (2011)

8. Jones, G., Leimgruber, W., Nel, E.: Issues in geographical marginality. General and Theoretical Aspects (Grahamstown: Rhodes University) (2007)

9. Legretto, A., Buono, P.: Poster: analyzing predictive models with the help of visualizations. In: womENcourage (Sep 2019)

10. Marucci, A., Fiorini, L., Di Dato, C., Zullo, F.: Marginality assessment: computational applications on Italian municipalities. Sustainability **12**(8), 3250 (2020)

11. Moretto, V., Elia, G., Schirinzi, S., Vizzi, R., Ghiani, G.: A knowledge visualization approach to identify and discovery inner areas: a pilot application in the province of Lecce. Manag. Decis. (2021). https://doi.org/10.1108/MD-01-2021-0104

12. Pister, A., Buono, P., Fekete, J.D., Plaisant, C., Valdivia, P.: Integrating prior knowledge in mixed-initiative social network clustering. IEEE Trans. Vis. Comput. Graphics **27**(2), 1775–1785 (2021). https://doi.org/10.1109/TVCG.2020.3030347

13. Tempestai, T., Bazzani, G.M., Thiene, M.: Le conseguenze della riforma della politica agricola comunitaria sul paesaggio rurale. Le conseguenze della riforma della Politica Agricola Comunitaria sul paesaggio rurale, pp. 79–95 (2006)

14. Zolin, M.B., Ferretti, P., Grandi, M.: Sustainability in peripheral and ultra-peripheral rural areas through a multi-attribute analysis: the case of the Italian insular region. Sustainability **12**(22), 9380 (2020)

Use and Even Recommend? Acceptance Modeling of a Smartphone Launcher App for Elderly Users

Andreas Sackl[1(✉)], Raimund Schatz[1(✉)], and Manfred Tscheligi[1,2(✉)]

[1] AIT Austrian Institute of Technology, Vienna, Austria
{andreas.sackl,raimund.schatz,manfred.tscheligi}@ait.ac.at
[2] University of Salzburg, Salzburg, Austria

Abstract. In this paper, we demonstrate how to utilize acceptance modeling in UX optimization via an adapted Technology Acceptance Model (TAM), which was applied in an industrial software development context. We evaluated a new Android launcher application that changes the user interface of smartphones to better match the needs of elderly users. Our findings show, that the factor "Usefulness" has the highest relevance and should be prioritized in both further product improvements and marketing processes. Furthermore, it is necessary to include the additional acceptance output variable "Intention to recommend" to determine successful communication strategies. We encourage researchers and practitioners to use context-specific technology acceptance models in software development processes to ensure adaption in the relevant target group.

Keywords: Acceptance model · User study · Smartphone · Elderly users

1 Introduction

Emporia, an Austrian company which produces feature phones and smartphones for seniors, developed an elderly-friendly Android launcher application that changes the UI of common off-the-shelf smartphones in order to better match the special needs of elderly users, see Fig. 1 (a) and (b). The Android launcher application was already in a late stage of the development process. However, previous market research by the company has shown that adoption of such a launcher typically happens via younger relatives who download and install the launcher on a smartphone (often an older model being reused), which is then handed over to the older family member. For the company, these younger relatives constituted a novel yet critical target group. Thus, it was necessary to obtain reliable information about how this group perceives and evaluates the product and as a consequence, how likely they would accept and adopt it. In this paper, we describe how we addressed this challenge by adapting Venkatesh's

© IFIP International Federation for Information Processing 2021
Published by Springer Nature Switzerland AG 2021
C. Ardito et al. (Eds.): INTERACT 2021, LNCS 12936, pp. 290–294, 2021.
https://doi.org/10.1007/978-3-030-85607-6_24

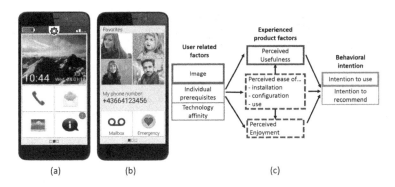

Fig. 1. (a) Home screen of the Android launcher. (b) Dial screen of the Android launcher. (c) Adapted TAM model for elderly-friendly smartphone applications. Bold borders indicate original TAM factors, whereas factors with thin borders were context specific and dashed ones were adapted ones.

technology acceptance model (TAM) [6] and by utilizing it via a user study designed to obtain empirical data on acceptance-related factors related to the launcher application.

TAMs were originally developed in the context of Information Systems with the purpose of quantitatively describing how different system and user related factors influence end-user adoption behavior, e.g. [4]. Although TAMs have the potential to provide substantial input in modern software development (cf. [1]), its practical application has been largely neglected so far. Similar to other end user studies (e.g. [1]), the underlying model needed to be adapted and extended to fulfill the requirements of the product and the target group. Hence, in our adapted TAM for elderly-friendly smartphone applications, we separated the original TAM factor *Behavioral intention* into *Behavioral intention to use* and *Behavioral intention to recommend* because recommendation to others (beyond mere usage) has become a critical factor in the context of acceptance and adoption in various contexts, e.g. [2]. We used the Net Promoter Score NPS [5] to determine this intention to recommend. For intention to use, we asked our study participants, if they would provide their older family members with a smartphone which has the launcher installed.

Whereas *Perceived usefulness* remained unchanged (e.g. whether the elderly family members would save time by using the launcher, and whether the software would support their daily life), we extended the original TAM factor *Perceived ease of use* with *Perceived ease of installation* and *Perceived ease of configuration*, since these are critical for applications like UI launchers (installation and configuration will be done by the younger relatives). Additionally, the younger relatives had to indicate how easy the daily usage would be for their older family members. We used the original TAM factor *Image* to determine the perceived social status of smartphones, i.e., younger relatives indicated if elderly people should use smartphones from a social point of view. Furthermore, we added the factors *Individual prerequisites* to determine if elderly users are able to interact with the UI from a physiological (i.e. cognitive, motoric and visual capabilities) point of view. A subset of the technology affinity questionnaire TA-EG [3] was used to determine the affinity of the elderly family members regarding new technology products. Furthermore, we understand *Perceived enjoyment* as key factor for user satisfaction and acceptance. We asked the study participants if their older family members would enjoy the usage of the launcher. Figure 1 (c) displays our adapted acceptance model. Except NPS, all factors were covered by several items rated on 7-point Likert scales ranging from 1 *strongly disagree* to 7 *strongly agree*.

We conducted a laboratory user study to provide participants with hands on experience with the close-to-final prototype. The goal of the user study was to evaluate our acceptance model and to derive specific recommendations for software development marketing strategies for our industrial partner. Overall, 25 participants ($f = 14$, $m = 11$), all taking care of elderly relatives, took part in our study, with age between 33 and 59 years and a mean age of 47. Study participants were asked to download, install and configure the Android Launcher including the granting of several android permissions, setting up WhatsApp, creating family contacts with photos and setting up the weather app. Then, the participants had to fulfill typical smartphone tasks, e.g., dialing, making a photo and sending it via WhatsApp, etc. All steps were evaluated via questionnaires accompanied by open questions to gather qualitative data about the investigated factors.

2   Findings

Table 1 displays the mean and SD values of all factors, Cronbach's alpha values (0.7–0.98) indicate a high internal consistency of the different items. The high mean values of the factors indicate, that the expectations of the target group regarding an easy to use and useful Android launcher for elderly relatives were fulfilled. The calculated NPS is 38%, which is comparable to the NPS of Apple in Austria with 39%[1].

Table 2 shows which factors are most relevant for *Behavioral intention to use/recommend* by depicting correlations (level of significance: $* = p < 0.05$, $** = p < 0.01$, $*** = p < 0.001$). The factor *Perceived usefulness* has the highest correlation for both *Intention to use* ($r = 0.84$, $p < .001$) and *Intention to recommend* ($r = 0.84$, $p < .001$), i.e., for further product optimizations we advised our industrial partner to focus on this aspect and to communicate, e.g., how using the launcher saves time (for both elderly users and their younger relatives) and how the launcher enables older user to interact with the smartphone. Furthermore, our participants provided some ideas how to increase the usefulness of the launcher, e.g., by providing the possibility to set alerts for individual intakes of pills. Surprisingly, *Perceived ease of use* has rather low impact on *Behavioral*

---

[1] http://www.marktmeinungmensch.at/studien/der-net-promoter-score-nps-von-smartphone-marken-i/, last access: 14.04.2021.

Table 1. Acceptance factor results

	Mean	SD
Techn. affinity	3.51	1.94
Prerequirements	6.07	0.84
Status	4.15	1.39
Easiness of ...		
... installation	5.95	0.92
... configuration	5.81	1.21
... usage	5.81	0.89
Usefulness	5.97	1.08
Enjoyment	5.06	1.25
Intention to use	5.88	1.49

Table 2. Relevance of factors

Factors targeting intention to use
1. usefulness (r=.84***)
2. easy config (r=.52**)
3. easy usage (r=.49*)
4. enjoyment (r=.44*)

Factors targeting intention to recommend
1. usefulness (r=.69***)
2. enjoyment (r=.61**)
3. easy config (r=.52**)
4. easy usage (r=.45*)

intention to use ($r = 0.49$, $p < .05$) and on *Behavioral intention to recommend* ($r = 0.45$, $p < .05$). However, the ratings themselves show that the launcher is easy to use. Although *Perceived ease of installation* was evaluated very positively, it doesn't exert significant impact on *Behavioral intention to use* or *Behavioral intention to recommend*. Some participants mentioned, that launcher installation is performed only once in the application life-cycle, which resulted in higher tolerance towards irritations like granting several Android permissions.

The average ratings about the *Image* of smartphones, that smartphones are perceived as becoming relevant for this user group from a social perspective. The ratings about the *Technology affinity* of elderly relatives is rather widespread (Inter Quantile Range = 3.83), e.g., this user group is diverse regarding the readiness to explore new technologies. The high ratings about the *Individual prerequisites* show, that - according to the younger relatives - the elderly target group has all necessary capabilities to handle a smartphone with the installed launcher.

3   Conclusion

In this paper, we discussed the integration of acceptance modelling in an industrial software development context. We demonstrated how practitioners benefit from context-specific acceptance models in both software development and marketing processes. Our findings show, that conducting an acceptance user study in a late stage of a software product development process provides valuable input for marketing strategies and defines a clear prioritization for final product improvements, e.g., in our case *Easiness of installation* seems to have only a minor impact on intention to use. Therefore, the industrial partner was advised to focus on improving the usefulness of the software and not putting res sources into enhancing the installation process.

Especially for software products that are bought online in app stores, online recommendations and Word-of-Mouth-Marketing are highly relevant for commercial success. Hence, it is crucial to understand the motivation and attitudes of potential customers. In our use case, *Behavioral intention to recommend* and

Behavioral intention to use need to be considered separately. For example, *Perceived enjoyment* is more important for *Behavioral intention to recommend* than for *Behavioral intention to use.*

References

1. Diamond, L., Busch, M., Jilch, V., Tscheligi, M.: Using technology acceptance models for product development: case study of a smart payment card. In: Proceedings of the 20th International Conference on Human-Computer Interaction with Mobile Devices and Services Adjunct, MobileHCI 2018, pp. 400–409. ACM, New York (2018). https://doi.org/10.1145/3236112.3236175. http://doi.acm.org/10.1145/3236112.3236175
2. Hosany, S., Witham, M.: Dimensions of cruisers' experiences, satisfaction, and intention to recommend. J. Travel Res. **49**(3), 351–364 (2010). https://doi.org/10.1177/0047287509346859
3. Karrer, K., Glaser, C., Clemens, C., Bruder, C.: Der Mensch im Mittelpunkt technischer Systeme. 8. Berliner Werkstatt Mensch-Maschine-Systeme (ZMMS Spektrum), vol. 22, chap. Technikaffinität erfassen – der Fragebogen TA-EG, pp. 196–201. VDI Verlag GmbH, Düsseldorf (2009)
4. Pai, F.Y., Huang, K.I.: Applying the technology acceptance model to the introduction of healthcare information systems. Technol. Forecasting Soc. Change **78**(4), 650–660 (2011). https://doi.org/10.1016/j.techfore.2010.11.007. http://www.sciencedirect.com/science/article/pii/S0040162510002714
5. Reichheld, F.F.: The One Number You Need to Grow. Harvard Business Review (2003)
6. Venkatesh, V., Bala, H.: Technology acceptance model 3 and a research agenda on interventions. Decis. Sci. **39**(2), 273–315. https://doi.org/10.1111/j.1540-5915.2008.00192.x. https://onlinelibrary.wiley.com/doi/abs/10.1111/j.1540-5915.2008.00192.x

User Feedback to Improve the Performance of a Cyberattack Detection Artificial Intelligence System in the e-Health Domain

Carmelo Ardito[1], Tommaso Di Noia[1]⦿, Eugenio Di Sciascio[1]⦿,
Domenico Lofù[1,2(✉)]⦿, Andrea Pazienza[2]⦿, and Felice Vitulano[2]⦿

[1] Politecnico di Bari, Via E. Orabona 4, 70125 Bari, Italy
{carmelo.ardito,tommaso.dinoia,eugenio.disciascio,
domenico.lofu}@poliba.it
[2] Innovation Lab, Exprivia S.p.A., Via A. Olivetti 11, 70056 Molfetta, Italy
{domenico.lofu,andrea.pazienza,felice.vitulano}@exprivia.com

Abstract. New and evolving threats emerge every day in the e-Health industry. The safety of e-Health's telemonitoring systems is becoming a prominent task. In this work, starting from a CADS (Cyberattack Detection System) model that uses artificial intelligence techniques to detect anomalies, we focus on the activity of interacting with data. Using a User Interaction Engine, a dashboard allows you to visually explore and view data from suspected attacks on healthcare professionals for a threat reaction. In particular, a User Feedback module is presented to interact with healthcare personnel and ask for a response on the anomaly detected.

Keywords: User interaction · User feedback · Artificial intelligence for security · Internet of medical things · e-Health

1 Introduction

In the e-Health sector, the protection of patient telemonitoring systems is essential to ensure that they follow their clinical path without any kind of external intrusion. In particular, Artificial Intelligence (AI) and Machine Learning (ML) have become critical technologies in information security, as they are capable of rapidly analyzing millions of events and identifying many different types of threats.

Intrusion analysts infer the context of a security breach by using prior knowledge to discover events relevant to the incident and understand why it happened [1]. Although security tools have been developed that provide visualization techniques and minimize human interaction to simplify the analysis process, too little attention has been paid to humanizing the interpretation of security incidents. Simply reporting a cyberattack is not sufficient to allow the healthcare

C. Ardito et al. (Eds.): INTERACT 2021, LNCS 12936, pp. 295–299, 2021.
https://doi.org/10.1007/978-3-030-85607-6_25

professional to correct the patient's clinical path. These data must be represented graphically, which can be understood by the healthcare professional. The detection of the cyberattack must therefore be supported by systems that provide different forms of visualization and interaction, according to the different end-users, and that allows them to have the possibility to interactively manipulate graphical representations based on Visual Data Mining (VDM) techniques.

This paper is organized as follows. Section 2 provides an overview of related work and technologies which were investigated as background knowledge. Section 3 provides the main contribution of the paper regarding the user interaction with a Cyberattack Detection System (CADS). Finally, Sect. 4 concludes the paper, outlining future works.

2   Background and Related Work

Cyberattack Detection System (CADS) is software that automates the cyberattack detection process and detects possible cyberattacks. Anomaly detection typically works on monitored network traffic data. Indeed, the integration of healthcare-based devices and sensors within the Internet of Things (IoT) has led to the evolution of the Internet of Medical Things (IoMT) [12]. In particular, ML-based anomaly detection systems are critical for ensuring security and mitigating threats such as bogus data injection attacks [7]. Therefore, designing a distributed security framework for distributed IoMT applications is a challenging task due to the dynamic nature of IoMT networks such as IoT devices, edge devices, and the cloud. The line of research in this way is moving towards building robust anomaly-based intrusion detection systems that efficiently distinguish attack and normal observations in the IoMT environment, consisting of interconnected devices and sensors. For this reason, works in [3,8,9] has dealt with a clinical and operational context to develop integrated solutions for continuous care in which AI and IoMT are used at the Edge, with a people-centered approach that fit the needs of healthcare professionals and is incorporated into their workflows.

Figure 1 depicts the architecture of the CADS proposed in [2]. It focuses on the security of data transmitted from IoMT sensors to three different interconnected processing modules: a Clinical Pathway Anomaly Detection (CPAD), an Explainer module, and an User Interaction Engine. The latter is made up of three sub-modules, i.e.: a Visualization Framework, an User Interface, and an User Feedback system. The activity of interacting with the data is carried out by means of the User Interaction Engine, which provides a dashboard through which to visually explore the data to get a clearer view of what happened over a period of time. In particular, thanks to the *User Feedback* module, it is possible to implement a continuous improvement of the classification performance, and consequently of the anomaly detection, thus obtaining a more effective identification of threats. In this way, CADS is increasingly accurate in identifying threats and therefore more robust from a security point of view.

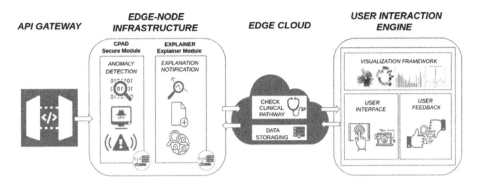

Fig. 1. Cyberattack detection system architecture

Below is a case study, where an e-Health telemonitoring system is, in turn, monitored by a CADS at the Edge. Let's consider a smart ECG device, which collects heartbeat information from a patient in remote assistance.

3   ECG User Interaction and User Feedback

The Interactive Machine Learning (IML) research domain incorporates human feedback into the model training process to develop high-performance ML models [4]. It is experience research again momentum [5].

Thanks to the use of examples provided by the system and human feedback [10,11], it is possible to allow the algorithm to learn how best to behave when faced with a given ECG detection. In our case study, the contribution of the User Feedback to the system is the evaluation of the detected anomaly and the embedding of a doctor's feedback. The User Feedback module will generate for each detection ECG_i a feedback coefficient ϕ_i that represents the doctor's feedback on a given instance.

Definition 1. *Let ECG be the set of the heartbeat detections received from a smart ECG monitoring end-device, ECG_i be the i-th heartbeat detection. Then, the feedback coefficient is a function $\phi \colon ECG \mapsto \{-1, 1\}$ such that any i-th user feedback related to the heartbeat detection ECG_i, is defined as follows:*

$$\phi_i = \begin{cases} +1 & \text{if } ECG_i \text{ is false positive or false negative} \\ -1 & \text{if } ECG_i \text{ is true positive or true negative} \end{cases} \tag{1}$$

Therefore, the User Feedback UF is a set of tuples such that, for any i-th pair of arguments (ECG_i, ϕ_i), a single element UF_i is defined as:

$$UF_i = (ECG_i, \phi_i) \tag{2}$$

In this way, the CADS will become more robust to external cyberattacks, since the User Feedback would report the opinion of the caregiver which will confirm or not whether the i-the ECG detection is abnormal or not. In the User Interaction Engine, the *Visualisation Framework* represents the data orchestrator, handling and visualizing processed data coming from the various modules. It uses algorithms of VDM [6] that allow, through different visualization techniques, to interactively group data in a more efficient way, improving the data insight process. Afterwards, the *User Interface (UI)* included in the User Interaction Engine allows the user to interact with the data. In the case study, the UI allows the caregiver to interact with the ECG instances. In the CADS architecture, an Explanation module displays useful classification information, with which it is possible to visually manage each ECG detection. For instance, one would be able to no longer consider an ECG instance as an anomaly, or, more specifically, to improve the classifier performances by indicating the correct class of anomaly when a wrong one has been predicted. The interaction with the user, in this case a doctor, helps the system to be more and more reliable, as well as secure from cyberattacks.

Through the integration of CPAD, Explainer, and User Interaction Engine modules, the Visualization Framework will be able to manage anomalies detected as threat insights. These will be appropriately displayed on the UI which, in addition to allowing interaction with the anomalous data (in this case the ECG detection), will be able to display the threat representation through a dashboard. Thanks to the threats graphical representation in the dashboard, the user's reaction to the threat is improved. The visual process, whereby the healthcare professional is able to mark a detection as true or not, is a key scenario in which ML methods are combined with human feedback through interactive visualization. This process enables the fast prototyping of the ML model that can improve both the performance of the algorithm and human feedback. It will be also able to complete tasks where anomaly identification was not yet possible. The system then uses User Feedback to refine detection results and guide further analysis. Caregiver Feedback is therefore used as an essential source of ever-improving anomaly detection of ECG, which means that labeling the local environment will trigger global updates and thus guide further analysis.

4   Conclusion

An e-Health telemonitoring system cannot always have a security expert managing the security of the system. The proposed User Interaction and, in particular, User Feedback modules introduced in an AI-based CADS provide a visual representation of the results to the expert user engaged in a feedback response, determining whether the detected anomalous data are truly atypical by assessing the detection with positive feedback. Otherwise, the user provides negative feedback. Such interaction with a CADS has an impact on the processed health data, adjusting the visualization reports with the corrected measurements, shown in a useful dashboard. Future works will focus on the development of a further visual interface in which, thanks to the use of ML and VDM algorithms, it is possible to graphically represent both machine capability and human intelligence.

Acknowledgments. This work was partially funded by the European Union, Horizon 2020 research and innovation programme, through the ECHO project (grant agreement no 830943) and by the Italian P.O. Puglia FESR 2014–2020 (project code 6ESURE5) SECURE SAFE APULIA.

References

1. AfzaliSeresht, N., Liu, Q., Miao, Y.: An explainable intelligence model for security event analysis. In: Liu, J., Bailey, J. (eds.) AI 2019. LNCS (LNAI), vol. 11919, pp. 315–327. Springer, Cham (2019). https://doi.org/10.1007/978-3-030-35288-2_26
2. Ardito, C., Di Noia, T., Di Sciascio, E., Lofù, D., Pazienza, A., Vitulano, F.: An artificial intelligence cyberattack detection system to improve threat reaction in e-health. In: Proceedings of Italian Conference on Cybersecurity (ITASEC 2021) (2021, to be published)
3. Ardito, C., et al.: Towards a situation awareness for ehealth in ageing society. In: Proceedings of the Italian Workshop on Artificial Intelligence for an Ageing Society (AIxAS 2020), pp. 40–55 (2020)
4. Fails, J.A., Olsen Jr., D.R.: Interactive machine learning. In: Proceedings of the 8th International Conference on Intelligent User Interfaces, pp. 39–45 (2003)
5. Koch, J., Taffin, N., Beaudouin-Lafon, M., Laine, M., Lucero, A., Mackay, W.E.: ImageSense: an intelligent collaborative ideation tool to support diverse human-computer partnerships. Proc. ACM Hum.-Comput. Interact. 4(CSCW1), 1–27 (2020)
6. Kreuseler, M., Nocke, T., Schumann, H.: A history mechanism for visual data mining. In: IEEE Symposium on Information Visualization. pp. 49–56 (2004)
7. Luo, Y., Xiao, Y., Cheng, L., Peng, G., Yao, D.D.: Deep learning-based anomaly detection in cyber-physical systems: progress and opportunities. arXiv preprint arXiv:2003.13213 (2020)
8. Pazienza, A., et al.: Adaptive critical care intervention in the internet of medical things. In: 2020 IEEE International Conference on Evolving and Adaptive Intelligent Systems (EAIS), pp. 1–8. IEEE (2020)
9. Pazienza, A., Mallardi, G., Fasciano, C., Vitulano, F.: Artificial intelligence on edge computing: a healthcare scenario in ambient assisted living. In: Proceedings of the 5th Italian Workshop on Artificial Intelligence for Ambient Assisted Living 2019, AI*AAL@AI*IA 2019, pp. 22–37 (2019)
10. Shi, Y., Xu, M., Zhao, R., Fu, H., Wu, T., Cao, N.: Interactive context-aware anomaly detection guided by user feedback. IEEE Trans. Hum.-Mach. Syst. 49(6), 550–559 (2019)
11. Stumpf, S., et al.: Toward harnessing user feedback for machine learning. In: Proceedings of the 12th International Conference on Intelligent User Interfaces, pp. 82–91 (2007)
12. Yang, G., Jan, M.A., Menon, V.G., Shynu, P., Aimal, M.M., Alshehri, M.D.: A centralized cluster-based hierarchical approach for green communication in a smart healthcare system. IEEE Access 8, 101464–101475 (2020)

VRQUEST: Designing and Evaluating a Virtual Reality System for Factory Training

Khanh-Duy Le[1]([⊠]), Saad Azhar[1], David Lindh[2], and Dawid Ziobro[1]

[1] ABB Research, Västerås, Sweden
duy.le@se.abb.com
[2] Linköping University, Linköping, Sweden

Abstract. Training is vital in factories to ensure the quality of workers' technical expertise but can be costly due to various physicality constrains. The emergence of virtual reality (VR) opens the opportunities to address this issue by providing affordable solutions where workers can freely learn by doing without compromising safety or risking damage. This paper presents an industrial research project carried out in a company, focusing on designing and evaluating a VR application for training a procedural task in factories. Insights from the evaluation suggest multiple design considerations that need to be taken into account in designing future VR interfaces for factory training in the company.

Keywords: VR · Factory training · Immersive environment

1 Introduction

Technical training plays an important role in manufacturing industries. Both experienced or newly-hired workers need to be trained regularly to ensure up-to-date technical knowledge and skills for reliable and timely operation or troubleshooting in factories. However, technical training can be costly. In traditional training approaches, trainees need to typically work directly on a piece of real equipment in order to help them acquire hands-on experience. This might be impractical in many scenarios where the real equipment is expensive, thus economically difficult for trainees to freely explore. Sometimes trial-and-error exploration with actual devices should even be avoided as they may cause life-threatening accidents. Traditional approaches also typically require experts to be locally present to supervise, assist or teach trainees, which is becoming challenging due to the shortage of experts as well as difficulties of traveling.

Electronic supplementary material The online version of this chapter (https://doi.org/10.1007/978-3-030-85607-6_26) contains supplementary material, which is available to authorized users.

C. Ardito et al. (Eds.): INTERACT 2021, LNCS 12936, pp. 300–305, 2021.
https://doi.org/10.1007/978-3-030-85607-6_26

Recent developments of VR technologies promise novel low-cost solutions for technical training in factories. Modern VR headsets can provide powerful visualization capabilities and intuitive interactions based on hand gestures conveyed through handheld controllers, in a relatively compact form factor with affordable prices. Intuitive gesture-based interactions currently supported on modern VR systems might also allow to simulate user interactions with virtual artefacts similarly as in the real world, thus helping train necessary motor skills for the tasks. This opens opportunities for industry to easily simulate complex and costly systems and environments at a high fidelity in virtual worlds, where trainees can freely explore, manipulate, make errors and learn without taking risks.

ABB is a global manufacturer and supplier of complex industrial systems including industrial robotics, power and heavy electrical equipment. Technical training is thus a crucial part in the organization's business, not only in securing the company's production but also in supporting the company's customers. With recent advancements of VR, ABB was interested in exploring the applicability of this technology to benefit technical training activities in and offered by the company. We thus carried out a research project focusing on designing, developing and evaluating a VR application called *VRQUEST* to support training of a technical task in factories. The main goal was to examine the advantages and disadvantages of currently common VR devices for industrial technical training.

2   Design and Development of VRQuest

To frame design and research problems, we interviewed several subject matter experts (SMEs) in the company to understand more about their current training practices. The SMEs were managers and engineers from different departments such as electrical, mechanical, system design, installation, site management and maintenance with various levels of experience working for the company. We also reviewed multiple research articles on training, learning and instructional design [1,2] to understand more about what should be scientifically considered when designing a system for training. Based on contextual understandings gathered from the SMEs and knowledge from the literature review, we ran a design workshop to ideate on different design features of the system. We chose a maintenance task where a user needs to procedurally perform multiple steps to change a filter of a cooling system as an exemplary use-case for the *VRQUEST* system. This task was chosen because it was a common one found in the literature as well as currently existing in the company. The design features were iteratively refined during the prototyping process following the five aspects below.

Physical Fidelity: This aspect includes: *representational fidelity* - describing how the virtual environment should resemble the look and even the feel of the environment, and *interaction fidelity* - describing that users interact with virtual artefacts as if they were in the real world [3]. This aspect is to familiarize users with the visual appearance of the corresponding real environment and the necessary psychomotor skills to perform the actual task. *VRQUEST* implements this by presenting a virtual room that resembles an existing cooling substation.

Fig. 1. Overview of *VRQUEST* system (a) 1:1 scale 3D model of the cooling system (b) a virtual screen allowing the user to choose the training mode (*Tutorial* or *Practice*) and view the instructions in *Tutorial* mode (c) summary of user performance when completing the task in *Practice* mode (d) a participant bending down and reaching his hand over a virtual pipe to turn a valve located close to the floor.

Fig. 2. Examples of user interactions in *VRQUEST*. (a) An arrow helps the user locate a switch (b) the user's virtual hand forming a pointing gesture with the index finger placed on the switch (c) then flicks down to turn it off (d) an arrow indicating the location and the rotation direction of a valve (e) grabbing the valve handle to rotate it (f) removing the nut of the filter using a wrench, the arrow indicates the rotation direction (g) the user turning the wrench in the indicated direction.

A 1:1 scale 3D model of a standard cooling system of ABB was also placed in the virtual room (Fig. 1a). *VRQUEST* also tries to ensure that the gestures used to operate different components of the cooling system should be as close to reality as possible, given the commercial VR hardware (i.e. 6-DOF touch controllers) that we had (see Fig. 1d and Fig. 2). Haptic feedback like vibrations and sound effects were also strategically employed to improve the realism of user interactions with virtual artefacts.

Sequential Task Description: *VRQUEST* describes the main goal users need to achieve by the end of the training task, followed by step-by-step descriptions of the sub-tasks needed to be completed to reach the main goal. The descriptions are presented as texts on a virtual screen placed at a corner in the virtual room (Fig. 1b).

Attention Guidance: In technical training, it is important to guide trainees to focus their attention in order to reduce frustration and tiredness caused by open exploration. *VRQUEST* supports this by employing visual indicators such as colored arrows to hint users about which artefacts they should interact with at the moment and how to interact with them (e.g. turn a valve in a particular direction) (Fig. 2).

Practice: After completing the task with guidance, users need to be able to repeatedly practice it, with or without guidance, to build the psychomotor memories needed for the task. *VRQUEST* supports this by offering two training modes: *Tutorial* mode, allowing users to practice with guidance provided by the system, and *Practice* mode, allowing users to practice without guidance so that they have to recall the steps by themselves.

Motivating Trainees: VRQUEST employs gamification features such as badges of seniority level or experience scores to motivate users to keep practicing. Once completing a training session in the *Practice* mode, the user will see a summary of their performance such as task completion time or the number of errors, coupled with the corresponding experience score and seniority badge.

The prototype of *VRQUEST* was developed using Unity and Steam VR and running on an Oculus Rift VR heaset connected to a Windows 10 Enterprise gaming PC.

3   Evaluation and Insights

Research insights from this project needed to be transferred to ABB businesses to be employed in the company's potential products and services in the future. Because of that, *VRQUEST* needed to be evaluated to holistically examine the advantages and disadvantages of common off-the-shelf VR technologies in their application for factory training. Design considerations also needed to be distilled based on these findings so that designers and developers in the company can take over and implement in future systems.

We conducted a user study with 10 participants working at ABB to evaluate if *VRQUEST* can help users effectively learn to perform a factory task as well as how the design affects users' experience. Each participant performed the filter changing task of *VRQUEST* in two trials, first in *Tutorial* mode and then in *Practice* mode with a 30-min coffee break in between. Our intention was to examine if participants can recall correctly by themselves all the steps to successfully complete the task after learning it once with guidance and especially being distracted from the task during the break. We collected the task completion times of the participants in both trials, the numbers of errors (e.g. missed steps, changed orders of steps in the task) the participants made when performing the task in the second trial, participants' perceived usability (using System Usability Scale (SUS) questionnaire) and their qualitative feedback after finishing both trials.

In general, we saw that *VRQUEST* could help participants successfully learn to perform a factory task. In the second trial, participants spent significantly less time than in the first one (on average, 4.7 ± 1.1 min vs 12.2 ± 1.1 min, pair-wise t-test showed $p < 0.001$)). On average, each participant made $0.8(\pm 0.4)$ errors (over 21 steps in total to complete the task) when performing it in the second trial. Regarding usability, *VRQUEST* received $65.8(\pm 3.1)$ on average for SUS scores, which can be considered as marginally acceptable [4].

Participants' qualitative feedback provided us better understandings on the quantitative data as well as the benefits of VR for factory training and how VR training systems can be better in the future. Participants reported that compared to training using user-manual printouts they traditionally had, the immersive environment of *VRQUEST* using 1:1 virtual copies of the real artefacts allowed them to easily grasp the overall picture of where to locate the cooling system's components as well as how to manipulate them. Hands-on experiences as well as the spatiality and immersion provided by VR helped users efficiently remember the operations of the task. Besides that, VR encouraged participants to interact and explore, helping them remember the training contents better. Knowing the artefacts were virtual made the participants feel more confident to interact, manipulate and explore without the fear of causing damages. The gamification features also had positive effects on users. Most of the participants reported that they liked the task-completion time and the number of errors index as it kept them informed about their performance. After finishing the task in the second trial, three participants tried performing the task again to beat their current results. However, experience scores and seniority badges received little attention from participants.

Even though VR can visually and spatially provide immersive experience, participants reported the lack of certain haptic feedback such as weight or heat, which were often important for them to sense where they are relative to an equipment (e.g. a heated pipe) or to feel the tool they are holding (e.g. a wrench or a screw driver). Currently it is difficult for developers to integrate those features in similar systems due to the lack of off-the-shelf supportive technologies. However, with enormous on-going academic research efforts in this topic and rapid industrial adoptions, we believe such an integration would be soon feasible. Besides that, even though it is important to replicate the real environment in the virtual world to ensure physical fidelity, VR training systems should also leverage the strengths of virtual environments to visualize certain information that is not visible in the real world to benefit training outcomes. For example, the system can provide an on-demand visualization of the flow of water in the pipes to help trainees understand deeply why they should turn off a valve before another. This can be further enhanced by providing pre-recorded videos of experts explaining or giving tips to remember at critical points in the training task. Furthermore, having effective tools for users to take and review notes directly in VR is also important for trainees to personalize their learning process.

4   Conclusion

In this paper, we present an industrial research project exploring the applicability of common off-the-shelf VR technologies into factory training. We designed an exemplary VR training system supporting a representative maintenance task called *VRQUEST* based on design considerations distilled from interviews with SMEs and literature reviews. We then conducted a user study to examine the strengths and the limitations of current VR technologies in supporting factory training. Design insights derived from this research project were delivered to different internal businesses of the company for adoptions in the future.

References

1. Sawyer, T., et al.: Learn, see, practice, prove, do, maintain: an evidence-based pedagogical framework for procedural skill training in medicine. Acad. Med. **90**(8), 1025–1033 (2015)
2. Jamet, E., Gavota, M., Quaireau, C.: Attention guiding in multimedia learning. Learn. Instr. **18**(2), 135–145 (2008)
3. Pence, T.B., Dukes, L.C., Hodges, L.F., Meehan, N.K., Johnson, A.: The effects of interaction and visual fidelity on learning outcomes for a virtual pediatric patient system. In: 2013 IEEE International Conference on Healthcare Informatics, pp. 209–218. IEEE (2013)
4. Bangor, A., Kortum, P.T., Miller, J.T.: An empirical evaluation of the system usability scale. Int. J. Hum.-Comput. Interact. **24**(6), 574–594 (2008)

Interactive Demos

A Biofeedback System to Compose Your Own Music While Dancing

Carmelo Ardito[✉] ⓘ, Tommaso Colafiglio ⓘ, Tommaso Di Noia ⓘ,
and Eugenio Di Sciascio ⓘ

Politecnico di Bari, Via E. Orabona 4, 70125 Bari, Italy
{carmelo.ardito,tommaso.colafiglio,tommaso.dinoia,
eugenio.disciascio}@poliba.it

Abstract. Brain Computer Interfaces can enable engaging interactions between different art forms such as music, dance, painting. Building on this, we present a demo of a biofeedback system: a dancer wearing a NeuroSky headset adapts her performance according to the music she listens to. The same music has been generated by a music-composition software depending on her own real-time mental status represented by different fluctuations of some EEG parameters.

Keywords: Brain computer interface · Biofeedback · Music

1 Introduction

The relationship between various art forms is one of the fields of investigation that crosses all artistic disciplines, from musicians/composers to choreographers and theater

Fig. 1. An actual implementation of the proposed biofeedback system.

C. Ardito et al. (Eds.): INTERACT 2021, LNCS 12936, pp. 309–312, 2021.
https://doi.org/10.1007/978-3-030-85607-6_27

or cinema directors. The interplay between music and dance has profoundly influenced composers of every era by creating new technical-compositional models both in the world of music and in the world of dance itself. At the same time, in Computer Science, the interest in Brain Computer Interfaces (BCIs) has significantly increased in recent years, because it represents a possibility for implementing a more intrinsic human-machine relationship. Also biofeedback systems [1] are gaining momentum, characterized by the continuous loop between users wearing a BCI and computers.

In this paper, we propose the demonstration of a biofeedback system that puts in a choreographic/compositional relationship a dancer with a music composition software developed on purpose and two musicians (Fig. 1). The dancer wears a NeuroSky MindSet device [2] that detects some neurologic parameters, in particular her attention values [3]. Depending on these values, the software generate a music polyphony that is presented on an electronic score to musicians, who play it. In turn, the music thus produced influences the mental status of the dancer, who will adapt her choreography according to what she hears, generating new polyphonic musical bars (Fig. 2).

Fig. 2. Dancer wearing the BCI headset during a live performance[1].

2   System Architecture and Operation

The hardware part of the system is based on the NeuroSky MindSet, i.e. a device that can detect the brain EEG signal through a dry electrode placed on the forehead at the Fp1 position (see [4] for further details). It translates electrical impulses related to brain neuronal activity into digital numerical signals that can then be processed by a computer. The electrical signals can be measured by placing the electrode of the device on the forehead. The NeuroSky MindSet headset returns two parameters, namely attention (similar to concentration) and meditation (similar to relaxation) [3, 5] (Fig. 3).

---

[1] The cables connected to the dancer's wrists, as well as the light strips on the headset are only for choreographic reasons and do not have any further technical implication.

Fig. 3. The NeuroSky MindWave Mobile 2 used in the system.

The general workflow of the system usage is schematized in Fig. 4. The *dancer*, wearing the NeuroSky MindSet headset, starts dancing. The device transmits every second her values of attention. The algorithm of *Polyphony Generator* module, depending on the intensity of the attention value, generates strings of rhythmic musical figures. For an high attention status, polyphonic voices are generated with smaller musical values such as quarter note, eighth note and sixteenth note and relative pause value. For low attention status, polyphonic voices with larger musical values such as whole note, half note and quarter note and relative pause values are generated. Given the attention value, the algorithm selects a set of rhythmic values and generates strings of rhythmic figures in a randomized modality.

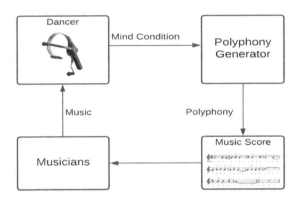

Fig. 4. System workflow.

The software is provided with a graphical interface that permits to choose on which musical scales model the polyphony is generated (see Fig. 5). All possible scales that can be calculated within an octave interval can be selected. Finally, the generated rhythmic sequences are superimposed on the previously selected scalar model. The process is repeated for all four voices of the polyphony texture. The music score reporting the resulting polyphony is displayed and continuously updated on a screen, so that musicians can play it.

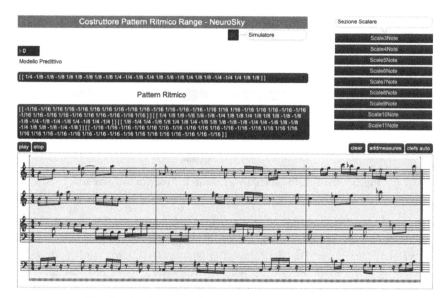

Fig. 5. User interface of the Polyphony Generator module.

3   Conclusion

We presented a biofeedback system useful for the interaction between music and dance in a BCI context. A possible evolution of this work could be to implement emotion recognition techniques to further improve the interaction between different art forms.

Acknowledgments. The authors acknowledge partial support of the following projects: PON Casa delle tecnologie emergenti di Matera "CTEMT" (CUP I14E20000020001), Servizi Locali 2.0, PON ARS01_00876 Bio-D, PON ARS01_00821 FLET4.0, PON ARS01_00917 OK-INSAID, H2020 PASSPARTOUT.

References

1. Wagner, M.J.: Brainwaves and BioFeedback. A brief history-implication for music research. J. Music Therapy **12**(2), 46–58 (1975)
2. NeuroSky EEG device. http://neurosky.com/biosensors/eeg-sensor
3. Neurosky: NeuroSky's eSense™ Meters and Detection of Mental State (2009)
4. Tyagi, A., Semwal, S., Shah, G.: A review of EEG sensors used for data acquisition. Int. J. Comput. Appl. (2012)
5. Bronzino, J.D.: Principles of electroencephalography. In: Bronzino, J.D. (ed,) The Biomedical Engineering – Handbook, Second Edition. CRC Press LLC, Boca Raton (2000)

A Personalised Interactive Mobile App for People with Autism Spectrum Disorder

Federica Cena[1](✉), Amon Rapp[1], Claudio Mattutino[1], Noemi Mauro[1],
Liliana Ardissono[1], Simone Cuccurullo[1], Stefania Brighenti[3], Roberto Keller[3],
and Maurizio Tirassa[2]

[1] Department of Computer Science, University of Torino, 10149 Torino, Italy
{federica.cena,amon.rapp,claudio.mattutino,noemi.mauro,
liliana.ardissono,simome.cuccurullo}@unito.it
[2] Department of Psychology, University of Torino, 10124 Torino, Italy
{stefania.brighenti,maurizio.tirassa}@unito.it
[3] Adult Autism Center, ASL Torino, Torino, Italy
roberto.keller@aslcittaditorino.it

Abstract. The PIUMA app aims at allowing users with autism to explore their city, finding new places that can be interesting for them but at the same time do not annoy them. Users can navigate the city through an interactive map that is both personalized and crowdsourced.

Keywords: Autism · Mobile app · Crowdsourcing · Recommender systems

1 Introduction

Autism Spectrum Disorder (ASD) is characterized by the presence of persistent deficits in social communication and interaction, and deficits in social-emotional reciprocity, accompanied by the presence of restricted, repetitive behavior, interests or activities and hypo/hyper reactivity to sensory stimuli [4]. Moreover, several studies [2,3] reported that people with autism tend to avoid places that may negatively impact on their senses. Sight, smell and hearing are relevant with reference to mobility in urban environments. Such sensory aversions may result in anxiety, fatigue, disgust, sense of oppression or distraction [2].

In this paper, we describe the app resulting from the PIUMA project (Personalized Interactive Urban Maps for Autism)[1], which aims to support ASD people in moving and living their city by means of an interactive map. The map

---

[1] The project involves a collaboration among Computer Science and Psychology Departments of the University of Torino and Adult Autism Center of Torino, Italy.

Supported by Compagnia di San Paolo.

guides everyday movements by providing tailored suggestions, i.e., by recommending items (Points of Interest - PoIs) suitable to ASD people according to their interests and aversions. Moreover, the map is crowdsourced. In other words, it is populated with PoIs, comments, and reviews by people with autism, and caregivers, as well as by anyone wishing to contribute to make ASD people's lives easier. The app provides the user with different modalities of content fruition. The user can navigate the map to find interesting places for her/him, or (s)he can use the search tool or apply filters for category and sensory features.

In the following, we discuss three main aspects of the app: the recommendations (Sect. 2), the crowdsourcing features (Sect. 3), and exploration modalities (Sect. 4). Section 5 concludes the paper with technical details.

2   Personalization

A key feature of our app is the possibility to provide the user with personalized recommendations (as you can see in Fig. 1a). We consider both user preferences, and item compatibility in the identification of the most relevant items for a user. We assume that the overall compatibility of a user with a PoI depends on her/his compatibility with each of the PoI's sensory features. Regarding preferences, we assume that the user's interest in a PoI depends on her/his preference for the category to which the item belongs [1]. We combine the compatibility ($comp$) and preference ($pref$) evaluation of an item to estimate its rating ($\hat{r}$) by means of a weighted model that balances these two components in a way that is personalized to the individual user. For this purpose we introduce the α parameter, which takes takes decimal values from 0 to 1:

$$\hat{r} = \alpha * comp + (1 - \alpha) * pref \tag{1}$$

In order to receive any recommendations, a user has to fill in a short questionnaire where (s)he declares which category of place (s)he likes, and which sensory features of places bother her/him. This step is not mandatory: if the user decides to skip it, (s)he is still able to use all the functions of the app, but without the personalized suggestions.

3   Crowdsourcing

The app enables users to extend the knowledge about places by adding evaluations of their sensory features. This is crucial for two very different reasons:

- The first one concerns user empowerment. Enabling users to provide their opinions does not only improve their life, favouring independent living, but also their participation in urban life. This can impact on the sense of self-efficacy and empowerment of persons with cognitive problems who, by contributing to the crowdsourced data collection, can actively work for a collective goal that may bring benefits to other people as well as to themselves.

(a) Visualization of recommendations with compatibility values.

(b) Features evaluations of item "Piazza Castello".

Fig. 1. User interface of the PIUMA app - personalized recommendations.

- The second reason is technical, i.e., in order to recommend places that are compatibile with the user's aversions, we need sensory information about items. As the Open Data made available by geo websites like OpenStreetMap[2] lack such information, a possible solution is that of acquiring sensory features directly from people, a task that perfectly fits the previously discussed user empowerment goal.

The user interface of our app is thus designed to gather sensory features of places [2]. For each place, the user can rate each of its features, and in particular its level of i) brightness, ii) crowding, iii) noise, iv) smell and v) openness; see Fig. 1b. Ratings take values from 1 to 5. These features have been defined based on findings collected in a user study carried out by some of the authors of the present paper [2], and of state-of-art research [3]. By interacting with the app, the user can also provide a global evaluation of the place. For each PoI, the system returns the average of the collected evaluations. Such information represents the domain knowledge base to be used as a source for the generation of personalized recommendations. Finally, people can insert new places. In the case of Torino (Italy), more than 200 markers were placed on the map by real users.

4   Filters

We provide users with different content fruition modalities. They can navigate the map to discover interesting places (by clicking on a marker of the map, the app shows information about the place, and the values of its sensory features),

---

[2] https://www.openstreetmap.org/.

(a) Categories (top) and sensory (bottom) filters.

(b) Map with PoIs based on the filters of Fig. 2a.

Fig. 2. User interface of the PIUMA app - filters.

they can use the topside search box to find specific locations, or they can apply filters to select the PoIs to be displayed in the map. Users can customize the content of the map concerning PoIs that are near to their current location by applying filters. We provide two types of filters: by category and by sensory features. Using the category filter, the user can select the types of places to be shown in the map (e.g., bars, and parks), while sensory filters are used to select PoIs conforming to them (e.g., in relation to noise, light, etc.). See Fig. 2a. Multiple filters can be jointly applied. For instance, users can search for low-crowded, bright and large squares and parks, as in Fig. 2b.

5   Technical Details

The PIUMA app has been developed to run on Android smartphones and tablets. The minimum supported Android version is 7.0 Nougat (API Level 24) that, according to the latest data from Google[3], can bring PIUMA to 73.3% of Android devices. Users' data are stored into a MongoDB server.

References

1. Mauro, N., Ardissono, L., Cena, F.: Personalized recommendation of PoIs to people with autism. In: Proceedings of the 28th ACM Conference on User Modeling, Adaptation and Personalization. p. to appear. UMAP 2020, ACM, New York, NY, USA (2020). https://doi.org/10.1145/3340631.3394845
2. Rapp, A., Cena, F., Schifanella, C., Boella, G.: Finding a secure place: a map-based crowdsourcing system for people with autism. IEEE Trans. Hum.-Mach. Syst. **50**(5), 1–10 (2020). https://doi.org/10.1109/THMS.2020.2984743

---

[3] https://developer.android.com/about/dashboards.

3. Robertson, C.E., Baron-Cohen, S.: Sensory perception in autism. Nat. Rev. Neurosci. **18**(11), 671 (2017). https://doi.org/10.1038/nrn.2017.112
4. Tavassoli, T., Miller, L.J., Schoen, S.A., Nielsen, D.M., Baron-Cohen, S.: Sensory over-responsivity in adults with autism spectrum conditions. Autism **18**(4), 428–432 (2014). https://doi.org/10.1177/1362361313477246

Cooking in the Dark: Exploring Spatial Audio as MR Assistive Technology for the Visually Impaired

Renan Guarese[1]([✉]) [iD], Franklin Bastidas[2] [iD], João Becker[2],
Mariane Giambastiani[2], Yhonatan Iquiapaza[2], Lennon Macedo[2] [iD],
Luciana Nedel[2] [iD], Anderson Maciel[2] [iD], Fabio Zambetta[1] [iD],
and Ron van Schyndel[1] [iD]

[1] Royal Melbourne Institute of Technology, Melbourne, VIC, Australia
renan.martins.guarese@student.rmit.edu.au,
{fabio.zambetta,ron.vanschyndel}@rmit.edu.au
[2] Federal University of Rio Grande do Sul, Porto Alegre, RS, Brazil
lennon.macedo@ufrgs.br,
{fgbcuya,jcbecker,mtgiambastiani,yjiccama,nedel,amaciel}@inf.ufrgs.br

Abstract. In the context of raising awareness to assistive technologies, we propose a gaming experience that allows users to embody having a visual impairment. By occluding the user's vision and providing spatialized audio and passive haptic feedback, allied with a speech recognition digital assistant, our goal is to present a multi-sensory experience that offers the user a sense of embodiment inside a mixed reality blindness simulation. Inside the game environment, the player is required to cook a meal completely in the dark. Being aided solely by their remaining senses and a digital assistant with spatialized audio capabilities.

Keywords: Mixed and Augmented reality · Assistive technologies · Accessibility · Embodiment · Spatial audio · Passive haptics

1 Introduction

Recently, researchers have claimed that the responsibility of addressing disability should be placed on everyone collectively, including technology designers [1,11]. In that line of thought, works have focused XR (augmented and virtual reality) applications towards the Blind and Visually Impaired (BVI) [2–4]. Specifically working with audio, these rely on the notion that current spatialized audio technologies allow for a decent accuracy on estimating a sound source, especially

Electronic supplementary material The online version of this chapter (https://doi.org/10.1007/978-3-030-85607-6_29) contains supplementary material, which is available to authorized users.

Fig. 1. Left: blindfolded user putting on the HMD. Right: user interacting with the game via voice command and receiving spatialized sound feedback.

when head movement is being tracked [2]. Considering assistive technologies in particular, domotics [8,9] and virtual assistants [10,12] have also shown their potential to help day-to-day activities of people with disabilities.

2   Related Work

Exploring the spatiality of indoor environments, Iravantchi et al. introduced the concept of Digital Ventriloquism [6]. Everyday objects are given a voice via sound projections in a highly directional pan-tilt ultrasonic array. In a different project particularly focusing on BVI users, Ferrand et al. [2,3] developed a navigation device to guide users in everyday activities with sounds using binaural techniques, which proved to be viable for walking and even roller-skating. Among their approaches, specifically Head-related transfer functions (HRTF) and Inertial Measurement Unit (IMU) sensors were similarly used in the current project for the synthesis of spatial sound beacons positioned according to everyday objects in the game, guiding players towards them.

3   Game Scenario and Tasks

The game portrays a smart home kitchen environment. The player has a dinner date planned with a guest and the lights go out. In order to complete the game, a meal needs to be prepared and served before the guest arrives, completely in the dark. A digital voice assistant guides the user throughout the experience, reminding them of the recipe, cooking procedures, time constraints and how to find each required ingredient and utensil. The smart home enables sound to be projected from different objects, in a digital ventriloquism manner [6], aiding the user to find the necessary resources without any visual cues. The voice assistant is capable of speech recognition, understanding and replying to player questions related to the tasks.

All user tasks require a sense of micro-navigation by the user, i.e. sensing of the immediate environment for obstacles and hazards [13], which is provided by the smart home via an assistive technology manner. Most tasks are simply based on finding and reallocating objects, such as putting spaghetti into a pot. The difficulty relies on the lack of vision: resources will need to be found solely on sound and tactile guidance. The majority of objects represented in the game are real, such as the food, water and kitchen utensils, improving the player's sense of presence via passive haptics [5].

4   Materials and Methods

Being supervised by a Visually Impaired researcher in its development, the game is meant to explore the different senses BVI people rely on. Considering the total darkness in the game scenario, a regular blindfold is used to occlude any real or virtual visual aspects, as depicted in Fig. 1-left. Besides that, several tools were used to convey the player with audio and haptic experiences.

Spatial Audio: As users are required to locate objects solely on sound and passive tactile feedback, a reliable spatial audio system is necessary. This navigation method relies on the natural ability of humans to localize directions of a sound. As to virtually synthesize these binaural sounds, transfer functions that characterize how ears receive sound from different points in space can be used [2]. These are known as HRTFs, and they're based on physical models and measurements of human head, torso, and ear shapes. The human brain responds to these differences to provide perceived direction in sound. As a device that already implements an approximation of these based on the current user's inter-pupilary distance coupled to inside-out head-tracking, the Microsoft HoloLens was chosen as the main platform for the game.

Passive Haptics: Given that people might not be confident enough to make precise judgements on object locations based solely on sound, players are also expected to reach out their arms in order to understand the environment in front of them. By having real objects and props placed in the game, the user's sense of presence may be elevated [5]. Feeling the textures of, weighing and smelling ingredients are typical actions expected from cooking a meal. Thus, using the passive haptics of real kitchen utensils, wind from a fan, water from a sink and even real food [7] might arguably help the player in embodying the game protagonist.

Digital Assistant: As a means to interface the smart-home elements of the game towards the virtually blind main character, a digital voice assistant was implemented. According to recent studies, people with disabilities - particularly the BVI - have been widely benefited by the use of commercially available virtual assistants in daily tasks [10]. Even specifically within MR experiences, preliminary results indicated that the presence of a speech-based virtual assistant improved user performance in the execution of MR activities [12]. By taking advantage of the speech input features of the HoloLens, voice commands related to the game tasks were implemented. Allying that to text-to-speech synthesis, a conversational agent named Axela was created, being able to respond to users' demands and inquiries.

5   Conclusions and Future Work

This work demonstrates an innovative way of raising awareness to assistive technologies for the BVI through a game. Along with the passive haptics, narrative, and voice interface of the virtual assistant, it was possible to create a game in which a protagonist is simulated with a total loss of vision. For further works, we aim to compare the performances of BVI and sighted users within the simulation. We hypothesize that BVI users are likely to have behaviors in place facilitating themselves in the kitchen. By observing these behaviors, we aim to optimize our micro-guidance methods for BVI users, so that these can be used in real-life scenarios, besides gaming environments.

References

1. Branham, S.M., Kane, S.K.: Collaborative accessibility: how blind and sighted companions co-create accessible home spaces. In: Proceedings of the 33rd Annual ACM Conference on Human Factors in Computing Systems. CHI 2015 (2015)
2. Ferrand, S., Alouges, F., Aussal, M.: Binaural Spatialization methods for indoor navigation. In: Audio Engineering Society Convention 142 (2017)
3. Ferrand, S., Alouges, F., Aussal, M.: An augmented reality audio device helping blind people navigation. In: Computers Helping People with Special Needs (2018)
4. Grayson, M., Thieme, A., Marques, R., Massiceti, D., Cutrell, E., Morrison, C.: A dynamic ai system for extending the capabilities of blind people. In: Extended Abstracts of the 2020 CHI Conference on Human Factors in Computing Systems. CHI EA 2020 (2020)
5. Insko, B.E.: Passive Haptics Significantly Enhances Virtual Environments. Ph.D. thesis (2001)
6. Iravantchi, Y., Goel, M., Harrison, C.: Digital ventriloquism: giving voice to everyday objects. In: Proceedings of the 2020 CHI Conference on Human Factors in Computing Systems. CHI 2020 (2020)
7. Khot, R.A., Mueller, F.: Human-food interaction. Found. Trends Hum.-Comput. Interact. **12**(4), 238–415 (2019)
8. Navarro-Tuch, S.A., et al.: Emotional domotics: inhabitable space variable control for the emotions modulation. In: Proceedings of SAI Intelligent Systems Conference 2016 (2018)
9. de Oliveira, G.A.A., de Bettio, R.W., Freire, A.P.: Accessibility of the smart home for users with visual disabilities: an evaluation of open source mobile applications for home automation. In: Proceedings of the 15th Brazilian Symposium on Human Factors in Computing Systems. IHC 2016 (2016)
10. Storer, K.M., Judge, T.K., Branham, S.M.: "All in the same boat": tradeoffs of voice assistant ownership for mixed-visual-ability families (2020)

11. Thieme, A., Bennett, C.L., Morrison, C., Cutrell, E., Taylor, A.S.: "I can do every-thing but see!" - how people with vision impairments negotiate their abilities in social contexts (2018)
12. Vona, F., Torelli, E., Beccaluva, E., Garzotto, F.: Exploring the potential of speech-based virtual assistants in mixed reality applications for people with cognitive disabilities (2020)
13. Zöllner, M., Huber, S., Jetter, H.C., Reiterer, H.: Navi - a proof-of-concept of a mobile navigational aid for visually impaired based on the Microsoft Kinect. In: Human-Computer Interaction - INTERACT 2011 (2011)

Engagement is the Key: A New Journey for ADHD Treatment

Pierpaolo Di Bitonto[1], Ada Potenza[1]([⊠]), Annamaria Schena[2,3],
and Antonio Ulloa Severino[1]

[1] Grifo Multimedia Srl, via B. Zaccaro, 17-19, 70126 Bari, BA, Italy
{p.dibitonto,a.potenza,a.ulloa}@grifomultimedia.it
[2] Iamhero Srl, via Torino 47, 80040 Volla, NA, Italy
[3] Villa Delle Ginestre Srl, via Torino 47, 80040 Volla, NA, Italy

Abstract. Attention deficit hyperactivity disorder (ADHD) is one of the most common neurodevelopmental disorders diagnosed in children, for which Cognitive Behavioral Therapy (CBT) represents the main standard treatment used worldwide, despite its pedantic approach negatively affects both patients' engagement and improvement. In this work we aim to renovate ADHD treatment with a new approach for cognitive, behavioral, and emotional patient rehabilitation. Iamhero is a first prototype of hi-tech multisensorial therapeutic environment, that bases its strength on patients physical and emotional engagement, leading therefore to cognitive and behavioral skills improvement. The first results show encouraging improvement in learning skills in patients that have steadily used the system for six months. In this paper we explain Iamhero main features, and the first experimental results obtained.

Keywords: Digital therapeutics · ADHD · Engagement

1 Digital Therapeutics and ADHD Treatment

Social and demographic changes that modern society is facing make ever more timely and urgent healthcare sector enhancement, with smarter solutions allowing a better therapy delivery and management, but most of all a full end-user engagement, in order to improve its empowerment and therapeutic compliance. Among the solutions that embrace both technology and medicine Digital Therapeutics (DTx) are emerging, namely as a "deliver evidence-based therapeutic interventions that are driven by high quality software programs to prevent, manage, or treat a medical disorder or disease".[1] DTx can be applied on a wide range of pathologies, especially those whose cure or treatment have a psychological basis or are enhanced by a proper patient behavior, such as neurodevelopmental disorders, anxiety, depressive disorder, substance abuse, obesity, diabetes, etc. Within

Electronic supplementary material The online version of this chapter (https://doi.org/10.1007/978-3-030-85607-6_30) contains supplementary material, which is available to authorized users.

the framework of DTx, we present in this article a hi-tech multisensorial therapeutic environment called Iamhero, that aims to help young ADHD patients to improve their cognitive and behavioral skills.

According to the main guidelines [2], Attention Deficit Hyperactivity Disorder (ADHD), is a neurodevelopmental disorder characterized by a persistent pattern of inattention and/or hyperactivity/impulsivity that are often associated with other psychiatric comorbidities. The main treatments can be divided in pharmacological (stimulant or not stimulant) treatments or non-pharmacological treatments, such as Cognitive Behavioral Therapy (CBT); such options are often combined with personalized educational plan at school and parental training. Although CBT represents a gold standard, it still has clear limits, as the scholastic and repetitive approach of some of the activities realized with the young patients may lead to frustration and refusal of the treatment, or more generally to a low level of engagement, with consequent negative influence on the treatment efficacy [3]. At the same time, such approach presents limits also for the therapist, as it does not allow a real-time evaluation of patients progresses. Iamhero system set itself as a key to resolve these challenges, aiming at improving patient's engagement and therapist's therapy management.

2   Iamhero: A New Boost for ADHD Treatment

Iamhero is a game-based therapeutic environment that bases its strength on patients physical and emotional engagement, leading therefore to cognitive and behavioral skills improvement. The system has been developed in collaboration with a pool of ADHD experts and end-users that - in a user-centred design approach – not only have highlighted the therapeutic goals to pursue but have also provided feedback throughout the development and test phase. Another key factor for Iamhero development is represented by Emotional Design. According to Norman [4], emotions are a crucial component that affects cognitive process. Each component of Iamhero games – such as the use of challenges, self-consistent tasks, use of positive or negative feedbacks, a consistent narrative, an age-tuned graphic design - has been designed to work on patient's engagement and trigger emotions.

Iamhero is composed by three macroelements: **Applied games**: *Topological categories, Infinite runner* and *Space adventure* are three games used in clinical environments under therapist supervision. "*Topological categories*" (Fig. 1) is a 6-levels VR-based game that allows to incrementally train one or several topological categories and simultaneously work on attention, planning, focus, memory, and the ability to wait and stand still. "*Infinite runner*" is an 11-levels exergame in which the player will simulate the game character movement by running on

Fig. 1. Game session of topo-logical categories game

the spot and shifting laterally, to avoid obstacles and capture specific items. Through the game is possible to work on semantic categories, motor coordination, attention, ability to wait and respect of the rules. *"**Space adventure**"* is a 7-levels game (with 3 difficulty modes) that can be played by means of a motion-sensing device or mouse. The game allows to work on the ability to work on the patient's attention, memory, ability to solve complex problems and to reflect on the cause-effect relationship resulting from actions. **Gamification app**: contains four minigames that aim to enhance the same skills acquired by the patients during the clinical sessions. The app can be used both on iOS and Android tablets or smartphone under parent supervision, therefore continuing the therapy beyond the clinical sessions. **Dashboard**: platform that allow the therapist to administer the applied game in clinic, assign tasks to be executed at home on the gamification app, monitor patients' performances, evaluate goals achievement and accordingly personalize the therapy.

The advantages of Iamhero are multiple: 1) the system allows a holistic training, as the presence of increasing degrees of complexity in the different game levels enables to train little by little more skills simultaneously. 2) the system constantly provides reinforcement or warning. 3) Whenever a task is completed, the game analyzes it on the basis of specific parameters (e.g., comprehension of topological or semantic categories, attention, planning, environmental stress, etc.), based on which a score is elaborated. 4) Each score, as well as the progress trend are available in real-time within the dashboard, allowing the therapist to personalize both the session and the treatment in the short-to-medium term.

First Results

The games here presented have been experimented for six months in a private clinic in the framework of a national research project (Progetto BRAVO) [5]. An experimental sample of 60-patients group has been selected, ranging from 5 to 12 years old and with a diagnosis of ADD or ADHD in comorbidity with language and learning disabilities. Patients have been sorted in Control Group (CG) that attended only standard therapy session in clinic, and an Experimental Group (EG), in which standard treatment where interspersed with session with applied games (plus the use of the gamification app at home in time between the clinic appointments).

In order to evaluate the system usability and to conduct the first efficacy assessments, standardized tests have been administered at the beginning (T0) and end (T1) of the experimental period. The efficacy resulting from combining traditional therapy with applied games has been verified through a repeated-measurement Analysis of Variance (ANOVA-MR) of standardized tests scores, evaluating from statistical perspective not only the differences between the two administration timings (pre and post experimental period) but also to analyze possible differences between the control and experimental group. The analysis has been conducted specifically form the tests mostly administered among the experimental sample for the purpose of ensuring compliance with the statistic assumptions at the basis of the theoretical framework. Results highlight an overall average improvement of cognitive performance of patients and underline the statistical significance ($p < .05$) of the differences between T0 and T1 as regards the following cognitive skills: ability to select in the mental lexicon target words belonging to specifical semantic categories, lexical, concentration, inhibition, and selection abilities, Visual Motor Integration ability, Performance-related age in relation to child IQ and improvement measures. These results (Table 1) confirm that both groups have experienced an improvement of the abovementioned abilities, but in some cases the improvement is stronger in the experimental group, suggesting a positive effect of Iamhero system, the satisfaction, engagement, and positive emotions felt during the game.

Table 1. Standardized tests ANOVA-MR results

Test	CG	EG	CG		EG		F (p value)		
			Pre	Post	Pre	Post	Time	P Interaction	p Group
BVL – Grammar comprehension	17	25	21.32	20.79	21.62	25.90	3.54 (.07)	**5.82 (.02)**	0.53 (.47)
BVL Phonological fluency	17	26	5.28	6.58	4.41	7.14	**10.21 (.01)**	1.30 (.26)	0.01 (.93)
BVL Semantic fluency	17	25	13.33	15.92	13.98	17.34	**12.35 (.01)**	0.21 (.65)	0.21 (.65)
BVL Phrases rep.	17	23	7.97	9.38	7.36	9.10	**7.49 (.01)**	0.08 (.78)	0.08 (.78)
BVL Non-words rep.	16	25	8.58	9.20	7.90	10.18	**11.95 (.01)**	3.88 (.06)	0.01 (.93)
GOODENOUGH DRAW	11	12	5.20	5.81	5.44	6.03	**16.52 (.01)**	0.01 (.95)	0.43 (.52)
VMI	11	10	14.39	16.39	13.53	14.93	**4.67 (.04)**	0.14 (.71)	0.37 (.55)

3 Conclusions

In conclusion, Iamhero system shows promising results when applied in combination with ADHD non pharmaceutical therapies. More investigation will be carried out in the following months within a clinical trial, to confirm the first results obtained. At the same time, the system is open for new development in order to enrich the applied game set and the related trained skills, as well as exploring neurodevelopmental disorders that can benefit from the same game-based approach.

References

1. https://dtxalliance.org/wp-content/uploads/2019/11/DTA_DTx-Definition-and-Core-Princi ples.pdf
2. American Psychiatric Association: Diagnostic and Statistical Manual of Mental Disorders: Diagnostic and Statistical Manual of Mental Disorders, Fifth Edition. American Psychiatric Association, Arlington (2013)

3. Raja Sree, M.S., Subramaniam, R.: Strengths and limitations of using cognitive behavioral therapy (CBT) as treatment for psychotic disorders, Munich, GRIN Verlag (2013). https://www.grin.com/document/313308
4. Norman, D.A.: Emotional Design: Why We Love (or Hate) Everyday Things. Basic Books, New York (2004)
5. BRAVO: a Gaming Environment for the Treatment of ADHD Salento AVR 2019 Conference (2019). https://doi.org/10.1007/9783030259655_30

Wearable Confidence — Concept and Prototype Design

Yulia Zhiglova[1,2]([✉]) [ID], Kristi Kuusk[1,2] [ID], David Lamas[1,2] [ID], Ilja Smorgun[1,2] [ID], and Paul Seitlinger[1,2] [ID]

[1] Tallinn University, Tallinn, Estonia
yzhigl@tlu.ee
[2] Estonian Academy of Arts, Tallinn, Estonia
kristi.kuusk@artun.ee

Abstract. We present Wearable Confidence - a vibrotactile display for facilitating self-confidence through applying emotionally resonant vibrotactile feedback generated from natural soundscapes and music pieces. The short-term research objective is to test how emotionally resonant vibrotactile stimuli influence the physiological parameters of a person correlated with various affective states. The objective of the demonstration is to offer the first-hand experience of the interaction with the Wearable Confidence prototypes and contribute conversations around designing vibrotactile body-centric technologies for self-perception change.

Keywords: Body-centric · Vibrotactile display · Affect

1 Introduction

The importance of touch for humans has been demonstrated in numerous studies [6,7]. One of the powerful properties of touch is to communicate and influence the emotional state of a person. The researchers from the field of affective vibrotactile technologies utilize the knowledge about physiological aspects of tactile sense in the design of novel affective touch technologies for the purposes of emotion regulation, enhancing remote communication and more [2].

Prior research shows some consistent results on how various combinations of engineering parameters (e.g., amplitude, frequency, placement) influence the affective state of a person, specifically the levels of arousal and valence [4,5]. We also know how to simulate types of touch to elicit various sensations (e.g., pleasant touch) [3]. While some knowledge about the design space of vibrotactile stimuli and their effect on perception is well-established [10], there are many remaining areas worth investigating further. One of them includes understanding how to achieve (or influence) a specific affective state by using different emotionally resonant natural sounds in the form of vibration [4]. We plan to investigate this question in our research. Here we present Wearable Confidence - a conceptual dress and a functional jacket meant to facilitate self-confidence

© IFIP International Federation for Information Processing 2021
Published by Springer Nature Switzerland AG 2021
C. Ardito et al. (Eds.): INTERACT 2021, LNCS 12936, pp. 328–331, 2021.
https://doi.org/10.1007/978-3-030-85607-6_31

through implicit vibrotactile sensations applied to the body. The sensations are generated from various emotionally resonant natural sounds and music pieces (Fig. 1).

Fig. 1. Wearable Confidence concept dress. Photo credit: Marin Sild.

2   Envisioned Applications

We envision that the concept of Wearable Confidence can be used in two main scenarios—for the purposes of emotion regulation and immersive experiences.

In the case of emotion regulation, imagine such a situation. You are about to go for an important interview and feel nervous and even insecure. Your "Wearable Confidence" jacket that you currently wear knows about it because it has access to your daily calendar. It also knows your current physiological parameters and decides (or you give an explicit command to it) to make you feel more confident. The jacket does it by applying specific emotionally resonant tactile stimulation for a specific duration so that by the time you reach your interview destination, you feel ready to conquer the world!

In the case of an immersive experience, we envision a wearable that can make one feel what others feel. In this case, we name the display "Wearable Emotion". Imagine you are watching an online performance. During this performance, both spectators and the performer wear an affective vibrotactile display. Such displays can translate the emotional state of the performer back to the audience and the other way around, making everyone's heart and soul beat in unison.

These are only two examples. If we know how to influence specific affective states with emotionally resonant vibrotactile stimuli, the applications are endless. We can enrich remote communication, help the elderly feel less lonely, influence our mood, and even become more empathic.

3   Design Rationale

In the first stage of our research, the primary goal is to design and test a body-centric vibrotactile display that allows a person to feel more confident in various contexts. For that, we developed two prototypes - a concept dress and a functional jacket. Follow this link https://www.youtube.com/watch?v=tg166Rj9O1k to get more details on our design process.

The dress is meant to showcase visually how a discrete stimulation of the body can make a person feel more confident and evoke discussion around the topic. The dress as a fashion piece is meant to not attract attention. The confidence, in this case, comes not from the visual forms, but from the inside, by means of vibrotactile stimulation sensed by the wearer only. The functional prototype is designed in a form of a sleeveless jacket, constructed of thin stretchy material.

A grid of six (2 by 3) miniature voice-coil vibrotactile actuators (model: TEAX13C02, Tectonic Elements, UK) are attached between two thin layers on the upper rear of the jacket. We chose these particular actuators because they provide a wide range of frequencies and the ability to manipulate the amplitude and frequency separately (as in LRA type of vibration motors) as has been proven in prior research [3]. We chose to place the actuators on the wearer's upper back because it allows more space for stimulation as well as placement by the shoulder blades may provide greater radiance of the sensation. Also, as we plan to apply a longer duration (20 s) of stimulation, the lower sensitivity of skin receptors on the back may be beneficial. The rationale behind the longer duration of stimulation was based on the prior work that showed that longer duration elicits a stronger emotional response to the vibrotactile stimuli [4].

4   Future Work

We are currently preparing for a study to categorize natural sounds and music pieces to be perceived as vibrotactile feedback to elicit various combinations on the arousal and valence circumplex model [8]. The goal of this study is to select the most effective vibrotactile stimulations to influence the extreme states within the arousal and valence dimension. We will use an existing open-source database of sounds, DEAM [1] where each sound has a specific arousal and valence rating, assigned through a self-report by the participants. We will select several sounds that represent opposites in terms of valence-arousal parameters and will transform them into vibration. In addition to self-report, we will gather physiological data [9] to see how the applied stimuli influence the skin conductance level (an indicator of arousal), facial tension (an indicator of valence), and heart rate variability (an indicator of stress).

5   Engaging with Wearable Confidence Prototypes

Both the dress and the jacket will be demonstrated. The dress is meant to evoke a discussion around the topic and the jacket will serve as a testbed for exploring how emotionally resonant vibrotactile stimuli may influence affective states. Specifically, during the interaction, a participant will have an opportunity to wear a jacket and feel various sensations on the back while his or her physiological data is taken. We will also ask the participants to report on their experiences. The physiological data will be gathered through a skin conductance sensor and heart rate sensor. The output will be predefined and controlled by the researcher. The participants will be asked to fill out a consent form. We anticipate that participants will get the following insights by interacting with the Wearable Confidence prototypes:

- Getting an awareness about their bodily signals when exposed to emotionally resonant vibrotactile sensations;
- Getting an awareness about the key vibrotactile parameters that influence the affective state of a person;
- The demonstration may spark curiosity in the topic, produce discussion and result in future research cooperations.

References

1. Aljanaki, A., Yang, Y.H., Soleymani, M.: Developing a benchmark for emotional analysis of music. PloS One **12**(3), e0173392 (2017). https://doi.org/10.1371/journal.pone.0173392. https://pubmed.ncbi.nlm.nih.gov/28282400
2. Eid, M.A., Al Osman, H.: Affective haptics: current research and future directions. IEEE Access **4**, 26–40 (2016). https://doi.org/10.1109/ACCESS.2015.2497316
3. Israr, A., Abnousi, F.: Towards pleasant touch: vibrotactile grids for social touch interactions. In: Extended Abstracts of the 2018 CHI Conference on Human Factors in Computing Systems, p. LBW131. ACM (2018)
4. Macdonald, S.A., Brewster, S., Pollick, F.: Eliciting emotion with vibrotactile stimuli evocative of real-world sensations. In: Proceedings of the 2020 International Conference on Multimodal Interaction, ICMI '20, pp. 125–133. Association for Computing Machinery, New York (2020). https://doi.org/10.1145/3382507.3418812
5. Mazzoni, A., Bryan-Kinns, N.: Mood glove: a haptic wearable prototype system to enhance mood music in film. Entertain. Comput. **17**, 9–17 (2016). https://doi.org/10.1016/j.entcom.2016.06.002. http://www.sciencedirect.com/science/article/pii/S1875952116300209
6. Montagu, A.: Touching: The Human Significance of the Skin. Perennial library, HarperCollins (1986). https://books.google.ee/books?id=XU7Z_aqCYggC
7. Morrison, I., Löken, L.S., Olausson, H.: The skin as a social organ. Exp. Brain Res. **204**(3), 305–314 (2010). https://doi.org/10.1007/s00221-009-2007-y
8. Russell, J.A.: A circumplex model of affect. J. Pers. Soc. Psychol. **39**(6), 1161–1178 (1980). https://doi.org/10.1037/h0077714
9. Wagner, J., Jonghwa Kim, Andre, E.: From physiological signals to emotions: implementing and comparing selected methods for feature extraction and classification. In: 2005 IEEE International Conference on Multimedia and Expo, pp. 940–943 (2005). https://doi.org/10.1109/ICME.2005.1521579
10. Yoo, Y., Yoo, T., Kong, J., Choi, S.: Emotional responses of tactile icons: effects of amplitude, frequency, duration, and envelope. In: 2015 IEEE World Haptics Conference (WHC), pp. 235–240 (2015). https://doi.org/10.1109/WHC.2015.7177719

Panels

Artificial Intelligence for Humankind: A Panel on How to Create Truly Interactive and Human-Centered AI for the Benefit of Individuals and Society

Albrecht Schmidt[1](✉), Fosca Giannotti[2], Wendy Mackay[3], Ben Shneiderman[4], and Kaisa Väänänen[5]

[1] Ludwig-Maximilians-Universität of München, Munich, Germany
`albrecht.schmidt@ifi.lmu.de`
[2] ISTI-CNR, Pisa, Italy
[3] LISN, Université Paris-Sud, CNRS, Inria, Université Paris-Saclay, Paris, France
[4] University of Maryland College Park, College Park, MD, USA
[5] Human-Centered Technology, Computing Sciences, Tampere University, Tampere, Finland

Abstract. This panel discusses the role of human-computer interaction (HCI) in the conception, design, and implementation of human-centered artificial intelligence (AI). For us, it is important that AI and machine learning (ML) are ethical and create value for humans - as individuals as well as for society. Our discussion emphasizes the opportunities of using HCI and User Experience Design methods to create advanced AI/ML-based systems that will be widely adopted, reliable, safe, trustworthy, and responsible. The resulting systems will integrate AI and ML algorithms while providing user interfaces and control panels that ensure meaningful human control.

Keywords: AI and society · Explainable AI · Human-centered artificial intelligence · Interactive machine learning · Intelligent systems · Intelligent user interfaces · Trust and bias in AI

1 Motivation

AI is promising revolutions in many areas of our lives. We have observed major advances in machine learning (ML) algorithms over the last years, leading to impressive systems for example in image understanding and natural language recognition. Data is collected at scale and the number of available data sets (public or inside companies) is growing rapidly, as many understand the fundamental value of data. Many applications are, however, not focusing on people, they are not human-centered. In the following, we discuss why advancing AI and ML algorithms and technologies is not sufficient and why it will not be enough

© IFIP International Federation for Information Processing 2021
Published by Springer Nature Switzerland AG 2021
C. Ardito et al. (Eds.): INTERACT 2021, LNCS 12936, pp. 335–339, 2021.
https://doi.org/10.1007/978-3-030-85607-6_32

to create the AI revolution. In order to make real progress that is meaningful for humans, as individuals as well as for society, we have to understand how to fundamentally change the design of interactive systems with the new potential and capabilities of AI.

2   Understanding the Challenges

This preview of the panel conversation includes a set of statement made by the authors. The challenges that are discussed range from fundamental questions on the impact of AI on humankind to specific issues that relate to the design of tools and systems that are useful for people. One core question is about the role of HCI. Why is HCI key to making AI valuable for individuals and society?

> *"HCI is the forward-thinking research field that considers not only the quality of technological artifacts but their purpose, value, user experience, and fit for the individual and the society."*
>
> *"HCI emphasises the human side of the interaction between people and AI: rather than highlighting algorithmic performance, HCI emphasises how to create a positive impact on human users and society."*

How does HCI add innovation to AI research? What skills are there, that researchers and practitioners in interaction design will bring to the table?

> *"AI research focuses on the design and evaluation of algorithms, which is important, but a complete system includes some form of user interface and control panel. HCI complements and advances AI research by studying the design and conducting the evaluation of user interfaces. The User Experience Design approach suggests that the goal can be more than autonomous intelligent humanoid robots. IXD [interaction Design] opens the door to supertools, active appliances, tele-bots, and control centers."*
>
> *"HCI generates and evaluates simpler, yet more powerful ways to interact with intelligent systems that not only improve human performance, but also satisfaction and control."*
>
> *"HCI's key approaches are creativity, involving different people in the design and research process, and critical thinking. This combination is the essence of innovation, that also benefits AI application research."*
>
> *"In addition to strong design and technical skills, they must master diverse qualitative and quantitative methods for designing and assessing the effect of intelligent systems on human users."*

Systems based on AI, machine learning algorithms, and data driven applications have a direct impact on people's lives. There were many cases that reported bias - in data as well as in algorithms. However, systems should be fair. Is bias inevitable in intelligent systems?

"Biases are not totally inevitable and they may also reflect some existing phenomena. However, we have to put on the table all the needed safeguards to avoid undesirable effects and/or to discover/control direct and hidden bias. Transparency and explainability play an important role in highlighting. Then we have to decide how to manage them."

There is the hope that artificial intelligence will help us to address and solve the grant challenges of our times. How can we as HCI researchers address sustainability with AI in mind?

"We can design and research persuasive and ethically sound interactive systems that utilise AI for the benefit of different target groups and related stakeholders. All facets of sustainability can be advanced, i.e. ecological, economic and social sustainability, by using AI's proactive, optimising and bias-free characteristics."

Another significant challenge is to foster an inclusive society. Here participation is key. How can we ensure eParticipation on a societal level with more and more AI systems available in our lives?

"Various AI systems can proactively bring into people's attention societally relevant issues. For example, youths' eParticipation can be advanced by context-sensitive digital services or even embodied agents such as social robots. Such AI systems can use persuasive techniques to nudge people to participate and hence advance inclusion of all people."

Currently there is generally a separation between creating basic AI technologies and the user experience created. However, this does lead to solutions that are not putting the human at the center. Why is it not possible to separate research in AI-algorithms and in AI-UX?

"If we are going to have explainable AI, then there may be a need to modify and improve the algorithms to make them more explainable. Visual interfaces to support explainability leads to improved algorithms, because developers will get a better understanding of what their algorithms are doing and what happens when their algorithms are incorrect, biased, or vulnerable to adversarial attacks."

Related to this is the question, are we still in control or if AI is taking over more and more of our choices. How can we balance human control and the need for high levels of automation?

"We want to do more than balance human control and automation. HCAI [Human-Centred AI] can lead designers to high levels of human control and high levels of automation."

We have to question the way we interact with computer on a fundamental level. Why do should we move from human-computer interaction to a human-computer partnership?

"Human-computer partnerships take advantage of the best human and AI capabilities, while minimizing their limitations, making it possible to upskill humans, not deskill or replace them."

Rethinking the relationship between computational devices, algorithms, data, individuals, and society is a prerequisite to a potential AI revolution.

3   Reading List in Human Centered AI

With the following reading list We like to highlight a broad view of "Human Centered Artificial Intelligence". The articles are a starting point to offer different perspectives on interactive intelligent systems and the role of human-computer interaction in their development. We have included basic definitions for the topics, considerations how this can change design, and how we develop new interaction paradigms. Further, we highlight issues related to trust and explanations, as well as societal aspects of the impact on people's lives. We also included several concrete examples.

- Human-centered Artificial Intelligence: Three fresh ideas [13].
- Interactive Human Centered AI: A Definition and Research Challenges [10]
- Human-Centred Machine Learning [3]
- Design Lessons From AI's Two Grand Goals: Human Emulation and Useful Applications [14].
- How Might Design Practice Change in the AI Era? [6]
- Intervention UIs: a New Interaction Paradigm for Automated Systems [12]
- How do People Train a Machine? Strategies and (Mis)Understandings [9]
- Human-Centered Artificial Intelligence: Reliable, Safe & Trustworthy [15]
- Opening the black box: a primer for anti-discrimination [8]
- Meaningful explanations of Black Box AI decision systems [7]
- ImageSense: An Intelligent Collaborative Ideation Tool to Support Diverse Human-Computer Partnerships [4]
- Expressive Keyboards: Enriching Gesture-Typing on Mobile Devices [1]
- Fieldward and Pathward: Dynamic Guides for Defining Own Gestures [5]
- The End of Serendipity: Will Artificial Intelligence Remove Chance and Choice in Everyday Life? [11]
- GreenLife: A Persuasive Social Robot to Enhance the Sustainable Behavior in Shared Living Spaces [2].
- CivicBots: Chatbots for Supporting Youth in Societal Participation [16].

4   Conclusions

Advancing AI technologies and improving ML algorithms will not lead to an AI revolution. We argue that human-computer interaction is the key discipline for creating meaningful tools, systems, applications, and devices that incorporate AI. HCI offers the skills and tools to make use of AI and ML to create meaningful and valuable experiences for individuals and society.

References

1. Alvina, J., Malloch, J., Mackay, W.E.: Expressive keyboards: enriching gesture-typing on mobile devices. ACM, New York (2016). https://doi.org/10.1145/2984511.2984560
2. Beheshtian, N., Moradi, S., Ahtinen, A., Väänanen, K., Kähkonen, K., Laine, M.: Greenlife: a persuasive social robot to enhance the sustainable behavior in shared living spaces. In: Proceedings of the 11th Nordic Conference on Human-Computer Interaction: Shaping Experiences, Shaping Society. NordiCHI '20. ACM, New York (2020). https://doi.org/10.1145/3419249.3420143
3. Gillies, M., et al.: Human-centred machine learning. ACM, New York (2016). https://doi.org/10.1145/2851581.2856492
4. Koch, J., Taffin, N., Beaudouin-Lafon, M., Laine, M., Lucero, A., Mackay, W.E.: Imagesense: an intelligent collaborative ideation tool to support diverse human-computer partnerships. Proc. ACM Hum.-Comput. Interact. 4(CSCW1) (2020). https://doi.org/10.1145/3392850
5. Malloch, J., Griggio, C.F., McGrenere, J., Mackay, W.E.: Fieldward and pathward: Dynamic guides for defining your own gestures. ACM, New York (2017). https://doi.org/10.1145/3025453.3025764
6. Olsson, T., Väänänen, K.: How might design practice change in the AI era? Interactions (2021). https://doi.org/10.1145/3466154
7. Pedreschi, D., Giannotti, F., Guidotti, R., Monreale, A., Ruggieri, S., Turini, F.: Meaningful explanations of black box AI decision systems
8. Ruggieri, S., Giannotti, F., Guidotti, R., Monreale, A., Pedreschi, D., Turini, F.: Opening the black box: a primer for anti-discrimination (2020). http://hdl.handle.net/11568/1088440
9. Sanchez, T., Caramiaux, B., Françoise, J., Bevilacqua, F., Mackay, W.: How do people train a machine? Strategies and (Mis)Understandings. In: CSCW 2021 - The 24th ACM Conference on Computer-Supported Cooperative Work and Social Computing, Virtual, United States (2021). https://hal.inria.fr/hal-03182950
10. Schmidt, A.: Interactive human centered artificial intelligence: a definition and research challenges. ACM, New York (2020). https://doi.org/10.1145/3399715.3400873
11. Schmidt, A.: The end of serendipity: will artificial intelligence remove chance and choice in everyday life? In: CHItaly 2021: 14th Biannual Conference of the Italian SIGCHI Chapter (2021). https://doi.org/10.1145/3464385.3464763
12. Schmidt, A., Herrmann, T.: Intervention user interfaces: a new interaction paradigm for automated systems, 24(5) (2017). https://doi.org/10.1145/3121357
13. Shneiderman, B.: Human-centered artificial intelligence: three fresh ideas. AIS Trans. Human-Comput. Interact. https://doi.org/10.17705/1thci.00131
14. Shneiderman, B.: Design lessons from AI's two grand goals: human emulation and useful applications. IEEE Trans. Technol. Soc. 1(2), 73–82 (2020). https://doi.org/10.1109/TTS.2020.2992669
15. Shneiderman, B.: Human-centered artificial intelligence: reliable, safe & trustworthy. Int. J. Human-Comput. Interact. 36(6), 495–504 (2020). https://doi.org/10.1080/10447318.2020.1741118
16. Väänänen, K., Hiltunen, A., Varsaluoma, J., Pietilä, I.: CivicBots – chatbots for supporting youth in societal participation. In: Følstad, A., et al. (eds.) CONVERSATIONS 2019. LNCS, vol. 11970, pp. 143–157. Springer, Cham (2020). https://doi.org/10.1007/978-3-030-39540-7_10

Artificial Intelligence versus End-User Development: A Panel on What Are the Tradeoffs in Daily Automations?

Fabio Paternò[1]([✉]), Margaret Burnett[2], Gerhard Fischer[3], Maristella Matera[4], Brad Myers[5], and Albrecht Schmidt[6]

[1] CNR-ISTI, HIIS Laboratory, Pisa, Italy
fabio.paterno@isti.cnr.it
[2] Oregon State University, Corvallis, OR, USA
[3] University of Colorado, Boulder, USA
[4] Politecnico di Milano, Milan, Italy
[5] Carnegie Mellon University, Pittsburgh, USA
[6] Ludwig Maximilian University of Munich, Munich, Germany

Abstract. Artificial Intelligence (AI) and End-User Development (EUD) look at automation from two different perspectives. The former tends to provide fully automatic solutions, the latter aims to empower users to directly create what they want. We need both, but it is still unclear how to combine them to obtain effective every-day automations that meet the flexible and dynamic user needs. The panel aims to stimulate the Human-Computer Interaction community to think more carefully about such aspects and the possible approaches to address them.

Keywords: Artificial intelligence · End-user development · Automations

1 Motivations

Automation is finding its way into many parts of everyday life. This is manifested by the increasing opportunities for end users to offload decisions to their home appliances, to hand over control to their cars, or to go shopping at self-checkout stores. Supported by Artificial Intelligence (AI), emerging automated services integrating analysis and decisions based on the processing of large information sets are becoming widespread. In anticipation of the broad impact that these emerging technologies will have on our life, a reflective and systematic consideration is necessary that leverages their full potential in terms of user experience.

While there is a long human factors research tradition on automation, such research has long been concentrated on highly specialized professional work tasks for highly trained and specialized personnel, such as control centre operators or pilots. However, the analysis of technological trends indicates that more than 30 billion devices currently make up the Internet of Things (IoT) demonstrating its pervasiveness. With such technological innovations and new use cases in domains such as industry, home automation

© IFIP International Federation for Information Processing 2021
Published by Springer Nature Switzerland AG 2021
C. Ardito et al. (Eds.): INTERACT 2021, LNCS 12936, pp. 340–343, 2021.
https://doi.org/10.1007/978-3-030-85607-6_33

and retail, the goal of designing automation for a broader population has become crucial. This transition of automation technology towards everyday life has thus brought people's experience to the centre of attention, thereby making it the mediator between humans and the surrounding technologies [5].

In everyday automation usage situations, continuous interaction is typically not as central as with manually operated systems. The relationships of users to automation in everyday contexts can be described as forms of "implicit interaction" [9] or "peripheral interaction" [3]. However, while implicit and peripheral interaction is often thought to imply that users provide inputs to a system, automated systems can often go further by taking the initiative in addressing user needs. The associated challenges include how to make users understand "when it is their turn", when they can override, and where it is best that they follow the recommendation of a system. Supported by these new forms of implicit interaction, many automated systems no longer feature prominent displays, and they are merging into the users' surroundings. In a sense, everyday automation is thus a strong driver for putting into practice the visions of "ubiquitous computing", "disappearing computer", as well as "ambient intelligence". The ambient nature of automated systems and their interwovenness in mundane, repetitive routines also supports the ordinariness of the involved user experience [4].

There is an increasing number of automations that are activated through the use of AI techniques, but they sometimes provide undesired effects and people have difficulties in understanding why they are generated, and how they can be modified and controlled [8]. AI systems in the user's surroundings can be enabled to learn and consequently change their behaviour. While the adaptation to user preferences can increase ease-of-use, this may have an impact on their intelligibility. Issues to be addressed include thresholds for perceivability and acceptance factors of system adaptation over longer time periods, and the possibility of modifying adaptations when they are not effective. In many usage contexts, manual interventions have to be supported, in order to better adapt the system behaviour to the respective context and preferences [10].

Such interventions require the user to switch from a passive mode towards an active one in both using the system and understanding the domain in which the system is operating. Related challenges regard designing environments able to allow users to understand what interventions they can perform, and which associated effects their actions will entail. Apart from situation-dependent interventions, people can also take on quite an active role when it comes to the customization of automated systems. In fact, automation offers the potential for the creative planning and customization of system behaviours even to people who have never programmed before. Many services, such as IFTTT ("If-This-Then-That"), offer means for the configuration of routines but they have limited capabilities, and thus often are inadequate to express user needs. A central question in this regard is how to enable people with no or little programming skills to customize the automation behaviour.

End-User Development (EUD) [1] represents the objective to empower all stakeholders (designers, users, workers, learners, teachers) to actively participate and make their voices heard in personally meaningful problems. EUD methods and techniques should allow users to understand what they can customize and whether what they specify actually corresponds to the desired behaviour. In both cases, it is crucial to adopt meaningful metaphors and related interactive paradigms [2]. The resulting solutions should be available for immediate and easy use, for example by allowing users to specify their desired personalisation rules through direct interactions with the objects involved in the automation (which is a form of Programming by Demonstration (PBD)). Here, the AI might help the users generalize the demonstration to create reusable automations [7]. However, when non-programmers are supported, some mechanisms are needed to safeguard the correct functioning of the system. Additionally, there is the need to address the challenge of both enabling informal EUD languages while still maintaining formality on the system's side. One further challenge is to allow end users to understand the actual effects consequent to the automations that they create or modify. While most approaches in explainable AI (see for example [6]) focus on providing indications on the outcome of some machine learning algorithms, in this panel we aim to discuss ways to allow people to both understand and control the algorithms, the dynamic effects that the resulting automations might have and their interference with other existing ones.

Enabling end-users to control automation [11] thus raises important research questions in terms of adequate modelling abstractions that can lead to incorporating the notion of explainability, configurability, user control from the beginning of the design process, rather than to add these dimensions when the systems are already in place. New design approaches, based on a human-centered perspective and intrinsically accounting for user intervention and control, are needed to let the end users make sense of automation capabilities.

2 Discussion

Given the background described in the previous section, several points can be discussed in the panel, for example:

- What are the dark patterns of AI and those of EUD, examples of cases where such disciplines provide effects that conflict with users' ability to actually obtain and control the desired daily automations?
- What are the application domains and associated scenarios where everyday automations actually controlled by end users can have high impact (possible candidates: smart homes, ambient assisted living, retail, industry 4.0, …)?
- What are the most suitable technologies, metaphors, interactive paradigms, programming styles to allow people to easily control, create, modify the automations most relevant for them in their daily activities (e.g., wizards, chatbots, block-based, data flow, process-oriented, PBD)?
- What are the principles, design practices, and methodologies available in Human-Computer Interaction (HCI) that could be adopted to empower the end-users to control automation in AI systems?
- What can the role of recommendation systems be in smart environments that users can control? When, how, and for what purpose can recommendations be useful and usable?
- What are the most effective ways to explain the automations that populate surrounding environments as well as their actual effects to users with limited technological knowledge?

References

1. Lieberman, H., Paterno, F., Wulf, V. (eds.): End User Development. Kluwer Publishers, Dordrecht (2006)
2. Ardito, C., Desolda, G., Lanzilotti, R., Malizia, R., Matera, M.: Analysing trade-offs in frameworks for the design of smart environments. Behav. Inf. Technol. **39**(1), 47–71 (2020)
3. Bakker, S., Elise Hoven, E., Berry, E.: Peripheral interaction: characteristics and considerations. Pers. Ubiquit. Comput. **19**(1), 239–254 (2015). https://doi.org/10.1007/s00779-014-0775-2
4. Clemmensen, T., Hertzum, M., Abdelnour-Nocera, J.: Ordinary user experiences at work: a study of greenhouse growers. ACM Trans. Comput.-Human Interact. **27**(3), 1–31 (2020). https://doi.org/10.1145/3386089
5. Fröhlich, P., Baldauf, M., Meneweger, T., Tscheligi, M., de Ruyter, B., Paternó, F.: Everyday automation experience: a research agenda. Pers. Ubiquit. Comput. **24**(6), 725–734 (2020). https://doi.org/10.1007/s00779-020-01450-y
6. Guidotti, R., Monreale, A., Ruggieri, S., Turini, F., Giannotti, F., Pedreschi, D.: A survey of methods for explaining black box models. ACM Comput. Surv. (CSUR) **51**(5), 1–42 (2018)
7. Jia-Jun Li, T., Radensky, M., Jia, J., Singarajah, K., Mitchell, T.M., Myers, B.A.: PUMICE: a multi-modal agent that learns concepts and conditionals from natural language and demonstrations. In: Proceedings of the 32nd Annual ACM Symposium on User Interface Software and Technology (UIST 2019), pp. 577–589 (2019)
8. Shneiderman, B.: Human-centered artificial intelligence: reliable, safe & trustworthy. Int. J. Human-Comput. Interact. **36**(6), 495–504 (2020)
9. Schmidt, A.: Implicit human computer interaction through context. Pers. Technol. **4**(2), 191–199 (2000). https://doi.org/10.1007/BF01324126
10. Schmidt, A., Herrmann, T.: Intervention user interfaces: a new interaction paradigm for automated systems. Interactions **24**(5), 40–45 (2017)
11. Manca, M., Paternò, F., Santoro, C., Corcella, L.: Supporting end-user debugging of trigger-action rules for IoT applications. Int. J. Hum. Comput. Stud. **123**, 56–69 (2019)

Experiencing Contemporary Art at a Distance

Barbara Rita Barricelli[1]([✉]) [ID], Antonella Varesano[2], Giuliana Carbi[3],
Torkil Clemmensen[4] [ID], Gian Luca Foresti[2] [ID], José Abdelnour Nocera[5,6] [ID],
Maja Ćirić[7], Gerrit van der Veer[8] [ID], Fabio Pittarello[9] [ID], Nuno Jardim Nunes[6,10] [ID],
Letizia Bollini[11] [ID], and Alexandra Verdeil[12]

[1] Department of Information Engineering, Università degli Studi di Brescia, Brescia, Italy
barbara.barricelli@unibs.it
[2] Department of Mathematics, Computer Science and Physics, Università degli Studi di Udine,
Udine, Italy
{antonella.varesano,gianluca.foresti}@uniud.it
[3] Trieste Contemporanea, Trieste, Italy
giuliana.carbi@triestecontemporanea.it
[4] Copenhagen Business School, Copenhagen, Denmark
tc.digi@cbs.dk
[5] School of Computing and Engineering, University of West London, London, UK
jose.nocera@iti.larsys.pt, jose.abdelnour-nocera@uwl.ac.uk
[6] ITI/Larsys, Madeira, Portugal
nunojnunes@tecnico.ulisboa.pt, nuno.nunes@iti.larsys.pt
[7] Independent Curator – Art Critic, Belgrade, Serbia
curator@majaciric.com
[8] Department of Computer Science, Vrije Universiteit (VUA), Amsterdam, The Netherlands
g.c.vander.veer@vu.nl
[9] Department of Environmental Sciences, Informatics and Statistics, Università Ca' Foscari,
Venice, Italy
pitt@unive.it
[10] Instituto Superior Técnico, Lisbon, Portugal
[11] Faculty of Design and Art, Free University of Bozen-Bolzano, Bolzano, Italy
letizia.bollini@unibz.it
[12] Tactile Studio UG, Berlin, Germany
hello@tactilestudio.de

Abstract. This panel wants to start a discussion about the importance of designing new ways of Contemporary Art digitization and digitalization to foster the creation of successful user experiences for its remote fruition.

Keywords: Contemporary art · Extended reality · Digitization · Digitalization · Cross-disciplinary collaboration · Digital job skills

1 Topic of the Panel

The perception of Contemporary Art experienced remotely, at a distance, forces us to put a screen between us and the artworks. This makes us lose all those physical sensations that stem when seeing, living, feeling, sensing, and interacting with art in presence [1].

C. Ardito et al. (Eds.): INTERACT 2021, LNCS 12936, pp. 344–347, 2021.
https://doi.org/10.1007/978-3-030-85607-6_34

All these sensory aspects are all superimposed and intertwined with the memories, inferences, and sensations that we have experienced in similar situations and this whole complex system strictly depends on the presence of the body within a space.

This panel wants to start a discussion about the importance of designing new ways of Contemporary Art digitization and digitalization to foster the creation of successful user experiences for its remote fruition. To do so, first of all, the differences between the live and the remote (digitalized) experiences of Contemporary Art fruition need to be identified [2]. Then, it is also fundamental to distinguish between digital objects and digital user experience: when speaking of digitization and digitalization, most of the attention is given to the chosen technologies, but very little attention is usually given to the humanists' knowledge about the objects that are digitalized. Location, time, social context, senses involved (sight, touch, hearing, smell – some of all of them are often entangled) are the aspects that need to be taken care of when designing for experiencing Contemporary Art at a distance.

We are facing two precise ways of thinking about this process, which led towards two distinct ways of interaction and user experience design. The first one is lean to enhance and increase the existing online experiences of art fruition with techniques able to fill the void left by the lack of physicality and senses, using hybrid and multilevel technology implementations. The second one is oriented toward the modification of the state-of-the-art paradigm and the creation of new forms of experience, free from the body and previous inferences, memories, and perceptions [3].

From a technological perspective, the first approach results in the exploitation of Extended Reality (e.g., Virtual Reality, Augmented Reality, Mixed Reality), while the second one is meant to adopt new and old technologies in disruptive and even unpredictable ways, not yet experimented in the Contemporary Art field [4]. In both cases, the process to design for these new user experiences needs to consider the contribution of three main elements: the mind of the designer, the technological tools at hand, and the context/environment in which the idea is developed and capable of being accepted. This diversity needs to be represented in the processes of digitalization by enabling a cross-disciplinary collaboration of domain experts: Contemporary Art curators, HCI/Interaction Design researchers, and Multimedia Software Engineers.

To address all audiences in the widest way possible and allow inclusion in art, the mediation tools are multiple and involve sensory experiences such as hybrid exhibits combining haptic and digital interactions. We believe that the definition of a new model, a new idea of creative design in Contemporary Art, emerges by the coexistence of three aspects: the mind of the designer, the technological tools at hand, and the context/environment in which the idea is developed and capable of being accepted.

This panel aims to bring together professionals in different disciplines and practices but who have in common active experiences in the artistic application field and the expertise in developing new services, software, and devices attentive to the sensible use of digital archives for Contemporary Art.

2 Interdisciplinary Perspective

The six panelists have been selected to represent the diversity of experts who are today involved in the field of Art Digitization and Digitalization. Their backgrounds and viewpoints will provide the audience with different points of view, leading to an interdisciplinary perspective, and will make the discussion stimulating. *Maja Ćirić* will discuss the point of view of the curators within art critic's perspective; *Gerrit C. van der Veer* will bring to the discussion the perspective of user-centered design experts and specifically will explain the influence of individual differences and cultural diversity, applied to cultural heritage and visualization; *Fabio Pittarello* will contribute by pointing out the challenges that exist in the field of Digital Humanities for Arts and Cultural Heritage; *Nuno Jardim Nunes* will provide insights that emerged from the Bauhaus of the Seas manifesto; *Letizia Bollini* will provide her point of view as architect expert in interaction and user experience design for Digital Archives and Cultural Heritage; *Alexandra Verdeil*, manager of Tactile Studio, will be carrying a voice from the industry of this sector.

3 Challenges and Open Issues to Be Discussed

Several challenges and open issues affect this research and application domain. The intent of this panel is to exploit the expertise of the panelists and the audience to investigate how to apply academic and industry competencies for advancing the field.

There are mainly eight questions that will be guiding this panel:

1. How can we improve digital experiences of Contemporary Art through innovative digitization and digitalization processes?
2. How can be technology used for increasing, integrating, or even creating a new experience of Contemporary Art artworks?
3. Is it sufficient to enhance the experience or do we need to shift the paradigm and completely freeing experience from senses and inferences?
4. What are the possible development models to get beyond the standardized digital vision of archives, producing multilevel and hybrid user experiences?
5. What forms of design are needed to produce new forms of user experience?
6. To help to move from a cultural elite appropriation of Contemporary Art to a more universal and open access digital experience, a shift in Arts education is desirable. How could this be made, considering the Arts education done in schools (for children and young adults)?
7. Which skills in the field of Contemporary Art and Arts, in general, should be acquired by an interaction designer to be able at designing products and services for an audience of both experts and novices?
8. In the light of this shift we are proposing, in digitization and digitalization of Contemporary Art, what skills, profiles, attitudes should a manager in the cultural heritage domain have, for being able to supervise these new design processes?

References

1. Turkle, S.: Life on the Screen: Identity in the Age of the Internet. Simon & Schuster Paperback, New York (1995)
2. Gobble, M.: Digitalization, digitization, and innovation. Res.-Technol. Manag. **61**(4), 56–59 (2018)
3. Lippard, L.R., Chandler, J.: The dematerialization of art. Art Int. **12**(2), 31–36 (1968)
4. Longo, G.O.: Simbionte: prove di umanità futura, Melteni, Sesto San Giovanni, Italy (2003)

Posters

A Case Study of Navigation System Assistance with Safety Purposes in the Context of Covid-19 Pandemic

Stefano Galantucci[1]($\boxtimes$) , Paolo Giglio[1] , Vincenzo Dentamaro[1] ,
and Giuseppe Pirlo[1,2]

[1] Department of Computer Science, University of Bari, Bari, Italy
Stefano.galantucci@uniba.it
[2] Digital Innovation S.R.L, via Orabona 4, 70126 Bari, Italy

Abstract. The standards defined by the human-computer interaction discipline highlight the need for renewed interpretation of services for the customer. Indeed the increasing number of original applications based on the progression of technology and the spread of sensors in almost every space (private and public) is the ground of potential benefits for the end users. Nevertheless every new advance in this scenario should take into account how technology is able to connect and be interfaced with the user natural language. In this regard, the following work proposes an analysis of the feasibility of a smart city public safety application in the context of Covid 19 exposure prevention. Particularly it will be observed how even a necessary service could be enhanced on its effectiveness if designed according to the human-computer-interaction standards.

Keywords: Human-computer interaction · Signal processing · Smart cities urban safety

1 Proposal

As the IoT technology is spreading in almost every aspect of users' life [1, 2], it becomes a priority to analyze how it is changing the way it interfaces with users [3]. Indeed several critical aspects arise from this, such as the safety of end users [4] and the optimization of the interaction between users and technological devices when a service is supplied [5]. One field of paramount importance in this regard is the connection of the urban environment with the end user who is interacting with it [6, 7], concerning the complexity of all services and dynamics related to it [8]. Indeed aspects of paramount importance are those of safety with regard to user interaction with surrounding entities and systems (public transportation systems, points of interests) and the ability to provide all the necessary information in order to help to satisfy its needs. This conjugation of the research field is even more demanding if the recent Covid-19 pandemic is considered: the overall urban environment presents itself as profoundly transformed, not from a structural point of view, rather by a risk-factor aspect, especially regarding its inhabitants'

C. Ardito et al. (Eds.): INTERACT 2021, LNCS 12936, pp. 351–354, 2021.
https://doi.org/10.1007/978-3-030-85607-6_35

conduct. From this perspective, the city could progressively become a smart system that recognizes its inhabitants and "behaves" in a cooperative way with them. The way this relation is developing is a central subject of what is generally referred as human-computer-interaction (Fig. 1).

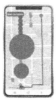

Fig. 1. An example of the front end design of the application: the red areas are indicative of the presence of crowded roads. The navigation systems determines an alternative route to reach the destination based on the objective of minimizing the potential exposure to crowded places.

This study aims to provide an ensemble of services that collectively contribute to create an enhanced user experience when using an application for safety assistance, specifically in the context of Covid 19 avoidance of crowded areas: in order to provide such a service it is developed a system of cluster recognition of humans in public spaces: the goal is to provide prompt advice to the user (which could be obliged to go to its workplace or to go food shopping) in order to avoid the most crowded places. For this purpose, an effective system should analyze the pattern of spatial distribution of people in a crowded environment. This application comes from the need to assess the covid related risk for those places that are naturally interested by a huge traffic of subjects (such as supermarkets or public transportation vehicles). A cautious user (who may also possess a delicate health condition) would be assisted in the decision of selecting the right places to fulfill its personal needs. This service has been implemented in a user-friendly app that allows the user to select a desired destination in order to receive the best route to reach the location with full safety. The overall work can be split into two main phases: a preliminary phase concerning the study of feasibility of the project along with its technical development and a secondary phase of refinement and design of the overall final technological product. As stated before, the core of this work concerns the recognition of dangerous clusters of people in public spaces and it is part of a broader technology aimed to refine the synergic interaction between the user and the public environment. In order to obtain a prompt response to the dynamical condition of the city, the method adopted was based on exploiting the video surveillance public network of a place of interest in order to gather up-to-date videos of the current state of the streets. Due to the prohibitive amount of data and to their typology, artificial intelligence algorithms, particularly Convolutional Neural Networks, were adopted. Indeed their suitability to give fast results according to input data was of paramount importance to give prompt answers regarding the potential risks a user could face during its route to a final destination.

2 Experiments

The classification features were performed by using the aforementioned algorithms, particularly the employment of Convolutional Neural Networks.

Neural Network Engineering: The CNN adopted was designed starting from the Inception V3 architecture [9]. The bulk of the network was trained on the ImageNet dataset [10]. The final fully connected layers of the network were trained with the Violent-Flows-Crowd [11, 12]. The resulting classification output is a score in the range [0, 1], with "crowded" attribute belonging to the range [0, 0.5] and "not crowded" attribute to the range (0.5, 1].

Datasets: The bulk of the Inception V3 inspired CNN was trained on the ImageNet dataset. The final layers of the CNN were trained on the Violent-Flows-Crowd dataset. This dataset was preprocessed in order to obtain all the videos with the same number of frames.

Front-End Development: The second phase of the project consisted on designing the front-end apparatus of an application that would respond to the following needs: a navigation system to be questioned about the route to reach a specific destination. A clear and easy-to-use list of all possible routes and vehicles needed to reach the destination. A real time updating system that would dynamically alert the customer about changing on the profile of risk, i.e. some transportation system or some location could be occupied by a prohibitive amount of other users.

3 Execution and Results

In the context of usability and human-computer-interaction the system should also be able to be personalized with respect to the specific users, i.e. adapting to its health condition or other specific needs whose satisfaction would result in an overall increment of its wellness. Additionally it should be designed to interact in a seamless and natural way in order to provide a human-like experience. Finally, it should be able to dynamically change with respect to the users' needs and changes of habits over time, without losing the fundamental objective of providing wellness and safety. The front-end development was performed mostly on the readability aspect, with particular attention to the requirement of a natural communication pattern. The main functionalities of the application were developed, i.e. the navigation system with the alert system and the priority matching of the best routes in terms of safety and specific needs of the customer. Once the AI algorithms were trained and the feasibility of the process was verified, the system was applied on a set of videos gathered from the video surveillance system of a location of interest. The process resulted in obtaining an up-to-date indicator of how much "crowdy" the areas under analysis are. The classification process was performed constantly in order to get multiple outcomes of the same areas. The results for each location were averaged in time in order to get a robust evaluation of the "crowded" attribute of the place. Once applied to real world videos, the Inception V3 based Convolutional neural network had a performance above the 70% on recognizing risky situations, i.e. the presence of dangerous clusters of people in the same place. In order to compute the accuracy, 3 real world videos on pedestrian locations were manually labeled with respect to a scale of gravity (very crowded, crowded, not crowded) in terms of how much crowd a place is on each photogram. When employed over time, this accuracy has proved to be sufficient to classify a set of points of interest with respect to the likelihood of being exposed to the presence of other subjects in small areas, i.e. under the minimal safety distance. The overall technology was installed into a user-friendly application able to be easily set-up for the basic customer needs. A prototype of a hypothetical application for the user assistance on a specific topic (navigation system) was developed. The project shall be located into a broader perspective, i.e. an ensemble of services designed to assist the user in a broader series of needs in the context of smart cities. An interesting following development would be to manage the available routes of the end users in order to distribute the traffic while minimizing dangerous agglomerates of people.

References

1. Lo, F.Y., Campos, N.: Blending Internet-of-Things (IoT) solutions into relationship marketing strategies. Technol. Forecast. Soc. Chang. **137**, 10–18 (2018)
2. Van Kranenburg, R., Bassi, A.: IoT challenges. Commun. Mobile Comput. **1**(1), 1–5 (2012)
3. Nuamah, J., Seong, Y.: Human machine interface in the Internet of Things (IoT). In: 2017 12th System of Systems Engineering Conference (SoSE), pp. 1–6. IEEE (2017)
4. Zalewski, J.: IoT safety: state of the art. IT Prof. **21**(1), 16–20 (2019)
5. Straker, L., Pollock, C.: Optimizing the interaction of children with information and communication technologies. Ergonomics **48**(5), 506–521 (2005)
6. Parker, C., Caldwell, G.A., Fredericks, J.: The impact of hyperconnectedness on urban HCI: challenges and opportunities. In Proceedings of the 31st Australian Conference on Human-Computer-Interaction, pp. 480–484 (2019)
7. Farkas, P.: Defining HCI/UX principles for urban environment. In: Marcus, A. (ed.) DUXU 2015. LNCS, vol. 9188, pp. 346–356. Springer, Cham (2015). https://doi.org/10.1007/978-3-319-20889-3_33
8. Zhou, Y., Jiang, N.: The research and co-creation model for urban interaction design and practices. In: Rau, P.-L.P. (ed.) CCD 2018. LNCS, vol. 10912, pp. 444–454. Springer, Cham (2018). https://doi.org/10.1007/978-3-319-92252-2_35
9. Szegedy, C., Vanhoucke, V., Ioffe, S., Shlens, J., Wojna, Z.: Rethinking the inception architecture for computer vision. In: Proceedings of the IEEE Conference on Computer Vision and Pattern Recognition, pp. 2818–2826 (2016)
10. Deng, J., Dong, W., Socher, R., Li, L.-J., Li, K., Fei-Fei, L.: ImageNet: a large-scale hierarchical image database. In: 2009 IEEE Conference on Computer Vision and Pattern Recognition, pp. 248–255 (2009)
11. Hassner, T., Itcher, Y., Kliper-Gross, O.: Violent flows: real-time detection of violent crowd behavior. In: 2012 IEEE Computer Society Conference on Computer Vision and Pattern Recognition Workshops, pp. 1–6. IEEE (2012)
12. Sumon, S.A., Shahria, M.D.T., Goni, M.D.R., Hasan, N., Almarufuzzaman, A.M., Rahman, R.M.: Violent crowd flow detection using deep learning. In: Nguyen, N.T., Gaol, F.L., Hong, T.-P., Trawiński, B. (eds.) ACIIDS 2019. LNCS (LNAI), vol. 11431, pp. 613–625. Springer, Cham (2019). https://doi.org/10.1007/978-3-030-14799-0_53

A Multi-planar Approach to Encoding Story Worlds for Dynamic Narrative Generation

David John Tree[1]($\boxtimes$) (iD) and Alessio Malizia[2]($\boxtimes$) (iD)

[1] Games and Visual Effects Research Lab, School of Creative Arts, University of Hertfordshire, Hatfield, UK
darmilatron@protonmail.com
[2] Computer Science Department, University of Pisa, Pisa, Italy

Abstract. Tabletop Role-Playing Games transport the player to a fantastical fictional world. This world is inhabited by characters, players and objects. Prior to the commencement of play, the Dungeon Master prepares not only the rules of the world but an account of historical events and the current world state. While the rules provide the player with boundaries of play, the character sheets store the current player state, and the back story provides context for the happenings during the game session.

Consider how often a story is told where, "In a land far away lived…". Rarely does a story rely on a universe where all existents are spontaneously spawned into being. Instead, vast historical worlds with cultures, histories and languages are created. This context provides the reader/viewer/player with an understanding of the world in which they find themselves. Players learn of warring factions, key artefacts, and are introduced to key drivers of the worlds drama. When Non-Playing Characters (NPC) are introduced into the game, the dungeon master draws on this history to form quests and to feed the players a view of this world.

These behavioural systems, however, react to a player's moves with little consideration for the world context. This lack of context leads to the trope of the robotic NPC with little awareness of the world. How do we ingrain this knowledge of a contextual world?

Keywords: Model-based design of interactive systems · Human-centred artifical intelligence · Dynamic storytelling generation

1 Background

Early approaches to populating game worlds approximated agent behaviour through the simulation of individual behavioural agents [1]. Individual agent simulation does produce high fidelity approximations, however at a high computational cost. This high computational cost limited the utilisation of individual agent simulation within video games. Instead of computing crowds as a collection of individual agents, Flow fields presented tread crowds as a fluid which is later sampled to produce character direction

© IFIP International Federation for Information Processing 2021
Published by Springer Nature Switzerland AG 2021
C. Ardito et al. (Eds.): INTERACT 2021, LNCS 12936, pp. 355–358, 2021.
https://doi.org/10.1007/978-3-030-85607-6_36

and speed. Flow fields indeed presented a significant step-change in the size of crowds and saw wide adoption within commercial videogames [2].

Voxel-based approaches furthered the success of flow-field, addressing the limitation of handling overlapping environments. McCarthy [3] outlines the design of a voxel-based crowd simulation engine developed for Planet Coaster [4]. The goal of the engine was to enable the population of 10,000 NPCs within the theme park simulation game Planet Coaster. This highlights that traditional approaches to crowd simulation would not enable the crowd's density to be generated due to the complex interactions and number of agents involved. The approach used combines voxel representations of the game world with flow/potential fields to simulated crowds as a singular entity. The paper also briefly outlines some of the considerations for audio and animation that were taken into account during the system's design. It is clear from the paper that balancing system resources and performance were key to achieving the real-time objective. The author highlights that an advantage of the flow system used was that the calculations could be performed asynchronously to the game thread.

While crowd simulation focuses on the movement of characters through game worlds, Vonnegut was interested in how characters traverse complex emotional curves. When examining fairy stories, Vonnegut [5] posited that the emotional curves of the majority of stories conformed to six archetypes. These archetypes were defined by plotting emotional highs and lows against time. Unlike Freytag's triangle [6], which describes the rise and fall of action within drama, Vonnegut's hypothesis instead focused on what he describes as high and low emotional states. The concept of story shapes was later ratified by applying big data analytics and sentiment analysis to Project Gutenberg's library [7].

The ludo-narrative debate is longstanding within the field of videogames critical studies [8–11]. A central factor to this debate was the role of narratives within games. While early contemplation on this field was divisive, as the discussion has matured, the investigation into the concept of ludo-narrative resonance is currently underway. Ludo-narrative resonance seeks to combine game mechanics with narrative elements to enhance the overall ability of the game to tell a story [12]. Open world games encourage the exploration of a game world in an unrestricted fashion. This freedom leads to a fundamental challenge to the telling of stories. In which order will the player encounter the story events?

2   Model

Our main research question then is: "How can game developers build, store and control dynamic story worlds?" This question forms a component of the more significant question of how human authors can work alongside Artificially Intelligent systems to tell stories in games that adapt based on player action. Fundamental to this challenge is a unified model of story worlds that is comprehensible to human and machine alike. The necessity to model whole worlds is a challenge that has previously been undertaken in the field of crowd simulation, where we draw our inspiration.

Existing approaches to world generation for games either lean towards Procedurally Generated worlds or Computational Narratives. Our model bridges these domains by providing a single unified contextual model through multiple voxel layers. These layers include terrain, masking layers and more central to this paper, drama driver layers Fig. 1. Drama driver layers store values for the world's current emotional state, with each one storing a single feeling and its counterparts such as happiness, sadness, peril, or safety. These layers are then stacked and combined to generate a drama state for the respective location in the game world.

The stacked nature of these drivers allows the author to add the complexity required for a specific project. Additional local grids can be dynamically created during gameplay by the system and human authors in response to an event, providing players with a greater sense of consequence within the world.

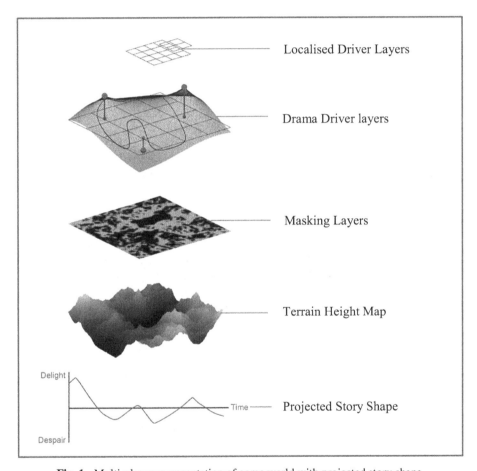

Fig. 1. Multi-planar representation of game world with projected story shape.

Author interaction with the layer is through the placement of attractors and repulsors, which are then manipulated in real-time. Synchronously the layers are computed, player trajectories are projected, and their story shapes estimated. This eventual visualisation allows the author to adjust the dramatic drivers to produce the intended story shape.

3 Future Work

This poster presented some of the early design considerations for the development of the Open world Dynamic Interactive Narrative framework (O.D.I.N). Future work includes the construction of a working prototype to validate the hypothesis that computational storytelling can be better with a final goal of democratising the creation of Dynamic Interactive narratives to enable expert authors and amateurs alike to tell their story in this form.

References

1. Champandard, A.J.: AI Game development: synthetic creatures with learning and reactive behaviors. new riders (2003). In: Banerjee, B., et al. (eds.) 2008 22nd Workshop on Principles of Advanced and Distributed Simulation. Advancing the Layered Approach to Agent-Based Crowd Simulation, pp. 185–192 (2008). https://doi.org/10.1109/PADS.2008.13
2. McCarthy, O.: Game design deep dive: creating believable crowds in planet coaster. https://www.gamasutra.com/view/news/288020/Game_Design_Deep_Dive_Creating_believable_crowds_in_Planet_Coaster.php. Accessed 06 Apr 2021
3. Fletcher, A.: Planet coaster. Frontier Developments (2016)
4. Vonnegut, K.: Shape of stories. https://www.youtube.com/watch?v=GOGru_4z1Vc
5. Freytag, G.: Freytag's Technique of the Drama: An Exposition of Dramatic Composition and Art. Scott, Foresman, Chicago (1900). An authorised translation from the 6th German ed. Elias J. MacEwan
6. Reagan, A.J., Mitchell, L., Kiley, D., Danforth, C.M., Dodds, P.S.: The emotional arcs of stories are dominated by six basic shapes. EPJ Data Sci. **5**(1), 1–12 (2016). https://doi.org/10.1140/epjds/s13688-016-0093-1
7. Aarseth, E.: Genre trouble: narrativism and the art of simulation. First Person New Media as Story Performance and Game, pp. 45–55 (2004)
8. Murray, J.H.: The last word on ludology v narratology in game studies. In: 05–Proceedings of the 2005 DiGRA International Conference, Vancouver, Canada (2005).
9. Juul, J.: The definitive history of games and stories, ludology and narratology – the ludologist. https://www.jesperjuul.net/ludologist/2004/02/22/the-definitive-history-of-games-and-stories-ludology-and-narratology/. Accessed 17 Dec 2020
10. Frasca, G.: Simulation versus narrative: introduction to ludology. In: The Video Game Theory Reader. Routledge (2003)
11. Brice, M.: Ludonarrative Resonance. http://www.mattiebrice.com/ludonarrative-resonance/. Accessed 16 Apr 2021

A Systematic Review of Usefulness Design Goals of Occupational Mobile Health Apps for Healthcare Workers

Nurha Yingta[1(✉)], José Abdelnour Nocera[1,2], Obed Brew[1], and Ikram Ur Rehman[1]

[1] University of West London, St Marry, Ealing, UK
`21363511@student.uwl.ac.uk`, {`Jose.Abdelnour-Nocera,Obed.brew,`
`Ikram.Rehman`}`@uwl.ac.uk`
[2] ITI/Larsys, Funchal, Portugal

Abstract. To improve healthcare professionals' health and wellbeing at work, many available effective treatments including meditation, and workplace intervention, have been developed. However, the utilisation of these interventions is still limited. Currently, various mobile health applications (mHealth Apps) exist to help a wide range of users with different occupational health issues, such as stress, anxiety, and burnout. Despite their advantages, post-download uptake of mHealth apps by end-users remains low. Some of the reasons for this are poor usability, irrelevant or missing user-desired features, and poor user experience. This review paper explores the usefulness of mHealth Apps for the early detection of occupational-related ill-health among healthcare workers. Science Direct, ACM Digital Library, IEEE Xplore, and SAGE Journal were searched comprehensively to identify relevant research articles. A total of 9546 reviewed papers were primarily identified through the systematic search on the databases. 2546 articles were removed from them, by duplication check on a RefWorks software. Titles and abstract screening of the remaining 126 led to 50 relevant articles being selected for full text screening. Of these 76 were excluded based on exclusion criteria. Finally, 19 articles were selected for a final inclusion to identify the relevant usefulness design goals, including usability, utility and user experience, deemed as critical for apps' adoption and use. These goals include provide contextually relevant information, which is easy to understand for usability; support self-help guidance and in-depth knowledge for occupational health and wellbeing for utility: reinforced trust and perceived security in m-Health apps for user experience.

Keywords: Occupational health · Usability · Utility · User experience · Healthcare workers

1 Occupational Mobile Health and Usefulness

Occupational-related ill-health (ORIH) is a major health concern for successful economic growth. In UK, the rate of ORIH is 4.8 thousand per 100,000 workers [1], and it is commonly associated with any physical and mental health conditions that result from organisational factors as well as an imbalance of demands, skills and social support at

© IFIP International Federation for Information Processing 2021
Published by Springer Nature Switzerland AG 2021
C. Ardito et al. (Eds.): INTERACT 2021, LNCS 12936, pp. 359–363, 2021.
https://doi.org/10.1007/978-3-030-85607-6_37

work [2]. Current data suggests most ORIH in UK are mental health related (51% of 1.6 million cases), followed by musculoskeletal (30%) – other types of illness make up 19% [3].

Workers in the medical sector are at increased risk of occupational-related ill-health due to the extraordinary stressors in this environment [4]. Stressors related to the healthcare profession include long work hours, dealing with pain, loss and emotional suffering, disease outbreak, and providing support to families [5, 6]. These stressors can trigger physical and mental health issues, such as stress, burnout and anxiety.

Despite the advantages of mHealth apps, it remains a huge challenge to find effective ones supporting the prevention and management of occupational ill-health as not much has been done to identify and assess the factors impacting the usefulness and adoption in the contexts of usability, utility and user experience terms. Therefore, the review focuses on the usefulness design goals of mobile mHealth apps to support occupational ill-health in HCWs.

Most of the research on usefulness and mHealth has been focused on perceived usefulness and based on acceptance models such as the Technology Acceptance Model (TAM) and e- Commerce Acceptance Model (EAM) [7, 8]. Several authors in previous studies have addressed the terms "usefulness" in different ways. For example, Nielsen [9] defines a useful interactive system as compounded with the attribution of usability and utility. In addition to usability and utility, usefulness is influenced by the emotional feelings with a system, including enjoyment to provide a richer experience of continued use [10, 11]. Overall, the literature on usefulness reflects that this is a complex construct defined by usability, utility and user experience (UX) factors contingent on users' contexts and sociocultural backgrounds. Having a consideration of HCW's real-world experiences is vital to designing integrated and useful mHealth solutions [12].

2   Review Methodology and Findings

Four resources including ACM digital Library, IEEE Xplore, SAGE journal, and Science Direct were searched in December 2020, and repeated in February 2021, to identify relevant studies. The search terms relating to occupational "mHealth apps", "wellbeing health apps", "usefulness", "usability", "utility", "user experience", and "healthcare workers" in different Boolean operator ("AND" and "OR") were used to identify relevant literature. Screening for inclusion was then carried out to extract relevant studies identifying the key design goals that enhance the adoption and continued use of such mHealth apps. A PRISMA Flowchart was created to identify the following points; (1) studies that use occupational health apps or wellbeing health apps; (2) studies that relevant to usability, utility and user experience; (3) studies that were conducted with healthcare workers or workers. We excluded studies that reported on health apps used only by patient (s), abstract, posters, and studies with no full text available.

A total of 9546 reviewed papers were primarily identified through the systematic search on the databases. 2546 articles were removed from them, by duplication check on a RefWorks software. Titles and abstract screening of the remaining 126 led to 50 relevant articles being selected for full text screening. Of these 76 were excluded based on exclusion criteria. Finally, 19 articles were selected for a final inclusion to identify the relevant usefulness of mHealth apps. We cannot list all reviewed papers here due to space limitations of the poster paper, but we have provided at least the most important reference for each goal in Table 1.

Table 1. Identified usefulness design goals of occupational m-Health apps proven to be relevant or often lacking.

Concept	Goals (position statement)	Goal definition	Reference
Usability goals	Provide contextually relevant information, which is easy to understand	Healthcare workers have mentioned apps should reflect their own work domain context and roles	[13]
	Match user expectations about the type of app: prevention or management	Help the user access the information they need whether the app helps them prevent or manage work-related ill-health	[14]
Utility goals	Support self-help guidance and in-depth knowledge for occupational health and wellbeing	The reviewed literature reveals this is a feature that is lacking or not sufficiently developed	[15]
	Promote social connectedness	The app should include some communication and information sharing features such as a group collaboration among app users and with clinicians	[16]
User experience goals	Reinforced trust and perceived security in m-Health apps	It is necessary for users to feel confident that the system will behave as intended. This has resulted in increased collaboration with the system securely and willingly	[17]
	Manage the performance expectancy of m-Health apps	The app design should be consistent with its intended goal, e.g. if it is presented as a prevention app then its features should be consistent with this aim	[18]

3   Discussion and Conclusions

The findings presented here provide an enhanced understanding of usefulness design goals that should be considered in designing an mHealth app to support healthcare workers health and wellbeing in healthcare work setting. The identified design goals highlight not only the key dimensions of usefulness, but also the key insights needed to inform design to improve adoption and continued use of such occupational mHealth apps. For instance, in relation to usability and user experience goals, given the fast-paced nature of healthcare work, workers' everyday usage and associated experiences should be considered in the design of such health apps. This is in line with previous study by [19], which suggests that understanding ordinary users' experience, cognitive challenges and demands from the workplace context will ensure the design of relevant and useful mHealth solution. Moreover, in relation to utility goals, mHealth apps will have the potential to provide healthcare workers with a better health and wellbeing if the crucial features are effectively incorporated in such apps. This suggests that having a consideration of user desired features could lead to the increased adoption and continued used of the system [20].

The review presented in this paper provides insightful knowledge for the design of occupational mHealth apps to enhance the usefulness of such health apps. Due to the nature of healthcare professionals work contexts and environments, future occupational mHealth apps should be designed differently following domain-relevant and distinct design goals such as those identified in this review. The proposed goals address these aspects and are contributions to the literature on mHealth by advancing knowledge on the user-centred design of this genre of apps, focusing on healthcare workers [16, 21].

References

1. Hse.gov.uk.: Health and safety statistics (2021)
2. Rajgopal, T.: Mental well-being at the workplace. Indian J. Occup. Environ. Med. **14**, 63–65 (2010). https://doi.org/10.4103/0019-5278.75691
3. New, long-standing cases of work-related ill health by type, 2019/20: The Labour Force Survey (LFS)
4. Ravalier, J.M., McVicar, A., Boichat, C.: Work stress in NHS employees: a mixed-methods study. Int. J. Environ. Res. Public Health **17**, 6464 (2020). https://doi.org/10.3390/ijerph171 86464
5. Solano Lopez, A.L.: Effectiveness of the mindfulness-based stress reduction program on blood pressure: a systematic review of literature. Worldviews Evid.-Based Nurs. **15**, 344–352 (2018). https://doi.org/10.1111/wvn.12319
6. Alameddine, M., Dainty, K.N., Deber, R., Sibbald, W.J.B.: The intensive care unit work environment: current challenges and recommendations for the future. J. Crit. Care. **24**, 243–248 (2009). https://doi.org/10.1016/j.jcrc.2008.03.038
7. Schnall, R., Higgins, T., Brown, W., Carballo-Dieguez, A., Bakken, S.: Trust, perceived risk, perceived ease of use and perceived usefulness as factors related to mHealth technology use. Stud. Health Technol. Inf. **216**, 467–471 (2015)
8. Alsswey, A., Al-Samarraie, H.: Elderly users' acceptance of mHealth user interface (UI) design-based culture: the moderator role of age. J. Multimodal User Interfaces **14**(1), 49–59 (2019). https://doi.org/10.1007/s12193-019-00307-w
9. Nielsen, J.: Usability inspection methods. In: Conference Companion on Human Factors in Computing Systems, pp. 413–414 (1994)
10. Koufaris, M.: Applying the technology acceptance model and flow theory to online consumer behavior. Inf. Syst. Res. **13**, 205–223 (2002). https://doi.org/10.1287/isre.13.2.205.83

11. MacDonald, C., Atwood, M.: What does it mean for a system to be useful?: an exploratory study of usefulness. Presented at the (2014). https://doi.org/10.1145/2598510.2598600
12. Aryana, B., Brewster, L., Abdelnour-Nocera, J.: Design for mobile mental health: an exploratory review (2018)
13. Yassaee, M., Mettler, T., Winter, R.: Principles for the design of digital occupational health systems. Inf. Organ. **29**, 77–90 (2019). https://doi.org/10.1016/j.infoandorg.2019.04.005
14. Torquati, L., Kolbe-Alexander, T., Pavey, T., Leveritt, M.: Changing diet and physical activity in nurses: a pilot study and process evaluation highlighting challenges in workplace health promotion. J. Nutr. Educ. Behav. **50**, 1015–1025 (2018). https://doi.org/10.1016/j.jneb.2017.12.001
15. Richert, J., Lippke, S., Ziegelmann, J.P.: Intervention-engagement and its role in the effectiveness of stage-matched interventions promoting physical exercise. Res. Sports Med. **19**, 145–161 (2011). https://doi.org/10.1080/15438627.2011.583164
16. Torous, J., Nicholas, J., Larsen, M.E., Firth, J., Christensen, H.: Clinical review of user engagement with mental health smartphone apps: evidence, theory and improvements. Evid. Based Ment. Health **21**, 116–119 (2018)
17. Rajan, J.V., et al.: Understanding the barriers to successful adoption and use of a mobile health information system in a community health center in São Paulo, Brazil: a cohort study. BMC Med. Inform. Decis. Mak. **16**, 146 (2016). https://doi.org/10.1186/s12911-016-0385-1
18. Liew, M.S., Zhang, J., See, J., Ong, Y.L.: Usability challenges for health and wellness mobile apps: mixed-methods study among mHealth experts and consumers. JMIR Mhealth Uhealth **7**, e12160 (2019). https://doi.org/10.2196/12160
19. Clemmensen, T., Hertzum, M., Abdelnour-Nocera, J.: Ordinary user experiences at work: a study of greenhouse growers. ACM Trans. Comput.-Hum. Interact. **27**, 1–31 (2020). https://doi.org/10.1145/3386089
20. Chandrashekar, P.: Do mental health mobile apps work: evidence and recommendations for designing high-efficacy mental health mobile apps. mHealth **4**, 6 (2018). https://doi.org/10.21037/mhealth.2018.03.02
21. Yen, P.-Y., Bakken, S.: Review of health information technology usability study methodologies. J. Am. Med. Inf. Assoc.: JAMIA **19**, 413–422 (2012). https://doi.org/10.1136/amiajnl-2010-0000

An Exploration of Potential Factors Influencing Trust in Automated Vehicles

Hatice Şahin[(✉)], Sarah Vöge, Benjamin Stahr, Nina Trilck, and Susanne Boll

University of Oldenburg, Oldenburg, Germany
{hatice.sahin,sarah.voge,benjamin.stahr,nina.trilck,
susanne.boll}@uni-oldenburg.de

Abstract. Trust, which is one of the main components for acceptance of automated vehicles could be affected by different factors. We have investigated the influence of prior information regarding the safety of Automated Vehicles, different light conditions and the malfunction of external Human-Machine Interfaces on trust. Despite a small sample, we have found that trust is reduced when malfunctions occur and it is immediately recovered back. Prior information regarding safety and different light conditions didn't have a significant effect on trust.

Keywords: Automated vehicles · eHMI · Overtrust · VR · VRU · Acceptance · Malfunction

1 Introduction and Background

During the last years, an increasing interest in the research of autonomous and automated vehicles (AV) could be observed [9]. Besides the technical challenges, human acceptance is an important aspect deciding about the deployment of AVs. In the public opinion, often only the acceptance by passengers of the AV seems to be important [6]. However, the acceptance by other road users is also important. Therefore, a focus should also be on the perception of vulnerable road users (VRUs) [6]. Especially for VRUs, it is hard to understand the intentions of AVs which leads to acceptance problems [6]. This problem is mainly based on the lack of interpersonal communication via gaze, gestures and/or facial expressions between VRUs and the driver [6]. Hence, the effective communication between VRUs and AVs is still an open challenge [6]. Trust, which is one of the main components for acceptance [11], can be influenced by different aspects [7]. Trust and the level of knowledge on AVs has been found to be linked with acceptance of AVs [11]. In this work, trust is to be understood as the trust towards the correct, error-free behavior of AVs, thereby in the whole system. Not only the absence of trust is problematic, but sometimes also its presence [6]. One reason of the latter is overtrust. Overtrust can be defined as the false estimation of risk when interacting with a machine [10].

© IFIP International Federation for Information Processing 2021
Published by Springer Nature Switzerland AG 2021
C. Ardito et al. (Eds.): INTERACT 2021, LNCS 12936, pp. 364–367, 2021.
https://doi.org/10.1007/978-3-030-85607-6_38

For the communication between VRUs and AVs, the different modalities of communication such as body language, auditory, haptic, and the visual modality could be considered [4]. The visual modality has been explored the most often and it has been considered as the most intuitive modality for the majority of potential users. It can include texts, symbols, abstract visual shapes and forms or anthropomorphic elements [4]. One of the ways to use this modality is via external Human-Machine Interfaces (eHMI). eHMIs can be integrated on the surface of the AVs in order to present different types of information [4]. They may contain the intention of the AV, automation state, advice, time-to-cross, situational awareness, danger/safety zone and warnings [4]. Some studies have already explored the idea of using eHMIs for the necessary communication in an ambiguous crossing situation. They have mainly focused on single pedestrians [4–6,8]. Some other studies also included malfunctions and/or system errors. For example, Holländer et al. [6] conducted a study concerning overtrust towards AVs in virtual reality. The study showed that the initial trust and perceived safety were negatively affected by a single malfunction, but it recovered fast, which indicates overtrust.

2   User Study

To further investigate the role of trust and overtrust in the interaction between VRUs and AVs, a user study was conducted in a VR environment. Seven participants were recruited (one female), aged between 21–85 ($M = 41$, $SD = 25.5$). Three factors with two levels were tested for their potential influence on VRU's trust on AVs. These factors were

- Prior information regarding the safety of AVs as between subjects variable (positive and negative information) [11].
- Different light conditions as within subject variable (day and night). To our knowledge, this factor hasn't been explored in previous research before.
- Influence of experiencing a collision based on an intentional malfunction of the eHMI as within subject variable (match and mismatch) [6]. Whereas, the collision itself would be a between subject variable.

The task was to cross the road in front of an AV. Participants used bluetooth controllers in order to move the virtual world. The experiment consisted of two blocks with five trials each and a training. Before the start of VR trials, participants received an information sheet regarding the safety of AVs. One group received only positive information while the other one received only negative information. The light condition was changed after the first block and the starting condition was counter-balanced among participants. The malfunction which could lead to a potential collision occurred in the third and the eighth trial.

Participants started with filling out the informed consent and a Demographic Questionnaire [3]. It is part of the PRQF which further contains the Pedestrian Behavior Questionnaire, Pedestrian Receptivity Questionnaire, and a Scenario-based Questionnaire. In order to capture trust and possible changes, Pedestrian

Receptivity Questionnaire was used before and after reading the information sheet, and after the VR part. Moreover, for differences in trust, the Scenario-based Questionnaire [3] and the STS-AD [2] were examined. The Scenario-based Questionnaire of two questions were handed out after the information and after each VR trial block. The STS-AD was implemented in the VR to measure trust after each single trial. It is a set of five items of which one is directly about trust. Additionally, the IPQ [1] was used to measure the sense of presence.

3   Initial Results

Starting with the first factor, the trust items of the Pedestrian Receptivity Questionnaire [3] were used in order to answer whether positive or negative information regarding the safety of AVs affected the trust. For this, the results from the PRQ after reading the information were used. No significant differences in trust between positive and negative information groups were found with Mann-Whitney U test ($p = 0.5$). Scores from STS-AD yielded similar results ($p = 0.45$).

The second factor was explored for the purpose of investigating the effect of different light conditions on trust in AVs. By using trust values from STS-AD, Wilcoxon signed-rank test was performed. The p-value of 0.40 indicated no significant differences between the two light conditions. Further, the Scenario-based questionnaire from the PRQF [3] was analyzed. The first question asks the type of behavior on a crosswalk with an AV approaching. The most participants chose to "wait until AV stops", followed by "wait until AV brakes" and only one participant chose to "hurry to cross". Conducting a Wilcoxon signed-rank test, a p-value of 1 underlines the similar choices for the dark and the daylight conditions. The second question asked about the acceptance of presence of AVs in the participants' area. Wilcoxon signed-rank test indicated no significant differences between different light conditions ($p = 1$).

The third potential factor which could affect trust was the influence of experiencing a collision based on a malfunction. Only a single collision occurred among all trials in all participants. This collision led to a high decrease in trust scores of STS-AD and it was observed that the trust of the affected participant was lower than the median trust of other participants.

To test the effect of malfunctions, a Wilcoxon signed-rank test was performed in STS-AD scores, which indicated a significant difference in trust between trials with and without eHMI malfunctions ($p < 0.001$).

4   Discussion and Future Work

The results of the effect of malfunction in STS-AD trust scores are in line with the results of Holländer et al. [6], where the occurrence of a malfunction directly influenced the trust. Our participants had high trust into the system from the beginning and their trust recovered directly in the next trial after the occurrence of a malfunction as in Holländer et al. However, in terms of the effect of the collision, we cannot derive a meaningful outcome since we had a small sample.

Moreover, two participants had some prior knowledge about automated driving, its current status and possible future developments, which could have influenced the results. The use of a VR environment could have increased situational trust, as users would not be harmed even in the event of a collision. However, this is necessary, because collisions could have and did occur in the experiment due to car malfunction. Furthermore, the VR helped us to provide a controlled setting, so the influence of other potentially trust-influencing factors, such as weather conditions or other pedestrians, could be avoided. Some improvements could be made in the future in the VR itself, such as better integration with the world of questionnaires presented in VR, a more complex crossing task with mixed traffic situations, or adding 6 DoF support to allow participants to walk in reality.

References

1. igroup presence questionnaire (IPQ) overview. http://www.igroup.org/pq/ipq/index.php
2. Situational trust scale for automated driving (STS-AD): development and initial validation. In: 12th International Conference on Automotive User Interfaces and Interactive Vehicular Applications, pp. 40–47 (2020)
3. Deb, S., Strawderman, L., Carruth, D.W., DuBien, J., Smith, B., Garrison, T.M.: Development and validation of a questionnaire to assess pedestrian receptivity toward fully autonomous vehicles. Transp. Res. Part C: Emerg. Technol. **84**, 178–195 (2017)
4. Dey, D., et al.: Taming the eHMI jungle: a classification taxonomy to guide, compare, and assess the design principles of automated vehicles' external human-machine interfaces. Transp. Res. Interdisc. Perspect. **7**, 100174 (2020)
5. Faas, S.M., Kao, A.C., Baumann, M.: A longitudinal video study on communicating status and intent for self-driving vehicle-pedestrian interaction. In: Proceedings of the 2020 CHI Conference on Human Factors in Computing Systems, pp. 1–14 (2020)
6. Holländer, K., Wintersberger, P., Butz, A.: Overtrust in external cues of automated vehicles: an experimental investigation. In: Proceedings of the 11th International Conference on Automotive User Interfaces and Interactive Vehicular Applications, pp. 211–221 (2019)
7. Lee, J.D., See, K.A.: Trust in automation: designing for appropriate reliance. Hum. Factors **46**(1), 50–80 (2004)
8. Otherson, I., Conti-Kufner, A.S., Dietrich, A., Maruhn, P., Bengler, K.: Designing for automated vehicle and pedestrian communication: perspectives on eHMIs from older and younger persons. In: Proceedings of the Human Factors and Ergonomics Society Europe, pp. 135–148 (2018)
9. Tango, F., Montanari, R.: Shaping the drivers' interaction: how the new vehicle systems match the technological requirements and the human needs. Cogn. Technol. Work **8**(3), 215–226 (2006)
10. Wagner, A.R., Borenstein, J., Howard, A.: Overtrust in the robotic age. Commun. ACM **61**, 22–24 (2018)
11. Ward, C., Raue, M., Lee, C., D'Ambrosio, L., Coughlin, J.F.: Acceptance of automated driving across generations: the role of risk and benefit perception, knowledge, and trust. In: Kurosu, M. (ed.) HCI 2017. LNCS, vol. 10271, pp. 254–266. Springer, Cham (2017). https://doi.org/10.1007/978-3-319-58071-5_20

Brain Computer Interface, Visual Tracker and Artificial Intelligence for a Music Polyphony Generation System

Carmelo Ardito$^{(\boxtimes)}$ ⓘ, Tommaso Colafiglio ⓘ, Tommaso Di Noia ⓘ,
and Eugenio Di Sciascio ⓘ

Politecnico di Bari, Via E. Orabona 4, 70125 Bari, Italy
{carmelo.ardito,tommaso.colafiglio,tommaso.dinoia,
eugenio.disciascio}@poliba.it

Abstract. In the Brain Computer Interface domain, studies on EEG represent a huge field of interest. Interactive systems that exploit low cost electroencephalographs to control machines are gaining momentum. Such technologies can be useful in the field of music and assisted composition. In this paper, a system that aims to generate four-part polyphonies is proposed. An artificial intelligence algorithm permits to generate polyphonies based on the N. Slonimsky's theory by elaborating data coming from a Leap Motion device, to detect user's hand movement, and a five-channel EEG signal detection device.

Keywords: EEG · Brain computer interface · Leap motion · Slonimsky

1 Introduction

A music composer continuously develops music models that represent her idea of music. Such models can be intended as musical materials useful in the construction of the final piece. Thus, composers explore multiple combinations of pitches, rhythmic profiles, dynamics, and all the other parameters that represent sound in general. In 1947, the composer N. Slonimsky published a treaty entitled "Thesaurus of Pattern and Melodic Scale" [1], in which he presented a technique for constructing melodic patterns based on dividing one or more octaves into equal parts. According to Slonimsky, the construction of melodic patterns can be made systematic by inserting notes below, within and above a musical interval-axis (see Fig. 1). Once the type of interval division of the octave is chosen[1], notes can be inserted within (Interpolation), beyond (Ultrapolation) and below the division interval (Infrapolation). By combining these techniques for filling interval-axes, sinusoidal profiles of Infra-Interpolation, Infra-Ultrapolation and Infra-Inter-Ultrapolation are obtained.

---

[1] In Fig. 1, the octave between the C note under the pentagram and the C note in the second upper space has been chosen and is represented in the Principal Tones section.

C. Ardito et al. (Eds.): INTERACT 2021, LNCS 12936, pp. 368–371, 2021.
https://doi.org/10.1007/978-3-030-85607-6_39

Fig. 1. Techniques for inserting notes within interval axes

In this research work, a technological tool is presented that exploits Artificial Intelligence algorithms, a Leap Motion controller [2], and a five-electrode Emotive headset [3] to support composers in exploring melodic profiles that represent the basis for composing new music pieces via the Slonimsky's Infra-Inter-Ultrapolation technique.

2   The Polyphony Generation System

The system architecture is schematized in Fig. 2. The *Pitch Profile Generator* module on the left side is based on an algorithm that transforms into note pitches the coordinates of the composers' fingers detected by the Leap Motion device. The result is a pitch profile, i.e. a sequence of notes without indications about their duration. The module on the right side is characterized by *FeedForward Net Classifier* that, with a Deep Network algorithm, analyzes the EEG signal coming from the five electrodes of the Emotiv headset worn by the composer and classifies her mental status as "focused" or "relaxed". Here, a mental status is intended a sequence of power spectrum values obtained from the EEG signal. The algorithm has been previously trained by the specific composer's mental status dataset. The *Polyphonic Structure Generator*: 1) receives the pitch profile, 2) multiplies it by four to have a draft polyphony, 3) according to the composer's mental state, gives a duration to the notes of the four pitch profiles, which are differentiated by means of a scramble method.

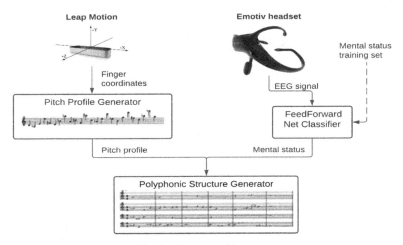

Fig. 2. System architecture

By means of the Cortex API SDK [4], the system derives a series of numerical values in the overall frequency 1–43 Hz, classified in different bands of the power spectrum of interest, i.e., Delta (0–4 Hz), Theta (4–8 Hz), Alpha (8–12 Hz), Beta (12–35 Hz) and Gamma (>35 Hz). The Keras framework [5] is used to implement the Deep Network algorithm as shown in Fig. 3.

```
model = Sequential()
model.add(Dense(50, input_dim = X_train.shape[1], activation="relu"))
model.add(Dense(1, activation="sigmoid"))
model.compile(optimizer='sgd', loss='binary_crossentropy', metrics=['accuracy'])
model.summary()
model.fit(X_train, Y_train, epochs=100)
accuracy = model.evaluate(X_test, Y_test)
```

Fig. 3. Deep network algorithm implemented in Keras with Python

Before using the system for composing, it has to be trained to the mental states of a specific composer, so that the underlying network can adapt to the bandwidth variation characteristics, which is a specific function of each user. Such a "calibration" has to be done once for each user. The composer wears the BCI headset and samples herself in two different mental states, i.e., focused and consciously relaxed. Focused mental status means a higher amplitude of high frequencies in the range 13–40 Hz, which corresponds to the Beta and Gamma frequency bands. Consciously relaxed means a greater activation of low frequencies and specifically the Alpha band between 8–13 Hz.

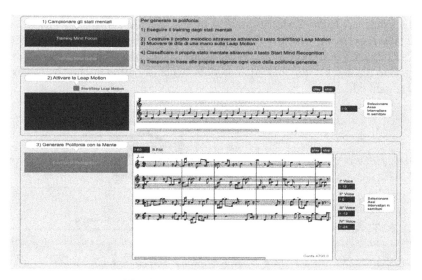

Fig. 4. User interface of the system.

If the mental status is classified as Focus, the polyphony is generated with rhythmic figures such as quarter note, height notes, sixteenth notes, and their corresponding pauses. If, on the contrary, the mental status is Consciously relaxed, the polyphony generated has rhythmic values of short, whole notes, half notes, quarter notes and their corresponding pause values. In addition, each bandwidth value received in real-time from the BCI headset is used to assign a dynamic value to each generated note.

Figure 4 shows the system user interface, which is divided in three sections, as for the main phases of the polyphony composition process. Starting from the top, the first section is devoted to the two mental states training; a summary of the overall process is provided in the green box, which also acts as user guide. The second section is dedicated to generating the pitch profile using the Leap Motion visual tracker; a graph of finger positions is drawn in the black panel, while on the right the composer can see in real-time the pentagram with the sequence of generated notes. By means of the field on the right, the composer can possibly change the interval-axis. The third section shows how, in real-time, the pitch profile is transformed in the resulting polyphony according to the composer's EEG. A few further parameters can be set by using the other widgets in this section of the interface.

The generated polyphony can be saved in a format compatible with popular software tools, e.g. MAX/Msp [6], that the composer can use for refining it and transform in the final piece of music.

3   Conclusions

In this paper we presented an approach aimed at generating complex polyphonic structures related to the theoretical model of Slonimsky, useful for the composer who wants to optimize her compositional process. The polyphonic material obtained is deliberately not complete in a strict musical sense, because we want to leave to the composer the possibility to work and perfect it according to her artistic needs. The creative process is a process that involves different technical and emotional aspects and in this sense, the final goal is to demonstrate that the BCI, in our opinion, could be useful as a support, and not as a substitute, tool for the composer. The system can be evolved by expanding the compositional theoretical models, thus providing a wider support to the work of contemporary musicians/composers.

Acknowledgments. The authors acknowledge partial support of the following projects: PON Casa delle tecnologie emergenti di Matera "CTEMT" (CUP I14E20000020001), Servizi Locali 2.0, PON ARS01_00876 Bio-D, PON ARS01_00821 FLET4.0, PON ARS01_00917 OK-INSAID, H2020 PASSPARTOUT.

References

1. Slonimsky, N.: 1984 – Thesaurus of Scales and Melodic Patterns. C. Scribner, New York (1947). Schirmer Books, s division of Macmillan Publishing Co., Inc., New York
2. Ultraleap. Leap Motion Controller. https://www.ultraleap.com/product/leap-motion-controller/. Accessed April 2021
3. Emotiv Insight 5-channel mobile EEG. https://www.emotiv.com/product/emotiv-insight-5-channel-mobile-eeg/. Accessed April 2021
4. Emotiv Cortex API. https://emotiv.gitbook.io/cortex-api/. Accessed April 2021
5. Keras Framework. https://keras.io/. Accessed April 2021
6. Max/Msp. https://cycling74.com/. Accessed April 2021

Charting Experience Categories for Museum Exhibitions

Siiri Paananen$^{(\boxtimes)}$ [ID], Mari Suoheimo [ID], and Jonna Häkkilä [ID]

University of Lapland, Yliopistonkatu 8, 96300 Rovaniemi, Finland
{siiri.paananen,mari.suoheimo,jonna.hakkila}@ulapland.fi
https://www.ulapland.fi/EN/Webpages/User-Experience-Research-Group-LUX

Abstract. In this poster, we chart and identify user experience categories with museum experiences. The experience categories were searched from narratives people provided in a survey-based user study (n = 48), where people reflected their positive and negative experiences, technology use and possible ethical concerns in museum exhibitions they had visited. Cultural heritage is a special design domain, as it can involve not only fragile old materials but also cultural sensitivities related to the events in history. The paper highlights the role of interactivity and multi-sensory experiences in museums, and our research contributes background knowledge for designers and practitioners working with museum exhibits.

Keywords: Cultural heritage · User experience · Museums · Experience design · Design sensitivities

1 Introduction

There has been a vast HCI research on cultural heritage [4], and prior art has presented a great number of examples how interactive technologies can be applied to museum exhibitions. It has been regarded that in general, interactive technologies can enhance museum experiences (e.g. [5]) and enable new ways of story-telling and experiencing the exhibitions [7].

In our research, we seek to dig deeper in understanding the user experience elements of museum exhibitions. Whereas most of the prior art has focused on single installations or exhibitions, we wish to take a more general approach, charting the experiences that people have had in museums, and analyse and identify the experience categories that can be found. We are interested in how people remember technology in relation to their visits to the museums. We also seek to gain more understanding about the ethics and cultural sensitivities with the museum experiences from the visitor viewpoint, as it is important that designers pay attention to those issues in the cultural heritage design context [2].

User experience is defined by Hassenzahl as "a momentary, primarily evaluative feeling (good-bad) while interacting with a product or service" [3]. His definition highlights the user's subjective experience and feelings, instead of focusing

© IFIP International Federation for Information Processing 2021
Published by Springer Nature Switzerland AG 2021
C. Ardito et al. (Eds.): INTERACT 2021, LNCS 12936, pp. 372–376, 2021.
https://doi.org/10.1007/978-3-030-85607-6_40

on the product. In the big picture of ubiquitous computing research, studies addressing the user experience design are still scarce [9]. Nikolakopoulou and Koutsabasis present a review of UX research conducted on interactive systems with cultural heritage [4], but they do not seek to identify experience categories.

2   Online Survey

In order to chart the experiences with museum visits, we organised an online survey. A similar approach of collecting written experience narratives has been user earlier [6]. The online survey consisted of four different parts. In the first part, it collected background information of the participants as age, gender and how often one would visit museums before COVID-19 pandemic and restrictions. Second section had open ended questions related to a memorable museum experience (2A) and the use of technologies (2B). The third section asked if any museum exhibition had made participants think about ethical issues. In the fourth section the participants could choose five adjectives that presented for them the most desired museum experience. We used Desmet's framework for product experience categories for the options [1]. The open ended questions of the survey were coded in three cycles [8] and the codes created were discussed in peer-review style meetings. Two researchers coded the answers separately and a third researcher analysed these answers and gave a final code.

In total 48 people participated, 62% women, 27% men and 11% other/did not wish to answer. The largest age group was 26–35 years (42%) then and 36–45 years with 21% of the answers. Largest part of the people 46%, selected that they visit museums 1–4 times per year, 21% answered 5–8 times per year and 19% answered that they visit less often than once per year.

3   Findings

Memorable Museum Experiences. In the second Sect. 2A participants described a memorable museum experience and told what made it a positive or a negative experience. The codes in the Fig. 1 show how these experience in the order of importance visual aspect (33), sense of realisation or impact (16), participation (11), immersion (10), technology (7) and social aspect (6). Issues relating to senses as touch (4), auditory (3) and smell (0) were not often recognised. Majority found the experiences positive (36) and the ones that felt it was negative (5) often had a visit to a museums with a sensitive historical context as a mental hospital or a concentration camp.

Technology Enhancing Museums Experiences. In the second Sect. 2B participants described how technologies had enhanced their museum experience. The most mentioned categories were auditory experiences as headphones or sound (16), interactivity (13), films (12) and technological installations (9). One participant described the experience as follows: *"The technology was a seamless* *part of the exhibition. It didn't feel like it was added simply because they wanted to use technology. It helped to create the mood for the exhibition"* (#26). Most felt that the experience had been positive (31) and only few as negative (4). The reasons for being negative was similar as in the previous question.

Ethical Themes. In the third section the participants described what ethical issues the exhibitions have raised from their perspective. Majority was worried about how vulnerable groups are being treated (8), unethically acquired pieces as the ones stolen in the colonial times (7), political orientation (7), death (6) and indigenous peoples issues (5). Only some were disturbed about the other people's behaviour in the museum, like disrespecting the sensitive museum exhibition pieces such as mummies (#20).

2A) Memorable museum experience		2B) How technology has enhanced a museum experience		3) Themes concerning ethics	
Visual / Seeing / Lighting	33	Headphones / Sound	16	Vulnerable groups	8
Impact / Realization	16	Interactive (like Kinect)	13	Unethically adquired pieces	7
Activity / Creating / Participating	11	Film / Video / Monitor / Projection	12	Political orientation	7
Immersion / Other World	10	Technological installation	9	Death	6
Technology	7	Augmented reality	5	Indigenous	5
Social Aspect	6	Virtual reality	3	War	4
Touch	4	Game with technology (like Wii)	3	Visitors' disrecpectful behaviour	3
Auditory / Hearing / Sound / Music	3	Light	3	Recognition of people	1
Smell	0				

Fig. 1. Three coded categories with the number of times it was discussed in the survey.

Desired User Experience. In the fourth section, where people had to choose five most desired museum experience emotions, the top five categories selected the most were Inspiration (41), Curiosity (39), Fascination (38), Admiration (23), Astonishment (18). The six least selected ones were Boredom (0), Alarm (1), Irritation (1), Jealousy (1), Contempt (1), Softened (1). People mentioned how these categories depend on the museum and topic, so they are not universal and static (#38). In some cases respondents reported that negative feelings could help to have a deeper understanding of a topic (#37).

4   Discussion

The experiences reported by the participants seem to go much with the traditional ways of experiences the museums pieces as the visual aspect gained most codes. None of the participants reported smell in their museum experiences, but this might be explained by it being rarely used in museums. Using the sense of smell in museums could be an interesting topic for future research. Touch was also another sensory aspect not much covered, but visual and auditory experiences were raised more, as they are most often used in many exhibitions. Many of the experiences (11) mentioned participating to an activity, such as creating something or a physical experience. Sound was one of the most mentioned when it comes to using technologies, as many museums have ambient sounds or audio guides, which many people found enjoyable, as it allowed them to feel immersed to the environment (#15) and feel autonomy and explore more content (#34).

On the basis of the results a lot of the positive museum experience descriptions (10) featured immersion, fantasy world or dream world. One participant described experience as follows *"It felt like I was in a dreamworld. It did not feel negative, the sensation was that it was surreal"* (#5). The results highlight that the museum experiences can have a long lasting impact, as one participant remembered an experience from when they were 7 years old (#26). Perhaps these immersive multi-sensory experiences at museums that have the possibility a to transfer the visitor to another world are a contrast to our everyday life.

Fig. 2. The top 5 selected (blue circles) and the 6 least selected emotions (red boxes) added on Desmet's (2007) model, which was adapted from Russel's (1980) model. (Color figure online)

Interactivity was another theme that raised by the visitors when describing a memorable museums experience and another with technology. The results confirm the previous research how technology is used to enhance the experience (e.g. [5]). When placed to Desmet's core affect model [1], the most desired museum experiences from the survey are positioned to the pleasant and activated axles, as can be seen in Fig. 2. The least selected emotions were spread out to either unpleasant the calm sectors, or combinations. Thus we can see how the results from the open ended questions and from the selection of adjectives emphasize the active or interactive participation of the visitor.

This study also confirms how ethical issues should be also considered when designing in the museums in order to create a positive experience for the visitor also in sensitive contexts [2]. Each of the different themes presented in this paper could offer topics to research separately as well. Other types of existing emotion and experience frameworks could be used for a similar study for comparison.

References

1. Desmet, P.M., Hekkert, P.: Framework of product experience. Int. J. Des. **1**(1), 57–66 (2007)
2. Häkkilä, J., et al.: Design sensibilities-designing for cultural sensitivity. In: Proceedings of the 11th Nordic Conference on Human-Computer Interaction: Shaping Experiences, Shaping Society, pp. 1–3 (2020)
3. Hassenzahl, M.: User experience (UX) towards an experiential perspective on product quality. In: Proceedings of the 20th Conference on l'Interaction Homme-Machine, pp. 11–15 (2008)
4. Nikolakopoulou, V., Koutsabasis, P.: Methods and practices for assessing the user experience of interactive systems for cultural heritage. In: Applying Innovative Technologies in Heritage Science, pp. 171–208. IGI Global (2020)
5. Pallud, J., Monod, E.: User experience of museum technologies: the phenomenological scales. Eur. J. Inf. Syst. **19**(5), 562–580 (2010)
6. Partala, T., Kallinen, A.: Understanding the most satisfying and unsatisfying user experiences: emotions, psychological needs, and context. Interact. Comput. **24**(1), 25–34 (2012)
7. Roussou, M., Katifori, A.: Flow, staging, wayfinding, personalization: evaluating user experience with mobile museum narratives. Multimodal Technol. Interact. **2**(2), 32 (2018)
8. Saldaña, J.: The Coding Manual for Qualitative Researchers. SAGE (2021)
9. Väänänen-Vainio-Mattila, K., Olsson, T., Häkkilä, J.: Towards deeper understanding of user experience with ubiquitous computing systems: systematic literature review and design framework. In: Abascal, J., Barbosa, S., Fetter, M., Gross, T., Palanque, P., Winckler, M. (eds.) INTERACT 2015. LNCS, vol. 9298, pp. 384–401. Springer, Cham (2015). https://doi.org/10.1007/978-3-319-22698-9_26

Collecting Qualitative Data During COVID-19

Vanessa Cesário[✉] [iD] and Valentina Nisi [iD]

ITI/LARSyS, IST University of Lisbon, Lisbon, Portugal
vanessa.cesario@iti.larsys.pt

Abstract. The current pandemic situation leads researchers to reflect on conducting qualitative research, completely changing how they conduct participatory research. As it became clear that the pandemic would last many months, researchers started to redesign their planned research in digital spaces through social media channels and participatory online tools. From communicating with participants over Zoom (or other similar applications) to sharing information on exclusive online groups, digital platforms have become, for many, the only way to work, learn, or be entertained. This situation offered a significant opportunity to think creatively about research engagement and reflect on which aspects truly require researchers to be "on the ground" to conduct face-to-face participatory sessions to gather qualitative data. Qualitative researchers must use this opportunity to reflect while using digital tools for distance research. This paper is inspired by the work the authors are conducting in MEMEX – a European-funded project promoting social inclusion by developing collaborative storytelling tools related to cultural heritage and at the same time facilitating encounters and interactions between communities at risk of social exclusion. Thus, the work here presented reflects on the digital tools and techniques to collect qualitative data when the researchers cannot meet the participants face-to-face due to pandemics safety measures or other restrictions.

Keywords: COVID-19 · Qualitative data · Focus groups · Collaboration · Digital tools · Co-design

1 Introduction

While collecting quantitative data has been used online for several decades, collecting qualitative data has been challenging. Yet the global pandemic has oddly helped to push technologies to make qualitative data collection more accessible to a wide range of users: COVID-19 imposed lockdowns and social distancing, changing how researchers collect qualitative data during these uncertain and stressful times. Much qualitative research usually relies on face-to-face interaction: ethnographic types of interviews (structured, semi or unstructured), focus groups, and fieldwork are typical methods to gather qualitative data that depend on face-to-face interaction. Researchers usually plan to conduct fieldwork using traditional in-person methods, but now they are reconsidering it because participants cannot meet them face-to-face. These traditional face-to-face methods are

© IFIP International Federation for Information Processing 2021
Published by Springer Nature Switzerland AG 2021
C. Ardito et al. (Eds.): INTERACT 2021, LNCS 12936, pp. 377–381, 2021.
https://doi.org/10.1007/978-3-030-85607-6_41

being transformed into a "distance" method not to put projects on hold. Back in 2017, Braun and colleagues [1] created helpful guidance on what digital techniques have to offer, what types of research questions are best suited to be answered through digital tools, as well as specific ethical questions that require consideration (practical, technical, and privacy challenges). While the ideal co-design face-to-face sessions may no longer be an option, the authors of this poster – researchers in the co-design field working in the MEMEX project – researched and reported techniques to collect qualitative data when the subjects cannot be face-to-face due to pandemics or other restrictions. This poster addresses some important questions and challenges regarding online methods for collecting qualitative data, raising more questions for future research.

2 Data Generation Techniques

Below we report on data generation techniques – focus group, co-creation tools, storing and analysing data, photo-taking, and visuals – inspired by the impossibility to run qualitative studies with participants from the MEMEX project. This section reads like a set of techniques that can be used in any qualitative research when participants have access to computers, internet access, and smartphones.

Focus Groups. This is a standard technique in qualitative research because they are helpful to track initial reactions to the form of a concept or product [2, 3]. Focused groups can be moved online, with the aid of videoconferencing tools such as *Zoom*, *Teams*, *GoToMeeting*, *Google Hangouts* or virtual environments such as *Virbela* and *Mozilla*. Even before pandemics, *WhatsApp* and *Facebook* started to be used to conduct interviews and sometimes focused groups. Online or virtual focused groups have increased in popularity to capture ideas and opinions from a wider demographic group [4], allow greater accessibility for specific populations, and minimise costs and programming issues. Videoconferencing is a close substitute to face-to-face interviews. It can enable the data to be collected over large geographical areas even when social distancing measures are not in place [5]. As long as participants can access a computer with reliable internet, these tools allow individuals to talk to each other, see the moderator, and view a shared picture or document on the screen. Ideally, participants can access the session by clicking on a link without installing any software. These tools allow groups into private spaces (breakout rooms) where the moderator can enter and exit; however, they require careful management. As a helpful note, it is always handy to have a phone number to call participants if they struggle to enter or re-enter the main session. Researchers can use online polling tools to keep participants engaged at critical points (e.g. *Pollev*, *Mentimeter*). The polls can be used as a mechanism to keep users engaged, alongside collaboration tools, and gather accurate data for discussion.

Co-creation Tools. In a certain way, digital tools such as *Miro*, *Mural*, *Padlet* replace the whiteboard or flipcharts used in face-to-face sessions. These tools can support videoconferencing and perform exercises with participants throughout the session. Also, the participant can group and collaborate on co-design sessions synchronously or asynchronously with a group of participants. Researchers can use these tools for collaborative brainstorm activities. Participants write down ideas as virtual post-it notes, keeping track of inspirations or solutions during the session by plotting post-it notes in a matrix or map to prioritise items. The researcher should send the participants a link to access a visual workspace where they can collaborate simultaneously.

Storing and Analysing Data. While it is an option in presential focused groups to record the session through video and audio, which allows a later checking of the non-verbal communication of the participants, it must be the norm in online ones. Researchers record online session to analyse the behaviours and the conversations of the participants. Recordings of videoconferences sessions provide more focused data than face-to-face sessions; the camera usually focuses on the upper part of the body, emphasising facial expression recording and gestures. These situations can provide a better understanding of how participants express and feel. Storing and analysing video data can require quite a lot of storage space and a reasonably powerful computer. Recording on smartphones quickly becomes problematic – even with the right app, storing and transferring recordings and file security quickly becomes a problem. However, if one is just concerned with the audio of the interview through a computer, one can do this with the native Voice Recorder app of the computer. Note that there are tools that automatically transcribe audio for us, but their accuracy is not always the best and is still not a substitute for professional transcription. As noted, there are many technical and practical challenges concerning videoconferencing and recordings.

Photo-Taking and Visuals. Pandemic constraints allow for a limited presence outside, wearing masks and strict rules about social distancing. These constraints affect photo-taking activities in various ways: (i) limited presence outdoors: depending on the country and pandemic gravity, people are not allowed to spend time outside their apartments, or limited during some hours of the day; (ii) the use of masks can influence expressivity of subjects or possibly their interest or ability in performing their routines; this can bias the observations collected through the photographic data; (iii) social distancing also affect behaviours of people and norms and their presence in public open and closed spaces. To make up for these shortcomings, participants should be allowed to use photos they have taken previously, by other people, or even allowed to find data on the internet. Participants should be encouraged to look through phone camera rolls, old photo albums to select photographs to discuss with others within the activity. However, it is not all about the digital. Methods such as drawings, paper diaries, collages, letters, cultural probes are not digital methods and can be used online. Asking participants to create such visuals or videos may help represent their feelings. The essential point is that the photographs or visuals represent participants' thoughts, experiences, and feelings, being in line with the activity's prompt.

3   Reflections

This poster questions the above set of tools for gathering qualitative data. We, as qualitative researchers, draw questions about trust and report, chat functionalities, technology training, and the digital divide. We believe these reflections will lead to a lively and productive discussion in the INTERACT community. It highlights challenges on the new possibilities for participation to inform the development of interactive technologies, raising more questions for future research on how remote research can have an enormous impact as time and technology progresses.

Trust and Rapport. Gaining trust and rapport with participants is a crucial part of getting valuable data. It helps both the researcher and the participant think about each other's feelings, making it easier to feel a human connection. It is more challenging to create this trust and rapport online as we are missing many social cues. Also, it might be more difficult to break the ice over videoconferencing when participants and the moderator never met face-to-face. Researchers have less option for ice-breaking activities, and sometimes for technical reasons, participants do not have access to the camera, and the interview just relies on audio.

Chat Functionalities. Interesting questions arise about the chat functionalities provided by such online tools. Does it enable participants to raise questions by allowing them time to reflect? Is it a space to share opinions that participants would not have shared in front of more experienced people? More studies are needed to answer these questions.

Technology Training. Technology provides new possibilities for participation, disrupting, and shifting power. Participants must be aware of using the technology to be used in the online session. Researchers should support this by providing training on the technology, running a "test run" to ensure everyone is comfortable with the actual data collection time frame. Nonetheless, researchers should make the process as welcoming as possible, have ice breakers, and plan to share a cup of tea/coffee virtually!

Digital Divide. The drawbacks of online tools are the influence of the digital divide and access to the internet and powerful devices. Do participants have access to these tools, and are they familiar with their use? Are all participants at the same tech-savvy level? Researchers should also be mindful of the participants and ensure that all the participants have equal access and opportunity to work with the requirements. If the aim is to prioritise the involvement of marginalised participants, qualitative researchers need to question what is really "rethinking participatory approaches" for the communities they work with. What lessons are we learning about digital participatory methods that can modify our research? Researchers should be highly cautious in celebrating the opportunities offered by the internet and digital devices because of the existing digital divide in some countries: marginalised groups that cannot have a voice due to their lack of availability and sophistication of broadband use. Infrastructural and socioeconomic disparities remain determined by geographic location, education, age, and income. The issue that participatory researchers face in embracing internet-powered participation is that it reinforces the gap between access to the internet and digital devices and deepens digital inequalities. Thus, it is crucial to make methodological negotiations in participatory approaches not to affect the core underpinnings of participatory methods and development ethics.

Acknowledgements. This project has received funding from the European Union's Horizon 2020 research and innovation programme under grant agreement No. 870743 and the ARDITI's postdoctoral scholarship M1420–09-5369-FSE-000002.

References

1. Braun, V., Clarke, V., Gray, D. (eds.): Collecting Qualitative Data: A Practical Guide to Textual, Media and Virtual Techniques. Cambridge University Press, Cambridge, New York (2017)
2. Cesário, V.: Guidelines for combining storytelling and gamification: which features would teenagers desire to have a more enjoyable museum experience? In: Extended Abstracts of the 2019 CHI Conference on Human Factors in Computing Systems, p. SRC03. ACM, New York (2019). https://doi.org/10.1145/3290607.3308462
3. Cesário, V., Matos, S., Radeta, M., Nisi, V.: Designing interactive technologies for interpretive exhibitions: enabling teen participation through user-driven innovation. In: Bernhaupt, R., Dalvi, G., Joshi, A., Balkrishan, D.K., O'Neill, J., Winckler, M. (eds.) INTERACT 2017. LNCS, vol. 10513, pp. 232–241. Springer, Cham (2017). https://doi.org/10.1007/978-3-319-67744-6_16
4. Del Carpio Ramos, H.A., Del Carpio Ramos, P.A., Tarrillo Carrasco, J.E., García-Peñalvo, F.J., Morante Dávila, M.A.: Online instrument: perception of virtual learning of the doctorate in the context of COVID-19. In: Eighth International Conference on Technological Ecosystems for Enhancing Multiculturality, pp. 211–218. Association for Computing Machinery, New York (2020). https://doi.org/10.1145/3434780.3436603
5. Wattenberg, T.L.: Online focus groups used as an accessible participatory research method. In: Proceedings of the 7th International ACM SIGACCESS Conference on Computers and Accessibility, pp. 180–181. Association for Computing Machinery, New York (2005). https://doi.org/10.1145/1090785.1090819

Contemporary Art Digitalization: An Opportunity for Designing New Experiences

Barbara Rita Barricelli[1](⊠) ⬤, Antonella Varesano[2], Giuliana Carbi[3],
Torkil Clemmensen[4] ⬤, and Fabio Pittarello[5] ⬤

[1] Università degli Studi di Brescia, Brescia, Italy
`barbara.barricelli@unibs.it`
[2] Università degli Studi di Udine, Udine, Italy
`antonella.varesano@uniud.it`
[3] Trieste Contemporanea, Trieste, Italy
`giuliana.carbi@triestecontemporanea.it`
[4] Copenhagen Business School, Copenhagen, Denmark
`tc.digi@cbs.dk`
[5] Università Ca' Foscari, Venice, Italy
`pitt@unive.it`

Abstract. CLOUDART is a cross-disciplinary working group that joins the forces of three specific domain expert communities: Contemporary Art, Human-Computer Interaction, and Multimedia Software Engineering, all experienced in socio-technical creative projects. CLOUDART initiative aims to investigate how to design new hybrid user experiences for the online fruition of Contemporary Art.

Keywords: Art digitalization · Human-computer interaction · Interaction design · User experience · Extended reality

1 Contemporary Art: Beyond Physical Presence and Bodily Experiences

Contemporary Art always anticipates society's visions and demands. Its field of action expands outside the physical outcome, going beyond something that can be seen, heard, or touched. Contemporary Art production is not composed of only paintings, drawings, or sculptures; the materials used come from different sources: tangible, intangible, or even dematerialized. This became obvious from the 1960s, when conceptual art, happenings and performances, land art, video art became central in the art discourse [1], and modes of their documentation, reproduction, and cataloging became hot archival issues [2]. The creation, maintenance, and distribution of digital art archives are the themes that mostly affect the field of Contemporary Art. This presents peculiar needs and issues to be addressed that originate from the large variety of the types of art that are put in place; e.g., site-specific installation art, participative art, public art (and their engagement in

C. Ardito et al. (Eds.): INTERACT 2021, LNCS 12936, pp. 382–385, 2021.
https://doi.org/10.1007/978-3-030-85607-6_42

the social and political sphere), technology-based art. In all these examples, problems that arise are related to the challenges that emerge from the conservation of the artistic contribution – sometimes very difficult if not impossible due to the intangible nature of their materials or because of the obsolescence of technological hardware used in the original artworks. In 1999 Nicholas Mirzoeff proposes an overturned definition of postmodernity: "the postmodern is the crisis caused by modernism and modern culture confronting the failure of its strategy of visualizing. In other words, it is the visual crisis of culture that creates postmodernity, not its textuality" [3]. Is it possible that today, our practices of looking – which increasingly continue swinging around the many images we encounter every day – are again in a new phase of transformation? We believe that Contemporary Art production can help us to understand that transformation because in its very realm such practices of human measurement constantly change [4]. Just a few decades before Mirzoeff's reflections, still the body was the only one constant of scale for sculpture: in the 1960s Bob Morris in his famous *Notes on Sculpture* articles used to link art objects' qualities to be either intimate or public (namely non-personal) to their relative size (smaller or larger) as compared to human body [5]. Till then and for centuries it has been an affair of Body and Space. Both of them vanished in the communicational and educational streams that flow through the Internet for most of our new days. So, proper digital measures enabling us to feel wonder as to when our body was in that real space should be studied or new practices of looking and the visualization through digital devices (to sympathetically and electively feel wonder) should be implemented.

CLOUDART is a cross-disciplinary working group that aims at joining the forces of three specific domain expert communities: Contemporary Art, Human-Computer Interaction, and multimedia software engineering, all experienced in socio-technical creative projects. CLOUDART aims to investigate the methodologies necessary to fill the gap of online fruition both by proposing techniques capable of increasing the fruition of art online and, in a more visionary way, to produce new types of experiences using disruptive technologies, producing new digital archives, trying to overcome the problem of the absence of body and shift toward a new paradigm. CLOUDART members' research is focused on the creation of a cross-media digitization able to design new use of digitalization experience, still unpredictable, but oriented to and implemented in the Contemporary Art field.

2 Digitalization of Contemporary Art: The CLOUDART Vision

In the Oxford English Dictionary, the term *digitization* refers to *the action or process of digitization; the conversion of analog data (especially in images, video and text for later use) into digital form*. By contrast, *digitalization* refers to *the adoption or increase in the use of digital or information technology by an organization, industry, country, etc.* By reflecting on the meaning of digitization and digitalization, it becomes clear that the future of a new digital market needs digitalization, in the sense of digitalization for precise purposes [6]. Today, to become available and known all over the world, artworks need to be appropriately dematerialized through the process of digitization, properly archived, and made available on the Internet.

The entire process of artwork management, evolved through centuries and consolidated in the last 50 years, needs to be rethought. A question arises: what should be the correct use of digitalization for the diverse artwork of Contemporary Art field? There must be awareness of the concept of immateriality and the relative disappearance of objects. The fruition of art through a computer screen leads to a new principle of reality, a vision that is free from physical bodily sensations. The perception of art assumes new dimensions, so new psychological attitudes need to be investigated: the perception of art through the Internet loses the physical sensation that stems from seeing, living, interacting with art in presence, and that is led by personal previous experience. Digitalization and dematerialization concepts assign to screen-mediated art fruition a new principle of reality, detached from physicality, that has not yet been thoroughly investigated. The key factor of the CLOUDART initiative is the establishment of a team of stakeholders with diverse backgrounds and professionalism from a variety of fields to cooperate and mutually inspire the conversation. Particularly, the challenging relationship between art and technology and human work needs to be explored. The design of interactive applications to support the human work of professionals needs to be appropriately informed [7]: new design methods, approaches, and techniques need to be defined, as well as the development of new technologies and the disruptive use of old ones must be tailored on the specific artistic application domain. Despite that CLOUDART is focused specifically on Contemporary Art, the results of such research are relevant to other fields. The introduction of new design techniques, that insert the point of view of technological humanism in the redesign of established but obsolescent knowledge management process, is also expected to have a stimulating effect on the job market: cross-disciplines and intersections are crucial elements for redesigning new digitization and digitalization skills and such effect will be consistent with other significant drivers of both successful business development and general European economic development. To influence the design of new hi-tech services and products it is fundamental to establish interdisciplinary communities of domain experts, capable of designing emotional services, shaped also on the principles of artistic interpretation.

CLOUDART intends to design a new way of digitization and archiving, able at exploiting both new and old technologies but focused more on the users and less on technological tools. Digitization does not just revolve around archiving and storage, but also on the fruition of content and experience development. Full exploitation of the digitalization process requires Human-Computer Interaction (HCI) experts to go far beyond the mere usable design of archive search engines and data visualization. It means to understand how to exploit multichannel and hybrid features of Contemporary Art and its dimensions, identified by the domain experts together with art-goers. In the context of CLOUDART, it is important to make a distinction between digital objects and digital user experience: when speaking about digital objects, the focus goes to the process of creating digital copies of real objects. This process takes into great account all the issues derived from technology, but very little attention is usually given to the humanists' knowledge about the objects that are digitalized.

CLOUDART vision considers the existence of different aspects to be considered: location, time, social context, senses involved (sight, touch, hearing, smell – some of all of them are often entangled). This calls for a further effort aimed at shifting the attention to these aspects from mere digital object creation to the design of complex hybrid digital user experience of Contemporary Art and the definition of proper evaluation methods.

To design for a new way of Contemporary Art digitalization at the service of new experience fruition not just focusing on the missing aspects but also investigating all new potentials. We are already accustomed to extended reality [8], virtual reality, and augmented reality applied to the art domain, but the fruition experience needs to be further improved, especially through the creative use of technologies, not just the new ones but also the most well-known (old) ones [9]. Technology is never neutral because it always transforms our experience of reality: a new way of acting produces a new way of thinking and the remote experience is a clear example of that [10]. However, there is a profound difference between designing to fill the lack of physical senses and designing a new experience free from body boundaries. Digital technology is no longer to be seen as just prostheses capable of increasing, extending, enhancing some sensory aspects [11] but can be a new frontier in the design of new experiences. The diversity of fields that are concerned by these questions reflect the plurality of expertise represented in the CLOUDART working group: Contemporary Art curators, HCI/Interaction Design researchers, multimedia software engineers.

References

1. Lippard, L.R.: Six Years: The Dematerialization of the art Object from 1966 to 1972. Praeger, New York (1973)
2. Lippard, L.R., Chandler, J.: The dematerialization of Art. Art Int. **12**(2), 31–36 (1968)
3. Mirzoef, N.: An Introduction to Visual Culture. Routledge, London and New York (1999)
4. Bourriaud, N.: Postproduction. La culture comme scénario: comment l'art reprogramme le monde contemporain. Les presses du réel, Dijon, France (2004)
5. Morris, R.: Notes on sculpture. Artforum **4**(6), 221–235 (1966)
6. Gobble, M.-A.M.: Digitalization, digitization, and innovation. Res.-Technol. Manage. **61**(4), 56–59 (2018)
7. Abdelnour-Nocera, J., Barricelli, B.R., Lopes, A., Campos, P., Clemmensen, T.: Preface. In: Human Work Interaction Design: Analysis and Interaction Design Methods for Pervasive and Smart Workplaces. IFIP AICT, vol. 468, p. V. Springer, Heidelberg (2015). https://www.scopus.com/record/display.uri?eid=2-s2.0-84952049326
8. Banfi, F., Brumana, R., Stanga, C.: Extended reality and informative models for the architectural heritage: from scan-to-BIM process to virtual and augmented reality. Virtual Archaeol. Rev. **10**(21), 14–30 (2019)
9. Minsky, M.: The society of Mind. Simon & Shuster, New York (1986)
10. Winograd, T., Flores, F.: Understanding Computers and Cognition: A New Foundation for Design. Addison-Wesley Professional, New York (1987)
11. De Kerchove, D.: Brainframes: Technology. Mind and Business. Bosch and Keuning, Utrecht (1991)

Design Students' Challenges in Individual Brainstorming Using a Design Fiction Method

Lu Liu[✉][iD], Tamara Hoveling[iD], and Panos Markopoulos[iD]

Eindhoven University of Technology, Eindhoven, Netherlands
{l.liu3,p.markopoulos}@tue.nl

Abstract. Design fiction (DF) is gaining ground as an approach that helps designers to explore possible futures. As a method founded upon critical attitudes and creative thinking, DF may be challenging for design students. In this study, we explore how design students use DF during creative design activities. Students engaged in an individual digital brainstorm and an in-depth, semi-structured interview about their experiences with the brainstorm based on DF. The results show that DF can be challenging for students who do not have a clear appreciation of what is technologically feasible for a particular time frame in the future and do not yet have the breadth of knowledge to argue about broader topics that DF is particularly attuned to into the discussion as, for example, economics and societal norms. This study contributes insights into how DF impacts the students' design thinking, as well as difficulties they had regarding their individual thinking process.

Keywords: Design fiction · Design thinking · Individual brainstorm · Design challenge · Design education

1 Introduction

Design Fiction (DF) is a new, creative methodology that may improve design thinking [5,14], and can be used to envision hypothetical products of tomorrow, by creating a speculative story-world told through designed artifacts [2,8]. The ability to engage in DF practices can help designers to think free from commercial and real-world constraints [2], and is therefore an important competency for design students to acquire. Currently, design student's design thinking processes usually rely deeply on group work [1,13], thus they seem to have difficulties overriding the boundaries of their own state of mind when brainstorming individually [13]. However, individual brainstorming can produce more original ideas than group work [7,10]. DF could potentially be a valuable addition to current thinking tools of individual brainstorming.

This qualitative study set out to explore the difficulties in design students' thinking processes when brainstorming individually using a DF framework. Previous work shows that DF-methods know challenges in constructing and understanding the future-bound ethics of technology in one's mind [9], and in terms

© IFIP International Federation for Information Processing 2021
Published by Springer Nature Switzerland AG 2021
C. Ardito et al. (Eds.): INTERACT 2021, LNCS 12936, pp. 386–389, 2021.
https://doi.org/10.1007/978-3-030-85607-6_43

of ethical vagueness, as the future concepts are not feasible and are difficult for design students to relate to [3].

2 Method

The study consisted of an online individual brainstorm and a semi-structured interview. The pre-study briefing and interview were done via Skype and the brainstorm session was done via mural.com [11]. The topic of this brainstorm was the appearance, functions, and uses of the interior of future self-driving cars.

The brainstorm session lasted approximately forty minutes and was based on the Approach of DF by the Near Future Laboratory [4]: a design company that specializes in the exploration of (unexpected) futures. Their prominence and impact in the field as evidenced by citations to their work motivated us to choose to use their method as a paradigmatic case. The brainstorm session consisted of the following four steps: 1) design brief with an explanation of the assignment and design challenge about self-driving cars, 2) participants were asked to write down their concerns, ambitions, fears and everyday needs of inhabitants of envisioned futures, with self-driving cars in mind, 3) participants were asked to consider all things that could change in the future with regards to, for example, law, norms, aesthetics, social and personal values, and habits, as changes in environmental factors might influence how suitable different design choices are, and 4) participants had to come up with different futuristic ideas or designs that would offer the possibility to discuss a different kind of future.

During the interview, participants were asked about their overall impressions, their feelings about different steps, the differences between DF and their regular design process in their design curriculum, the added value of DF in the future, and the ways in which DF helped them to look further ahead.

In total, ten design students were selected by means of purposive sampling [12]. The participants were bachelor (2) and master (8) students who are currently following different design curricula worldwide.

3 Results

The interview data were analyzed inductively, in a thematic analysis approach based on the guidance provided by Braun and Clarke [6]. To analyze and identify patterns in our interview transcriptions, themes within the data were developed bottom-up. We summarized and divided transcriptions into different data segments. By tagging the data segments, we generated initial codes and recognized common themes, to which we added other suitable codes. During the analysis, the themes were adapted repeatedly until all codes were combined into overarching themes: thinking from future, future potential, missing of external input, switching between steps, study setup, and thinking process.

The main challenges of the DF method itself are thinking from a future perspective and adopting DF in future projects. Most participants mentioned that they struggled with thinking of futuristic ideas, especially with abstract concepts. Although thinking from the future perspective is hard, nine participants mentioned that the DF method can be helpful in future projects because of the clear structure and the inspirational perspective it stimulates. Regarding their assignment, participants found the setup of our sessions difficult without external input, such as other research or input from users. Besides, most participants saw a link between the steps, but could not switch fluently between them, probably because they had not yet internalized the DF approach. Such challenges derive from the study setup but are not derived from the DF as such. Participants emphasized on differences between the regular and DF thinking processes. About step two (inhabitants of envisioned futures), participants mentioned getting insights from the keywords, and looking from a personal perspective made it easier to imagine future scenarios. Additionally, participants mentioned that step three (future environment) helped them look at the bigger picture: the societal and economical perspective, but also at the impact self-driving cars may have.

4   Conclusion and Discussion

This study provided insights into the challenges that students face while engaging in DF. Almost all participates felt challenged to think with a future perspective, which is consistent with the notion that the future concepts of DF are not feasible and relatable to students [3]. Additionally, this study showed why students regard DF as hard to apply. Abstract concepts such as economic models or social norms are beyond most students' knowledge, thus participants thought they missed external input. Therefore, it is important that in future DF-based ideation sessions, students first engage in some preparatory work that will allow them to inject into the design process substantive knowledge on topics related to the design challenge. While useful insights have been obtained, the study setup constrained the way DF practices were applied. Similar studies in the future should strive for more flexibility and realism in the design challenge.

Yet, not only challenges were mentioned. Most participants thought that the DF method made it easier to imagine future scenarios, due to its clear structure with questions and keywords and the personal perspective of the assignment. Especially, the step concerning the future environmental factors was perceived as a difficult but essential tool for thinking in-depth about the future and for looking at the 'bigger picture' of the future environment and its inhabitants. Because DF was new for most of our participants, they thought DF helped them to broaden their ideation. To extend the results of the study, we need to investigate how students use DF in real-life projects of longer duration. This study assessed only students' self-efficacy about the DF brainstorm, but future research may assess how well students apply DF methods from an expert perspective.

References

1. Amabile, T.M.: Componential theory of creativity (2012). https://www.hbs.edu/faculty/PublicationFiles/12-096.pdf

2. Auger, J.: Alternative presents and speculative futures designing fictions through the extrapolation and evasion of product lineages. In: Swiss Design Network Conference 2010, pp. 42–57 (2010). https://researchonline.rca.ac.uk/id/eprint/1093

3. Baumer, E.P., et al.: What would you do? Design fiction and ethics. In: Proceedings of the International ACM SIGGROUP Conference on Supporting Group Work, pp. 244–256. Association for Computing Machinery, Sanibel Island, January 2018. https://doi.org/10.1145/3148330.3149405

4. Bleecker, J.: Design fiction: a short essay on design, science, fact and fiction (2009). https://blog.nearfuturelaboratory.com/2009/03/17/design-fiction-a-short-essay-on-design-science-fact-and-fiction/

5. Blythe, M.: Research through design fiction: narrative in real and imaginary abstracts. In: Conference on Human Factors in Computing Systems - Proceedings, pp. 703–712. Association for Computing Machinery, Toronto (2014). https://doi.org/10.1145/2556288.2557098. http://dl.acm.org/citation.cfm?doid=2556288.2557098

6. Braun, V., Clarke, V.: Using thematic analysis in psychology. Qual. Res. Psychol. **3**(2), 77–101 (2006). https://doi.org/10.1191/1478088706qp063oa. /record/2006-06991-002

7. Harari, O., Graham, W.K.: Tasks and task consequences as factors in individual and group brainstorming. J. Soc. Psychol. **95**(1), 61–65 (1975). https://doi.org/10.1080/00224545.1975.9923234. https://www.tandfonline.com/doi/abs/10.1080/00224545.1975.9923234

8. Lindley, J., Coulton, P.: Back to the future: 10 years of design fiction. In: ACM International Conference Proceeding Series, pp. 210–211. Association for Computing Machinery, New York, July 2015. https://doi.org/10.1145/2783446.2783592. https://dl.acm.org/doi/10.1145/2783446.2783592

9. Lindley, J.G.: A thesis about design fiction. Thesis (Ph.D.), Lancaster University (2018). https://doi.org/10.17635/lancaster/thesis/449

10. Madsen, D.B., Finger, J.R.: Comparison of a written feedback procedure, group brainstorming, and individual brainstorming. J. Appl. Psychol. **63**(1), 120–123 (1978). https://doi.org/10.1037/0021-9010.63.1.120. /record/1979-21061-001

11. MURAL: MURAL - Online Brainstorming, Synthesis and Collaboration. https://www.mural.co/

12. Patton, M.Q.: Sampling, qualitative (purposive). In: The Blackwell Encyclopedia of Sociology. Wiley, Oxford, February 2007. https://doi.org/10.1002/9781405165518.wbeoss012. http://doi.wiley.com/10.1002/9781405165518.wbeoss012

13. Paulus, P.B., Nijstad, B.A.: Group Creativity: Innovation through Collaboration. Oxford University Press (2003). https://doi.org/10.1093/acprof:oso/9780195147308.001.0001. /record/2003-88061-000

14. Tanenbaum, J., Pufal, M., Tanenbaum, K.: The limits of our imagination: design fiction as a strategy for engaging with dystopian futures. In: Proceedings of the Second Workshop on Computing within Limits, pp. 1–9. Association for Computing Machinery, Irvine, June 2016. https://doi.org/10.1145/2926676.2926687. https://dl.acm.org/doi/10.1145/2926676.2926687

Discreet Interactive Wallpaper Concepts Study

Damien Brun$^{(\boxtimes)}$, Saara Lehtinen, and Jonna Häkkilä

Lapland University, Rovaniemi, Finland
{damien.brun,saara.lehtinen,jonna.hakkila}@ulapland.fi

Abstract. In this paper, we address the design of discreet interactive wallpapers. We chart the initial user perceptions with a simulation-based user study (n = 14), where we evaluate different concepts specifically designed for electrochromic ink, ranging from ambient information delivery to gamification. Our research contributes background knowledge for designers and practitioners working with interactive environments.

Keywords: Interactive walls · Ambient displays · Electrochromic

1 Introduction

Smart and interactive environments are one of the main themes of ubiquitous computing, and research has addressed them from various viewpoints. For instance, the concept of interactive wallpapers has been explored to provide either useful, engaging or entertaining ambient experiences.

First, Huang and Waldvogel [4] defined the interactive wallpaper in four points: (1) operate in everyday life, (2) open, (3) spatial and (4) alive. The authors showed a series of implementations, mostly projector-based, blending decorative art and useful science. In the same vein, Campbell *et al.* [1] explored the concept of interactive wallpaper at home, providing scene-setting for immersive drama or additional content, such as recipes while watching a TV cooking show. Hoare *et al.* [3] explored an interactive hide-and-seek children-oriented game with wallpapers. However, despite showing benefits of using interactive wallpapers, previous works were mostly agnostic of the technical implementation and many years or decades later remain far-fetched to be integrated.

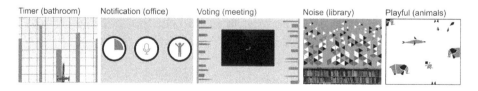

Fig. 1. Each abstract interactive wallpaper concept.

Published by Springer Nature Switzerland AG 2021
C. Ardito et al. (Eds.): INTERACT 2021, LNCS 12936, pp. 390–394, 2021.
https://doi.org/10.1007/978-3-030-85607-6_44

In this context, we address the topic of wallpapers with concepts based in the technical possibilities of interactive free-form graphics that can be manufactured with electrochromic inks, providing thin, transparent, flexible and low-power consuming displays. When an electric current is applied to the display, the ink moves from one place to the other, back and forth when reversing polarity. On the other hand, the displays have a limited number of colors and states and more importantly, do not emit light, thus, allowing visually discreet interactions, which are naturally integrated to indoor environments. The process of creating electrochromic displays is explained in detail by Jensen et al. [5].

We conducted a user study while specifically emulating the opportunities (low consumption, thus, blending solar panels into design) and limits (bi-state monochromatic graphical elements) of this technology as wallpapers. Each wallpaper concept (Fig. 1) aims to address different ideas:

- *Timer*, in our case taking place in the bathroom, with ink moving slowly decreasing one bar while increasing another. Multiple displays are stacked above each other, allowing a smooth transition.
- *Notification*, taking place in the office with the visual form of portholes. In this case, respectively (from left to right) alerting a future meeting, the microphone status and recall to move (or stand). When the notification is off, the ink is hidden around the border.
- *Voting* (more broadly the idea of communal expressing walls), with stacks of horizontal bars placed on opposite corners of a (meeting) room.
- *Noise* (ambient) with a colored repeated pattern showing its current level, in our case taking place in a library. The noisier the environment is, the higher (top) the displays are activated.
- *Playful*, taking the form of a hide-and-seek game with integrated solar panel elements (black shape) to a repeated pattern of animals. When an animal is hidden, the corresponding ink goes to a state placed behind the solar panel.

2   User Study

We conducted the exploratory study over seven sessions with the aim to collect preliminary user perceptions and qualitative feedback about our interactive wallpapers concepts.

Fourteen (n = 14) participants (9 female) were recruited at the university campus from students and administrative employees. They participated in the study by pair into a laboratory environment for service and design interaction. Two back-projected walls were used to display the wallpaper concepts, complemented with furniture (tables, chairs) and tangible artifacts (keyboards, tablets, books and a sanitizer dispenser) to improve the simulation (Fig. 2).

For each session, the participants first gave their consents and were introduced to real electrochromic displays as examples. Then, participants were invited to engage with a think-aloud protocol for each simulated concept presented in a specific coherent order (similar to this paper) to follow an imaginary short story. The narrative was such that they just arrived at work and had to

Fig. 2. User study setting for each wallpaper concept.

clean their hands in the bathroom with the *timer* concept. Then, they sat in an office with the *notification* concept and transitioned to a meeting room with the *voting* concept. Finally they stopped by the library with the *noise* concept (including simulated audio) before going home and engaging with the *playful* concept.

One instructor gave initial explanations of each concept while taking notes and another was changing the physical structure of the settings accordingly with the desired context. The *Wizard of Oz* method was used to simulate interactions, such as activity (e.g., washing hands) or touch detection.

Hassenzahl has defined user experience (UX) as "*a momentary, primarily evaluative feeling (good-bad) while interacting with a product or service*" [2]. Thus, before leaving, participants had to complete a questionnaire to assess their feeling (1–5 scale) toward each wallpaper concept, and to collect their least and most preferred (including explanations) as well as additional open comments. Each session was video-recorded for subsequent analysis and lasted around 45 min in total.

3 Findings

Participants' quantitative ratings are reported in Fig. 3. Two concepts were clearly favored: *Noise (library)* and *Playful (animals)*. Interestingly, these results

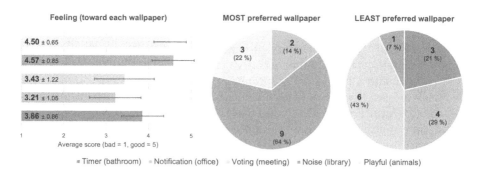

Fig. 3. Average score (including 95% confidence interval) of the participants' feelings toward each wallpaper as well as counts of the most and least preferred wallpapers.

also show a preference to adopt a repeating pattern design, which is more aligned with the mental representation of traditional wallpapers.

Timer. The low perceivability (n = 8) was the major drawback of this concept, either by taking time to notice the moving bars, or by considering them unclear. On the other hand, participants would like to exploit the *timer* concept with kids (n = 6) and in different contexts such as tooth-brushing (n = 4).

Notification. The lack of noticeability (n = 4) and usefulness (n = 4) were the main issues. Participants were also concerned to define the right placement (n = 8) and its visibility to others (n = 6), either to inform or to keep privacy.

Voting. The lack of usefulness (n = 5) was also the main issue with participants evoking the use of other technologies for the same context (n = 3).

Noise. This concept received a large amount of exclamatory positivity with participants evoking great usefulness and fit to its environment (n = 12), "*rather than looking like something hung on the wall*" (P2). However, some were also concerned about the noticeability (n = 8) and the inclination toward an opposite effect, considering it as a game for loudness (n = 8).

Playful. Even with a visually discreet interactive wallpaper, this concept received the same overall positive feedback as previous work [3] with participants also highlighting benefits for teaching (n = 6), physical exercise (n = 4) and memory activities (n = 4).

4 Future Work

Following our first findings, we considered a repeating pattern design (giving a flat or depth illusion effect). A prototype was made (Fig. 4) for the noise concept based on 3 flexible layers, blending solar panels, electrochromic displays and the circuitry to connect all of them. Other implementation approaches remain to be explored (such as multiple 2-layered standalone electrochromics) and studied over a series of experiments, measuring for instance their noticeability.

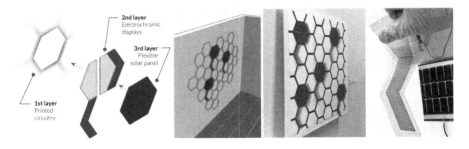

Fig. 4. Early interactive wallpaper conceptual implementation and real prototype.

Acknowledgements. This project has received funding from the European Union's Horizon 2020 research and innovation programme under Grant Agreement No. 760973.

References

1. Campbell, R., Felton, R., Hoarse, C.: Smart wallpaper. In: Proceedings of the 2014 ACM International Conference on Interactive Experiences for TV and Online Video, Industry Track-TVX, vol. 14. Citeseer (2014)
2. Hassenzahl, M.: User experience (UX) towards an experiential perspective on product quality. In: Proceedings of the 20th Conference on l'Interaction Homme-Machine, pp. 11–15 (2008)
3. Hoare, C., Campbell, R., Felton, R., Betsworth, L.: Hide and seek: exploring interaction with smart wallpaper. In: Proceedings of the 2015 Annual Symposium on Computer-Human Interaction in Play, pp. 129–133 (2015)
4. Huang, J., Waldvogel, M.: Interactive wallpaper. In: ACM SIGGRAPH 2005 Electronic Art and Animation Catalog, pp. 172–176 (2005)
5. Jensen, W., Colley, A., Häkkilä, J., Pinheiro, C., Löchtefeld, M.: TransPrint: a method for fabricating flexible transparent free-form displays. In: Advances in Human-Computer Interaction 2019 (2019)

Do Animation Direction and Position of Progress Bar Affect Selections?

Kota Yokoyama[1(✉)], Satoshi Nakamura[1], and Shota Yamanaka[2]

[1] Meiji University, Nakano-ku, Tokyo, Japan
cs212018@meiji.ac.jp
[2] Yahoo Japan Corporation, Chiyoda-ku, Tokyo, Japan

Abstract. Web sites and applications show visual feedback such as a progress bar or a throbber to signal that users should wait. These moving objects guide the eye. We hypothesized that users would end up looking near the end position of the visual feedback after waiting. As a result that users might be more likely to select an object near the end position of the visual feedback. This study focused on using a progress bar as visual feedback for waiting and on the design to influence the users' subsequent choice. We tested our hypotheses using a progress bar with different display positions and animation directions. The results suggest that changing the progress bar's position on a display or the animation's direction may bias the subsequent selection position.

Keywords: Choice behavior · Visual feedback · Progress bar · Fairness

1 Introduction

People usually face situations where they have to make various choices. Past research has shown that human habits and psychological effects influence their choices. Therefore, when users make choices, systems need to be adapted to handle various intentions. For example, in Web-based questionnaires, if a factor causes bias in the selection, the survey's reliability is also affected. Therefore, identifying the factors that cause bias in selection is crucial because such factors may affect the survey's credibility.

When customers use a computer, they sometimes have to wait while reading media files and layout designs displayed on the screen. This waiting time always exists even if the computer's processing speed and the Internet's communication speed are excellent. A long waiting time may annoy the user to make him/her misrecognize it as an error [1]. Bouch et al. [2] clarified that a feeding back extended users' time that they would be willing to wait. In particular, many users prefer a progress bar to be used in Web sites and applications [3] because they can easily estimate the time in which a task is

Electronic supplementary material The online version of this chapter (https://doi.org/10.1007/978-3-030-85607-6_45) contains supplementary material, which is available to authorized users.

C. Ardito et al. (Eds.): INTERACT 2021, LNCS 12936, pp. 395–399, 2021.
https://doi.org/10.1007/978-3-030-85607-6_45

completed. However, because such visual feedback may induce a users' line of sight, it may affect their behavior when making a selection after the waiting period is over.

Previous studies researched the relationship between the user gaze and selection behavior. Simonson [4] suggested that users tended to complete the selection process when they found the appropriate product. Shimojo et al. [5] found that users tended to prefer choices with long gaze time. These results suggest that if a progress bar guides a user's gaze and changes the order of viewing and gazing time for each option, the option near the end of the progress bar animation will be the one more likely to be selected.

In this study, we focus on the effect of the progress bar animation before presenting a user interface for selections. We also speculate that gender differences may exist in the effects of animated progress bars because a previous study [6] reported that men were more sensitive to moving objects and rapid changes than women. Therefore, we hypothesized the following.

- Hypothesis 1: When a system presents a progress bar before the user interface, the user may be more likely to choose near the animation's end.
- Hypothesis 2: The effect of hypothesis 1 would be more pronounced by men than women.

In this study, we prepared two animation directions (leftward or rightward) and two positions (upper or lower) of the progress bar and compared their effects on the location of users' selection. In addition, we implemented an experimental system to test these effects in crowdsourcing platforms.

2 Experiment

In this study, we designed the experiment based on online shopping on the Internet to clarify the relationship between the design of the progress bar and the users' selection behavior after the waiting period ends.

We recruited participants for this experiment using Yahoo! Crowdsourcing, a major crowdsourcing platform in Japan. This experiment was limited to PC users. Our system asked each participant to select one of eight options after a waiting period. Our system repeated this selection process nine times and asked participants to answer questionnaires after the experiment.

We prepared five types of waiting screens (see Fig. 1). Four conditions combined the display position of the progress bar (upper, lower) and the animation's direction (rightward, leftward). One condition involved the background color changing from black (RGB value: 55) to white (RGB value: 255) without displaying the progress bar. We prepared three kinds of waiting times of 2 s, 5 s, and 10 s and experimented with three times for each condition. We also prepared nine product categories (vacuum cleaners, water, mice, dumbbells, Web cameras, teacups, chairs, tissues, and batteries) for the selections. In addition, we prepared eight kinds of product images for each category.

Figure 1 shows one trial example in which a paritcipant assigned to each condition to select a bottle of water. Product images were randomly placed in 2 (rows) by 4 (columns) squares each time. The system first instructed participants not to look away from the screen while waiting and asked the questionnaire after the experiment how long they looked away.

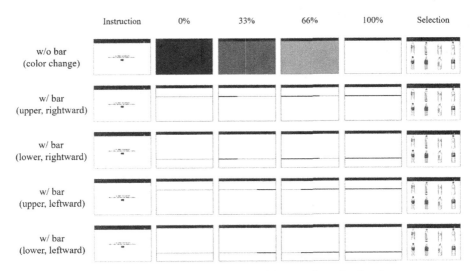

Fig. 1. Examples of one trial in each condition to select a bottle of water.

3 Results and Discussion

We recruited 1,000 participants (500 men and 500 women). Among them, we excluded 380 participants who did not follow the instructions and whose data were incorrect. Finally, we obtained 620 participants' data (330 men, 290 women) to analyze. The results enabled us to collect at least 909 selection data in each condition.

Figure 2 shows the selection rate at each position in each condition. Figure 3 shows the men's selection rate, and Fig. 4 shows the women's selection rate at each position in each condition. These figures correspond to 2 (rows) by 4 (columns) squares in which the choices were displayed in the experiment. The arrows in these figures indicate the animation direction of the progress bar and its display position. Figure 2 showed no trend in selection at the end of the animation. Therefore, hypothesis 1 was not well-supported at this stage. Figure 3 and 4 revealed no trend like that of hypothesis 1, so hypothesis 2 was also rejected.

However, in the lower-rightward, lower-leftward, and upper-rightward display conditions, the selection rate of the center two rows tended to be high. Because the product images' arrangement was random, the deviation should not have arisen in the selected position unless other factors caused it. Therefore, we analyzed the degree to which bias was substantial in the selection rate in each condition. As a result, we found that the lower-rightward, lower-leftward, and upper-rightward display conditions may have specifically caused bias in the selected position. We did the same analysis in accordance with the time condition. The result suggests that the 10-s condition may not affect the bias of the selected position under any waiting screen conditions.

These results suggest that when designers incorporate a progress bar into a survey site, they may want to apply the progress bar on the upper side and the direction of the animation leftward to obtain fair results.

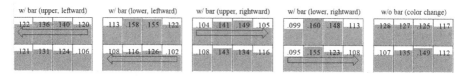

Fig. 2. Results of the selection rate at each position in each condition.

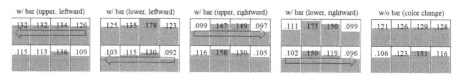

Fig. 3. Results of the selection rate at each position in each condition for men.

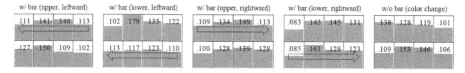

Fig. 4. Results of the selection rate at each position in each condition for women.

4 Conclusion

In this work, we investigated the effect of the design of a progress bar on the selecting behavior after a waiting period ended by conduting the experiment test. In the future, we will investigate how the difference in the shape or the difference in the animation speed affects users' selections after the waiting period ends.

References

1. Nah, F.: A study on tolerable waiting time: how long are Web users willing to wait? Behav. Inf. Technol. **23**(3), 153–163 (2004)

2. Bouch, A., Kuchinsky, A., and Bhatti, N.: Quality is in the eye of the beholder: meeting users' requirements for internet quality of service. In: Proceedings of the SIGCHI Conference on Human Factors in Computing Systems. ACM, The Hague (2000)
3. Branaghan, R.J., Sanchez, C.A.: Feedback preferences and impressions of waiting. Hum. Factors **51**(4), 528–538 (2009)
4. Simonson, I.: The effect of product assortment on buyer preferences. J. Retail. **75**(3), 347–370 (1999)
5. Shimojo, S., Simion, C., Shimojo, E., Scheier, C.: Gaze bias both reflects and influences preference. Nat. Neurosci. **6**(12), 1317–1322 (2003)
6. Abramov, I., Gordon, J., Feldman, O., Chavarga, A.: Sex & vision I: spatio-temporal resolution. Biol. Sex Differ. **3**(1), 20 (2012)

Don't Touch Me! A Comparison of Usability on Touch and Non-touch Inputs

Kieran Waugh$^{(\boxtimes)}$ and Judy Robertson

The University of Edinburgh, Edinburgh, Scotland, UK
{Kieran.Waugh,Judy.Robertson}@ed.ac.uk

Abstract. Public touchscreens are filthy and, regardless of how often they are cleaned, they pose a considerable risk in the transmission of bacteria and viruses. While we rely on their use, we should find a feasible alternative to touch devices. Non-touch interaction, via the use of mid-air gestures, has been previously labelled as not user friendly and unsuitable. However, previous works have extensively compared such interaction to precise mouse movements. In this paper, we investigate and compare the usability of an interface controlled via a touchscreen and a non-touch device. Participants (N = 22) using a touchscreen and the Leap Motion Controller, performed tasks on a mock-up ticketing machine, later evaluating their experience using the System Usability and Gesture Usability scales. Results show that, in contrast to the previous works, the non-touch method was usable and quickly learnable. We conclude with recommendations for future work on making a non-touch interface more user-friendly.

Keywords: Non-touch · Gesture · Touchless · Leap motion controller

1 Introduction

Public information kiosks and self-service displays are becoming common in public life, but there are some negative aspects to these types of public displays. Such devices have been found to have 1,475 times more bacteria than the average toilet seat [4,6]. Similarly, the average supermarket self-service contains 5.9 times more bacteria than found on hospital displays [3]. One possible solution to these issues is to remove the touch aspect of public devices and instead enable interaction through non-touch gestures. There is currently limited research on the relative usability of mid-air interactions in a public setting and few controlled studies that compare the Leap Motion Controller (LMC) and touchscreen for public interaction design. Our work explores the usability of non-touch technologies to replace public touchscreens.

This paper documents a user study where participants compared and evaluated a mock-up ticket machine using both a touchscreen and a LMC which allows interaction via mid-air gestures. We measure participant success and errors when interacting with both devices as well as task time for the different inputs and system/gesture usability scores.

© IFIP International Federation for Information Processing 2021
Published by Springer Nature Switzerland AG 2021
C. Ardito et al. (Eds.): INTERACT 2021, LNCS 12936, pp. 400–404, 2021.
https://doi.org/10.1007/978-3-030-85607-6_46

2   Methodology

We used a within-subjects study design where participants were asked to imagine they were at a train station. Tasks were then completed on both a touchscreen and LMC using on-screen point-and-push. To prevent step memorisation, the tasks in the two conditions differed slightly. The order of the touch and non-touch conditions was randomised between participants and tasks were ordered so they increased in difficulty (Table 1). The system recorded an activity log for each participant and after completing each condition, participants were asked to fill out the System and Gesture Usability Scale surveys [2,11] (SUS/GUS). After both conditions, they also filled out demographics, interface preference, and overall system feedback questions. Finally, we provided information about the cleanliness of the screen and asked for their preference again.

Table 1. Tasks performed by the participants for both the touchcreen and LMC

	Touch	Non-touch
Task 1	Buy a return ticket to Edinburgh Zoo for two adults and one child	Buy a return ticket to Princes Street for one adult and one child
Task 2	Buy a one way ticket to The University of Edinburgh for one adult and one child	Buy a one way ticket to Botanic Garden for two adults and one child
Task 3	Print a prepaid ticket using the code XBLPZ. After, complete the survey	Print a prepaid ticket using the code PRSGM. After, complete the survey

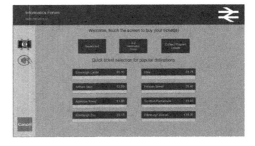

Fig. 1. Study setup with touch monitor and LMC placed below.

Fig. 2. Interface shown to participants.

3   Results

22 people participated in the study, ranging from (self-reported) low to advanced technical backgrounds and an age range of 18 to 44. 8/22 participants preferred using non-touch over the touchscreen and 20/22 participants would use the system again in public. 12/14 people who preferred using the touchscreen changed

preference after learning about the disease/bacteria spread on the average screen. Participants using the LMC took longer to complete the tasks (Table 2). Task 3, which required manipulating a UI slider, recorded the most time as the affordance suggested it should be draggable but a selection at a scale point was needed. On average, across the three tasks, participants made 2.09 errors with the LMC and 1.18 with the touchscreen with more errors made during task 2 and 3 (see Fig. 3). 10/22 participants made 0 errors when using the LMC.

Table 2. Mean time in seconds and clicks per task with standard deviation (SD)

	Mean time (SD)		Mean clicks (SD)	
	Touch	Non-touch	Touch	Non-touch
Task 1	23.9 (8.3)	35.2 (11.5)	7.68 (1.39)	6.91 (1.06)
Task 2	32.0 (10.0)	53.9 (31.0)	7.73 (1.35)	9.27 (1.98)
Task 3	34.4 (8.1)	64.8 (16.5)	11.09 (2.31)	14.73 (2.69)

As shown in Table 3, the touchscreen was rated higher in both scales, with a larger variance in the ratings for the non-touch scores. The post-experiment feedback was coded using open coding by the first author and later checked through discussion with the second author. Three categories were created: 1) user interface changes, 2) sensor tracking, and 3) general comments. 13 participants expressed a need to change the user interface (1), 11 identified issues with sensor tracking (2), and 3 participants provided further general comments (3). The participants identified specific points that could improve the system: clearer visual prompts, gesture pointers, bigger user interface elements and more space between them, and less use of the display corners. "Bigger buttons may help too", "keyboard keys were a bit close together", "More difficult to select buttons in corners/edges could be improved".

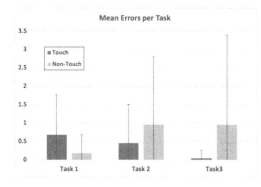

Fig. 3. Mean errors per task with standard deviation

Table 3. Mean SUS and GUS scores for both touch and non-touch with standard deviation

	Touch		Non-touch	
	Mean	SD	Mean	SD
SUS	90.34	10.33	70	18.39
GUS	95.3	8.38	64	24.33

4 Discussion

Previous research comparing the LMC with traditional mouse actions found the LMC to have poor usability [1,8,10]. In contrast to these previous works, in our study the LMC shows promising usability with participants scoring their experience highly. As shown in Table 4, our SUS score is not only higher than the published average but also far higher than those in previous works. A possible explanation for these higher scores may be a more mature technology with better tracking. Having a high SUS/GUS score in this experiment along with a relatively low error rate suggests poor usability may no longer be the case.

The qualitative feedback indicates that design changes to the user interface could improve usability as also highlighted by Bachmann et al. [1]. Participants highlighted difficulties with the gesture set. Particularly, they were frustrated at the accuracy of point and push required by the LMC. These gestures are problematic as they attempts to follow touchscreen conventions, further supporting the idea of creating non-touch designed gesture sets [8]. There is a clear gap in research on user interfaces designed for public use with non-touch devices.

Table 4. Comparison of previous studies of LMC and other input devices.

	SUS LMC	SUS other	Device compared
Sauro [9]	–	68	Published average
Pirker et al. [7]	55	75	Keyboard
Škrlj et al. [5]	56.5	88.7	3D mouse
Our study	70	90.3	Touchscreen

5 Conclusions and Future Work

An exploration into touchless technology is an important first step to creating a feasible alternative to touch devices. Our results indicate that a non-touch approach is usable in a public setting and quickly learnable. While participants overall preferred the touchscreen, the resulting data for the LMC is significantly more promising than those in previous works, signalling considerable improvements in the gesture tracking technology. Further investigation is required with a more diverse user group to help build an accessible user interface for non-touch systems. Two areas need to be addressed in further research:

1. A user interface specifically designed for a non-touch environment. Given the feedback from this study, potential areas of improvement are the size and location of UI buttons/objects and clearer calls to interact.

2. Exploration of alternative interaction gestures. The gesture set chosen for this experiment did not work for all elements. The user interface must be designed with consideration to the limitations of the input range. For example, in this study, a UI slider not working with a point and push gesture.

Further investigation into specialised user interfaces and gesture sets can advance the potential of non-touch systems, facilitating the adoption of this technology into public spaces.

Acknowledgements. The authors would like to thank everyone who took time to participate in the study and Kate Farrell for supplying equipment. We would also like to thank Kami Vaniea for their advice and my colleagues and friends for their help proof-reading.

References

1. Bachmann, D., Weichert, F., Rinkenauer, G.: Evaluation of the leap motion controller as a new contact-free pointing device. Sensors **15**(1), 214–233 (2014). https://doi.org/10.3390/s150100214
2. Brooke, J.: SUS: A 'Quick and Dirty' Usability Scale, pp. 207–212. CRC Press (1996). https://doi.org/10.1201/9781498710411-35
3. Gerba, C.P., Wuollet, A.L., Raisanen, P., Lopez, G.U.: Bacterial contamination of computer touch screens. Am. J. Infect. Control **44**(3), 358–360 (2016). https://doi.org/10.1016/j.ajic.2015.10.013
4. InsuranceQuotes: Germs at the airport, looking at the microorganisms that travel with us (2018). https://www.insurancequotes.com/health/germs-at-the-airport. Accessed 13 June 2020
5. Krlj, P., Bohak, C., Guna, J., Marolt, M.: Usability evaluation of input devices for navigation and interaction in 3D visualisation. Int. SERIES Inf. Syst. Manage. Creat. eMedia (CreMedia) **1**(2014), 19–23 (2015)
6. National-Science-Foundation: International household germ study (2011). https://www.nsf.org/knowledge-library/2011-nsf-international-household-germ-study-exectutive-summary. Accessed 13 June 2020
7. Pirker, J., Pojer, M., Holzinger, A., Gütl, C.: Gesture-based interactions in video games with the leap motion controller. In: Kurosu, M. (ed.) HCI 2017. LNCS, vol. 10271, pp. 620–633. Springer, Cham (2017). https://doi.org/10.1007/978-3-319-58071-5_47
8. Saalfeld, P., Mewes, A., Luz, M., Preim, B.: Comparative evaluation of gesture and touch input for medical software, pp. 143–152. Tagungsbände/Proceedings (2015). https://doi.org/10.1515/9783110443929-016
9. Sauro, J.: A Practical Guide to the System Usability Scale: Background, Benchmarks & Best Practices. CreateSpace Independent Publishing Platform (2011). https://books.google.co.uk/books?id=BL0kKQEACAAJ
10. Seixas, M.C.B., Cardoso, J.C.S., Dias, M.T.G.: The leap motion movement for 2D pointing tasks - characterisation and comparison to other devices (2015). https://doi.org/10.5220/0005206100150024
11. Wickeroth, D., Benoelken, P., Lang, U.: Manipulating 3D content using gestures in design review scenarios. Int. J. Inf. Stud. **1**, 243–251 (2009)

Effects of Audio-Visual Information on Interpersonal Distance in Real and Virtual Environments

Azusa Yamazaki, Naoto Wakatsuki, Koichi Mizutani⬤, Yukihiko Okada⬤, and Keiichi Zempo⁽⊠⁾⬤

University of Tsukuba, Tsukuba, Japan
`zempo@iit.tsukuba.ac.jp`

Abstract. In this study, interpersonal distances were measured in a real environment (RE) and an immersive virtual environment (VE) under each audiovisual condition (bimodal (V-A), visual-only (V/o), and auditory-only (A/o)), in order to design interpersonal services in a VEs and experiments in a VEs that are usually difficult to set up in REs. The experiment revealed the interpersonal distances in the VE that can be converted to the RE and the audiovisual conditions that cause them.

1 Introduction

Personal space is one of the most important factors for the smooth operation of social life. Leslie Hayduk described personal space as the area around a person where the intrusion of others causes discomfort [1]. The length of interpersonal distance that forms personal space changes accordingly as the environment changes [2] and affects the quality of service [3].

The virtual reality market is currently growing, with more and more services such as stores and offices communicating through avatars in a virtual environments (VEs) [4]. Therefore, there is a need to communicate at an appropriate interpersonal distance in VEs, just as in real environments (REs). In addition, the study of interpersonal distance in a VE has great potential for research applications. Experiments in a VE make it possible to perform experiments that are difficult to perform in an RE [5], while maintaining external validity and taking many factors into account [6]. From the above, it is important to clarify the interpersonal distance in the VE, and it is also effective to compare it with that in the RE, where much knowledge is available.

Studies on interpersonal distance in VE include the study which revealed the existence of interpersonal distance in VE [7], and the study which revealed the length of interpersonal distance and its difference by gender and age [8,9]. In those studies, the information used to perceive the approaching person is only visual information, not auditory information. However, in two-way communication, it is necessary to examine interpersonal distance when both visual and auditory information is available. Additionally, the interpersonal distance

ⓒ IFIP International Federation for Information Processing 2021
Published by Springer Nature Switzerland AG 2021
C. Ardito et al. (Eds.): INTERACT 2021, LNCS 12936, pp. 405–410, 2021.
https://doi.org/10.1007/978-3-030-85607-6_47

when only auditory information is used to perceive the approaching person is unknown. Therefore, it is necessary to study the interpersonal distance when the perceived information is visual and auditory, visual only, and auditory only. The purpose of this study is to measure the interpersonal distance in the VE under each audiovisual condition and to compare the results with those of the RE.

2   Experimental Design

2.1   Setup

To investigate the effects of RE and VE, as well as visual and auditory information, on interpersonal distance, the same space and the same confronting mannequin/avatar were prepared in an RE and a VE. Additionally, the visual and auditory conditions were restricted. Three within-subject factors were manipulated: the environment, approach direction, and perceived audiovisual condition.

Two environments were prepared: an RE and a VE. For the RE, a 7.2 m × 7.5 m × 3.1 m room was used. A 3D scan of the room used in the RE was taken by a 12.9-inch iPad Pro with Light Detection and Ranging (LiDAR) and imported into Unity. This allowed us to recreate the real room in a VE as shown in the Fig. 1. LiDAR is an optical sensor technology that identifies the distance to an object and its properties. For sound output in VE, the audio environment "Steam audio" is used, and the sound is heard in three dimensions. In the VE experiment, video and audio were presented using a head-mounted display (HMD; Dell Visor VR118, Dell Inc., resolution: 1440 × 1440 on each side, 590 g) and headphones (SONY, MDR-CD900 ST). To match the viewing angle, the viewing angle was standardized to 110°, the same as the HMD, by wearing goggles that limited the viewing angle during the experiment in the RE.

Three audiovisual conditions were prepared: a bimodal condition in which the subject could see the approaching person and hear his voice (V-A condition), a visual-only condition in which the subject could see the approaching person but not hear his voice (V/o condition), and an auditory-only condition in which the subject was blindfolded and could not see the approaching person but could hear his voice (A/o condition). As an approaching person, an avatar was used in VE, and a mannequin with an iPad Pro showing an image of the avatar's face fixed on its face was used in RE. The voice of the approaching person was a recording of a voice saying "Hello".

Approach directions were 8 directions of 45° each, with the front direction being 0°. Each subject was tested in a random order concerning the experimental conditions. The experiment was conducted under the scenario that the approaching person was a shopkeeper who had never met the subject before.

2.2   Procedure

In the experiment, the RE and VE were calibrated to match in size, the interpersonal distance was determined by the stop-distance method, and the egocentric

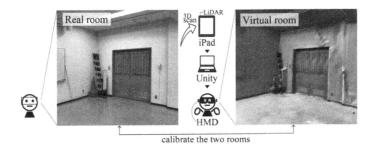

Fig. 1. The real room and the virtual room used in the experiment.

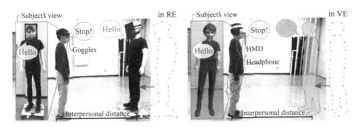

Fig. 2. Scene of the experiment in the case of approach from the front direction under V-A conditions.

distance was measured by the blind walking task. Initially, calibration was performed to align the perceived size of the RE and VE. This is because it has been shown that distances are perceived as reduced in VEs compared to REs [10,11], and the degree of reduction depends on the viewing angle and image quality of the device used [12]. The subject stood facing forward with his heels aligned with the markings in the center of the room in the RE and wore the HMD. Subjects alternately looked at or listened to the RE and the VE for room size, eye level, and the appearance and loudness of the approaching person. And if they differed, the VE's were matched by adjusting their sizes. The next step was to determine the interpersonal distance using the stop-distance method as shown in the Fig. 2 [13,14]. The approaching person gradually approached from a distance of 2.5 m from the subject, and when the subject felt uncomfortable if the person approached any closer, the subject signaled the approaching person to stop. Next, interpersonal distance was measured in a blind walking task [15,16]. The subject grasped the position of the approaching person based on the audiovisual information. They then closed their eyes and walked to the position where they thought the approaching person was. The distance walked was measured. This made it possible to measure the egocentric distance, which is the distance that is perceived.

The subjects were 8 males between the ages of 22 and 25 with no problems in walking, vision, or hearing. Since the length and characteristics of the interper-

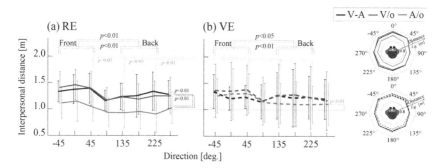

Fig. 3. Graphs comparing the interpersonal distance for each audiovisual condition in the RE and the VE.

sonal distance vary depending on gender [8,9], the subjects in this study were standardized as males.

3   Result and Discussion

In this section, the results and a discussion of the experiment are presented. A comparison of the interpersonal distance between each audiovisual condition in the RE and VE is shown in Fig. 3. A t-test was conducted at a significance level of 5%. The experiment revealed the interpersonal distances in the VE that can be converted to the RE and the audiovisual conditions that cause them.

In the VE, there was no significant difference between the front ($-45°$, $0°$, $45°$) and rear ($135°$, $180°$, $225°$) interpersonal distances in the V-A condition, and the front interpersonal distance was significantly greater than the rear interpersonal distance in the V/o and A/o conditions, respectively. The same tendency was observed in each audiovisual condition in the RE. The fact that the front distance is greater than the rear distance is consistent with previous studies [7,17]. This suggests that the appearance of the shopkeeper with a greeting in front (V-A condition) is natural, but the silent appearance of the shopkeeper (V/o condition) or with only a voice (A/o condition) is unnatural, which may have caused greater discomfort and a desire for greater interpersonal distances.

Besides, in the RE, the A/o condition, the interpersonal distance was significantly smaller than that in the V-A condition, but it was not significantly different compared to the V/o condition. These results suggest that the interpersonal distance in the V-A condition in the RE is caused by the interpersonal distance in the V/o condition rather than the interpersonal distance in the A/o condition. In the VE, there was no significant difference between the V-A, V/o, and A/o conditions. Most of the subjects were accustomed to having a sound image nearby in the RE but were not accustomed to the presence of a sound image in the VE. Therefore, the range of alertness in the A/o condition is wider in the VE, and the interpersonal distance may be greater than in the RE.

Furthermore, in the V-A and V/o conditions, there was no significant difference in the interpersonal distance between the VE and RE. In the A/o condition, the interpersonal distance was significantly greater in the VE than in the RE, especially in the 45°, 135°, and 225° directions. This indicates that the interpersonal distance in the VE is significantly greater than that in the RE, especially when approaching from a diagonal direction.

In this study, the experiments were conducted with the same appearance and voice of the approaching person with the same resolution and viewing angle of the HMD, but the effects of these factors on the interpersonal distance should be studied in the future.

References

1. Hayduk, L.: Personal space: an evaluative and orienting overview. Psychol. Bull. **85**(1), 117–134 (1987)
2. Iachini, T., Coello, Y., Frassinetti, F., Ruggiero, G.: Body space in social interactions: a comparison of reaching and comfort distance in immersive virtual reality. PLoS One **9**(11), e111511 (2014)
3. Arai, T., Chida, Y., Okada Y., Zempo, K.: Sensor network to measure MAAI on value co-creation process. In: Adjunct Proceedings of UbiComp/ISWC 2019 Adjunct (2019)
4. Meißner, M., Pfeiffer, J., Peukert, C., Dietrich, H., Pfeiffer, T.: How virtual reality affects consumer choice. J. Bus. Res. **117**, 219–231 (2020)
5. Uzzell, D., Horne, N.: The influence of biological sex, sexuality and gender role on interpersonal distance. Br. J. Soc. Psychol. **45**, 579–597 (2006)
6. Bailenson, J.N., Blascovich, J., Beall, A.C., Loomis, J.M.: Interpersonal distance in immersive virtual environments. Pers. Soc. Psychol. Bull. **29**(7), 819–833 (2003)
7. Bailenson, J.N., Blascovich, J., Beall, A.C., Loomis, J.M.: Equilibrium theory revisited: mutual gaze and personal space in virtual environments. Presence Teleoper. Virtual Environ. **10**(6), 583–598 (2001)
8. Evans, G.W., Howard, R.B.: Personal space. Psychol. Bull. **80**(4), 334–344 (1973)
9. Aliakbari, M., Faraji, E., Pourshakibaee, P.: Investigation of the proxemic behavior of Iranian professors and university students: effects of gender and status. J. Pragmat. **43**(5), 1392–1402 (2011)
10. Jones, A.J., Swan, J.E., Singh, G., Ellis, S.R.: Peripheral visual information and its effect on distance judgments in virtual and augmented environments. In: Proceedings of the 8th Symposium on Applied Perception in Graphics and Visualization, APGV 2011, pp. 29–36. ACM, France (2011)
11. Piryankova, I.V., Rosa, S., Kloos, U., Bülthoff, H.H., Mohler, B.J.: Egocentric distance perception in large screen immersive displays. Displays **34**(2), 153–164 (2013)
12. Buck, L. E., Young, M.K., Bodenheimer, B.: A comparison of distance estimation in HMD-based virtual environments with different HMD-based conditions. ACM Trans. Appl. Percept. **15**(3), Article 21 (2018)
13. Miller, H.C., Chabriac, A.S., Molet, M.: The impact of facial emotional expressions and sex on interpersonal distancing as evaluated in a computerized stop- distance task. Can. J. Exp. Psychol. **67**(3), 188–194 (2013)
14. Hecht, H., Welsch, R., Viehoff, J., Longo, M.R.: The shape of personal space. Acta Physiol. **193**, 113–122 (2019)

15. Sahm, C.S., Creem-Regehr, S.H., Thompson, W.B., Willemsen, P.: Throwing versus walking as indicators of distance perception in similar real and virtual environments. ACM Trans. Appl. Percept. **2**(1), 35–45 (2005)
16. Andre, J., Rogers, S.: Using verbal and blind-walking distance estimates to investigate the two visual systems hypothesis. Percept. Psychophys. **68**(3), 353–361 (2006)
17. Bönsch, A., Radke, S., Ehret, J., Habel, U., Kuhlen, T.W.: The impact of a virtual agent's non-verbal emotional expression on a user's personal space preferences. In: IVA 2020: Proceedings of the 20th ACM International Conference on Intelligent Virtual Agents, pp. 1–8. ACM, Virtual Event, Scotland (2020)

Exploring Button Design for Low Contrast User Interfaces

Ashley Colley[1], Çağlar Genç[1(✉)], Markus Löchtefeld[2], Heiko Mueller[3],
Walther Jensen[2], and Jonna Häkkilä[1]

[1] University of Lapland, Rovaniemi, Finland
[2] Aalborg University, Aalborg, Denmark
[3] University of Oldenburg, Oldenburg, Germany

Abstract. Mainstream display technologies have progressed towards higher resolutions and contrast levels. However, for IoT applications, where displays are embedded in the environment, there are requirements to optimize displays for lower power consumption or minimal environmental impact, potentially sacrificing contrast or switching time. We approach this issue by considering the spatial design of UI components. As a first step, we explore switch type UI components (e.g., check box, toggle switch) and evaluate the performance of 4 alternative spatial designs at low contrast levels. As a contribution, we open the issue of spatial UI design for low contrast and demonstrate an approach for its evaluation.

Keywords: Low contrast · UI components · Visibility · Design

1 Introduction

The evolution of display technologies has witnessed ever increasing performance in terms of resolution, contrast levels and refresh rates. However, for Internet of Things (IoT) applications, displays may need to sacrifice parameters such as resolution, contrast and refresh rate to achieve low power consumption.

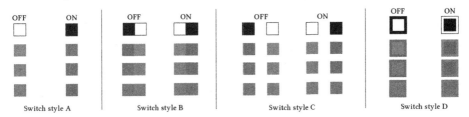

Fig. 1. The four graphical styles of switch UI component, with the 6 low contrast variants of each tested in the study

Several 'low-contrast' display technologies exist, e.g., the chemical lateral flow displays used in cheaper pregnancy tests. Other technologies such as electrochromic [5] and thermochromic displays [6,9] provide opportunities for the

© IFIP International Federation for Information Processing 2021
Published by Springer Nature Switzerland AG 2021
C. Ardito et al. (Eds.): INTERACT 2021, LNCS 12936, pp. 411–415, 2021.
https://doi.org/10.1007/978-3-030-85607-6_48

display designer to optimise the display design to minimise power consumption at the expense of e.g. switching time and contrast.

Decreased display contrast may lead to situations where the state of the display is not clear to users [2, 8, 10]. Similar contrast issues can also occur due to environmental factors, e.g. reduced contrast caused by reflection on smartphone screens [3]. For people with degraded visual performance, e.g. due to macular degeneration, cataracts or glaucoma, display contrast is even more critical.

We approach the issue of low-contrast visual displays from a UI design perspective by exploring the impact of visual design on the usability one of the most basic UI components, a simple switch button, when rendered at low contrast levels. Through a smartphone app based user study with 25 participants we report on the influence of 4 different switch designs when presented at low contrast levels (Fig. 1). As a contribution, we open the issue of design for low contrast user interfaces and demonstrate an experimental approach for its evaluation.

2   Concept

To explore the impact of visual design on usability at low contrast levels we created 4 alternative designs for the *on/off* switch UI component. This was selected as it is one of the most basic of UI components, common to all formats of GUI. As a design criteria, the active visual areas of each of the component designs were identical, only the spatial arrangement was changed between the cases. The evaluated switch component designs were (see Fig. 1): (A) a 'checkbox' style switch, with white indicating the *off* state and black the *on* state without any visual reference for comparison. This case was included as a baseline. (B) a left-right toggle switch style design. - similar in design to switch components of the Apple iOs or Google's Material Design. (C) a variant of switch style B, but with a visual gap separating the two areas of the switch. (D) a variant of switch style B, but with one graphical areas surrounding the other. The area of the surrounding area being identical to the central area.

Six levels of greyscale were selected for the components, with the following percentages of black (k value): 44%, 46%, 48%, 52%, 54%, 56%. These levels were selected based on initial exploration to provide the right level of challenge when viewed on a smartphone screen. In components with two filled areas (styles B - D), the greyscale colors were used in pairs balanced around a k value of 50%, i.e., [44%, 56%], [46%, 54%],[48%, 52%]. To explore the effect of orientation, e.g. left-right, the greyscale color pairs were applied in both orientations, resulting in a total of 6 variations per component style (Fig. 1).

3   User Study

A test application running on Android smartphones was developed, this included a test to evaluate the contrast capabilities of the test device/participant, as well as evaluation of the four switch component styles.

3.1   Test Proceedure

To identify any issues with either the performance of the smartphones used for testing, or the participant's low contrast vision, we implemented a sine wave grating test based on the Functional Acuity Contrast Test (FACT) [4] to our test app. The test consisted of 25 sine wave gratings with between 1.5 and 18 cycles per degree (assuming a 45 cm viewing distance from a 5″ device screen) and contrasts between 0.6% and 8.3%. Each of the 25 grating patterns was presented once, and randomly inclined at an angle of either $-15°$, $0°$ or $+15°$. This test aimed to identify outliers due to, e.g., issues with the participant's test configuration or participants with poor low contrast vision.

As training, the test app presented an initial screen showing images of the 4 styles of switch and then one test case of each style of component was tested, the results of which were discarded. The test application then presented the 24 test cases (see Fig. 1) in random order. For each case, the model illustrating the switch in *off* and *on* states was first shown, then after a delay of 1.5 s, the test case image was shown The participant then assessed if the presented case represented the *off* state or *on* state of the component, pressing a button to indicate their selection.

Test participants, recruited through the authors' personal networks, installed the test app on their own devices, and after completing the test, sent a log file of the test data to the facilitator. Altogether 28 participants returned data in the study. After validation with the 1.5IQR rule data from 3 participants were removed as outliers. Hence data from 25 participants (14 female, $\overline{age} = 27.2, SD = 4.6$) was further analyzed.

3.2   Results

Of the 25 contrast test images, the mean number correctly identified participants was 23.0, $SD = 1.3$, with participants identifying between 20 and 25 correctly. Hence it was deemed that all participant/test configuration combinations provided a normal level of contrast differentiation. The mean correct response rate across the 4 test cases in each style completed by each participant was calculated (Fig. 2. A within-subjects ANOVA identified a significant effect of style on correct response rate at the $p < .05$ level [$F(3, 4) = 96.197, p < .001$]. Pair-wise t-tests, with a Holm corrected p level, identified significant difference in the correct response rate between Style A (correct response rate $= 0.46$) and the other Styles; B (0.99), C (0.96) and D (0.90) [all $p < .001$].

Task completion times were first processed using the 1.5IQR rule, by which times above 6536 ms were identified as outliers and removed from further analysis. Figure 2 shows the median and quartile distribution of the task times. A within-subjects ANOVA test identified a significant effect of style on task time at the $p < .05$ level [$F(3, 4) = 8.032, p < .001$]. Pair-wise t-tests, with a Holm corrected p level, identified significant difference in the task times between Style A (1960 ms) and the other Styles; B (2434 ms), C (2452 ms) and D (2704 ms) [all $p < .001$]. No other significant differences in task times were identified.

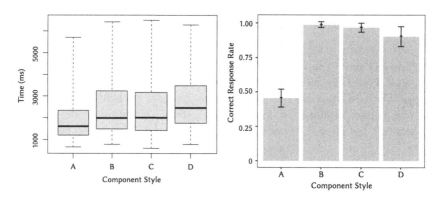

Fig. 2. Left: task time per component (Outliers removed). Right: mean percentage correct answers per component style. Error bars indicate standard error of the mean

The results were further analyzed to identify if any bias towards *on* or *off* state was present, e.g., bias in spatial perception due to left-to-right reading direction [1], or, in the case of Style D, inner-outer bias. For Styles B and C the observed differences were negligible, whilst for Style D a Chi-square tests of independence for showed that there was no significant association between component state and correct response, $\chi^2(1, N = 150) = 1.4, p = .23$. For component Style A there was a clear bias towards perception that the switch was in the *on* state, with 111/150 (74%) of answers responding in the positive sense.

4   Discussion and Conclusion

Compared to the other component styles, switch style A presented a much more challenging case to participants, requiring the absolute estimation of a grayscale shade without any reference. When displayed on a white background, participants tended to overestimate the darkness of the shade, with 74% of answers reporting the switch to be in the *on* state, rather than the expected 50%. The primary cause of this phenomena is the influence of the white background. Prior works have mitigated such issues by presenting grayscale samples on a grayscale noise pattern background [7]. However, our use of a white background is more representative of actual usage within a UI and highlights a potential problem when using this style of component.

We acknowledge that our study was limited by the number of participants. Although our study design represented a good initial approach, it lacked the sensitivity needed to identify subtle differences between the performance of the alternative UI component designs. In future this could be improved, e.g. by limiting the amount of time each component is visible.

Acknowledgements. This work has been supported by the European Union's Horizon 2020 Programme under grant no. 760973, DecoChrom.

References

1. Afsari, Z., Ossandón, J.P., König, P.: The dynamic effect of reading direction habit on spatial asymmetry of image perception. J. Vis. **16**(11), 8 (2016)
2. Buchner, A., Baumgartner, N.: Text-background polarity affects performance irrespective of ambient illumination and colour contrast. Ergonomics **50**(7), 1036–1063 (2007)
3. Colley, A., Tikka, P., Huhtala, J., Häkkilä, J.: Investigating text legibility in mobile ui: a case study comparing automated vs. user study based evaluation. In: Proceedings of International Conference on Making Sense of Converging Media, pp. 304–306 (2013)
4. Stereo Optical Company, Inc.: Functional acuity contrast test (FACT), March 2018
5. Jensen, W., Colley, A., Häkkilä, J., Pinheiro, C., Löchtefeld, M.: TransPrint: a method for fabricating flexible transparent free-form displays. In: Advances in Human-Computer Interaction 2019 (2019)
6. Liu, L., Peng, S., Wen, W., Sheng, P.: Paperlike thermochromic display. Appl. Phys. Lett. **90**(21), 213508 (2007)
7. Matejka, J., Glueck, M., Grossman, T., Fitzmaurice, G.: The effect of visual appearance on the performance of continuous sliders and visual analogue scales. In: Proceedings of the 2016 CHI Conference on Human Factors in Computing Systems, CHI 2016, pp. 5421–5432. ACM, New York (2016). https://doi.org/10.1145/2858036.2858063
8. Mayr, S., Buchner, A.: After-effects of TFT-LCD display polarity and display colour on the detection of low-contrast objects. Ergonomics **53**(7), 914–925 (2010)
9. Peiris, R.L., Nanayakkara, S.: PaperPixels: a toolkit to create paper-based displays. In: Proceedings of the 26th Australian Computer-Human Interaction Conference on Designing Futures: The Future of Design, OzCHI 2014, pp. 498–504. ACM, New York (2014). https://doi.org/10.1145/2686612.2686691. http://doi.acm.org/10.1145/2686612.2686691
10. Wang, A.H., Chen, M.T.: Effects of polarity and luminance contrast on visual performance and VDT display quality. Int. J. Ind. Ergon. **25**(4), 415–421 (2000)

Factors Influencing Trust Assessment in Technology

Sonia Sousa[1,2($\boxtimes$)] and Gabriela Beltrão[1]

[1] School of Digital Technologies, Tallinn University, Tallinn, Estonia
scs@tlu.ee, gbeltrao@tlu.ee
[2] University of Trás-os-Montes e Alto Douro (UTAD), Vila Real, Portugal

Abstract. This study presents exploratory research on how to measure perceived Trust in technology across culture. Builds from a validated Human-Computer Trust Model (HCTM) questionnaire (12 items) to efficiently measure users' predispositions to trust a technological artefact (e.g. WhatsApp). This approach aims to provide results that are not tied to a specific context while also focusing on underexplored populations. Two central research questions guided this research: RQ1: Can the Human-Computer Trust Scale (HCTS) be used to map trust behaviors across different cultures? And RQ2: Can the Human-Computer Trust scale be used to support trustworthy design practices? This research aimed first to gain new insights on how to measure users Trust in technology across-culture and second, reflect how useful the trust scale is to map user's Trust in a system. The study contemplates designers (n = 5) and users (n = 91). Results indicate that the Human-Computer Trust scale (HCTS) can be a useful, easy-to-use tool to map users trust predispositions but needs to be complemented with additional guidance on how to analyze and interpret the results. Same regards on mapping trust behaviors across culture if analyzed with complementary indicators like gender differences, privacy perception.

Keywords: Trust in technology · User research · Human factors · User experience

1 Introduction

In this fast-changing post-truth era context [12] trust plays a decisive role. Trusting can affect users' acceptance, and uptake [10] of technology and determine its adoption. Although one of the major issues in trust research in technology is the failure to recognize the construct's subjective and multi-dimensional nature [14,22]. Trust, in fact, can be interpreted from different lenses affecting how we assess its characteristics and influences in users interactions. Despite that, few insights highlight that difference or focus on the effects of trust when studying a human-artefact relationship [1,15,20]. More, detrimentally of the default mainstream attention given to ethics, privacy and security, we continue to feel threatened and not know how our data is being used or misused [17,21].

© IFIP International Federation for Information Processing 2021
Published by Springer Nature Switzerland AG 2021
C. Ardito et al. (Eds.): INTERACT 2021, LNCS 12936, pp. 416–420, 2021.
https://doi.org/10.1007/978-3-030-85607-6_49

This has given more importance to studying the trust effects in technology. For instance, on how to identify gender differences [2,3,23] or what characteristics can affect propensity trust among individuals. In the literature since Muir & Moray [16] study on how to measure trust in automation other studies emerged like: Empirically derived (ED) [9], Human-Computer Trust (HTC) [13], SHAPE Automation Trust Index (SATI) [4,11]. However, the oversupply of model and a "mixed conceptualization" makes it difficult for non-experts to choose and apply the adequate measurement. The Human-Computer Trust Scale (HCTS) analyzed in this study, besides being recent (2019), demonstrated to be reliable as it went through a rigorous empirical testing process [8]. Assessing the scale validity in four distinctive technological applications - E-Voting, Siri and two futuristic scenarios home for life and futures schools [6,7,22]. It portrays perceived trust in technology through 3 main attributes: Risk Perception, Competence, and Benevolence. Thus the reason for adopting it in this study.

2   Method

This study is guided by two central research questions: RQ1: Can the Human-Computer Trust scale (HCTS) be used to map trust behaviors across different cultures? along with RQ2: Can the Human-Computer Trust scale (HCTS) be used to support trustworthy design practices? Two main research focuses were taken in consideration here: (1) deploying a cross-cultural online survey focused on mapping trust behaviors across three countries, Brazil, Portugal, and Mozambique. (2) measuring the usefulness of the HCTS to support trustworthy design practices.

The survey aim was on assessing users' trust in a single object, WhatsApp. The technological object was present as a journey map usage scenario. The reason for choosing WhatsApp included it popularity, and since Facebook owned it in 2016, some concerns raised regarding recent privacy changes and its potential use for phishing and misinformation. The survey included a total of 31 questions. The HTCS psychometric instrument (12 items) in Portuguese [18] and complementary questions like demographics (e.g. country, age range, gender, and WhatsApp usage); and questions measuring users? adoption [5] and Privacy concerns and awareness [19]. Convenience sampling was used for data collection during April and May 2021. A total of 91 responses were analysed. The majority of the respondents are from Portugal (58.2%), then from Brazil (23,1%) and Mozambique (18.7%). 59,3% were females, 34,6% males and 1,1% non-binary respondent, not considered in the analysis because of low representativeness. Their age ranges grouped according to generations ranges - 62,6% from Generation Z (up to 24 years old), 25,3% Millennials (between 25 and 40 years old), 10,9% from Generation X (41 to 56 years old), and 1,1% Baby Boomer (57 or more years old), which was also not considered.

The design study aim was to understand to what extend the HCTS can be useful to support design practices. We invited five designers to apply the instrument and observed how well they understood the trust assessment mechanism and reasoning for their evaluation choices, goal, stimuli. Including how easy it was for them to report the results and gather insights on user's trust in a system for their design process. Those observation procedures were followed by contextual laddering interviews. Among the participants, the majority had at least two or more years of design experience in the Human-Computer Interaction field. Their tasks included using the HCTS to evaluate users trust in a technological artefact, for instance, voice user interface systems (e.g. Google Home), contact tracing app (e.g. Hoia.me), social media applications (e.g. Facebook).

3   Results and Discussion

To understand the extent that the HCTS can be used to map trust behaviors across different cultures (RQ1). The cross-cultural survey results revealed that the overall score on trust in WhatApp among the 91 responses was considered low but satisfactory [M = 3.24 in a 5 points Likert scale, SD = .79; CV = .79]. Also helped to identify the most problematic construct - the Risk Perception (RP) [M = 1.09; SD = 1.09; CV1.19], that score very low rate, followed by Benevolence (BEN) [M = 3.06; SD = 1.16; CV = 1.13] and Competence (COM) [M = 4.00; SD = .96; CV = .92] is consider the less concerning. Then the detailed analyzis by country revealed no significant differences, although Portugal [M = 3.50, SD = .53] and Mozambique [M = 3.50, SD = .53] had a significantly higher Trust Score than Brazil [M = 3.12, SD = .64]. It should be noted that during the analyzis as the sample included more Participants from Portugal, and to ensure that each country surveyed had an equivalent representation, the sample (n = 91) was weighted by country of approximately one third. Regarding the trust difference across genders, results indicated that female's trust was slightly higher than males. However, the difference was not statistically significant (t(87) = 0.95, p = .34). Results per generation confirm that although not all groups indicated significant differences, an independent t-tests, revealed that Generation Z (M = 3.51, SD = .70) has the highest Trust Score, which is significantly higher than Millennials' (M = 2.90, SD = .73), t(73) = 3.66, p ≤ .01. Generation Z had also higher Trust Scores than Generation X (M = 3.11, SD = .94), but the difference was not statistically significant, nor was the difference between Generation X and Millennials. Still, these results are enough to demonstrate that there are significant differences in trust scores between the groups.

Additionally, the design study results helped generate new insights on the individual necessities of the instrument to support trustworthy design practices (RQ2). When asked how the instrument helped gain new insights on users trust in technology, the majority agreed that it was helpful, practical and easy to apply. However, some consider the results analyzis to be confusing and difficult to interpret. The instrument needs additional explanation on how to perform the data analyzis and interpretation of the results. Including more guidance on how the overall trust score and each construct results can guide them through their design in build trustworthy design processes.

4   Conclusion

In conclusion, although some designers considered to be challenging to understand and interpret the results, the majority agreed that the scale is easy to use and valuable. Highlighted points are the fact of being not technical in nature, practical, and simple to apply. Results also revealed that the HCTS could be used to map trust behaviors across cultures if analyzed with complementary indicators. Findings also highlighted the complex nature of the topic and the need to provide reliable and simple to use methods to facilitate further explorative studies that can explore cross cultural factor like gender and generation differences. The cross-cultural survey results, for example, contradicted the authors' expectations that the Portuguese population trusts more the Whatsapp application when compared with Brazilians. Also indicated a link between contextual factors like gender and user generations and their willingness to trust a specific object [3]. In light of this, designers and technologists should consider users' mapping user's Trust in a system during their design process.

References

1. Benbasat, I., Wang, W.: Trust in and adoption of online recommendation agents. J. Assoc. Inf. Syst. **6**(3), 4 (2005)
2. Buchan, N.R., Croson, R.T., Solnick, S.: Trust and gender: an examination of behavior and beliefs in the investment game? J. Econ. Behav. Organ. **68**(3/4), 466–76 (2008)
3. Byrnes, J.P., Miller, D.C., Schafer, W.D.: Gender differences in risk taking: a meta-analysis. Psychol. Bull. **125**(3), 367 (1999)
4. Goillau, P., Kelly, C., Boardman, M., Jeannot, E.: Guidelines for trust in future ATM systems-measures (2003)
5. Goldsmith, R.E., Freiden, J.B., Eastman, J.K.: The generality/specificity issue in consumer innovativeness research. Technovation **15**(10), 601–612 (1995)
6. Gulati, S., Sousa, S., Lamas, D.: Modelling trust: an empirical assessment. In: Bernhaupt, R., Dalvi, G., Joshi, A., K. Balkrishan, D., O'Neill, J., Winckler, M. (eds.) INTERACT 2017. LNCS, vol. 10516, pp. 40–61. Springer, Cham (2017). https://doi.org/10.1007/978-3-319-68059-0_3
7. Gulati, S., Sousa, S., Lamas, D.: Modelling trust in human-like technologies. In: Proceedings of the 9th Indian Conference on Human Computer Interaction, pp. 1–10 (2018)
8. Gulati, S., Sousa, S., Lamas, D.: Design, development and evaluation of a human-computer trust scale. Behav. Inf. Technol. **38**(10), 1004–1015 (2019)
9. Jian, J.Y., Bisantz, A.M., Drury, C.G.: Foundations for an empirically determined scale of trust in automated systems. Int. J. Cogn. Ergon. **4**(1), 53–71 (2000)
10. Kassim, E.S., Jailani, S.F.A.K., Hairuddin, H., Zamzuri, N.H.: Information system acceptance and user satisfaction: the mediating role of trust. Procedia Soc. Behav. Sci. **57**, 412–418 (2012)
11. Kelly, C., Boardman, M., Goillau, P., Jeannot, E.: Guidelines for trust in future ATM systems: a literature review (2003)
12. Lewandowsky, S., Ecker, U.K., Cook, J.: Beyond misinformation: understanding and coping with the "post-truth" era. J. Appl. Res. Mem. Cogn. **6**(4), 353–369 (2017)

13. Madsen, M., Gregor, S.: Measuring human-computer trust. In: 11th Australasian Conference on Information Systems, vol. 53, pp. 6–8. Citeseer (2000)
14. Mayer, R.C., Davis, J.H., Schoorman, F.D.: An integrative model of organizational trust. Acad. Manag. Rev. **20**(3), 709–734 (1995)
15. Mcknight, D.H., Carter, M., Thatcher, J.B., Clay, P.F.: Trust in a specific technology: an investigation of its components and measures. ACM Trans. Manage. Inf. Syst. **2**(2), 12:1–12:25 (2011). https://doi.org/10.1145/1985347.1985353. http://doi.acm.org/10.1145/1985347.1985353
16. Muir, B.M., Moray, N.: Trust in automation. Part II. Experimental studies of trust and human intervention in a process control simulation. Ergonomics **39**(3), 429–460 (1996)
17. Oper, T., Sousa, S.: User attitudes towards Facebook: perception and reassurance of trust (Estonian case study). In: Stephanidis, C., Antona, M. (eds.) HCII 2020. CCIS, vol. 1226, pp. 224–230. Springer, Cham (2020). https://doi.org/10.1007/978-3-030-50732-9_30
18. Pinto, A., Sousa, S., Silva, C., Coelho, P.: Adaptation and validation of the HCTM scale into human-robot interaction Portuguese context: a study of measuring trust in human-robot interactions. In: Proceedings of the 11th Nordic Conference on Human-Computer Interaction: Shaping Experiences, Shaping Society, pp. 1–4 (2020)
19. Rogers, E.M., Singhal, A., Quinlan, M.M.: Diffusion of Innovations. Routledge (2014)
20. Söllner, M., Leimeister, J.M.: What we really know about antecedents of trust: a critical review of the empirical information systems literature on trust. Psychology of Trust: New Research, D. Gefen, Verlag/Publisher: Nova Science Publishers (2013)
21. Sousa, S., Bates, N.: Factors influencing content credibility in Facebook's news feed. Hum.-Intell. Syst. Integr. 1–10 (2021)
22. Sousa, S., Lamas, D., Dias, P.: Value creation through trust in technological-mediated social participation. Technol. Innov. Educ. (2014)
23. Yamagishi, T., Yamagishi, M.: Trust and commitment in the United States and Japan. Motiv. Emot. **18**(2), 129–166 (1994)

FGFlick: Augmenting Single-Finger Input Vocabulary for Smartphones with Simultaneous Finger and Gaze Flicks

Yuki Yamato$^{(\boxtimes)}$, Yutaro Suzuki, and Shin Takahashi

University of Tsukuba, Tsukuba, Ibaraki, Japan
{yamato,ysuzuki,shin}@iplab.cs.tsukuba.ac.jp

Abstract. *FGFlick* is an interactive technique featuring simultaneous single-finger operation and a gaze. The user flicks a smartphone and moves their gaze linearly. FGFlick thus augments the single-finger input vocabulary. As a result of the evaluation of the FGFlick gestures, we achieved success rates of 84.0%.

Keywords: FGFlick · Single-finger input vocabulary · Flick gesture · Gaze input · Interaction techniques · Mobile devices

1 Introduction

Smartphone users favor one-handed operation [4], but it causes the limited thumb reach problem—distant bezels and physical buttons are hard to reach [1]. The one-handed operation also restricts multi-finger inputs. It is necessary to increase the single-finger input vocabulary to allow one-handed operation with a stable grip.

Fig. 1. FGFlick overview. The user flicks with a finger on a smartphone while he also moves his gaze linearly.

In this work, we developed *FGFlick*, an interactive technique that simultaneously uses a single-finger operation and an explicit gaze (Fig. 1). The user flicks a smartphone and moves their gaze linearly. By combining finger and gaze flicks, FGFlick augments the single-finger input vocabulary. Here, we briefly describe the design and implementation of FGFlick.

© IFIP International Federation for Information Processing 2021
Published by Springer Nature Switzerland AG 2021
C. Ardito et al. (Eds.): INTERACT 2021, LNCS 12936, pp. 421–425, 2021.
https://doi.org/10.1007/978-3-030-85607-6_50

2   Related Work

Previous work proposed combined hand and eye movements to improve the manipulation of laptop computers and wearable devices [3,8]. The works of Pfeuffer et al. [5–7] forwarded a touch to a gazed point on a tablet; this permitted point selection and cursor manipulation around the point. They sought principally to attain unreachable areas of the screen. However, we sought to augment the input vocabulary.

The work of Elleuch et al. [2] proposed a method to interact with mobile devices using a combination of gazes and static hand gestures; we employed finger flicks instead. Wang et al. [9] developed the BlyncSync gesture set (synchronous blinks and touches); we employed simple gaze gestures.

3   FGFlick

FGFlick is an interactive technique featuring simultaneous single-finger operation and a gaze (Fig. 1). The user flicks a smartphone while moving the gaze. We have designated this gaze gesture as a "gaze flick". Because finger and gaze flicks must be performed simultaneously, they are distinguished from conventional flicks and involuntary eye movements. A gaze flick is a linear gaze. Compared with compound gazes, a gaze flick is rapid and does not require visual guidance. By combining the directions of finger and gaze flicks, FGFlick augments the single-finger input vocabulary of smartphones.

FGFlick has various interaction examples. As an alternative to a physical button, an FGFlick gesture is used to capture screenshots; the user is not required to hold the power button and the volume button simultaneously to get screenshots, as one of the traditional ways. FGFlick can also be employed to manipulate unreachable targets. We assign FGFlick gestures in the same direction to "Back" and "Open". The user can navigate back to a photo gallery from a screen displaying a selected image by executing *Flick-Right-Gaze-Right*. The user can open the Notification Center by executing *Flick-Left-Gaze-Left*.

4   Prototype Implementation

We used an iPhone X and ARKit[1] to implement eye-tracking and the FGFlick recognition system.

4.1   Recognition of FGFlick Gestures

The system starts FGFlick recognition when it detects a finger flick. Figure 2 shows the finger flick and simultaneous gaze flick. When the system detects a finger flick, it notes the start and end times. It then calculates the start and end times of a possible gaze flick: $G_{\text{start}} = F_{\text{start}} - \textit{offset}_{\text{start}}$, and $G_{\text{end}} =$

---

[1] https://developer.apple.com/documentation/arkit.

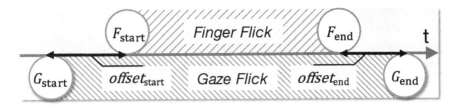

- F_{start} / F_{end}: the start and the end position of the finger flick on the screen.
- G_{start}: the start position of the gaze flick before offset$_{start}$ from F_{start}.
- G_{end}: the end position of the gaze flick after offset$_{end}$ from F_{end}.
- offset$_{start}$ / offset$_{end}$: the offset between F_{start} and G_{start} and between F_{end} and G_{end}.

Fig. 2. A part of FGFlick recognition parameters.

F_{end} + $offset_{end}$. Based on preliminary experiments, we set $offset_{start}$ to 0 ms and $offset_{end}$ to 66.8 ms.

Next, the system decides whether the finger flick is an FGFlick gesture or a conventional flick, depending on whether the gaze flick is explicit or simply an involuntary eye movement. In preliminary experiments, we found that a gaze flick (an explicit gesture) was longer than involuntary eye movements during conventional flicks. Thus, we distinguish gaze flicks by the length of eye movement during the finger flick (d_{gaze}; the linear distance travelled from G_{start} to G_{end}). If the length is shorter than a threshold (d_{th}), the system regards the eye movement as involuntary and the finger flick is thus a conventional flick; otherwise, the system regards the eye movement as a gaze flick. We set d_{th} to 218 pt based on preliminary experiments.

The FGFlick gestures are classified by the directions of the finger and gaze flicks. For finger flicks, the system calculates the angle (θ_{finger}) of F_{start} to F_{end} and assigns it to one of four directions. For gaze flicks, the system calculates the angle (θ_{gaze}) of G_{start} to G_{end} and assigns it to one of four directions.

4.2   Preliminary Evaluation

We evaluated the accuracy of the FGFlick recognition system. We enlisted eight volunteers (P1–P8; mean age, 23.0 years [range, 21–25 years]; six males). We asked them to perform 20 types of FGFlick gestures, four finger flicks (up, down, left, right) multiplied by four gaze flicks (up, down, left, right) + "Keep." All volunteers grasped an iPhone X and performed each FGFlick gesture once in one session; they completed five sessions in total. We thus obtained 800 gestures: $= 8_{volunteers} \times 5_{sessions} \times 20_{gestures}$.

Figure 3 shows the confusion matrix. The success rate was 84.0%. "Down" was often mistaken for "Keep" because many volunteers positioned the device lower than the face. Thus, they initially looked down and lacked the ability to gaze "Down" further. We plan to change the "Down" distance threshold.

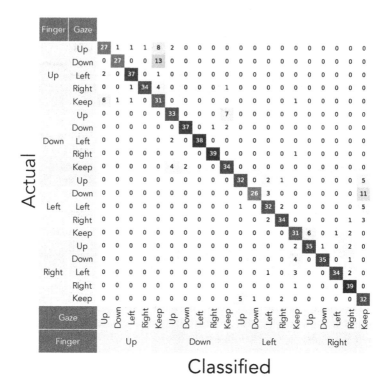

Fig. 3. The confusion matrix of the FGFlick gestures.

5 Conclusion and Future Work

FGFlick is an interactive technique featuring simultaneous single-finger operation and a gaze. The user flicks a smartphone and moves their gaze linearly. FGFlick thus augments the single-finger input vocabulary. We will further evaluate accuracy and usability, then explore whether users develop eye fatigue.

References

1. Bergstrom-Lehtovirta, J., Oulasvirta, A.: Modeling the functional area of the thumb on mobile touchscreen surfaces. In: Proceedings of the SIGCHI Conference on Human Factors in Computing Systems, CHI 2014, pp. 1991–2000. Association for Computing Machinery, New York (2014). https://doi.org/10.1145/2556288.2557354
2. Elleuch, H., Wali, A., Samet, A., Alimi, A.M.: Interacting with mobile devices by fusion eye and hand gestures recognition systems based on decision tree approach. In: Verikas, A., Radeva, P., Nikolaev, D.P., Zhang, W., Zhou, J. (eds.) Ninth International Conference on Machine Vision (ICMV 2016), vol. 10341, pp. 62–66. International Society for Optics and Photonics, SPIE (2017). https://doi.org/10.1117/12.2269010

3. Nagamatsu, T., Yamamoto, M., Sato, H.: MobiGaze: development of a gaze interface for handheld mobile devices. In: CHI 2010 Extended Abstracts on Human Factors in Computing Systems, CHI EA 2010, pp. 3349–3354. Association for Computing Machinery, New York (2010). https://doi.org/10.1145/1753846.1753983

4. Ng, A., Brewster, S.A., Williamson, J.H.: Investigating the effects of encumbrance on one- and two- handed interactions with mobile devices. In: Proceedings of the SIGCHI Conference on Human Factors in Computing Systems, CHI 2014, pp. 1981–1990. Association for Computing Machinery, New York (2014). https://doi.org/10.1145/2556288.2557312

5. Pfeuffer, K., Alexander, J., Chong, M.K., Gellersen, H.: Gaze-touch: combining gaze with multi-touch for interaction on the same surface. In: Proceedings of the 27th Annual ACM Symposium on User Interface Software and Technology, UIST 2014, pp. 509–518. Association for Computing Machinery, New York (2014). https://doi.org/10.1145/2642918.2647397

6. Pfeuffer, K., Alexander, J., Chong, M.K., Zhang, Y., Gellersen, H.: Gaze-shifting: direct-indirect input with pen and touch modulated by gaze. In: Proceedings of the 28th Annual ACM Symposium on User Interface Software & Technology, UIST 2015, pp. 373–383. Association for Computing Machinery, New York (2015). https://doi.org/10.1145/2807442.2807460

7. Pfeuffer, K., Gellersen, H.: Gaze and touch interaction on tablets. In: Proceedings of the 29th Annual Symposium on User Interface Software and Technology, UIST 2016, pp. 301–311. Association for Computing Machinery, New York (2016). https://doi.org/10.1145/2984511.2984514

8. Rivu, S., Abdrabou, Y., Mayer, T., Pfeuffer, K., Alt, F.: GazeButton: enhancing buttons with eye gaze interactions. In: Proceedings of the 11th ACM Symposium on Eye Tracking Research & Applications, ETRA 2019, pp. 1–7. Association for Computing Machinery, New York (2019). https://doi.org/10.1145/3317956.3318154

9. Wang, B., Grossman, T.: BlyncSync: enabling multimodal smartwatch gestures with synchronous touch and blink. In: Proceedings of the 2020 CHI Conference on Human Factors in Computing Systems, CHI 2020, pp. 1–14. Association for Computing Machinery, New York (2020). https://doi.org/10.1145/3313831.3376132

Field of View Limitation-Driven Design of a Mixed Reality Game for Heritage Sites

Giuseppe Caggianese[(⊠)] and Luigi Gallo

Institute for High Performance Computing and Networking,
National Research Council of Italy, Naples, Italy
{giuseppe.caggianese,luigi.gallo}@icar.cnr.it

Abstract. In this work, we describe the design of a customized user interface (UI) for a mixed reality application in a heritage site. The visuals, widgets and spatial interaction techniques have been customized to improve the user experience without diverting the user's attention by minimizing the effect of the limited field of view (FOV) of the see-through head-mounted display (HMD) used, Microsoft HoloLens v1. The approach consists in using diegetic elements that are coherent with the narrative of the heritage site, and widgets and augmented layers always entirely included in the FOV of the see-through display.

Keywords: Mixed reality · User interface design · Limited FOV

1 Introduction and Background

Emerging Mixed Reality (MR) technologies, which aim at a symbiotic blending of the real world with the virtual world [7], present many exciting opportunities for the cultural heritage (CH) sector. Such a merging of the real and the virtual, combined with the opportunity to realize immersive and interactive experiences, allows a creative enhancement, extension and dissemination of cultural content. In this context, curators often want to provide visitors to the physical exhibition spaces with a new way to engage with their collection. MR technologies, based on innovative interaction paradigms, could enrich these spaces as shown by the studies of Chrysanthi et al. [3], Okura et al. [8] and Brancati et al. [2] In addition, serious games could improve the knowledge transfer in the CH, since they offer the possibility of realizing cultural content personalized by age group and of enhancing motivation towards acquiring new knowledge about the heritage site [5,6].

Supported by the project Parco Archeologico Urbano di Napoli (RIPA-PAUN), POR Campania FESR 2014/2020.

Electronic supplementary material The online version of this chapter (https://doi.org/10.1007/978-3-030-85607-6_51) contains supplementary material, which is available to authorized users.

Fig. 1. (left to right, top to bottom) Used HMD's narrow FOV able to shows only a portion of the scene which for this reason was hidden under the physical floor; the sphere widget, fully visible in the FOV of the device, that collides the floor opening a breach over the archaeological excavations; manipulation of the collected finding, the text shows the finding name *Puleggia di bozzello* and the question *Do you think it could belong to the ship?*; interactive panels for the presentation of cultural information related to the artifacts collected.

This paper describes some of the compelling opportunities and challenges involved in realizing a MR game to improve knowledge transfer in the CH. In particular, certain strategies aimed at mitigating the adverse effects associated with the narrow FOV of most commonly used see-through HMDs are proposed and discussed. We have chosen to use Microsoft HoloLens v1 which, according to Hammady et al. [4] exhibits a FOV of 34° that must be considered in the design of a spatial UI. This work aims at leveraging custom design strategies to improve the user's sense of presence, reducing the effect of the FOV limitation, regardless of the HMD used.

2   MR Game Overview

The MR game recreates the setting of the archaeological excavations of the ancient Roman port of Naples, where archaeologists have found the artifacts displayed in the exhibition. The exhibition includes objects of daily life and equipment of the ship to maneuver the sails. 3D digitized scans of some of these artifacts have been used in the game together with reconstruction data from one of the Roman ships found nearby [1].

The game is a location-aware applications in which the synthetic scene has been incorporated into the surrounding environment and the cultural information proposed has been organized in diegetic elements adaptive to the real environment, the user's position, and the achievement of the game objectives. The game's mission is to spatially explore the augmented archaeological site to identify and group together all the digital reproductions of the artifacts displayed, so as to create a personal collection of the individual findings to enhance an understanding of their functions and uses in the past time period. The virtual environment designed to augment the physical one has been realized with a double functionality, aimed at mitigating the limited FOV of the visor and at introducing engaging game strategies. The digital reconstruction of the archaeological excavation (see Fig. 1 on top left) is hidden from the user because it is situated under the line of the floor. The user can explore the digital environment, one section at a time, by manipulating a widget, a digital sphere that, when placed in contact with the physical floor, opens a breach through which it is possible to gain a glimpse of the reconstruction of the underlying archaeological excavation (see Fig. 1 on top right). Through the sphere widget, the visitor is also able to locate and group together reconstructions of the findings. Each time one of the objects is found by the user, it can be acquired and placed in the collection. However, before being placed in the collection, the artifact needs to be catalogued as belonging, or not, to the shipwreck that can be glimpsed at the base of the excavation reconstruction (see Fig. 1 on bottom left).

Finally, for any of the collected artifacts, it is possible to request additional information at a virtual desk. The desk also shows the search progress (e.g., how many objects have been found), the cataloguing work already carried out correctly during the game and, among those already found, the objects that belong to the ship (see Fig. 1 on bottom right).

3   Interaction Techniques Design and Widgets

The user can use the gaze to point to an element in the scene and the air tap gesture to perform the click and to grab and move the interactive elements. The most compelling aspect of the design phase involved identifying an interaction mechanism that could combine gaming mechanisms with the need to mitigate the limited FOV offered by the device employed. As mentioned, the game settings are initially hidden under the physical floor, and the user has to interact with a sphere widget provided to explore them. The designed interaction technique binds the vision to the virtual object's position. The sphere becomes a manipulable tool used to access cultural information. The advantage is that, when the user manipulates this tool, she/he naturally places it at the center of his FOV, without perceiving its limitations in space. The user can move the sphere in the physical environment until it collides with the part of the floor where she/he wants to open a breach. At that point, along the section of the sphere that intersects with the floor, the scene below will become visible and the user can start exploring it. To interact with the sphere and move it along the physical environment, the user should point at it with her/his gaze and maintain the air tap gesture to simulate a grab of the object. Once grabbed, the sphere will follow the user's hand movements. The sphere pointed at with the gaze can be enlarged or reduced by increasing or decreasing, respectively, the distance between the two hands used to maintain the air tap gesture. The maximum size of the sphere is continuously monitored to ensure that it is always completely visible within the FOV of the MR HMD. In a preliminary evaluation of the system, we observed that the use of the sphere widget leads the user to interact with it also in an indirect way. Users alternate the movement of the sphere with the variation of her/his point of view: the former action in order to start the exploration of an area; the latter to refine the search for findings by looking in the surrounding area.

Finally, the information submitted to the user is organized in interactive information panels linked to the user position or anchored into the physical space. Using panels is coherent with the methods of presenting information usually adopted by museums. Moreover, the panels have been chosen because, thanks to the contrast between text and background, they are easily readable, even in the presence of cluttered backgrounds.

4 Conclusions

In this paper we have introduced a novel MR serious game for the exploration of a heritage site. The focus has been on the design of a custom UI, based on the HoloLens device, aimed at minimizing the limitations of the FOV of the device itself. Empirical studies on the perceived effectiveness of the FOV-aware widgets are currently ongoing.

References

1. Boetto, G., Poveda, P.: La restitution de napoli c. un navire romain à tableau. Dossiers d'Archéologie (364), 64–65 (2014)
2. Brancati, N., Caggianese, G., Frucci, M., Gallo, L., Neroni, P.: Experiencing touchless interaction with augmented content on wearable head-mounted displays in cultural heritage applications. Pers. Ubiquit. Comput. **21**(2), 203–217 (2016). https://doi.org/10.1007/s00779-016-0987-8
3. Chrysanthi, A., Papadopoulos, C., Frankland, T., Earl, G.: 'Tangible pasts': user-centred design of a mixed reality application for cultural heritage. In: Archaeology in the Digital Era, pp. 31–39. Amsterdam University Press (2014)
4. Hammady, R., Ma, M., Strathearn, C.: User experience design for mixed reality: a case study of Hololens in museum. Int. J. Technol. Mark. **13**(3–4), 354–375 (2019)
5. Liarokapis, F., Petridis, P., Andrews, D., de Freitas, S.: Multimodal serious games technologies for cultural heritage. In: Ioannides, M., Magnenat-Thalmann, N., Papagiannakis, G. (eds.) Mixed Reality and Gamification for Cultural Heritage, pp. 371–392. Springer, Cham (2017). https://doi.org/10.1007/978-3-319-49607-8_15

6. Malegiannaki, I.A., Daradoumis, T., Retalis, S.: Teaching cultural heritage through a narrative-based game. J. Comput. Cultural Heritage (JOCCH) **13**(4), 1–28 (2020)
7. Milgram, P., Kishino, F.: A taxonomy of mixed reality visual displays. IEICE Trans. Inf. Syst. **77**(12), 1321–1329 (1994)
8. Okura, F., Kanbara, M., Yokoya, N.: Mixed-reality world exploration using image-based rendering. J. Comput. Cultural Heritage (JOCCH) **8**(2), 1–26 (2015)

Human Olfactory Interface for Odor Modulation Utilizing Gas Adsorption and Desorption: Evaluation of Separation Performance of Odorous Substances in Adsorption Process

Kento Honda[1]([⊠]) [ID], Haruka Matsukura[2] [ID], Daisuke Iwai[1] [ID], Hiroshi Ishida[3] [ID], and Kosuke Sato[1] [ID]

[1] Osaka University, Osaka 560-8531, Japan
honda@sens.sys.es.osaka-u.ac.jp, {daisuke.iwai,sato}@sys.es.osaka-u.ac.jp
[2] The University of Electro-Communications, Tokyo 182-8585, Japan
matsukura@uec.ac.jp
[3] Tokyo University of Agriculture and Technology, Tokyo 184-8588, Japan
h_ishida@cc.tuat.ac.jp

Abstract. This paper proposes a human olfactory interface that modulates airborne odors and enables the users to selectively sniff only the odors that they want. Air containing odors is collected and exposed onto plural types of adsorbents for separation and concentration of odorous substances contained in the odors. The desorbed substances from the adsorbents are mixed at different ratios from the original odors for modulation. This paper describes preliminary work on the evaluation of separation performance of odorous substances in adsorption process. As a provisional target, two kinds of odorous substances, 1-Nonanol and (−)-Carvone, were selected. 1-Nonanol smells like citronella oil and (−)-Carvone smells like spearmint. An odor generated by mixing these two substances smells a similar odor of (+)-Carvone which smells like sweet caraway. In order to separate each substance from the mixture, adsorbents were selected based on the molecular diameters and adsorption capability. Sensory tests with the triangle test were conducted to assess the separation capability of the selected adsorbents. An expected performance was not observed. More detail investigation including quantitative measurement with a gas chromatography will be needed for future work.

Keywords: Olfactory interface · Olfaction · Odor

This work was supported in part by JSPS KAKENHI Grant Number 19K14947 and 19H02103.

1   Introduction

Odors affect human psychological status and performance [1]. Taking preferable odors for individuals into their daily life has great potential to improve the quality of life. On the contrary, there are many variety of products to remove unfavorable odors, including air purifiers and refresher sprays. However, as far as the authors know, there are no attempts to dynamically modulate odors by adjusting the proportion of chemical substances contained in the odors.

This research aims to develop a human olfactory interface system that can modulate airborne odors so as to allow the users to selectively sniff only the odors that they want. The development of the proposed system is inspired by our previous research on an odor amplifier using an adsorbent [2]. Figure 1 shows a conceptual diagram of the proposed system. An airborne odor including multiple odorous substances is introduced into multiple types of adsorbents with different adsorption characteristics for separation. When presenting a modulated odor, the proportion of the odorous substances contained in the odor are changed by controlling the amount of desorbed odorous substances from each adsorbent. This paper describes preliminary work on the evaluation of the separation performance in the adsorption process.

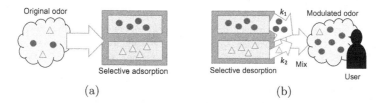

Fig. 1. Conceptual diagram of odor modulation. (a) Odorous substances in airborne odor are separated using multiple adsorbents with different adsorption characteristics. (b) Odor is modulated by adjusting each amounts of desorbed odorous substance.

2   Outline of Proposed System

The schematic diagram of the system is shown in Fig. 2. In the adsorption process of odorous substances, the airborne odor sucked using an air pump passes

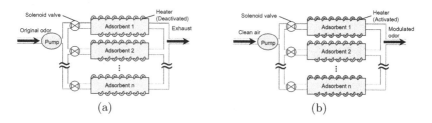

Fig. 2. Schematic diagram of the proposed system (a) in adsorption process to separate odorous substances and (b) in desorption process to presented a modulated odor.

through all adsorbents as shown in Fig. 2(a). In the desorption process, the flow rate of clean air sent into each adsorbrent is adjusted with a solenoid valve as shown in Fig. 2(b) in order to modulate the original odor by changing the proportion of odorous substances contained in the odor.

3   Selection of Adsorbents

As a provisional target, two kinds of chemical substances, 1-Nonanol and $(-)$-Carvone, were selected. 1-Nonanol smells like citronella oil and $(-)$-Carvone smells like spearmint. An odor generated by mixing these two substances smells a similar odor of $(+)$-Carvone which smells like sweet caraway. In order to separate each substance from the mixture of 1-Nonanol and $(-)$-Carvone, we decided to use synthetic zeolites because of availability and affordability.

Zeolites are microporous crystalline aluminosilicates that adsorb surrounding molecules [3]. Each zeolite has a specific size pores and can only adsorb molecules smaller than the size of the pores. The adsorbed molecules on zeolites can be desorb by heating them. As a result of manual calculation by the authors, the effective diameters of 1-Nonanol and $(-)$-Carvone are 0.18–1.33 nm and 0.62–1.11 nm, respectively. We selected a pellet type of commercially available synthetic zeolites, Molecular Sieves 3A, which is sold by Nacalai Tesque, Inc. The effective diameter of adsorbable molecules on to Molecular Sieves 3A is less than 0.3 nm. Therefore, we estimated that Molecular Sieves 3A adsorbs only 1-Nonanol.

4   Evaluation of Separation Performance

To examine the separation in the adsorption process, a mixture gas was generated by bubbling the mixture of liquid phase of 15 mL each of 1-Nonanol and $(-)$-Carvone with air at a flow rate of 2.0 L/min. The mixture gas was introduced through 2.0 g of Molecular Sieve 3A contained in a polyethylene tube (ϕ 20 mm, length 50 mm). We expected that the exhaust through the adsorbent contains $(-)$-Carvone only.

Sensory tests with the triangle odor bag method were conducted to check if our expectation is correct. The method is commonly used in Japan for olfactory-related sensory evaluation including determination of odor detection threshold [4]. Subjects of the method are instructed to compare the smell in each odor bag and to pick a bag that is different from the other two bags. The probability of the subjects' selections is statistically checked using the binomial test compared with that of random choice. Although chemical analysis equipment such a gas chromatograph is able to accurately quantify the contents of the exhaust, we chose conducting sensory tests for the evaluation in this research because the execution is relatively easier for us.

If there is no difference between the adsorption rate of 1-Nonanol and that of $(-)$-Carvone onto Molecular Sieves 3A, the exhaust is the same as the diluted mixture gas at a rate. We conducted sensory tests in which participants were instructed to compare the exhaust gas with diluted mixture gases. The diluted mixture gas was generated by bubbling the diluted liquid mixtures of 1-Nonanol and (−)-Carvone with liquid paraffin at four volume concentration levels, 10%, 1%, 0.5% and 0.1%.

Three odor bags were prepared for each trial. One contains the exhaust through the adsorbent, and the others contain the diluted mixture gas at one of the four concentration levels. A subject did the comparison with the three odor bags at each concentration level, which means that a subject conducted four trials each. The order of presented concentration were adjusted among the subjects to reduce the order effect. 8 subjects (21–25 years old) participated.

The identification rate of the exhaust at each concentration level is shown with the blue dot in Fig. 3. The subject significantly distinguished the exhaust at all the concentration levels, which suggests that adsorption characteristic of Molecular Sieves 3A differs between 1-Nonanol and (−)-Carvone.

For further investigation, we conducted other sensory tests using either 1-Nonanol or (−)-Carvone with the same procedure as the sensory test using the mixture gas as described above. The number of the subjects who participated in the sensory test was also 8. Several subjects participated in multiple tests. The age range of the subjects were also 21–25 years old. The identification rates are also shown in Fig. 3 as red triangles and orange rhombuses. We performed the binomial test under each condition to see if the accuracy rate was significantly higher than when the odors were indistinguishable. The identification rates of 1-Nonanol and (−)-Carvone are similar, although we expected that the identification rates of 1-Nonanol are similar to those of the mixture gas.

As a result of the sensory tests, an expected separation performance was not observed. However, the separation performance has not been denied with the results. We will continue further investigation including well-designed sensory tests and quantitative measurement using a gas chromatography.

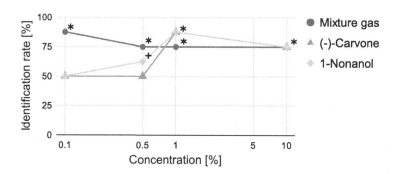

Fig. 3. Identification rates of the exhaust through adsorbent when comparing it with gas generated using diluted liquid substances. (∗: $p < 0.05$, +: $p < 0.1$)

5   Conclusions

The authors have attempted to develop an olfactory interface that can modulate airborne odors. This paper describes the experiments to evaluate the separation performance of odorous substances in the adsorption process. An estimated separation performance was not confirmed with the provisional adsorbent selected by the authors. Further investigation including measurement using a experimental equipment to obtain quantitative evaluation should be needed for future work.

References

1. Diego, M.A., et al.: Aromatherapy positively affects mood, EEG patterns of alertness and math computations. Int. J. Neurosci. **96**(3–4), 217–224 (1998). https://doi.org/10.3109/00207459808986469
2. Matsukura, H., Ishida, H.: Review on development of devices for amplifying human olfaction: approaches using real and virtual concentration method. Electron. Commun. Jpn. **102**, 55–60 (2018). https://doi.org/10.1002/ecj.12143
3. Davis, M.E., Lobo, R.F.: Zeolite and molecular sieve synthesis. Chem. Mater. **4**, 756–768 (1992). https://doi.org/10.1021/cm00022a005
4. Daikoku, S., Mitsuda, M., Tanamura, T., Uchiyama, K.: Measuring odor threshold using a simplified olfactory measurement method. J. Hum.-Environ. Syst. **21**(1), 1–8 (2019). https://doi.org/10.1618/jhes.21.1

Human-Centered Visual Interfaces for Image Retrieval: An Exploratory Study

Diogo Cruz[1](✉), Diogo Cabral[2], and Pedro F. Campos[1]

[1] ITI/LARSyS, University of Madeira, Funchal, Portugal
2030115@student.uma.pt, pedro.campos@iti.larsys.pt
[2] ITI/LARSyS, IST, University of Lisbon, Lisbon, Portugal
diogo.n.cabral@tecnico.ulisboa.pt

Abstract. The widespread use of digital cameras in mobile phones has led to an increase in the number of pictures captured and shared. However, the development of interfaces for visualizing image collections has not matched that growth. Most search methods are based on text descriptions and retrieve a large number of results on thumbnail 2D grids, which can be hard to analyze. Therefore, it is crucial to couple image retrieval with purposely designed interfaces. This paper covers the study of four different interfaces for the visualization of collections of images, including a regular 2D grid, a variable-size 2D grid, a pile of images, and a spiral. These interfaces were evaluated in a user test involving nine participants performing search tasks. We found that both grids exhibit higher usability and lower task times than the Pile and Spiral. The Variable Size Grid had lower usability scores than the Regular Grid, but it showed higher-quality task results and was preferred by the participants in this study.

Keywords: Visual search · Image visualization · Retrieval interfaces

1 Introduction

With the rise of digital cameras and the growing number of devices that use them, there has been a considerable increase in the number of images being captured. Thomee and Lew [17] claimed that finding optimal user interfaces for queries and results is one of the grand challenges for image retrieval. However, the study of novel ways to visualize collections of images has been quite limited. Most of the recent research has focused on improving search methods [1, 6, 19]. The works that proposed novel visualizations for image browsing and search [2, 8, 20] have failed to measure how the different visualizations affect human search and content analysis. While search methods can filter the images to retrieve, it is simply not enough in many cases. Therefore, it is crucial to couple image retrieval methods with purposely designed image visualization interfaces.

Electronic supplementary material The online version of this chapter (https://doi.org/10.1007/978-3-030-85607-6_53) contains supplementary material, which is available to authorized users.

C. Ardito et al. (Eds.): INTERACT 2021, LNCS 12936, pp. 436–441, 2021.
https://doi.org/10.1007/978-3-030-85607-6_53

2D grids with image thumbnails are the predominant interface in image search engines all these years but problematic for visualizing large datasets. André et al. [2] analyzed image browsing and concluded that interfaces should: support exploration; exploit thumbnail aesthetics; allow for search refinement and present its history; allow saving images for later.

Similarity functions can create a visualization of image sets [3, 10, 11]. Placing visually similar images close to each other has been proved to improve the time required to locate specific images [12]. Heesch and Rüger [8] present a visualization where the most relevant images are larger and near the center, and the least relevant are smaller and placed around. The authors also discuss another idea where the images are placed around a central point, forming a spiral. Additional research [7, 13, 18] has developed this idea further. More recent works [9, 14, 15, 21] have studied the possibility of visualizing images in virtual reality environments.

This work compares four different user interfaces for visualizing image collections: Regular Grid, Variable Size Grid, Pile and Spiral. Considering two different search tasks, we conducted a user test measuring the usability, the duration of each task, the quality of task results (Precision, Recall, and F-Measure), and users' preferences for each visualization.

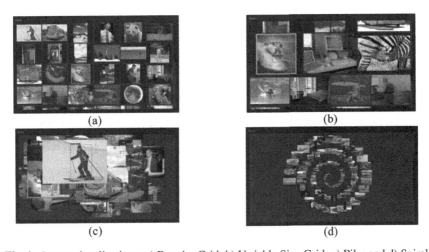

Fig. 1. Image visualizations: a) Regular Grid; b) Variable Size Grid; c) Pile; and d) Spiral

2   Visual Interfaces for Image Search

We developed four different user interfaces for visualizing collections of images as part of a visual search application: Regular Grid, Variable Size Grid, Pile and Spiral.

In a typical use case, the results are sorted by the confidence obtained from the visual search method. The sorting takes advantage of each interface to make sense according to their characteristics and make the most relevant results more prominent. Hovering over an image will show a tooltip with relevant information and a scaled-up version (also implemented in the other visualizations). The Regular Grid (Fig. 1a) is a standard scrollable 2D grid with image thumbnails and works as a baseline.

Then we developed a grid with thumbnails of different sizes (Fig. 1b), similar to the Regular Grid except that the rows towards the top have fewer and larger images. The number of images per row increases gradually along the y-axis, and the images are gradually smaller. The images are sorted by relevance in descending order, so the top results are more relevant and larger.

We also developed a visualization with overlap, called Pile (Fig. 1c). The images are placed in a randomized (x, y) position, and their depth is determined by their relevance, being the most relevant images displayed on top. The user can drag the images around freely. It is also possible to bring the images to the foreground and scale with the scroll wheel, zooming in/out and clear some space. Finally, we developed a visualization where the images are placed in a spiral (Fig. 1d), exploiting the aesthetics aspect of thumbnails. The images are placed in a spiral path according to a function based on an Archimedes spiral. The most relevant images are displayed towards the outside of the spiral as it is easier to look at multiple images simultaneously. The spiral can be zoomed in/out with the scroll wheel, always over the center. It is possible to drag any image towards it before zooming in, so any image can be looked at in a large size.

3 Evaluation

We conducted a user test following a within-subject design with seven males and two females (average age: M = 27.78 years; SD = 13.28). Users were asked to perform four sets of two tasks each, one task being a broad search and the other a specific search. A broad search consists of searching for objects that belong to a group: buses, balls, dogs, and apples. A specific search consists of searching for an object with specific characteristics: red buses, footballs, beige dogs, and green apples. The order of the visualizations used for each task was counterbalanced to minimize any possible learning and dataset biases. All tasks were properly timed.

Table 1. SUS scores and time in seconds for each visualization/task

	SUS		Broad search task	Specific search task	
	M (SD)	Mdn	M (SD)	M (SD)	Mdn
Regular Grid	94.69 (9.40)	98.75	87.93 (33.86)	30.78 (8.58)	31.14
Variable Size Grid	87.50 (11.50)	91.25	92.07 (31.31)	49.41 (37.59)	36.16
Pile	48.55 (13.69)	62.50	251.17 (61.90)	134.46 (37.15)	141.87
Spiral	53.75 (26.22)	48.70	185.29 (60.09)	96.48 (46.02)	106.96

Four collections (transportation, sports, animal, and food) of 100 images each were used, one for each set of tasks. These images were obtained from the COCO dataset [5]. Each visualization and each image collection were used to perform one set of tasks. The broad search task included 20 correct images, while the specific search included five correct images that the participants should select. Participants were not told how many images there were in total nor how many were correct. However, before each task, they were told which image theme they would be browsing and what to search for. The images were presented in random order (not sorted). To accomplish each task, users could select the images that they considered as having target objects with a double click.

To compare each visualization, we measured its usability through the SUS questionnaire [4] (Table 1); the time taken by each participant to accomplish each task (Table 1); the quality of task results, through Precision, Recall and F measure [16] (Table 2); user preference, through a final questionnaire. Regarding users' preferences, the Variable Size Grid was the most preferred visualization (Mdn = 1), followed by the Regular Grid (Mdn = 2), Pile (Mdn = 3), and the Spiral (Mdn = 4).

Table 2. Effectiveness: Precision, Recall, and F Measure

	Broad search task						Specific search task					
	Precision		Recall		F Measure		Precision		Recall		F Measure	
	M (SD)	Mdn	M (SD)	Mdn	M (SD)	Mdn	M (SD)	Mdn	M (SD)	Mdn	M (SD)	Mdn
Regular Grid	0.99 (0.4)	1.00	0.88 (0.20)	1.00	0.92 (0.15)	1.00	1.00 (0.00)	1.00	0.87 (0.14)	0.80	0.93 (0.09)	0.89
Variable Size Grid	1.00 (0.00)	1.00	0.93 (0.07)	0.95	0.96 (0.04)	0.97	1.00 (0.00)	1.00	0.93 (0.10)	1.00	0.96 (0.06)	1.00
Pile	0.98 (0.03)	1.00	0.97 (0.04)	1.00	0.97 (0.02)	0.98	0.98 (0.06)	1.00	1.00 (0.00)	1.00	0.99 (0.03)	1.00
Spiral	0.98 (0.05)	1.00	0.89 (0.12)	0.95	0.93 (0.07)	0.94	1.00 (0.00)	1.00	0.89 (0.18)	1.00	0.93 (0.11)	1.00

4 Discussion and Conclusions

We presented four interfaces for visualizing image collections and compared them in a user test with nine participants. Our results show that both Grids present higher usability scores when compared with the non-traditional visualizations like the Pile and Spiral. Participants also performed both tasks, broader and specific search, fastest using both Grids. It is interesting to note that the Pile, sometimes used to show collections of images or algorithm search results, is not recommended for human analysis and search tasks. Regarding the quality of results, no significant differences were found between the different visualizations. However, it is relevant to note that the Variable Size Grid presents a higher Recall and F-Measure score when compared with the Regular Grid, particularly on specific search tasks. This result suggests that combining both visualizations in an adaptive interface could be an interesting approach for future work, which is reinforced by participants' preference, which has selected the Variable Size Grid as the preferable interface.

Acknowledgments. This research was funded by FCT/MCTES by LARSyS (UIDB/50009/2020) and by CEECINST/00122/2018 (IST-ID/300/2019).

References

1. Alexander, M., Gunasekaran, S.: A Survey on Image Retrieval Methods (2014). https://doi.org/10.13140/2.1.2779.0723
2. André, P., Cutrell, E., Tan, D.S., Smith, G.: Designing novel image search interfaces by understanding unique characteristics and usage. In: Gross, T., et al. (eds.) INTERACT 2009. LNCS, vol. 5727, pp. 340–353. Springer, Heidelberg (2009). https://doi.org/10.1007/978-3-642-03658-3_40
3. Basalaj, W.: Proximity Visualisation of Abstract Data. No. UCAM-CL-TR-509. University of Cambridge, Computer Laboratory (2001)
4. Brooke, J.: SUS: a quick and dirty usability scale. Usability Eval. Ind. **189**(194), 4–7 (1996)
5. COCO - Common Objects in Context (2020). http://cocodataset.org/#home. Accessed 3 Aug 2020
6. Dureja, A., Pahwa, P.: Image retrieval techniques: a survey. Int. J. Eng. Technol. **7**(2), 215–219 (2017)
7. Goker, A., Butterworth, R., Macfarlane, A., Stumpf, S.: Presenting and visualizing results on an image retrieval user interface. In: Proceedings of the British HCI 2017 (2017)
8. Heesch, D., Rüger, S.: Three interfaces for content-based access to image collections. In: Enser, P., Kompatsiaris, Y., O'Connor, N.E., Smeaton, A.F., Smeulders, A.W.M. (eds.) CIVR 2004. LNCS, vol. 3115, pp. 491–499. Springer, Heidelberg (2004). https://doi.org/10.1007/978-3-540-27814-6_58
9. King, F., et al.: An immersive virtual reality environment for diagnostic imaging. J. Med. Robot. Res. **1**(01), 1640003 (2016)
10. Nguyen, G., Worring, M.: Optimization of interactive visual-similarity-based search. ACM TOMM **4**(1), 1–23 (2008)
11. Rodden, K.: Fd, Cambridge. Evaluating Similarity-Based Visualisations as Interfaces for Image Browsing (2002)
12. Rodden, K., Basalaj, W., Sinclair, D., Wood, K.: Evaluating a visualisation of image similarity as a tool for image browsing. In: Proceedings of the InfoVis 1999, pp. 36–43. IEEE (1999)
13. Rüger, S.: Putting the user in the loop: visual resource discovery. In: Detyniecki, M., Jose, J.M., Nürnberger, A., van Rijsbergen, C.J. (eds.) AMR 2005. LNCS, vol. 3877, pp. 1–18. Springer, Heidelberg (2006). https://doi.org/10.1007/11670834_1
14. Schaefer, G., Budnik, M., Krawczyk, B.: Immersive browsing in an image sphere. In: Proceedings of the IMCOM 2017. ACM, New York, NY, USA, Article 26, pp. 1–4 (2017)
15. Schaefer, G., Ruszala, S.: Hierarchical image database navigation on a hue sphere. In: Bebis, G., et al. (eds.) ISVC 2006. LNCS, vol. 4292, pp. 814–823. Springer, Heidelberg (2006). https://doi.org/10.1007/11919629_81
16. Schütze, H., Manning, C.D., Raghavan, P.: Introduction to information retrieval. Cam- bridge University Press, Cambridge (2008)

17. Thomee, B., Lew, M.: Interactive search in image retrieval: a survey. Int. J. Multimed. Inf. Retr. **1**(2), 71–86 (2012)
18. Torres, R., Silva, C., Medeiros, C., Rocha, H.: Visual structures for image browsing. In: Proceedings of the CIKM 2003. ACM, New York, NY, USA, pp. 49–55 (2003)
19. Wang, H., Mohamad, D., Ismail, N.: Approaches, Challenges and Future Direction of Image Retrieval, arXiv preprint arXiv:1006.4568 (2010)
20. Zhang, L., Chen, L., Jing, F., Deng, K., Ma, W.Y.: EnjoyPhoto: a vertical image search engine for enjoying high-quality photos. In: Proceedings of the ACM Multimedia 2006, ACM, New York, NY, USA, pp. 367–376 (2006)
21. Zheng, L., He, L., Yu, C.: Mobile virtual reality for ophthalmic image display and diagnosis. J. Mob. Technol. Med. **4**(3), 35–38 (2015)

InteractDiff: A 3D Sandbox Game for Online Teaching and Campus Life Experience

Davy P. Y. Wong[1](✉), Chia-Ming Hsu[2], Jie-Ke Pan[2], Man-Lin Huang[1], Yen Nee Chew[3], and Ju-Ting Chang[3]

[1] Institute of Information Systems and Applications, National Tsing Hua University, Hsinchu, Taiwan
davyw@gapp.nthu.edu.tw
[2] Department of Industrial Engineering and Engineering Management, National Tsing Hua University, Hsinchu, Taiwan
[3] Institute of Service Science, National Tsing Hua University, Hsinchu, Taiwan

Abstract. The coronavirus pandemic forced teachers to use online meeting software to teach courses remotely. However, without on-site supervision from teachers, students can get distracted and lead to learning inefficiencies. Distraction also leads to low interaction, and teachers may lose enthusiasm in teaching. In addition, social interaction is necessary for campus life. To address these problems, we present InteractDiff, a 3D sandbox game to improve the online teaching experience and interactivity. We designed several school scenarios and mechanisms where users act as an avatar inside to imitate real-life interactions in university. Our preliminary study shows potential feasibility and positive feedback from users.

Keywords: Gamification of learning · Online learning · Synchronous learning · Virtual worlds

1 Introduction

Almost all school activities are being cancelled or run in virtual due to the coronavirus pandemic. Teachers are forced to use online meeting software like Zoom[1] and Google Meet[2] to teach courses. Although this way reduces infection risk, it also brings new challenges in learning. We categorised three issues between teachers and students from the literature review, observation in online university classrooms and a user journey map we created.

1. In the synchronous online class, many students choose not to turn on the video camera and microphone [2]. Teachers cannot understand their learning status

---

[1] Zoom Video: https://zoom.us.
[2] Google Meet: https://meet.google.com.

© IFIP International Federation for Information Processing 2021
Published by Springer Nature Switzerland AG 2021
C. Ardito et al. (Eds.): INTERACT 2021, LNCS 12936, pp. 442–446, 2021.
https://doi.org/10.1007/978-3-030-85607-6_54

through observation [10]. They may lose enthusiasm in teaching because of lacking verbal and non-verbal feedback from students.
2. Without on-site supervision from teachers, some students feel hard to stay concentrated in the online class [10], which may affect their learning efficiency.
3. Interaction with peers plays a vital role in school life [6]. Current online meeting software only offers a one-to-many communication mode. It is difficult for students to discuss with others privately and deprive their belonging needs [1].

Inspired by gamified learning [9], we propose InteractDiff to tackle these problems. InteractDiff is a sandbox game for imitating different school scenarios. Every user in the system acts as an avatar to represent themselves, such as Second Life [5] and The Sims[3]. Teachers can switch to different scenes and adapt their purposes, such as a laboratory or exhibition hall. Students can express their thoughts and interact with peers by controlling the avatar.

Previous studies have been proven the feasibility of 3D virtual learning environments, especially in non-higher education [3]. Also, VR (Virtual Reality) technologies have been commonly used to improve the learning experience [4,7]. However, Circles [8] pointed out the accessibility concerns in VR classroom. Based on the popularity of head-mounted display, InteractDiff is designed to be a PC video game for university students instead of a VR application.

This work aims to explore the feasibility of popularising a 3D virtual environment in universities, combining learning and campus life into one virtual space. We believe that this gamified learning approach can improve the learning experience and disadvantages of online meeting software.

2 InteractDiff

We built InteractDiff by Unity[4] to realise the virtual campus. Users can control the avatar by mouse and keyboard to imitate real-life behaviours and campus life, including social activities, attending class and interact with NPCs (non-player character). Several school scenarios and functions were also designed:

Environment: In addition to traditional classrooms, two virtual environments were designed for teaching. Based on Savanna Preferences and Biophilia Effect, we provided an outdoor grassland (Fig. 1a) for multiple uses, such as exhibition and presentation. This greenery environment could reduce the anxiety of learning. In Fig. 1b, we also created a virtual laboratory and common room for experiment demonstration and social interaction. This is an alternative and cost-effective way to experience different lectures or occasions without spending time in commute.

Group Mode: When teachers need to hold a group discussion, Group Mode allows everyone to form a group by controlling their avatar close to each other

---

[3] The Sims 4: https://www.ea.com/games/the-sims/the-sims-4.
[4] Unity: https://unity.com.

in the classroom. Only group members can hear each other. Teachers can also join the discussion by moving the avatar to a specific group (see Fig. 1d). This feature imitated face-to-face discussion, offering a space for social interaction to makes students feel affiliated.

Draw Lots and Vote: Teachers can randomly select a student to answer questions using Draw Lots, which helps teachers know their understanding of the course content. In addition, teachers can also hold a vote and visualise the results. Floating bubbles on avatars (Fig. 1c) show the response from students. Students can express their emotion and idea through the bubble. Teachers can know their thoughts rapidly and avoid missing questions from students. These features not only enhance teacher-student interaction but also reduce distraction possibilities.

Incentive System: Teachers can grant badges or award Concentrate Points (CP) to students who achieve corresponding goals or give good responses. CP is the virtual currency in InteractDiff, allowing users to purchase the new outfit and dress up their avatar. This feature encourages class participation by fulfilling their different needs [1,6].

Fig. 1. Functions of InteractDiff (from left to right): (a) A outdoor grassland for class project presentation, (b) common room for gathering, (c) Voting and (d) Group Mode aim to improve in-class interaction.

3 Preliminary User Study

To evaluate the motivation for using InteractDiff, we recruited five university lecturer with online teaching experience. A long-term systematic user study is currently in progress. For the students, 50 participants between the ages of 20 and 30 were recruited, all university students. In the evaluation, each participant was asked to watch our demo video and assume they were simultaneously using our system. After the video section, participants were given ten minutes to operate our prototype and try all the functions mentioned above. Finally, participants completed a questionnaire in System Usability Scale (SUS) and a short interview that focuses on interactivity and concentration.

The average System Usability Scale score is 82. In Question 1, *"I think that I would like to use this system frequently"* and Question 9, *"I felt very confident using the system"*, we both received 4.4/5 points on average. For the interview results, we invited an expert to code the transcripts to identify obvious themes emerging from the conversations. Partial themes show in the following result. Regarding the motivation, 95% of participants showed their willingness to use InteractDiff: *"That's awesome, I can dress up my avatar and go to class."*; *"Can't wait to use this system (to have class)."* (P12, P46). About the interactivity, 86% of participants believed that students might have more interaction with teachers, *"I am afraid to ask questions in class, this (the system) is a great way to interact with the teacher."* (P27).

Consideration in using the system was also pointed out. Some participants (14%) are worried that InteractDiff may distract them during class: *"The system is fun. But I wonder if my class use this system, I might lose concentrate because there have many functions."* (P34). The results indicate that although the system received positive feedback, the distraction possibilities in using InteractDiff have to be evaluated in future. Future work also included an internet-connectable prototype, a comparison with traditional meeting software, and a comprehensive study between teacher and student.

References

1. Almquist, E., Senior, J., Bloch, N.: The elements of value. Harv. Bus. Rev. **94**(9), 47–53 (2016)
2. Castelli, F.R., Sarvary, M.A.: Why students do not turn on their video cameras during online classes and an equitable and inclusive plan to encourage them to do so. Ecol. Evol. (2021). https://doi.org/10.1002/ece3.7123
3. Cheng, A., Yang, L., Andersen, E.: Teaching language and culture with a virtual reality game. In: Proceedings of the 2017 CHI Conference on Human Factors in Computing Systems (2017). https://doi.org/10.1145/3025453.3025857
4. Liao, M.Y., Sung, C.Y., Wang, H.C., Lin, W.C.: Virtual classmates: embodying historical learners' messages as learning companions in a VR classroom through comment mapping. In: 2019 IEEE Conference on Virtual Reality and 3D User Interfaces (VR), pp. 163–171 (2019). https://doi.org/10.1109/VR.2019.8797708
5. Lorenzo-Alvarez, R., Rudolphi-Solero, T., Ruiz-Gomez, M. J., Sendra-Portero, F.: Game-based learning in virtual worlds: a multiuser online game for medical undergraduate radiology education within second life. Anatomical Sci. Educ. (2019). https://doi.org/10.1002/ase.1927
6. Nguyen, T.D., Cannata, M., Miller, J.: Understanding student behavioral engagement: importance of student interaction with peers and teachers. J. Educ. Res. (2018). https://doi.org/10.1080/00220671.2016.1220359

7. Oiwake, K., Komiya, K., Akasaki, H., Nakajima, T.: VR classroom: enhancing learning experience with virtual class rooms. In: 2018 Eleventh International Conference on Mobile Computing and Ubiquitous Network (ICMU), pp. 1–6 (2018). https://doi.org/10.23919/ICMU.2018.8653607

8. Scavarelli, A., Arya, A., Teather, R.J.: Circles: exploring multi-platform accessible, socially scalable VR in the classroom. In: 2019 IEEE Games, Entertainment, Media Conference (GEM), pp. 1–4 (2019). https://doi.org/10.1109/GEM.2019.8897532

9. Subhash, S., Cudney, E.A.: Gamified learning in higher education: a systematic review of the literature. Comput. Hum. Behav. **87**, 192–206 (2018). https://doi.org/10.1016/j.chb.2018.05.028

10. Vale, J., Oliver, M., Clemmer, R.M.: The influence of attendance, communication, and distractions on the student learning experience using blended synchronous learning. Can. J. Scholarship Teach. Learn. (2020). https://doi.org/10.5206/cjsotl-rcacea.2020.2.11105

Interacting with More Than One Chart: What Is It All About?

Angela Locoro[1]([⊠])([iD]), Paolo Buono[2], and Giacomo Buonanno[1]

[1] Università Cattaneo - LIUC, Corso G. Matteotti, 20, 21053 Castellanza, VA, Italy
{alocoro,buonanno}@liuc.it
[2] Università degli Studi di Bari Aldo Moro, Piazza Umberto I, 1, 70121 Bari, Italy
paolo.buono@uniba.it

Abstract. Visual objects made of multiple views, e.g., dashboards and small multiples, are taking the scene in information communication and visual patterns design, but still vague are the studies that try to abstract away from characterizing them at the level of their single charts, and rather focus on their structural characteristics and the resulting interactions with their multi-view ensemble seen as a whole. In this paper, we are proposing this unified view through a multi-dimensional wheel, on the strand of Cairo's wheel made for infographics, devised for the identification, the analysis, and the evaluation of design patterns for multiple views.

Keywords: Visualization techniques · Tools for design, modelling and evaluation · Multiple coordinated views · Dashboards · Small multiples

1 What are Dashboards and Multiple Views from an Interactionist Point of View

This paper moves from the current definitions and characterizations of MCVs such as dashboards [2] and small multiples [5] to provide a formal "middle layer" between the conceptual vagueness of their definition and the concrete details of their instantiation [3,4], so as to see whether new interaction challenges may emerge, be evaluated and designed starting from an *holistic* perspective.

In particular, we argue that the main kind of interaction with visual objects like dashboards seems to roughly correspond to a "tree-like graph visit": starting from the root (overview), and going deep into details. According to this formal structure, the interaction style of individuals with a dashboard may be defined as *recursive.*

To exemplify this kind of interactional recursive behavior, Fig. 1a depicts a recursive navigational style, where a person makes an operation o (e.g., a selection or a filter) on a dashboard d, through an interface operational functionality f_o until a bottom node (a leaf in the graph style metaphor) is not reached, which is still a meaningful level. A meaningful level of detail may be formally defined on hierarchical family of partitions P of a dataset [6], e.g., a dataset subset

© IFIP International Federation for Information Processing 2021
Published by Springer Nature Switzerland AG 2021
C. Ardito et al. (Eds.): INTERACT 2021, LNCS 12936, pp. 447–450, 2021.
https://doi.org/10.1007/978-3-030-85607-6_55

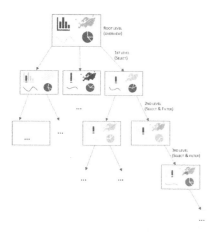

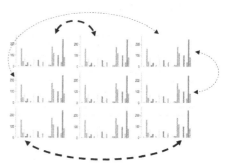

(b) An example of small multiple un-ordered, horizontal, network like compara-tive interactions. Dashed arrows of different thickness distinguish main from secondary virtual connections found by the user.

(a) An example of dashboard recursive ex-plorative interaction.

Fig. 1. Dual nature of multiple views interactions.

according to some other selection/filtering criteria, one category of a categorical dataset, one data point, and so on, which can still be displayed at the dashboard (whole)-view and where this view can be considered still meaningful. Formally:

$$\bigcup a_i, \bigcup a_j \in P, o \in O, d \in D, f_o : D_{ai} \to D_{aj}, ... f_o(f_o(d_a)) \tag{1}$$

On the opposite, interacting with small multiples roughly corresponds to navigating in a "network-like graphs", where charts (nodes) are of the same kind (when not the same "node" with a small variation, all the rest being equal) and the eyes go back and forth from one "node" to another one, in what can be called an *iterative* navigation style, until a meaningful relational pattern is reached in the eye of the user. Formally, a small multiple can be seen as a graph structure $G = (C, E, f_o)$, with charts c as nodes ($c \in C$), meaningful patterns as virtual edges ($e \in E$), and an operational goal f_o executed by a user iteratively to "visually connect" two charts by a meaningful virtual edge:

$$E = \{(c_1, c_2) \in C \mid c_1 \neq c_2\} \iff \exists f_o : C \to C \tag{2}$$

2   The Multiple Views Wheel: A Bird's View

What are the interaction properties that are recognizable for these two orthogo-nal interaction styles? We identify eight well known interaction dimensions that were applied partly to single charts and are also applicable to multiple views and viceversa. Starting from the previous work, we provide a formal definition, at the level of the multiple views visual construct, to which the structure of our wheel may be referred to (Fig. 2).

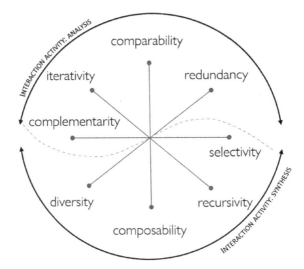

Fig. 2. The multi-chart wheel, inspired by Alberto Cairo's wheel on Infographics design dimensions [1]. This wheel depicts the interaction dimensions mainly with small multiples (upper emicycle) and mainly with dashboards (lower emicycle).

Given P as a dataset partition family and F, G, Z as visual mapping functions of a dataset partition into a chart, each dimension of the wheel, at the multiple views level, may be formally characterized as follows:

Iterativity: for any pair of a dataset partition elements, $\forall a_i, a_j \in P_z, a_i \neq a_j$, there may exist a relationship $\exists R : F \times F$, virtually connecting each pair of charts $F(a_i), F(a_j)$, from repeated observations by a user. For example, in a small multiples view we iterate the interaction on the same chart on each category of a categorical dataset, by repeatedly observing and finding connections.

Comparability: for any pair of a dataset partition elements, $\forall a_i, a_j \in P_z, a_i \neq a_j$, there exists a visual mapping of the same kind mapping each partition element to the same kind of chart, $F(a_i) \wedge F(a_j)$. This configuration allows the comparability of each pair of elements of a dataset partition during interaction.

Redundancy: for each element of a dataset partition $\forall a_i \in P_z$ there may exist two visual mapping functions F, G such that they are applied to the same element of the dataset partition, $F(a_i) \wedge G(a_i)$. In this way, the information of the container results redundant, and the interaction effort is meant to reinforce a pattern in data.

Recursivity: for each element of a hierarchical partition family $\forall b_i, b_j \in P$, such that $\bigcup b_i \in P_{h1}, \bigcup b_j \in P_{h2}$, and $P_{h2} \subset P_{h1}$ a visual mappings family of functions is applied recursively $F(F(P)) \wedge G(G(P))$, until a bottom (leaf) partition visualization is reached. In a dashboard, interacting with selections and filters generates a recursive application of the same charts (the dashboard) on a secondary partition of a dataset.

Composability: for each dataset partition $\forall P_z \in P$, a visual mappings family of functions is applied to the same dataset partition, by composing two visual mapping functions, $G(F(P_z))$. This interaction dimension is applicable to single charts containing more than one visualization principle. However, it can be also applied to dashboards charts.

Diversity: for each element of a partition family $P_{z1} \in P, P_{z2} \in P$, where $P_{z1} \neq P_{z2}$ a visual mapping family of functions is applied to each partition, $F(P_{z1}) \wedge G(P_{z1}) \wedge F(P_{z2}) \wedge G(P_{z2})$, so as to provide a variety of charts (as in dashboards) for the same dataset, and offering a variety of perspectives around its analysis.

Complementarity: for each element of a dataset partition $\forall a_i \in P_z$ there exists a visual mapping family, $F(a_i) \wedge G(\bigcup P_z \backslash a_i) \vee F(a_i) \wedge F(\bigcup P_z \backslash a_i)$, mapping the element and its complement to distinct charts. This configuration allows the interaction with a complete information on the same dataset element.

Selectivity: for each element of a partition family $P_{z1} \in P, P_{z2} \in P$, where $P_{z1} \neq P_{z2}$, there may exist only one between two visual mapping of the same kind, $F(P_{z1}) \vee F(P_{z2})$ applied to each dataset partition. This configuration allows to select one distinct view for each dataset partition, and allows interacting with one of them at a time (e.g., in dashboards).

What can be seen at this level of abstraction? The opposite poles should be incompatible, i.e., not present at the same time; nearby poles may be compatible, e.g., redundancy and comparability. Open questions remain, like for example: among these configurations, what are the more cognitively intense? What are the most effective when in combination? This should be regarded as future work.

References

1. Cairo, A.: The Functional Art: An Introduction to Information Graphics and Visualization. New Riders (2012)
2. Few, S.: Information Dashboard Design: The Effective Visual Communication of Data, vol. 2. O'reilly, Sebastopol (2006)
3. Javed, W., Elmqvist, N.: Exploring the design space of composite visualization. In: 2012 IEEE Pacific Visualization Symposium, pp. 1–8. IEEE (2012)
4. Qu, Z., Hullman, J.: Keeping multiple views consistent: constraints, validations, and exceptions in visualization authoring. IEEE Trans. Vis. Comput. Graph. **24**(1), 468–477 (2017)
5. Sarikaya, A., Correll, M., Bartram, L., Tory, M., Fisher, D.: What do we talk about when we talk about dashboards? IEEE Trans. Vis. Comput. Graph. **25**(1), 682–692 (2018)
6. de Soto, A.R., Recasens, J.: Modelling a linguistic variable as a hierarchical family of partitions induced by an indistinguishability operator. Fuzzy Sets Syst. **121**(3), 427–437 (2001)

Introducing Gestural Interaction on the Shop Floor: Empirical Evaluations

Salvatore Andolina[1], Paolo Ariano[2], Davide Brunetti[3], Nicolò Celadon[2], Guido Coppo[1], Alain Favetto[2], Cristina Gena[3], Sebastiano Giordano[2], and Fabiana Vernero[3(✉)]

[1] Synarea, Torino, Italy
{andolina,coppo}@synarea.com
[2] IIT, Torino, Italy
{Paolo.Ariano,Nicolo.Celadon,Alain.Favetto,Sebastiano.Giordano}@iit.it
[3] Università degli Studi di Torino, Corso Svizzera 185, 10149 Torino, Italy
{davide.brunetti,cristina.gena,fabiana.vernero}@unito.it

Abstract. This paper describes two empirical evaluations we carried out in the context of an Industry 4.0 project, where we explored the use of touchless gestural interaction on the shop floor.

Keywords: Gestural interaction · Empirical evaluation · Industry 4.0

1 Introduction

In the "smart factory" vision, industries are production-oriented cyberphysical systems [4] able to exploit emerging information technologies to guarantee flexible, efficient, environment-friendly, high-quality and low-cost production processes [5]. In this context, however, designing appropriate modalities to communicate, analyze and interact with all the information related to production processes can be challenging, especially in consideration of its many environmental and safety-related constraints. For example, keyboards or touch devices may be inconvenient for workers on the shop floor, who must wear protective gloves, while voice-based interaction may be impractical due to the background noise.

Guided by the requirements expressed by our industrial partners, in the HOME regional project[1] on Industry 4.0 we explored the use of large displays in combination with touchless gestural interaction. Based on previous work in the neuromotor rehabilitation field [2], the project consortium developed a smart armband which allows to detect gestures from movement and muscle biosignals,

---

[1] https://www.home-opensystem.org/.

This work was supported by HOME (Hierarchical Open Manufacturing Europe) Regional Project (POR FESR, code 319-50).

C. Ardito et al. (Eds.): INTERACT 2021, LNCS 12936, pp. 451–455, 2021.
https://doi.org/10.1007/978-3-030-85607-6_56

while a machine learning library allows to calibrate and recognize task-specific gestures. Notice that this *ad hoc* solution was preferred to the use of motion sensing input devices, in that these can raise a number of issues related to privacy and perceived surveillance. The definition of an appropriate set of gestures has undergone several steps, including a guessability study [1], in an attempt to balance the sometimes competing needs for gesture intuitiveness (end users) and recognizability (project consortium), combined with a preference for minimum calibration, due to the fact that the armband can be shared by several workers.

In this paper, we describe our final empirical evaluations with our industrial partner Galeasso s.r.l.[2], which specializes in sheet metal fabrication and is going to adopt the armband on its shop floor.

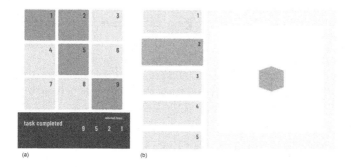

Fig. 1. The grid-like (a) and CAD-like (b) interfaces.

2   Empirical Evaluations

Two evaluations were carried out with the future users of the armband to assess its ease of use and elicit comments and suggestions on gestural interaction at the workplace. We focused on a specific scenario suggested by our partner Galeasso s.r.l., where welders frequently switch between their workbench and a nearby desktop computer to browse the tasks they have been assigned and visualize 3D models of the final product. Thus, we developed a prototype web application (Fig. 1) consisting in: 1) a grid-like interface to simulate selection tasks and 2) a CAD-like environment showing 3D objects. The application can be controlled through the armband and is to be shown on large displays installed on the shop floor. The main actions allowed by the application are point and select, which can be enacted through arm movements and the "close fist" gesture, respectively.

2.1   First Empirical Evaluation

The first empirical evaluation was carried out in June 2019. Participants were two skilled welders. One of them (P1, 32 y/o) used computers and other digital

---

[2] https://www.galeasso.com/.

devices for more than 14 h per week and was already familiar with gestural interfaces (Wii, X-Box), while the other (P2, 47 y/o) was less technology-savvy. Participants were asked to perform two tasks:

1. **Task 1 (grid-like interface):** select a series of tiles. Each user was assigned three sequences of four tiles each.
2. **Task 2 (CAD-like interface):** view a cube with differently-coloured facets; select the cube and rotate it, so as to make the blue facet visible.

We manually recorded the number of errors made by participants, as well as their comments, elicited through the thinking aloud protocol. After each task, participants were also invited to assess their user experience through a short survey, consisting of 4 questions which could be answered through a 1–4 scale[3].

Results. In the first task, both participants made two errors each, which consisted in selecting a certain tile twice. Such errors were probably due to the sensitivity setting of the armband, which might have caused small involuntary movements to be treated as selection gestures. Figure 2 reports our results for user experience evaluations. While P1, the participant having previous experience with gestural interaction, consistently expressed positive evaluations for both tasks, P2 was less positive, especially for the second task, where he had experienced most difficulties (see the free comments section for details).

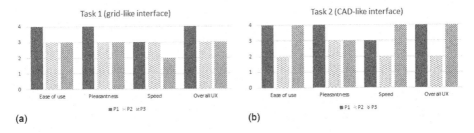

Fig. 2. User experience assessments for the first (a) and second (b) task.

Free Comments. P1 experienced no particular difficulties and only suggested that the application should cope with involuntary movements such as little tremors. On the whole, he looked forward to using gestural interaction to carry out his everyday activities at the workplace. P2 found the task of rotating objects especially difficult and pointed out some additional problems due to the specific implementation of the test interface. He was quite satisfied about both the comfort and the sensitivity settings of the armband, but he also observed that arms might get tired after prolonged use. On the whole, he was convinced that using gestural interaction might significantly improve his work experience.

---

[3] While quantitative measures are not significant due to the small number of participants, they were deemed to be useful to better interpret and understand free comments.

2.2   Second Empirical Evaluation

Based on the results of the first evaluation, the project consortium worked on an improved version of the armband, focusing in particular on its sensitivity setting. Taking into account the delays caused by the COVID-19 pandemic, a second and final empirical evaluation was carried out in October 2020, where we used the same procedure, tasks and measures as in the previous evaluation. The participant (P3, 30 y/o) was an accomplished 3D designer, with some welding skills and similar demographics as P1 and P2 (notice that we were unable to recruit the very same participants due to shift management issues). In particular, similarly to P1, he was also an heavy user of digital devices and had previous experience with gestural interaction (Kinect in particular).

Results. User experience evaluations are reported in Fig. 2. Although he made no errors, P3 expressed a slightly less positive evaluation for the first task, in comparison with P1 and P2. In particular, he complained that the interaction was too slow. His evaluation, however, was notably higher for the second task.

Free Comments. P3 observed that he had some difficulties in pointing to the desired part of the interface and in having his gestures recognized, which was probably due both to his initial lack of familiarity with the armband and to persisting problems in sensitivity settings. Coherently with his low evaluation for the "speed" dimension in the first task, he pointed out that his experience would have been more satisfying, had the application been more responsive.

2.3   Conclusion

Our results offer some insight on the adoption of gestural interaction in smart factories. Most importantly, all the participants were favourable to our solution and willing to use it in their everyday work activities. User experience evaluations were generally positive, even if free comments highlighted the importance of fine tuning sensitivity settings: in the second evaluation, there were no errors due to involuntary movements, but the application appeared less responsive.

An open issue is the evaluation of the long-term user experience, which might be negatively affected by a natural decrease in motivation, as the initial enthusiasm starts to fade, as well as by the insurgence of arm fatigue, as hypothesized by one of the participants. While we are quite confident that the identified gestures avoid highly fatiguing arm positions which might cause the well-known "gorilla arm syndrome" [3], these aspects should be assessed empirically in future studies.

Finally, we must point out that one of the limitations of the here presented work is the small number of participants. On the other hand, however, we were able to involve actual representatives of our end users and to carry out the evaluations in a natural setting, i.e., on the shop floor, thus gaining good ecological validity.

References

1. Andolina, S., et al.: Experimenting with large displays and gestural interaction in the smart factory. In: 2019 IEEE International Conference on Systems, Man and Cybernetics, SMC 2019, Bari, Italy, 6–9 October 2019, pp. 2864–2869. IEEE (2019). https://doi.org/10.1109/SMC.2019.8913900
2. Di Girolamo, M., Celadon, N., Appendino, S., Turolla, A., Ariano, P.: EMG-based biofeedback system for motor rehabilitation: a pilot study. In: 2017 IEEE Biomedical Circuits and Systems Conference (BioCAS), pp. 1–4 (2017). https://doi.org/10.1109/BIOCAS.2017.8325086
3. Hansberger, J.T., et al.: Dispelling the gorilla arm syndrome: the viability of prolonged gesture interactions. In: Lackey, S., Chen, J. (eds.) VAMR 2017. LNCS, vol. 10280, pp. 505–520. Springer, Cham (2017). https://doi.org/10.1007/978-3-319-57987-0_41
4. Riedl, M., Zipper, H., Meier, M., Diedrich, C.: Cyber-physical systems alter automation architectures. Annu. Rev. Control. **38**, 123–133 (2014)
5. Wang, S., Wan, J., Li, D., Zhang, C.: Implementing smart factory of Industrie 4.0: an outlook. Int. J. Distrib. Sensor Netw. **12**(1), 3159805 (2016). https://doi.org/10.1155/2016/3159805

Making Warning Messages Personal: A Big 5 Personality Trait Persuasion Approach

Joseph Aneke[1]([⊠]) [iD], Carmelo Ardito[2] [iD], and Giuseppe Desolda[1] [iD]

[1] Dipartimento di Informatica, Università degli Studi di Bari, Bari, Italy
{joseph.aneke,giuseppe.desolda}@uniba.it
[2] Dipartimento di Ingegneria Elettrica e dell'Informazione, Politecnico di Bari, Bari, Italy
carmelo.ardito@poliba.it

Abstract. Several mitigation strategies in form of warning messages against phishing attacks have continued to fail largely due to user negligence. Thus, it is important for researchers to focus not only on the accuracy of the provided recommendations but also on other factors that influence the acceptance of recommendations and the extent to which these recommendations are convincing or persuasive. In this paper, we present our ongoing approach that leverages on the *Big 5 Personality trait* model and users digital traces harvested from their social networks, thereafter, transformed into a personalized warning message. We argue that stimulating users through personal recommendations evokes an understanding of the implications of their actions or inaction.

Keywords: Personalized messages · Big 5 personality trait · Social Network Sites (SNSs)

1 Introduction

Recipients of a warning message in the event of a phishing attack are more likely to heed a warning if they believe they are the intended recipient [1] and perceive the content as applicable to their unique personality. In light of this, the issue of personalization becomes key in presenting warnings. In this work we are guided by the following research questions:

RQ1: How can we deploy human-related theories to enhance users' acceptance of warning recommendations?
RQ2: How can unique digital traces combined with persuasiveness as intrinsic characteristics be integrated into the design of a warning mechanism system to increase users' acceptance of the warning recommendations?

The impact of the Big 5 personality traits with reference to digital traces on social networks has been a subject of interest to researchers with a possible positive correlation been envisaged in recommendations [2]. For instance, authors in [1] through Facebook

© IFIP International Federation for Information Processing 2021
Published by Springer Nature Switzerland AG 2021
C. Ardito et al. (Eds.): INTERACT 2021, LNCS 12936, pp. 456–461, 2021.
https://doi.org/10.1007/978-3-030-85607-6_57

likes by users demonstrated that Computer-based personality judgments were more accurate and reliable than those made by humans or close friends.

In developing our personalized warning messages, we developed a framework consisting of two key approaches. First, there was the refinement of the warning message text to appeal to recommended individual personality trait preferences. Secondly, we exploited harvesting unique digital traces from already existing users' relationships in SNS to reinforce the acceptance of the warning advice. Thus, a variant of the warning text tailored to a user's personality trait, combined with inputs (e.g., profile picture) of a Phishing attack expert, makes the message personalized and easier to accept.

The rest of the paper is structured as follows: in Sect. 2 we present a background to related work, Sect. 3 discusses our conceptual framework. Conclusions and future work are provided in Sect. 4.

2 Background of Related Work

Personalization or customization of messages is a term used to describe different styles of tailoring strategies [3]. Its applications could be found in websites, emails, health campaigns, etc. [4]. The research community has tried to understand, among others, its structure and user interconnection, as well as interactions with Big 5 personality traits, in keeping persons glued for so long to messages [5].

The Big 5 Personality Traits model was developed by the psychologists Paul Costa and Robert McCray and it is one of the most common models used in modern research into information security behavioral analysis [6]. It consists of five factors that represent personality traits: conscientiousness, agreeableness, extroversion, neuroticism, openness to experiences [7].

With respect to information security, studies have shown that there is a significant relationship between conscientiousness personality and agreeableness personality as it pertains to security policy [8].

3 Design of Warning Text

In order to address RQ1, we adopted the Big 5 personality trait spectrum. In this spectrum, each of the individual personalities may fall anywhere either from Low (Negative), Neutral, or High (positive) [9], as depicted in Fig. 1. Hence, our designed warning texts were done to represent several variants that returned all possible emotional values within the spectrum range.

The generation of the explanations proposed in the text of our warning messages is based on a generic pattern purposely defined in [10–12] to instantiate each warning message. For example, for the Time life security indicator, a phishing warning message text reads as:

"This website was created recently. This is typical of fraudulent websites. Do not disclose private information on it.".

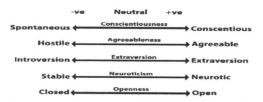

Fig. 1. Big 5 personality trait spectrum

According to the warning guidelines indicated in [13], we produced five variants of the above text message (see Table 1), which had the same objective but were expressed in different ways. We then subjected these messages to sentiment analysis and readability measures evaluations. The messages returned all possible spectrum values (−ve, Neutral and +ve), as reported in the sentiment analysis column.

Table 1. Warning message variant across spectrum range

Message variant	Sentiment analysis	Reach (%)	Word count	Smog Index
This website was created recently. This is typical of fraudulent websites. Do not disclose private information on it	−0.93	100	18	6.8
This website is young. It is typical of fake websites. Do not disclose your private information on it	−0.85	100	17	5
Young (New) websites are famous for criminal activities. There is a potential risk if you proceed	+0.39	100	17	7.2
Young websites are famous for criminal activities. It may be risky if you proceed	+0.46	100	14	6
Young websites are famous for criminal activities. There may be a potential risk if you proceed	0.0	100	15	7.2

3.1 Integration of Digital Traces in Warning Messages

In order to address RQ2, we adopted Cialdini's persuasion principles [14]. It states that when people are faced with a lifeline decision, they defer to experts or similar others, they are most likely inclined to accept requests made by somebody they like in a way, and usually have the tendency to commit to their previous or reported opinion or behaviour.

The conceptual framework, presented in Fig. 2, comprises of two stages: Identification and pre-processing and customization. At the *Identification and pre-processing phase*, three key activities take place: 1) the defiled security indicator is identified from the pool; 2) the personality traits of the user and the spectrum rage values for the warning text are marked; 3) the list of social networks that the user has subscribed to is also identified and ranked. At the *Customisation phase*, the best fit warning text and the most persuasive image (e.g., profile picture) selected from users frequently used social network is selected. The most persuasive image is determined through a possible relationship to a friend or friend of friends. Once a relationship graph has been derived, the shortest path is selected, and the resultant friends' picture is selected and uploaded on the tray for the warning message.

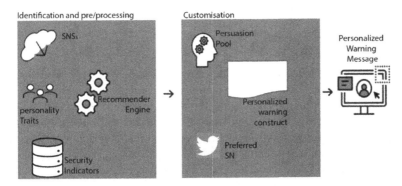

Fig. 2. Conceptualization of the proposed framework

Figure 3 shows how the mechanism has been implemented as a splash-screen displayed as soon as the user tries to access a deceptive website. On the left side, one of the variants of the warning message is shown, while the right panel aims at persuading the user to not proceed since the users' friends Joseph, Lucia, and Andrea strongly recommend that he should not proceed to the fake URL (www.bank.0f.america.com).

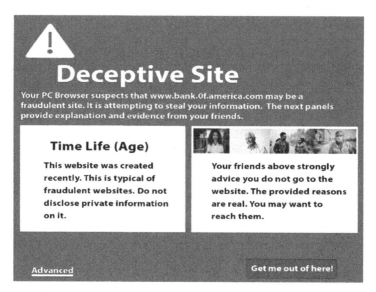

Fig. 3. Implementation of the personalized warning message mechanism

4 Conclusion

In this paper, we presented a mechanism that aims at drawing users' attention to phishing warning messages and help them to take the right decision about proceedings towards a website or not. Our contribution is novel in that we proposed an approach that tailors the warning text to suit the Big 5 personality trait. Also, the personalized warnings included referrals and pictures harvested from a user's SNS and recommendations from experts in security domains implicit or explicit to them. As a next step, we would evaluate our design with real users. Also, it could be extremely interesting to study the possible use of the multiple SNSs which users do not subscribe to.

References

1. Baker, E.J.: Hurricane evacuation behavior. Int. J. Mass Emerg. Disasters **9**, 287–310 (1991)
2. Winter, S., Maslowska, E., Vos, A.L.: The effects of trait-based personalization in social media advertising. Comput. Hum. Behav. **114**, 106525 (2021)
3. Houghton, D., Pressey, A., Istanbulluoglu, D.: Who needs social networking? An empirical enquiry into the capability of Facebook to meet human needs and satisfaction with life. Comput. Hum. Behav. **104**, 106153 (2020)
4. Kocaballi, A.B., Berkovsky, S., Quiroz, J.C., Laranjo, L.: The personalization of conversational agents in health care: systematic review. J. Med. Internet Res. **21**, e15360 (2019)
5. Viswanath, B., Mislove, A., Cha, M., Gummadi, K.P.: On the evolution of user interaction in Facebook. In: Proceedings of the 2nd ACM Workshop on Online Social Networks, pp. 37–42 (2009)

6. Wang, J.-L., Jackson, L.A., Zhang, D.-J., Su, Z.-Q.: The relationships among the big five personality factors, self-esteem, narcissism, and sensation-seeking to Chinese University students' uses of social networking sites (SNSs). Comput. Hum. Behav. **28**, 2313–2319 (2012)

7. John, O.P., Srivastava, S.: The Big-Five Trait Taxonomy: History, Measurement, and Theoretical Perspectives, vol. 2. University of California Berkeley, Berkeley (1999)

8. Franke, U., Brynielsson, J.: Cyber situational awareness–a systematic review of the literature. Comput. Secur. **46**, 18–31 (2014)

9. Lim. https://www.simplypsychology.org/. Accessed 15 April 2021

10. Aneke, J., Ardito, C., Desolda, G.: Help the user recognize a phishing scam: the design of explanation messages in warning interfaces for phishing attacks, presented at the 23rd International Conference on Human-Computer Interaction, Washington DC, USA (2021)

11. Aneke, J., Ardito, C., Desolda, G.: Designing an intelligent user interface for preventing phishing attacks. In: Abdelnour Nocera, J., et al. (eds.) INTERACT 2019. LNCS, vol. 11930, pp. 97–106. Springer, Cham (2020). https://doi.org/10.1007/978-3-030-46540-7_10

12. Aneke, J., Ardito, C., Desolda, G.: Unpacking warning messages: towards mitigating phishing attacks, presented at the In Proceedings of the Italian Conference on ICT for Smart Cities and Communities (iCities 2019). 18–20 September 2019. Pisa, Italy (2019)

13. Bravo-Lillo, C., Cranor, L.F., Downs, J., Komanduri, S., Sleeper, M.: Improving computer security dialogs. In: IFIP Conference on Human-Computer Interaction, 2011, pp. 18–35 (2011)

14. Cialdini, R.B.: The science of persuasion. Sci. Am. **284**, 76–81 (2001)

Persona's Role in the Design of Future Technologies by Academics and Practitioners

Parisa Saadati[1]([✉]) [ID], José Abdelnour Nocera[1,2] [ID], and Torkil Clemmensen[3] [ID]

[1] University of West London, London, UK
{abdejos,parisa.saadati}@uwl.ac.uk
[2] ITI/Larsys Portugal, Funchal, Portugal
[3] Copenhagen Business School, Frederiksberg, Denmark
tc.digi@cbs.dk

Abstract. Automation and the introduction of Industry 4.0 interactive technologies have imposed novel challenges and burdens on academics and industrial practitioners. Developing systems for future workplaces need sufficient knowledge and understanding of the trends and technological developments and their viability from both industry and academic experts before introducing the general population. Utilizing co-design ideation workshops supported by various design tools can provide better ideation for designing future scenarios. We conducted a qualitative study to analyze academics' and industrial practitioners' points of view on persona as a design tool during a conference workshop. These participants empirically test the co-creation of personas and find conceptual differences between the groups in their tool use. We used pre and post-workshop surveys and workshop transcripts to code and clustered our findings. The conclusion is that the differences in academics' and industrial practitioners' perspectives and use of design tools for ideation are substantial but combined in a team can lead to designing positive experiences in future workplaces.

Keywords: Future technologies · Personas · Design · Academics · Practitioners

1 Introduction

Automation and the introduction of Industry 4.0 interactive technologies in industrial work systems have brought new ambiguities in the challenges and burdens on interactive systems designers. The analysis presented in this article has been developed to elicit different perspectives from academics and industry practitioners in understanding the nature and influence of using personas as a design tool in professional design work for future technologies. Industry practitioners seldom use tools [1] validated by academics [2]. Instead, they use a collection of their own tools, methods, and systems to externalize their ideas [3]. Industry practitioners may use material with qualities that challenge their idea's accurate representation and externalization [4]. In comparison, academics create more insights on selecting and evaluating design ideas as fundamental skills. In practice,

C. Ardito et al. (Eds.): INTERACT 2021, LNCS 12936, pp. 462–466, 2021.
https://doi.org/10.1007/978-3-030-85607-6_58

the success of the industry practitioners is based on experience rather than theoretical knowledge [2].

Using tangible design tools can establish a shared 'language' through physical form when verbal communication fails due to professional terminology and misalignments between different professional working cultures [1, 5, 6]. Using these design tools is often developed on a trial-and-error basis, resulting in low engagement, trust, and interaction with the participating stakeholders [1]. On the other hand, there are different views on using these design tools among academics and industry practitioners. Using these design tools enables innovation and success in designing interaction designs [2]. Personas in co-design projects have begun to include users and others in either persona inceptions or assemblies or deployment. Personas in co-design are typically used as objects of conversation in design and validation [7]. In this paper, we ask the research question: *What are the main differences in academics' and industrial practitioners' views on common design tools for ideation?* We empirically test the co-creation of personas and find conceptual differences between the groups in their tool use.

2   Workshop and Methods

We investigated a selection of design tools with particular attention to personas for co-designing [8] workshops for future scenarios. The selection criteria for these tools are based on suitability with the work domains of the designer, namely Industry 4.0, and automation, and convenience for the type, space, and duration of the workshops. To gather this input, we conducted a 5-h online workshop in one of the International Conferences on Co-Designing Personas for User Experience and Engagement in Automation. Consistent with the goal of the workshop, participants discussed:

- A more robust understanding of how design tools can be used by practitioners and academics to ideate and co-design emergent future technologies.
- Presenting different views on using idea management workshops as a fundamental practice for future scenarios for industry practitioners and academics.

The participants in this workshop were 3 industry practitioners from different companies, 1 doctoral student, 3 active researchers, and 1 post-doctorate researcher. All participants were either from an HCI background or were knowledgeable as an active working in this discipline. All participants had experience in developing and utilizing personas in the research or real scenarios. The first author of this paper served as the workshop facilitator. We employed the Nominal Group Technique [9] for data collection during the workshop. This method is a structured method for group brainstorming that encourages contribution from everyone and quicker decision-making on the relative important issue, problem, or solutions.

The workshop was unfolded as follows: (1) most participants presented the findings of their contribution, while others could ask questions and discuss their opinion on utilizing personas in the design process; (2) the facilitator shared a personas template [10] and invited the participants to co-design two personas for a defined scenario while raising any issues they considered relevant; (3) the persona template allowed the participant to share and cluster their ideas under each relevant heading and voted on new features; (4) finally, we clustered similar insights/findings under the initial categories presented in Tables 1, 2 and 3.

3 Workshop Result

In Table 1, we summarize the observation, workshop survey, recorded discussion, and findings related to use and popularity of persona based on three criteria: how both types of academics and industry practitioners used the tools, how they valued the design tools and how the design tool is applicable is in their fields.

Table 1. Main differences between the academics and industry practitioners' point of view on using Personas as a common design tool.

	How designers used the tool	Value	Applicability of the design tool
Industry practitioners	To generate assumption-based personas based on field observations or design within the operation team	Fast spreading, valuable and easy tool to use before the design process or during the design iterations. Also applicable for testing the systems	Personas provide narratives for different types of users based on clusters of behaviors for design inspiration
Academics	To generate both data-driven and assumption-based personas. They are preferably using data-driven personas	Can provide insights by capturing the different behaviors without expressing a defined personality or socio-demographics	Persona can be used alongside other user stories and user scenarios to understand users' final designs better

In Table 2, participants' disagreements were grouped and outlined from the transcripts under the initial categories we have created. We also added the participants' insights from the post-workshop survey to this table.

Table 2. Academics and industry practitioners' disagreements on the designing personas.

Academics	Industry practitioners
Data driven persona vs proto personas	
Incorrect practices on personas by industry. 3 votes	Proto personas and reverse engineering as a common practice. 4 votes
Helpfulness of personas in designing future scenarios	
Co-designing for future scenarios better than the current ones. 6 votes	Not easy to create personas for new segments. 2 votes
The number of personas to design	
Businesses should prioritize the number of personas. 3 votes	No particular number to follow; the team will decide on this number. 4 votes
Type of data collection for personas	
Data for personas can come from different sources and forms. (Various votes and ideas)	Using segmentation in busy domains is impossible, but alternative sources are available. (Agreement on some of the alternative sources)

Table 3. Academics and industry practitioners' agreements on the designing personas.

Insights agreed
Personas can be used in iterative design and for testing the systems
A.I. personas should consider future scenarios, specifically for technologies with livelihood about their jobs and work alongside the human worker (e.g., Robots, A.I. engines)
Photo personas can transfer pre-conceptions about the users to the developers, or they can touch cultural sensitivity
Data collection is not always accessible, but having a context, situation, obstacles, and a scenario is essential for co-designing personass
A shared, engaging environment that people can design together is important for co-designing the personas and increasing practicable personas

4   Conclusion

We explored empirical differences in academics' and industry practitioners' perspectives and the use of persona as a design tool for ideation of future scenarios. To do this, we analysed the collected data from a conference co-design workshop for future scenarios in different platforms and environments. Our findings support other studies findings of the dissimilar views between academics and industry practitioners' for idea generation process and design tools [2].

Our analysis indicated that while these two groups may, on the behavioural level, use common design tools in the same fashion, there are important differences between them in the thinking, ideation, prototyping, and overall design process. We can see how practitioners follow a 'reverse engineering' approach using design tools such as personas in terms of thinking and ideation. Similarly, as discussed in the workshop, industry practitioners will 'try' design tools (e.g. Proto-persona) with more confidence in the workshops once concrete details about scenarios and examples from other domains were presented. In contrast, academics' preferred initial approach was to think of the available data, principles, and conceptual models before engaging in ideation and applied design practice.

The identified differences may have implications for how to feed information to industry decision-makers. Specifically, we can argue that (1) there is a need to involve both academics and industry practitioners in co-design ideation workshops for emergent future systems, (2) design tools usage should be linked explicitly to specific contexts, scenarios, or situations to provide decision information relevant to the specific domain and environment, (3) using data-driven design tools based on the current trends and events may facilitate consensus about a design reality, and the facilitators of co-design ideation workshops have a critical role in leading the various designers and the overall session to an optimal outcome.

References

1. Rygh, K., Clatworthy, S.: The use of tangible tools as a means to support co-design during service design innovation projects in healthcare. In: Pfannstiel, M.A., Rasche, C. (eds.) Service Design and Service Thinking in Healthcare and Hospital Management, pp. 93–115. Springer, Cham (2019). https://doi.org/10.1007/978-3-030-00749-2_7
2. Inie, N., Dalsgaard, P.: How interaction designers use tools to manage ideas. ACM Trans. Comput.-Hum. Interact. **27**, 7:1–7:26 (2020). https://doi.org/10.1145/3365104
3. Kaye, J., et al.: To have and to hold: exploring the personal archive. In: Proceedings of the SIGCHI Conference on Human Factors in Computing Systems - CHI 2006, p. 275. ACM Press, Montréal, Québec, Canada (2006). https://doi.org/10.1145/1124772.1124814
4. Runco, M.A., Dow, G., Smith, W.R.: Information, experience, and divergent thinking: an empirical test. Creat. Res. J. **18**, 269–277 (2006). https://doi.org/10.1207/s15326934crj 1803_4
5. Jenkins, T., Boer, L., Brigitta Busboom, J., Simonsen, I.Ø.: The future supermarket: a case study of ethnographic experiential futures. In: Proceedings of the 11th Nordic Conference on Human-Computer Interaction: Shaping Experiences, Shaping Society, pp. 1–13. ACM, Tallinn Estonia (2020). https://doi.org/10.1145/3419249.3420130
6. Kymalainen, T., et al.: Evaluating future automation work in process plants with an experience-driven science fiction prototype. In: 2016 12th International Conference on Intelligent Environments (IE), pp. 54–61. IEEE, London, United Kingdom (2016). https://doi.org/10.1109/IE.2016.17
7. Cabrero, D.G., Winschiers-Theophilus, H., Abdelnour-Nocera, J., Kapuire, G.K.: A hermeneutic inquiry into user-created personas in different Namibian locales. In: Proceedings of the 14th Participatory Design Conference: Full papers-volume 1, pp. 101–110 (2016)
8. Simonsen, J., Robertson, T. (eds.): Routledge International Handbook of Participatory Design. Routledge, London (2012)
9. Delbecq, A.L., Van De Ven, A.H., Gustafson, D.H.: Group Techniques for Program Planning: A Guide to Nominal Group and Delphi Processes. Scott, Foresman (1975)
10. Nielsen, L.: Personas - User Focused Design. Springer London, London (2019). https://doi.org/10.1007/978-1-4471-7427-1

Planning Smart Social Distancing - Mobile Application Concept Design and Evaluation

Eveliina Heikkilä, Mari Suoheimo, and Jonna Häkkilä[✉]

University of Lapland, Yliopistonkatu 8, 96300 Rovaniemi, Finland
{eveliina.heikkila,mari.suoheimo,jonna.hakkila}@ulapland.fi
https://www.ulapland.fi/EN/Webpages/User-Experience-Research-Group-LUX

Abstract. The COVID-19 crisis has caused social distancing practices to be part of everyday life. We present the concept and user interface design of a smart phone application that enables planning daily schedules in a manner which seeks to optimise the social distancing. We present the application UI design and its evaluation in two focus groups (n = 8). The findings highlight the need for and positive attitude towards a mobile application that supports avoiding crowds during and after the pandemic time.

Keywords: Covid-19 · Social distancing · Mobile application · Calendar · Location based services

1 Introduction

In spring 2020, the world faced the global Covid-19 pandemic. Society had to adapt to restrictions, including social distancing practices. The pandemic caused lock-downs and mobility restrictions, bringing a shift to home offices [7], and causing many practical challenges for everyday life in families [2]. The social distancing measures to stem the pandemic included both government set restrictions, as well as voluntary recommendations. Mobile applications, such as Crowdless or Mind the Gap, have been adopted as a tool for helping people to keep safe while conducting their mandatory everyday mobility and interactions with people, and to minimise the social encounters with people exposed to Covid-19 [1,4]. Mobile tracing applications have been introduced in several countries, and their nationwide use has been promoted in order to prevent Covid-19 from spreading.

We introduce a mobile application concept and user interface (UI) design that aims to help people to avoid crowded places during pandemic outbreaks. The design target is to support people to conduct their daily activities whilst minimising the probability to become exposed to, or transmit, the disease. We organized a user study with two focus groups to evaluate the application concept and to discuss the ideas of mobile app supported social distancing. Whereas prior

© IFIP International Federation for Information Processing 2021
Published by Springer Nature Switzerland AG 2021
C. Ardito et al. (Eds.): INTERACT 2021, LNCS 12936, pp. 467–470, 2021.
https://doi.org/10.1007/978-3-030-85607-6_59

art has evaluated an asocial hiking app for avoid people on a hiking route [6], we address the UI design and concept of supporting social distancing in everyday mobility.

2   Social Distancing Mobile App Concept

The Smart Social Distancing mobile app concept supports users to foresee possible crowded places on a map, and plan how to schedule and navigate from one place to another more safely, Fig. 1. The design process started from defining the main functions, exploring different information visualization techniques, studying existing applications, and then proceeding to drafting the UI design flows, wireframes, and finally the UI graphics.

The features in Fig. 1 present the main functions of the Smart Social Distancing (SSD) mobile app concept. A heatmap function shows the crowded areas on a city map. The user can plan a daily schedule by adding calendar events. Figure 1-right illustrates the application menu. Route recommendations create an optimized route to navigate by avoiding crowds, and the 3D map shows the hotspot map in 3D. In addition, the user can search how crowded a specific place is. Risk notifications give the user warnings about, e.g., which of the frequently visited places are crowded during the day.

Fig. 1. The Smart Social Distancing application concept main functions.

3   Focus Group Study

3.1   Set-Up of the Study

To study user perceptions of social distancing and evaluate the SSD mobile app concept, two of the focus groups sessions were organized. Each focus group included three female and one male participant (total n = 8), age between 20 and 45 (mean 28) years. Each focus group session lasted for one hour. The focus group session had three main sections with specific questions. First, the participants were asked what kind of applications they have been using to prevent themselves being in crowded places now during the time of Covid-19, and what other means they had applied to maintain physical distance to other people. The answers were collected using post-it notes. First, the participants got to see and try out the prototype. After that they received a paper questionnaire, where each of the eight main application functions were rated on a scale from 1 (not useful) to 7 (most useful). After this, the participants reflected, using post-it notes, which features they liked most, which ones the least, and how they would use the application after the pandemic time. Finally, the participants answered questions relating to their anticipated future behavioural changes after the pandemic. Also here, post-it notes were used to support the discussion.

3.2 Findings

The participants had been using applications such as video calls, food ordering, sending messages, social media tools, and generally tools to help them to take care of everyday practicalities remotely. However, they had not used applications where the main use case was to avoid crowds. Such applications are hardly available to Finnish users in particular. Therefore, participants had used other ways to avoid crowds, such as planning to run errands outside of the assumed crowded hours, or checking peak times from Google search. They had to come up with new rhythms for their day while trying to avoid crowds.

As the most useful feature of the application, the participants perceived the hotspot map, where the red color illustrated how crowded a place was, see Fig. 1. This feature was voted to the most useful by 62,5% of the participants in the evaluation questionnaire, and it also gained the most comments with the post-it notes. After the hotspot map, the most liked functions were the risk notifications, how to avoid crowds by scheduling the day, and the ability to see the busiest hours of different places.

When ideating how they would use the application after the pandemic, the answers focused mostly on avoiding crowds and rush hours. Recognizing the most visited places was also suggested, as well as organizing Pokémon Go type games, which would include moving from one place to another. As a long term behavior change, participants estimated generally a bigger desire to avoid crowds, even after the pandemic. Altogether, the Smart Social Distancing application was seen to have potential. A mobile app to support social distancing while planning everyday tasks requiring mobility was embraced.

4 Discussion

In our work, we have presented a mobile application concept and UI design for a Smart Social Distancing application to support avoiding crowds while conducting normal everyday mobility, and evaluated it with focus groups. The participants found the concept of Smart Social Distancing mobile app useful, and especially seeing the crowded areas with one glance on a map was embraced. Even though Koronavilkku, a Finnish government supported app for notifying if the user had been exposed to Covid-19, is widely used, an application which would generally guide avoiding crowds is not, to the best of our knowledge, available in Finland. The participants were not using any specific mobile apps to guide them for social distancing, although they generally used tools that supported remote operations, such as ordering food. Prior art has introduced different concepts of that relate to avoiding crowds, and utilizing context information [3] has gained a strong foothold in application design. Recognizing crowd density and movement patterns in urban events has been addressed by prior art [8], as well as automatically adjusting navigation to avoid traffic jams [5].

Considering their behavior after the pandemic, most of the participants answered that they would continue to use the proposed mobile application to avoid crowds. This may indicate that the pandemic time has caused a permanent change in social behavior, and that life routines adopted during pandemic might actually remain in people's everyday lives. This would be an interesting topic for future research.

Acknowledgments. This research has been supported by the Smart Social Distancing project, funded by Business Finland.

References

1. Collado-Borrell, R., Escudero-Vilaplana, V., Villanueva-Bueno, C., Herranz-Alonso, A., Sanjurjo-Saez, M.: Features and functionalities of smartphone apps related to COVID-19: systematic search in app stores and content analysis. J. Med. Internet Res. **22**(8), e20334 (2020)
2. Häkkilä, J., Karhu, M., Kalving, M., Colley, A.: Practical family challenges of remote schooling during COVID-19 pandemic in Finland. In: NordiCHI 2020, pp. 1–9. ACM (2020)
3. Häkkilä, J., Schmidt, A., Mäntyjärvi, J., Sahami, A., Åkerman, P., Dey, A.K.: Context-aware mobile media and social networks. In: Proceedings of the 11th International Conference on Human-Computer Interaction with Mobile Devices and Services, pp. 1–3 (2009)
4. Kondylakis, H., et al.: COVID-19 mobile apps: a systematic review of the literature. J. Med. Internet Res. **22**(12), e23170 (2020)
5. Liebig, T., Sotzny, M.: On avoiding traffic jams with dynamic self-organizing trip planning. In: 13th International Conference on Spatial Information Theory (COSIT 2017). Schloss Dagstuhl-Leibniz-Zentrum fuer Informatik (2017)
6. Posti, M., Schöning, J., Häkkilä, J.: Unexpected journeys with the HOBBIT: the design and evaluation of an asocial hiking app. In: Proceedings of the 2014 Conference on Designing Interactive Systems, pp. 637–646 (2014)
7. Von Gaudecker, H.M., Holler, R., Janys, L., Siflinger, B., Zimpelmann, C.: Labour supply in the early stages of the COVID-19 pandemic: empirical evidence on hours, home office, and expectations (2020)
8. Zomer, L.B., Daamen, W., Meijer, S., Hoogendoorn, S.P.: Managing crowds: the possibilities and limitations of crowd information during urban mass events. In: Geertman, S., Ferreira, J., Goodspeed, R., Stillwell, J. (eds.) Planning Support Systems and Smart Cities. LNGC, pp. 77–97. Springer, Cham (2015). https://doi.org/10.1007/978-3-319-18368-8_5

Raya: A Tangible Exercise Buddy Reminding Oneself of the Commitment to Exercise

Daphne Menheere[1(✉)], Alynne de Haan[1], Steven Vos[1,3], and Carine Lallemand[1,2]

[1] Industrial Design Department, Eindhoven University
of Technology, Eindhoven, The Netherlands
d.s.menheere@tue.nl

[2] HCI Research Group, University of Luxembourg, Esch-sur-Alzette, Luxembourg

[3] School of Sport Studies, Fontys University of Applied Sciences, Eindhoven, The Netherlands

Abstract. Although many people have a positive intention to be more active, a key challenge remains to turn this intention into action. Social support as a motivational strategy can increase adherence in exercise and can be provided by relational agents as a substitute for human coaches. We first conducted an exploratory two-week user study, to explore how emotional design and tangible interaction influences experience and motivation to exercise. We then designed a propositional research object Raya, a tangible exercise buddy that helps one to realize their workout by reminding them of their goals and self-commitment. We invite designers to bridge the gap in the design space of sport-related technologies by designing tangible artefacts embedding supportive and qualitative aesthetics of interaction rather than focusing on performance.

Keywords: Exercise motivation · Empathic virtual agent · Tangible interaction

1 Introduction and Related Work

Many people aim to incorporate exercising into their daily life. Yet a key challenge is to transform these positive intentions into exercise behavior, eventually creating a long-term exercise habit. This phenomenon is the exercise intention-behavior gap [12]. Social support as a motivational strategy can increase adherence in exercise [14], and numerous studies thus advocate for including social features in sport-related technology [13]. A way to do so is the use of relational agents also called Embodied Conversational Agents. These anthropomorphic characters are designed to build social-emotional relationships with their users, and are often used in behavior change [3]. Within this context, relational agents can take the role of coaches and are sometimes even preferred to human trainers because of the convenience and permanence of the interaction [3]. In this paper, we describe Raya, a propositional object to investigate a qualitative way to design for motivation. Raya is designed as a tangible relational agent entailing human characteristics, aiming to help overcome barriers experienced before exercise.

Over recent years, the trend in sport-related interventions is to use quantification to give exercising feedback and support people in implementing their intentions. Although

© IFIP International Federation for Information Processing 2021
Published by Springer Nature Switzerland AG 2021
C. Ardito et al. (Eds.): INTERACT 2021, LNCS 12936, pp. 471–475, 2021.
https://doi.org/10.1007/978-3-030-85607-6_60

this feedback type speaks to some people, it does not necessarily reach all who would benefit from exercising regularly [7], especially those who like social support [15]. Social support as a motivational strategy to increase adherence in exercise has proven to be effective [13, 14], yet many interventions enable social support during the training session and not before. Lack of social support is also experienced prior to exercising, preventing one from initiating exercise [8, 11], resulting in an intention-behavior gap. Enabling social support outside of the training is a gap to investigate.

Embodied Conversational Agents (ECA) are used as a substitute for tasks which usually involve human interaction and are often designed to mimic the role of companions or coaches in behavior change interventions. Providing social support is an essential skill of these virtual characters, who rely on emotional design and communication strategies to achieve that aim. One of the primary goals for designers is to "*create agents capable of having natural and effective interactions with users that can produce some desirable of beneficial outcome*" [2, p. 755]. To reach this objective, extensive research on the expression of synthetic human emotions has been conducted, exploring dimensions such as speech content and tone, body language or facial expressions. Examples of relational agents supporting physical activity can be found in several studies [3, 4]. Currently ECA are majorly represented as screen-based entities having human characteristics [2]. Examples can take the form of robots, virtual pets, or other interactive devices. The effectiveness of interventions using ECA [1, 15] might result from a humanization of the user's interaction: "*Whereas computer-based interventions might be considered dehumanizing and lacking the empathy necessary for delivering intervention content, when coupled with avatars or virtual agents there are advantages that might re-humanize the user's interaction with the intervention*" [5].

2 Exploratory Study

We propose the design of a tangible relational agent that helps people realize their exercise intentions by guiding them in goal setting and self-commitment. To investigate how motivating such an agent can be, we set up an exploratory user study wizard of ozing the buddy via text messages. Findings are used to inform the buddy design.

2.1 Participants and Procedure

Five women (aged 22 to 60) participated in a two-weeks study, after obtaining informed consent. Their activity level was slightly active (exercising 1–2 per week), to moderately active (3 times a week). Five participants indicated to plan their workout upfront, and four indicated to often experience doubts to exercise. Before the study, participants filled out an initial questionnaire, including questions about their lifestyle and physical activity habits. We then asked the participants to send a text message to the (virtual) buddy when they thought of doing a workout. They thus planned their exercising goals with the buddy and explained their intention, either through a voice or text message. After planning, we invited the participants to fill out questions about their feelings telling their plans to the buddy. Before the workout, multiple messages are sent by the buddy reminding them of their planned workout and goals. Two hours after the messages, participants are asked to fill in a questionnaire about their feelings, if the reminder came at an opportune or non-opportune moment, if they went exercising or not, and whether the messages were motivating or not. Finally, we investigated how they experienced the virtual buddy and how this affected their goal setting and motivation. Participants were also asked about the ideal look and feel of a buddy in terms of communication, relatedness, friendship and motivation.

2.2 Results

In total, the virtual buddy sent 17 reminders to the participants when they indicated having the intention to exercise that day.

Dialogue with Buddy. A first observation is an interplay between monologue and dialogue conversations between the buddy and the participant. The participants indicated, for example, being able to thank the buddy for their messages or to confirm they went for a workout. For practical reasons, a dialogue is necessary to sketch a complete overview of the planned workout. One participant mentioned that she expected to receive more messages from the buddy, and as this would be valuable in order not to forget it. Another participant felt the buddy was always there because you could talk to it at any time. One of the six participants mentioned that the spoken messages felt personal. Although the participants found it easy to communicate with the buddy over WhatsApp, it lacked a personal touch as compared to communicating in real-life. They admitted that a more personal social interaction would be more motivating than just receiving a text.

Impact on Motivation. Eleven out of 17 reminders were reported as motivating: "*It was in writing what I wanted to achieve, it helped me with extra motivation*" (P3), "*It shed light on what I found important*" (P1). The remaining six did not motivate participants, most of the time due to poor timing of the reminder. One participant indicated to prefer several messages spread out over an extended period to get support more often. Five out of six participants indicated to feel more actively involved in their exercise planning, making them more aware of what they had planned. The reminders sent by the buddy were considered positive, since it contributed to the commitment they made and to the awareness that they were on the 'right' track, making them more likely to go.

3 Design: Raya

Raya is a tangible exercise buddy designed for people who have the intention to exercise but experience doubts before doing it. Raya helps one to plan a workout and asks the user for their personal motivation to exercise that day. When the user eventually is in doubt about going or not, Raya sparks a dialogue and triggers emotions, remembering why one initially wanted to go exercising and stimulating the actual intended behavior: "*Guess what? It is almost time to [activity]! You said you wanted this because you want to [reason]. It is [date] [time] already, so go get dressed!*".

Compared to a classical voice UI system, tangible aspects are key in the interaction with Raya. The buddy's voice is medium pitched and its heart beats faster to notify the user it wants to talk. Raya starts to speak when it detects laying on the user's hand. Raya has a silent mode by shaking it. Raya is designed as an empathic and life-like animal-shaped buddy, entailing human characteristics (heartbeat, warm touch). It intends to act as a companion capable of eliciting emotional responses. The buddy is customizable, allowing each person to adopt their preferred animal. Raya integrates multiple sensors. To detect if it is being held, we used an Hexiwear with integrated accelerometer and vibration motor to simulate a heartbeat. To enable a dialogue between the buddy and user, we used the API of Google Dialogflow (Small Talk) (Fig. 1).

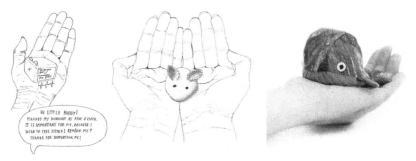

Fig. 1. Left, the heartbeat cube, which discusses with the user her plans and goals. Middle, first version of the tangible sport buddy in the shape of a mouse. Right, the final design of Raya.

4   Discussion and Conclusion

We explored the integration of tangible human attributes within a relational agent for exercise encouragement. We aimed to trigger a bond between the user and the buddy, which could support an increased motivation to exercise. Positioning this work away from quantification [6] and 'in-the-moment' interventions [9], we question current approaches of motivational design through our propositional object Raya.

Our findings showed the benefits of a supportive communication style, where a coach is perceived as an ally rather than a persuader [10]. Previous research on conversational agents highlights a concern for repetitive interactions, which reduce the engagement of the user [3] and effectiveness of the intervention. The richness of dialogue should thus be a central point of focus in the design of agents. The conversation should progress, as the buddy provides information and emotional support, also using multiple types of social support [15]. A challenge identified is to define the opportune interaction moment. When should the buddy communicate to motivate the users? When is it the 'right moment' to send a reminder or to engage in a conversation? It depends on individual preferences and contextual factors. Different implementation strategies might be adopted, from a self-report of preferences to the use of contextual data to determine the opportune timing. Further research is needed, with a larger field study and experimental variations in the buddy's attitudes to confirm these findings.

References

1. Ahn, S.J.G., et al.: Using virtual pets to promote physical activity in children: an application of the youth physical activity promotion model. J. Health Commun. **20**(7), 807–815 (2015). https://doi.org/10.1080/10810730.2015.1018597
2. Beale, R., Creed, C.: Affective interaction: how emotional agents affect users. Int. J. Hum.-Comput. Stud. **67**(9), 755–776 (2009)
3. Bickmore, T.W.: Relational agents: Effecting change through human-computer relationships. Massachusetts Institute of Technology (2003)
4. Feltz, D.L., Forlenza, S.T., Winn, B., Kerr, N.L.: Cyber buddy is better than no buddy: a test of the Köhler motivation effect in exergames. Games Health J. **3**(2), 98–105 (2014). https://doi.org/10.1089/g4h.2013.0088
5. LeRouge, C., Dickhut, K., Lisetti, C., Sangameswaran, S., Malasanos, T.: Engaging adolescents in a computer-based weight management program: avatars and virtual coaches could help. J. Am. Med. Inform. Assoc. **23**(1), 19–28 (2016)
6. Lockton, D., Ricketts, D., Chowdhury, S.A., Lee, C.H.: Exploring qualitative displays and interfaces. In: Proceedings of the CHI Conference Extended Abstracts on Human Factors in Computing Systems, pp. 1844–1852 (2017)
7. Menheere, D., van Hartingsveldt, E., Birkebæk, M., Vos, S., Lallemand, C.: Laina: dynamic data physicalization for slow exercising feedback. In: DIS 2021, p. 26, 28 June–2 July 2021, Virtual Event, USA (2021). https://doi.org/10.1145/3461778.3462041
8. Menheere, D., et al.: The runner's journey: identifying design opportunities for running motivation technology. In: Proceedings of the 11th Nordic Conference on Human-Computer Interaction: Shaping Experiences, Shaping Society, pp. 1–14. https://doi.org/10.1145/3419249.3420151
9. Mueller, F., Vetere, F., Gibbs, M.R., Edge, D., Agamanolis, S., Sheridan, J.G.: Jogging over a distance between Europe and Australia. In: Proceedings of the 23nd Annual ACM Symposium on User Interface Software and Technology - UIST 2010, p. 189 (2010). https://doi.org/10.1145/1866029.1866062
10. Ntoumanis, N., Quested, E., Reeve, J., Cheon, S.H.: Need supportive communication: implications for motivation in sport, exercise, and physical activity. Persuas. Commun. Sport Exerc. Phys. Act. **2018**, 155–169 (2018)
11. Pridgeon, L., Grogan, S.: Understanding exercise adherence and dropout: an interpretative phenomenological analysis of men and women's accounts of gym attendance and non-attendance. Qual. Res. Sport Exerc. Health. **4**(3), 382–399 (2012). https://doi.org/10.1080/2159676X.2012.712984
12. Rhodes, R.E., De Bruijn, G.J.: How big is the physical activity intention-behaviour gap? A meta-analysis using the action control framework. British J. Health Psychol. 18(2), 296–309 (2013). https://doi.org/10.1111/bjhp.12032
13. Ryan, R., Frederick, C., Lepes, D., Rubio, N., Sheldon, K.: Intrinsic motivation and exercise adherence. Int. J. Sport Psychol. **28**(4), 335–354 (1997)
14. Scarapicchia, T.M.F., Amireault, S., Faulkner, G., Sabiston, C.M.: Social support and physical activity participation among healthy adults: a systematic review of prospective studies. Int. Rev. Sport Exerc. Psychol. 10(1), 50–83 (2017). https://doi.org/10.1080/1750984X.2016.1183222
15. Vos, S., Walravens, R., Hover, P., Borgers, J., Scheerder, J.: Voor de pret of de prestatie? Typologieen van evenementenloopsters. Vrijetijdsstudies. **32**(2), 19–34 (2014)

Regenerative Swiping: A Hybrid Vision for Improved Sustainability with "Free" Energy Harvesting

José Luís Silva^(✉) (iD)

ITI/LARSyS and Instituto Universitário de Lisboa (ISCTE-IUL), ISTAR, Lisboa, Portugal
jose.luis.silva@iscte-iul.pt

Abstract. In a world facing climate change emergency, energy harvesting must be improved. Future interactive devices (with new materials) and a move of energy harvesting from devices to users can trigger this improvement. This paper presents a vision on how (many) future interactive devices should be powered. Beyond the benefits of a self-powered and ultra-low power interactive devices vision, a complementary one with self-powered users and "free" energy harvesting is essential. For example, harvesting user's energy (e.g. heart rate pulsations) and/or enabling him/her to produce (e.g. kinetic/inertial energy harvesting) and store (e.g. wearables) energy for future interactions. Self-powered users can then perform interactions with devices (that require only power during interaction or extra power during interaction) powering them through direct contact interaction. This will allow the removal of built-in batteries on these devices and a global reduction of batteries. The proposed hybrid vision combines self-powered devices/users and "free" energy harvesting.

Keywords: Human-centered computing · Human computer interaction · Interaction techniques · Interaction devices · Self-powered users · "Free" energy harvesting · Interaction-powered devices

1 Introduction

The world desperately needs an energy paradigm shift for an improved sustainability. The energy used by interactive devices is electricity, considered clean energy if obtained exclusively from renewable sources. However, electricity is still highly reliant on burning fossil fuels [2] and/or nuclear activity. There is a pressing need to increase energy harvesting from renewable sources to improve sustainability.

In chemistry, the well-known law of conservation of mass[1] discovered by Lavoisier states that "nothing is lost, nothing is created, everything is transformed". Similarly, the conservation of energy[2] law state that energy can neither be created nor destroyed;

---

[1] https://en.wikipedia.org/wiki/Conservation_of_mass (last accessed June 1st, 2021).
[2] https://en.wikipedia.org/wiki/Conservation_of_energy (last accessed June 1st, 2021).

© IFIP International Federation for Information Processing 2021
Published by Springer Nature Switzerland AG 2021
C. Ardito et al. (Eds.): INTERACT 2021, LNCS 12936, pp. 476–480, 2021.
https://doi.org/10.1007/978-3-030-85607-6_61

rather, it can only be transformed or transferred from one form to another. Therefore, we still have nowadays an immense waste of energy because most of them is not transferred where needed.

For instance, focusing on interactive devices, when users interact with them (e.g. pressing a button or swiping) there is "free" energy (from pressure and/or friction) that could be transferred back to the device.

The trend to an increasing number of electronic devices demands novel directions such as ultra-low power devices, interaction, and ambient energy harvesting but also novel low maintenance power schemes to decrease the burden of maintaining this huge number of devices.

2   The Vision

To achieve a successful paradigm shift, a hybrid approach should be followed. This means that efforts should be made in different directions. First, the number of batteries should be reduced to diminish the burden of maintaining a huge and increasing number of devices. This can be accomplished moving batteries from devices to users [1] (see Fig. 1a). Users with (wearable) batteries enable additional energy harvesting that can be obtained from users and their activities (e.g. Energy Harvesting Footwear [11]). Second, ultra-low power devices associated with ambient energy harvesting (e.g. some wristwatches are powered by kinetic energy) will tend to make devices self-sustainable. And, devices' functionalities or states with additional energy requirements could be powered with energy from self-powered users while interacting with the device. Finally, energy from the interaction should also be harvested. For example, when a user is interacting with a touchscreen the frictional energy resulting from the interaction should be transferred back to the device or to the user for future interactions (regenerative swiping).

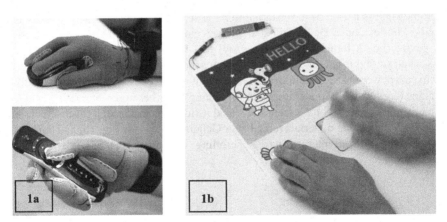

Fig. 1. a. A user wears the user-end of TouchPower and uses a mouse and TV remote controller without batteries [1]. **b.** Paper Generator harvests energy from rubbing and activates the e-paper display, revealing the word "hello" [5].

According to Karagozler et al. [5] these interactions are in a microjoule and milliwatt order of magnitude. There are few thousand of Joules in a smartphone battery however, as billions of users interact daily with touch screens (according to the study of the *dScout* company our screen phones are touched more than 2 thousand of time a day [12]) this simple additional energy harvesting could globally save an immense number of Joules. Furthermore, recent advances in hypersurfaces[3] enable the conversion of any material of any shape into an intelligent surface that will recognize gestures. Each gesture on the surface creates a distinctive vibration pattern that is identified and converted into a command. This leads to believe that touch interactions will not decrease in near future. Therefore, friction/pressure energy harvesting will have a huge impact.

The move of battery from devices to user (as proposed in the work of Zhang et al. [1]) enables a lower maintenance power scheme and an increasing potential source of energy to harvest available. Reducing battery per user to one and being able to harvest energy from both users (their activities and interactions) and environment are advantages that became possible.

Self-powered users will foster power-as-needed devices (i.e., devices that only require power during interaction) and the removal of built-in batteries, but other devices will continue to be required. Therefore, self-powered and sustainable devices must also be fostered. However, some of these devices might require more energy while being interacted that might not be available. This falls in the benefits of this proposed hybrid vision (see Fig. 2) that merges both:

1. Self-powered devices - able to manage power requirements of devices while "idle" (nonbeing interacted);
2. Self-powered users - provide power to power-as-needed devices and extra power to other devices to deal with additional power requirements associated with interactions;
3. "Free" energy harvesting - provides a source of energy to self-powered users.

Some authors [3, 4, 13] have started to harvest "free" energy from common human activities. For example, De Winkel et al. [13] recently developed an interactive battery-free device (i.e., a Battery-Free Game Boy) that harvests energy from gamer button presses and sunlight. This energy together with a move to lower-power devices pave the way to self-powered and sustainable users fueled with "free" energy from their common activities (e.g., walking, opening a door, breathing). Furthermore, interaction-powered interactive devices can complement the stated vision. For instance, a touchscreen built with energy harvesting materials (e.g., Paper Generator [5] – see Fig. 1b) and being able to harvest energy from interaction (e.g., scrolling) can increase the usage efficiency of "free" energy.

---

[3] https://www.hypersurfaces.com (last accessed June 1st, 2021).

reuse energy harvested
from friction/pressure

Fig. 2. Proposed hybrid vision - regenerative swiping with self-powered users, "free" energy harvesting and interaction-powered Devices.

3   Discussion and Conclusions

The proposed vision presents potential benefits in terms of sustainability however, with potential implications in terms of User Experience. For instance, current ultra-low energy devices provide less attractive interfaces [6, 7]. Furthermore, some devices might require more pressure to harvest more energy from the interaction and/or might be unable to provide a colorful interface. Another disadvantage of the proposed vision is the required use of a glove by self-powered users to transfer energy to devices. However, as stated by Zhang et al. [1] some techniques such as skin electronics [8, 9] and intrabody [10] can help get rid of the glove.

Future research should focus on harvesting more "free" energy from user interaction. The effectiveness of the presented vision might imply changes in users' interactions and behavior. For example, more vigorous interactions might be needed to harvest enough energy or a need for a more active users' lifestyle. This might be mitigated by designing solutions focusing on users' needs instead of users' wants.

This paper presents a hybrid vision aiming to improve energy sustainability. The approach focusses on the intersection of three points:

1. powering users;
2. harvesting "free" energy;
3. low powered, self/interaction-powered and sustainable devices.

Acknowledgements. This work was supported from Fundação para a Ciência e a Tecnologia (FCT, Portugal), through LARSyS (project UIDB/50009/2020) and through projects UIDB/04466/2020 and UIDP/04466/2020.

480   J. L. Silva

References

1. Zhang, T., Yi, X., Yu, C., Wang, Y., Becker, N., Shi, Y.: TouchPower: interaction-based power transfer for power-as-needed devices. Proc. ACM Interact. Mob. Wearable Ubiquitous Technol. **1**(3), 1–20 (2017)

2. Strezov, V., Evans, T.J. (eds.): Biomass Processing Technologies. CRC Press, Boca Raton (2014)

3. Gorlatova, M., Sarik, J., Grebla, G., Cong, M., Kymissis, I., Zussman, G.: Movers and shakers: kinetic energy harvesting for the internet of things. IEEE J. Sel. Areas Commun. **33**(8), 1624–1639 (2015)

4. Gorlatova, M., Sarik, J., Grebla, G., Cong, M., Kymissis, I., Zussman, G.: Movers and shakers: kinetic energy harvesting for the internet of things. In: 2014 ACM International Conference on Measurement and Modeling of Computer Systems, pp. 407–419 (June 2014)

5. Karagozler, M.E., et al.: Paper generators: harvesting energy from touching, rubbing and sliding. In: Proceedings of the 26th Annual ACM Symposium on User Interface Software and Technology (2013)

6. Grosse-Puppendahl, T., et al.: Exploring the design space for energy-harvesting situated displays. In: Proceedings of the 29th Annual Symposium on User Interface Software and Technology, pp. 41–48 (2016)

7. Jensen, W., Colley, A., Häkkilä, J., Pinheiro, C., Löchtefeld, M.: TransPrint: A method for fabricating flexible transparent free-form displays. Advances in Human-Computer Interaction, 2019 (2019)

8. Weigel, M., Lu, T., Bailly, G., Oulasvirta, A., Majidi, C., Steimle, J.: Iskin: flexible, stretchable and visually customizable on-body touch sensors for mobile computing. In: Proceedings of the 33rd Annual ACM Conference on Human Factors in Computing Systems, pp. 2991–3000 (April 2015)

9. Kawahara, Y.: Digital fabrication technologies for on-skin electronics. In: Proceedings of the 2016 ACM International Joint Conference on Pervasive and Ubiquitous Computing: Adjunct, pp. 946–949 (September 2016)

10. Partridge, K., et al.: Empirical measurements of intrabody communication performance under varied physical configurations. In: Proceedings of the 14th annual ACM symposium on User interface software and technology, pp. 183–190 (November 2001)

11. Akay, H., Xu, R., Seto, K., Kim, S.G.: U.S. Patent No. 10,973,276. Washington, DC: U.S. Patent and Trademark Office (2021)

12. Nelson, P.: We touch our phones 2,617 times a day, says study. Netw. World **7**, 353 (2016)

13. De Winkel, J., Kortbeek, V., Hester, J., Pawełczak, P.: Battery-free game boy. Proc. ACM Interact. Mob. Wearable Ubiquitous Technol. **4**(3), 1–34 (2020)

Robotic Emotion Monitoring for Mental Health Applications: Preliminary Outcomes of a Survey

Marat Rostov[1], Md Zakir Hossain[1,2(✉)] (iD), and Jessica Sharmin Rahman[1]

[1] Research School of Computing, Australian National University (ANU), Canberra, Australia
zakir.hossain@anu.edu.au

[2] Research School of Biology, ANU & Agriculture and Food, The Commonwealth Scientific and Industrial Research Organization (CSIRO), Black Mountain, Canberra, Australia

Abstract. Maintaining mental health is crucial for emotional, psychological, and social well-being. Currently, however, societal mental health is at an all-time low. Robots have already proven useful in medicine, and robot assisted mental therapies through emotional monitoring have great potential. This paper reviews 60 recent papers to determine how accurately robots can classify human emotions using the latest sensor technologies. Among 18 different signals, it was determined that EDA sensors are best for this application. Our findings also show that CNN outperforms SVM, SVR, KNN and LDA for classifying EDA data with an average of 79% accuracy. This is further improved with the addition of RGB sensor data.

Keywords: Emotion recognition · Machine learning · Physiology · Robots · Sensors

1 Introduction

In 2017, Twenge et al. [1] surveyed 600,000 people living in the U.S for exploring societal mental health. Their goal was to determine self-reported depression rates amongst the current youth. During 2009–2017, they found the proportion of adolescents reporting a depressive episode had doubled. These results were a sobering reminder of the times we live in. Social isolation has been linked to a plethora of mental issues [2, 3]. This is especially a problem, when developed countries are finding that the number of single-person households is increasing. In some countries these make up 60% of residences [4]. Loneliness is not limited to millennials either, an aging and busier population is resulting in our elders having less familial support. Hence, our society is one of great loneliness and mental health is sure to degrade if nothing is done.

We believe that robots will play a crucial role in maintaining our mental health. Not by replacing practicing professionals, but as an aid to improve mental therapies. Assistive robots have already seen widespread success in healthcare [5, 6]. In addition, facial expression analysis found useful for detecting doubt effect, subjective beliefs, differentiating between observed real and posed smiles, and assessing mental health [7, 8]. Thus, it is possible to use robots for monitoring mental health of patients and report them

C. Ardito et al. (Eds.): INTERACT 2021, LNCS 12936, pp. 481–485, 2021.
https://doi.org/10.1007/978-3-030-85607-6_62

back to a professional therapist. Currently, detailed mental health monitoring is done through patients recounting their days. However, people often face difficulties remembering events accurately. Robots can help us achieve this through emotion monitoring. As an example, sadness is found highly correlated with depression for clinical diagnoses [9]. As such, recognizing emotions through robots could provide an objective account of patients' mental states. It is worthwhile to note that without AI or machine learning (ML) methods, robots must use a hard-coded program to achieve emotion recognition. Thus, our aim is to determine which non-invasive physiological signals and ML methods are most appropriate for emotion monitoring through robots.

2   Method

We searched six academic databases, namely IEEE Xplore, Google Scholar, University SuperSearch, Scopus, Pubmed Central, and ResearchGate. Three keywords were derived in consultation with University librarians: **robot***, **emotion recognition**, and **sensor*** (where * denotes wildcard characters). The key words cover the area related to robotic, emotional, and physiological contexts where 'sensor' term is used to find related physiological based papers. The search results were kept between 1 June 2015 to 31 May 2020 for finding most up-to-date papers. If there were more than 200 results (Google Scholar, University SuperSearch, and Scopus), the results were sorted by the engine's definition of relevance for accumulating most relevant papers of interest, and the top 200 results were added to the screening pool. This resulted in a collection of 805 papers in total, of which 619 were unique.

Then, articles were excluded if they were either: 1) publications that were not original peer-reviewed papers, 2) papers not related to emotion recognition, 3) papers that do not mention applicability of research to improving robots or machines, or 4) papers that do not state research applicability in a mental therapy context. For validation of excluded results, two reviewers acted independently on the 619 unique papers. There were 17% mismatched papers from each reviewer. By discussing with third reviewer, 60 papers were finally included for detail analyses.

3   Results

We found 18 different signals were studied in 60 included papers. They are categorized into *physiological* and *physical* signals[1]. Figure 1 (left) shows the distribution of sensors used in experiments. In total, 112 sensors were studied across the 60 papers. The heart signal category makes up the largest fraction at 28.6%. RGB was the most common signal studied across the 60 papers (15.2%). The RGB is followed by EDA (14.3%), EEG (13.4%), and others. Overall, the physiological and the physical signals make up 70.5% and 29.5% of the total signals studied respectively.

---

[1] *Physiological*: BVP, PPG, HR, ECG, EDA (electrodermal activity), EEG, EOG, ST (skin conductance), HDR (hemodynamic response), motion (accelerometers and positional information), resp. (respiratory signals).*Physical*: 3D, RGB, Text, env. (environmental), radio signal, SA (speech audio), Tactile (pressure sensor).

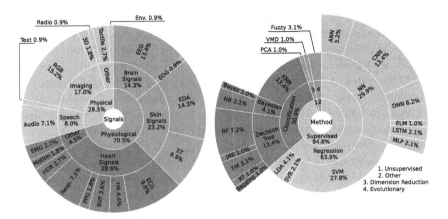

Fig. 1. Signals (See footnote 1) studied (left) and used ML (See footnote 2) methods (right) in the included papers.

The distribution of used ML[2] classifiers is displayed in Fig. 1 (right). The classifiers have been categorized into supervised, unsupervised, and others. The supervised methods are subcategorized into classification and regression. It has been seen that SVM is a highly representative method with 27.8% usability followed by KNN (13.4%) and CNN (13.4%). Methods involving artificial neural networks accounted for 29.9% cases. The overwhelming majority, 94.8%, of classifiers are supervised. Meanwhile dimensionality reduction methods were the only unsupervised methods used, at 2.1% usability.

4   Discussion and Conclusion

Emotion classification from facial images or video data appeared six times in the top 15 papers with highest classification accuracies, for example [10, 11]. However, top three highest scoring scores reported from four or less sample sizes. EEG appeared twice in the top 15 papers with an average accuracy of 92.0% between the two. HR, EDA, ECG, body temperature, motion data, speech audio, EMG, BVP were also appeared in the list of top 15 papers. The 'top 15 papers' represents the highest accuracies among the included 60 papers. This is highly important as it means that the majority of commonly studied non-invasive physiological signals have the potential to be very accurate in emotion recognition.

The highest scoring method was found CNN, applied on RGB data. However, Fig. 1 (right) shows that the most common classifier was SVM (27.8%). We believe there are two reasons for the low number of papers for CNN. Firstly, training CNNs or any deep networks require huge data. This is hard to come from physiological signals, and even the

---

[2] *ML methods*: ANN (artificial neural network), Bagging, Bayes, LDA, KNN, PCA, VMD (variational mode decomposition), MLP, CNN (convolutional neural network), DNN (deep neural network), ELM (extreme learning machine), LSTM, NB, SVM, SVR, Fuzzy, RF (random forest), J48 (J48 decision tree), EM (ensemble methods), RT (regression tree).

largest sample size in the included 60 papers was 457 for an EDA experiment. However, image sets can have potentially thousands of faces, and this does not count video datasets. Computational effort could be another factor as SVM is faster than CNNs.

Initially, RGB cameras appeared to be the best single sensor for emotion recognition. EEG, ECG, and other physiological sensors are also found viable for high accuracy emotion recognition. However, these fall short on comfort and ease of use due to longer setup times. Future work should analyses the sensors long term comfort and ease of implementation. This way, we will have a better idea of which sensors are better implementable in the mental therapy application.

EDA was determined to be best suited towards mental health monitoring robots. Out of the 60 papers, 14 papers considered some form of EDA in emotion recognition. Of these, only two used standalone EDA [12, 13], while others used a fusion of sensors. It has been found that even standalone EDA has great potential for emotion recognition tasks. Thus, an inbuilt EDA sensor [14, 15] on robot can be used for the tasks. Furthermore, CNN-classified EDA provided an average of 79.0% accuracy over six papers. Hence, CNN appears to be the best classifier for EDA data if the sample size is sufficient to allow it. In addition, robot would have a microphone and RGB camera to pick up speech and facial expressions. The fusion of EDA, RGB and speech audio would provide accuracy well above standalone CNN classified EDA data of 79.0%. Overall, we found which sensors we can use in robots to assist in mental health monitoring. Evaluating the accessibility, accuracy, and applicability on 18 unique sensors over 60 papers, EDA was the single-best sensor for this application. Our findings also show that CNN performs better than other ML classifiers.

This research helps pave the way towards improved social robotics and robot assisted mental health solutions. We have shown that using new classifiers with even standalone EDA provides accurate and objective emotion recognition. But in combination with camera and microphone data, we can attain very high emotion recognition accuracy, as required for clinical depression diagnosis. Minimizing the number of sensors required allows cost effective robots with less failure points. Hence, a robot with a camera and microphone feed providing support to a patient wearing an EDA wristband could be the emotion monitoring robot that helps to keep us all in good mental health.

Due to the lack of space in here, our future work will explore the overall process to conduct the literature review as proposed by Kitchenham [16], which includes, but not limited to, detailed planning, execution and data synthesis, the sample size used, the gender of the participants, suitable EDA sensors, RGB data collection and classification, different research dimensions, and broad future challenges.

References

1. Twenge, J.M., Joiner, T.E., Rogers, M.L., Martin, G.N.: Increases in depressive symptoms, suicide-related outcomes, and suicide rates among U.S. adolescents after 2010 and links to increased new media screen time. Clin. Psychol. Sci. **6**(1), 3–17 (2017)
2. Mushtaq, R., Shoib, S., Shah, T., Mushtaq, S.: Relationship between loneliness, psychiatric disorders and physical health? A review on the psychological aspects of loneliness. J. Clin. Diagn. Res. **8**(9), WE01-4 (2014)

3. Loades, M.E., et al.: Rapid systematic review: the impact of social isolation and loneliness on the mental health of children and adolescents in the context of COVID-19. J. Am. Acad. Child Adolesc. Psychiatry **59**(11), 1218–1239 (2020)
4. Snell, K.D.M.: The rise of living alone and loneliness in history. Soc. Hist. **42**(1), 2–28 (2017)
5. M. Simon. "This Incredible Hospital Robot Is Saving Lives. Also, I Hate It". WIRED (2015). https://bit.ly/34JHZxR. Accessed October 2020
6. C. W. R. University. "5 Medical Robots Making a Difference in Healthcare" Case Western Reserve University (2020). https://bit.ly/3iggbZP. Accessed Oct 2020
7. Zhu, X., Qin, Z., Gedeon, T., Jones, R., Hossain, M.Z., Caldwell, S.: Detecting the doubt effect and subjective beliefs using neural networks and observers' pupillary responses. In: Cheng, L., Leung, A.C.S., Ozawa, S. (eds.) ICONIP 2018. LNCS, vol. 11304, pp. 610–621. Springer, Cham (2018). https://doi.org/10.1007/978-3-030-04212-7_54
8. Hossain, M.Z., Gedeon, T., Sankaranarayana, R.: Using temporal features of observers' physiological measures to distinguish between genuine and fake smiles. IEEE Trans. Affect. Comput. **11**(1), 163–173 (2018)
9. Mouchet-Mages, S., Baylé, F.J.: Sadness as an integral part of depression, (in Eng). Dialogues Clin. Neurosci. **10**(3), 321–327 (2008)
10. Ruiz-Garcia, A., Elshaw, M., Altahhan, A., Palade, V.: Deep learning for emotion recognition in faces. In: Villa, A.E.P., Masulli, P., Pons Rivero, A.J. (eds.) ICANN 2016. LNCS, vol. 9887, pp. 38–46. Springer, Cham (2016). https://doi.org/10.1007/978-3-319-44781-0_5
11. Yang, J., Wang, R., Guan, X., Hassan, M.M., Almogren, A., Alsanad, A.: AI-enabled emotion-aware robot: the fusion of smart clothing, edge clouds and robotics. Futur. Gener. Comput. Syst. **102**, 701–709 (2020)
12. Boccanfuso, L., et al.: A thermal emotion classifier for improved human-robot interaction. In: 25th IEEE International Symposium on Robot and Human Interactive Communication, pp. 718–723 (2016)
13. Yin, G., et al.: User independent emotion recognition with residual signal-image network. In: International Conference on Image Processing, pp. 3277–3281 (2019)
14. FitBit. "Fitbit Debuts Sense, Its Most Advanced Health Smartwatch; World's First with EDA Sensor for Stress Management, Plus ECG App, SpO2 and Skin Temperature Sensors". FitBit (2020)
15. Hossain, M.Z., Gedeon, T., Sankaranarayana, R.: Observer's galvanic skin response for discriminating real from fake smiles. In: 27th Australasian Conference on Information Systems, pp. 1–8 (2016)
16. Kitchenham, B.: Procedures for performing systematic reviews. Keele Univ. **33**, 1–26 (2004)

Safe-to-Touch: Tracking Touched Areas in Public Transport

Linda Hirsch$^{(\boxtimes)}$ (ID), Yanhong Li$^{(\boxtimes)}$, Hendrik Geiger$^{(\boxtimes)}$, and Andreas Butz$^{(\boxtimes)}$

LMU Munich, Munich, Germany
{linda.hirsch,yanhong.li,butz}@ifi.lmu.de, h.geiger@campus.lmu.de

Abstract. Risk areas for smear infections in public transport stay generally unnoticeable for passengers. However, touching a handrail can be similar to shaking hands with a thousand people. Although prior research looked into self-cleaning materials to tackle such issues, little has been done to make touched areas more transparent to passengers. In this work-in-progress, we present our idea of "Safe-to-Touch", a handrail indicating prior touch points until completed self-cleaning. We prototyped a first interactive version and introduced the idea, including photos of it, in an online survey with 52 participants. Our preliminary results showed that 98.1% of participants would probably change their touch behaviors according to our handrails' indications and would appreciate the increased transparency.

Keywords: Touch surfaces · Public transport · Interactive handrail

1 Introduction

Handrails in public transports are touched daily by thousands of people. Hence, these shared touch surfaces pose a high risk for smear infections. In a study with undergraduate students, Fierer et al. found that each student carried a minimum of 150 different bacteria species on one hand alone [3], which can be distributed via common touch surfaces. Prior work in material science and engineering approached the topic by researching self-cleaning materials and infection risk-reducing mechanisms [1]. However, little has been done to communicate increased risk areas to passengers and to enable them to consciously avoid previously touched areas.

In this work-in-progress, we introduce our idea for "Safe-to-Touch", a handrail coated with copper, a material with self-cleaning properties. In addition to being self-cleaning, the handrail can track touched areas for 120 min and indicate its increased smear infection risk with light indications. According to Querido et al. [2], 120 min is the time frame in which copper self-cleans 99% of its surface. In this first step, we aimed to build a simple setup that only communicates its touched areas and their state to its passengers. The idea is to enable passengers to make a more active, conscious choice about where to touch public

Published by Springer Nature Switzerland AG 2021
C. Ardito et al. (Eds.): INTERACT 2021, LNCS 12936, pp. 486–489, 2021.
https://doi.org/10.1007/978-3-030-85607-6_63

transport. It could increase passengers' socio-spatial awareness of other passengers' touch behaviors by making touch traces visible, potentially decreasing the smear infection risk. We see the relevance of this topic in the recently increased awareness of hygiene and the insecurity in recognizing infection sources, which have evolved throughout the COVID-19 pandemic.

We approached this topic in a user interface design course with "revealing human traces" as an overarching project theme. Considering the motivation mentioned above, we applied a user-centered design approach beginning with desk research about passengers' behaviors and infection risks in public transport. Based on our findings, we developed the idea of "Safe-to-Touch". We developed an interactive prototype, which we evaluated in an online survey ($N = 52$) to gather feedback on the concept and its design. The results showed that all participants who used handrails in public transport would probably adapt their touch behavior according to our prototype's indication. Below, we give a short overview of prior research about public transport measurements before presenting "Safe-to-Touch" and our online study results in more detail.

2   Related Work

Prior work discovered that the infection risk via shared touch surfaces in public transport is high and exponentially increasing [4,5]. The majority of work focused on tracking and identifying the infection risk, excluding potential counter-measurements. Others explored potential solutions in the form of self-cleaning materials [1], mechanisms[1] or behavioral guidelines[2] for passengers.

Regarding handrails, Vargas-Robles et al. [6] showed that the majority of passengers (99%) interacted with handrails during their rides, contributing to the bacteria exchange. The mass of bacteria even resettled already 5 to 30 min after cleaning handrails. Therefore, this leaves a small time frame for passengers not to get in contact with others' bacteria in public transport.

However, only very few studies approach the topic from a Human-Computer Interaction (HCI) perspective, which focuses on passengers as end-users in a real-time and in-situ interaction. Hence, we see a gap in the current research discourse, which opens a broader range of design opportunities.

3   *Safe-to-Touch*: Development and Testing

We applied a user-centered design approach, beginning with desk research. This was followed by the concept development and prototyping of "safe-to-touch". Finally, we evaluated it in an online survey with 52 participants.

Our desk research revealed a gap in communicating areas of increased smear infection risks to passengers. We decided to focus on handrails in particular, because more than 99% of passengers are touching them.

---

[1] https://bit.ly/39tOEyR, last accessed March, 28th 2021.
[2] https://bit.ly/31tQag0 and https://bit.ly/3sC0K0t, last accessed March, 28th 2021.

3.1   Safe-to-Touch Prototype

Based on our prior desk research, we defined some requirements to be considered in the prototyping: 1) Using anti-bacterial materials to reduce infection risks. 2) Revealing touched areas until the completion of the self-cleaning process. 3) Creation of sub-sections so that passengers can vary touch positions according to the indication. 4) Applying an easy-to-understand indication to enable immediate decision making and touch reaction.

Based on those requirements, we built the first low-fidelity prototype to iterate on the indication design. We compared color choices, positions, and sizes using modeling clay and cardboard. After making several grip tests, we decided to create a pole with three subsections. Each included an independent indication consisting of an LED strip that changes color according to the current touch state. The handrail differentiates between three states: 1) default, untouched, 2) "currently-touched" and 3) "in-cleaning-mode" state, each representing a different phase of touch interaction. We considered the ISO 22324 guidelines for color-coded alerts[3], and chose green for the default, a neutral color for the second touch state, and red for the third. The LED strip was attached along the handrail's length with a slightly raised profile. This made it visible from many angles while leaving as much area as possible for actually gripping the handrail. An Arduino microcontroller measured the time passed since the last registered touch on each section.

3.2   Online Survey

We conducted an online survey with 52 participants of mixed age groups. 32 of them were 18 to 28 years old, ten were from 29 to 45, and another ten were 46 and older. All were or had been (before COVID-19) frequent users of either subway, bus, or city trains. We introduced photos of our prototype with the concept idea descriptions to participants, asking them to give their opinions on its design and functionality and their perceptions of hygiene in public transport (on a Likert-scale from 1: negative perception to 5: positive perception).

3.3   Preliminary Results

Thirty-one participants reported on an increasingly negative perception of hygiene in public transport since the beginning of the COVID-19 pandemic. Another 13 remained neutral, and the remaining 8 slightly positive. Considering the handrail, a vast majority (94.1%) indicated that they would feel more comfortable with "Safe-to-Touch" compared to current handrail solutions. Also, 98.1% stated that they would change their touch behavior according to our prototype's indication. The remaining 1.9% explained that they already avoided handrails and hence, would not change their behavior. Participants further indicated that our proposed color combination was understandable.

---

[3] https://www.iso.org/standard/50061.html, last accessed March 28th, 2021.

4 Conclusion, Limitations and Next Steps

The current status of "Safe-to-Touch" satisfied participants' interest and needs to be better informed of potential risk areas for smear-infection. The topic is essential because of the increased hygiene awareness, especially with the global pandemic of COVID-19. Prior research focused on automated, nontransparent measurements or behavioral guidelines handed out to passengers. However, little research was looking into real-time, real-place feedback, which is a contribution of our poster. However, our study also has some limitations. First, our concept and prototype are still in an initial state, even though they can be further improved by, e.g., integrating self-cleaning mechanisms that speed up the process. Also, our evaluation approach did not make people interact directly with the prototype but relied on the provided pictures and the description. For future steps, it might be helpful to use thermochromic paint or other touch-reacting materials to indicate touched areas more precisely and leave more surface as alternative touch places for passengers. Also, to properly test the color indications' effect, we will try the handrail in an actual usability study with users approaching the handrail from different angles. Finally, we wish to spark an interesting discussion about the design opportunities for revealing passenger-to-passenger touch interactions in public transport with this poster.

Acknowledgements. We want to thank Abdullah Tayyab, Lennat Grigoleit and Till Wagner from our user interface design course. They initiated the idea and developed the prototype.

References

1. Michels, H., Moran, W., Michel, J.: Antimicrobial properties of copper alloy surfaces. Adv. Mater. Processes **166**, 57–58 (2008)
2. Querido, M.M., et al.: Self-disinfecting surfaces and infection control. Colloids Surf. B: Biointerfaces **178**, 8–21 (2019)
3. Fierer, N., Hamady, M., Lauber, C.L., Knight, R.: The influence of sex, handedness, and washing on the diversity of hand surface bacteria. Proc. Natl. Acad. Sci. **105**(46), 17994–17999 (2008)
4. Birteksöz Tan, A., Erdogdu, G.: Microbiological burden of public transport vehicles. Istanb. J. Pharm. **47**, 52–56 (2017)
5. Zhou, J., Koutsopoulos, H.: Virus transmission risk in urban rail systems: a microscopic simulation-based analysis of spatio-temporal characteristics (2020)
6. Vargas-Robles, D., Gonzalez-Cedillo, C., Hernandez, A.M., Alcaraz, L.D., Peimbert, M.: Passenger-surface microbiome interactions in the subway of Mexico City. PLoS ONE **15**(8), e0237272 (2020)

Sign Language GIFs Exchange Communication System: A PECS-Based Computer-Mediated Communication Tool for the Deaf

Celeste Zhilla, Giulio Galesi[✉], and Barbara Leporini

ISTI-CNR, Pisa, Italy
{giulio.galesi,barbara.leporini}@isti.cnr.it

Abstract. Thanks to technological advances, Sign Language (SL), which is used by most deaf people, has gradually been freed from the need for face-to-face interaction. Deaf people used to communicating via SL may experience many problems in writing and reading text contents. Considering those difficulties, we propose a messaging system that integrates a Graphics Interchange Format (GIF) gallery representing phrases and words in SL to promote written communication closer to the needs of this user category.

Keywords: Deaf · Sign language · CMC · GIF · Chat

1 Introduction

According to the World Health Organization (WHO), around 466 million people worldwide currently have disabling hearing loss, and around 95% of deaf/hard of hearing children are born to hearing-impaired parents. Based on the estimation of WHO, 900 million people will be suffering from hearing loss in 2050[1].

Many hearing-impaired people use Sign Language (SL) for communication. SL is a linguistic system, consisting of a structured and organized set of signs, with a precise grammar, syntax, and morphology of its own. However, SL communication is not universal. Differences exist between countries and there are even regional variations of SL [1].

SL is the preferred choice for people who have totally lost their hearing capability. SL users rarely use hearing aids, write notes or lip read. So, SL communication leads to several issues for deaf people when interacting with non-deaf people that cannot understand SL. The development of methods that provide some types of ICT solutions for deaf-hearing and hearing-deaf communication has increased. In order to ease their communication, there is considerable research activity in the development of possible supporting tools. These tools have a wide range from systems of Speech to Text (which translates verbal speech into written words and vice versa with Text to Speech), Display System, Haptic or Visual Feedback (e.g., applications focused on multimodal approach,

---

[1] https://www.who.int/news-room/fact-sheets/detail/deafness-and-hearing-loss.

© IFIP International Federation for Information Processing 2021
Published by Springer Nature Switzerland AG 2021
C. Ardito et al. (Eds.): INTERACT 2021, LNCS 12936, pp. 490–494, 2021.
https://doi.org/10.1007/978-3-030-85607-6_64

able to convert speech to visual contexts and vibrations, and similarly, the contexts and vibrations can be converted to speech [2]) up to Mobile support [3].

There are also wearable technologies but, that often means that the deaf person must wear numerous very visible devices (e.g., gloves with sensors, helmet with infra-red filters camera). This could potentially represent a stigma for the hearing-impaired person.

Computer-mediated SL communication involves new ways to manipulate language structure and performance, including experimentation of new proposed language forms. Thanks to the developments of new tools, for the first time, hearing-impaired people can communicate using manual visual language, which in many cases is their native language, across space and time zones [4]. Also, the animation capabilities of modern screens offer an exciting opportunity to create a new communication system for people who use SL to communicate. So, SL communication needs to be further investigated to support it through tools and applications.

This work is focused on a component proposed in a project aimed at developing a remote video application to support SL interpreting. A messaging system prototype that makes use of Augmentative Alternative Communication (AAC) methodology is presented. SL is a movement-based language without a standard written form; because of this, deaf people communicating via SL may face several difficulties, including the use of the written form [5]. In order to support chat communication between SL users, in our prototype, we propose the integration of a gallery of Graphics Interchange Format (GIF) representing phrases and words in SL format to promote written communication closer to the needs of the deaf or hard-hearing people.

2 Design Approach

Communication is one of the most important aspects affecting the social interaction for the deaf. Additional methods such as the use of AAC may be used to overcome communication problems and barriers for deaf people [6]. AAC is an area of clinical practice that seeks to reduce, moderate, and compensate for the temporary or permanent difficulties of people with severe communication disorders both on the expressive and receptive fronts and help them in their social needs of life [7]. For deaf people, one of the possible used AAC-based practices are representational systems [8]. The best known is the Picture Exchange Communication System (PECS), which is a communication strategy based on the exchange of several PECS images that make up a sentence. PECS is used to remedy the mismatch in the communication methods of people with deafness and one or more intellectual disabilities (mild or moderate) who communicate through the SL and those who do not use it. In this way, studies - proposing illustrated dictionaries to facilitate message writing intended for their communication partners - have shown that, with adequate preparation regarding the rules of use, the subjects were able to use these tools with success and they have had the role of facilitating writing [9].

Following the representational assisted AAC methodology, in this work, we propose the use of short and silent moving images, the GIFs with the aim to facilitate text-based computer-mediated communication for the deaf. The idea is proposing a chat component based on the AAC communication system. To prepare the aforementioned GIFs, videos provided by the Spread the Sign's website were converted through a special app.

3 Chat Prototype

The chat component is part of a remote communication tool designed for those deaf people who use SL interpretation. Similar characteristics and tasks offered by typical popular chat systems for the communication between users are provided by the proposed chat component (see Fig. 1). To support chat communication for the deaf user, in addition to the traditional text editing via keyboard, a series of GIFs is shown when the specific button "GIF SL" is hit. Those GIFs representing sentences and words expressed in SL can be selected by the user to edit the message to be sent via chat.

Fig. 1. Chat prototype window.

The GIFs set developed for the chat prototype contains a limited number of GIFs images, but it was enough to test the proposed approach. Therefore, the main limitation is that the user may not find the appropriate SL GIF needed to compose and send a certain word/phrase. On the other hand, the main benefit of GIFs is that they can automatically play short, non-audio "looping" video clips [10]. Thanks to these characteristics, the GIF format is well suited as a representation system for assisted AAC. GIFs, in fact, as non-audio contents, are a very suitable medium for the SL rendering, because they can show SL characteristics like: (1) the area where the sign is made, showing part of the signer's body; (2) the configuration of the hands in executing the sign, that is the shape it assumes by positioning the fingers; (3) the orientation of the palm of the hand in making the sign concerning the signer's body; (4) the movement of the hand or hands in carrying out the sign [11]. The GIF format can play animations in an endless silent loop, so it is suitable for learning new signs.

The GIFs gallery layout is in line with the common grid outline used for the AAC systems, in which the symbols are in specific positions within a grid (see Fig. 2). As each symbol is isolated, it supports the recall of the individual contents of each cell [12]. The use of GIFs representing SL movements grouped in a gallery is an interesting PECS-based methodology that can be great benefit to the Deaf community.

Fig. 2. A subset of a SL GIFs gallery

4 Conclusions and Future Work

This paper presents a potential assistive technology to support chat communication by the deaf. The chat prototype was designed to be used by deaf people who use SL to communicate and have difficulty with written production. The proposed system differs from existing solutions in (1) no advanced digital skills are required and (2) only a few clicks are required to write SL messages.

The current chat prototype has the sign language limitation which needs to be considered in the future work. In fact, our proposed system has been designed for the Italian Sign Language (LIS), and so it needs to be adapted to the various existing sign languages. So, further future development will have to consider the interface localization so that the gif gallery will be shown in the selected language.

In addition, future studies will further develop the chat tool so that the system provides automatic translation from text messages to GIFs (i.e. to SL) and vice versa, thus also allowing communication between a person who uses SL to communicate and one who does not.

References

1. Tilano-Vega, L.M., et al.: Tools facilitating communication for the deaf. Educación y Educadores **17**, 468–480 (2014)
2. Sobhan, M., Chowdhury, M.Z., Ahsan, I., Hasan, M., Kamrul, H.: A communication aid system for deaf and mute using vibrotactile and visual feedback, pp. 184–190 (2019). https://doi.org/10.1109/ISEMANTIC.2019.8884323
3. Dhanjal, A.S., Singh, W.: Tools and techniques of assistive technology for hearing impaired people. In: International Conference on Machine Learning, Big Data, Cloud and Parallel Computing (COMITCon), Faridabad, India, pp. 205–210 (2019)
4. Keating, E., Mirus, G.: American sign language in virtual space: interactions between deaf users of computer-mediated video communication and the impact of technology on language practices. Lang. Soc. **32**(5), 693–714 (2003)
5. Marschark, M., Mouradian, V., Halas, M.: Discourse rules in the language productions of deaf and hearing children. J. Exp. Child Psychol. **57**(1), 89–107 (1994). ISSN 0022-0965
6. Davis, T.N., Barnard-Brak, L., Dacus, S., Pond, A.: Aided AAC systems among individuals with hearing loss and disabilities. J. Dev. Phys. Disabil. **22**, 241–256 (2010)

7. Koul, R.K., Lloyd, L.L.: Survey of professional preparation in augmentative and alternative communication (AAC) in speech-language pathology and special education programs. Am. J. Speech Lang. Pathol. **3**(3), 13–22 (1994)
8. Malandraki, G.A., Okalidou, A.: The application of PECS in a deaf child with autism: a case study. Focus Autism Other Dev. Disab. **22**(1), 23–32 (2007)
9. Allgood, M., Kathryn, H., Easterbrooks, S., Fredrick, L.: Use of picture dictionaries to promote functional communication in students with deafness and intellectual disabilities. Commun. Disord. Q. **31**, 56–64 (2009)
10. Morris, S., Vollmer, T.: A comparison of picture and GIF-based preference assessments for social interaction. J. Appl. Behav. Anal. **53** (2020). https://doi.org/10.1002/jaba.680
11. Goldin-Meadow, S., Brentari, D.: Gesture, sign, and language: the coming of age of sign language and gesture studies. Behav. Brain Sci. **40**, e46 (2017)
12. Cooper, A., Ireland, D.: Designing a chat-bot for non-verbal children on the autism spectrum. Stud. Health Technol. Inform. **252**, 63–68 (2018)

Spatial Layout Versus List Layout: A Comparative Study

Daniel Roßner[1]([⊠]) [iD], Claus Atzenbeck[1] [iD], and Tom Gross[2] [iD]

[1] Institute of Information Systems, Hof University, Alfons-Goppel-Platz 1,
95028 Hof, Germany
{daniel.rossner,claus.atzenbeck}@iisys.de

[2] Human-Computer Interaction Group, University of Bamberg,
Kapuzinerstraße 16, 96047 Bamberg, Germany
tom.gross@uni-bamberg.de

Abstract. Information retrieval systems support users in finding relevant information in data sets. List layouts are wide-spread, but spatial layouts are catching up. User studies that systematically show their benefits for users are missing. We report on a comparative between-subject study with 43 participants comparing a spatial layout with a list layout. One group performed a task with a system providing semantic visualization, and the other group performed the same task with a system without semantic visualization. The results show that the users of the spatial layout had significantly more interaction with the system in shorter time, with a slightly higher outcome and higher satisfaction.

Keywords: Spatial hypertext · Spatial layout · List layout · User study

1 Motivation

Spatial hypertext promises to discover "the missing link" [5], bridging the gap between human beings' associative thinking and machines explicit structures. On a 2D screen, spatial context can be derived, e.g. by interpreting size, shape, hue or spatial arrangement of nodes. Interpretation of the spatial context happens naturally for humans, but need specialized algorithms when done by machines. So-called *spatial parsers* [7] analyze the visual cues mentioned above and produce a weighted graph of the human organized layout. The resulting graph may be utilized in various cases, e.g. supporting hierarchical selection [1] or user interaction in general [4]. This process of parsing human generated layouts to an explicit structure can be inverted as well, often with the goal of making complex information structures visually accessible. Such *meaningful layout* generation "works well in iterative systems, in which the collection of elements is not defined a priori" [2]. An example of such a layout generation is explained in [6], where authors argue that the positioning and dynamic behavior support users' browsing and understanding of the spatial hypertext. Klouche et al. [3] identified "a

C. Ardito et al. (Eds.): INTERACT 2021, LNCS 12936, pp. 495–498, 2021.
https://doi.org/10.1007/978-3-030-85607-6_65

lack of understanding on the end-user benefits of interactive visualization in multi-aspect search scenarios", especially in comparison to conventional search interfaces with a ranked result list. Effects of interactive, spatial visualizations in such information retrieval scenarios are still not well studied. For this purpose we conducted a user study with 43 computer science students and discuss the first results in the following sections.

2   Experiment

We had an experimental design with a spatial variant (Mother) and a list variant (List). Both were tested remotely, with the same knowledge base, offering the same suggestions. 43 students in computer science (26% female, two not specified) with a mean age of 22.6 (ranging from 19 to 30) were asked to participate in a voluntary user study. Participants should imagine the following situation: "Close to your residence, it is planned to build new wind turbines. Find as many potential advantages, disadvantages and other personally relevant topics you want to ask questions about at a soon to be held citizens' meeting, as possible."

The task is completed, when participants think, they have gathered enough information for the citizens' meeting. Right after, they should write down the topics, which they will ask questions about. The experiment used two systems, one based on a spatial suggestion visualization and a reference system which shows results in a ranked list. Participants got randomly assigned to one of the systems. The underlying data is German, and the participants were native speakers. In both cases, the system shows an initial keyword, suitable for an open search task given to the users. In turn, they get suggestions based on this keyword and all other selected suggestions.

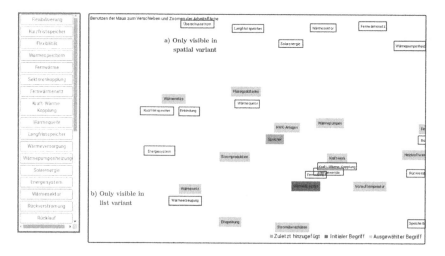

Fig. 1. Comparison of spatial layout (a) and ranked list (b); suggestions are identical (Color figure online)

The knowledge base is a weighted graph with keywords, formed around the topics of sustainability and renewable energy. All keywords are extracted nouns of ten Wikipedia pages, like "Windenergie" (wind power), "Passivhaus" (passive house) or "Fernwärmespeicher" (steam accumulator). Weight calculation is done by accumulating how often these keywords appear in the same context.

To make results comparable with a list-based variant, the spatial one does not allow users to alter position and size of nodes. Focus is given on how suggestions are represented, not how users interact with already selected nodes. An example is shown in Fig. 1a. Colorized keywords are nodes selected by the user, with *green* denoting the initial (given) keyword, which cannot be deselected. *Light Blue* marks selected keywords, that can be deselected and *dark blue* highlights the last selected keyword. Suggestions do not have any colorization and are positioned with the algorithm from [6]. In short, the authors describe a physics based approach, utilizing a simulated, annealing spring network to represent parts of a weighted graph.

Selected keywords appear at the position where they were suggested to be. The number of suggestions grows with the number of selected nodes linearly. Panning and zooming the viewport helps look into details or gaining an overview. Both actions are triggered by the computer mouse, the latter with the mouse wheel. The baseline system is very similar to the spatial one, as can be seen in Fig. 1b, and is inspired by the baseline system of [3], where results are shown in a ranked list. Suggestions are not visible in the space until they get selected from the ranked list on the left. With selecting an entry from the list, the keyword appears in the space, positioned as in the spatial variant.

During the test, any interaction with the system is recorded, such that a detailed replay of a session could be created. For the analyses we examined those which are relevant to the effectiveness, efficiency, and satisfaction of the users. In this study effectiveness is defined as the outcome in the number of chosen topics, written down right after task completion, and efficiency as the task duration in seconds. Satisfaction is the subjective assessment of how helpful the system was, on a scale from 0 to 10. Additionally, we want to characterize the respective interaction of the participants with either variant. For this purpose we measured the number of pans and zooms as well as the number of de-/selections.

3   Results and Future Work

The results for both test scenarios are summarized in Table 1. Overall, the collected data shows a higher efficiency for the spatial variant, as participants did finish in less time, while the rating of the helpfulness is equal for both test variants. The quantity and quality (the latter estimated by authors) of chosen topics suggest, that both groups performed similar, thus the variants were equally effective. While not statistically significant, both the effectiveness and satisfaction measure tend to be better for the spatial variant.

Adding and deleting nodes are the necessary actions to browse the knowledge graph. Participants with the spatial visualization seem to interact less, but the differences are not significant (Wilcoxon: $p = 0.089$). Yet, due to the faster task completion, there are significantly more interactions per time frame. As expected, spatial variant participants used the 2D space considerably more to explore the knowledge base, measured by the amount of pans and zooms.

Table 1. Summarized results for list and spatial variants; bold values indicate $p < 0.05$

	Baseline (B)		Mother (M)		B vs. M	
	M	SD	M	SD	Test	
Chosen topics	2.5	1.5	3.3	2.8	$p = 0.2465$	(t-test)
Task duration (seconds)	251.6	147.2	162.5	133.4	$\boldsymbol{p = 0.02265}$	(Wilcoxon)
Helpful rating (0–10)	5.7	2	6.2	1.9	$p = 0.2504$	(t-test)
Navigation (pan+zoom)	21.8	27.1	50.2	37.6	$\boldsymbol{p = 0.000741}$	(Wilcoxon)
Interactions (de-/selections)	25.3	12.4	20.3	14.8	$p = 0.08811$	(Wilcoxon)

In the end, this and comparable studies suggest advantages of spatial visualizations in information retrieval scenarios, compared to typical list-based interfaces. We plan to investigate the data into more detail: Did the interaction rate change during the test? How does another layout algorithm influence the result? *How* do users browse the 2D space? Furthermore, this study utilized a reduced feature set of the positioning algorithm. Especially the possibility to move nodes, while suggestions re-position themselves may influence the results, as there are more opportunities to interact with the system.

References

1. Francisco-Revilla, L., Shipman, F.: Parsing and interpreting ambiguous structures in spatial hypermedia. In: 16th ACM Conference on Hypertext and Hypermedia, HT 2005, pp. 107–116. ACM Press (2005)
2. Kerne, A., Koh, E., Sundaram, V., Mistrot, J.M.: Generative semantic clustering in spatial hypertext. In: Proceedings of the 2005 ACM Symposium on Document Engineering, pp. 84–93. ACM Press (2005)
3. Klouche, K., Ruotsalo, T., Micallef, L., Andolina, S., Jacucci, G.: Visual re-ranking for multi-aspect information retrieval. In: Proceedings of the 2017 Conference on Conference Human Information Interaction and Retrieval, CHIIR 2017, pp. 57–66. ACM (2017)
4. Lyon, K., Nürnberg, P.J.: Applying information visualisation techniques to spatial hypertext tools. In: Wiil, U.K. (ed.) MIS 2004. LNCS, vol. 3511, pp. 85–93. Springer, Heidelberg (2005). https://doi.org/10.1007/11518358_7
5. Marshall, C., Shipman, F., III: Searching for the missing link: discovering implicit structure in spatial hypertext. In: Proceedings of the Fifth ACM Conference on Hypertext, pp. 217–230, November 1993
6. Roßner, D., Atzenbeck, C., Gross, T.: Visualization of the relevance: using physics simulations for encoding context. In: Proceedings of the 30th ACM Conference on Hypertext and Social Media, HT 2019, pp. 67–76. ACM Press (2019)
7. Shipman, F., Moore, J.M., Maloor, P., Hsieh, H., Akkapeddi, R.: Semantics happen: knowledge building in spatial hypertext. In: Proceedings of the ACM Conference on Hypertext, pp. 25–34. ACM Press (2002)

The Impact of Culture on Visual Design Perception

Ioana D. Visescu[✉]

Department of Business Development and Technology, Aarhus University, Aarhus, Denmark
201911148@post.au.dk

Abstract. This paper questions the concept of universal users, taking a first step in looking at design perception differences between cultures, opening a discussion about culture in the context of HCI and more specifically interface interaction. This is done through a short study assessing participants from 3 cultures and their perception of interface by looking at 3 mobile payment applications with the help of remote eye-tracking technology (iMotions), and AI predictive analysis software (EyeQuant). Results show considerable differences between the two software solutions as well as between cultures, diverging in preference over text vs icons, with little consistent patterns as ground for speculation further than what the data shows.

Keywords: Culture · Eye tracking · HCI · Interface design

1 Introduction

In a continuous race to have an edge in the sales and marketing sectors, several companies have emerged promising a shortcut to interaction analysis, allowing companies to assess their websites or applications faster and with impressive numbers as promises. This shortcut has been pushed even further given the current state of the world under the current pandemic and thus the need of remote analysis. We can see similar reasons evoked when justifying the need of these tools "associated costs, running user studies might become extremely challenging due to health, travel, and financial constraints", etc. [1]. While some tools approach interaction analysis through methods such as cursor patterns or go as far as to have their users interact with a website or page while describing the process out loud, other companies have taken it a step further and offer an analysis based on previously collected data and a set of algorithms bound to create an analysis of a universal experience [2].

This of course raises the question of the existence of a universal user. While more and more companies go global with their products and content, it is important to understand whether there are objective design approaches that will be accepted internationally, or whether accommodating and catering to a regional culture is a worthy investment. Papers show cultural differences can have an impact as deep as usefulness perception [3], and while a call for the creation of cultural personas exists in the current literature [4], is

© IFIP International Federation for Information Processing 2021
Published by Springer Nature Switzerland AG 2021
C. Ardito et al. (Eds.): INTERACT 2021, LNCS 12936, pp. 499–503, 2021.
https://doi.org/10.1007/978-3-030-85607-6_66

there really a segregation in market needs regarding visual design and functionality, or is the seemingly utopian universal user a reality?

2   Methods

The concept of a universal user is being questioned throughout this study by comparing the heatmap of a software providing the perspective of a universal user [2], with heatmaps from a software analyzing the eye movement of participants from 3 distinct countries and cultures – the Chinese, the Danish, and the Kenyan one, in order to see any potential discrepancies between them.

The participants were split in 3 studies, based on nationality, and were asked to look at the interfaces of their local application, as well as the other two foreign applications, while their eye movements were tracked with the help of the iMotions software mentioned in the Software section.

2.1   Participants

In the Kenyan study, out of 16 participants, 11 were considered valid. In the Chinese study, out of the 11, 8 were considered valid. In the Danish study, out of 11, 9 were considered valid. Some data was considered invalid due to a variety of factors, including: poor light conditions, the inability of the software to identify the eye, study participants being engaged in other activities (for example looking away from the computer during the time their eye motion was analyzed), etc.

The ages of the participants vary from 20 to 55 year old, all participants are familiar with the concept of mobile payment applications, and have previously used their local application. The participants had not previously interacted with the other two applications. The local application are considered to be: WeChat Pay for China, MobilePay for Denmark, and M-Pesa for Kenya.

2.2   Software

The software used in this project is by Eyequant and iMotions. Eyequant provides a software using AI to predict what users focus on regarding visual designs. The software makes use of predictive algorithms and provides feedback on the design of a chosen page, allowing companies to optimize their websites, ads, or other promotional material.

iMotions provides a software meant for remote eye tracking, among other services. The software is currently limited to eye tracking and uses the remote access hardware such as computer/laptop cameras. The software version used during this study was in its initial stages, and since this study, iMotions has debugged and optimized its software for a more inclusive and overall improved performance.

2.3   Procedure

The Eyequant study has been performed through their main service, providing a fast solution in the form of heatmapping predicted attention spots.

The iMotions study was performed remotely, accessing the laptop/PC's camera, and it included several steps of calibration. The test has a duration of less than 5 min including the calibration, includes 92 slides, out of which 9 are direct stimuli for the study, and out of which 3 have been analyzed directly in this project. The stimuli are kept on the screen for a duration of 6 s, which was considered similar to other studies of this kind [5], and the calibration slides were on the screen for 5 s each. The participants are presented with the interface slides in a random order. The approximated distance of the participants from the screen is of 60 to 90 cm. The resulting heatmaps were compared by software and culture of provenience.

3   Results and Discussion

Below are presented the side-by-side heatmaps from both software companies, Eyequant on the left of each of the 3 sets of images, and iMotions above and to the right of the application name in each set. WeChat Pay, the Chinese local payment application is the first interface shown on the left side, followed by the one of MobilePay – the local Danish application on the bottom, and finally by the M-pesa one on the righ – the local Kenyan application.

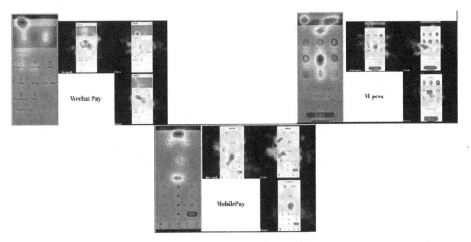

The Eyequant heatmap (on the left of each image batch) seems to show a preference for text and general titles over icons, which can seem contra intuitive for image/icon heavy designs such as the Wechat and M-pesa interfaces. The iMotions analysis (above and to the right of the text of each image batch) seems to overlap the Eyequant one when reduced to the center focal point, but does not show a strict user preference of the text/titles. The Eyequant and iMotions analyses diverge the most in the case of Wechat, where Eyequant shows little to no interest to icons, while the iMotions study shows the users' eyes are generally attracted to icons and more visually telling, or crowded parts of the interface. The two platforms diverge as well in their MobilePay heatmaps, but as the general interface of this application is rather plain and the numbers are occupying a fair share of the screen, it is surprising to see such little interest on the bottom part of the screen, where the icons are placed. This might be due to the muted colours and what can be considered a weaker call to action.

The pattern is kept consistent with the M-pesa heatmaps too, showing a focus on the middle third of the screen, and little to no interest for the text over the icons, with the inconsistent occurrence of the Chinese users.

As Eyequant has no clearly defined data gathering and processing patterns and processes, it is rather difficult to assess the accuracy of the software, and none of the nationalities mentioned in the iMotions analysis above seem to replicate the Eyequant one, their overlapping consistently leaving out the preference Eyequant as a software shows for text.

The data gathered throughout this project can show meaningful differences dictated by culture and context, and that it is important to understand and acknowledge the existence and importance of cultural spectrums in user perception of interfaces and their usability.

4   Conclusion

The main concern of the study – the existence of a universal user, was approached through comparison and data analysis techniques and according to the findings presented in this project, a definite effect of cultural nature can be seen on visual perception. From gender norms to cultural differences, the concluding aspect of this project is that the universal user is far from being a current reality.

However, while the literature sometimes emphasizes a clear and defined gap in between cultures, the reality seems, however, to be more nuanced. While cultural differences exist and cannot and should not be denied, the truth is that this information should be approached rather as a spectrum than as a defined block.

With more and more technologies emerging promising a shortcut to user studies, we must not forget that software, as well as products in their general sense, should be approached through a cultural lens too, and companies have nothing but to gain from adapting their products to local markets.

Finally, the discrepancy in understanding of user needs and cultural values and general cultural impact shows the need for an increased funding in research as well as in general product and software development. While universal users may well become a norm in future years, the current global situation seems to be far from homogenous, and companies and research centers should act accordingly. This first attempt at defining distinctive interface perceptions in visual design is to be followed by more extensive studies, both in the number of participants, as well as in the nature of separation. Future works should take into account age groups focus, as well as gender, and can be extended to include more cultures for a better understanding of where the lines of interaction blur, and where they become more defined patterns.

References

1. How | EyeQuant – Data Driven Design. EyeQuant – Data Driven Design (2021). https://www.eyequant.com/how/. Accessed 08 June 2021

2. Hashmi, W., Chaqfeh, M., Subramanian, L., Zaki, Y.: PQual: automating web pages qualitative evaluation. In: Adjunct Publication of the 33rd Annual ACM Symposium on User Interface Software and Technology UIST 2020 Adjunct, New York, NY, USA, pp. 148–150. Association for Computing Machinery (2020). https://doi.org/10.1145/3379350.3416163
3. Evers, V., Day, D.: The role of culture in interface acceptance. In: Howard, S., Hammond, J., Lindgaard, G. (eds.) Human-Computer Interaction INTERACT '97. ITIFIP, pp. 260–267. Springer, Boston (1997). https://doi.org/10.1007/978-0-387-35175-9_44
4. Lachner, F., von Saucken, C., 'Floyd' Mueller, F., Lindemann, U.: Cross-cultural user experience design helping product designers to consider cultural differences. In: Patrick Rau, P.L. (ed.) CCD 2015. LNCS, vol. 9180, pp. 58–70. Springer, Cham (2015). https://doi.org/10.1007/978-3-319-20907-4_6
5. Online Data Collection – iMotions. Imotions Publish, 19 May 2021. https://imotions.com/online-data-collection/. Accessed 08 June 2021
6. Wilming, N., Onat, S., Ossandón, J., et al.: An extensive dataset of eye movements during viewing of complex images. Sci. Data 4, 160126 (2017). https://doi.org/10.1038/sdata.2016.126

Think-Aloud Surveys

A Method for Eliciting Enhanced Insights During User Studies

Lene Nielsen[1]([⊠]), Joni Salminen[2], Soon-Gyo Jung[2], and Bernard J. Jansen[2]

[1] IT University Copenhagen, 2300 Copenhagen S, Denmark
Lene@itu.dk
[2] Qatar Computing Research Institute, HBKU, Doha, Qatar

Abstract. In a user experiment, we tried out a novel data collection approach consisting of combining surveys with the think aloud method. We coin the phrase "think-aloud survey method", where participants think-aloud while completing a questionnaire. We analyzed the transcripts and found that the think aloud survey provides deeper insights into the reasoning behind the participants' Likert scale choices and responses to open-ended questions, along with an enhanced understanding of the tasks and prompting the participants to explicate their choices. All resulting in more insights for design. The think- aloud survey method further offers other insights into usability issues and encourages the participants to provide system improvement proposals. The think-aloud survey method is useful for researchers and practitioners applying a large number of usability evaluations and wanting to dig deeper into the motivations for choice.

Keywords: Surveys · Tests · Interface design

1 Introduction

This work reports from an instance of combining two well-known data collection techniques: surveys and the think aloud (TA) method resulting in something greater than the sum of its parts. Alongside an experiment testing of the interactive persona analytics system [1] in a real-world setting of an organization that uses the system for marketing and communication, we applied what we dub the "think aloud survey" (TAS) that combines quantitative and qualitative research by the use of the think-aloud protocol with a questionnaire. The novelty of the method is that, typically, user experiment participants are asked to complete surveys in silence. In contrast, our suggestion is to ask the participants to explicate their cognitive processes verbally while completing the survey, which we found have multiple benefits for data richness and quality.

In our experience, the TAS method provides nuanced insights into the participants' understanding of the questions and spurs them to reflect upon their scale choices and open answers, providing perceptions into why a certain answer was given. This encouraged us to look into if this method can provide information otherwise difficult to access. In the following, we report on our experiences of employing the TAS in an actual user study. We introduce the TAS as an additional qualitative analysis that answers the why of questionnaires while conducting a user study.

© IFIP International Federation for Information Processing 2021
Published by Springer Nature Switzerland AG 2021
C. Ardito et al. (Eds.): INTERACT 2021, LNCS 12936, pp. 504–508, 2021.
https://doi.org/10.1007/978-3-030-85607-6_67

2   Surveys in Small Scale Research

As stated by [8], surveys are a frequently used method within HCI research. The self-reported data provides information about the users' perception of the system, their interaction with it [14], understanding of the different user groups, and what opinions they hold [4]. It enables researchers to gather information from a small set of users and infer to a larger group [9]. The advantages of surveys are that they are relatively easy to generate and analyze. The challenges lie mainly in research mistakes and participant misunderstandings of survey questions and scales [10]. A common criticism of surveys is that the questions are subject to misinterpretation and fail to measure what is intended [12]. To eliminate the misinterpretations it is suggested to do a few initial tests of participants' understanding of the questions using the TA protocol [11, 13] and let subjects verbalize their thoughts as they attempt to answer the survey questions. The proposed survey response process involves testing the comprehension, retrieval of information, judgment or estimation, and selection of a response to the question [15].

3   The Think Aloud Method in Usability Evaluation

TA in HCI is known as one of the protocols for usability testing [2, 6]. The participant is asked to vocalize his or her thoughts, feelings, and opinions while interacting with a system [7]. The concurrent TA method is expected to provide information during the participant's interaction with a system to identify the areas or features that cause problems for the user [3].

We propose to use the TA protocol to capture the active scale decision (qualitative analysis) and at the same time measure the participants' attitude towards and willingness to use, in this case, the interactive persona system (quantitative analysis). In our experimental setting, we found that the combination can provide answers to both how many have a particular attitude and why they express the attitude, as well as the reasoning and context behind a specific quantitative answer the participant gives.

4   Data Collection

Our data collection site is a large non-profit organization with employees of multiple nationalities. In total, there were 37 participants, of which ten (27%) were women. The average age of the participants was 32.9 years (SD = 6.9). The participants' experience of personas included 'Conceptual experience' (71%, n = 26), 'Some practical experience' (27%, n = 10), and 'Extensive experience' (3%, n = 1).

In an experimental setting, we wanted to test a persona analytics system. The participants were encouraged to speak during the completion of the questionnaire, thus providing richness to the participant survey responses. The survey questions (SQs) were applied in a questionnaire using a seven-point Likert scale with 1 = Strongly disagree, 7 = Strongly agree. After the survey were completed, participants were asked questions about the process and the survey responses retrospectively. All of this was recorded and later transcribed for analysis. The questionnaire resulted in initial research on the participant's understanding of the system and its usefulness.

For the purpose of this research and to analyze the TA transcripts, one researcher applied a coding process focusing on the questions reported above. NVivo, a software package for qualitative analysis, was used for the coding.

5 Findings

Overall, we identified nine possible benefits associated with the use of the TAS to complement the quantitative survey results. In the following sections, we present the benefits.

1. **Correcting Misunderstandings**
   Participants in doubt about a question, can ask the researcher to explain the question. The ambiguity of a question becomes visible.
   Individual perceptions of the Likert scale becomes visible.
2. **Forcing Argumentation and Affecting Scoring**
   Upon what the participants base their judgment, becomes clear as the contextual judgement is vocalized. The researchers, get an understanding of the reasoning behind a score.
3. **Revealing Same Arguments for Different Scores**
   Different participants might have the same argument but provide different scores. The difficulty of relying on the value without the contextual information becomes clear.
4. **Providing Information Beyond the Scale**
   Participants elaborate on the middle score, as weighing between the positive and the negative sides, but also something missing. The answers open for much more information than a neutral value.
5. **Providing Contextual Information about Participants' Understanding of the System**
   In surveys, it can be difficult to access if the participants understand what it is they are evaluating. An example shows that the participant have a fairly accurate understanding of the persona method, what personas are, and what to expect from the persona method. Thus providing information about the understanding of the system.
6. **Understanding Use Contexts**
   The information that the participants provide, makes the use context known to the researchers, thus enables them to improve the IT system. These insights adds richness to the findings and actions that occurred during the actual user study preceding the questionnaire.
   It becomes clear that if the participant lacks something that the system should be able to provide for their daily tasks.
7. **Identifying Missing Content for Design**
   The TAS includes issues concerning the interface and the content that is not provided in an unmoderated survey. This is valuable for the further development of the interactive system.

8. **Exposing Interface Issues**
   The TAS method exposes problems in the interface design and how participants relate to and their expectations of an interface. In this case that parts of system are confusing.

9. **Yielding Proposed Solutions**
   A critique often leads to suggestions for improvement and the participant suggests improvement.

In summary: The analysis of the TAS transcripts revealed different patterns that connects to the participants misunderstanding survey questions, revealing arguments for the scores they gave and at the same time forcing the participants to consider their motivation for scoring. It uncovered that the same argument can result in different scores, providing the researchers with information beyond the scores. Results also tested if the participants understood the persona analytics system, and provided information about a future use context and uncovered usability issues, as well as suggestion for solutions.

The positive effect of the TAS is the possibility to do both a qualitative analysis of the transcripts and a quantitative analysis of the quantitative scoring carried out by the participants. This provides information on the participants understanding of the system, information needs and use context, usability issues, and solutions to design. A quantitative analysis of the scores provides where the main problems are, and is relatively fast to extract.

The downside is that it requires a moderator and is time consuming.

6   Conclusion and Future Work

The proposed method of combining surveys with the think aloud protocol – the think aloud survey – provides insights similar to usability testing and insights into survey questions and responses. The method provides in-depth insights into the survey questions and can answer the why that is typically difficult to elicit from quantitative research. For practitioners, this method can be a faster way to get both quantitative and qualitative data, and it can be a test bed for setting up large surveys. In this research, we did not anticipate the usefulness of the method in terms of enhanced system design. In the future, it will be necessary to set up studies that are designated to investigate the application of the think aloud survey.

References

1. An, J., et al.: Imaginary people representing real numbers: generating personas from online social media data. ACM Trans. Web **12**(4) (2018). https://doi.org/10.1145/3265986
2. Ericsson, K.A., Simon, H.: Protocol Analysis: Verbal Reports as Data. MIT Press (1984)
3. Frandsen-Thorlacius, O., et al.: Non-universal usability? In: Proceedings of the 27th International Conference on Human Factors in Computing Systems - CHI 09, New York, New York, USA, p. 41 (2009)
4. Goodman, E., et al.: Observing the user experience: a practitioner's guide to user research (Second Edition). IEEE Trans. Prof. Commun. (2013)

5. Haeger, H., et al.: Cognitive Interviews to Improve Survey Instruments. Annual Forum of the Association for Institutional Research (2012)
6. Hertzum, M.: Usability Testing: A Practitioner's Guide to Evaluating the User Experience (2020)
7. Mack, R., Nielsen, J.: Usability inspection methods. ACM SIGCHI Bull. (1993)
8. Müller, H., et al.: Designing unbiased surveys for HCI research. In: Proceedings of the Extended Abstracts of the 32nd Annual ACM Conference on Human Factors in Computing Systems - CHI EA 2014, New York, New York, USA, pp. 1027–1028 (2014)
9. Müller, H., Sedley, A., Ferrall-Nunge, E.: Survey research in HCI. In: Olson, J.S., Kellogg, W.A. (eds.) Ways of Knowing in HCI, pp. 229–266. Springer, New York (2014). https://doi.org/10.1007/978-1-4939-0378-8_10
10. Ozok, A.A.: Survey design and implementation in HCI. In: The Human–Computer Interaction Handbook (2020)
11. Padilla, J.-L., Leighton, J.: Cognitive interviewing and think aloud methods. In: Zumbo, B.D., Hubley, A.M. (eds.) Understanding and Investigating Response Processes in Validation Research. SIRS, vol. 69, pp. 211–228. Springer, Cham (2017). https://doi.org/10.1007/978-3-319-56129-5_12
12. Schwarz, N.: The psychology of survey response. In: Tourangeau, R., Rips, L.J., Rasinski, K. (eds.) p. 401. Cambridge University Press, New York (2000). ISBN 0-521-57246-0 (cloth) and 0-521-57629-6 (paper). International Journal of Public Opinion Research (2001). https://doi.org/10.1093/ijpor/13.1.80
13. Tourangeau, R.: Cognitive Sciences and Survey Methods. Cognitive Aspects of Survey Methodology: Building a Bridge Between Disciplines (1984)
14. Between Disciplines
15. Tullis, T., Albert, B.: Measuring the User Experience: Collecting, Analyzing, and Presenting Usability Metrics: Second Edition (2013)
16. Willis, G.B., Artino, A.R.: What Do Our Respondents Think We're Asking? Using Cognitive Interviewing to Improve Medical (2013)
17. Willis, G.B., Artino, A.R.: What do our respondents think we're asking? using cognitive interviewing to improve medical education surveys. J. Graduate Med. Educ. (2013). https://doi.org/10.4300/jgme-d-13-00154.1

Towards a Design Space for Shadows as Ambient Displays

Özge Raudanjoki$^{(\boxtimes)}$ and Jonna Häkkilä

University of Lapland, 96300 Rovaniemi, Finland
{ozge.raudanjoki,jonna.hakkila}@ulapland.fi

Abstract. In this paper, we present a design space for using shadows in interactive systems. The main elements of the design space are optical properties, dynamicity, reality, temporality, and projection surface. The paper contributes a systematic approach for designing interactive systems with shadows, adding to the prior art, which consists mostly of focused case studies.

Keywords: Shadows · Design space · Ambient displays · User experience

1 Introduction

Shadow is caused by a local and relative deficiency of visible light [1]. Since classical times shadows have been associated with different meanings. The examples of shadow as a communicative metaphor are found in Plato's Republic. In his Allegory of the Cave dialogues, the prisoners chained in the cave can see only shadow-beings, which represent the erroneous vision of truth [7]. Being an integral part of our physical world, shadows surround us everywhere, their shape and appearance changing depending on the illumination and the surface they are cast to. Despite their omnipresence, we are so accustomed to shadows that we hardly notice their presence.

Designing with shadows appears in various domains. The natural phenomenon of shadows is employed in architecture and product design, to create spatial effects, for aesthetics, or for function, e.g. in sundials. Art has explored the visual effects and illusions with shadows, properties which have also been applied in user interface design. Today, a growing domain of digital entertainment demands designing with virtual representations of light and shadows.

In our research, we are interested in the concept of using shadows as part of the design of interactive systems. In addition to a large body of work in performative arts [4], interactive shadow display concepts have been studied in human-computer interaction (HCI) research. Due to their nature, existing at the periphery of our attention, shadows offer interesting design opportunities as ambient displays. Ambient displays have been defined to locate at the periphery

© IFIP International Federation for Information Processing 2021
Published by Springer Nature Switzerland AG 2021
C. Ardito et al. (Eds.): INTERACT 2021, LNCS 12936, pp. 509–512, 2021.
https://doi.org/10.1007/978-3-030-85607-6_68

of the user's attention and present non-critical information in abstract and aesthetic ways [9]. As ambient displays, shadows have been demonstrated in HCI in the context of plants [2], human shadows [11], candles [6], and lamps [8]. In addition, shadows have been integrated as an input method with mobile projector phones [3], and suggested to function as a user guidance [11]. However, the prior art in HCI has been rather scattered and focused more on single design cases.

In this paper, we wish to approach the topic of designing shadow UIs in a more systematic way and present a design space for using shadows as displays in interactive systems.

2   Design Space

The proposed design space for using shadow as an ambient display is presented in Fig. 1.

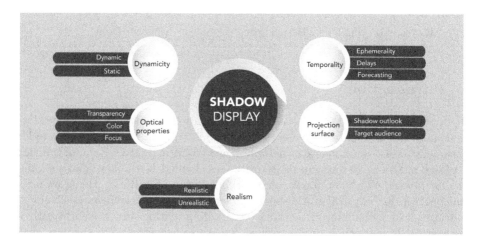

Fig. 1. Design space for shadow displays.

Optical Properties. In the context of its use as a design element, the main characteristics of shadow is its unique optical properties. Shadows in the physical world are affected by optical properties, such as *transparency, color,* and *optical focus.* The specific shades of colors can be associated with the type of information, urgency, or intensity. Besides that, color could create a coherency with a change of atmosphere in the physical space, e.g. depending on the time of day.

The transparency, or the opacity of shadow is determined by how well the object blocks light. If the light source is colored, e.g., yellow light, the light area surrounding the shadow is yellow. If there are artificial shadow silhouettes created with projected images, they can be colorful instead of black. Minomo et al. utilized colorful patterns, animations, textual information, photos, and live videos to make shadows colorful more naturally [10].

Dynamicity. Another aspect of the design space is the choice between the dynamic and static representation of shadow. While a dynamic change in shadow can provide information about an ongoing process, a static interpretation can be associated with instant events. The dynamic representation of information might include a stage of the process or abrupt indications of a specific event. Choice of expression is one of the challenges of the design space, depending on the type of information or notification to be conveyed.

Realism. Shadows created artificially may not always have a realistic outlook, but can give a distorted sense of reality. Perhaps one of the most compelling aspects of the artificial shadow metaphor is its consistency with real objects.

Temporality. Another consideration when thinking about the design is to understand the temporality of the display. Visualization of artificial shadows can have temporal elements that change with time. *Ephemerality* is a state of the temporary existence of things only for a short period of time [5]. It is an important part of our experiences with our surroundings. Nature is filled with unique, expressive examples of ephemeral materials. Most of these ephemeral materials are perceived as poetic [5] due to their meaningful, expressive nature.

Projection Surface. The surface where a shadow is cast affects primarily two aspects, the *outlook of the shadow*, and its *visibility*, which is important if we think to whom, or to which audience, the shadow display is targeted. Shadows are cast within an architectural space e.g. walls, doors, windows, desktops, floors, ceilings, which might provide different functionality of usability. A shadow that is displayed on the surface of water or onto a rough stone paving might provide different aesthetic modalities and modes of interaction.

3   Discussion and Conclusion

In this paper, we have described properties and other factors which we considered as creating the design space of shadows. Our design space for shadow as an ambient information display aims to describe broad application areas for shadows as a design element that can provide interesting opportunities and experience-rich applications. Especially the aesthetic, semiotic, and functional qualities of shadow make it a viable option for an ambient information display element. Based on prior research, it is known that temporal aspects in the movement of shadows [11], the movement dynamics [11], and the level of realism in the shape of the shadow [2, 11] influence the user experience with shadow displays. In future work, we aim to gain more insight into quantifying the UX with shadow displays through a systematic empirical study.

Acknowledgements. This research has been partially supported by the Smart Social Distancing project, funded by Business Finland.

References

1. Baxandall, M.: Shadows and Enlightenment. Yale University Press, London (1997)
2. Colley, A., Raudanjoki, Ö., Mikkonen, K., Häkkilä, J.: Plant shadow morphing as a peripheral display. In: Proceedings of the 18th International Conference on Mobile and Ubiquitous Multimedia, pp. 1–5 (2019)
3. Cowan, L.G., Li, K.A.: Shadowpuppets: supporting collocated interaction with mobile projector phones using hand shadows. In: Proceedings of the SIGCHI Conference on Human Factors in Computing Systems, pp. 2707–2716. CHI 2011, ACM, New York, NY, USA (2011)
4. Currell, D.: Shadow Puppets and Shadow Play. Crowood, Marlborough (2015)
5. Döring, T., Sylvester, A., Schmidt, A.: A design space for ephemeral user interfaces. In: Proceedings of the 7th International Conference on Tangible, Embedded and Embodied Interaction, pp. 75–82 (2013)
6. Häkkilä, J., Lappalainen, T., Koskinen, S.: In the candle light: pervasive display concept for emotional communication. In: Proceedings of the 5th ACM International Symposium on Pervasive Displays, pp. 161–167. PerDis 2016, ACM, New York, NY, USA (2016)
7. Heidegger, M.: The Essence of Truth: on Plato's Cave Allegory and Theaetetus. Bloomsbury Publishing, London (2013)
8. Jensen, W., Löchtefeld, M., Knoche, H.: Shadowlamp: an ambient display with controllable shadow projection using electrochromic materials. In: Extended Abstracts of the 2019 CHI Conference on Human Factors in Computing Systems, p. LBW1510. ACM (2019)
9. Mankoff, J., Dey, A.K., Hsieh, G., Kientz, J., Lederer, S., Ames, M.: Heuristic evaluation of ambient displays. In: Proceedings of the SIGCHI Conference on Human Factors in Computing Systems, pp. 169–176. CHI 2003, ACM, New York, NY, USA (2003)
10. Minomo, Y., Kakehi, Y., Iida, M.: Transforming your shadow into colorful visual media: multi-projection of complementary colors. In: Proceedings of the 2005 ACM SIGCHI International Conference on Advances in Computer Entertainment Technology, pp. 61–68 (2005)
11. Raudanjoki, Ö., Häkkilä, J., Hurtig, K., Colley, A.: Perceptions of human shadow manipulation as an ambient display. In: Proceedings of the 9TH ACM International Symposium on Pervasive Displays, pp. 71–77 (2020)

Towards Identifying Augmented Reality Unique Attributes to Facilitate Chemistry Learning

Sandra Câmara Olim[1,3]([✉]) [iD], Valentina Nisi[1,2] [iD], and Teresa Romão[3] [iD]

[1] ITI/LARSys, 9020-105 Funchal, Portugal
sandra.olim@iti.larsys.pt
[2] Instituto Superior Técnico, Lisbon, Portugal
valentina.nisi@tecnico.Ulisboa.pt
[3] NOVA LINCS, FCT, Universidade Nova de Lisboa, Lisbon, Portugal
tir@fct.unl.pt

Abstract. Augmented Reality (AR) applications have the potential to improve students' Chemistry learning performance. By identifying the unique features and affordances of this technology, we can design more effective tools to facilitate the learning process of abstract concepts. We developed Periodic Fable in the Wild, an AR serious game as an instrument to conduct design-based research. The game aims to facilitate the learning of abstract concepts related to the Periodic Table by children (9 to 13 years old). We intend to optimize our game by continuing our research with our target audience, analysing their feedback, making refinements and continuing testing.

Keywords: Augmented Reality · Serious games · Spatial skills · Chemistry

1 Introduction

Children, as young as nine years old, have already a perception of Chemistry as complex, not so attractive, less relevant to everyday life and a challenging domain [1,2]. Some of the factors that contribute to a negative perception of Chemistry are that it demands imagination, since there is no visible or physical referent; translating 2D information into 3D mental models can lead to cognitive overload and students with low spatial skills struggle with mental models [2].

Augmented Reality (AR) uniqueness of superimposing digital information within the real environment provides children's opportunities to:

1. Engage with educational content in digital format [3] while relating them to the actual physical world [4].
2. Provide visualization of abstract and complex concepts through animations, 3D modeling and other digital information.
3. Develop broader spatial skills by using activities with 3D objects (virtual or physical), providing an effective context for teaching [5].

© IFIP International Federation for Information Processing 2021
Published by Springer Nature Switzerland AG 2021
C. Ardito et al. (Eds.): INTERACT 2021, LNCS 12936, pp. 513–516, 2021.
https://doi.org/10.1007/978-3-030-85607-6_69

By developing an AR serious game to conduct design-based research, we intend to identify AR features and affordances towards facilitating the learning of abstract concepts in Chemistry. We also intend to change the negative perspective of this domain by using game design elements to engage children toward the learning content.

2   Periodic Fable in the Wild Systems Designs

Periodic Fable (PF) in the Wild is an AR serious game targeting 9 to 13-year-old children, designed to teach them basic chemistry concepts of the Periodic Table of Elements in formal and non-formal educational settings. The game's sub-theme evolves around the chemical composition of some products and substances (verified and validated by a chemistry teacher and a chemistry researcher). The AR game uses a marker-based system that operates with images/patterns (scan by the mobile device) to trigger the upload of virtual information (in our case, tridimensional models, animations, text, sound and a 2D minigame). The app was developed for android mobile devices using ARCore SDK for Unity 3D.

PF in the Wild was also developed with the aim to integrate every day routine products, that children are accustomed to (water bottle, bleach, batteries, balloons), as part of the game-play mechanics. The game's situated learning approach allows our target group to gain scientific knowledge about the chemical compounds that form the products. The goal is to achieve this by interacting with physical objects, AR technology and collaborating with other colleagues. PF in the Wild contributes to the learning process by creating meaningful connections between the content and the context.

The game starts with a tutorial that guides the user through the different game components:

1. The gathering of chemical atoms composing the product in question. The atoms are collected by scanning markers allocated in the products displayed on shelves (see Fig. 1 - number 1). All the collected atoms are displayed afterward on a 2D grid (see Fig. 1 - number 2). The application indicates the player when it has collected enough atoms by blocking the capture button. An animation of a character that represents an element with such atoms will also be showcase (see Fig. 1 - number 1).
2. Reconstruction of chemical composition of the selected product by combining the atoms identified in the screen's chemical structures (using a mini word puzzle kind of game). The collected atoms' icons are aligned on a simple grid and need to be connected by the participant's tip of the finger from one atom to the next. The player is guided in the sliding action by the chemical formula, which shows the order of the atoms, and it is displayed on the right side of the screen (see Fig. 1 - number 2).
3. Anchoring the AR visualization in the real world. The player has to use the device camera to scan and recognize a pattern in the real-world player surrounding. The AR application will build the AR experience around that location and allow the visualization of the tridimensional AR compound/molecular structure created by the player (see Fig. 1 - number 3).

4. Conclusion of the game experience. Congratulation message and player score display appear after the AR experience. The player's score is calculated by the time they spend on each activity within the game (see Fig. 1 - number 4).
5. Game reward. A Reward- Selfie screen is displayed at the end of the experience inviting the player to take a picture with all the game characters to share with family and friends (see Fig. 1 - number 5).

Fig. 1. PF in the Wild game flow

To get an overall understanding of the game, we conducted a pilot study with five participants (three female and two male). Children with ages ranging from 11 to 13 played the game for about 10 min. Some of the comments that we gather from post-game experience interviews point to the learning potential of the game "I think this is good for learning since I need to use the right compound to keep going"; usability "it is easy and good for learning"; the repetitiveness of the game mechanics "mini-game is too repetitive". We also asked the players to think aloud and took observation notes. In this note, we observed one of the players seems lost in collecting the elements and manifested frustration by saying, "I forgot which compound I was trying to form". Nevertheless, when asked: Will you play again? all of the participants answered "yes".

3   Conclusion and Future Work

We developed an AR serious game to evaluate the features and affordance of the technology towards facilitating the learning of abstract concepts of the Periodic Table. After a preliminary pilot study with the five children, we identify game-play elements that need refinements, such as the game's repetitiveness, which we plan to address by incorporating new elements, like animations and visual feedback between each task. Also as to better guide the user towards the compound that needs to be created at the different stages of the game, we will implement the display of UI with an images of the compounds structure until the tasks are accomplished (see Fig. 1, number 2 - right corner). Nevertheless, the overall players' assessment was positive and the comments oversee the app's potential as a tool to engage children with the content knowledge, in order to validate the game, further research is needed. This research's next step is concept and usability testing of the AR serious game with larger sample groups in formal and non-formal settings.

Acknowledgement. This work has been supported by MITIExcell (M1420-01-0145-FEDER-000002), MADEIRA 14–20 FEDER funded project Beanstalk (2015–2020), LARSyS-FCT Pluriannual funding 2020–2023 (UIDB/50009/2020), FCT Ph.D. Grant PD/BD/150286/2019, and by FCT/MCTES NOVA LINCS PEst UID/CEC/04516/2019.

References

1. Luraschi, M., Rezzonico, R., Pellegri, G.: The chemist, that madman! How children perceive science. CHIMIA Int. J. Chem. **66**(11), 820–825 (2012)
2. Osborne, J., Simon, S., Collins, S.: Attitudes towards science: a review of the literature and its implications. Int. J. Sci. Educ. **25**(9), 1049–1079 (2003)
3. Thamrongrat, P., Law, E.L.-C.: Design and evaluation of an augmented reality app for learning geometric shapes in 3D. In: Lamas, D., Loizides, F., Nacke, L., Petrie, H., Winckler, M., Zaphiris, P. (eds.) INTERACT 2019. LNCS, vol. 11749, pp. 364–385. Springer, Cham (2019). https://doi.org/10.1007/978-3-030-29390-1_20
4. Cesário, V., Trindade, R., Olim, S., Nisi, V.: Memories of Carvalhal's palace: haunted encounters, a museum experience to engage teenagers. In: Lamas, D., Loizides, F., Nacke, L., Petrie, H., Winckler, M., Zaphiris, P. (eds.) INTERACT 2019. LNCS, vol. 11749, pp. 554–557. Springer, Cham (2019). https://doi.org/10.1007/978-3-030-29390-1_36
5. Fowler, S., Cutting, C., Kennedy, J., Leonard, S.N., Gabriel, F., Jaeschke, W.: Technology enhanced learning environments and the potential for enhancing spatial reasoning: a mixed methods study. Math. Educ. Res. J. 1–24 (2021). https://doi.org/10.1007/s13394-021-00368-9

Usability Evaluation of a VibroTactile API for Web-Based Virtual Reality Experiences

José Canelha[1] , Jorge C. S. Cardoso[2](✉) , and André Perrotta[3]

[1] DEI, University of Coimbra, Coimbra, Portugal
[2] CISUC, DEI, University of Coimbra, Coimbra, Portugal
`jorgecardoso@dei.uc.pt`
[3] CITAR, Catholic University of Portugal, Porto, Portugal
`avperrotta@dei.uc.pt`

Abstract. This paper presents the Vibrotactile Editor System for designing and programming Vibrotactile (VT) feedback for Virtual Reality (VR) experiences. We describe the system and a usability evaluation of the programmatic component for the A-Frame web-based VR framework through a set of programming tasks. The resolution of the tasks showed some difficulty in understanding the state of the component when developing without the VT hardware present. The results show a number of potential improvements that we discuss.

Keywords: Vibrotactile feedback · Virtual Reality · Usability evaluation · API

1 Introduction

Providing Vibrotactile (VT) feedback for VR experiences is often complex, involving custom hardware with several actuators. An inherent challenge in the use of VT in this context is the technical expertise in designing and programming the different VT patterns to be used in VR experiences [1]. Different combinations of vibration patterns across the various actuators and across time must first be designed and iterated, and then the final sequences must be programmed into the VR framework.

Motivated by the technical requirements of the Thertact-Exo project[1], whose objective is to improve a neurorehabilitation training protocol that induces partial neurological recovery in paraplegic patients through long-term training with a brain-machine interfaced exoskeleton and an immersive VR system enhanced with visual-tactile feedback, the aim of this work was to develop a Graphical

---

[1] *Thertact-Exo: A brain controlled exoskeleton for spinal cord regeneration*, funded by Prêmio Melo e Castro - Santa Casa da Misericórdia de Lisboa, reference: MC-12-18.

© IFIP International Federation for Information Processing 2021
Published by Springer Nature Switzerland AG 2021
C. Ardito et al. (Eds.): INTERACT 2021, LNCS 12936, pp. 517–521, 2021.
https://doi.org/10.1007/978-3-030-85607-6_70

User Interface (GUI) for editing VT patterns and a high-level VR component that allows easier programming of VT feedback.

In this paper, we describe the proposed system, an initial evaluation of the Application Programming Interface (API) of the VR framework component, and the insights we gathered from this evaluation.

2   Vibrotactile Editor System

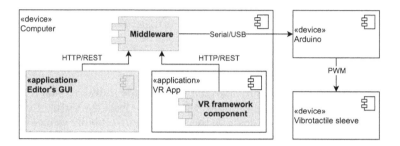

Fig. 1. Architecture of the vibrotactile editor system

The Vibrotactile Editor system (Fig. 1) is composed of 1) middleware, 2) editor's GUI for editing, and 3) VR framework components.

The middleware component is responsible for interpreting the commands issued from either the GUI or from the VR framework components and translating them into Arduino commands to control the VT sleeve. The middleware exchanges information with Arduino via a serial connection, controlling the vibration motors through Pulse Width Modulation (PWM). It exposes an HyperText Transfer Protocol (HTTP) API that is used by the VR framework components and the editor's GUI. Additionally, the middleware stores user's configurations as well as custom and default vibration patterns.

The editor's GUI is a desktop application for creating and testing vibration patterns across a number of actuators. The editor allows playing the timeline directly on the VT device for testing purposes, but its main output is a configuration file (*.json*) that can be used by the VR components.

The VR framework components provide high-level programming abstractions to programmers of VR applications. We currently support the web-based VR framework A-Frame (http://aframe.io) and Unity (http://unity3d.com/). The VR components also expose a number of JavaScript functions that can be used directly by programmers such as $sin()$ to send a sinusoidal waveform vibration, $ramp()$ to send a ramp vibration, $sendVibrations()$ to vibrations defined in a configuration file, and $customVibrations()$ to send a custom timeline.

3   Vibrotactile Component API Usability Testing

We evaluated the A-Frame implementation of the VR framework component through a remote, API task-based usability test approach.

Eight participants completed the test, all were students of Informatics Engineering in our department, with 3+ years of programming experience. We sent out the test tasks through email, as a shared Google Doc. We asked participants to leave comments in their code, pointing out unclear issues with the API's documentation, and suggestions to improve the API. We also asked them to fill in a post-test questionnaire after completing the tasks and requested users to send their solutions through email. The test consisted of four programming tasks (https://bit.ly/3fykqye), with increasing difficulty. The questionnaire was based on the structured interview presented by [2]. The complete set of questions can be seen in Fig. 2.

3.1   Results

The source code of each participant was analysed to verify the correctness of each solution. Table 1 shows the main issues that were found. The main issues were related to the entity that the component was attached to, the event associated with triggering the vibration, the use of an incorrect vibration file, and extra or incorrect parameters in calling the vibration functions. The results from the post-test questionnaire are shown in Fig. 2. In general, the results for each question are positive, or neutral.

Table 1. A-Frame component API usability tests results

Task	Issues
#1 Attach the vibrotactile component to an entity	Attaching component to wrong entity; Not associating event; Associating wrong event
#2 Vibrations after animation	Using wrong animation event; Not associating event; Associating wrong event; Incorrect vibration file
#3 Use JavaScript methods	Sending extra vibrations; Incorrect ramp; Associating wrong event
#4 Vibrotactile GPS	Vibrations in area transition only

4   Discussion

Given the mistakes that we identified in participants' code, we identified opportunities for improving the usability of the VR framework component:

- Provide more complete log messages. In particular, when vibrations are triggered from events, the log message is not explicit enough. This may have

	Question	Strongly Disagree	Disagree	Neutral	Agree	Strongly Agree
Understandability	hat the API types map to the domain concepts in the way you expected?			1	5	2
	keep track of information not represented by the API to solve the tasks?		5	3		
	Does the code required to solve the tasks match your expectations?			1	5	2
Learnability	ed the first task, was it easier to perform the remaining tasks / subtasks?			1	5	2
	Do you feel you had to learn many dependencies to solve the tasks?	1	5	2		
Abstraction	Do you find the API abstraction level appropriate to the tasks?			1	6	1
	erriding default behaviors, providing non-API types) to meet your needs?	2	5	1		
	d to understand the underlying implementation to be able to use the API?	2	5	1		
Readability	Do you find the API understandable, accessible, and readable ?				4	4
	Do you find able to use the API logically ?				4	4

Fig. 2. A-Frame component API usability questionnaire results

caused some of the mistakes we found in the source code from the various participants. For example, they may have assumed they had configured the correct event.

– Provide a visual debug mode where the entities to which the component is attached are visually highlighted and visually represent (e.g., through animation) when a vibration is triggered. This would make it easier to detect when the vibrations are attached to the wrong entities.
– Provide an audio debug mode where vibrations are automatically rendered as audio. This would make it easier to understand the vibrations being triggered even in case they are attached to non-visible entities. This would make it obvious, for example in the last task, whether the vibrations were being triggered continuously as the user moved through the virtual environment. Audio representations can also make it easier to notice when wrong (or more than expected) vibrations are being triggered.

5   Conclusion

Having a VT system for designing and programming vibration patterns is an important aspect for the creation of rich VR experiences that rely on VT feedback.

Our system provides not only a GUI for editing the VT patterns, but also programmatic components for the A-Frame and Unity VR frameworks. We have evaluated the VR framework component and are in the process of revising its implementation according to the findings.

Funding. Funded by national funds through the FCT - Foundation for Science and Technology, I.P., within the scope of the project CISUC - UID/CEC/00326/2020 and by European Social Fund, through the Regional Operational Program Centro 2020.

References

1. Burdea, G.C.: Virtual rehabilitation–benefits and challenges. Methods Inf. Med. **42**(5), 519–23 (2003). https://doi.org/10.1267/METH03050519. http://www.ncbi. nlm.nih.gov/pubmed/14654886
2. Piccioni, M., Furia, C.A., Meyer, B.: An empirical study of API usability. In: International Symposium on Empirical Software Engineering and Measurement, pp. 5–14 (2013). https://doi.org/10.1109/ESEM.2013.14

Workshops

2nd International Workshop on Empowering People in Dealing with Internet of Things Ecosystems (EMPATHY)

Giuseppe Desolda[1]([✉]), Vincenzo Deufemia[2], Maristella Matera[3], Fabio Paternò[4], Fabiana Vernero[5], and Massimo Zancanaro[6]

[1] University of Bari Aldo Moro, Bari, Italy
giuseppe.desolda@uniba.it
[2] University of Salerno, Salerno, Italy
deufemia@unisa.it
[3] Politecnico di Milano, Milan, Italy
maristella.matera@polimi.it
[4] CNR-ISTI, Pisa, Italy
fabio.paterno@isti.cnr.it
[5] University of Turin, Turin, Italy
fabiana.vernero@unito.it
[6] University of Trento, Trento, Italy
massimo.zancanaro@unitn.it

1 Motivation and Objectives

The design and development of the so-called smart objects have become a huge trend in the last decade, thanks to the proliferation of low-cost technologies embedded with sensors and actuators. A major role in further fostering this tendency has been played by the Internet of Things (IoT), which connects the physical world with the Internet via ubiquitous sensors and actuators.

In this scenario, end-users who may often lack specific technical skills are provided with the opportunity to configure the behavior of their smart objects, as well as their interactions with other objects and online services, thanks to novel interaction paradigms. Depending on the solution adopted, "IoT ecosystems" can leave their users completely free and unsupported in their configuration task, exploit intelligent techniques to automatically determine how smart objects should behave, or implement an intermediate approach. To this respect, a prominent example is represented by social and humanoid robots, i.e., integrated sets of sensors and actuators which can exhibit human-like behavior, which can guide and support end users in their configuration tasks.

The technological landscape, therefore, appears extremely variegated, with existing solutions offering different levels of user control and automation. Such possibilities can be exploited in a wide variety of application domains that can have an impact on our daily life, such as industry 4.0, ambient-assisted living, retail, smart home, cultural heritage, and education. In this perspective, it is also important to understand how to

© IFIP International Federation for Information Processing 2021
Published by Springer Nature Switzerland AG 2021
C. Ardito et al. (Eds.): INTERACT 2021, LNCS 12936, pp. 525–529, 2021.
https://doi.org/10.1007/978-3-030-85607-6_71

combine methods and tools from the artificial intelligence field and those developed in the area of End-User Development (EUD) to help users understand, control and modify the automation available in the surrounding context of use.

Given the diffusion and the relevance that these approaches have been gaining, this workshop aims to serve as a venue for discussing ongoing research and sharing ideas for researchers and practitioners working on solutions to personalize the behavior of IoT ecosystems.

Topics include, but are not limited, to: End-User Development (EUD) for IoT; Interaction Paradigms for IoT; Usability of IoT Systems; Interface Design for IoT; Intelligent Interface for IoT Systems; Accessibility for IoT Systems; Virtual and Augmented Reality for EUD in IoT settings, Conversational User Interfaces for EUD, Usable Privacy and Security in IoT systems, Personalisation and Recommendations for IoT.

2   Workshop Format and Participants

It is a one-day workshop, oriented towards discussions, hands-on sessions, and presentations. The number of workshop participants is limited to 30, mainly from academia and companies. Participants were informed about the workshop via the most known international mailing lists (e.g., DBWORLD, CHI-Announcements, etc.). Workshop papers are made available on CEUR Workshop Proceedings while workshop results are published on the workshop website (https://empathy-ws.github.io/2021/).

Table 1. Workshop Schedule

Time	Phase
09.00–09.15	Welcome and Introduction
09.15–10.30	Paper Presentations I
10.30–11.00	Coffee Break
11.00–12.30	Paper Presentations II
12.30–13.00	Future directions and wrap up
13.00–14.30	Lunch with all participants
14.30–15.00	Presentation of challenges
15.00–16.00	Creative thinking
16.00–16.30	Coffee Break
16.30–17.00	Result presentation
17.00–17.45	Agenda Definition & Wrap-Up

Table 1 shows the workshop schedule. At the beginning of the workshop, participants are welcomed and introduced to the workshop's goals and organizers. Then the accepted papers are presented in two sessions. Participants are encouraged to provide short but provoking presentations that tackle questions in line with the workshop goals. They are granted 10/15 min for presentation and Q&A. The workshop thus continues with a discussion on the main challenges, future directions, and controversial aspects that characterize the current landscape for the EUD of IoT systems.

In the afternoon, after lunch, the organizers present the challenges and future directions that emerged during the previous discussion, inviting the participants to use them as a ground for a creative thinking session. This activity takes 60 min and participants are divided into small groups; participants are provided with material for the illustrations of their ideas. Due to the COVID-19 prevention procedures recommended by the World Health Organization (https://www.who.int/emergencies/diseases/novel-cor onavirus-2019), interaction among participants is supported both online, thanks to virtual collaborative environments, and in presence, considering appropriate distances. Participants are provided with digital tools to collaboratively sketch their ideas and to prepare posters, videos, or 'Wizard-of-Oz' prototypes, or use storytelling or role-playing. After the coffee break, each group presents their solution to the workshop audience. Finally, the workshop organizers and participants consolidate results and ideas into the production of a structured map of topics to be addressed in future research.

The workshop is wrapped by identifying ways to move forward, including the initiation of joint publications, the organization of a new edition of the workshop (e.g., at CHI 2022, or IS-EUD 2023), and journal special issues on the topic.

3   Previous History

Looking at the recent history of significant workshops in the same research area, at CHI 2019 two workshops have been organized on IoT for non-technical people [1, 2], while a workshop on the interaction with smart objects [3], which led to a TOCHI special on "End User Development for the Internet of Things", was organized at CHI 2018. A workshop on "Intelligent User Interfaces for Internet of Things" took place at IUI 2019. Last year at CHI 2020 a workshop on Automation experience across domains: designing for intelligibility, interventions, interplay and integrity was organized [4].

The first EMPATHY workshop was held at AVI 2020, it was well attended, and the discussion was stimulating and interesting. Thus, we felt useful proposing a new edition that includes the same topics of the previous one, and addresses also further aspects that can raise interest and participation.

4   Organizers

The organizing team is a group of researchers with different disciplinary training and experience levels. They are involved in the EMPATHY project, which has been funded by the Italian Ministry of Education, Universities and Research (MIUR) troughs a three-year basis, research projects of national interest (PRIN). Their interdisciplinary nature allows the team to appreciate the diverse backgrounds of workshop attendees and to stimulate a critical discussion during the workshop.

Giuseppe Desolda is Assistant Professor at the Computer Science Department of the University of Bari "Aldo Moro" (email: giuseppe.desolda@uniba.it, website: http://ivu. di.uniba.it/people/desolda.htm). His research interests lie in HCI, specifically Interaction with Ubiquitous Systems, IoT, EUD, and Usable Security. Among others, he chaired the "Human-centered cybersecurity" (CHItaly 2019) and the "SERVE: Smart Ecosystems cReation by Visual dEsign" (AVI'16) workshops.

Vincenzo Deufemia is Associate Professor at the Department of Computer Science of the University of Salerno (email: deufemia@unisa.it, website: http://docenti.unisa.it/vincenzo.deufemia). His research interests include data science, pattern recognition and Human-Computer Interaction, with emphasis on usable privacy and security for end users. He has been a member of the organizing committee of several international conferences.

Maristella Matera is Associate Professor at the Department of Electronics, Information and Bioengineering (DEIB) of Politecnico di Milano (email: maristella.matera@polimi.it, website: http://matera.faculty.polimi.it/). Her research focuses on aspects at the intersection between Web Engineering and Human-Computer Interaction, with emphasis on design methods and tools for Web application development. She has been a member of the organizing committee of several international events - among others, she was program co-chair of AVI 2016. She is an associate editor for the journals "Future Generation Computer Systems" (FGCS) and ACM Transactions on Web (TWeb). She is chair of the Italian chapter of the ACM SIGCHI.

Fabio Paternò is Research Director at CNR-ISTI, where he leads the laboratory on Human Interfaces in Information Systems (http://hiis.isti.cnr.it/Users/Fabio/). His research activity has mainly been carried out in the Human-Computer Interaction (HCI) field, with the goal to introduce computational support to improve usability, accessibility, and user experience for all in the various possible contexts of use. For this purpose, he has continuously led for several years numerous interdisciplinary and international projects. He has been co-organiser of several workshops in international conferences.

Massimo Zancanaro is a professor of Human-Computer Interaction at the Department of Psychology and Cognitive Science at the University of Trento (email: massimo.zancanaro@unitn.it; https://webapps.unitn.it/du/it/Persona/PER0004568/). His research interests are in the field on Human-Computer Interaction and specifically on the topic of Intelligent Interfaces for which he is interested in investigating aspects related to the design as well as to study the reasons for use and non-use. At present, he serves as vice-chair for the Italian Chapter of the ACM Special Interest Group in Computer-Human Interaction and as Associated Editor for the journal Behavior and Information Technology.

Fabiana Vernero is a Lecturer at the Department of Computer Science, University of Turin (email: fabiana.vernero@unito.it, website: https://www.unito.it/persone/fvernero). She is part of the PhD committee in Modeling and Data Science, University of Turin. Her research interests include intelligent user interfaces, recommender systems and persuasive technologies.

The primary contact person is Giuseppe Desolda. All the organizers plan to attend the workshop.

References

1. Fröhlich, P., et al.: Everyday automation experience: non-expert users encountering ubiquitous automated systems. In: Extended Abstracts of the 2019 CHI Conference on Human Factors in Computing Systems (CHI EA 2019). ACM, New York (2019)
2. Fuentes, C., et al.: New directions for the IoT: automate, share, build, and care. In: Extended Abstracts of the 2019 CHI Conference on Human Factors in Computing Systems (CHI EA 2019). ACM, New York (2019)
3. Müller, F., et al.: SmartObjects: sixth workshop on interacting with smart objects. In: Extended Abstracts of the 2018 CHI Conference on Human Factors in Computing Systems (CHI EA 2018). ACM, New York (2018)
4. Fröhlich, P., et al.: Automation experience across domains: designing for intelligibility, interventions, interplay and integrity. In: Extended Abstracts of the 2020 CHI Conference on Human Factors in Computing Systems (2020)

Control Rooms in Safety Critical Contexts: Design, Engineering and Evaluation Issues
IFIP WG 13.5 Workshop at INTERACT 2021

Tilo Mentler[1], Philippe Palanque[2(✉)], Susanne Boll[3], Chris Johnson[4], and Kristof Van Laerhoven[5]

[1] Trier University of Applied Sciences, Trier, Germany
T.Mentler@inf.hochschule-trier.de
[2] Université Toulouse III – Paul Sabatier, Toulouse, France
palanque@irit.fr
[3] University of Oldenburg, Oldenburg, Germany
susanne.boll@uni-oldenburg.de
[4] Queen's University Belfast, Belfast, UK
c.w.johnson@qub.ac.uk
[5] University of Siegen, Siegen, Germany
kvl@eti.uni-siegen.de

Abstract. Human-Computer Interaction (HCI) research has been focussing on the design of new interaction techniques and the understanding of people and the way they interact with computing devices and new technologies. The ways in which the work is performed with these interactive technologies has arguably been less of a focus. This workshop aims at addressing this specific aspect of Human-Computer Interaction in the control rooms domain. Control rooms are crucial elements of safety-critical infrastructures (e.g., crisis management, emergency medical services, fire services, power supply, or traffic management). They have been studied in terms of Human-Computer Interaction with respect to routine and emergency operations, human-machine task allocation, interaction design and evaluation approaches for more than 30 years. However, they are dynamic and evolving environments with, for instance, the gradual introduction of higher levels of automation/autonomy. While state of the art control rooms are still characterized by stationary workstations with several smaller screens and large wall-mounted displays, introducing mobile and wearable devices as well as IoT solutions could enable more flexible and cooperative ways of working. The workshop aims at understanding how recent technologies in HCI could change the way control rooms are designed, engineered and operated. This workshop is organized by the IFIP WG 13.5 on Human Error, Resilience, Reliability and Safety in System Development.

Keywords: Control room · Pervasive computing · Safety · Usability · UX · Security · Resilience · Dependability

© IFIP International Federation for Information Processing 2021
Published by Springer Nature Switzerland AG 2021
C. Ardito et al. (Eds.): INTERACT 2021, LNCS 12936, pp. 530–535, 2021.
https://doi.org/10.1007/978-3-030-85607-6_72

1 Overview and Goals

While Human Factors approaches [1] and User-Centered Design [19] have been used to design and evaluate control rooms for a long time, the interaction technologies they offer are usually several steps behind what can be found in other areas such as home entertainment or gaming. Control rooms are deployed in very different domains such as crisis management, emergency medical services, intensive care units, fire services, power supply, maritime navigation, or traffic management.

More recent work has been focussing on the use of new technologies in the context of control rooms exploiting new interaction techniques and new interaction technologies introduced in research contributions from the Human-Computer Interaction area. Speech was considered early as an input modality [6] while the issues raised by its deployment was questioned in [8]. Auditory information was used as an alerting system in addition to the traditional display of information in [11] even though studies have shown [9] that human brain filters out that information in case of high workload or stress. Tactile feedback was introduced in cockpits more recently [12] (but this feedback directly used in combination with information displays) while tangible interactions were introduced as a mean to bring interactions closer to the ones on physical knobs [7]. Multi-touch interactions have also been recently studied both in control rooms [15] and interactive cockpits [16] raising multiple issues. Ambient displays [20] [ref] and head mounted displays [21] [ref] have been used to add a digital layer of information on top of control room elements to support situation awareness and attention in safety critical environments. This introduction of nonstandard (at the time) modalities, led to multimodal interactions (both in terms of input and output) but they are still considered a challenge in 2016 [2] while the early work from Bolt in that domain was introduced more than 25 years earlier [3]. Multimodality as input was however introduced successfully in industrial control rooms [5] or military aircraft cockpits [14] while multimodal output was largely used for alerting flying crews [13].

Beyond interaction technologies, the centralised nature of control rooms was questioned [10] and mobile solutions were proposed to support control and monitoring activities on the move. However, the introduction of these technologies in critical systems raised immediately the issue of their dependability and their security as soon as the environment loses its closeness nature.

While state of the art in deployed control rooms is still characterized by stationary workstations with several smaller screens and large wall-mounted displays, introducing mobile and wearable devices as well as IoT solutions could enable more flexible and cooperative ways of working. However, turning control rooms into pervasive computing environments raises user-related challenges such as usability and user experience, system-related ones such as reliability and dependability and more global ones such as safety and security [17]. However, it is clear that control rooms must evolve and integrate advanced interaction technologies [18] so that operations can be improved.

This workshop promotes sharing of experiences in designing, implementing, and evaluating interactive systems in control rooms. We are especially interested by contributions presenting theories, methods, and approaches for considering them as pervasive computing environments and interdependencies between all the properties listed above. In this workshop we consider control rooms in their broader sense including (ship) bridges, cockpits, and operating rooms. This workshop is organized by the IFIP Working Group 13.5 on Human Error, Resilience, Reliability, Safety and System Development.

2   The Specificities of Control Rooms

These control rooms are characterized by their operations that must be resilient to adverse events and unforeseen situations including human errors, system failures, environmental adversary conditions and malicious attacks. One of the specific challenges in their development is the demonstration that they meet requirements imposed by regulatory authorities.

As discussed in [4] control rooms present very specific aspects that make them very different from other interactive systems:

- They allow monitoring and control of complex cyber-physical systems;
- Their operations are usually defined and regularly assessed by regulatory authorities;
- They are operated by trained professional users that are usually qualified by dedicated organizations;
- They usually involve multiple operators who have to coordinate their actions to reach their goals;
- Operators have different levels of authority which grant different access to functions and data;
- Operator errors might have catastrophic consequences on people and goods;
- Failures in the display and control system might have catastrophic consequences on people and goods;
- Their deployment requires the acquisition of a certification from external organizations;
- They are operated in close worlds reducing security risks.

This list is far from being exhaustive but it gives a set of characteristics to be taken into account when considering the design of new types of control rooms and the constraints that have to be addressed.

3   Target Audience and Expected Outcomes

This workshop is open to everyone who is interested in the aspects related to the design, the engineering, the evaluation, the deployment, the maintenance and the certification of control rooms. We expect a high participation of IFIP working group 13.5 members. We invite participants to present position papers describing real-life case studies that illustrate, if possible, how a new technology would enhance control room operations. They could also highlight the trade-offs between two or more properties of interactive systems such as user experience and dependability or usability and security. The way the new technology will be addressing some known or envisioned problem in a control should be presented in the contribution. We are also interested in methods, theories and tools for control rooms development as long as they address some user interface properties. Accepted position papers are published in INTERACT 2021 adjunct conference proceedings. We also expect to discuss at the workshop how to disseminate individual contributions to the community in a special issue in a journal or in an edited volume.

4 Structure of the Workshop

This proposal encompasses a full-day workshop organized around presentation of position papers and working activities in small groups. From the set of contributions, a subset of selected case studies is invited to be presented at the beginning of the workshop and is used to support the discussion that follows. The morning sessions are dedicated to welcoming participants and presenting case studies. Participants are invited to comment the case studies and to report similar experiences. The afternoon sessions are devoted to interactive sessions, where participants are engaged to work in small groups to propose solutions to the issues raised by the case studies presented in the morning. Proposed solutions will be compiled and compared. Based on the lessons learned, participants will draft an agenda of future work that can be accomplished.

5 Workshop Organizers

Tilo Mentler is a professor of Human Computer Interaction and User Experience at Trier University of Applied Sciences. His research is focused on human-centered design in safety-critical contexts (e.g. mobile devices and mixed reality in healthcare, novel approaches to critical infrastructure). Currently, he works on control rooms as pervasive computing environments and examines the role of user experience in safety-critical settings. Prof. Mentler is chair of the special interest group "Usable Safety & Security" within the German Informatics Society (GI), member of the IFIP Advisory Board of GI and has been the GI representative in the IFIP Domain Committee on IT in Disaster Risk Reduction.

Philippe Palanque is Professor in Computer Science at University of Toulouse 3, where he leads the Interactive Critical Systems research group. Since the late 1980s he has been working on the development and application of formal description techniques for interactive systems. He has worked on research projects at the Centre National d'Études Spatiales (CNES) for more than 10 years and on software architectures and user interface modelling for interactive cockpits in large civil aircraft (funded by Airbus). The main driver of Philippe's research over the last 20 years has been to address in an even way usability, safety and dependability in order to build trustable safety-critical interactive systems. As for conferences he is TPC co-chair of EICS 2021 and is a member of the ACM CHI steering committee. He is a member of CHI academy, the chair of the IFIP TC 13 committee on Human-Computer Interaction, and secretary of IFIP WG 13.5.

Susanne Boll is a full professor for Media Informatics and Multimedia Systems at the University of Oldenburg and a member of the board of the OFFIS-Institute for Information Technology. Her research focus lies in the field of human-computer interaction (HCI). In her ongoing research, she is designing novel interaction technology for a respectful and beneficial cooperation of human and technology in a future automated world. She works on novel interaction methods for a safe cooperation and humans in safety-critical automated environments such as automated driving, health care and production. Her scientific results have been published in top venues in her field such as ACM CHI, MobileHCI, AutomotiveUI, as well as internationally recognized journals.

Prof. Boll was named a Fellow of the German Informatics Society in October 2020. She was named a Distinguished Member of the ACM in 2019 and is an elected member of acatech, The German National Academy of Science and Engineering.

Chris Johnson is Professor and Pro Vice Chancellor of Engineering and Physical Sciences at Queen's University Belfast. Over the last 20+ years, he has authored more than 200 peer reviewed publications, including one of the first textbooks on Accident and Incident Reporting. He has held fellowships from NASA, the US Air Force and Navy. He is a Scientific Advisor to the EC SESAR JU on the future of air traffic management and helped author guidelines on incident reporting for EUROCONTROL and for the European Railway Agency. He also helped the UK Department for Transport to develop the national cyber security strategy for aviation. In 2021, he is one of some fifteen expert witnesses retained to support the public inquiry into the Grenfell Tower fire.

Kristof Van Laerhoven is Professor in Ubiquitous Computing at the University of Siegen, Germany. His research interests span the areas of wearable and distributed sensing systems that focus on machine learning challenges, such as recognising what human users are doing, what they are focusing on, and how stressed they are. He is wearable department co-editor at IEEE Pervasive, is co-editor of Springer Adaptive Environments, associate editor for ACM IMWUT, and was general co-chair for ACM UbiComp/ISWC in 2020. More information can be found on http://ubicomp.eti.uni-siegen.de.

References

1. Carvalho, P.V.R., dos Santos, I.L., Gomes, J.O., Borges, M.R.S., Guerlain, S.: Human factors approach for evaluation and redesign of human–system interfaces of a nuclear power plant simulator. Displays **29**(3), 273–284 (2008)
2. Heimonen, T., Hakulinen, J., Sharma, S., Turunen, M., Lehtikunnas, L., Paunonen, H.: Multimodal interaction in process control rooms: are we there yet? In: Proceedings of the 5th ACM International Symposium on Pervasive Displays (PerDis 2016), pp. 20–32. ACM DL (2016)
3. Bolt, R.A.: "Put-that-there": voice and gesture at the graphics interface. In: Proceedings of the 7th annual conference on Computer graphics and interactive techniques (SIGGRAPH 1980). Association for Computing Machinery, pp. 62–270, New York, NY, USA (1980)
4. Boring, R.L., Hugo, J., Richard, C.M., Dudenhoeffer, D.D.: SIG: the role of human-computer interaction in next-generation control rooms. In: CHI 2005 Extended Abstracts on Human Factors in Computing Systems (CHI EA 2005), pp. 2033–2034. ACM DL (2005)
5. Fagerlönn, J., Hammarberg, K., Lindberg, S., Sirkka, A., Larsson, S.: Designing a multimodal warning display for an industrial control room. In: 12th International Audio Mostly Conference on Augmented and Participatory Sound and Music Experiences (AM 2017), pp. 1–5. ACM DL, Article 46 (2017). https://doi.org/10.1145/3123514.3123516
6. Baber, C., Usher, D.M., Stammers, R.B., Taylor, R.G.: Feedback requirements for automatic speech recognition in the process control room, Int. J. Man-Mach. Stud. **37**(6), 703–719 (1992). https://doi.org/10.1016/0020-7373(92)90064-R. ISSN 0020-7373
7. Müller, J., Schwarz, T., Butscher, S., Reiterer, H.: Back to tangibility: a post-WIMP perspective on control room design. In: International Working Conference on Advanced Visual Interfaces (AVI 2014), pp. 57–64. ACM, DL (2014)

8. Huber, K.: Does speech technology have a place in the control room? IEEE Power Eng. Soc. Gen. Meet. **3**, 2702–2703 (2005)

9. Dehais, F., Causse, M., Vachon, F., Régis, N., Menant, E., Tremblay, S.: Failure to detect critical auditory alerts in the cockpit: evidence for inattentional deafness. Hum. Factors **56**(4), 631–44 (2014). https://doi.org/10.1177/0018720813510735. PMID: 25029890

10. Juhlin, O., Weilenmann, A.: Decentralizing the control room: mobile work and institutional order. In: Prinz, W., Jarke, M., Rogers, Y., Schmidt, K., Wulf, V. (eds.) ECSCW 2001, pp. 379—397 (2001). Springer, Dordrecht. https://doi.org/10.1007/0-306-48019-0_20

11. Patterson, R.D., Mayfield, T.F.: Auditory Warning Sounds in the Work Environment [and Discussion]. Philosophical Transactions of the Royal Society of London. Series B, Biological Sciences, vol. 327, no. 1241, 1990, pp. 485–492. JSTOR. www.jstor.org/stable/55320. Accessed 10 March 2021

12. Nojima, T., Funabiki, K.: Cockpit display using tactile sensation. In: First Joint Eurohaptics Conference and Symposium on Haptic Interfaces for Virtual Environment and Teleoperator Systems, pp. 501–502. World Haptics Conference, Pisa, Italy (2005). https://doi.org/10.1109/WHC.2005.27

13. Selcon, S.J., Taylor, R.M., Shadrake, R.A.: Multi-modal cockpit warnings: pictures. words. or both? Pro. Hum. Factors Soc. Ann. Meet. **36**(1), 57–61 (1992)

14. Bastide, R., Navarre, D., Palanque, P., Schyn, A., Dragicevic, P.: A model-based approach for real-time embedded multimodal systems in military aircrafts. In: 6th International Conference on Multimodal Interfaces (ICMI 2004), pp. 243–250. ACM DL (2004)

15. Selim, E., Maurer, F.: EGrid: supporting the control room operation of a utility company with multi-touch tables. In: ACM International Conference on Interactive Tabletops and Surfaces (ITS 2010), pp. 289–290. ACM (2010)

16. Cockburn, A., et al.: Turbulent touch: touchscreen input for cockpit flight displays. In: Proceedings of the 2017 CHI Conference on Human Factors in Computing Systems (CHI 2017), pp. 6742–6753. ACM DL (2017)

17. Palanque, P., Basnyat, S., Bernhaupt, R., Boring, R., Johnson, C., Johnson, P.: Beyond usability for safety critical systems: how to be sure (safe, usable, reliable, and evolvable)? In: CHI 2007 Extended Abstracts on Human Factors in Computing Systems (CHI EA 2007). ACM DL, 2133–2136 (2007)

18. Roth, E., O'Hara, J.: Integrating digital and conventional human system interface technology: lessons learned from a control room modernization program. NUREG/CR-6749). Washington, DC: US Nuclear Regulatory Commission (2002)

19. Ulrich, T.A., Boring, R.L.: Example user centered design process for a digital control system in a nuclear power plant. In: Proceedings of the Human Factors and Ergonomics Society 57th Annual Meeting, pp. 1727–1731 (2013)

20. Cobus, V., Heuten, W., Boll, S.: Multimodal head-mounted display for multimodal alarms in intensive care units. In: Proceedings of the 6th ACM International Symposium on Pervasive Displays (PerDis 2017), pp. 1–2. Association for Computing Machinery, New York, NY, USA, Article 26 (2017). https://doi.org/10.1145/3078810.3084349

21. Stratmann, T.C., Kempa, F., Boll, S.: LAME: light-controlled attention guidance for multi-monitor environments. In: Proceedings of the 8th ACM International Symposium on Pervasive Displays (PerDis 2019), pp. 1–5. Association for Computing Machinery, New York, NY, USA, Article 7 (2019). https://doi.org/10.1145/3321335.3324935

Geopolitical Issues in Human Computer Interaction

José Abdelnour Nocera[1,2]([✉]), Torkil Clemmensen[3], Anirudha Joshi[4], Zhengjie Liu[5], Judy van Biljon[6], Xiangang Qin[7], Isabela Gasparini[8], and Leonardo Parra-Agudelo[9]

[1] School of Computing and Engineering, University of West London, London, UK
Jose.Abdelnour-Nocera@uwl.ac.uk
[2] ITI/LARSyS, Funchal, Portugal
[3] Copenhagen Business School, Frederiksberg, Denmark
tc.digi@cbs.dk
[4] IIT Bombay, Industrial Design Centre, Mumbai, India
anirudha@iitb.ac.in
[5] Sino-European Usability Center, Dalian Maritime University, Dalian, China
liuzhj@dlmu.edu.cn
[6] School of Computing, University of South Africa, Pretoria, South Africa
Vbiljja@unisa.ac.za
[7] Beijing University of Posts and Telecommunications, Beijing, China
qinxiangang@aliyun.com
[8] UDESC, Department of Computer Science, Joinville, SC, Brazil
isabela.gasparini@udesc.br
[9] Department of Design, University of Los Andes, Bogota, Colombia
leonardo.parra@uniandes.edu.co

Abstract. This workshop will explore and discuss geopolitical issues in Human Computer Interaction (HCI) as a field of knowledge and practice. These issues are mainly seen at two levels: (1) on discourses surrounding motivations and value of HCI as a sociotechnical field, and (2) on discourses surrounding concepts of HCI diffusion, maturity and diversity as articulated by global and local knowledge networks. Since the beginning of HCI, discussions of democracy have been around. It may even be fair to say that the key notion of usability aims to support the citizens of a democratic society. Obviously, exactly how HCI should do this remains open for discussion. HCI has several roots deep in military needs from the world wars of the 20th century. It was also born out of the sociotechnical traditions with its emancipatory ambitions, aiming at creating conditions for supporting human agency that facilitates the realization of people's needs and potential. There's an inherent contradiction between these traditions. Thus, we're interested in exploring the following question: how to reconcile such diverse discourses as military power and emancipatory ambitions in a geopolitical analysis of HCI research and associated discourses? Moreover, the diffusion of HCI as field of knowledge and practice is dominated by political and post-colonial discourses that pervade local and global knowledge networks shaping what is considered useful and relevant research and practice. In this workshop we understand these issues as geopolitical in nature and aim to trace the cultural and sociotechnical dynamics that construct the field of HCI.

© IFIP International Federation for Information Processing 2021
Published by Springer Nature Switzerland AG 2021
C. Ardito et al. (Eds.): INTERACT 2021, LNCS 12936, pp. 536–541, 2021.
https://doi.org/10.1007/978-3-030-85607-6_73

Keywords: Geopolitical issues · Sociotechnical · HCI knowledge · HCI practice · Diffusion · Maturity · Diversity

1 Introduction

This workshop will explore and discuss geopolitical issues in Human Computer Interaction as a field of knowledge and practice. These issues are mainly seen at two levels: (1) on discourses surrounding motivations and value of HCI as a sociotechnical field; (2) on discourses surrounding concepts of HCI diffusion, maturity and diversity as articulated by global and local knowledge networks.

Since the beginning of HCI, discussions of democracy have been around, e.g. [1, 2]. It may even be fair to say that the key notion of usability aims to support the citizens of a democratic society or one that could be co-designed by its citizens. Originally, usability and the larger field of HCI was conceived for western democracies. Acknowledging that the meaning of emancipatory sociotechnical HCI depends on our ideas about the ideal society, models of democracy and participation becomes important. A review of studies of HCI and policy recapped basic models of democracy found in the literature [3]. Their models of democracy included a deliberative democracy, which is a system of governance that uses arguments in discussions until consensus is reached (Denmark may be an example); a Marxist system of governance that sees decision-making on policy as related to the economic system (China may be an example); and a cosmopolitan democracy [4] system of governance that highlights citizens', no matter their geographical location, rights to political participation in global affairs (UN may be an example). For HCI design approaches, the government system in its wider societal context is thus both a context for design and the ultimate end-goal of the design activities. HCI is both shaped by and may contribute to design of particular Marxist, deliberate, and cosmopolitan systems of governance. Policy makers and researchers may therefore benefit from knowing about and considering sociotechnical HCI approaches when they study and perform "democracy".

Obviously, exactly how HCI should shape and is shaped by these and other models of democracy and governance remains open for discussion. The influence of different models can be seen in the fact that HCI has several roots deep in military needs from the world wars of the 20th century [5], but it was also born out of the sociotechnical traditions with its emancipatory ambitions, that is, creating conditions for human workers, managers, etc. that facilitate the realization of their needs and potential [4, 5]. In addition, the tension between the focus on the individual and on the social dimensions surrounding interaction is inherent in critical analyses of HCI, e.g. [6, 7]. How military power and emancipatory ambitions are related in a geopolitical analysis of HCI research? How do these ambitions influence or are influenced by globalization and economic development? How does the inherent tensions operate within the field? These are all tensions of geopolitical nature as they are underpinned by contrasting models of democracy and governance.

Moreover, the diffusion of HCI as field of knowledge and practice is dominated by political and post-colonial discourses that pervade local indigenous and global knowledge networks shaping what is considered useful and relevant research and practice [8,

9]. The post-colonial analyses of HCI diffusion are fundamentally framed as set of inter-cultural and potentially uneven power relations in these 'design' situations of encounters [8]. However, there is also a need to focus on local and indigenous HCI concepts and methods [9] that are often invisible to professional and academic spaces of knowledge exchange [10]. The potential contribution of explicitly local or indigenous perspectives, approaches, and experiences with HCI tends to remain unknown, e.g. [11].

Last but not least, there are attempts to understand HCI maturity and diversity levels through origins, frequencies and levels of participation in conferences such as CHI or CSCW, e.g. [12]; through organizational adoption, e.g. [13, 14] or through regional institutionalizing efforts, e.g. [15]. The problem we identified is that HCI's maturity and diversity are placed on a continuum where western models of value, quality and participation reinforce political configurations of exclusion and inclusion, which regulate human and knowledge mobility in the field. Thus, limiting its potential to integrate other views, forms of being, living and understanding the world and the field itself.

2 Workshop Objectives

In this workshop we understand the above issues as geopolitical in nature and aim to trace the cultural and political dynamics that construct the field of HCI. More concretely, we will pursue the following objectives:

- To help develop a frame of understanding of geopolitical issues in HCI.
- To collect examples and experiences that show political discourses shaping HCI's motivations and values.
- To collect examples and experiences of HCI diffusion, maturity and diversity as articulated by global and local knowledge networks.
- To formulate a research agenda for future work on geopolitical research on HCI.

3 Expected Outcomes

The workshop will produce a research agenda for studying geopolitical issues through a HCI lens, and how best to understand and analyze them. The aim with this research agenda is to stimulate further research interest and provide direction for critical research on HCI. In addition, extended versions of the workshop papers will be published by Springer in the LNCS series as a volume collecting papers from the INTERACT2021 workshops.

4 Target Audience

The target audience for this workshop includes researchers and practitioners working on topics related to HCI diffusion, education, capacity building, and social studies of science and technology and critical research on HCI. Early-stage researchers and PhD students are also encouraged to submit work-in-progress papers.

5   Organizing Committee

The workshop is organized by IFIP TC13 WG13.8 – Interaction Design for International Development. The organizers are:

José Abdelnour Nocera is professor in Sociotechnical Design and Head of the Sociotechnical Centre for Innovation and User Experience at the University of West London. He is the current Chair for IFIP TC13 WG13.8 and the British Computer Society Sociotechnical Specialist Group. His interests lie in the sociotechnical and cultural aspects of systems design, development and use.

Torkil Clemmensen is professor at the Department of Digitalization, Copenhagen Business School, Denmark. His research interest is in psychology as a science of design. His research focuses on cultural and psychological perspectives on usability, user experience, and the digitalization of work. He contributes to Human-Computer Interaction, Design, and Information Systems. He is a vice-chair of IFIP TC13 WG8.

Anirudha Joshi is professor in the interaction design stream in the IDC School of Design. He works in the area that can be described as "Interaction Design for Indian Needs", which aims to solve some age-old problems by leveraging new technologies. Anirudha has worked in diverse domains including healthcare, literacy, Indian language text input, banking, education, and accessibility.

Zhengjie Liu, Professor at Dalian Maritime University, China, has been working in HCI since 1989. He founded the Sino European Usability Center in 2000 as the first research center dedicated to usability in China. He is a co-founder of SIGCHI China and CCF TC-HCI. He is awardee of ACM SIGCHI Lifetime Achievement in Service Award (2017) and IFIP TC13 Pioneers Award (2013).

Judy van Biljon holds the National Research Foundation's Chair in Information and Communication for Development (ICT4D) hosted by the School of Computing at the University of South Africa (Unisa). She has contributed to the body of academic knowledge by publishing on Human-Computer Interaction evaluation and interaction design for marginalised groups, technology adoption, and sustainability in digital learning for resource-constrained environments. She serves as Associate Editor of Information Technology for Development and as a Senior Editor of the Electronic Journal of Information Systems in Developing Countries.

Xiangang Qin is currently a lecturer in the School of Digital Media and Design Arts at Beijing University of Posts &Telecommunications. Prior to current job, Xiangang Qin used to work in the Department of Digitization at Copenhagen Busi-ness School as postdoctoral and international incoming fellowship, Lenovo, China Mobile and Siemens. His research interests include issues of UX in context-aware systems, UX measurement and culturability issue of HCI.

Isabela Gasparini received her Ph.D. degree from the Federal University of Rio Grande do Sul (UFRGS - Brazil) with a sandwich period at TELECOM Sud Paris (France). She is currently an Associate Professor at the Santa Catarina State University (UDESC), where she is involved in Human-Computer Interaction and Technology-Enhanced Learning fields, with a special interest in adaptive e-learning systems, gamification, learning analytics, recommender systems, infoviz, and cultural issues. She is the editor-in-chief of the Brazilian Journal of Computers in Education (2019–2021), and the coordinator of the Special Human-Computer Interaction committee of the Brazilian Computer Society.

Leonardo Parra-Agudelo is a part of the team that constitutes the school of Architecture and Design at Universidad de los Andes (Bogota, Colombia). Leonardo finished a PhD in urban matters and social transformation at QUT, holds an MFA in design and technology from Parsons the New School for Design, studied design in Colombia, and is also a certified motorbike technician and everything-two-wheel rider. He believes in in-disciplinary and disobedient research and creative practice, and explores how to blur disciplinary boundaries, through care-full interactions.

References

1. Bjørn-Andersen, N., Clemmensen, T.: The shaping of the scandinavian socio-technical IS research tradition. Scand. J. Inf. Syst. **29**, 79–118 (2017)
2. Bødker, S., Ehn, P., Sjögren, D., Sundblad, Y.: Co-operative design—perspectives on 20 years with 'the scandinavian IT design model. In: proceedings of NordiCHI, pp. 22–24 (2000)
3. Nelimarkka, M.: A Review of Research on Participation in Democratic Decision-Making Presented at SIGCHI Conferences. Toward an Improved Trading Zone Between Political Science and HCI. Proceedings of the ACM on Human-Computer Interaction, vol. 3, pp. 1–29 (2019)
4. Archibugi, D., Koenig-Archibugi, M., Marchetti, R.: Introduction: Mapping global democracy (2011)
5. Shackel, B.: Human-computer interaction—whence and whither? J. Am. Soc. Inf. Sci. **48**, 970–986 (1997)
6. Dillon, A.: Group dynamics meet cognition: applying socio-technical concepts in the design of information systems. In: The New SocioTech: Graffiti on the Long Wall, pp. 119–125. Springer Verlag, London (2000)
7. Abdelnour-Nocera, J., Clemmensen, T.: Theorizing about socio-technical approaches to HCI. In: Barricelli, B.R., et al. (eds.) HWID 2018. IAICT, vol. 544, pp. 242–262. Springer, Cham (2019). https://doi.org/10.1007/978-3-030-05297-3_17
8. Irani, L., Vertesi, J., Dourish, P., Philip, K., Grinter, R.E.: Postcolonial computing: a lens on design and development. In: Proceedings of the SIGCHI Conference on Human Factors in Computing Systems, pp. 1311–1320. ACM, New York, NY, USA (2010). https://doi.org/10.1145/1753326.1753522
9. Abdelnour-Nocera, J., Clemmensen, T., Kurosu, M.: Reframing HCI through local and indigenous perspectives. Int. J. Hum.-Comput. Interact. **29**, 201–204 (2013). https://doi.org/10.1080/10447318.2013.765759
10. Suchman, L.: Located accountabilities in technology production. Scand. J. Inf. Syst. **14**, 91–105 (2002)
11. Kurosu, M., Kobayashi, T., Yoshitake, R., Takahashi, H., Urokohara, H., Sato, D.: Trends in usability research and activities in Japan. Int. J. Hum.-Comput. Interact. **17**, 103–124 (2004)
12. Sturm, C., Oh, A., Linxen, S., Abdelnour Nocera, J., Dray, S., Reinecke, K.: How WEIRD is HCI? Extending HCI principles to other countries and cultures. In: Proceedings of the 33rd Annual ACM Conference Extended Abstracts on Human Factors in Computing Systems, pp. 2425–2428. Association for Computing Machinery, New York, NY, USA (2015). https://doi.org/10.1145/2702613.2702656
13. Guidini Gonçalves, T., Marçal de Oliveira, K., Kolski, C.: HCI in practice: an empirical study with software process capability maturity model consultants in Brazil. J. Softw.: Evol. Process **30**, e2109 (2018)

14. Lacerda, T.C., von Wangenheim, C.G.: Systematic literature review of usability capability/maturity models. Comput. Stand. Interfaces **55**, 95–105 (2018). https://doi.org/10.1016/j.csi.2017.06.001

15. Smith, A., Joshi, A., Liu, Z., Bannon, L., Gulliksen, J., Li, C.: Institutionalizing HCI in Asia. In: Baranauskas, C., Palanque, P., Abascal, J., Barbosa, S.D.J. (eds.) INTERACT 2007. LNCS, vol. 4663, pp. 85–99. Springer, Heidelberg (2007). https://doi.org/10.1007/978-3-540-74800-7_7

HCI-E²: HCI Engineering Education
For Developers, Designers and More

Konrad Baumann[1] , José Creissac Campos[2](✉) , Alan Dix[3] ,
Laurence Nigay[4] , Philippe Palanque[5] , Jean Vanderdonckt[6] ,
Gerrit van der Veer[7] , and Benjamin Weyers[8]

[1] FH Joanneum University of Applied Sciences, Graz, Austria
[2] University of Minho & HASLab/INESC TEC, Braga, Portugal
jose.campos@di.uminho.pt
[3] Computational Foundry, Swansea Universty, Wales, UK
[4] University Grenoble Alpes, Grenoble, France
[5] University of Toulouse, Toulouse, France
[6] Université catholique de Louvain, Louvain-la-Neuve, Belgium
[7] Vrije Universiteit Amsteredam, Amsterdam, The Netherlands
[8] University of Trier, Trier, Germany

Abstract. This workshop aims at identifying, examining, structuring and sharing educational resources and approaches to support the process of teaching/learning Human-Computer Interaction (HCI) Engineering. The broadening of the range of available interaction technologies and their applications, many times in safety and mission critical areas, to novel and less understood application domains, brings the question of how to address this ever-changing nature in university curricula usually static. Beyond, as these technologies are taught in diverse curricula (ranging from Human Factors and psychology to hardcore computer science), we are interested in what the best approaches and best practices are to integrate HCI Engineering topics in the curricula of programs in software engineering, computer science, human-computer interaction, psychology, design, etc. The workshop is proposed on behalf of the IFIP Working Groups 2.7/13.4 on User Interface Engineering and 13.1 on Education in HCI and HCI Curricula.

Keywords: Human-computer interaction · Engineering · Education

1 Workshop Topics and Scope

Engineering interactive systems is a multidisciplinary endeavour positioned at the intersection of Human-Computer Interaction (HCI), software engineering, usability engineering, interaction design, visual design and other disciplines. The field of Human-Computer Interaction Engineering (HCI-E) is concerned with providing methods, techniques, and tools for the systematic and effective design; development, testing, evaluation, and deployment of interactive systems in a wide range of application domains.

ⓒ IFIP International Federation for Information Processing 2021
Published by Springer Nature Switzerland AG 2021
C. Ardito et al. (Eds.): INTERACT 2021, LNCS 12936, pp. 542–547, 2021.
https://doi.org/10.1007/978-3-030-85607-6_74

The aim of such contributions is threefold:

- Improve the process of designing, developing, and evaluating interactive systems;
- Improve the quality of the user interface of interactive systems, including usability and user experience properties and software properties (also known as external and internal properties, respectively [3]);
- Adapt these contributions to the specific requirements and needs of the various application domains.

In recent years, the range of interactive techniques and applications has broadened considerably and can be expected to grow even further in the future. While new interaction techniques offer the prospect of improving the usability and user experience of interactive systems, they pose new challenges, not only for methods and tools that can support their design, development, and evaluation in a systematic engineering-oriented manner, but also to the designers and developers that must use them. This is aggravated by the fact that they are increasingly being applied in safety and mission critical, novel and less understood application domains (e.g., wearable medical devices and AI-based systems).

The techniques, methods and tools mentioned above, as well as many other novel forms of interaction, involve aspects that need to be adequately addressed in the curricula of programs in software engineering, computer science and HCI [1,2,4,5]. This begs the question of how best to address these topics in those curricula, and what the best approaches to address them are. Particularly relevant in the current context are approaches that support the educational process in an online context. When considering education about HCI Engineering, we need to think about who is being educated as there is likely to be different curriculum scope and educational methods for different types of learners. There are two main distinctions that are likely to influence these methods:

Technical vs. non-technical – Computer science and similar students are likely to be the main consumers of detailed HCIE education. However, it is also important for those who are likely to have a more interface design or user research role to be able to appreciate the limits of technology and the potential impacts of architectural design choices.

Student vs. practitioner – It is likely that the primary interest of many participants will be university education. However, developers are often involved in lively online discussions about different frameworks, and even the use of monads in interactive JavaScript. Interaction Design Foundation courses attract tens of thousands of UX practitioners worldwide, evidencing the desire for on-the-job learning in both communities.

Participants may target one or other of these types of learners, have interests that cover several, or indeed may address other groups.

2   Goals and Expected Outcomes

The workshop aims at identifying, examining and structuring educational resources and approaches to support the teaching/learning of HCI Engineering.

It aims to cover a range of areas from challenges related to novel forms of interaction to emerging themes stemming from new application domains. Another goal is to consider the variety of students' skills and experiences. For instance, how to incorporate and teach HCI engineering in computer science curricula or in UI/UX design curricula? How to teach HCI engineering to students with different skills (e.g., engineers, designers)? The goal is also to consider different lecturing modalities, ranging from on-site lectures, project-based pedagogy to online/remote lecturing.

The intended outcome of the workshop is a structured overview of educational resources. This shall be structured according to the topics identified in the roadmap. This overview will take the form of an online resource, built around a wiki-style system, which will be made available to the community. We expect that, through this resource, educational materials (e.g., from slides and reference materials to exercises and exams) will be made available. It is expected that the workshop will result in the definition of a first instance of this resource and that this work will be continued in follow-up workshops, as well as in the context of IFIP Working Group 2.7/13.4 on User Interface Engineering[1], where external participants are welcome. Depending on the quality of the submissions and the workshop results, revised versions of the contributions will be published on an edited volume. Alternatively, we will produce a journal paper summarizing and consolidating the contributions, in the form of an HCI Engineering Education roadmap. These results shall serve as a basis for drafting a roadmap for a curriculum for the engineering of advanced interactive computing systems and for identifying quality lecturing modalities.

3   Target Audience

Achieving the workshop's goals means bringing together expertise both on the Engineering of HCI and on education. Hence, we will solicit contributions from the HCI-E related communities and we will be very interested to welcome members of the educational community, for a fruitful discussion. To do so we will dispatch the call to the usual channels including announcements in mailing lists, conferences, and personal contacts.

4   Submission

Position papers (6–10 pages in LNCS format) must report experiences related to HCI Engineering education. Submissions could report software engineering units including some aspects of HCI-E, curricula or teaching units dedicated to HCI-E, case studies/projects demonstrating aspects of HCI-E, evaluation of students' skills related to HCI-E, training non-technical and mixed students in HCI-E, training appropriate aspects of HCI-E to professionals/practitioners, a new teaching modality promising for teaching HCI-E, introducing HCI-E into

---

[1] http://ui-engineering.org.

existing curricula, etc. Authors could also provide in their submission a short summary of their experience in the field and their motivation to participate in this workshop.

Submissions will be processed via the workshop web pages that will be hosted at the IFIP WG 13.4 web site. Position papers will be reviewed by the organizers, and participants will be invited to attend the workshop based on review results. All selected contributions will appear in the workshop proceedings that will be either an edited volume or a submission to a journal.

5 Organisers Background and Experience

The workshop is proposed on behalf of IFIP Working Groups 2.7/13.4 on User Interface Engineering and 13.1 on Education in HCI and HCI Curricula, and intends to further work ongoing within the groups.

WG 2.7/13.4 aims at advancing the state of the art in all aspects of designing, developing, and evaluating interactive computing systems with a particular focus on principled methodological engineering approaches. The scope of investigation comprises, among others, methods and tools for modelling, prototyping, developing and evaluating user interfaces (UI), quality models for interactive systems, and new interface technologies suitable to improve user interaction.

The WG understands UI Engineering as the creation and application of scientific knowledge and systematic, structured design and development methods to predictably and reliably improve the consistency, usability, scalability, economy and dependability of practical problem solutions. UI Engineering addresses all aspects related to methods, processes, tools, technologies, and empirical studies involved in the invention, design and construction of interactive systems. The techniques addressed concern all types of applications, for example, business applications, social media, smart environments, medical devices, automotive and aeronautics applications, and others.

The identification and organisation of educational resources for the topic has raised interest within the group in recent meetings. This interest was strengthened by the current pandemic crisis that requires novel approaches to support the teaching and learning process.

WG 13.1 aims at improving HCI education at all levels of higher education, coordinate, at coordinating and uniting efforts to enhance the development of HCI curricula, at recommending fundamental structures for curricula and course materials and for their adaptation to various national educational systems, at advancing international recognition of qualifications in this field, and at promoting the teaching of HCI. Since it is interested to gather all resources which can be effectively used in such HCI curricula, it is particularly interested in collecting, analyzing, and comparing models, methods, and tools for supporting the development of interactive applications and their UIs.

Konrad Baumann is chair of IFIP WG 13.1 Education in HCI and HCI Curricula. As a professor at University of Applied Sciences FH Joanneum in Graz, Austria, his teaching and research interests focus on HCI-related topics like usability testing, user-centred design, user interface design, information design, user experience design, interaction design and evaluation of exhibitions. He has been supervising more than 100 theses. He is co-author of two books, an editorial board member of the Information Design Journal (IDJ) and served as a board member of the International Institute for Information Design (IIID). He received his PhD in 2004 at the Institute for Design and Assessment of Technology at TU Vienna. Before that, he also worked in industry as a product manager.

José Creissac Campos is the chair of IFIP WG 2.7/13.4 on User Interface Engineering. He is an associate professor at the informatics department of the University of Minho, and a senior researcher at HASLab/INESC TEC. José chairs the Steering Committee of the ACM SIGCHI Symposium on Engineering Interactive Computing Systems (EICS) and is a member of the Editorial Board of the ACM Proceedings in Human-Computer Interaction journal. He has served in several organizing committees, including several ACM SIGCHI EICS, IFIP TC13 INTERACT 2011 and Formal Methods Week 2019. He regularly serves on the Program Committees of EICS, INTERACT and IUI, among others.

Alan Dix is Director of the Computational Foundry at Swansea University. He is author of one of the principle textbooks in Human Computer Interaction as well as many other research publications and a recent book on Statistics for HCI. He was the general chair of HCI-Educators 2007 as well as several more recent workshops in the area, including a series of Covid-related virtual workshops on video in HCI education early in 2020. He has worked in a number of commercial roles in addition to his academic posts and contributes to courses at Interaction Design Foundation. Alan still designs and codes interactive systems.

Laurence Nigay is a full Professor (Exceptional class) in Computer Science at the University of Grenoble Alpes (UGA) and is also an elected senior member of the Academic Institute of France (IUF). She is the director of the Engineering Human-Computer Interaction (EHCI) research group of the Grenoble Informatics Laboratory (LIG), comprised of 11 faculty members and more than 20 non-permanent members. From 1998-2004, she was vice-chair of the IFIP working group 2.7/13.4. She has been regularly involved in the ACM SIGCHI Symposium on Engineering Interactive Computing Systems (EICS): reviewer since 2009, member of the Editorial Board, program co-chair at EICS 2015, doctoral consortium co-chair at EICS 2014 and 2012. From 2005 to 2019 she was the director of the Masters of Computer Engineering at the University of Grenoble.

Philippe Palanque is a professor in Computer Science at the University Toulouse 3 and is head of the ICS (Interactive Critical Systems) research group at IRIT. Since the early 90's his research focus is on interactive systems engineering proposing notations, methods and tools to integrate multiple properties such as usability, dependability, resilience and more recently user experience. These contributions have been developed together with industrial partners from various application domains such as civil aviation, air traffic management or satellite ground segments. He is currently one of the head of the Master of HCI in Toulouse (www.masterihm.fr) that was created in 2000. He was steering committee chair of the CHI conference series at ACM SIGCHI, is a member of the CHI academy and chair of IFIP Technical Committee on HCI (TC13).

Jean Vanderdonckt is a full professor in Computer Science at Université catholique de Louvain where he leads the Louvain Interaction Lab, which is located midway between software engineering, HCI, and usability engineering. He is Vice-Chair of WG 13.1 Education in HCI and HCI curricula. He is co-editor-in-chief of Springer's HCI series of books and holder of the Francqui Chair in Computer Science 2020.

Gerrit van der Veer has been teaching at the Vrije Universiteit Amsterdam since 1961. He started in Cognitive Psychology, moved to Ergonomics, and into Computer Science, where he specialized in the design of interactive systems. He has been developing education in interaction design in many European countries, including Belgium, Germany, Spain, Italy, Romania, and the Netherlands, as well as in China. He is currently working for the Dutch Open University Department Human-Computer-Society, the Dutch University of Twente, Department of Human-Media Interaction, the University of Sassari (Italy) Faculty of Architecture and Design, the Luxun Academy of Fine Arts (China) Department of Multimedia and Animation, and the Maritime University of Dalian (China) Faculty of Computer Science. Gerrit has been President of ACM SIGCHI, the world leading international society for HCI, from 2009-2015.

Benjamin Weyers is currently Assistant Professor at University of Trier and Head of the Human-Computer Interaction Group. Before, he was PostDoc at the Virtual Reality and Immersive Visualization group at RWTH Aachen University. He received his PhD in 2011 at the University of Duisburg-Essen and joined the RWTH in 2013. He is interested in the research and development of interactive analysis methods for abstract and scientific data using immersive systems as well as the integration of VR and AR into the control of technical systems for the support of human users in semi-automated control scenarios. An integral element in this research is the application of modeling method as part of the engineering process. Therefore, Benjamin focuses on the development and use of formal methods for the description of interactive systems. He is member of IFIP WG 2.7/13.4 on User Interface Engineering.

References

1. ACM/IEEE-CS Joint Task Force on Computing Curricula: Computer science curricula 2013. Technical report, ACM Press and IEEE Computer Society Press, December 2013
2. Churchill, E.F., Bowser, A., Preece, J.: Teaching and learning human-computer interaction: past, present, and future. Interactions **20**(2), 44–53 (2013)
3. Gram, C., Cockton, G. (eds.): Design Principles for Interactive Software. Chapman & Hall (1996)
4. Hewett, T.T., et al.: ACM SIGCHI curricula for human-computer interaction. Technical report. ACM, New York (1996)
5. The Joint Task Force on Computing Curricula: Software Engineering 2014: Curriculum guidelines for undergraduate degree programs in software engineering. Technical report. ACM & EEE-Computer Society, New York (2015)

Human-Centered Software Engineering
for Changing Contexts of Use
IFIP WG 13.2 Workshop at INTERACT 2021

Stefan Sauer[1]([⊠]) [ID], Regina Bernhaupt[2] [ID], and Carmelo Ardito[3] [ID]

[1] Paderborn University, Paderborn, Germany
sauer@uni-paderborn.de
[2] Eindhoven University of Technology, Eindhoven, The Netherlands
r.bernhaupt@tue.nl
[3] Politecnico di Bari, Bari, Italy
carmelo.ardito@poliba.it

Abstract. The context of use plays an important role in Human-Centered Software Engineering (HCSE). Typically, user, environment, and platform are considered to make up the core aspects of the context of use. Changing the context of use has significant impact on how to design and develop with a user-centered perspective and how usage of these systems changed for example in the current pandemic situation with a focus on remote work. New kinds of work environments in industry providing different types of user assistance evolve, new settings for remote and distributed work styles are required to account for social distancing, or the trends towards autonomous and AI-based systems demand for new ways of thinking about socio-technical interaction and systems. This workshop promotes sharing of knowledge and experiences that address how to deal with evolving contexts of use in today's and future application domains and its influence on human-centered socio-technical system design and development practices. Beyond the traditional themes of IFIP Working Group 13.2 workshops, the main focus lies on theories, methods, and approaches for dealing with the context of use, its influence on HCSE, and factors for its change over time.

Keywords: Human-Centered Software Engineering · Context of use · Change · Adaptive user interfaces

1 Overview and Goals

The context of use plays an important role in Human-Centered Software Engineering (HCSE) and Human-Computer Interaction (HCI) research [1, 2]. Typically, user, environment, and platform are considered to make up the core aspects of the context of use [3]. Changing the context of use, for example due to unplanned circumstances like the current pandemic situation, has significant impact on how we use systems, and how we adapt and adopt them even if the systems were not designed for such usages. In HCSE research we have to account for this change, making interactive system development

C. Ardito et al. (Eds.): INTERACT 2021, LNCS 12936, pp. 548–552, 2021.
https://doi.org/10.1007/978-3-030-85607-6_75

context-aware or design and develop in a way that systems can adapt for novel forms of usage. Recently, we observe developments that strongly change contexts of use. For example, in the area of industrial automation (Industry 4.0) work environments change, new kinds of user assistance evolve, and workers are going to be supported by innovative types of devices and digital assistance tools to accomplish their working tasks. Typical examples are augmented, virtual, and mixed reality (AR, VR, MR) applications in training or support situations. The COVID-19 pandemic has drastically changed where and the way how we work, particularly in collaboration with others to keep distance and increase personal safety. In contrast, the trend towards increasingly autonomous systems and systems that use and provide artificial intelligence gives rise to new kinds of interaction, particularly, human-machine interaction (HMI), in areas such as autonomous driving or human-robot collaboration in different domains such as industrial production, logistics, or health. These trends should be accounted for in the way we design and build such interactive systems, possibly coming to evolutionary or even revolutionary solutions. For example, expected or unforeseen changes of usage scenarios and their context of use may be accounted for by flexible and more resilient system solutions and be reflected in the development practices and technical frameworks. Specific kinds of interaction such as HMI, but also social and socio-technical interaction may demand for more prominent and explicit consideration. Quality aspects such as ubiquity, security, and safety may be seen in a different light. Changing contexts of use may even have an impact on the way we think about user motivation and user experience, away from short-term notions like emotions towards long-term traits like users' values. We want to specifically account for these developments in addition to the general concerns of HCSE. Discussions and interactive working sessions in the course of the HCSE@INTERACT 2021 workshop will particularly deal with these concerns.

In this workshop, we aim to broaden the traditional scope of the workshop series of IFIP Working Group 13.2 [4–6]. We focus on the study of context of use, its long-term evolutionary trends as well as its short-term design and management in a user-centered design process, from a social and user-centered methodological viewpoint as well as from a technical viewpoint. Our aim is to cover a large set of user interface perspectives, aspects, and properties and fuel new ideas and approaches for research and practice. The long-term perspective of this workshop is to foster the development of theories, methods, tools and approaches for dealing with the changing context of use and its impact on HCI and collaboration that should be taken into account when developing interactive and socio-technical systems.

This workshop is a follow-up of the successful workshops organized at INTERACT 2017 in Mumbai, India [5] and INTERACT 2019 in Paphos, Cyprus [6].

2 Target Audience and Expected Outcomes

This workshop is open to everyone who is interested in aspects of human-computer interaction from a user-centered perspective. Typical contributions to this workshop focus on user interface properties while designing and building interactive systems and study associated methods, processes and approaches. We expect a high participation of IFIP Working Group 13.2 members. We invited participants to present position papers proposing novel solution ideas and describing real-life case studies that illustrate the role of the context of use in HCI and its impact on the system design and use. Any perspective and related aspects of user interface design were welcome. However, we were especially interested in work that deals with current trends that change the way humans use, interact and collaborate with technical components in socio-technical systems. We were also interested in methods, theories and tools for managing context of use at design and run-time. Submitted position papers were reviewed and selected for presentation in the workshop by an international program committee comprising the organizers and selected members of IFIP Working Group 13.2 who are experts in the field. Accepted papers were made available through the workshop website. Furthermore, an extended version of selected papers was considered for inclusion in a Springer LNCS post-proceedings volume published in conjunction with the other INTERACT workshops organized by the IFIP TC13 Working Groups.

3 Workshop Contributions

Nine contributions have been accepted for presentation at the workshop. They are briefly described in the following.

How to Identify Changing Contexts of Use With Creativity Workshops – An Experience Report, presented by Wasja Brunotte, Lukas Nagel, Kurt Schneider and Jil Klünder, reports their experiences with a multi-stakeholder requirements elicitation workshop method that combines the 6-3-5 Method with the Walt-Disney Method to ensure that a broad range of requirements can be elicited while ensuring equal contribution from different stakeholders and improving the number of perspectives on the future context of use of a software that is developed.

Describing Digital Work Environment Through Contextual Personas, presented by Ruochen Wang, Marta Larusdottir and Åsa Cajander, reports the results from a study involving student software developers using personas that were enriched to represent physical work context, organisational work environment, social work environment aspects as well as the cognitive load. Interesting insights regarding improvements are identified: the ability of representing diversity of user groups especially when it comes to aging populations or non-tech savvy user groups, and, more generally, personas that evolve with the project and over time.

Towards Flexible Interaction Design for Operator Assistance Systems, presented by Jan Van den Bergh and Florian Heller. The authors present an approach to assess the usability of Operator Assistance Systems, such as hoist, lifts, cranes, and robotic arms. Such systems help operators in handling components of various weights in order to reduce ergonomic stress and are currently evaluated based on ergonomic criteria. However, the acceptance of such systems by the operator does not only depend on the amount of support it generates, but also on basic usability factors. Based on the observations of a contextual inquiry, the authors designed a simple scoring sheet to evaluate and compare the usability aspects of such systems.

Creating a Post-Sedentary Work Context for Software Engineering, presented by Martin Hedlund, Cristian Bogdan and Gerrit Meixner, presents a research agenda on how to address the sedentary work style of software engineers by re-structuring tasks to be performed and supported by for example visual programming and providing associated technological solutions including virtual reality (VR), augmented reality, and haptic interaction within VR to perform these tasks. The research agenda addresses the possible study set-ups for such types of interventions and how to investigate aspects like program comprehension, code creation or novel types of interaction techniques.

Coping with Changing Contexts: A Healthcare Security Perspective, presented by Bilal Naqvi and Carmelo Ardito. The authors aim at stimulating a discussion on how to cope with changing contexts while considering the threats posed by phishing and ransomware attacks in the context of healthcare infrastructures. Indeed, phishing has been the most prevalent attack mechanism on the healthcare infrastructures during the ongoing COVID-19 pandemic, which increased the pace of digitization of the healthcare industry. The authors propose three ways to cope with these threats in the perspective of healthcare, i.e., i) training and supporting developers at work; ii) initiating cross-disciplinary education and training mechanisms; iii) application of existing HCI principles.

Privacy Knowledge Base for Supporting Decision-Making in Software Development, presented by Maria Teresa Baldassarre, Vita Santa Barletta, Danilo Caivano, Antonio Piccinno and Michele Scalera. The authors propose an approach to support software developers in integrating security and privacy requirements at every stage of the software development cycle, which is critical to guarantee the confidentiality, integrity and availability of the system and consequently of the data. In particular, they define a Privacy Knowledge Base (PKB) that encompasses the key elements to support decision-making in privacy-oriented software development. An industrial case study shows preliminary results on how PKB provides the guidance needed for privacy-oriented software development.

bRIGHT – A Framework for Capturing and Adapting to Context for User-Centered Design, presented by Rukman Senanayake and Grit Denker, deals with user context modeling and adaptation. Particular challenges of creating and maintaining an accurate model of the user context are incomplete and uncertain information. The proposed HCI framework bRIGHT is capable of creating an accurate context model as the user engages with the computer system. In this paper, the authors discuss the new architectural design of bRIGHT for improving knowledge representation and base type system and its expected benefits.

Affordance-derived Declarative Interaction Models for Context Adaptation, presented by Cristian Bogdan, proposes an approach to achieving fully declarative interactive applications. A concrete user interface is sketched and the interaction function is derived from the UI's form through affordance mechanisms. As a result, a declarative model of the dynamic interaction aspects of the application is obtained. This model can be used to complement existing solutions for declaratively describing the static aspects of the user interface to make a fully declarative application. This is an important prerequisite for such an application to be automatically adapted to its context of use.

On the Consistency of UI Adaptations, presented by Kai Biermeier, Enes Yigitbas, Nils Weidmann and Gregor Engels, looks at employing Triple Graph Grammars (TGGs) as a sophisticated mechanism for controlling the consistency of user interface (UI) adaptations to the current context-of-use. To prevent the undesirable application of conflicting UI adaptations and ease the specification of UI adaptation rules, they introduce their notion of adaptation consistency based on TGGs augmented with a 0–1 priority system. TGGs are an established formalism for consistency maintenance in model-driven engineering. TGG semantics are extended with a priority system to control the rules' application order. The authors also outline the implementation of a prototypical TGG interpreter as a design and run-time solution for ensuring consistency of UI adaptations.

4   Workshop Format

This full-day workshop is designed to be held in hybrid format, i.e., allowing participants to either attend in person on-site or just remotely/virtually. It is organized around presentation of position papers and working activities in small groups. In the morning sessions, after welcoming the participants and setting the frame for the workshop, the selected position papers are presented. In addition, further position statements can be contributed by the workshop participants. Participants are also invited to comment on the propositions and case studies and to report similar experiences. Position papers and statements together are used to support the discussion that follows. The afternoon sessions are thus devoted to interactive sessions, where participants will be engaged to work in small groups, discuss and propose solutions to the identified challenges seen in the morning. Due to the hybrid workshop format, on-site and virtual group discussions are run in parallel. Solutions proposed by the participants are compiled and compared. Based on the lessons learned, participants are encouraged to draft an agenda of future work that can be accomplished.

References

1. Abowd, G.D., Dey, A.K., Brown, P.J., Davies, N., Smith, M., Steggles, P.: Towards a better understanding of context and context-awareness. In: Gellersen, H.-W. (ed.) HUC 1999. LNCS, vol. 1707, pp. 304–307. Springer, Heidelberg (1999). https://doi.org/10.1007/3-540-48157-5_29
2. Dey, A.: Understanding and using context. Pers. Ubiquit. Comput. **5**, 4–7 (2001)
3. Calvary, G., Coutaz, J., Thevenin, D., Limbourg, Q., Bouillon, L., Vanderdonckt, J.: A unifying reference framework for multi-target user interfaces. Interact. Comput. **15**(3), 289–308 (2003)
4. Winckler, M., Bernhaupt, R., Forbrig, P., Sauer, S.: IFIP WG 13.2 workshop on user experience and user-centered development processes. In: Abascal, J., Barbosa, S., Fetter, M., Gross, T., Palanque, P., Winckler, M. (eds.) INTERACT 2015. LNCS, vol. 9299, pp. 661–662. Springer, Cham (2015). https://doi.org/10.1007/978-3-319-22723-8_90
5. Winckler, M., Larusdottir, M., Kuusinen, K., Bogdan, C., Palanque, P.: Dealing with conflicting user interface properties in user-centered development processes. In: Bernhaupt, R., Dalvi, G., Joshi, A.K., Balkrishan, D., O'Neill, J., Winckler, M. (eds.) Human-Computer Interaction, INTERACT 2017, IFIP WG 13.2 + 13.5 Workshop at INTERACT 2017. LNCS, vol. 10516, pp. 521–523. Springer, Cham (2017)
6. Ardito, C., Bernhaupt, R., Palanque, P., Sauer, S.: Handling security, usability, user experience and reliability in user-centered development processes. In: Lamas, D., Loizides, F., Nacke, L., Petrie, H., Winckler, M., Zaphiris, P. (eds.) INTERACT 2019. LNCS, vol. 11749, pp. 759–762. Springer, Cham (2019). https://doi.org/10.1007/978-3-030-29390-1_76

Human-Centred Technology for Sustainable Development Goals: Challenges and Opportunities

Lara S. G. Piccolo[1]([⊠]) [iD], Vânia Neris[2] [iD], Kamila Rios Rodrigues[3] [iD],
and Masood Masoodian[4] [iD]

[1] Knowledge Media Institute - The Open University, Milton Keynes, UK
lara.piccolo@open.ac.uk
[2] Federal University of São Carlos, São Carlos, Brazil
vania@dc.ufscar.br
[3] University of São Paulo, São Paulo, Brazil
kamila.rios@icmc.usp.br
[4] School of Arts, Design and Architecture, Aalto University, Espoo, Finland
masood.masoodian@aalto.fi

Abstract. A human-centred approach to technology design for addressing sustainable development goals demands rethinking the way technological solutions are developed and deployed, taking into account situated design solutions and their impact on the social, economic and environmental aspects. For technology designers, this provides an opportunity to bridge the gap between the real and the ideal worlds. This workshop aims at building an agenda that defines challenges and opportunities for the design of interactive technologies, which promote fairness and prosperity on the planet, and contribute towards one or more of the United Nations' Sustainable Development Goals.

Keywords: Sustainability · Sustainable development goals · Human-centred design · Human-centred technologies

1 Context

The 2030 Agenda for Sustainable Development adopted by the United Nations (UN) Members calls for global partnerships to achieve significant advances in fairness and prosperity in the world. This includes equal access to, and management of resources such as water, energy, climate, oceans, urbanization, transport, science and technology. These themes are addressed as a set of 17 UN Sustainable Development Goals (SDGs)[1] intended to be achieved by the year 2030. These goals should be achieved uniformly across the nations, dissolving the well-established dichotomy of *developed* and *developing* contexts [2].

---

[1] https://sdgs.un.org/goals.

© IFIP International Federation for Information Processing 2021
Published by Springer Nature Switzerland AG 2021
C. Ardito et al. (Eds.): INTERACT 2021, LNCS 12936, pp. 553–557, 2021.
https://doi.org/10.1007/978-3-030-85607-6_76

In line with this agenda, we understand *sustainability* more broadly, beyond the environmental aspects related to solutions that do not harm the environment, to include also the social aspects related to human rights, respecting differences, and the dissemination of values that are the basis of the continuance of life in society for future generations [3–5].

According to [1], sustainability can, and should be, a central focus of interaction design. Initially, Blevis [1] believes that for a perspective of sustainability, "design is defined as an act of choosing among or informing choices of future ways of being. This perspective of sustainability is presented in terms of design values, methods, and reasoning".

Addressing technology design for sustainable development goals with a human-centred approach demands rethinking the way technological solutions are developed and consumed, and considering the situated design solutions and their impact in the social, economic and environmental aspects. As stated in [3], this should be used by designers as an opportunity to establish a bridge between the real-life, with its inequalities and injustices, and the ideal world, as aspired by the UN SDGs.

2   Objectives

With this broad perspective of *sustainability* in mind, the objective of this workshop is to build an agenda which aims to define challenges and opportunities for design of interactive technologies that address one or more SDGs with a holistic view.

Topics of interest include, but are not limited to:

- IoT and smart communities
- Environmental monitoring
- Design solutions that support sustainable behaviour
- Green computing
- Ethical aspects of green computing
- Equality and fairness in access to technology
- Sustainable design
- Design for sustainability

The workshop will engage the participants in:

- Discussing challenges and obstacles related to creating human-centred technology towards advancing the sustainable development goals;
- Mapping some key stakeholders, and questioning the relationships between them;
- Co-creating future scenarios where human-centred technology support individuals and communities to advance on fairness and prosperity.

2.1   Participation

The workshop is of interest to researchers and practitioners who aim to impact society through the design and development of technologies that attempt to advance fairness and prosperity through equal access to, and management of resources such as water, energy, climate, oceans, urbanization, transport, science and technology.

The call for papers will be distributed via the network of the workshop organisers, HCI-related mailing lists, IFIP mailing lists, and social media in general.

Participants are encouraged to submit a motivation paper describing their approach to design of technology aimed at advancing the society towards one or more Sustainable Development Goals, by addressing related challenges and/or opportunities.

As travelling may not be possible to everyone, online participation will also be possible.

The number of participants should be between 8 to 15, in order to keep group activities feasible and interesting.

2.2   Overall Structure

This one day workshop is structured to be engaging, practice-oriented, hands-on, and participatory.

The workshop starts with the participants' presentations, focusing on their design approaches to advance the SDGs. This is followed by a set of activities designed to create discussion of challenges and barriers, and envisioning future scenarios.

The workshop includes plenty of time for the exchange of ideas and experiences among the participants. The main parts of the workshop are:

– Short presentations of the accepted papers;
– A follow-up interactive session to allow further discussions and map the main points raised in the presentations;
– Collaborative activities, facilitated by the organisers, and involving all the participants to map challenges and barriers;
– Concluding discussions and planning of future directions and outcome.

More details on the workshop program and call for papers are available at the workshop website: https://lifes.dc.ufscar.br/HCT4SDG.

3   Organisers

Lara Piccolo is a Research Fellow at the Knowledge Media Institute (KMi) at the Open University, UK. She investigates the role of technology to engage people and communities with some global challenges, including inequalities, universal access to technology and climate change. She worked for 10 years in Brazil bridging academia, policy making and industry in Research and Development projects targeting digital inclusion, accessibility and energy literacy and smart monitoring.

Vânia Neris is an Associate Professor working in the Department of Computing at the Federal University of São Carlos (UFSCar) in Brazil. She has been researching on Human-Computer Interaction since 1999 and now she leads the Flexible and Sustainable Interaction Lab (LIFeS). Her main current research interests include: (1) computer support for mental health and well-being, (2) sustainability in computing and (3) computer science education.

Kamila Rodrigues is an Assistant Professor at the Institute of Mathematical and Computer Sciences at the University of São Paulo (ICMC/USP) in Brazil. Her research interests include usability, user experience, accessibility, sustainability aspects, and also the study of the emotional responses of users during the interaction with interactive multimedia systems, mainly serious games. She works as a collaborator in research developed at the LIFeS lab (Federal University of São Carlos/Brazil) with digital therapeutic applications for different pathologies and in research at the Intermídia-ICMC/USP lab on data collections and remote interventions using technological infrastructure.

Masood Masoodian is a Professor of Visual Communication Design at Aalto University, Finland. His research interests include visual design, interaction design and visualization, specializing in visualization of time-based data (e.g., energy, health and environment) particularly for non-expert users. He has served as a programme chair, programme committee member, and reviewer for numerous international conferences and workshops.

4   Expected Outcome

The accepted position papers will be published in the official adjunct conference proceedings. Furthermore, the main workshop results will be further disseminated to a wider audience during the conference.

The possibility of a joint publication reflecting the workshop outcomes will be suggested and discussed with the participants.

Acknowledgment. This workshop is supported by the IFIP Working Group 13.10 on Human-Centred Technology for Sustainability. For more information please visit, it4se.hs-augsburg.de/wg13-10/.

References

1. Blevis, E.: Sustainable interaction design: invention & disposal, renewal & reuse. In: Proceedings of the SIGCHI Conference on Human Factors in Computing Systems, pp. 503–512. CHI 2007, Association for Computing Machinery, New York, NY, USA (2007). https://doi.org/10.1145/1240624.1240705

2. Kumar, N., et al.: HCI across borders and sustainable development goals. In: Extended Abstracts of the 2020 CHI Conference on Human Factors in Computing Systems, pp. 1–8. CHI EA 2020, Association for Computing Machinery, New York, NY, USA (2020). https://doi.org/10.1145/3334480.3375067, https://doi-org.libezproxy.open.ac.uk/10.1145/3334480.3375067

3. Neris, V., Rodrigues, K., Silva, J.: The future, smart cities and sustainability. In: I GranDIHC - BR Grand Research Challenges in Human-Computer Interaction in Brazil. Human-Computer Interaction Special Committee (CEIHC) of the Brazilian Computer Society (SBC) (2015)

4. Neris, V.P., Rodrigues, K.R., Silva, J.: Futuro, cidades inteligentes e sustentabilidade. GranDIHC-BR–Grandes Desafios de Pesquisa em Interação Humano-Computador no Brasil, pp. 16–18 (2012)

5. de Santana, V.F., Neris, V.P.A., Rodrigues, K.R.H., Oliveira, R., Galindo, N.: Activity of Brazilian HCI community from 2012 to 2017 in the context of the challenge 'future, smart cities, and sustainability'. In: Proceedings of the XVI Brazilian Symposium on Human Factors in Computing Systems. IHC 2017, Association for Computing Machinery, New York, NY, USA (2017). https://doi.org/10.1145/3160504.3160562

Multisensory Augmented Reality

Kasun Karunanayaka[1]([✉]) [iD], Anton Nijholt[2] [iD], Thilina Halloluwa[1] [iD],
Nimesha Ranasinghe[4] [iD], Manjusri Wickramasinghe[1] [iD], and Dhaval Vyas[3] [iD]

[1] School of Computing, University of Colombo, Colombo, Sri Lanka
{ktk,tch,mie}@ucsc.cmb.ac.lk
[2] University of Twente, Enschede, Netherlands
a.nijholt@utwente.nl
[3] University of Queensland, St Lucia, Australia
d.vyas@uq.edu.au
[4] School of Computing and Information Science, University of Maine, Orono, USA
r.ranasinghe@maine.edu

Abstract. Multisensory augmented reality enables content developers to generate more realistic, sensory rich user experiences. Applications and research related to multisensory augmented reality expands through several areas such as education, medicine, human-machine interactions, human-food interactions, marketing, and neuroscience. Aim of this workshop is to gather researchers and industry representatives who are involved in multisensory augmented reality research to discuss the current state-of-the-art in the field, define future research directions, form new collaborations, and come up with future publication plans. We believe that this workshop would enhance the participants' experience of the Interact 2021 and encourage more participants to attend the main conference.

Keywords: Multisensory augmented reality · Multisensory internet ·
Multimodal interfaces · HCI · Multisensory user experiences

1 Introduction

Augmented Reality (AR) research is usually based on a definition provided by Ronald Azuma [2]: AR (1) combines real and virtual objects in a real environment, (2) registers (aligns) real and virtual objects, (3) and runs interactively, in three dimensions, and in realtime. This definition does not limit AR to specific technologies and neither does it limit AR to the sight sense. The definition applies to all senses. That is, AR systems can provide artificially generated visual, auditory, tactile, olfactory, and gustatory experiences or combinations of these experiences superimposed on reality (Multisensory AR). Although we often speak of virtual 'imagery' that is overlaid on a user's 'view' of the physical environment, the other senses and their cross-modal properties can be addressed as well to design useful, convincing, and attractive AR environments. When, according to the definition, we want to register or align real and virtual objects we should take into account that the virtual objects have other than visual properties or don't have

© IFIP International Federation for Information Processing 2021
Published by Springer Nature Switzerland AG 2021
C. Ardito et al. (Eds.): INTERACT 2021, LNCS 12936, pp. 558–563, 2021.
https://doi.org/10.1007/978-3-030-85607-6_77

visual properties at all. We can have virtual touch, sound, smell, and taste objects that are superimposed on reality and define an augmented reality world that is experienced by a user's senses.

During the past decades, Multisensory Augmented Reality (MAR) have been used to deliver immersive user experiences in different areas. Traditional Internet communication was previously dominated by text, images, audio and video. However, digitization of other sensory modalities such as touch [24], taste [4, 17], and smell [4, 16] transforming the current Internet communication into a multisensory Internet communication. In relation to teaching and training, MAR can be used to provide enhanced interactions using virtual objects, user guidance, and force feedback [9, 10, 19]. Some previous research related to human-food Interaction suggested that multisensory augmented reality can be used to generate or modify our perceptions by altering color, textures, shapes, taste, and smell of food and beverages that we eat and drink [4, 17, 21, 22]. On the other hand, digital sensory marketing can be considered as another important area where MAR can be used to create and enhance customer experiences [15]. MAR has also been used to develop new interactions and communication methods related to smart cities and smart communities [1, 12–14, 17]. MAR can also enhance our gaming experiences [23] as well as it can be used to improve industry and automation activities [8, 11].

At present, the field of MAR is primarily focused on technology developments, such as developing new ways to simulate multiple senses and create new interactions by combining AR and human senses. However, little is known about the impact of the addition of each stimulus, let alone multiple stimuli in MAR experiences. Future explorations of MAR, apart from expanding into different application areas, will help study technology-mediated perception, cognition, and human behaviors. These studies will assist in uncovering secrets in the human brain, behavior, neuroscience, and physiology.

2 Workshop Objectives, Target Audience, and Topics

The first workshop on Multisensory Augmented Reality (http://usehci.org/mar2021/) for Interact 2021 was proposed to gather researchers from diverse disciplines such as human-computer interaction, augmented reality, virtual reality, interaction design, gaming, psychology, and neuroscience. This workshop will be held on 30th August 2021 as a one-day workshop in conjunction with the Interact 2021 conference in Bari, Italy.

The structure of this workshop is focused on creating research partnerships and identifying collaborative projects. During the workshop, recent advances in Multi-sensory Augmented Reality will be discussed, which will be the key trends, challenges, and opportunities in conducting research in these intersections. Our overall goal is to have a focused workshop that will initiate projects which will extend beyond the workshop itself. We believe that the intimate nature of workshops at INTERACT is an ideal venue for this type of workshop.

Submissions were sought on the topics including MAR interfaces, applications of MAR, new sensing and actuation Technologies, multimodal or crossmodal perception in AR, smart wearable technologies, MAR based digital and sensory marketing, MAR in human food interaction, and communication protocols for MAR. The workshop's Call for Participation were distributed via several mailing lists related to HCI, UX, and related areas interested in multisensory research. Additionally, the call for participation was distributed via various social media channels and media arts groups. The workshop website (http://usehci.org/mar2021/) was used to share more information and update interested participants.

3 Summary of Position Papers

We have received eight submissions for the workshop. Submissions were reviewed by the workshop organizers and after careful consideration, five position papers were accepted. Either full paper versions or abstracts of those position papers are published on the MAR2021 website (https://usehci.org/mar2021/proceedings). Key contributions of those position papers are described below.

Thomas and Holmquist have proposed a 'Generalised Architecture for Multisensory Augmented Reality' [19]. This approach would entail three components: data to be displayed, preferred modality in which it is to be displayed, and a transformation function between first and second. As a result of the literature review and outcomes of their focus group findings, authors have suggested that audio, visual, haptics, and temperature modalities are the most desirable modalities for future devices, although they have suggested further investigation on smell and taste as well.

'The Value of Sound within a Multisensory Approach to AR in the Arts' by Bilbow, Kiefer, and Chevalier [3] discussed the potential of using sound in creating coherent, immersive, and embodied multisensory AR experiences. First, this paper explains a theoretical framework which investigates sensory modalities afforded by AR. Second, it describes two artworks which investigates embodied experiences in AR artworks. Authors suggested that DIY approaches to augmented reality are essential for creative work, and they further speculate on how art can contribute to future theory, technologies and practice in the field.

Guedes's (2021) paper is about 'Designing Multisensory Experiences in Museums for People with Disabilities' [6]. This position paper questioned about how accessible and feasible current museums are for people with disabilities. Then the paper discussed how technology can support different forms of interacting, understanding, and sensemaking of artworks and multimedia content before, during, and after a museum visit. One example application proposed by the author is called AIMuseum, which provides an accessible and inclusive solution that seeks to enhance museums and exhibitions with Augmented Reality and Screen Readers. In addition to that it discusses several available opportunities for designing, implementing, and evaluating tools for and with people with disabilities to support their experience in museums while catering to different abilities.

'Beyond visual guidance in semi-manual industrial assembly of wooden house sections' by Tobisková, Malmsköld, and Pederson [20] proposed a multimodal AR based guidance system for semi-manual industrial assembly of wooden house sections. This proposed system incorporate vision, hearing, touch, smell senses together with guidance through subtle cues for supporting the truss assembly operations. Authors have reported the findings of their brainstorming sessions related to the process of assembling wood trusses and mapping AR guidance modalities which is useful.

The paper titled 'The use of Augmented Reality to deliver enhanced user experiences in fashion industry' by Jayamini et. al. [7] reviewed how the fashion design industry has acquired novel technologies such as AR, VR, Mixed Reality, and Machine learning to address the limitations of traditional fashion experience and user experience. Literature review section of this paper provides a detailed overview of the recent developments related to fashion design, apparel self-customization, and enhancing customer shopping experiences. They argue that MAR has a huge potential in transforming the fashion industry towards digitalization by introducing the applications such as virtual fashion shows, virtual showrooms, virtual fitting rooms, virtual fit-or-sizing tools, digital jewelry, virtual stylists, and magazine catalogs.

4 Expected Outcomes and Future Plan

One of the main expected outcomes of this workshop is to gather researchers who are working on similar research topics, present each other's research and research interest, discuss improvements to current research, form new research ideas, and start new research collaborations. In this way, it is possible to build multidisciplinary research teams and plan future research work and publications. We expect that this workshop would serve the purpose of knowledge gathering and dissemination related to MAR and enhance Interact 2021 participation and experience. To stimulate additional discussions, all accepted submissions to the workshop, presentations, and inspiring discussions will be made public on the website (http://usehci.org/mar2021/).

5 Workshop Organizers

Kasun Karunanayaka is a Senior Lecturer at the University of Colombo School of Computing, Sri Lanka. Kasun obtained his PhD in Electrical and Computer Engineering from the National University of Singapore (NUS) in 2014. He conducts research related to Mixed Reality, Multisensory Communication, and Physical Computing.

Anton Nijholt received his PhD in computer science from the Vrije Universiteit in Amsterdam. He held positions at various universities, inside and outside the Netherlands. In 1989 he was appointed full professor at the University of Twente in the Netherlands. His main research interests are multimodal interaction with a focus on entertainment computing, affect, humour and brain-computer interfacing.

Thilina Halloluwa is a Senior Lecturer at the University of Colombo School of Computing. He has a PhD from the Science and Engineering Faculty at the Queensland University of Technology, Brisbane. Within the fields of Human-Computer Interaction (HCI) and Computer-Supported Cooperative Work (CSCW), his research focuses on Designing for Underserved Communities, Smart Agriculture, Gamification, and Technology Enhanced Education.

Nimesha Ranasinghe is an Assistant Professor at the School of Computing and Information Science and directs the Multisensory Interactive Media lab (MIM lab - www. mimlab.info/) at the University of Maine. He completed his Ph.D. at the Department of Electrical and Computer Engineering, National University of Singapore (NUS), in 2013. His research interests include Multisensory Interactive Media, Human-Computer Interaction, Augmented and Virtual Reality.

Manjusri Wickramasinghe is a Senior Lecturer at the University of Colombo School of Computing, Sri Lanka. He obtained his PhD in Information Technology from Monash University in 2016. His research interests are Machine Learning, Computer Vision and Graphics, and Serious Games.

Dhaval Vyas is an ARC DECRA Fellow (2018–2021) and a Senior Lecturer in the School of Information Technology and Electrical Engineering, at the University of Queensland, Australia. He received a PhD in Human-Computer Interaction from the University of Twente, the Netherlands. His research spans across the areas of Human-Computer Interaction (HCI) and Computer-Supported Cooperative Work (CSCW).

References

1. Arsovski, S., Osipyan, H., Cheok, A.D., Muniru, I.O.: Internet of speech: a conceptual model. In: 3rd International Conference on Creative Media, Design and Technology (REKA 2018), pp. 359–363. Atlantis Press (2018)
2. Azuma, R.: A survey of augmented reality. Pres.: Teleoper. Virtual Environ. **6**(4), 355–385 (1997)
3. Bilbow, S., Kiefer, C., Chevalier, C.: The value of sound within a multisensory approach to AR in the arts. In: Proceedings of the Multisensory Augmented Reality Workshop, Interact (2021). https://usehci.org/mar2021/proceedings/
4. Cheok, A.D., Karunanayaka, K.: Virtual taste and smell technologies for multisensory internet and virtual reality. Springer, Cham (2018). https://doi.org/10.1007/978-3-319-73864-2
5. Edirisinghe, C., Podari, N., Cheok, A.D.: A multi-sensory interactive reading experience for visually impaired children; a user evaluation. Pers. Ubiquit. Comput. 1-13 (2018). https://doi.org/10.1007/s00779-018-1127-4
6. Guedes, L.S.: Designing multisensory experiences in museums for people with disabilities. In: Proceedings of the Multisensory Augmented Reality Workshop, Interact (2021). https://usehci.org/mar2021/proceedings/
7. Jayamini, C., Sandamini, A., Pannala, T., Kumarasinghe, P., Perera, D., Karunanayaka, K.: The use of augmented reality to deliver enhanced user experiences in fashion industry. In: Proceedings of the Multisensory Augmented Reality Workshop, Interact (2021). https://usehci.org/mar2021/proceedings/
8. Karunanayaka, K., Saadiah, H., Shahroom, H., Cheok, A.D.: Methods to develop a low-cost laboratory olfactometer for multisensory, psychology, and neuroscience experiments. In: IECON 2017–43rd Annual Conference of the IEEE Industrial Electronics Society, pp. 2882–2887. IEEE (2017)
9. Liyanage, S.U., Jayaratne, L., Wickramasinghe, M., Munasinghe, A.: Towards an affordable virtual reality solution for cardiopulmonary resuscitation training. In: 2019 IEEE Conference on Virtual Reality and 3D User Interfaces (VR), pp. 1054–1055. IEEE (2019)
10. Lu, J., Li, L., Sun, G.P.: A multimodal virtual anatomy e-learning tool for medical education. In: Zhang, X., Zhong, S., Pan, Z., Wong, K., Yun, R. (eds.) Edutainment 2010. LNCS, vol. 6249, pp. 278–287. Springer, Heidelberg (2010). https://doi.org/10.1007/978-3-642-14533-9_28
11. Malý, I., Sedláček, D., Leitao, P.: Augmented reality experiments with industrial robot in Industry 4.0 environment. In: 2016 IEEE 14th International Conference on Industrial Informatics (INDIN), pp. 176–181. IEEE (2016)
12. Nijholt, A.: Making Smart Cities More Playable. Springer, Singapore (2020). https://doi.org/10.1007/s00779-018-1127-4

13. Nijholt, A.: Virtual and augmented reality animals in smart and playful cities (invited paper). In: 2020 IEEE Joint 9th International Conference on Informatics, Electronics & Vision (ICIEV) and 2020 4th International Conference on Imaging, Vision & Pattern Recognition (icIVPR), Kitakyushu, Japan, pp. 1–7 (2020)

14. Nijholt, A.: Humorous and playful social interactions in augmented reality. In: Contribuciones a la Lingüística y a la Comunicación Social. Tributo a Vitelio Ruiz Hernández. Sixteenth International Symposium on Social Communication, Centro de Lingüística Aplicada, Santiago de Cuba, Cuba, pp. 167–173 (2021)

15. Petit, O., Cheok, A.D., Spence, C., Velasco, C., Karunanayaka, K.T.: Sensory marketing in light of new technologies. In: Proceedings of the 12th International Conference on Advances in Computer Entertainment Technology, pp. 1–4 (2015)

16. Ranasinghe, N., Nguyen, T.N.T., Liangkun, Y., Lin, L.Y., Tolley, D., Do, E.Y.L.: Vocktail: a virtual cocktail for pairing digital taste, smell, and color sensations. In: Proceedings of the 25th ACM International Conference on Multimedia, pp. 1139–1147 (2017)

17. Ranasinghe, N., et al.: Season traveller: multisensory narration for enhancing the virtual reality experience. In: Proceedings of the 2018 CHI Conference on Human Factors in Computing Systems, pp. 1–13 (2018)

18. Tache, R., et al.: Command center: authoring tool to supervise augmented reality session. In: 2012 IEEE Virtual Reality Workshops (VRW), pp. 99–100. IEEE (2012)

19. Thomas, T., Holmquist, L.E.: The value of sound within a multisensory approach to AR in the arts. In: Proceedings of the Multisensory Augmented Reality Workshop, Interact (2021). https://usehci.org/mar2021/proceedings/

20. Tobisková, N, Malmsköld, L., Pederson, T.: Beyond visual guidance in semi-manual industrial assembly of wooden house sections. In: Proceedings of the Multisensory Augmented Reality Workshop, Interact (2021). https://usehci.org/mar2021/proceedings/

21. Velasco, C., Karunanayaka, K., Nijholt, A.: Multisensory human-food interaction. Front. Psychol. **9**, 796 (2018)

22. Velasco, C., et al.: Multisensory approaches to human-food interaction. In: Proceedings of the 2020 International Conference on Multimodal Interaction (ICMI 2020). ACM, New York, pp. 878–880 (2020)

23. Yamabe, T., Nakajima, T.: Playful training with augmented reality games: case studies towards reality-oriented system design. Multimed. Tools Appl. **62**(1), 259–286 (2013)

24. Zhang, E.Y., Cheok, A.D., Arsovski, S., Muniru, I.O.: Exploring the role of robotic kissing "kissenger" in digital communication through Alan Turing's imitation game. In: IECON 2017–43rd Annual Conference of the IEEE Industrial Electronics Society, pp. 2870–2875. IEEE (2017)

Participatory Design Landscape for the Human-Machine Collaboration, Interaction and Automation at the Frontiers of HCI (PDL 2021)

Wiesław Kopeć[1] , Cezary Biele[2] , Monika Kornacka[3] ,
Grzegorz Pochwatko[4] , Anna Jaskulska[5] , Kinga Skorupska[1,3](✉) ,
Julia Paluch[1] , Piotr Gago[1] , Barbara Karpowicz[1] , Marcin Niewiński[1] ,
and Rafał Masłyk[1]

[1] Polish-Japanese Academy of Information Technology, Warsaw, Poland
kinga.skorupska@pja.edu.pl
[2] National Information Processing Institute, Warsaw, Poland
[3] SWPS University of Social Sciences and Humanities, Warsaw, Poland
[4] IP Polish Academy of Sciences, Warsaw, Poland
[5] KOBO Association, Warsaw, Poland

Abstract. We propose a one-day transdisciplinary creative workshop in the broad area of HCI focused on multiple opportunities of incorporating participatory design into research and industry practice. This workshop will become a venue to share experiences and novel ideas in this area. At the same time, we will brainstorm and explore frontiers of HCI related to engaging end users in design and development practices of established and emerging ICT solutions often overlooked in terms of co-design. We welcome a wide scope of contributions in HCI which explore sustainable opportunities for participatory design and development practices in the context of interconnected business, social, economic and environmental issues. The contributions ought to explore challenges and opportunities related to co-design at the frontiers of HCI - participatory design of newest and complex technologies, not easily explainable or intuitive, novel collaborative (remote or distributed) approaches to empowering users to prepare them to contribute as well as to engaging them directly in co-design.

Keywords: Participatory design · Human-computer interaction · Robotic process automation · Collaborative interactive machine learning · Business process management systems · Crowdsourcing · Natural language processing

Supported by Human Aspects in Software Engineering (HASE) Research Initiative.

© IFIP International Federation for Information Processing 2021
Published by Springer Nature Switzerland AG 2021
C. Ardito et al. (Eds.): INTERACT 2021, LNCS 12936, pp. 564–569, 2021.
https://doi.org/10.1007/978-3-030-85607-6_78

1   Theme and Topics

1.1   Theme

Our workshop on participatory design landscape for the human-machine collaboration, interaction and automation welcomes contributions in the broad area of Human-Computer Interaction. We focus on facilitating end-users involvement in a sustainable and ethical way in the context of the novel ICT solutions, remote co-design participation and accelerating digital transformation touching both the professional and the private spheres. This transformation presents multiple opportunities for addressing complex interdependent problems with co-designed ICT-based solutions using remote or distributed collaboration and novel empowerment approaches, to enable all users to fully participate in co-designing even complex solutions, which are not easy to relate to or intuitive.

1.2   Contributions

The contributions ought to explore challenges and opportunities related to co-design at the frontiers of HCI - participatory design of newest and complex technologies, not easily explainable or intuitive, novel collaborative (remote or distributed) approaches to empowering users to prepare them to contribute as well as to engaging them directly in co-design. Therefore, we welcome reports of interdisciplinary projects, studies and potential research initiatives which use (or would like to benefit from) various participatory approaches. These can, for example, include cases of user empowerment [1,5,7,10] or engaging users in diverse co-design contexts, such as Living Labs [6,8], design probes, and other creative co-design methods (Fig. 1).

1.3   Topics

These studies, while necessarily focusing on participatory design practices, can touch upon various aspects of applied computer science (including data science, artificial intelligence, social informatics and human-computer interaction) alongside with current state-of-the-art in psychology, social science and economics (such as neuroscience, psychophysiology and cognitive studies). The interdisciplinary and participatory approach they ought to describe can be applied in the context of interconnected business, social, economic and environmental issues, as our focus is on the use of co-design approaches in a wide scope of novel contexts. Therefore, in the workshop we will explore the opportunities related to participatory design of both established and emerging solutions and interfaces like Voice Assistants (VA), Virtual (VR), Augmented (AR) and Mixed Reality alongside with major underlying trends like Artificial Intelligence (AI), Machine Learning (ML), Natural Language Processing (NLP) or Complex Event Processing (CEP) in the context of multiple areas of interest to science and industry where co-design can be particularly beneficial. One example of such area of interest is related to creating health solutions using technologies that are new

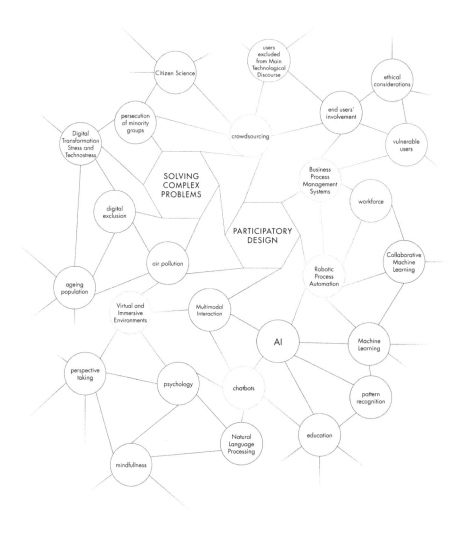

Fig. 1. Example topics for this workshop in relation to its key co-design theme.

to end users - patients - but that have already been proven to be effective at improving the efficiency of mental health therapy, such as VR or AR. Another opportunity is related to the co-development of self-help mobile applications or games [3] for health (including mental health) [2] and of wearable monitoring solutions. The development and increased access to wearable, mobile and robotic technology brings novel opportunities for using IT-based solutions in everyday life, including personal spaces and workplaces. Such solutions make it possible to measure psychological processes and to provide treatment in ecological conditions of patients' everyday life. Yet, research and practice show that functionality and ergonomics of the proposed solutions are crucial for acceptability and compliance. Thus, participatory design may be an adequate way to address those challenges. Especially the design of social robots, which heavily rely on expectations based on social interaction norms, stands to greatly benefit from participatory design [9].

2   Organizers

We are a multidisciplinary group of scientists, researchers, IT professionals and activists whose key focus is on multiple positive applications of ICT through engaging in participatory practices[1], especially focused on engaging the users excluded from the technological discourse [5] (for example, with games[2] or hackathons[3] or through inviting stakeholders to take part in educational and capacity building projects[4]).

Key Organizers

- Wiesław Kopeć, PhD, MBA, (Google Scholar Profile)
  Head of XR Lab, Computer Science Department,
  Polish-Japanese Academy of Information Technology (PJAIT)
- Cezary Biele, PhD, (Google Scholar Profile)
  Head of Laboratory of Interactive Technologies,
  National Information Processing Institute (NIPI)
- Monika Kornacka, PhD, (Google Scholar Profile)
  Head of Emotion Cognition Lab, Institute of Psychlogy,
  SWPS University of Social Sciences and Humanities (SWPS)
- Grzegorz Pochwatko, PhD, (Google Scholar Profile)
  Head of Virtual Reality and Psychophysiology Lab, Institute of Psychology,
  Polish Academy of Sciences (IP PAS)

Program Committee. Jakub Możaryn, PhD, Warsaw University of Technology (Google Scholar Profile); Jacek Lebiedź, PhD, Gdansk University of Technology (University Profile); Marzena Wojciechowska, PhD, PJAIT Resarch Center (ResearchGate Profile); Dominika Tkaczyk, PhD, Crossref (Google Scholar Profile); Sebastian Zagrodzki, Google (LinkedIn Profile) Łukasz Czarnecki, Amazon (LinkedIn Profile); Anna Jaskulska, Kobo Association and Living Lab (Kobo Profile); Ewa Makowska, Business and System Analyst and IT Project Manager (LinkedIn Profile).

Paper Co-Chairs. Kinga Skorupska, XR Lab PJAIT, (Google Scholar Profile) and Julia Paluch, XR Lab PJAIT (ResearchGate Profile).

---

[1] Participatory Design Workshops.
[2] Location-Based Game.
[3] Hackathon.
[4] ALIEN Project.

Technical Chairs. Rafał Masłyk, XR Lab PJAIT; Barbara Karpowicz, XR Lab PJAIT; Maciej Krzywicki, XR Lab PJAIT; Piotr Gago, XR Lab PJAIT.

3 Objectives

In organizing this workshop we have three key objectives:

1. Exchanging experiences, ideas, best practices and guidelines for co-designing at the transdisciplinary frontiers of HCI.
2. Outlining the participants' aspirations and opportunities for breaking new ground in the area of HCI and exploring ideas for innovative project proposals and practices involving participatory design.
3. Establishing common ground and voice for the discussion of the challenges and opportunities related to the future of participatory practices at the frontiers of HCI.

4 Target Audience

We invite researchers and practitioners in the broad area of HCI, who want to explore the opportunities of incorporating participatory practices in their work, including design, collaborative ML, RPA, and crowdsourcing in an ethical and sustainable way. At the same time we want to find new areas where co-design of ICT-based solutions may work towards improving social cohesion and addressing complex business, social, economic and environmental issues.

5 Methodology

We propose a one-day exploratory workshop combining sharing best practices as interactive presentations and discussions with a creative flair of a collaborative design-inspired toolbox geared towards exploring opportunities at the frontiers of co-design and HCI. In the course of the workshop we want to use creative tools to aid free thinking, instead of stifling it with over-formalized "creative" methodology focused on structured results. We believe that allowing for a degree of ambiguity at the beginning of the creative process is a must, while the outlines of our combined expertise are sufficient to work as bounds that limit the scope of our imagination. In this vein, the workshop will be led in a friendly atmosphere, without formalized introductions or strict presentation formats. Our workshop facilitators have diverse creative tools and practices at their disposal, which they can adjust accordingly to the number and needs of the participants and their levels of energy.

6   Expected Outcomes

As our key motivation is to explore the opportunities related to participatory design at the frontiers of HCI, while grounding these firmly in established and emerging practices, the most important outcome will be a post-workshop multi-author publication. Its format will be the result of issues discussed during the workshop, but the idea for it is inspired by Kittur et al. [4] whose paper "The Future of Crowd Work" clearly outlined the aspects, trends and opportunities related to crowdsourcing. We feel the same is needed in the area of participatory design and human factors at the frontiers of HCI, as such design ought to take into account ethics, preferences and motivations as well as the broad user experience and visual design. Especially now, that more remote tools and approaches are needed to engage users, and novel forms of empowerment ought to emerge to let co-designers really understand the context of the complex co-designed solutions. Additionally, we would be happy to invite our participants to look for opportunities to publish a collection of extended papers from the workshop.

References

1. Davidson, J.L., Jensen, C.: Participatory design with older adults: an analysis of creativity in the design of mobile healthcare applications. In: Proceedings of the 9th ACM Conference on Creativity & Cognition, pp. 114–123. ACM (2013)
2. Jessen, S., Mirkovic, J., Nes, L.S.: Mystrengths, a strengths-focused mobile health tool: participatory design and development. JMIR Form Res. 4(7), e18049 (2020). https://doi.org/10.2196/18049
3. Jessen, S., Mirkovic, J., Ruland, C.M.: Creating gameful design in mHealth: a participatory co-design approach. JMIR Mhealth Uhealth 6(12), e11579 (2018). https://doi.org/10.2196/11579
4. Kittur, A., et al.: The future of crowd work. In: Proceedings of the 2013 Conference on Computer Supported Cooperative Work, pp. 1301–1318. ACM (2013)
5. Kopeć, W., Nielek, R., Wierzbicki, A.: Guidelines towards better participation of older adults in software development processes using a new spiral method and participatory approach. In: Proceedings of the CHASE 2018: International Workshop on Cooperative and Human Aspects of Software, ICSE 2018. ACM, New York (2018). https://doi.org/10.1145/3195836.3195840
6. Kopeć, W., Skorupska, K., Jaskulska, A., Abramczuk, K., Nielek, R., Wierzbicki, A.: Livinglab PJAIT: towards better urban participation of seniors. In: Proceedings of the International Conference on Web Intelligence, WI 2017, pp. 1085–1092. ACM, New York (2017). https://doi.org/10.1145/3106426.3109040
7. Ladner, R.E.: Design for user empowerment. Interactions 22(2), 24–29 (2015)
8. Pallot, M., Trousse, B., Senach, B., Scapin, D.: Living lab research landscape: from user centred design and user experience towards user cocreation. In: First European Summer School "Living Labs" (2010)
9. Piçarra, N., Giger, J.C., Pochwatko, G., Możaryn, J.: Designing social robots for interaction at work: socio-cognitive factors underlying intention to work with social robots. J. Autom. Mob. Robot. Intell. Syst. 10 (2016)
10. Sanders, E.B.N.: From user-centered to participatory design approaches. In: Design and the Social Sciences: Making Connections, pp. 1–8 (2002)

Pilot Implementation: Testing Human-Work Interaction Designs

Morten Hertzum[1]([✉]) [ID], Torkil Clemmensen[2] [ID], Barbara Rita Barricelli[3] [ID], Pedro F. Campos[4], Frederica Gonçalves[4], José Abdelnour Nocera[4,5], Ganesh Bhutkar[6] [ID], and Arminda Guerra Lopes[4,7]

[1] University of Copenhagen, Karen Blixens Plads 8, 2300 Copenhagen, Denmark
hertzum@hum.ku.dk
[2] Copenhagen Business School, Howitzvej 60, 2000 Frederiksberg, Denmark
tc.digi@cbs.dk
[3] Università degli Studi di Brescia, Via Branze 38, 25123 Brescia, Italy
barbara.barricelli@unibs.it
[4] ITI/LARSyS and University of Madeira, Funchal, Portugal
{pedro.campos,frederica.goncalves}@iti.larsys.pt
[5] University of West London, London, UK
Jose.Abdelnour-Nocera@uwl.ac.uk
[6] Vishwakarma Institute of Technology, Pune, India
ganesh.bhutkar@vit.edu
[7] Polytechnic Institute of Castelo Branco, Castelo Branco, Portugal
aglopes@ipcb.pt

Abstract. Pilot implementations are field tests of properly engineered, yet unfinished, systems. In contrast to lab tests, the users in a pilot implementation use the system for performing real work. In contrast to full-scale implementations, the objective of a pilot implementation is to learn. The workshop on pilot implementation aims to (a) help mature this technique for evaluating human-work interaction designs during the process of their development and implementation, (b) collect case studies that analyze experiences with conducting and learning from pilot implementations, and (c) formulate a research agenda for future work on pilot implementations – addressing their strengths, limitations, conduct, impact, and so forth. The target audience for the workshop is researchers and practitioners working on topics related to work analysis, interaction design, system-organization fit, organizational implementation, benefits realization, and in-the-wild evaluation.

Keywords: Pilot implementation · Field test · Human-work interaction design

1 Introduction

The integration of work analysis and interaction design methods is pivotal to the successful development and implementation of systems for pervasive and smart workplaces [13]. With this workshop, the IFIP TC13.6 working group on Human Work Interaction

© IFIP International Federation for Information Processing 2021
Published by Springer Nature Switzerland AG 2021
C. Ardito et al. (Eds.): INTERACT 2021, LNCS 12936, pp. 570–574, 2021.
https://doi.org/10.1007/978-3-030-85607-6_79

Design (HWID) aims to create a forum for investigating and discussing how pilot implementations can – and cannot – contribute to this integration. The workshop builds on prior research documenting the value of in situ methods in working to ensure and improve system usefulness [e.g., 3, 6, 14].

A pilot implementation is *"a field test of a properly engineered, yet unfinished system in its intended environment, using real data, and aiming – through real-use experience – to explore the value of the system, improve or assess its design, and reduce implementation risk"* [7]. This definition positions pilot implementation in between predictive usability tests and full-scale implementation. In contrast to usability tests, which are conducted in the lab to evaluate mockups or prototypes, pilot implementations are conducted in the field and necessarily involve users performing their real work using the pilot system. In contrast to full-scale implementation, which is intended to result in continued use, pilot implementations are temporary and aim to feed information about the finalization and implementation of the system back into the development process.

Pilot implementations recognize that systems are sociotechnical and that their social, organizational, and contextual qualities can only be evaluated thoroughly in the field. This recognition of a need for extending the iterative design process beyond the lab is not exclusive to pilot implementations. It is also at the fore in, for example, design in use [4], living labs [1], technology probes [9], digital twins [12], and breaching experiments [5]. However, some of these other methods are mainly used by researchers who study technology use. In contrast, pilot implementations are widely used by practitioners within the resource limitations of development and implementation processes.

2   Workshop Objectives

The HWID workshop on pilot implementation has three main objectives:

- To help mature pilot implementation as a technique for evaluating human-work interaction designs during the process of their development and implementation.
- To collect case studies that analyze experiences – good and bad – with conducting and learning from pilot implementations.
- To formulate a research agenda for future work on pilot implementations – addressing their strengths, limitations, conduct, impact, and so forth.

3   Pilot Implementation

Prior work emphasizes that a pilot implementation is not just the period during which a system is in pilot use. Hertzum et al. [7] propose that pilot implementation involves five interrelated activities:

- *Planning and design*, during which the pilot implementation is defined. This activity involves deciding where and when the pilot implementation will take place, how lessons learned during the pilot implementation will be collected, and so forth.

- *Technical configuration*, during which the pilot system is configured for the pilot site. As part of this activity, data must be migrated to the system and interfaces to other systems at the pilot site must be developed or simulations set up.
- *Organizational adaptation*, during which the pilot site revises work procedures to benefit from the pilot system. This activity also involves user training and, possibly, temporary safeguards against pilot-system breakdowns.
- *Use*, during which the system is used for real work at the pilot site. This activity involves striking a balance between integrating the system in normal procedures and maintaining a focus on the system as an object under evaluation.
- *Learning*, which is the overarching objective of pilot implementation. This activity runs in parallel with the four other activities and collects data and insights about the system, its use, and the associated organizational changes.

The three first activities are preparations, which may consume more time than the period of pilot use. During the period of pilot use, the consequences of the system become salient to the users because it begins to influence their daily work and requires them to change their practices. This salience motivates the users to voice their concerns [15]. They will often be more motivated to participate at this stage than during requirements specification and usability tests, which may be experienced as a distraction that takes time away from getting their daily work done. Finally, learning occurs during the preparations as well as during the period of pilot use. The collection and analysis of the learnings require work. This work may involve measuring whether specified benefits are realized, interviewing users about their user experience, and having managers discuss additional visions for changes associated with the system.

Pilot implementations create room for innovative experimentation [2], help align the stakeholders on whom system adoption is dependent [11], provide valuable feedback about system finalization [7], identify important discrepancies in how different user groups perceive a system [16], and create a decision point for discontinuing systems that face too many obstacles [8]. These strengths are important arguments for conducting pilot implementations. However, multiple challenges have also been identified, including the following [7, 8, 10, 11, 16]:

- Pilot implementations tend to be either too early or too late. When they are too early, the system and organization are not yet ready. When they are too late, the benefits to be realized from full-scale implementation are unduly delayed.
- The boundaries of pilot implementations are continuously negotiated because any choice comes with difficult-to-handle interactions across the boundary between the pilot site and its surroundings, which have not yet implemented the system.
- The focus on learning is difficult to maintain in the midst of getting the daily work done. Some users may see the pilot implementation as the first stage of full-scale implementation and fail to notice the learning objective altogether.
- Pilot implementations involve special precautions to safeguard against critical errors and to encourage system use. There is a tension between the presence of these precautions and their absence when the system is released for full-scale use.

- The learning may be situated and difficult to transfer from the pilot site to other sites. Specifically, it is difficult to distinguish consequences that are local to the pilot implementation from consequences that are inherent in the system and its use.
- Pilot implementations are not final statements about the fit between system and organization. They add realism (compared to lab tests), but the realism increases salience rather than terminates discussion about what using the system will be like.
- Pilot implementations are generative; they are not merely tests. A pilot implementation fosters alignment, reveals tension, shifts power, and otherwise affects users and organizations. All these effects must be contended with post pilot.

Pilot implementations are recognized among practitioners for their contributions to system finalization, organizational implementation, and project de-escalation. However, the extant research on pilot implementations leaves lots of open questions about common experiences with conducting pilot implementations, about how best to organize them, about their pitfalls, and about which questions the research on pilot implementation needs to address.

4 Expected Outcomes

The workshop will produce a research agenda for studying pilot implementations and how best to conduct them. The aim of this research agenda is to stimulate further research interest and provide direction for research on pilot implementation. At the workshop, the organizers will invite the workshop participants to co-author a paper that presents the research agenda and discusses it on the basis of the cases and insights contributed by the participants.

5 Target Audience

The target audience for the HWID workshop on pilot implementation includes researchers and practitioners working on topics related to work analysis, interaction design, system-organization fit, organizational implementation, benefits realization, and in-the-wild evaluation. Because pilot implementations are common in practical development and implementation projects, we pay special attention to attracting practitioners from various work environments to discuss real-life case studies. Participation in the workshop requires the submission and acceptance of a position paper, which is limited to a maximum of four pages. Early-stage researchers and PhD students are encouraged to submit papers describing work in progress.

References

1. Alavi, H.S., Lalanne, D., Rogers, Y.: The five strands of living lab: a literature study of the evolution of living lab concepts in HCI. ACM Trans. Comput.-Hum. Interact. **27**(3), article 10 (2020)

2. Bakker, R.M., Cambré, B., Korlaar, L., Raab, J.: Managing the project learning paradox: a set-theoretic approach toward project knowledge transfer. Int. J. Project Manage. **29**(5), 494–503 (2011)

3. Bannon, L.J.: From human factors to human actors: the role of psychology and human-computer interaction studies in system design. In: Greenbaum, J., Kyng, M. (eds.) Design at Work: Cooperative Design of Computer Systems, pp. 25–44. Erlbaum, Hillsdale (1991)

4. Bjögvinsson, E., Ehn, P., Hillgren, P.-A.: Design things and design thinking: contemporary participatory design challenges. Des. Issues **28**(3), 101–116 (2012)

5. Crabtree, A.: Taking technomethodology seriously: hybrid change in the ethnomethodology-design relationship. Eur. J. Inf. Syst. **13**(3), 195–209 (2004)

6. Fields, B., Amaldi, P., Wong, W., Gill, S.: In use, in situ: extending field research methods. Int. J. Hum.-Comput. Interact. **22**(1 & 2), 1–6 (2007)

7. Hertzum, M., Bansler, J.P., Havn, E., Simonsen, J.: Pilot implementation: learning from field tests in IS development. Commun. Assoc. Inf. Syst. **30**(1), 313–328 (2012)

8. Hertzum, M., Manikas, M.I., Torkilsheyggi, A.: Grappling with the future: the messiness of pilot implementation in information systems design. Health Inf. J. **25**(2), 372–388 (2019)

9. Hutchinson, H., et al.: Technology probes: inspiring design for and with families. In: Proceedings of the CHI2003 Conference on Human Factors in Computing Systems, pp. 17–24. ACM Press, New York (2003)

10. Korn, M., Bødker, S.: Looking ahead - How field trials can work in iterative and exploratory design of ubicomp systems. In: Proceedings of the UbiComp2012 Conference on Ubiquitous Computing, pp. 21–30. ACM Press, New York (2012)

11. Mønsted, T., Hertzum, M., Søndergaard, J.: A socio-temporal perspective on pilot implementation: bootstrappng preventive care. Comput. Support. Coop. Work **29**(4), 419–449 (2020)

12. Nikolakis, N., Alexopoulos, K., Xanthakis, E., Chryssolouris, G.: The digital twin implementation for linking the virtual representation of human-based production tasks to their physical counterpart in the factory-floor. Int. J. Comput. Integr. Manuf. **32**(1), 1–12 (2019)

13. Nocera, J.A., Barricelli, B.R., Lopes, A., Campos, P., Clemmensen, T. (eds.): Human Work Interaction Design: Work Analysis and Interaction Design Methods for Pervasive and Smart Workplaces. IFIP AICT. vol. 468. Springer, Cham (2015). https://doi.org/10.1007/978-3-319-27048-7

14. Nocera, J.A., Dunckley, L., Sharp, H.: An approach to the evaluation of usefulness as a social construct using technological frames. Int. J. Hum.-Comput. Interact. **22**(1 & 2), 153–172 (2007)

15. Wagner, E.L., Piccoli, G.: Moving beyond user participation to achieve successful IS design. Commun. ACM **50**(12), 51–55 (2007)

16. Winthereik, B.R.: The project multiple: enactments of systems development. Scand. J. Inf. Syst. **22**(2), 49–64 (2010)

Remote Conference in the Times
of the Pandemic

Julio Abascal[1] ⓘ, Cezary Biele[2], Daniel Cnotkowski[2], Gabriela Górska[2],
Jarosław Kowalski[2], Effie Lai-Chong Law[3] ⓘ, Bartosz Muczyński[4(✉)] ⓘ,
Abiodun Afolayan Ogunyemi[5] ⓘ, Mariusz Wierzbowski[2],
and Aldona Zdrodowska[2] ⓘ

[1] Informatika Fakultatea, University of the Basque Country (UPV/EHU), Manuel Lardizabal 1,
20018 Donostia, Spain
julio.abascal@ehu.eus
[2] National Information Processing Institute, al. Niepodległości 188B, 00-608 Warsaw, Poland
{cezary.biele,daniel.cnotkowski,gabriela.gorska,
jaroslaw.kowalski,mariusz.wierzbowski,
aldona.zdrodowska}@opi.org.pl
[3] University of Leicester, Leicester LE1 7RH, UK
elaw@mcs.le.ac.uk
[4] Maritime University of Szczecin, Wały Chrobrego 1-2, 70-500 Szczecin, Poland
b.muczynski@am.szczecin.pl
[5] Tallinn University, Narva mnt 25, 10120 Tallinn, Estonia
abnogn@tlu.ee

Abstract. The COVID-19 pandemic forced a sudden increase of remote activities including work, learning and also scientific conferences. Almost a year of experience in remote work, remote meetings and remote conferences clearly showed that these events are markedly different from their traditional counterparts. The aim of this workshop is to analyse factors influencing the user experience of remote conferences, thereby creating a set of guidelines for their future organizers. Patterns may be identified from personal experiences shared by HCI researchers as participants or organizers of remote conferences. Methodologically, the methods of Design Thinking combined with the auto-ethnographic approach will be employed for the workshop. Participants will be able to find new insights into the process of the organization of remote conferences and transform such insights into an actionable set of guidelines for future remote conference organization.

Keywords: Remote conferences · Virtual meetings · Social experiences

1 Introduction

While remote conferences are much more accessible and cheaper than traditional conferences they provide some new challenges in many areas: social, organizational and technical. Without proper planning any remote conference can feel like a series of disconnected webinars with very limited, almost anonymous contact between presenters

© IFIP International Federation for Information Processing 2021
Published by Springer Nature Switzerland AG 2021
C. Ardito et al. (Eds.): INTERACT 2021, LNCS 12936, pp. 575–578, 2021.
https://doi.org/10.1007/978-3-030-85607-6_80

and participants. In order to provide every participant with a meaningful experience it is important to understand their diverse expectations and limitations, and plan and organize the conference accordingly.

It may be argued that the COVID-19 pandemic is close to its end and with it scientific conferences will return to a traditional face-to-face format. We believe that even if it is true, probably remote conferences will remain popular events in the scientific world as researchers have already witnessed the advantages of remote participation (e.g., environmental friendliness). This workshop is proposed not only because there is not enough evidence to predict how the scientific conference landscape will evolve but also because authors believe that the current situation may impact all future conferences, making them more accessible and open. There is also a perspective for a new model of hybrid conferences, that will have to meet with the same challenges as any other online conferences.

2   Objectives

Due to the mixed experiences of participants and organizers of remote conferences it is important to search for effective solutions for such events. The aim of this workshop is to create a platform for HCI researchers to explore issues pertaining to the remote conference organization and practices in the times of COVID pandemic. This in effect will allow creation of guidelines outlining the best approach to effectively organize remote conferences. To achieve this the workshop will bring together people that have personal experience in attending and organizing remote conferences and researchers specializing in social and human-computer interactions. Being members of HCI community we believe that HCI researchers in this community are the group with the most suitable knowledge and experience to be able to prepare guidelines that are the goal of this workshop. A typical HCI research methods used in developed areas of HCI like Participatory Design or Computer Supported Cooperative Work could be described as 'objective ethnography' where researchers observe or cooperate with users in order to get to know their perspective. In the course of searching for a new method of describing reality the use of auto-ethnographic approach is gaining popularity in the last years in the area of HCI. This approach focuses on the reflexive self-analysis of the researchers' personal perspectives [1].

3   Target Audience and Expected Interest

The workshop is intended mainly for people that are or will be organizing any remote conference or online event but also for researchers interested in areas of social interaction, HCI, virtual reality. We plan to draw on both the experience and expertise of HCI researchers, who may be both actors and designers in the situation of planning the remote conference. The personal experience in the area of remote conferences will be definitely a very valuable asset for the participants but we'd like to stress that it is not necessary.

4   Overall Structure

Before the workshop, participants will be asked to prepare a position paper (min. 1 page) describing their experiences with remote conferences or/and their expectations. In order to facilitate this process workshop organizers will provide template containing a set of possible topics to consider when preparing such a paper, in the form of a set of open questions or mental exercises. The goal of this part will be for each of the participants to evaluate their experiences and realize their attitudes towards particular elements of the remote conference experience.

Such input from participants will ensure the effectiveness of the following main part of the workshop, that is the design session of the 'remote conference' understood as an innovative product, according to the five steps of typical Design Thinking methodology.

1. **Empathy** - on the basis of the material collected from the participants, Empathy Maps and Personas (a short description of a fictional person and their needs - quotes from the collected material will be used here) will be created. Thanks to the described personas, participants will be able to empathise with their needs and design solutions tailored to those needs. Participants of the workshop will be divided into smaller groups of 4–6 persons. The next steps are implemented separately in each group, which works on solutions for one persona.
2. **Problem definition** - after reading the description of the persona and its Empathy Map, each group reflects on what main problems/needs have emerged. Then participants formulate the main problem/issue regarding this persona. Solutions designed in further steps will be tailored for this specific need. Writing down an exact challenge/problem gives the group a sense of responsibility for solving this issue.
3. **Generation of ideas** - the next step is about generating ideas for concrete solutions. The brainstorming methodology is applied here. This stage participants do not care about the feasibility of the solutions, but about generating a large number of them. Thanks to this, when the obvious solutions are written down, it is possible to use natural creativity and generate ideas that are not obvious. During the group work participants are not allowed to criticize solutions, nor to discuss them. Then, from the large pool of all generated ideas (usually several dozen), the group chooses 2–3 to work on in further stages.
4. **Creation of a prototype** - the two or three most promising ideas selected in the previous stage are subjected to prototyping. The prototype is created quickly (5–10 min) from simple and cheap materials (paper, glue, newspapers, etc.). It can be a drawing, a model, or even a scene performed by the group. By building a prototype we achieve two goals: firstly, a different type of thinking is activated - about the specific properties and functions of a given solution. On the other hand the idea acquires a more tangible shape which is easier to present and discuss with other groups.
5. **Testing** - prototypes are presented to other groups in a simple form. Quick feedback is collected on the advantages and disadvantages of the solution. Then the group, enriched by the comments of the other groups, selects one of the two or three prototypes and develops its next more detailed version. The second version is also

discussed, feedback is collected and amendments are made. After the next stage of corrections the prototype is ready to be proposed as the final solution to the problem.

During the design process participants will also focus on the valuable characteristics not directly connected to the scientific course of the face-to-face conferences, like social contact, open discussion, creation of trust, etc. that are markedly more difficult to ensure during the remote conference. Especially those issues that make attending–and presenting to–a remote conference different to publishing a paper in a journal or presenting in a traditional way. During the workshop new ways of dealing with such areas of the conference will be proposed.

The last part of the workshop will consist of discussing the application of the technical solutions to the innovative 'remote conference' created in the Design Thinking session. We believe that this part will be very important in order to ground the ideas created during the design session in the available technical solutions, which will increase the chances that the ideas created during the workshop will be implemented in real life scenarios. During this part participants will get a broad overview of available free and paid software tools that can be used for video transmission, video and audio editing, streaming, chatting etc., learn what are the most critical elements of a remote conference and what measures should be taken to prepare for worst-case scenarios. We hope that in this part we will also be able to draw on the experiences of participants, but as the organizers of the workshop have the experience of conducting an effective remote conference (8th Machine Intelligence Digital Interaction 2020 [3]) this will also be an opportunity to share the best technical practices that we've tested during the conference.

5   Expected Outcomes

Following outcomes are expected after this workshop:

1. Creation of a set of guidelines for the organizers of future remote conferences, that will allow them to create the events that will be both effective and pleasurable experiences for researchers, not only in the HCI field.
2. Providing an outline for new, interesting research areas related to networking and interaction during online events during COVID-19 pandemic.
3. Building a small community that can provide support to each other and will help conducting broad study in the mentioned areas.

References

1. Rapp, A.: Autoethnography in human-computer interaction: theory and practice. In: Filimowicz, M., Tzankova, V. (eds.) New Directions in Third Wave Human-Computer Interaction: Volume 2 - Methodologies. HIS, pp. 25–42. Springer, Cham (2018). https://doi.org/10.1007/978-3-319-73374-6_3
2. Stickdorn, M., Lawerence, A., Hormess M., Schneider, J.: This is Service Design Doing. Applying Service Design Thinking in the Real World. O'Reilly (2018)
3. 8th Machine Intelligence and Digital Interaction – MIDI Conference. https://midi2020.opi.org.pl/

Remote User Testing
- Experiences and Trends

Lars Bo Larsen[1](✉), Tina Øvad[2], Lene Nielsen[3], and Marta Larusdottir[4]

[1] Aalborg University, Aalborg, Denmark
lbl@es.aau.dk
[2] Preely, Copenhagen, Denmark
tina@preely.com
[3] IT University, Copenhagen, Denmark
lene@itu.dk
[4] Reykjavik University, Reykjavik, Iceland
marta@ru.is

Abstract. This paper describes a one-day INTERACT 2021 workshop on remote testing with users as participants. Remote user testing has been around since the mid-nineties, but the Covid-19 pandemic has boosted the interest in remote working in general and thus also remote testing. The workshop aim is to present and discuss the current state-of-the-art of remote testing methods and identify emerging trends. Subjects that will be discussed include, but are not restricted to: Remote testing methods and platforms; capturing of quantitative as well as qualitative data; moderated, unmoderated and remotely moderated tests; testing of physical products; and remote testing of participants with special needs.

Keywords: Remote user testing · Usability · Remote user studies

1 Introduction

Remote user testing has been around for quite a long time. Early studies were carried out about 25 years ago in the mid-nineties [1–3] and have since evolved significantly. While the 00'ies witnessed many academic studies and methods, this is particularly evident over the recent decade with the arrival of numerous commercial tools and platforms for automated remote testing. However, the Covid-19 pandemic has put an even greater focus on remote work and the paradigm is more relevant now than ever before.

The basic idea of remote user testing is that a facilitator is not physically present at the same place as the participant in the user test. Instead, the participant accesses a product, a service or a prototype via a web browser or an app on a computer or a mobile device. In some cases, a facilitator may be (remotely) available to guide the user though the test scenarios, debriefing, etc. This is called supervised remote testing or remote moderated testing [4]. An alternative is to carry out the remote test unsupervised. This will in part save manpower

© IFIP International Federation for Information Processing 2021
Published by Springer Nature Switzerland AG 2021
C. Ardito et al. (Eds.): INTERACT 2021, LNCS 12936, pp. 579–583, 2021.
https://doi.org/10.1007/978-3-030-85607-6_81

and in part make the logistics of the test much easier as the test participant can perform the test any time and place s/he wishes. Unsupervised tests tend to mostly collect quantitative data, whereas supervised tests can capture a larger degree of qualitative data.

1.1   Supervised Remote Testing

Supervised remote testing is also referred to as synchronous testing, as it requires the test participants and the facilitator to be present at the same time. Supervised remote testing was described by e.g. Dray and Siegel in 2004 [5]. They discussed various possibilities for remote usability testing and made a comparison to usability test conducted in a lab setting. 10 years later, Brush et al. investigated differences in the participants' and facilitator' qualitative experience between lab and remote tests [6]. They had assumed that "participants would be more comfortable talking to the facilitator and would find it easier to think aloud and concentrate on tasks in the local condition". Contrary to the assumption, they found that most participants preferred the convenience of the remote testing approach. The findings suggested the remote test participants contributed to the results as much as in the lab-based test [6]. A special case is supervised testing with remote conductor - i.e. when an assistant or moderator participates at the user's side. This could e.g. be when the participant have special needs, such as children, persons with physical or cognitive impairments, the elderly, or those not comfortable with the digital solutions surrounding us. In such cases a local conductor, typically from the participant's household may be recruited to help execute the test.

1.2   Unsupervised Remote Testing

Unsupervised user testing is also referred to as asynchronous testing, as it does not require the test participants and the facilitator to be present at the same time. Bruun et al. compared three different methods in an unsupervised remote testing scenario: user-reported critical incidents; forum-based online reporting and diary-based user reporting [7]. They found that the results gathered by conducting the unsupervised testing were significantly sparser compared to results gathered by conducting lab-based usability tests. Despite this, unsupervised remote testing has gained a large foothold during recent years, due to its ease of deployment and corresponding cost-efficiency. As with supervised remote testing, this could also be carried out with a remote conductor.

1.3   Remote Testing Platforms

A number of companies have built platforms to facilitate remote user testing over the recent decade. One such platform supplier is the Danish company Preely [8]. The platform lets the interaction designer develop prototypes using a variety of tools, such as Sketch, Figma, Invision or Adobe XD [9–12] and then deploy them for test via the platform. Preely will import and execute the prototype and do all the bookkeeping and logging of user test data etc. for any number of test participants.

Other similar platforms are online services such as: Maze, UserTesting and UseBerry [13–15] for unsupervised testing. Similarly, consultancy services, like UserTribe, UserZoom and LookBack offer supervised remote tests [16–18]. These platforms are insight-based and qualitative and demands more resources post-test to make the analysis than the unsupervised ones.

1.4   Remote Testing of Physical Products

However, the present state-of-the-art of remote user testing methods and platforms are restricted to software products. At the present time it is relatively straight-forward to distribute software products, but if the product being tested is a physical device or a service, a number of new issues arise. Many have to do with the costs and logistics of distributing and later collecting the test products or prototypes. Others are directly concerned with the test session itself, such as making sure the user's camera is pointed towards the product being tested.

2   Workshop Scope and Aim

The purpose of the workshop is to assess the latest trends within remote user testing. In particular, to record and review the present state-of-the-art of methods and tools and asses the experiences gained during the Covid-19 pandemic. We will seek to answer the following questions:

- Which new experiences have the Covid-19 pandemic brought with regards to remote testing?
- Has the greatly increased focus on remote work during the pandemic also brought new ideas and methods to the field of remote testing?
- Have new requirements emerged, to which no solution yet exists?
- Are existing platforms and tools sufficient for the future demands?
- Will remote testing extend from software to physical products?
- How can unsupervised remote testing to a higher degree than now provide qualitative insights?
- Does remote testing cater sufficiently for user groups with special needs – such as children, persons with physical or cognitive impairments, the elderly, or those not comfortable with the digital solutions surrounding us?

The workshop invites papers sharing remote testing experiences as well as position papers bringing up a particular issue or focus. Contributions from industry are particularly welcome and could be in the form of a paper or a one-two page industry abstract. The workshop layout will be a mix of presentations from participants and group and plenary discussions (as described below).

The goal of the workshop will be to achieve an overview of the present state and challenges and provide a roadmap for the coming years' advances of remote testing.

3   Expected Outcome

We expect that the workshop will identify the current state-of-the-art and trends of remote user testing. In particular, the workshop will aim to pinpoint the challenges and unresolved problems facing the remote testing paradigm in the future and provide a proposal for a roadmap to address these.

3.1   Review Process and Proceedings

The paper contributions to the workshop will be peer reviewed by the organisers. Abstracts and industry contributions will be screened for relevance to the workshop topic. These will form the proceedings of the workshop and will be shared among participants prior to the workshop via the workshop website. The proceedings will be made public after the workshop for those authors who want that. The organisers will invite the participants who are interested to collaborate to publish a joint paper on the workshop results in a recognised peer-reviewed open access journal.

4   Organisation of the Workshop

The workshop will be based on active participation and discussions. Presentations will be organised in two main sessions, with a priority for discussions.

The aim is for 10 to 15 participants, to ensure a workshop atmosphere and informal style, where all have a chance to share viewpoints and engage actively in discussions. The workshop will take place in mixed-mode physically and virtually, due to expected Covid-19 travel restrictions, at the time of the workshop. The workshop will be split into two main sessions:

- **The morning session** will be devoted to presentations by the particpants and discussions based on the shared experiences and challenges given by the facilitators. All participants are expected to take active part in this and contribute with stories about good/bad experiences of remote user testing.
- **The afternoon session** will focus on identifying trends and creating a set of expectations and challenges for remote user testing for the upcoming years.

The participants will form smaller groups for parts of the discussions with one representative from each group to give a brief account of what has been discussed. To ensure the interactions between the participants, the groups will present their conclusions in plenum and be reformed after each session. To accommodate those present virtually, emphasis will be made to draw them into discussion and tools such as Miro [19] will be employed for notes and documentation instead of whiteboards and post-its.

The workshop will be moderated by the organisers, who are all experienced facilitators and expect to be present at the conference. They will act as presenters and session chairs, moderate the discussions, etc. As a follow-up, the findings and conclusions reached at the workshop will be published.

References

1. Castillo, J.C., Hartson, H.R., and Hix, D.: Remote usability evaluation at a glance * (Technical report) (1997). https://doi.org/10.1145/286498.286736
2. Hammontree, M.L., Weiler, P., Nayak, N.P.: Remote usability testing. Interactions **1**, 21–25 (1994)
3. Hartson, H.R., Castillo, J.C., Kelso, J., Neale, W.C., Kamler, J.: Remote evaluation: the network as an extension of the usability laboratory. In: Conference on Human Factors in Computing Systems - Proceedings, pp. 228–235. ACM Press, New York (1996). https://doi.org/10.1145/238386.238511
4. Safire, M.: Remote moderated usability: what, why and how. In: 12th Annual Usability Professionals Association Conference, Phoenix, AZ (2003)
5. Dray, S., Siegel, D.: Remote possibilities? International usability testing at a distance. Interactions. **11**, 10–17 (2004)
6. Bernheim Brush, A. J., Ames, M., and Davis, J.: A comparison of synchronous remote and local usability studies for an expert interface. In: Conference on Human Factors in Computing Systems - Proceedings, pp. 1179–1182, April 2015. https://doi.org/10.1145/985921.986018
7. Bruun, A., Gull, P., Hofmeister, L., Stage, J.: Let your users do the testing: a comparison of three remote asynchronous usability testing methods. In: Conference on Human Factors in Computing Systems - Proceedings, pp. 1619–1628. ACM Press, New York (2009). https://doi.org/10.1145/1518701.1518948
8. Preely. https://preely.com
9. Sketch. https://www.sketch.com/
10. Figma. https://www.figma.com/
11. InVision. https://www.invisionapp.com/
12. Adobe XD. https://www.adobe.com/products/xd.html
13. Maze. https://maze.co/
14. UserTesting. https://www.usertesting.com/
15. UseBerry. https://www.useberry.com/
16. UserTribe. https://usertribe.com/
17. UserZoom. https://www.userzoom.com/
18. LookBack. https://lookback.io/
19. Miro. https://miro.com/online-whiteboard/

Author Index

Printed in the United States
by Baker & Taylor Publisher Services